Interactive Reader

GRADE 10

HOLT McDOUGAL
a division of Houghton Mifflin Harcourt

TABLE OF CONTENTS

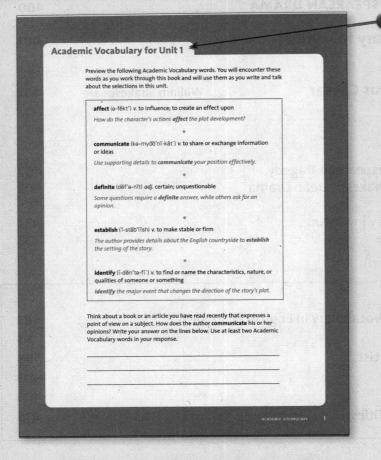

Academic Vocabulary for the Unit

Academic vocabulary is the language you use to talk and write about the subjects you are studying, including math, science, social studies, and language arts. Understanding and using academic vocabulary will help you succeed in school and on assessments.

Each unit in this book introduces five academic vocabulary words. You will have the opportunity to practice using these words after each selection.

Before Reading

The Before Reading pages introduce you to the text-analysis and reading skills you will practice as you read. Vocabulary words for the selection are introduced here as well.

Big Question

This activity gets you thinking about the real-life questions that literature addresses. Sometimes you'll work in a group or with a partner to complete this activity. After reading, you'll return to this activity. Don't be surprised if you have a different perspective.

Text Analysis

This section presents a brief, easy-to-understand lesson that introduces an important literary element and explains what to look for in the selection you are about to read.

Reading Skill: Make Inferences

Because writers don't always tell you everything you need to know about a character, you must make **inferences**, or logical guesses, about the character based on story details and your own experience. For example, you might infer that the mother in this story prefers the outdoors from her comment "A yard like this is more comfortable than most people know.... it is like an extended living room." As you read, notice what the characters' words and actions tell you about their personalities and attitudes. See below for an example.

	Story Details	Inferences
Dee	thinks orchids are tacky flowers	is stuck-up
Mama		
Maggie		

Vocabulary in Context

Note: Words are listed in the order in which they appear in the story.

furtive (fûr′tĭv) *adj.* sneaky, secretive
*The **furtive** child would not reveal his hiding spot.*

recompose (rē′kəm-pōz′) *v.* to restore to calm, to settle again
*She was quick to **recompose** herself after the argument.*

doctrine (dŏk′trĭn) *n.* a set of rules, beliefs, or values held by a group
*Many religions share similar **doctrines**.*

heritage (hĕr′ĭ-tĭj) *n.* something passed down through generations, such as tradition, values, property
*Students made a scrapbook that reflected aspects of their family **heritage**.*

Vocabulary Practice

Review the vocabulary words and their meanings. Then think about a situation in which two family members might oppose each other in a conflict about a family heirloom. Write a sentence or two describing the conflict, using at least two of the vocabulary words.

_____

_____

_____

EVERYDAY USE **17**

Reading Skill or Strategy

This lesson presents a reading skill or strategy that will help your reading comprehension. Opportunities to practice these skills will be provided as you read the selection.

Vocabulary in Context

Vocabulary words for the selection are introduced before reading. Each entry gives the pronunciation and definition of the word as well as a context sentence. Occasional **Vocabulary Practice** activities will give you a chance to practice using selection vocabulary.

Monitor Your Comprehension

SET A PURPOSE FOR READING
Read to find out how different ideas of family heritage lead to conflict.

Everyday Use

Short Story by
ALICE WALKER

BACKGROUND "Everyday Use" takes place during the 1960s, when many African Americans were discovering their heritage. The "black pride" movement, which grew out of the civil rights campaigns, called upon African Americans to celebrate their African roots and affirm their cultural identity. Many adopted African clothing, hairstyles, and names; some studied African languages.

MAKE INFERENCES
Reread lines 8–12. What can you infer about Maggie and her sister from this description? Underline the details that lead to your inferences.

_____

_____

_____

_____

_____

I will wait for her in the yard that Maggie and I made so clean and wavy yesterday afternoon. A yard like this is more comfortable than most people know. It is not just a yard. It is like an extended living room. When the hard clay is swept clean as a floor and the fine sand around the edges lined with tiny, irregular grooves, anyone can come and sit and look up into the elm tree and wait for the breezes that never come inside the house.

Maggie will be nervous until after her sister goes: she will stand hopelessly in corners, homely and ashamed of the burn scars down 10 her arms and legs, eying her sister with a mixture of envy and awe. She thinks her sister has held life always in the palm of one hand, that "no" is a word the world never learned to say to her.

You've no doubt seen those TV shows where the child who has "made it" is confronted, as a surprise, by her own mother and

18 INTERACTIVE READER / UNIT 1: PLOT, SETTING, AND MOOD

Reading the Selection

Notes in the side columns guide your interaction with the selection. Many notes ask you to underline or circle in the text itself. Others provide lines on which you can write your answers.

Set a Purpose for Reading

This feature gives you a reason for reading the selection.

Background

This paragraph gives you important information about the selection you are about to read. The background helps you understand the context of the literature by providing additional information about the author, the subject, or the time period during which the selection was written.

How to Use This Book

Side notes provide a variety of activities for you to complete as you read the selection.

Text Analysis or Reading Skill

These notes help you identify and analyze the literary element or reading skill you learned about on the Before Reading page.

Pause & Reflect

Notes in the side column allow you a chance to pause from your reading and think about what you have read.

Vocabulary

Definitions for vocabulary words are provided in the side margin at point of use. Occasional activities offer opportunities for you to use the vocabulary words.

After Reading

The After Reading pages help you assess the skills you have practiced throughout the selection.

Text Analysis

Demonstrate your knowledge of the text-analysis skill by filling out the organizer on this page and answering the question that follows.

Excerpt from the sample page:

would not flicker for minutes at a time. Often I fought off the temptation to shake her. At sixteen she had a style of her own: and knew what style was.

I never had an education myself. After second grade the school was closed down. Don't ask me why: in 1927 colored asked fewer questions than they do now. Sometimes Maggie reads to me. She stumbles along good-naturedly but can't see well. She knows she is not bright. Like good looks and money, quickness passed her by. She will marry John Thomas (who has mossy teeth in an earnest face) and then I'll be free to sit here and I guess just sing church songs to myself. Although I never was a good singer. Never could carry a tune. I was always better at a man's job. I used to love to milk till I was hooked in the side in '49. Cows are soothing and slow and don't bother you, unless you try to milk them the wrong way. **PAUSE & REFLECT**

I have deliberately turned my back on the house. It is three rooms, just like the one that burned, except the roof is tin; they don't make shingle roofs any more. There are no real windows, just some holes cut in the sides, like the portholes in a ship, but not round and not square, with rawhide holding the shutters up on the outside. This house is in a pasture, too, like the other one. No doubt when Dee sees it she will want to tear it down. She wrote me once that no matter where we "choose" to live, she will manage to come see us. But she will never bring her friends. Maggie and I thought about this and Maggie asked me, "Mama, when did Dee ever *have* any friends?"

She had a few. Furtive boys in pink shirts hanging about on washday after school. Nervous girls who never laughed. Impressed with her they worshiped the well-turned phrase, the cute shape, the scalding humor that erupted like bubbles in lye. She read to them.

When she was courting Jimmy T she didn't have much time to pay to us, but turned all her faultfinding power on him. He *flew*

Monitor Your Comprehension

CHARACTER AND CONFLICT
Why do you think Mama has "fought off the temptation to shake" Dee? Explain.

PAUSE & REFLECT
How has Mama's life experience differed from Dee's?

furtive (fûr′tĭv) *adj.* sneaky, secretive

EVERYDAY USE   21

After Reading

Text Analysis: Conflict and Character

The central conflict in "Everyday Use" is resolved at the end of the story. However, the characters are also faced with other minor conflicts—some of which are left unresolved. Identify additional conflicts in the chart below. Then tell whether or not each conflict is resolved. For each conflict that is resolved, explain how.

Description of Conflict	Resolved? If so, how?

Review your notes from "Everyday Use" and your completed conflict chart. Why do you think Alice Walker chooses to end the story with lingering conflicts?

EVERYDAY USE   29

After Reading

Reading Skill: Make Inferences

Think about what you learned about each character in "Everyday Use." Review the notes you took as you read and write a sentence describing each character in the chart below.

My Inferences
Dee
Maggie
Mama

What makes something VALUABLE?

Why might people disagree over why an object is valuable? Describe different possible reasons for disagreements.

_____

_____

Vocabulary Practice

Write T for true or F for false for each statement below.

_____ 1. Sneaking around is an example of furtive behavior.

_____ 2. When you recompose after a traffic accident, you become more upset.

_____ 3. If you believe in a certain group's doctrine, you follow their set of rules.

_____ 4. If you deny your heritage, you refuse to acknowledge your cultural history.

Reading Skill

The Reading Skill activity follows up on the skill you used as you read the text.

Big Question

The Big Question is followed up here with an opportunity for you to think about what you learned about life as you read.

Vocabulary Practice

Your knowledge of the vocabulary words is assessed with a variety of activities.

Academic Vocabulary in Writing

affect	communicate	definite	establish	identify

How does Dee identify her cultural heritage in "Everyday Use"? How does Mama? Write a few sentences about each character on the lines below. Use at least one Academic Vocabulary word in your response. Definitions for these terms are listed on page 1.

_____

_____

_____

_____

Assessment Practice

DIRECTIONS Use "Everyday Use" to answer questions 1–4.

1 Which word would Mama use to describe herself?
- (A) tough
- (B) quick-witted
- (C) educated
- (D) self-conscious

2 The most likely cause of Dee's conflict with her family is that —
- (A) she burned down the family house
- (B) she sees herself as better than they are
- (C) Mama refuses to call her by her new name
- (D) Mama has always preferred Maggie to Dee

3 The quilts are valuable to Mama because they —
- (A) are worth a lot of money
- (B) reflect her African heritage
- (C) were made for her by relatives
- (D) remind her of her family history

4 The main conflict of the story is resolved when —
- (A) Dee expresses appreciation for her family home
- (B) Maggie tells Mama that Dee can have the quilts
- (C) Mama takes the quilts from Dee and gives them to Maggie
- (D) Mama tells Dee that Maggie is going to marry John Thomas

---

Academic Vocabulary

The academic vocabulary words are followed up here. You will be asked to use at least one of the words in a speaking or writing activity about the selection.

Assessment Practice

To help you on your state tests, each selection is followed up by multiple-choice questions that test your comprehension of the selection.

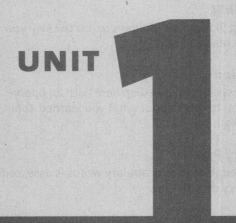

UNIT 1

The World of a Story

PLOT, SETTING, AND MOOD

Be sure to read the Text Analysis Workshop on pp. 28–35 in *Holt McDougal Literature*.

Academic Vocabulary for Unit 1

Preview the following Academic Vocabulary words. You will encounter these words as you work through this book and will use them as you write and talk about the selections in this unit.

affect (ə-fĕkt′) *v.* to influence; to create an effect upon

*How do the character's actions **affect** the plot development?*

•

communicate (kə-myōō′nĭ-kāt′) *v.* to share or exchange information or ideas

*Use supporting details to **communicate** your position effectively.*

•

definite (dĕf′ə-nĭt) *adj.* certain; unquestionable

*Some questions require a **definite** answer, while others ask for an opinion.*

•

establish (ĭ-stăb′lĭsh) *v.* to make stable or firm

*The author provides details about the English countryside to **establish** the setting of the story.*

•

identify (ī-dĕn′tə-fī′) *v.* to find or name the characteristics, nature, or qualities of someone or something

***Identify** the major event that changes the direction of the story's plot.*

Think about a book or an article you have read recently that expresses a point of view on a subject. How does the author **communicate** his or her opinions? Write your answer on the lines below. Use at least two Academic Vocabulary words in your response.

_____

_____

_____

Harrison Bergeron

Short Story by Kurt Vonnegut Jr.

What if everyone were THE SAME?

What would the world be like if everyone were the same—average in intelligence, talents, appearance, and strength—and no one was better than anyone else? How do you think people would feel and act toward each other? Would they be happy and satisfied?

BRAINSTORM With your class, brainstorm possible advantages and disadvantages of a world in which everyone is the same—exactly average. List your ideas in the notebook at left.

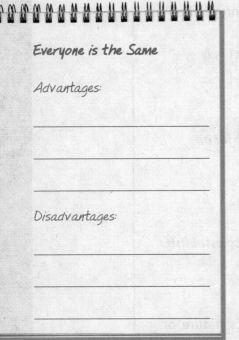

Everyone is the Same

Advantages:

_____

_____

_____

Disadvantages:

_____

_____

_____

Text Analysis: Plot and Conflict

Plot, or the chain of events in a story, usually includes these five stages:

- the **exposition,** or introduction
- the **rising action,** which reveals complications
- the **climax,** or turning point
- the **falling action,** or results of the climax
- the **resolution,** which reveals the final outcome

Conflict—the struggle between opposing forces—drives a story's plot. The chart below shows different types of conflicts.

As you read "Harrison Bergeron," look out for the conflicts the characters face.

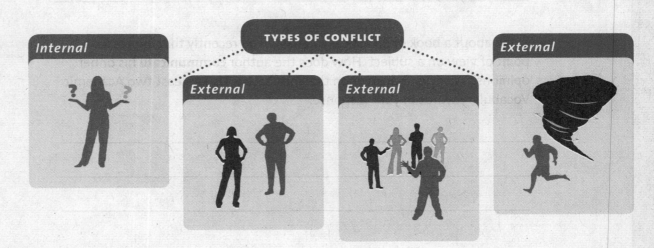

Internal

TYPES OF CONFLICT

External

External

External

Reading Skill: Draw Conclusions

When you **draw conclusions,** you make judgments based on story details and previous experiences in your own life. Use the following strategies to draw conclusions about the society depicted in "Harrison Bergeron":

- Note what results from the society's practices and laws.

- Apply your own prior knowledge to figure out why the society's officials act the way they do.

As you read, you will be prompted to make inferences like the one in the chart below.

Details About Society	My Reactions
Constitutional amendments make people equal in every way.	It would be hard to enforce equality.

Vocabulary in Context

Note: Words are listed in the order in which they appear in the story.

vigilance (vĭj′ə-ləns) *n.* alert attention, watchfulness
   *The teacher exercised **vigilance** as the children crossed the street.*

wince (wĭns) *v.* to shrink or flinch involuntarily, especially in pain
   *Most patients would **wince** in pain after the injection.*

consternation (kŏn′stər-nā′shən) *n.* confused amazement or fear
   *The thought of the ordeal filled her with **consternation.***

cower (kou′ər) *v.* to crouch down in fear
   *She tried to lure the kitten out, but it continued to **cower** in the corner.*

synchronize (sĭng′krə-nīz′) *v.* to match the timing of
   *Let's **synchronize** our watches so we arrive at the same time.*

neutralize (nōō′trə-līz′) *v.* to counteract or cancel the effect of
   *Preventive measures helped **neutralize** the impact of the storm.*

Vocabulary Practice

Review the vocabulary words and their meanings. Then use at least two vocabulary words to describe a conflict between two characters.

_____

_____

_____

Harrison Bergeron

Short Story by
KURT VONNEGUT JR.

BACKGROUND "Harrison Bergeron" is set in the year 2081. George and Hazel Bergeron are living in a society in which everyone is equal—by government order. But equality comes at a price. Many people are "handicapped" to bring them down to "average" levels. The Bergeron's genius son, Harrison, challenges the system in a daring move that society will never forget—or will it?

vigilance (vĭj′ə-ləns) *n.* alert attention, watchfulness

What is the purpose of the Handicapper General agents' **vigilance**?

_____

_____

_____

The year was 2081, and everybody was finally equal. They weren't only equal before God and the law. They were equal every which way. Nobody was smarter than anybody else. Nobody was better looking than anybody else. Nobody was stronger or quicker than anybody else. All this equality was due to the 211th, 212th, and 213th Amendments to the Constitution, and to the unceasing **vigilance** of agents of the United States Handicapper General.

Some things about living still weren't quite right, though.
10 April, for instance, still drove people crazy by not being springtime. And it was in that clammy month that the H-G men took George and Hazel Bergeron's fourteen-year-old son, Harrison, away.

It was tragic, all right, but George and Hazel couldn't think about it very hard. Hazel had a perfectly average intelligence, which meant she couldn't think about anything except in short bursts. And George, while his intelligence was way above normal, had a little mental handicap radio in his ear. He was required by law to wear it at all times. It was tuned to a government
20 transmitter.[1] Every twenty seconds or so, the transmitter would send out some sharp noise to keep people like George from taking unfair advantage of their brains. Ⓐ

George and Hazel were watching television. There were tears on Hazel's cheeks, but she'd forgotten for the moment what they were about.

On the television screen were ballerinas.

A buzzer sounded in George's head. His thoughts fled in panic, like bandits from a burglar alarm.

"That was a real pretty dance, that dance they just did," said
30 Hazel.

"Huh?" said George.

"That dance—it was nice," said Hazel.

"Yup," said George. He tried to think a little about the ballerinas. They weren't really very good—no better than anybody else would have been, anyway. They were burdened with sashweights[2] and bags of birdshot,[3] and their faces were masked, so that no one, seeing a free and graceful gesture or a pretty face, would feel like something the cat drug in. George was toying with the vague notion that maybe dancers shouldn't be handicapped.
40 But he didn't get very far with it before another noise in his ear radio scattered his thoughts.

George winced. So did two out of the eight ballerinas.

Hazel saw him wince. Having no mental handicap herself, she had to ask George what the latest sound had been.

"Sounded like somebody hitting a milk bottle with a ball peen hammer,"[4] said George.

---

1. **transmitter:** an electronic device for broadcasting radio signals.
2. **sashweights:** lead weights used in some kinds of windows to keep them from falling shut when raised.
3. **birdshot:** tiny lead pellets made to be loaded in shotgun shells.
4. **ball peen hammer:** a hammer with a head having one flat side and one rounded side.

Ⓐ **DRAW CONCLUSIONS**
Reread lines 1–22. Underline details that describe society in 2081. In the chart below, list the details and your opinion of the society so far.

Details About Society

↓

My Reaction

wince (wĭns) v. to shrink or flinch involuntarily, especially in pain

Why did two of the ballerinas **wince** at the same time as George?

_____

_____

_____

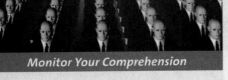
B DRAW CONCLUSIONS
Reread lines 29–49. Circle words and phrases that show how the society affects the thoughts and reactions of the people. What can you conclude about the different ways in which people are affected by the society?

_____

_____

_____

_____

_____

C PLOT AND CONFLICT
George's thoughts in lines 61–63 reveal more about the conflict between Harrison and the society. On the basis of what you've read so far, what behavior might be viewed as abnormal and illegal?

_____

_____

_____

_____

_____

_____

_____

"I'd think it would be real interesting, hearing all the different sounds," said Hazel, a little envious. "All the things they think up."

"Um," said George. **B**

50 "Only, if I was Handicapper General, you know what I would do?" said Hazel. Hazel, as a matter of fact, bore a strong resemblance to the Handicapper General, a woman named Diana Moon Glampers. "If I was Diana Moon Glampers," said Hazel, "I'd have chimes on Sunday—just chimes. Kind of in honor of religion."

"I could think, if it was just chimes," said George.

"Well—maybe make 'em real loud," said Hazel. "I think I'd make a good Handicapper General."

"Good as anybody else," said George.

60 "Who knows better'n I do what normal is?" said Hazel.

"Right," said George. He began to think glimmeringly about his abnormal son who was now in jail, about Harrison, but a twenty-one-gun salute in his head stopped that. **C**

"Boy!" said Hazel, "that was a doozy, wasn't it?"

It was such a doozy that George was white and trembling, and tears stood on the rims of his red eyes. Two of the eight ballerinas had collapsed to the studio floor and were holding their temples.

"All of a sudden you look so tired," said Hazel. "Why don't you stretch out on the sofa, so's you can rest your handicap bag on the 70 pillows, honeybunch." She was referring to the forty-seven pounds of birdshot in a canvas bag, which was padlocked around George's neck. "Go on and rest the bag for a little while," she said. "I don't care if you're not equal to me for a while."

George weighed the bag with his hands. "I don't mind it," he said. "I don't notice it any more. It's just a part of me."

"You been so tired lately—kind of wore out," said Hazel. "If there was just some way we could make a little hole in the bottom of the bag, and just take out a few of them lead balls. Just a few."

"Two years in prison and two thousand dollars fine for every 80 ball I took out," said George. "I don't call that a bargain."

"If you could just take a few out when you came home from work," said Hazel. "I mean—you don't compete with anybody around here. You just set around."

"If I tried to get away with it," said George, "then other people'd get away with it—and pretty soon we'd be right back to the dark ages again, with everybody competing against everybody else. You wouldn't like that, would you?"

"I'd hate it," said Hazel.

"There you are," said George. "The minute people start
90 cheating on laws, what do you think happens to society?" **D**

If Hazel hadn't been able to come up with an answer to this question, George couldn't have supplied one. A siren was going off in his head.

"Reckon it'd fall all apart," said Hazel.

"What would?" said George blankly.

"Society," said Hazel uncertainly. "Wasn't that what you just said?"

"Who knows?" said George. **PAUSE & REFLECT**

The television program was suddenly interrupted for a news
100 bulletin. It wasn't clear at first as to what the bulletin was about, since the announcer, like all announcers, had a serious speech impediment.[5] For about half a minute, and in a state of high excitement, the announcer tried to say, "Ladies and gentlemen—"

He finally gave up, handed the bulletin to a ballerina to read.

"That's all right—" Hazel said of the announcer, "he tried. That's the big thing. He tried to do the best he could with what God gave him. He should get a nice raise for trying so hard."

"Ladies and gentlemen—" said the ballerina, reading the bulletin. She must have been extraordinarily beautiful, because the
110 mask she wore was hideous. And it was easy to see that she was the strongest and most graceful of all the dancers, for her handicap bags were as big as those worn by two-hundred-pound men. **E**

---

5. **speech impediment** (ĭm-pĕd′ə-mənt): a physical defect that prevents a person from speaking normally.

D DRAW CONCLUSIONS
Reread lines 76–90. Underline George's reasons for not lightening his handicap bag. What are his beliefs about the society?

_____

_____

_____

_____

_____

PAUSE & REFLECT
Notice the difficulties Hazel and George experience in simply trying to have a conversation. What point does this help reinforce about the society?

_____

_____

_____

_____

E DRAW CONCLUSIONS
Circle words and phrases in lines 99–112 that tell you more about the society. How do the rules of the society affect people's job performance?

_____

_____

_____

_____

F PLOT AND CONFLICT
The **rising action** begins in lines 117–121. What do you learn about the conflict between Harrison and the society?

_____

_____

_____

_____

G PLOT AND CONFLICT
Underline details that describe Harrison's appearance in lines 124–141. Why has he been so handicapped by the government?

_____

_____

_____

consternation (kŏn′stər-nā′shən) *n.* confused amazement or fear

And she had to apologize at once for her voice, which was a very unfair voice for a woman to use. Her voice was a warm, luminous, timeless melody. "Excuse me—" she said, and she began again, making her voice absolutely uncompetitive.

"Harrison Bergeron, age fourteen," she said in a grackle[6] squawk, "has just escaped from jail, where he was held on suspicion of plotting to overthrow the government. He is a genius and an athlete, is under-handicapped, and should be regarded as extremely dangerous." **F**

A police photograph of Harrison Bergeron was flashed on the screen—upside down, then sideways, upside down again, then right side up. The picture showed the full length of Harrison against a background calibrated in feet and inches. He was exactly seven feet tall.

The rest of Harrison's appearance was Halloween and hardware. Nobody had ever born heavier handicaps. He had outgrown hindrances faster than the H-G men could think them up. Instead of a little ear radio for a mental handicap, he wore a tremendous pair of earphones, and spectacles with thick wavy lenses. The spectacles were intended to make him not only half blind, but to give him whanging headaches besides.

Scrap metal was hung all over him. Ordinarily, there was a certain symmetry, a military neatness to the handicaps issued to strong people, but Harrison looked like a walking junkyard. In the race of life, Harrison carried three hundred pounds.

And to offset his good looks, the H-G men required that he wear at all times a red rubber ball for a nose, keep his eyebrows shaved off, and cover his even white teeth with black caps at snaggle-tooth random. **G**

"If you see this boy," said the ballerina, "do not—I repeat, do not—try to reason with him."

There was the shriek of a door being torn from its hinges.

Screams and barking cries of **consternation** came from the television set. The photograph of Harrison Bergeron on the screen

_____

6. **grackle:** a blackbird with a harsh, unpleasant call.

jumped again and again, as though dancing to the tune of an earthquake.

150 George Bergeron correctly identified the earthquake, and well he might have—for many was the time his own home had danced to the same crashing tune. "My God—" said George, "that must be Harrison!"

The realization was blasted from his mind instantly by the sound of an automobile collision in his head.

When George could open his eyes again, the photograph of Harrison was gone. A living, breathing Harrison filled the screen.

Clanking, clownish, and huge, Harrison stood in the center of the studio. The knob of the uprooted studio door was still in his hand. Ballerinas, technicians, musicians, and announcers **cowered** 160 on their knees before him, expecting to die.

"I am the Emperor!" cried Harrison. "Do you hear? I am the Emperor! Everybody must do what I say at once!" He stamped his foot and the studio shook.

"Even as I stand here—" he bellowed, "crippled, hobbled, sickened—I am a greater ruler than any man who ever lived! Now watch me become what I *can* become!"

Harrison tore the straps of his handicap harness like wet tissue paper, tore straps guaranteed to support five thousand pounds.

Harrison's scrap-iron handicaps crashed to the floor.

170 Harrison thrust his thumbs under the bar of the padlock that secured his head harness. The bar snapped like celery. Harrison smashed his headphones and spectacles against the wall.

He flung away his rubber-ball nose, revealed a man that would have awed Thor, the god of thunder.

"I shall now select my Empress!" he said, looking down on the cowering people. "Let the first woman who dares rise to her feet claim her mate and her throne!" ⒣

A moment passed, and then a ballerina arose, swaying like a willow.

cower (kou′ər) *v.* to crouch down in fear

Ⓗ **PLOT AND CONFLICT**
Reread lines 161–177. Circle statements that reveal how Harrison views himself in relation to other people. How do his views put him in conflict with the government?

_____

_____

_____

_____

_____

_____

_____

_____

_____

_____

_____

180   Harrison plucked the mental handicap from her ear, snapped off her physical handicaps with marvelous delicacy. Last of all, he removed her mask.

She was blindingly beautiful.

"Now—" said Harrison, taking her hand, "shall we show the people the meaning of the word dance? Music!" he commanded.

The musicians scrambled back into their chairs, and Harrison stripped them of their handicaps, too. "Play your best," he told them, "and I'll make you barons and dukes and earls."

The music began. It was normal at first—cheap, silly, false.

190 But Harrison snatched two musicians from their chairs, waved them like batons as he sang the music as he wanted it played. He slammed them back into their chairs.

The music began again and was much improved.

PAUSE & REFLECT

The ballerina and the musicians risk punishment by cooperating with Harrison. Why would they take such a risk?

_____

_____

_____

PAUSE & REFLECT

Harrison and his Empress merely listened to the music for a while—listened gravely, as though **synchronizing** their heartbeats with it.

They shifted their weights to their toes.

Harrison placed his big hands on the girl's tiny waist, letting her sense the weightlessness that would soon be hers.

200 And then, in an explosion of joy and grace, into the air they sprang!

Not only were the laws of the land abandoned, but the law of gravity and the laws of motion as well.

They reeled, whirled, swiveled, flounced, capered, gamboled, and spun.

They leaped like deer on the moon.

The studio ceiling was thirty feet high, but each leap brought the dancers nearer to it.

It became their obvious intention to kiss the ceiling.

210 They kissed it.

And then, **neutralizing** gravity with love and pure will, they remained suspended in air inches below the ceiling, and they kissed each other for a long, long time. **❶**

It was then that Diana Moon Glampers, the Handicapper General, came into the studio with a double-barreled ten-gauge shotgun. She fired twice, and the Emperor and the Empress were dead before they hit the floor.

Diana Moon Glampers loaded the gun again. She aimed it at the musicians and told them they had ten seconds to get their 220 handicaps back on.

It was then that the Bergerons' television tube burned out. **❷**

Hazel turned to comment about the blackout to George. But George had gone out into the kitchen for a can of beer.

George came back in with the beer, paused while a handicap signal shook him up. And then he sat down again. "You been crying?" he said to Hazel.

synchronize (sĭng′krə-nīz′) *v.* to match the timing of

neutralize (nōō′trə-līz′) *v.* to counteract or cancel the effect of

❶ DRAW CONCLUSIONS
Underline words and phrases in lines 200–213 that indicate how the narrator views this rebellion against the laws. Then describe this view in your own words.

_____

_____

_____

_____

❷ PLOT AND CONFLICT
Reread lines 214–221. How is the conflict resolved?

_____

_____

_____

_____

_____

_____

PAUSE & REFLECT
How do George and Hazel react
to their son's death?

_____

_____

_____

_____

_____

"Yup," she said.

"What about?" he said.

"I forget," she said. "Something real sad on television."

230 "What was it?" he said.

"It's all kind of mixed up in my mind," said Hazel.

"Forget sad things," said George.

"I always do," said Hazel.

"That's my girl," said George. He winced. There was the sound of a riveting gun[7] in his head.

"Gee—I could tell that one was a doozy," said Hazel.

"You can say that again," said George.

"Gee—" said Hazel, "I could tell that one was a doozy."

PAUSE & REFLECT

---

7. **riveting** (rĭv′ĭ-tĭng) **gun:** a power tool used to hammer bolts (called rivets) that are used in construction work and manufacturing to fasten metal beams or plates together.

Text Analysis: Plot and Conflict

How does the conflict in "Harrison Bergeron" drive the plot? Describe the plot stages in the chart below.

Exposition (introductory information)
Rising Action (events that lead to the climax)
Climax (turning point)
Falling Action (results of climax)
Resolution (final outcome)

What was your reaction to the story's outcome?

_____

_____

_____

_____

_____

Reading Skill: Draw Conclusions

In your own words describe the society in "Harrison Bergeron." Then, think about how you would describe society today. What conclusion can you draw about the society in the story? Consider how most people function and what is considered normal.

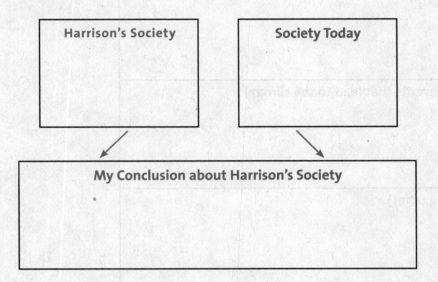

Harrison's Society	Society Today

My Conclusion about Harrison's Society

What if everyone were **THE SAME?**

Would you be happier if no one were better (or worse) than anyone else? Explain your answer.

_____

_____

_____

Vocabulary Practice

Circle the word that is most different in meaning from the others.

1. **(a)** vigilance, **(b)** attention, **(c)** alertness, **(d)** laziness

2. **(a)** grin, **(b)** flinch, **(c)** wince, **(d)** shrink

3. **(a)** joy, **(b)** consternation, **(c)** happiness, **(d)** elation

4. **(a)** tower, **(b)** crouch, **(c)** cower, **(d)** cringe

5. **(a)** time, **(b)** synchronize, **(c)** set, **(d)** separate

6. **(a)** neutralize, **(b)** worsen, **(c)** lessen, **(d)** decrease

Academic Vocabulary in Speaking

| affect | communicate | definite | establish | identify |

TURN AND TALK How did the laws of the society depicted in "Harrison Bergeron" **affect** its citizens? Discuss the different ways in which people were affected with a partner. Use at least two Academic Vocabulary words in your discussion. Definitions for these terms are listed on page 1.

Assessment Practice

DIRECTIONS Use "Harrison Bergeron" to answer questions 1–6.

1 The main conflict of the story revolves around Harrison Bergeron's resistance to —
- (A) the rules his parents have set
- (B) the authority of the government
- (C) the qualities he was born with
- (D) the appeals by others to rebel

2 Hazel does not wear a handicap transmitter because —
- (A) her intelligence is average
- (B) she is unusually attractive
- (C) her husband told her not to wear it
- (D) she broke the law and removed hers

3 The main conflict of the story is resolved when —
- (A) the Handicapper General takes Harrison to jail
- (B) the Handicapper General shoots and kills Harrison
- (C) a news reporter announces that Harrison has escaped from jail
- (D) Harrison declares himself emperor and removes his handicaps

4 In lines 66–67, two of the ballerinas collapse on the studio floor because —
- (A) the Handicapper General blasts them with noise
- (B) the Handicapper General shoots and kills them
- (C) Harrison Bergeron breaks down the studio door
- (D) Harrison Bergeron adds weight to their handicap bags

5 George does not lighten his handicap bag because —
- (A) his son is unable to untie it
- (B) his wife urges him to leave it on
- (C) he objects to his son becoming emperor
- (D) he worries about the risks of breaking the law

6 Which word best describes George and Hazel's reaction to their son's death?
- (A) annoyed
- (B) thrilled
- (C) unaware
- (D) hysterical

Everyday Use

Short story by **Alice Walker**

What makes something
VALUABLE?

The word *value* means different things to different people. For example, an old vase might have great historical, cultural, or artistic value. But others might think it's a useless piece of junk. Often people disagree over the value of an object. Or they may agree that it's valuable, but not for the same reason.

QUICKWRITE If you could save only one of your most precious possessions from being destroyed or left behind, what would you save? Write a sentence or two in the notebook at left identifying the item and telling why it is valuable to you.

Text Analysis: Conflict and Character

A story's plot progresses because of **conflict,** or the struggle between opposing forces. In "Everyday Use," the main conflict centers around two sisters, Dee and Maggie, and their mother, who narrates the story. This diagram illustrates the conflicts between the story's characters:

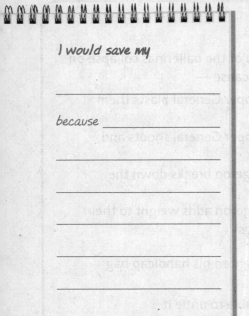

I would save my

_____

because _____

_____

_____

_____

_____

_____

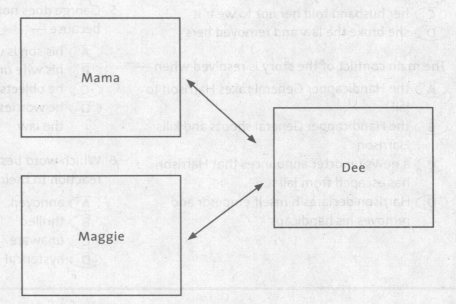

Mama

Dee

Maggie

As you read, think about what each character values and how these different values create tension between the characters. Pay attention to the reasons for the conflicts and whether they are resolved by the end of the story.

Reading Skill: Make Inferences

Because writers don't always tell you everything you need to know about a character, you must make **inferences,** or logical guesses, about the character based on story details and your own experience. For example, you might infer that the mother in this story prefers the outdoors from her comment "A yard like this is more comfortable than most people know. . . . It is like an extended living room." As you read, notice what the characters' words and actions tell you about their personalities and attitudes. See below for an example.

	Story Details	Inferences
Dee	thinks orchids are tacky flowers	is stuck-up
Mama		
Maggie		

Vocabulary in Context

Note: Words are listed in the order in which they appear in the story.

furtive (fûr'tĭv) *adj.* sneaky, secretive
   *The **furtive** child would not reveal his hiding spot.*

recompose (rē'kəm-pōz') *v.* to restore to calm, to settle again
   *She was quick to **recompose** herself after the argument.*

doctrine (dŏk'trĭn) *n.* a set of rules, beliefs, or values held by a group
   *Many religions share similar **doctrines.***

heritage (hĕr'ĭ-tĭj) *n.* something passed down through generations, such as tradition, values, property
   *Students made a scrapbook that reflected aspects of their family **heritage.***

Vocabulary Practice

Review the vocabulary words and their meanings. Then think about a situation in which two family members might oppose each other in a conflict about a family heirloom. Write a sentence or two describing the conflict, using at least two of the vocabulary words.

_____

_____

_____

Everyday Use

Short Story by
ALICE WALKER

BACKGROUND "Everyday Use" takes place during the 1960s, when many African Americans were discovering their heritage. The "black pride" movement, which grew out of the civil rights campaigns, called upon African Americans to celebrate their African roots and affirm their cultural identity. Many adopted African clothing, hairstyles, and names; some studied African languages.

Ⓐ **MAKE INFERENCES**
Reread lines 8–12. What can you infer about Maggie and her sister from this description? Underline the details that lead to your inferences.

_____

_____

_____

_____

_____

I will wait for her in the yard that Maggie and I made so clean and wavy yesterday afternoon. A yard like this is more comfortable than most people know. It is not just a yard. It is like an extended living room. When the hard clay is swept clean as a floor and the fine sand around the edges lined with tiny, irregular grooves, anyone can come and sit and look up into the elm tree and wait for the breezes that never come inside the house.

Maggie will be nervous until after her sister goes: she will stand hopelessly in corners, homely and ashamed of the burn scars down 10 her arms and legs, eying her sister with a mixture of envy and awe. She thinks her sister has held life always in the palm of one hand, that "no" is a word the world never learned to say to her. Ⓐ

You've no doubt seen those TV shows where the child who has "made it" is confronted, as a surprise, by her own mother and

father, tottering in weakly from backstage. (A pleasant surprise, of course: What would they do if parent and child came on the show only to curse out and insult each other?) On TV mother and child embrace and smile into each other's faces. Sometimes the mother and father weep, the child wraps them in her arms and leans
20 across the table to tell how she would not have made it without their help. I have seen these programs.

Sometimes I dream a dream in which Dee and I are suddenly brought together on a TV program of this sort. Out of a dark and soft-seated limousine I am ushered into a bright room filled with many people. There I meet a smiling, gray, sporty man like Johnny Carson who shakes my hand and tells me what a fine girl I have. Then we are on the stage and Dee is embracing me with tears in her eyes. She pins on my dress a large orchid, even though she has told me once that she thinks orchids are tacky flowers. **B**

30 In real life I am a large, big-boned woman with rough, man-working hands. In the winter I wear flannel nightgowns to bed and overalls during the day. I can kill and clean a hog as mercilessly as a man. My fat keeps me hot in zero weather. I can work outside all day, breaking ice to get water for washing; I can eat pork liver cooked over the open fire minutes after it comes steaming from the hog. One winter I knocked a bull calf straight in the brain between the eyes with a sledge hammer and had the meat hung up to chill before nightfall. But of course all this does not show on television. I am the way my daughter would want me
40 to be: a hundred pounds lighter, my skin like an uncooked barley pancake. My hair glistens in the hot bright lights. Johnny Carson has much to do to keep up with my quick and witty tongue. **C**

But that is a mistake. I know even before I wake up. Who ever knew a Johnson with a quick tongue? Who can even imagine me looking a strange white man in the eye? It seems to me I have talked to them always with one foot raised in flight, with my head turned in whichever way is farthest from them. Dee, though. She would always look anyone in the eye. Hesitation was no part of her nature.

B MAKE INFERENCES
Reread lines 13–29. Based on her dream, what inference can you make about what the narrator might want from Dee? Underline the details that lead to your inference.

_____

_____

_____

_____

_____

C CONFLICT AND CHARACTER
Underline details in lines 30–42 that tell you about Mama's character. Then circle the details that tell how Dee would like her mother to be. What does this reveal about their conflict?

_____

_____

_____

_____

_____

_____

_____

_____

_____

ⓓ MAKE INFERENCES
What inferences can you make about Dee, Maggie, and Mama based on the details in lines 50–71? Record them in the chart below.

Dee
Details
Inferences

Maggie
Details
Inferences

Mama
Details
Inferences

50 "How do I look, Mama?" Maggie says, showing just enough of her thin body enveloped in pink skirt and red blouse for me to know she's there, almost hidden by the door.

"Come out into the yard," I say.

Have you ever seen a lame animal, perhaps a dog run over by some careless person rich enough to own a car, sidle up to someone who is ignorant enough to be kind to him? That is the way my Maggie walks. She has been like this, chin on chest, eyes on ground, feet in shuffle, ever since the fire that burned the other house to the ground.

60 Dee is lighter than Maggie, with nicer hair and a fuller figure. She's a woman now, though sometimes I forget. How long ago was it that the other house burned? Ten, twelve years? Sometimes I can still hear the flames and feel Maggie's arms sticking to me, her hair smoking and her dress falling off her in little black papery flakes. Her eyes seemed stretched open, blazed open by the flames reflected in them. And Dee. I see her standing off under the sweet gum tree she used to dig gum out of; a look of concentration on her face as she watched the last dingy gray board of the house fall in toward the red-hot brick chimney. Why don't you do a dance

70 around the ashes? I'd wanted to ask her. She had hated the house that much. ⓓ

I used to think she hated Maggie, too. But that was before we raised the money, the church and me, to send her to Augusta[1] to school. She used to read to us without pity; forcing words, lies, other folks' habits, whole lives upon us two, sitting trapped and ignorant underneath her voice. She washed us in a river of make-believe, burned us with a lot of knowledge we didn't necessarily need to know. Pressed us to her with the serious way she read, to shove us away at just the moment, like dimwits, we seemed about

80 to understand.

Dee wanted nice things. A yellow organdy dress to wear to her graduation from high school; black pumps to match a green suit she'd made from an old suit somebody gave me. She was determined to stare down any disaster in her efforts. Her eyelids

---

1. **Augusta:** a city in Georgia.

would not flicker for minutes at a time. Often I fought off the temptation to shake her. At sixteen she had a style of her own: and knew what style was. **E**

I never had an education myself. After second grade the school was closed down. Don't ask me why: in 1927 colored asked fewer questions than they do now. Sometimes Maggie reads to me. She stumbles along good-naturedly but can't see well. She knows she is not bright. Like good looks and money, quickness passed her by. She will marry John Thomas (who has mossy teeth in an earnest face) and then I'll be free to sit here and I guess just sing church songs to myself. Although I never was a good singer. Never could carry a tune. I was always better at a man's job. I used to love to milk till I was hooked in the side in '49. Cows are soothing and slow and don't bother you, unless you try to milk them the wrong way. **PAUSE & REFLECT**

I have deliberately turned my back on the house. It is three rooms, just like the one that burned, except the roof is tin; they don't make shingle roofs any more. There are no real windows, just some holes cut in the sides, like the portholes in a ship, but not round and not square, with rawhide holding the shutters up on the outside. This house is in a pasture, too, like the other one. No doubt when Dee sees it she will want to tear it down. She wrote me once that no matter where we "choose" to live, she will manage to come see us. But she will never bring her friends. Maggie and I thought about this and Maggie asked me, "Mama, when did Dee ever *have* any friends?"

She had a few. <u>Furtive</u> boys in pink shirts hanging about on washday after school. Nervous girls who never laughed. Impressed with her they worshiped the well-turned phrase, the cute shape, the scalding humor that erupted like bubbles in lye. She read to them.

When she was courting Jimmy T she didn't have much time to pay to us, but turned all her faultfinding power on him. He *flew*

E CHARACTER AND CONFLICT
Why do you think Mama has "fought off the temptation to shake" Dee? Explain.

_____

_____

_____

_____

_____

PAUSE & REFLECT
How has Mama's life experience differed from Dee's?

_____

_____

_____

_____

_____

furtive (fûr′tĭv) *adj.* sneaky, secretive

recompose (rē'kəm-pōz') v. to restore to calm, to settle again

F MAKE INFERENCES
What do you learn about Dee from the way others respond to her? Underline details that reveal her personality in lines 111–119.

_____

_____

_____

_____

_____

_____

_____

_____

_____

PAUSE & REFLECT
What do you think Mama thinks of Dee's appearance?

_____

_____

_____

_____

_____

_____

_____

_____

to marry a cheap city girl from a family of ignorant flashy people. She hardly had time to **recompose** herself. **F**

120 When she comes I will meet—but there they are!

Maggie attempts to make a dash for the house, in her shuffling way, but I stay her with my hand. "Come back here," I say. And she stops and tries to dig a well in the sand with her toe.

It is hard to see them clearly through the strong sun. But even the first glimpse of leg out of the car tells me it is Dee. Her feet were always neat-looking, as if God himself had shaped them with a certain style. From the other side of the car comes a short, stocky man. Hair is all over his head a foot long and hanging from his chin like a kinky mule tail. I hear Maggie suck in her breath. "Uhnnnh," 130 is what it sounds like. Like when you see the wriggling end of a snake just in front of your foot on the road. "Uhnnnh."

Dee next. A dress down to the ground, in this hot weather. A dress so loud it hurts my eyes. There are yellows and oranges enough to throw back the light of the sun. I feel my whole face warming from the heat waves it throws out. Earrings gold, too, and hanging down to her shoulders. Bracelets dangling and making noises when she moves her arm up to shake the folds of the dress out of her armpits. The dress is loose and flows, and as she walks closer, I like it. I hear Maggie go "Uhnnnh" again. It 140 is her sister's hair. It stands straight up like the wool on a sheep. It is black as night and around the edges are two long pigtails that rope about like small lizards disappearing behind her ears.

PAUSE & REFLECT

"Wa-su-zo-Tean-o!" she says, coming on in that gliding way the dress makes her move. The short stocky fellow with the hair to his navel is all grinning and he follows up with "Asalamalakim,[2] my mother and sister!" He moves to hug Maggie but she falls back, right up against the back of my chair. I feel her trembling there and when I look up I see the perspiration falling off her chin.

_____

2. **Wa-su-zo-Tean-o!** (wä-sōō'zō-tē'nō) . . . **Asalamalakim!** (ə-säl'ə-mə-läk'əm): African and Arabic greetings.

150   "Don't get up," says Dee. Since I am stout it takes something of a push. You can see me trying to move a second or two before I make it. She turns, showing white heels through her sandals, and goes back to the car. Out she peeks next with a Polaroid. She stoops down quickly and lines up picture after picture of me sitting there in front of the house with Maggie cowering behind me. She never takes a shot without making sure the house is included. When a cow comes nibbling around the edge of the yard she snaps it and me and Maggie *and* the house. Then she puts the Polaroid in the back seat of the car, and comes up and
160   kisses me on the forehead. **G**

Meanwhile Asalamalakim is going through motions with Maggie's hand. Maggie's hand is as limp as a fish, and probably as cold, despite the sweat, and she keeps trying to pull it back. It looks like Asalamalakim wants to shake hands but wants to do it fancy. Or maybe he don't know how people shake hands. Anyhow, he soon gives up on Maggie.

"Well," I say. "Dee."

"No, Mama," she says. "Not 'Dee,' Wangero Leewanika Kemanjo!"[3]

170   "What happened to 'Dee'?" I wanted to know.

"She's dead," Wangero said. "I couldn't bear it any longer, being named after the people who oppress me."

"You know as well as me you was named after your aunt Dicie," I said. Dicie is my sister. She named Dee. We called her "Big Dee" after Dee was born.

"But who was *she* named after?" asked Wangero.

"I guess after Grandma Dee," I said.

"And who was she named after?" asked Wangero.

"Her mother," I said, and saw Wangero was getting tired.

180   "That's about as far back as I can trace it," I said. Though, in fact, I probably could have carried it back beyond the Civil War through the branches. **H**

"Well," said Asalamalakim, "there you are."

"Uhnnnh," I heard Maggie say.

---

3. **Wangero Leewanika Kemanjo** (wän-gär'ō lē-wä-nē'kə kĕ-män'jō).

G MAKE INFERENCES
In line 106 Mama thinks that Dee will want to tear her house down when she sees it. Yet in in lines 154–157 Dee makes sure the house is included in every picture she takes. What does this reveal about Dee?

_____
_____
_____
_____
_____
_____
_____
_____
_____
_____
_____

H CHARACTER AND CONFLICT
In lines 171–172, Dee refers to the fact that enslaved Africans lost their own names and were given the names of white people. What is Mama's opinion of Dee's name?

_____
_____
_____
_____

❶ MAKE INFERENCES
Reread lines 185–189. What can you infer about how Dee's friend views Mama?

_____

_____

_____

_____

_____

_____

_____

_____

_____

_____

_____

doctrine (dŏk′trĭn) *n.* a set of rules, beliefs, or values held by a group

"There I was not," I said, "before 'Dicie' cropped up in our family, so why should I try to trace it that far back?"

He just stood there grinning, looking down on me like somebody inspecting a Model A[4] car. Every once in a while he and Wangero sent eye signals over my head. ❶

190 "How do you pronounce this name?" I asked.

"You don't have to call me by it if you don't want to," said Wangero.

"Why shouldn't I?" I asked. "If that's what you want us to call you, we'll call you."

"I know it might sound awkward at first," said Wangero.

"I'll get used to it," I said. "Ream it out again."

Well, soon we got the name out of the way. Asalamalakim had a name twice as long and three times as hard. After I tripped over it two or three times he told me to just call him Hakim-a-barber.[5]

200 I wanted to ask him was he a barber, but I didn't really think he was, so I didn't ask.

"You must belong to those beef-cattle peoples down the road," I said. They said "Asalamalakim" when they met you, too, but they didn't shake hands. Always too busy: feeding the cattle, fixing the fences, putting up salt-lick shelters, throwing down hay. When the white folks poisoned some of the herd the men stayed up all night with rifles in their hands. I walked a mile and a half just to see the sight.

Hakim-a-barber said, "I accept some of their <u>doctrines</u>, but

210 farming and raising cattle is not my style." (They didn't tell me, and I didn't ask, whether Wangero (Dee) had really gone and married him.)

We sat down to eat and right away he said he didn't eat collards and pork was unclean. Wangero, though, went on through the chitlins and corn bread, the greens and everything else. She talked a blue streak over the sweet potatoes. Everything delighted her. Even the fact that we still used the benches her daddy made for the table when we couldn't afford to buy chairs.

---

4. **Model A:** an automobile manufactured by Ford from 1927 to 1931.
5. **Hakim-a-barber** (hä-kē′mə-bär′bər).

"Oh, Mama!" she cried. Then turned to Hakim-a-barber.
220 "I never knew how lovely these benches are. You can feel the
rump prints," she said, running her hands underneath her and
along the bench. Then she gave a sigh and her hand closed over
Grandma Dee's butter dish. "That's it!" she said. "I knew there
was something I wanted to ask you if I could have." She jumped
up from the table and went over in the corner where the churn
stood, the milk in it clabber[6] by now. She looked at the churn and
looked at it. **PAUSE & REFLECT**

"This churn top is what I need," she said. "Didn't Uncle Buddy
whittle it out of a tree you all used to have?"
230 "Yes," I said.
"Uh huh," she said happily. "And I want the dasher,[7] too."
"Uncle Buddy whittle that, too?" asked the barber.
Dee (Wangero) looked up at me.
"Aunt Dee's first husband whittled the dash," said Maggie so
low you almost couldn't hear her. "His name was Henry, but they
called him Stash."
"Maggie's brain is like an elephant's," Wangero said, laughing.
"I can use the churn top as a centerpiece for the alcove table," she
said, sliding a plate over the churn, "and I'll think of something
240 artistic to do with the dasher." **J**
When she finished wrapping the dasher the handle stuck out.
I took it for a moment in my hands. You didn't even have to look
close to see where hands pushing the dasher up and down to make
butter had left a kind of sink in the wood. In fact, there were a lot
of small sinks; you could see where thumbs and fingers had sunk
into the wood. It was beautiful light yellow wood, from a tree that
grew in the yard where Big Dee and Stash had lived.
After dinner Dee (Wangero) went to the trunk at the foot of
my bed and started rifling through it. Maggie hung back in the
250 kitchen over the dishpan. Out came Wangero with two quilts.
They had been pieced by Grandma Dee and then Big Dee and me

---

6. **clabber:** curdled milk.

7. **Dasher:** the plunger of a churn, a device formerly used to stir cream or milk to produce butter.

J MAKE INFERENCES
Reread lines 228–240. What do you learn about Dee and Maggie from these lines? Underline details that help you make inferences about their character.

K MAKE INFERENCES
What do you think the noises are
in lines 261–262?

_____

_____

_____

_____

_____

_____

_____

_____

_____

_____

had hung them on the quilt frames on the front porch and quilted
them. One was in the Lone Star pattern. The other was Walk
Around the Mountain. In both of them were scraps of dresses
Grandma Dee had worn fifty and more years ago. Bits and pieces
of Grandpa Jarrell's Paisley shirts. And one teeny faded blue piece,
about the size of a penny matchbox, that was from Great Grandpa
Ezra's uniform that he wore in the Civil War.

"Mama," Wangero said sweet as a bird. "Can I have these
260 old quilts?"

I heard something fall in the kitchen, and a minute later the
kitchen door slammed. **K**

"Why don't you take one or two of the others?" I asked.
"These old things was just done by me and Big Dee from some
tops your grandma pieced before she died."

"No," said Wangero. "I don't want those. They are stitched
around the borders by machine."

"That'll make them last better," I said.

"That's not the point," said Wangero. "These are all pieces of
270 dresses Grandma used to wear. She did all this stitching by hand.
Imagine!" She held the quilts securely in her arms, stroking them.

"Some of the pieces, like those lavender ones, come from old
clothes her mother handed down to her," I said, moving up to
touch the quilts. Dee (Wangero) moved back just enough so that
I couldn't reach the quilts. They already belonged to her.

"Imagine!" she breathed again, clutching them closely to
her bosom.

"The truth is," I said, "I promised to give them quilts to
Maggie, for when she marries John Thomas."

280 She gasped like a bee had stung her.

"Maggie can't appreciate these quilts!" she said. "She'd
probably be backward enough to put them to everyday use."

"I reckon she would," I said. "God knows I been saving 'em for long enough with nobody using 'em. I hope she will!" I didn't want to bring up how I had offered Dee (Wangero) a quilt when she went away to college. Then she had told me they were old-fashioned, out of style. **L**

"But they're *priceless*!" she was saying now, furiously; for she has a temper. "Maggie would put them on the bed and in five
290 years they'd be in rags. Less than that!"

"She can always make some more," I said. "Maggie knows how to quilt."

Dee (Wangero) looked at me with hatred. "You just will not understand. The point is *these* quilts, these quilts!"

"Well," I said, stumped. "What would *you* do with them?"

"Hang them," she said. As if that was the only thing you *could* do with quilts. **PAUSE & REFLECT**

Maggie by now was standing in the door. I could almost hear the sound her feet made as they scraped over each other.
300 "She can have them, Mama," she said, like somebody used to never winning anything, or having anything reserved for her. "I can 'member Grandma Dee without the quilts."

I looked at her hard. She had filled her bottom lip with checkerberry snuff and it gave her face a kind of dopey, hangdog look. It was Grandma Dee and Big Dee who taught her how to quilt herself. She stood there with her scarred hands hidden in the folds of her skirt. She looked at her sister with something like fear but she wasn't mad at her. This was Maggie's portion. This was the way she knew God to work.
310 When I looked at her like that something hit me in the top of my head and ran down to the soles of my feet. Just like when I'm in church and the spirit of God touches me and I get happy and shout. I did something I never had done before: hugged Maggie to me, then dragged her on into the room, snatched the quilts out of Miss Wangero's hands and dumped them into Maggie's lap. Maggie just sat there on my bed with her mouth open. **M**

L CONFLICT AND CHARACTER
How does the conflict between Dee and her family intensify in lines 278–287?

_____

_____

_____

_____

_____

PAUSE & REFLECT
Why doesn't Dee want Maggie to have the quilts?

_____

_____

_____

_____

_____

_____

M CHARACTER AND CONFLICT
How is the conflict over the quilts resolved?

_____

_____

_____

_____

heritage (hĕr'ĭ-tĭj) *n.* something passed down through generations, such as tradition, values, property

How do Dee and Mama view their **heritage** differently?

_____

_____

_____

"Take one or two of the others," I said to Dee.

But she turned without a word and went out to Hakim-a-barber.

"You just don't understand," she said, as Maggie and I came
320 out to the car.

"What don't I understand?" I wanted to know.

"Your **heritage**," she said. And then she turned to Maggie, kissed her, and said, "You ought to try to make something of yourself, too, Maggie. It's really a new day for us. But from the way you and Mama still live you'd never know it."

She put on some sunglasses that hide everything above the tip of her nose and her chin.

Maggie smiled; maybe at the sunglasses. But a real smile, not scared. After we watched the car dust settle I asked Maggie to
330 bring me a dip of snuff. And then the two of us sat there just enjoying, until it was time to go in the house and go to bed.

Text Analysis: Conflict and Character

The central conflict in "Everyday Use" is resolved at the end of the story. However, the characters are also faced with other minor conflicts—some of which are left unresolved. Identify additional conflicts in the chart below. Then tell whether or not each conflict is resolved. For each conflict that is resolved, explain how.

Description of Conflict	Resolved? If so, how?

Review your notes from "Everyday Use" and your completed conflict chart. Why do you think Alice Walker chooses to end the story with lingering conflicts?

_____

_____

_____

_____

_____

Reading Skill: Make Inferences

Think about what you learned about each character in "Everyday Use." Review the notes you took as you read and write a sentence describing each character in the chart below.

	My Inferences
Dee	
Maggie	
Mama	

What makes something **VALUABLE?**

Why might people disagree over why an object is valuable? Describe different possible reasons for disagreements.

_____

_____

_____

Vocabulary Practice

Write **T** for true or **F** for false for each statement below.

_____ 1. Sneaking around is an example of **furtive** behavior.

_____ 2. When you **recompose** after a traffic accident, you become more upset.

_____ 3. If you believe in a certain group's **doctrine**, you follow their set of rules.

_____ 4. If you deny your **heritage**, you refuse to acknowledge your cultural history.

Academic Vocabulary in Writing

affect	communicate	definite	establish	identify

How does Dee **identify** her cultural heritage in "Everyday Use"? How does Mama? Write a few sentences about each character on the lines below. Use at least one Academic Vocabulary word in your response. Definitions for these terms are listed on page 1.

_____

_____

_____

_____

Assessment Practice

DIRECTIONS Use "Everyday Use" to answer questions 1–4.

1 Which word would Mama use to describe herself?

- (A) tough
- (B) quick-witted
- (C) educated
- (D) self-conscious

2 The most likely cause of Dee's conflict with her family is that —

- (A) she burned down the family house
- (B) she sees herself as better than they are
- (C) Mama refuses to call her by her new name
- (D) Mama has always preferred Maggie to Dee

3 The quilts are valuable to Mama because they —

- (A) are worth a lot of money
- (B) reflect her African heritage
- (C) were made for her by relatives
- (D) remind her of her family history

4 The main conflict of the story is resolved when —

- (A) Dee expresses appreciation for her family home
- (B) Maggie tells Mama that Dee can have the quilts
- (C) Mama takes the quilts from Dee and gives them to Maggie
- (D) Mama tells Dee that Maggie is going to marry John Thomas

To Build a Fire
Short Story by **Jack London**

Should you trust your
INSTINCTS?

Birds build nests. Dogs bury bones. These behaviors are instincts, examples of unlearned, automatic behavior. Do people, like animals, have instincts? If they do, when are they likely to use them? Are a person's instincts as good as, say, a dog's? The story "To Build a Fire" tries to answer these questions.

DISCUSS In a small group, talk about whether or not humans have instincts. When have you used your instincts? List your ideas at left.

Human Instincts

1. *I shiver when I'm cold.*

2. _____

3. _____

4. _____

5. _____

Text Analysis: Setting and Conflict

The time and place of a story is its **setting.** In some stories, the setting can create the conflict the character faces. The setting can even act as the **antagonist,** or opponent, of the main character. In "To Build a Fire," the setting is the Yukon wilderness, and the main character must battle the crippling cold to survive. The chart below lists different ways in which the setting affects the story.

Creates Conflicts Can the man build a fire to warm his frozen limbs? He faces conflicts like this one as he struggles to survive.	**Influences Character** Overconfident and inexperienced in the cold, the man learns a life-or-death lesson.
Helps Create Mood The setting creates a mood of alienation and fear in the face of a natural world that is indifferent.	**Serves as a Symbol** The man's frozen surroundings symbolize death and the indifference of nature to what people want.

Setting in "To Build a Fire"

As you read, notice details about this harsh setting and think about the choices it forces the character to make.

Reading Strategy: Predict

When you **predict**, you use clues in the text to guess what will happen next. Predicting helps you become actively involved in what you are reading and gives you reasons to read on. To make predictions about what will happen in "To Build a Fire," use the following strategies:

- Think about the personality, actions, and thoughts of the main character to help you predict how he will respond to each new situation.

- Note passages of **foreshadowing,** or hints and clues about future plot events.

As you read, you will be prompted to make predictions in a chart like the one shown.

Predictions	Text Clues
The man will …	

Vocabulary in Context

Note: Words are listed in the order in which they appear in the story.

intangible (ĭn-tăn′jə-bəl) *adj.* unable to be perceived with the senses
*He could not describe the reason for his fear—it was **intangible.***

conjectural (kən-jĕk′chər-əl) *adj.* involving guesswork
*The only theories to explain what happened were **conjectural.***

apprehension (ăp′rĭ-hĕn′shən) *n.* fear and worry for the future
*The city expressed **apprehension** that budget constraints would limit their ability to fund new programs.*

reiterate (rē-ĭt′ə-rāt′) *v.* to repeat
*At an audience member's request, the speaker **reiterated** the question.*

smite (smīt) *v.* to inflict a heavy blow on; past tense—**smote** (smōt)
*Unable to open the door, he **smote** it with a sledgehammer.*

imperative (ĭm-pĕr′ə-tĭv) *adj.* urgently necessary
*It is **imperative** that you read the warning labels and closely follow the directions.*

conflagration (kŏn′flə-grā′shən) *n.* a large, destructive fire
*The firefighters fought hopelessly against the **conflagration.***

peremptorily (pə-rĕmp′tə-rə-lē) *adv.* in a commanding way that does not allow for refusal or contradiction
*To avoid confusion and disorder, the principal spoke **peremptorily** as she gave her instructions.*

TO BUILD A FIRE

Short Story by

JACK LONDON

BACKGROUND This story takes place in Canada's Yukon Territory. Jack London grew up in a poor neighborhood in Oakland, California, in the late 1800s. Fascinated by the rags-to-riches stories he heard about people mining gold in the Yukon, he sailed north at age 21. London did not find gold, but he did hear other gold prospectors tell stories about life in frozen northland. Many of London's stories were inspired by those tales and by his own experiences.

Day had broken cold and gray, exceedingly cold and gray, when the man turned aside from the main Yukon trail and climbed the high earth-bank, where a dim and little-travelled trail led eastward through the fat spruce timberland. It was a steep bank, and he paused for breath at the top, excusing the act to himself by looking at his watch. It was nine o'clock. There was no sun nor hint of sun, though there was not a cloud in the sky. It was a clear day, and yet there seemed an **intangible** pall over the face of things, a subtle gloom that made the day dark, and that
10 was due to the absence of sun. This fact did not worry the man. He was used to the lack of sun. It had been days since he had seen the sun, and he knew that a few more days must pass before that cheerful orb, due south, would just peep above the sky line and dip immediately from view.

intangible (ĭn-tăn′jə-bəl) *adj.* unable to be perceived with the senses

The man flung a look back along the way he had come. The
Yukon lay a mile wide and hidden under three feet of ice. On
top of this ice were as many feet of snow. It was all pure white,
rolling in gentle undulations where the ice jams of the freeze-up
had formed. North and south, as far as his eye could see, it was
20 unbroken white, save for a dark hairline that curved and twisted
from around the spruce-covered island to the south, and that
curved and twisted away into the north, where it disappeared
behind another spruce-covered island. This dark hairline was the
trail—the main trail—that led south five hundred miles to the
Chilcoot Pass, Dyea, and salt water; and that led north seventy
miles to Dawson, and still on to the north a thousand miles to
Nulato, and finally to St. Michael, on Bering Sea, a thousand
miles and half a thousand more. Ⓐ

But all this—this mysterious, far-reaching hairline trail,
30 the absence of sun from the sky, the tremendous cold, and the
strangeness and weirdness of it all—made no impression on the
man. It was not because he was long used to it. He was a newcomer
in the land, a *chechaquo*, and this was his first winter. The trouble
with him was that he was without imagination. He was quick and
alert in the things of life, but only in the things, and not in the
significances. Fifty degrees below zero meant eighty-odd degrees
of frost. Such fact impressed him as being cold and uncomfortable,
and that was all. It did not lead him to meditate upon his frailty as
a creature of temperature, and upon man's frailty in general, able
40 only to live within certain narrow limits of heat and cold; and from
there on it did not lead him to the <u>**conjectural**</u> field of immortality
and man's place in the universe. Fifty degrees below zero stood for
a bite of frost that hurt and that must be guarded against by the
use of mittens, ear flaps, warm moccasins, and thick socks. Fifty
degrees below zero was to him just precisely fifty degrees below
zero. That there should be anything more to it than that was a
thought that never entered his head.

As he turned to go, he spat speculatively. There was a sharp,
explosive crackle that startled him. He spat again. And again, in

Monitor Your Comprehension

Ⓐ **SETTING AND CONFLICT**
Reread lines 1–28. Underline
details about the setting. What
mood, or feeling, is created by
this description?

_____

_____

_____

_____

_____

_____

_____

_____

_____

_____

_____

conjectural (kən-jĕk′chər-əl) *adj.*
involving guesswork

What **conjectural** ideas does the
man not think about?

_____

_____

_____

_____

_____

_____

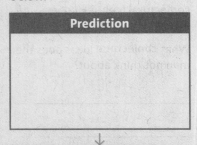

B SETTING AND CONFLICT
Reread lines 48–67. Why does the man spit on the snow? What conflict does the man face?

_____

_____

_____

_____

_____

_____

_____

_____

_____

C PREDICT
Do you think the man will get to camp by six o'clock? Write your prediction and the clues that helped you make it in the chart below.

Prediction

↓

Text Clues

50 the air, before it could fall to the snow, the spittle crackled. He knew that at fifty below spittle crackled on the snow, but this spittle had crackled in the air. Undoubtedly it was colder than fifty below—how much colder he did not know. But the temperature did not matter. He was bound for the old claim[1] on the left fork of Henderson Creek, where the boys were already. They had come over across the divide from the Indian Creek country, while he had come the roundabout way to take a look at the possibilities of getting out logs in the spring from the islands in the Yukon. He would be in to camp by six o'clock; a bit after dark, it was true,
60 but the boys would be there, a fire would be going, and a hot supper would be ready. As for lunch, he pressed his hand against the protruding bundle under his jacket. It was also under his shirt, wrapped up in a handkerchief and lying against the naked skin. It was the only way to keep the biscuits from freezing. He smiled agreeably to himself as he thought of those biscuits, each cut open and sopped in bacon grease, and each enclosing a generous slice of fried bacon. **B**

He plunged in among the big spruce trees. The trail was faint. A foot of snow had fallen since the last sled had passed over,
70 and he was glad he was without a sled, travelling light. In fact, he carried nothing but the lunch wrapped in the handkerchief. He was surprised, however, at the cold. It certainly was cold, he concluded, as he rubbed his numb nose and cheekbones with his mittened hand. He was a warm-whiskered man, but the hair on his face did not protect the high cheek-bones and the eager nose that thrust itself aggressively into the frosty air. **C**

At the man's heels trotted a dog, a big native husky, the proper wolf dog, gray-coated and without any visible or temperamental difference from its brother, the wild wolf. The animal was
80 depressed by the tremendous cold. It knew that it was no time for travelling. Its instinct told it a truer tale than was told to the man by the man's judgment. In reality, it was not merely colder than fifty below zero; it was colder than sixty below, than seventy below. It was seventy-five below zero. Since the freezing

---

1. **claim:** a tract of public land claimed by a homesteader or, as in this case, a miner.

point is thirty-two above zero, it meant that one hundred and seven degrees of frost obtained.[2] The dog did not know anything about thermometers. Possibly in its brain there was no sharp consciousness of a condition of very cold such as was in the man's brain. But the brute had its instinct. It experienced a vague

90 but menacing **apprehension** that subdued it and made it slink along at the man's heels, and that made it question eagerly every unwonted movement of the man as if expecting him to go into camp or to seek shelter somewhere and build a fire. The dog had learned fire, and it wanted fire, or else to burrow under the snow and cuddle its warmth away from the air. **D**

The frozen moisture of its breathing had settled on its fur in a fine powder of frost, and especially were its jowls, muzzle and eyelashes whitened by its crystalled breath. The man's red beard and mustache were likewise frosted, but more solidly, the deposit

100 taking the form of ice and increasing with every warm, moist breath he exhaled. Also, the man was chewing tobacco, and the muzzle of ice held his lips so rigidly that he was unable to clear his chin when he expelled the juice. The result was that a crystal beard of the color and solidity of amber was increasing its length on his chin. If he fell down it would shatter itself, like glass, into brittle fragments. But he did not mind the appendage. It was the penalty all tobacco chewers paid in that country, and he had been out before in two cold snaps. They had not been so cold as this, but by the spirit thermometer[3] at Sixty Mile he knew that they had been

110 registered at fifty below and at fifty-five. **PAUSE & REFLECT**

He held on through the level stretch of woods for several miles, crossed a wide flat . . . and dropped down a bank to the frozen bed of a small stream. This was Henderson Creek, and he knew he was ten miles from the forks. He looked at his watch. It was ten o'clock. He was making four miles an hour, and he calculated that he would arrive at the forks at half-past twelve. He decided to celebrate that event by eating his lunch there.

---

2. **obtained:** existed.

3. **spirit thermometer:** a thermometer in which temperature is indicated by the height of a column of colored alcohol.

apprehension (ăp'rĭ-hĕn'shən) *n.* fear and worry for the future

Why does the dog experience apprehension?

_____

_____

_____

D PREDICT
Reread lines 77–95 and underline the clues that help you predict what the man and the dog will do.

PAUSE & REFLECT
Do you think the man is prepared for the cold? Why or why not?

_____

_____

_____

_____

_____

_____

The dog dropped in again at his heels, with a tail drooping discouragement, as the man swung along the creek bed. The
120 furrow of the old sled trail was plainly visible, but a dozen inches of snow covered the marks of the last runners. In a month no man had come up or down that silent creek. The man held steadily on. He was not much given to thinking, and just then particularly he had nothing to think about save that he would eat lunch at the forks and that at six o'clock he would be in camp with the boys. There was nobody to talk to; and, had there been, speech would have been impossible because of the ice muzzle on his mouth. So he continued monotonously to chew tobacco and to increase the length of his amber beard.

130 Once in a while the thought **reiterated** itself that it was very cold and that he had never experienced such cold. As he walked along he rubbed his cheekbones and nose with the back of his mittened hand. He did this automatically, now and again changing hands. But, rub as he would, the instant he stopped his cheekbones went numb, and the following instant the end of his nose went numb. He was sure to frost his cheeks; he knew that, and experienced a pang of regret that he had not devised a nose strap of the sort Bud wore in cold snaps. Such a strap passed across the cheeks, as well, and saved them. But it didn't matter
140 much, after all. What were frosted cheeks? A bit painful, that was all; they were never serious. **E**

Empty as the man's mind was of thoughts, he was keenly observant, and he noticed the changes in the creek, the curves and bends and timber jams,[4] and always he sharply noted where he placed his feet. Once, coming around a bend he shied abruptly, like a startled horse, curved away from the place where he had been walking, and retreated several paces back along the trail. The creek he knew was frozen clear to the bottom—no creek could contain water in that arctic winter—but he knew also that there
150 were springs that bubbled out from the hillsides and ran along under the snow and on top the ice of the creek. He knew that the coldest snaps never froze these springs, and he knew likewise their

reiterate (rē-ĭt'ə-rāt') v. to repeat

E SETTING AND CONFLICT
Circle details in lines 130–141 that reveal a new problem. How does the man view this complication?

4. **timber jams:** piled-up masses of floating logs and branches.

danger. They were traps. They hid pools of water under the snow that might be three inches deep, or three feet. Sometimes a skin of ice half an inch thick covered them, and in turn was covered by the snow. Sometimes there were alternate layers of water and ice skin, so that when one broke through he kept on breaking through for a while, sometimes wetting himself to the waist.

That was why he had shied in such panic.

160 He had felt the give under his feet and heard the crackle of a snow-hidden ice skin. And to get his feet wet in such a temperature meant trouble and danger. At the very least it meant delay, for he would be forced to stop and build a fire, and under its protection to bare his feet while he dried his socks and moccasins. He stood and studied the creek bed and its banks, and decided that the flow of water came from his right. He reflected awhile, rubbing his nose and cheeks, then skirted to the left, stepping gingerly and testing the footing for each step. Once clear of the danger, he took a fresh chew of tobacco and swung along at 170 his four-mile gait.[5] **F**

In the course of the next two hours he came upon several similar traps. Usually the snow above the hidden pools had a sunken, candied appearance that advertised the danger. Once again, however, he had a close call; and once, suspecting danger, he compelled the dog to go on in front. The dog did not want to go. It hung back until the man shoved it forward, and then it went quickly across the white, unbroken surface. Suddenly it broke through, floundered to one side, and got away to firmer footing. It had wet its forefeet and legs, and almost immediately the water that 180 clung to it turned to ice. It made quick efforts to lick the ice off its legs, then dropped down in the snow and began to bite out the ice that had formed between the toes. This was a matter of instinct. To permit the ice to remain would mean sore feet. It did not know this. It merely obeyed the mysterious prompting that arose from the deep crypts of its being. But the man knew, having achieved a judgment on the subject, and he removed the mitten from his

F PREDICT
What do you think will happen to the man? Underline text clues in lines 142–170 that lead to your prediction.

_____

5. **four-mile gait:** walking pace of four miles per hour.

smite (smīt) *v.* to inflict a heavy blow on; *past tense*—**smote** (smōt)

G SETTING AND CONFLICT
Reread lines 191–214. How does the story's dangerous setting intensify the conflict?

_____

_____

_____

_____

_____

_____

_____

_____

_____

_____

_____

_____

_____

_____

_____

_____

_____

right hand and helped tear out the ice particles. He did not expose his fingers more than a minute, and was astonished at the swift numbness that **smote** them. It certainly was cold. He pulled on the mitten hastily, and beat the hand savagely across his chest.

At twelve o'clock the day was at its brightest. Yet the sun was too far south on its winter journey to clear the horizon. The bulge of the earth intervened between it and Henderson Creek, where the man walked under a clear sky at noon and cast no shadow. At half-past twelve, to the minute, he arrived at the forks of the creek. He was pleased at the speed he had made. If he kept it up, he would certainly be with the boys by six. He unbuttoned his jacket and shirt and drew forth his lunch. The action consumed no more than a quarter of a minute, yet in that brief moment the numbness laid hold of the exposed fingers. He did not put the mitten on, but, instead, struck the fingers a dozen sharp smashes against his leg. Then he sat down on a snow-covered log to eat. The sting that followed upon the striking of his fingers against his leg ceased so quickly that he was startled. He had had no chance to take a bite of biscuit. He struck the fingers repeatedly and returned them to the mitten, baring the other hand for the purpose of eating. He tried to take a mouthful, but the ice muzzle prevented. He had forgotten to build a fire and thaw out. He chuckled at his foolishness, and as he chuckled he noted the numbness creeping into the exposed fingers. Also, he noted that the stinging which had first come to his toes when he sat down was already passing away. He wondered whether the toes were warm or numb. He moved them inside the moccasins and decided that they were numb. **G**

He pulled the mitten on hurriedly and stood up. He was a bit frightened. He stamped up and down until the stinging returned into the feet. It certainly was cold, was his thought. That man from Sulphur Creek had spoken the truth when telling how cold it sometimes got in the country. And he had laughed at him at the time! That showed one must not be too sure of things. There was no mistake about it, it *was* cold. He strode up and down, stamping his feet and threshing his arms, until reassured by the returning warmth. Then he got out matches and proceeded to make a fire. From the under-growth, where high water of the previous spring had lodged a supply of seasoned twigs, he got his firewood. Working carefully from a small beginning, he soon had a roaring fire, over which he thawed the ice from his face and in the protection of which he ate his biscuits. For the moment the cold of space was outwitted. The dog took satisfaction in the fire,

230 stretching out close enough for warmth and far enough away to escape being singed. **PAUSE & REFLECT**

When the man had finished, he filled his pipe and took his comfortable time over a smoke, then he pulled on his mittens, settled the ear flaps of his cap firmly about his ears, and took the creek trail up the left fork. The dog was disappointed and yearned back towards the fire. This man did not know cold. Possibly all the generations of his ancestry had been ignorant of cold, of real cold, of cold one hundred and seven degrees below freezing point. But the dog knew; all its ancestry knew, and it had inherited the

240 knowledge. And it knew that it was not good to walk abroad in such fearful cold. It was the time to lie snug in a hole in the snow and wait for a curtain of cloud to be drawn across the face of outer space whence this cold came. On the other hand, there was no keen intimacy between the dog and the man. The one was the toil slave[6] of the other, and the only caresses it had ever received were the caresses of the whip lash and of harsh and menacing throat sounds that threatened the whip lash. So the dog made no effort to communicate its apprehension to the man. It was not concerned in the welfare of the man; it was for its own sake that

250 it yearned back toward the fire. But the man whistled, and spoke to it with the sound of whip lashes, and the dog swung in at the man's heels and followed after. **H**

The man took a chew of tobacco and proceeded to start a new amber beard. Also, his moist breath quickly powdered with white his mustache, eyebrows, and lashes. There did not seem to be so many springs on the left fork of the Henderson, and for half an

---

6. **toil slave:** a slave who performs hard labor.

PAUSE & REFLECT
How do you think the man feels at this point? Explain.

_____

_____

_____

H PREDICT
Once again, the narrator emphasizes the dog's unwillingness. Underline details in lines 232–252 that stress the severity of the situation. What do you think will happen next?

_____

_____

_____

_____

_____

_____

_____

_____

_____

_____

imperative (ĭm-pĕr′ə-tĭv) *adj.*
urgently necessary

Why is it **imperative** that the
man build another fire?

_____

_____

_____

_____

❶ SETTING AND CONFLICT
Reread lines 277–287. What new
conflict with the setting is the
man experiencing?

_____

_____

_____

_____

_____

_____

_____

hour the man saw no signs of any. And then it happened. At a
place where there were no signs, where the soft, unbroken snow
seemed to advertise solidity beneath, the man broke through.
It was not deep. He wet himself halfway to the knees before he
floundered out to the firm crust. He was angry, and cursed his
luck aloud. He had hoped to get into camp with the boys at six
o'clock, and this would delay him an hour, for he would have to
build a fire and dry out his footgear. This was **imperative** at that
low temperature—he knew that much; and he turned aside to the
bank, which he climbed. On top, tangled in the underbrush about
the trunks of several small spruce trees, was a high-water deposit[7]
of dry firewood—sticks and twigs, principally, but also larger
portions of seasoned branches and fine, dry, last year's grasses. He
threw down several large pieces on top of the snow. This served
for a foundation and prevented the young flame from drowning
itself in the snow it otherwise would melt. The flame he got by
touching a match to a small shred of birch bark that he took from
his pocket. This burned even more readily than paper. Placing it
on the foundation, he fed the young flame with wisps of dry grass
and with the tiniest dry twigs.

He worked slowly and carefully, keenly aware of his danger.
Gradually, as the flame grew stronger, he increased the size of
the twigs with which he fed it. He squatted in the snow, pulling
the twigs out from their entanglement in the brush and feeding
directly to the flame. He knew there must be no failure. When it
is seventy-five below zero, a man must not fail in his first attempt
to build a fire—that is, if his feet are wet. If his feet are dry, and
he fails, he can run along the trail for half a mile and restore his
circulation. But the circulation of wet and freezing feet cannot be
restored by running when it is seventy-five below. No matter how
fast he runs, the wet feet will freeze the harder. **❶**

All this the man knew. The old-timer on Sulphur Creek had
told him about it the previous fall, and now he was appreciating
the advice. Already all sensation had gone out of his feet. To
build the fire he had been forced to remove his mittens, and the

---

7. **high-water deposit:** debris left on the bank of a stream as the water recedes
from its highest level.

fingers had quickly gone numb. His pace of four miles an hour had kept his heart pumping blood to the surface of his body and to all the extremities. But the instant he stopped, the action of the pump eased down. The cold of space smote the unprotected tip of the planet, and he, being on that unprotected tip, received the full force of the blow. The blood of his body recoiled before it. The blood was alive, like the dog, and like the dog it wanted to hide away and cover itself up from the fearful cold. So long as
300 he walked four miles an hour, he pumped the blood, willy-nilly, to the surface; but now it ebbed away and sank down into the recesses of his body. The extremities were the first to feel its absence. His wet feet froze the faster, and his exposed fingers numbed the faster, though they had not yet begun to freeze. Nose and cheeks were already freezing, while the skin of all his body chilled as it lost its blood.

But he was safe. Toes and nose and cheeks would be only touched by the frost, for the fire was beginning to burn with strength. He was feeding it with twigs the size of his finger.
310 In another minute he would be able to feed it with branches the size of his wrist, and then he could remove his wet footgear, and, while it dried, he could keep his naked feet warm by the fire, rubbing them at first, of course, with snow. The fire was a success. He was safe. He remembered the advice of the old-timer on Sulphur Creek, and smiled. The old-timer had been very serious in laying down the law that no man must travel alone in the Klondike after fifty below. Well, here he was; he had had the accident; he was alone; and he had saved himself. Those old-timers were rather womanish, some of them, he thought. All a man had to do was to keep his head, and
320 and he was all right. Any man who was a man could travel alone. But it was surprising, the rapidity with which his cheeks and nose were freezing. And he had not thought his fingers could go lifeless in so short a time. Lifeless they were, for he could scarcely make them move together to grip a twig, and they seemed remote from his body and from him. When he touched a twig, he had to look and see whether or not he had hold of it. The wires were pretty well down between him and his finger ends. **J**

J PREDICT
Building the first fire soothed the man's fears about his situation. Notice how the details in lines 307–320 again soothe his fears and remind him of the man at Sulphur Creek again. The first fire was followed by a disaster. What do you think will happen this time? Circle clues in the text, and then write your prediction below.

_____

_____

_____

_____

_____

_____

_____

_____

conflagration (kŏn′flə-grā′shən)
n. a large, destructive fire

Ⓚ SETTING AND CONFLICT
How does the man further
complicate his conflict with the
setting?

_____

_____

_____

_____

_____

_____

Ⓛ PREDICT
Do you think the man will
be able to build a fire quickly
enough to save himself?
Underline clues in lines 351–360,
and then write your prediction
below.

_____

_____

_____

_____

_____

All of which counted for little. There was the fire, snapping
and crackling and promising life with every dancing flame. He
330 started to untie his moccasins. They were coated with ice; the
thick German socks were like sheaths of iron halfway to the
knees; and the moccasin strings were like rods of steel all twisted
and knotted as by some **conflagration**. For a moment he tugged
with his numb fingers, then, realizing the folly of it, he drew his
sheath knife.

But before he could cut the strings, it happened. It was his
own fault or, rather, his mistake. He should not have built the
fire under the spruce tree. He should have built it in the open.
But it had been easier to pull the twigs from the brush and drop
340 them directly on the fire. Now the tree under which he had done
this carried a weight of snow on its boughs. No wind had blown
for weeks, and each bough was full freighted. Each time he had
pulled a twig he had communicated a slight agitation to the
tree—an imperceptible agitation, so far as he was concerned, but
an agitation sufficient to bring about the disaster. High up in the
tree one bough capsized its load of snow. This fell on the boughs
beneath, capsizing them. This process continued, spreading out
and involving the whole tree. It grew like an avalanche, and it
descended upon the man and the fire, and the fire was blotted out!
350 Where it had burned was a mantle of fresh and disordered snow. Ⓚ

The man was shocked. It was as though he had just heard his
own sentence of death. For a moment he sat and stared at the
spot where the fire had been. Then he grew very calm. Perhaps
the old-timer on Sulphur Creek was right. If he had only had a
trail mate he would have been in no danger now. The trail mate
could have built the fire. Well, it was up to him to build the fire
over again, and this second time there must be no failure. Even if
he succeeded, he would most likely lose some toes. His feet must
be badly frozen by now, and there would be some time before the
360 second fire was ready. Ⓛ

Such were his thoughts, but he did not sit and think them. He
was busy all the time they were passing through his mind. He

made a new foundation for a fire, this time in the open, where no treacherous tree could blot it out. Next he gathered dry grasses and tiny twigs from the high-water flotsam. He could not bring his fingers together to pull them out, but he was able to gather them by the handful. In this way he got many rotten twigs and bits of green moss that were undesirable, but it was the best he could do. He worked methodically, even collecting an armful
370 of the larger branches to be used later when the fire gathered strength. And all the while the dog sat and watched him, a certain wistfulness in its eyes, for it looked upon him as the fire provider, and the fire was slow in coming.

When all was ready, the man reached in his pocket for a second piece of birch bark. He knew the bark was there, and though he could not feel it with his fingers, he could hear its crisp rustling as he fumbled for it. Try as he would, he could not clutch hold of it. And all the time, in his consciousness, was the knowledge that each instant his feet were freezing. This thought tended to put
380 him in a panic, but he fought against it and kept calm.

He pulled on his mittens with his teeth, and threshed his arms back and forth, beating his hands with all his might against his sides. He did this sitting down, and he stood up to do it; and all the while the dog sat in the snow, its wolf brush of a tail curled around warmly over its forefeet, its sharp wolf ears pricked forward intently as it watched the man. And the man, as he beat and threshed with his arms and hands, felt a great surge of envy as he regarded the creature that was warm and secure in its natural covering. **M**

After a time he was aware of the first faraway signals of
390 sensations in his beaten fingers. The faint tingling grew stronger till it evolved into a stinging ache that was excruciating, but which the man hailed with satisfaction. He stripped the mitten from his right hand and fetched forth the birch bark. The exposed fingers were quickly going numb again. Next he brought out his bunch of sulphur matches. But the tremendous cold had already driven the life out of his fingers. In his effort to separate one match from the others, the whole bunch fell into the snow. He tried to pick it out

M SETTING AND CONFLICT
How does the man's situation become more desperate in lines 374–388?

_____

_____

_____

_____

_____

_____

_____

_____

Ⓝ PREDICT

Reread lines 389–420. Underline events that complicate the man's attempts to light the fire. What do you think will happen next?

_____

_____

_____

_____

_____

_____

_____

_____

_____

_____

_____

_____

_____

_____

_____

_____

_____

_____

of the snow, but failed. The dead fingers could neither clutch nor touch. He was very careful. He drove the thought of his freezing
400 feet, and nose, and cheeks, out of his mind, devoting his whole soul to the matches. He watched, using the sense of vision in place of that of touch, and when he saw his fingers on each side the bunch, he closed them—that is, he willed to close them, for the wires were down, and the fingers did not obey. He pulled the mitten on the right hand, and beat it fiercely against his knee. Then, with both mittened hands, he scooped the bunch of matches, along with much snow, into his lap. Yet he was no better off.

After some manipulation he managed to get the bunch between the heels of his mittened hands. In this fashion he carried
410 it to his mouth. The ice crackled and snapped when by a violent effort he opened his mouth. He drew the lower jaw in, curled the upper lip out of the way and scraped the bunch with his upper teeth in order to separate a match. He succeeded in getting one, which he dropped on his lap. He was no better off. He could not pick it up. Then he devised a way. He picked it up in his teeth and scratched it on his leg. Twenty times he scratched before he succeeded in lighting it. As it flamed he held it with his teeth to the birch bark. But the burning brimstone[8] went up his nostrils and into his lungs, causing him to cough spasmodically. The
420 match fell into the snow and went out. Ⓝ

The old-timer on Sulphur Creek was right, he thought in the moment of controlled despair that ensued: after fifty below, a man should travel with a partner. He beat his hands, but failed in exciting any sensation. Suddenly he bared both hands, removing the mittens with his teeth. He caught the whole bunch between the heels of his hands. His arm muscles not being frozen enabled him to press the hand heels tightly against the matches. Then he scratched the bunch along his leg. It flared into flame, seventy sulphur matches at once! There was no wind to blow them out.
430 He kept his head to one side to escape the strangling fumes, and held the blazing bunch to the birch bark. As he so held it, he became aware of sensation in his hand. His flesh was burning.

_____

8. **brimstone:** sulfur, a chemical used in match heads.

He could smell it. Deep down below the surface he could feel it. The sensation developed into pain that grew acute. And still he endured it, holding the flame of the matches clumsily to the bark that would not light readily because his own burning hands were in the way, absorbing most of the flame.

At last, when he could endure no more, he jerked his hands apart. The blazing matches fell sizzling into the snow, but the birch bark was alight. He began laying dry grasses and the tiniest twigs on the flame. He could not pick and choose, for he had to lift the fuel between the heels of his hands. Small pieces of rotten wood and green moss clung to the twigs, and he bit them off as well as he could with his teeth. He cherished[9] the flame carefully and awkwardly. It meant life, and it must not perish. The withdrawal of blood from the surface of his body now made him begin to shiver, and he grew more awkward. A large piece of green moss fell squarely on the little fire. He tried to poke it out with his fingers, but his shivering frame made him poke too far, and he disrupted the nucleus of the little fire, the burning grasses and the tiny twigs separating and scattering. He tried to poke them together again, but in spite of the tenseness of the effort, his shivering got away with him, and the twigs were hopelessly scattered. Each twig gushed a puff of smoke and went out. The fire provider had failed. As he looked apathetically about him, his eyes chanced on the dog, sitting across the ruins of the fire from him, in the snow, making restless, hunching movements, slightly lifting one forefoot and then the other, shifting its weight back and forth on them with wistful eagerness. ◉

The sight of the dog put a wild idea into his head. He remembered the tale of the man, caught in a blizzard, who killed a steer and crawled inside the carcass, and so was saved. He would kill the dog and bury his hands in the warm body until the numbness went out of them. Then he could build another fire. He spoke to the dog, calling it to him; but in his voice was a strange note of fear that frightened the animal, who had never known the man to speak in such a way before. Something was

◎ **PREDICT**
As his situation becomes more desperate, it seems as if the man's only hope for survival would involve someone finding and helping him. Based on the clues in the text, what are the chances of this happening?

_____

_____

_____

_____

_____

_____

_____

_____

_____

_____

_____

---

9. **cherished:** tended; guarded.

the matter, and its suspicious nature sensed danger—it knew
not what danger, but somewhere, somehow, in its brain arose an
470 apprehension of the man. It flattened its ears down at the sound
of the man's voice, and its restless, hunching movements and the
liftings and shiftings of its forefeet became more pronounced; but
it would not come to the man. He got on his hands and knees
and crawled toward the dog. This unusual posture again excited
suspicion, and the animal sidled mincingly away. **P**

The man sat up in the snow for a moment and struggled for
calmness. Then he pulled on his mittens, by means of his teeth,
and got upon his feet. He glanced down at first in order to assure
himself that he was really standing up, for the absence of sensation
480 in his feet left him unrelated to the earth. His erect position in
itself started to drive the webs of suspicion from the dog's mind;
and when he spoke **peremptorily**, with the sound of whip lashes
in his voice, the dog rendered its customary allegiance and came
to him. As it came within reaching distance, the man lost his
control. His arms flashed out to the dog, and he experienced
genuine surprise when he discovered that his hands could not
clutch, that there was neither bend nor feeling in his fingers. He
had forgotten for the moment that they were frozen and that they
were freezing more and more. All this happened quickly, and
490 before the animal could get away, he encircled its body with his
arms. He sat down in the snow, and in this fashion held the dog,
while it snarled and whined and struggled.

But it was all he could do, hold its body encircled in his arms
and sit there. He realized that he could not kill the dog. There was

no way to do it. With his helpless hands he could neither draw nor hold his sheath knife nor throttle the animal. He released it, and it plunged wildly away, with tail between its legs, and still snarling. It halted forty feet away and surveyed him curiously, with ears sharply pricked forward.

500   The man looked down at his hands in order to locate them, and found them hanging on the ends of his arms. It struck him as curious that one should have to use his eyes in order to find out where his hands were. He began threshing his arms back and forth, beating the mittened hands against his sides. He did this for five minutes, violently, and his heart pumped enough blood up to the surface to put a stop to his shivering. But no sensation was aroused in the hands. He had an impression that they hung like weights on the ends of his arms, but when he tried to run the impression down, he could not find it. **PAUSE & REFLECT**

510   A certain fear of death, dull and oppressive, came to him. This fear quickly became poignant as he realized that it was no longer a mere matter of freezing his fingers and toes, or of losing his hands and feet, but that it was a matter of life and death with the chances against him. This threw him into a panic, and he turned and ran along the old, dim trail. The dog joined in behind and kept up with him. He ran blindly, without intention, in fear such as he had never known in his life. Slowly, as he plowed and floundered through the snow, he began to see things again—the banks of the creek, the old timber jams, the leafless aspens, and
520 the sky. The running made him feel better. He did not shiver.

PAUSE & REFLECT
How do you think the man feels at this point? Explain.

_____

_____

_____

_____

_____

_____

_____

Q SETTING AND CONFLICT
Reread lines 510–530. Notice the thoughts and fears that come into the man's head. What has his struggle now become?

_____

_____

_____

_____

_____

_____

R SETTING AND CONFLICT
Why does the man continue to run even though he knows he lacks the endurance to reach camp?

_____

_____

_____

_____

_____

_____

Maybe, if he ran on, his feet would thaw out; and, anyway, if he ran far enough, he would reach camp and the boys. Without doubt he would lose some fingers and toes and some of his face; but the boys would take care of him, and save the rest of him when he got there. And at the same time there was another thought in his mind that said he would never get to the camp and the boys; that he would soon be stiff and dead. This thought he kept in the background and refused to consider. Sometimes it pushed itself forward and demanded to be heard, but he thrust it
530 back and strove to think of other things. **Q**

It struck him as curious that he could run at all on feet so frozen that he could not feel them when they struck the earth and took the weight of his body. He seemed to himself to skim along above the surface, and to have no connection with the earth. Somewhere he had once seen a winged Mercury,[10] and he wondered if Mercury felt as he felt when skimming over the earth.

His theory of running until he reached camp and the boys had one flaw in it: he lacked the endurance. Several times he stumbled, and finally he tottered, crumpled up, and fell. When he tried to
540 rise, he failed. He must sit and rest, he decided, and next time he would merely walk and keep on going. As he sat and regained his breath, he noted that he was feeling quite warm and comfortable. He was not shivering, and it even seemed that a warm glow had come to his chest and trunk. And yet, when he touched his nose or cheeks, there was no sensation. Running would not thaw them out. Nor would it thaw out his hands and feet. Then the thought came to him that the frozen portions of his body must be extending. He tried to keep this thought down, to forget it, to think of something else; he was aware of the panicky feeling that it caused, and he was
550 afraid of the panic. But the thought asserted itself, and persisted, until it produced a vision of his body totally frozen. This was too much, and he made another wild run along the trail. Once he slowed down to a walk, but the thought of the freezing extending itself made him run again. **R**

---

10. **Mercury:** the messenger of the gods in Roman mythology, who flew about by means of wings on his helmet and sandals.

And all the time the dog ran with him, at his heels. When he fell down a second time, it curled its tail over its forefeet and sat in front of him, facing him, curiously eager and intent. The warmth and security of the animal angered him, and he cursed it till it flattened down its ears appeasingly. This time the shivering came

560 more quickly upon the man. He was losing in his battle with the frost. It was creeping into his body from all sides. The thought of it drove him on, but he ran no more than a hundred feet, when he staggered and pitched headlong. It was his last panic. When he had recovered his breath and control, he sat up and entertained in his mind the conception of meeting death with dignity. However, the conception did not come to him in such terms. His idea of it was that he had been making a fool of himself, running around like a chicken with its head cut off—such was the simile that occurred to him. Well, he was bound to freeze anyway, and he

570 might as well take it decently. With this newfound peace of mind came the first glimmerings of drowsiness. A good idea, he thought, to sleep off to death. It was like taking an anesthetic. Freezing was not so bad as people thought. There were lots worse ways to die. **PAUSE & REFLECT**

He pictured the boys finding his body the next day. Suddenly he found himself with them, coming along the trail and looking for himself. And, still with them, he came around a turn in the trail and found himself lying in the snow. He did not belong with himself any more, for even then he was out of himself, standing

580 with the boys and looking at himself in the snow. It certainly was cold, was his thought. When he got back to the States he could tell the folks what real cold was. He drifted on from this to a vision of the old-timer on Sulphur Creek. He could see him quite clearly, warm and comfortable, and smoking a pipe.

"You were right, old hoss;[11] you were right," the man mumbled to the old-timer of Sulphur Creek.

PAUSE & REFLECT
What has the man decided to do? What does this tell you about his character?

---

11. **old hoss:** old horse—here used as an affectionate term of address.

⑤ PREDICT

Do you think the dog will meet the same fate as the man? Why or why not?

_____

_____

_____

_____

_____

_____

_____

Then the man drowsed off into what seemed to him the most comfortable and satisfying sleep he had ever known. The dog sat facing him and waiting. The brief day drew to a close in a long, slow twilight. There were no signs of a fire to be made, and, besides, never in the dog's experience had it known a man to sit like that in the snow and make no fire. As the twilight drew on, its eager yearning for the fire mastered it, and with a great lifting and shifting of forefeet, it whined softly, then flattened its ears down in anticipation of being chidden by the man. But the man remained silent. Later the dog whined loudly. And still later it crept close to the man and caught the scent of death. This made the animal bristle and back away. A little longer it delayed, howling under the stars that leaped and danced and shone brightly in the cold sky. Then it turned and trotted up the trail in the direction of the camp it knew, where there were other food providers and fire providers. **⑤**

Text Analysis: Setting and Conflict

The main character of "To Build a Fire" makes a number of decisions that intensify his conflict with the natural setting. In the chart below, list decisions he made and tell how the story's outcome may have been different if he had made different choices.

Decision	Possible Different Outcome

Which decision do you think was the most crucial in determining the man's fate? Explain.

_____

_____

_____

_____

_____

Reading Strategy: Predict

Look back at the predictions you made as you read. Which predictions were correct? What clues helped you guess correctly or misled you?

Correct Predictions:	Incorrect Predictions:
Clues:	Clues:

Should you trust your INSTINCTS?

Did the man's personality lead him to ignore instincts that could have saved his life? Give details from the story in your answer.

_____

_____

_____

Vocabulary Practice

Decide whether the words in each pair are synonyms (words with similar meanings) or antonyms (words with opposite meanings). Write **A** if they are antonyms or **S** if they are synonyms.

_____ 1. intangible/touchable

_____ 2. conjectural/theorized

_____ 3. apprehension/anxiety

_____ 4. reiterate/restate

_____ 5. smite/caress

_____ 6. imperative/needless

_____ 7. conflagration/blaze

_____ 8. peremptorily/hesitantly

Academic Vocabulary in Writing

affect	communicate	definite	establish	identify

At what point in the story do you think the man's fate became **definite?** Describe when you realized the man would certainly not survive, using at least one Academic Vocabulary word in your answer. Definitions for these terms are listed on page 1.

_____

_____

_____

Assessment Practice

DIRECTIONS Use "To Build a Fire" to answer questions 1–4.

1 Which detail from lines 1–14 suggests how the setting will act as an opponent of the man?
- (A) "exceedingly cold"
- (B) "high earth-bank"
- (C) "not a cloud in the sky"
- (D) "cheerful orb"

2 The man is traveling alone because —
- (A) he is heeding the advice of the man from Sulphur Creek
- (B) he had a companion with him who died in an avalanche
- (C) he decided to take a different route to explore places for logging
- (D) he could not convince anyone to travel the Yukon at this time of year

3 Which word best characterizes the man's attitude toward his conflict in lines 317–320?
- (A) afraid
- (B) enthusiastic
- (C) desperate
- (D) overconfident

4 The climax, or turning point, of the man's conflict with the setting occurs when —
- (A) he freezes to death
- (B) he is able to build a fire
- (C) the snow puts out his fire
- (D) the dog breaks through the ice

UNIT 2

Word Portraits

CHARACTER DEVELOPMENT

Be sure to read the Text Analysis Workshop on pp. 176–181 in *Holt McDougal Literature*.

Academic Vocabulary for Unit 2

Preview the following Academic Vocabulary words. You will encounter these words as you work through this book and will use them as you write and talk about the selections in the unit.

---

dynamic (dī nam′ ik) *adj.* energetic; changing; in motion
*The actor played a **dynamic** character full of life and laughter.*

individual (ĭn′də-vĭj′ōō-əl) *adj.* existing as a single, separate thing or being
*Each **individual** action of the character tells readers something new about her.*

motive (mō′tĭv) *n.* incentive; inner drive or desire that causes someone to act
*His desire to get into college provided a **motive** for studying hard in high school.*

seek (sēk) *v.* to look for or try to find
*Throughout the story, the main character **seeks** answers to confusing questions.*

undergo (ŭn′dər-gō′) *v.* to endure, go through, or experience
*In books, characters often **undergo** difficult challenges.*

Think of a book you've read or a movie you've seen with **dynamic** characters who overcome challenges. Write a few sentences explaining what motivated the individual characters. Why were they believable? Include at least two Academic Vocabulary words in your response.

_____

_____

_____

The Possibility of Evil
Short Story by **Shirley Jackson**

How good are you at **JUDGING** people?

The main character in "The Possibility of Evil" believes she can read into the hearts of those around her. Do you think it is so easy to judge people? Are you confident that you would recognize evil if you came face to face with it?

DISCUSS With a group of classmates, fill in the chart at left with words and ideas that you associate with the word *evil*. Then use the ideas you have brainstormed to create a definition of the word.

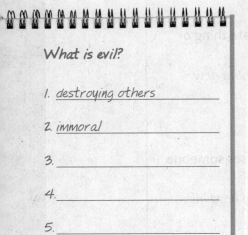

What is evil?

1. *destroying others*
2. *immoral*
3. _____
4. _____
5. _____

Text Analysis: Character Motivation

What might prompt a character in a book to steal a large sum of money? The character might steal money to feed his family or to achieve a lifelong dream of wealth. How do these reasons affect your opinion of him? When you consider the reasons behind a character's actions, you are learning about his or her **motivation.**

Possible motivation	
Need for money	→

Possible motivation	
Desire for wealth	→

Resulting Action

Sometimes, the narrator of a story will make direct comments about a character's motivation. However, in most cases you must figure out motivation by looking for clues and details such as

- the character's actions, thoughts, and values
- how other characters react to him or her
- your own insights into human behavior

In "The Possibility of Evil," Miss Strangeworth believes she acts in response to a **moral dilemma:** a difficult choice between two options, one of which violates her moral principles. A moral dilemma is often a choice between what is considered right and wrong. As you read, think about whether Miss Strangeworth is *really* motivated by moral principles, or if she has other reasons for her actions.

Reading Skill: Make Inferences

When you **make inferences** about a character, you apply your knowledge of human behavior to clues provided in the text. Learning to make inferences comes in handy when you are trying to figure out why a character acts a certain way. For example, if a character crosses to the other side of the street as another character approaches, you may infer that he or she doesn't like the other character.

As you read "The Possibility of Evil," you will be prompted to make inferences about the thoughts and feelings of characters. See the example below.

Details from Story	Inferences
After Tommy began working at the grocery, Miss Strangeworth called him Mr. Lewis.	She no longer thinks of Mr. Lewis as her friend or equal.

Vocabulary in Context

Note: Words are listed in the order in which they appear in the story.

infatuated (ĭn-făch′ōō-ā′tĭd) *adj.* intensely fond
*The child was **infatuated** with the television show and wanted to watch it every day.*

rapt (răpt) *adj.* fully absorbed; entranced
*The audience gave **rapt** attention to the performance of the play.*

negotiable (nĭ-gō′shə-bəl) *adj.* able to be bargained with
*Which terms of the contract are **negotiable**?*

degraded (dĭ-grā′dĭd) *adj.* corrupted, depraved
*The criminal's **degraded** behavior included lying and stealing.*

translucent (trăns-lōō′sənt) *adj.* allowing light to shine through
*The window curtains were **translucent** and allowed the sunshine into the room.*

reprehensible (rĕp′rĭ-hĕn′sə-bəl) *adj.* deserving blame and criticism
*The **reprehensible** actions of the politician were reported in the newspaper.*

Vocabulary Practice

Complete each phrase with a vocabulary word. Use the definitions above and context clues in the phrases.

1. stared with _____ attention

2. _____ with the hero of the novel

3. could almost see through the _____ bowl

4. _____ by trouble-seeking friends

5. a _____ act that deserves punishment

6. a decision that isn't _____

SET A PURPOSE FOR READING

As you read "The Possibility of Evil," look for the characters and events that explain the story's title.

THE POSSIBILITY *of* Evil

Short Story by
SHIRLEY JACKSON

BACKGROUND "The Possibility of Evil" and many of Shirley Jackson's other stories are set in small American towns that seem peaceful and friendly until their darker sides are revealed. The idea that ordinary humans are capable of great evil is a recurring theme in Jackson's writing.

Ⓐ MAKE INFERENCES
What inferences can you make about the type of town described in lines 1–6?

_____

_____

_____

_____

_____

_____

_____

Miss Adela Strangeworth stepped daintily along Main Street on her way to the grocery. The sun was shining, the air was fresh and clear after the night's heavy rain, and everything in Miss Strangeworth's little town looked washed and bright. Miss Strangeworth took deep breaths, and thought that there was nothing in the world like a fragrant summer day. Ⓐ

She knew everyone in town, of course; she was fond of telling strangers—tourists who sometimes passed through the town and stopped to admire Miss Strangeworth's roses—that she had
10 never spent more than a day outside this town in all her long life. She was seventy-one, Miss Strangeworth told the tourists, with a pretty little dimple showing by her lip, and she sometimes found herself thinking that the town belonged to her. "My grandfather built the first house on Pleasant Street," she would say, opening her blue eyes wide with the wonder of it. "This house, right here.

My family has lived here for better than a hundred years. My grandmother planted these roses, and my mother tended them, just as I do. I've watched my town grow; I can remember when Mr. Lewis, Senior, opened the grocery store, and the year the river
20 flooded out the shanties[1] on the low road, and the excitement when some young folks wanted to move the park over to the space in front of where the new post office is today. They wanted to put up a statue of Ethan Allen"[2]—Miss Strangeworth would frown a little and sound stern—"but it should have been a statue of my grandfather. There wouldn't have been a town here at all if it hadn't been for my grandfather and the lumber mill." **B**

Miss Strangeworth never gave away any of her roses, although the tourists often asked her. The roses belonged on Pleasant Street, and it bothered Miss Strangeworth to think of people
30 wanting to carry them away, to take them into strange towns and down strange streets. When the new minister came, and the ladies were gathering flowers to decorate the church, Miss Strangeworth sent over a great basket of gladioli; when she picked the roses at all, she set them in bowls and vases around the inside of the house her grandfather had built.

Walking down Main Street on a summer morning, Miss Strangeworth had to stop every minute or so to say good morning to someone or to ask after someone's health. When she came into the grocery, half a dozen people turned away from the shelves and
40 the counters to wave at her or call out good morning. **C**

"And good morning to you, too, Mr. Lewis," Miss Strangeworth said at last. The Lewis family had been in the town almost as long as the Strangeworths; but the day young Lewis left high school and went to work in the grocery, Miss Strangeworth had stopped calling him Tommy and started calling him Mr. Lewis, and he had stopped calling her Addie and started calling her Miss Strangeworth. They had been in high school together, and had gone to picnics together, and to high school dances and basketball

---

1. **shanties** (shăn′tēz): roughly built cabins; shacks.
2. **Ethan Allen:** a Revolutionary War hero who led a group of soldiers, called the Green Mountain Boys, from what is now Vermont.

THE POSSIBILITY OF EVIL 61

B MAKE INFERENCES
Reread lines 7–26. How does Miss Strangeworth feel about the contribution her family has made to the town? Underline the details that tell you this.

_____

_____

_____

_____

_____

_____

_____

_____

_____

_____

_____

C CHARACTER MOTIVATION
Why does Miss Strangeworth take time to greet so many people?

_____

_____

_____

_____

_____

games; but now Mr. Lewis was behind the counter in the grocery,
50 and Miss Strangeworth was living alone in the Strangeworth house
on Pleasant Street.

"Good morning," Mr. Lewis said, and added politely,
"lovely day."

"It is a very nice day," Miss Strangeworth said as though she
had only just decided that it would do after all. "I would like
a chop, please, Mr. Lewis, a small, lean veal chop. Are those
strawberries from Arthur Parker's garden? They're early this year."

"He brought them in this morning," Mr. Lewis said.

"I shall have a box," Miss Strangeworth said. Mr. Lewis looked
60 worried, she thought, and for a minute she hesitated, but then she
decided that he surely could not be worried over the strawberries.
He looked very tired indeed. He was usually so chipper, Miss
Strangeworth thought, and almost commented, but it was far too
personal a subject to be introduced to Mr. Lewis, the grocer, so
she only said, "And a can of cat food and, I think, a tomato."

Silently, Mr. Lewis assembled her order on the counter and
waited. Miss Strangeworth looked at him curiously and then said,
"It's Tuesday, Mr. Lewis. You forgot to remind me."

"Did I? Sorry."

70 "Imagine your forgetting that I always buy my tea on Tuesday,"
Miss Strangeworth said gently. "A quarter pound of tea, please,
Mr. Lewis."

"Is that all, Miss Strangeworth?"

"Yes thank you, Mr. Lewis. Such a lovely day, isn't it?"

"Lovely," Mr. Lewis said.

Miss Strangeworth moved slightly to make room for Mrs.
Harper at the counter. "Morning, Adela," Mrs. Harper said,
and Miss Strangeworth said, "Good morning, Martha."

PAUSE & REFLECT

"Lovely day," Mrs. Harper said, and Miss Strangeworth said,
80 "Yes, lovely," and Mr. Lewis, under Mrs. Harper's glance, nodded.

PAUSE & REFLECT
Reread lines 52–78. What does
Miss Strangeworth notice about
Mr. Lewis?

_____

_____

_____

_____

_____

_____

_____

_____

_____

_____

_____

_____

_____

_____

_____

_____

"Ran out of sugar for my cake frosting," Mrs. Harper explained. Her hand shook slightly as she opened her pocketbook. Miss Strangeworth wondered, glancing at her quickly, if she had been taking proper care of herself. Martha Harper was not as young as she used to be, Miss Strangeworth thought. She probably could use a good, strong tonic.[3]

"Martha," she said, "you don't look well."

"I'm perfectly all right," Mrs. Harper said shortly. She handed her money to Mr. Lewis, took her change and her sugar, and went
90 out without speaking again. Looking after her, Miss Strangeworth shook her head slightly. Martha definitely did *not* look well. **D**

Carrying her little bag of groceries, Miss Strangeworth came out of the store into the bright sunlight and stopped to smile down on the Crane baby. Don and Helen Crane were really the two most **infatuated** young parents she had ever known, she thought indulgently, looking at the delicately embroidered baby cap and the lace-edged carriage cover.

"That little girl is going to grow up expecting luxury all her life," she said to Helen Crane.
100 Helen laughed. "That's the way we want her to feel," she said. "Like a princess."

"A princess can be a lot of trouble sometimes," Miss Strangeworth said dryly. "How old is her highness now?"

"Six months next Tuesday," Helen Crane said, looking down with **rapt** wonder at her child. "I've been worrying, though, about her. Don't you think she ought to move around more? Try to sit up, for instance?"

"For plain and fancy[4] worrying," Miss Strangeworth said, amused, "give me a new mother every time."
110 "She just seems—slow," Helen Crane said.

"Nonsense. All babies are different. Some of them develop much more quickly than others."

"That's what my mother says." Helen Crane laughed, looking a little bit ashamed. **E**

---

3. **tonic:** a medicine for restoring and energizing the body.
4. **plain and fancy:** every kind of.

D MAKE INFERENCES
What can you infer from the way Mrs. Harper reacts to Miss Strangeworth's comment?

_____

_____

_____

_____

_____

infatuated (ĭn-făch′ōō-ā′tĭd) *adj.* intensely fond

Underline the details in lines 92–101 that show that Don and Helen Crane are **infatuated** with their baby.

rapt (răpt) *adj.* fully absorbed; entranced

E CHARACTER MOTIVATION
Reread lines 100–114. Why does Helen Crane speak about her worries to Miss Strangeworth?

_____

_____

_____

_____

_____

PAUSE & REFLECT

Reread lines 102–131. Does Miss Strangeworth seem like a reasonable person? Explain your answer.

_____

_____

_____

_____

_____

_____

_____

_____

_____

_____

_____

_____

_____

_____

_____

"I suppose you've got young Don all upset about the fact that his daughter is already six months old and hasn't yet begun to learn to dance?"

"I haven't mentioned it to him. I suppose she's just so precious that I worry about her all the time."

"Well, apologize to her right now," Miss Strangeworth said. "*She* is probably worrying about why you keep jumping around all the time." Smiling to herself and shaking her old head, she went on down the sunny street, stopping once to ask little Billy Moore why he wasn't out riding in his daddy's shiny new car, and talking for a few minutes outside the library with Miss Chandler, the librarian, about the new novels to be ordered, and paid for by the annual library appropriation. Miss Chandler seemed absentminded and very much as though she were thinking about something else. Miss Strangeworth noticed that Miss Chandler had not taken much trouble with her hair that morning, and sighed. Miss Strangeworth hated sloppiness. **PAUSE & REFLECT**

Many people seemed disturbed recently, Miss Strangeworth thought. Only yesterday the Stewarts' fifteen-year-old Linda had run crying down her own front walk and all the way to school, not caring who saw her. People around town thought she might have had a fight with the Harris boy, but they showed up together at the soda shop after school as usual, both of them looking grim and bleak. Trouble at home, people concluded, and sighed over the problems of trying to raise kids right these days.

From halfway down the block Miss Strangeworth could catch the heavy scent of her roses, and she moved a little more quickly. The perfume of roses meant home, and home meant the Strangeworth House on Pleasant Street. Miss Strangeworth stopped at her own front gate, as she always did, and looked with deep pleasure at her house, with the red and pink and white roses

massed along the narrow lawn, and the rambler[5] going up along the porch; and the neat, the unbelievably trim lines of the house itself, with its slimness and its washed white look. Every window sparkled, every curtain hung stiff and straight, and even the

150 stones of the front walk were swept and clear. People around town wondered how old Miss Strangeworth managed to keep the house looking the way it did, and there was a legend about a tourist once mistaking it for the local museum and going all through the place without finding out about his mistake. But the town was proud of Miss Strangeworth and her roses and her house. They had all grown together. **F**

Miss Strangeworth went up her front steps, unlocked her front door with her key, and went into the kitchen to put away her groceries. She debated having a cup of tea and then decided that

160 it was too close to midday dinnertime; she would not have the appetite for her little chop if she had tea now. Instead she went into the light, lovely sitting room, which still glowed from the hands of her mother and her grandmother, who had covered the chairs with bright chintz[6] and hung the curtains. All the furniture was spare and shining, and the round hooked rugs on the floor had been the work of Miss Strangeworth's grandmother and her mother. Miss Strangeworth had put a bowl of her red roses on the low table before the window, and the room was full of their scent.

Miss Strangeworth went to the narrow desk in the corner,

170 and unlocked it with her key. She never knew when she might feel like writing letters, so she kept her notepaper inside, and the desk locked. Miss Strangeworth's usual stationery was heavy and cream-colored, with "Strangeworth House" engraved across the top, but, when she felt like writing her other letters, Miss Strangeworth used a pad of various-colored paper, bought from the local newspaper shop. It was almost a town joke, that colored paper, layered in pink and green and blue and yellow; everyone in town bought it and used it for odd, informal notes

F MAKE INFERENCES
Underline the details in lines 140–156 that help you make the inference that Miss Strangeworth is hardworking.

---

5. **rambler:** a rose plant that grows upward like a vine, by clinging to a support.
6. **chintz:** a colorful printed cotton fabric.

G MAKE INFERENCES
Reread lines 169–176. What inference can you make about Miss Strangeworth's "other letters"?

_____

_____

_____

_____

_____

_____

H MAKE INFERENCES
What is Miss Strangeworth suggesting in this letter to Mrs. Harper?

_____

_____

_____

_____

_____

_____

_____

_____

negotiable (nĭ-gō′shə-bəl) *adj.* able to be bargained with

and shopping lists. It was usual to remark, upon receiving a note
180 written on a blue page, that so-and-so would be needing a new
pad soon—here she was, down to the blue already. Everyone used
the matching envelopes for tucking away recipes, or keeping odd
little things in, or even to hold cookies in the school lunch boxes.
Mr. Lewis sometimes gave them to the children for carrying home
penny candy. **G**

Although Miss Strangeworth's desk held a trimmed quill pen,
which had belonged to her grandfather, and a gold-frost fountain
pen, which had belonged to her father, Miss Strangeworth
always used a dull stub of pencil when she wrote her letters, and
190 she printed them in a childish block print. After thinking for a
minute, although she had been phrasing the letter in the back of
her mind all the way home, she wrote on a pink sheet: DIDN'T
YOU EVER SEE AN IDIOT CHILD BEFORE? SOME
PEOPLE JUST SHOULDN'T HAVE CHILDREN, SHOULD
THEY?

She was pleased with the letter. She was fond of doing things
exactly right. When she made a mistake, as she sometimes did,
or when the letters were not spaced nicely on the page, she had to
take the discarded page to the kitchen stove and burn it at once.
200 Miss Strangeworth never delayed when things had to be done.

After thinking for a minute, she decided that she would like
to write another letter, perhaps to go to Mrs. Harper, to follow
up the ones she had already mailed. She selected a green sheet
this time and wrote quickly: HAVE YOU FOUND OUT YET
WHAT THEY WERE ALL LAUGHING ABOUT AFTER
YOU LEFT THE BRIDGE CLUB ON THURSDAY?
OR IS THE WIFE REALLY ALWAYS THE LAST ONE TO
KNOW? **H**

Miss Strangeworth never concerned herself with facts; her
210 letters all dealt with the more **negotiable** stuff of suspicion.
Mr. Lewis would never have imagined for a minute that his
grandson might be lifting petty cash[7] from the store register if he

---

7. **petty cash:** a small fund of money kept handy for miscellaneous expenses.

had not had one of Miss Strangeworth's letters. Miss Chandler, the librarian, and Linda Stewart's parents would have gone unsuspectingly ahead with their lives, never aware of possible evil lurking nearby, if Miss Strangeworth had not sent letters to open their eyes. Miss Strangeworth would have been genuinely shocked if there *had* been anything between Linda Stewart and the Harris boy, but, as long as evil existed unchecked in the world, it was

220 Miss Strangeworth's duty to keep her town alert to it. It was far more sensible for Miss Chandler to wonder what Mr. Shelley's first wife had really died of than to take a chance on not knowing. There were so many wicked people in the world and only one Strangeworth left in town. Besides, Miss Strangeworth liked writing her letters. ❶

She addressed an envelope to Don Crane after a moment's thought, wondering curiously if he would show the letter to his wife, and using a pink envelope to match the pink paper. Then she addressed a second envelope, green, to Mrs. Harper. Then

230 an idea came to her and she selected a blue sheet and wrote: YOU NEVER KNOW ABOUT DOCTORS. REMEMBER THEY'RE ONLY HUMAN AND NEED MONEY LIKE THE REST OF US. SUPPOSE THE KNIFE SLIPPED ACCIDENTALLY. WOULD DOCTOR BURNS GET HIS FEE AND A LITTLE EXTRA FROM THAT NEPHEW OF YOURS?

She addressed the blue envelope to old Mrs. Foster, who was having an operation next month. She had thought of writing one more letter, to the head of the school board, asking how a

240 chemistry teacher like Billy Moore's father could afford a new convertible, but all at once she was tired of writing letters. The three she had done would do for one day. She could write more tomorrow; it was not as though they all had to be done at once.

She had been writing her letters—sometimes two or three every day for a week, sometimes no more than one in a month— for the past year. She never got any answers, of course, because she

❶ CHARACTER MOTIVATION

What moral issue does Miss Strangeworth say motivates her to write her letters? What other reason for writing the letters is given in lines 209–225?

degraded (dĭ-grā′dĭd) *adj.*
corrupted, depraved

J **CHARACTER MOTIVATION**
Miss Strangeworth calls the letters she sends "trash." If she sees them as trash, why does she send them?

_____

_____

_____

_____

_____

translucent (trăns-lōō′sənt) *adj.*
allowing light to shine through

PAUSE & REFLECT
In line 264, Miss Strangeworth thinks that "people must live graciously." Does Miss Strangeworth live graciously? Why or why not?

_____

_____

_____

_____

never signed her name. If she had been asked, she would have said that her name, Adela Strangeworth, a name honored in the town for so many years, did not belong on such trash. The town where she lived had to be kept clean and sweet, but people everywhere were lustful and evil and **degraded**, and needed to be watched; the world was so large, and there was only one Strangeworth left in it. Miss Strangeworth sighed, locked her desk, and put the letters into her big, black leather pocketbook, to be mailed when she took her evening walk. **J**

She broiled her little chop nicely, and had a sliced tomato and good cup of tea ready when she sat down to her midday dinner at the table in her dining room, which could be opened to seat twenty-two, with a second table, if necessary, in the hall. Sitting in the warm sunlight that came through the tall windows of the dining room, seeing her roses massed outside, handling the heavy, old silverware and the fine, **translucent** china, Miss Strangeworth was pleased; she would not have cared to be doing anything else. People must live graciously, after all, she thought, and sipped her tea. Afterward, when her plate and cup and saucer were washed and dried and put back onto the shelves where they belonged, and her silverware was back in the mahogany silver chest, Miss Strangeworth went up the graceful staircase and into her bedroom, which was the front room overlooking the roses, and had been her mother's and her grandmother's. Their Crown Derby dresser set[8] and furs had been kept here, their fans and silver-backed brushes and their own bowls of roses; Miss Strangeworth kept a bowl of white roses on the bed table.

She drew the shades, took the rose-satin spread from the bed, slipped out of her dress and her shoes, and lay down tiredly. She knew that no doorbell or phone would ring; no one in town would dare to disturb Miss Strangeworth during her afternoon nap. She slept, deep in the rich smell of roses. **PAUSE & REFLECT**

---

8. **Crown Derby dresser set:** a hairbrush, comb, and hand mirror made of fine china.

After her nap she worked in her garden for a little while, sparing herself because of the heat; then she came in to her supper. She ate asparagus from her own garden, with sweet-butter sauce, and a soft-boiled egg, and, while she had her supper, she listened to a late-evening news broadcast and then to a program of classical music on her small radio. After her dishes were done and her kitchen set in order, she took up her hat—Miss Strangeworth's hats were proverbial in the town; people believed that she had inherited them from her mother and her grandmother—and, locking the front door of her house behind her, set off on her evening walk, pocketbook under her arm. She nodded to Linda Stewart's father, who was washing his car in the pleasantly cool evening. She thought that he looked troubled. **Ⓚ**

There was only one place in town where she could mail her letters, and that was the new post office, shiny with red brick and silver letters. Although Miss Strangeworth had never given the matter any particular thought, she had always made a point of mailing her letters very secretly; it would, of course, not have been wise to let anyone see her mail them. Consequently, she timed her walk so she could reach the post office just as darkness was starting to dim the outlines of the trees and the shapes of people's faces, although no one could ever mistake Miss Strangeworth, with her dainty walk and her rustling skirts.

There was always a group of young people around the post office, the very youngest roller-skating upon its driveway, which went all the way around the building and was the only smooth road in town; and the slightly older ones already knowing how to gather in small groups and chatter and laugh and make great, excited plans for going across the street to the soda shop in a minute or two. Miss Strangeworth had never had any self-consciousness before the children. She did not feel that any of them were staring at her unduly or longing to laugh at her; it would have been most **reprehensible** for their parents to permit

Ⓚ MAKE INFERENCES
In lines 289–290, why would Miss Strangeworth be interested in whether Linda Stewart's father looked troubled? Look back at lines 212–220 for help in answering the question.

_____

_____

_____

_____

_____

_____

_____

reprehensible (rĕp′rĭ-hĕn′sə-bəl) *adj.* deserving blame and criticism

Underline the text that the adjective **reprehensible** describes.

their children to mock Miss Strangeworth of Pleasant Street. Most of the children stood back respectfully as Miss Strangeworth passed, silenced briefly in her presence, and some of the older children greeted her, saying soberly, "Hello, Miss Strangeworth."

Miss Strangeworth smiled at them and quickly went on. It had been a long time since she had known the name of every child in town. The mail slot was in the door of the post office. The children stood away as Miss Strangeworth approached it,
320 seemingly surprised that anyone should want to use the post office after it had been officially closed up for the night and turned over to the children. Miss Strangeworth stood by the door, opening her black pocketbook to take out the letters, and heard a voice which she knew at once to be Linda Stewart's. Poor little Linda was crying again, and Miss Strangeworth listened carefully. This was, after all, her town, and these were her people; if one of them was in trouble, she ought to know about it. **L**

"I can't tell you, Dave," Linda was saying—so she *was* talking to the Harris boy, as Miss Strangeworth had supposed—"I just
330 *can't*. It's just *nasty*."

"But why won't your father let me come around anymore? What on earth did I do?"

"I can't tell you. I just wouldn't tell you for *any*thing. You've got to have a dirty dirty mind for things like that."

"But something's happened. You've been crying and crying, and your father is all upset. Why can't *I* know about it, too? Aren't I like one of the family?"

"Not anymore, Dave, not anymore. You're not to come near our house again; my father said so. He said he'd horsewhip
340 you. That's all I can tell you: You're not to come near our house anymore."

"But I didn't *do* anything."

"Just the same, my father said . . ."

L CHARACTER MOTIVATION
What motivates Miss Strangeworth to listen to Linda Stewart's conversation?

_____

_____

_____

_____

_____

_____

_____

_____

_____

Miss Strangeworth sighed and turned away. There was so much evil in people. Even in a charming little town like this one, there was still so much evil in people. ⓜ

She slipped her letters into the slot, and two of them fell inside. The third caught on the edge and fell outside, onto the ground at Miss Strangeworth's feet. She did not notice it because she was

350 wondering whether a letter to the Harris boy's father might not be of some service in wiping out this potential badness. Wearily Miss Strangeworth turned to go home to her quiet bed in her lovely house, and never heard the Harris boy calling to her to say that she had dropped something.

"Old lady Strangeworth's getting deaf," he said, looking after her and holding in his hand the letter he had picked up.

"Well, who cares?" Linda said. "Who cares anymore, anyway?"

"It's for Don Crane," the Harris boy said, "this letter. She dropped a letter addressed to Don Crane. Might as well take it on

360 over. We pass his house anyway." He laughed. "Maybe it's got a check or something in it and he'd be just as glad to get it tonight instead of tomorrow."

"Catch old lady Strangeworth sending anybody a check," Linda said. "Throw it in the post office. Why do anyone a favor?" She sniffed. "Doesn't seem to me anybody around here cares about us," she said. "Why should we care about them?"

"I'll take it over, anyway," the Harris boy said. "Maybe it's good news for them. Maybe they need something happy tonight, too. Like us."

370 Sadly, holding hands, they wandered off down the dark street, the Harris boy carrying Miss Strangeworth's pink envelope in his hand. **PAUSE & REFLECT**

Miss Strangeworth awakened the next morning with a feeling of intense happiness and, for a minute, wondered why, and then remembered that this morning three people would open her letters. Harsh, perhaps, at first, but wickedness was never easily banished, and a clean heart was a scoured heart. She washed her

PAUSE & REFLECT

What do you think happened to
Miss Strangeworth's roses?

_____

_____

_____

_____

_____

_____

_____

_____

soft, old face and brushed her teeth, still sound in spite of her
seventy-one years, and dressed herself carefully in her sweet, soft
380 clothes and buttoned shoes. Then, going downstairs, reflecting
that perhaps a little waffle would be agreeable for breakfast in
the sunny dining room, she found the mail on the hall floor, and
bent to pick it up. A bill, the morning paper, a letter in a green
envelope that looked oddly familiar. Miss Strangeworth stood
perfectly still for a minute, looking down at the green envelope
with the penciled printing, and thought: It looks like one of
my letters. Was one of my letters sent back? No, because no one
would know where to send it. How did this get here?

Miss Strangeworth was a Strangeworth of Pleasant Street.
390 Her hand did not shake as she opened the envelope and unfolded
the sheet of green paper inside. She began to cry silently for the
wickedness of the world when she read the words: LOOK OUT
AT WHAT USED TO BE YOUR ROSES. **PAUSE & REFLECT**

Text Analysis: Character Motivation

The narrator offers more than one reason for Miss Strangeworth's activity. Complete the chart below with Miss Strangeworth's motivations for her actions. Include both her stated and her unstated motivations. In the Actions box, write a summary of the actions that Miss Strangeworth takes.

Motivation Chart

Miss Strangeworth's Motivations:	Examples:

Actions:

Review your notes for "The Possibility of Evil" and your Motivation Chart. Do you think Miss Strangeworth's main motivation is to address a moral dilemma—or is it something else? Use examples from the selection and your own experience to support your response.

_____

_____

_____

_____

_____

_____

Reading Skill: Make Inferences

Look at the chart you completed while reading "The Possibility of Evil." Now make an inference about each character based on details from the story.

Dave Harris	My Inference:
Details: He decides to take Miss Strangeworth's letter to Don Crane. (lines 367–369) →	
Mrs. Harper	My Inference:
Details: Her hands are shaking and she replies very briefly to Miss Strangeworth. (lines 81–88) →	
Miss Strangeworth	My Inference:
Details: She thinks that there is a great deal of evil in people, even in her small town. (lines 344–346) →	

How good are you at **JUDGING** people?

What can people do to avoid misjudging others?

_____

_____

_____

Vocabulary Practice

Circle the word that is most different in meaning from the others.

1. **(a)** disinterested, **(b)** infatuated, **(c)** lovesick, **(d)** smitten

2. **(a)** rapt, **(b)** inattentive, **(c)** absorbed, **(d)** immersed

3. **(a)** negotiable, **(b)** certain, **(c)** indisputable, **(d)** inarguable

4. **(a)** uplifted, **(b)** elevated, **(c)** honored, **(d)** degraded

5. **(a)** clear, **(b)** translucent, **(c)** dense, **(d)** transparent

6. **(a)** reprehensible, **(b)** admirable, **(c)** respectable, **(d)** praiseworthy

Academic Vocabulary in Writing

dynamic	individual	motive	seek	undergo

What is Miss Strangeworth's **motive** behind writing the letters? What is she **seeking** to accomplish? Use at least two Academic Vocabulary words in your response. Definitions for these terms are listed on page 57.

_____

_____

_____

_____

Assessment Practice

DIRECTIONS Use "The Possibility of Evil" to answer questions 1–4.

1 How does Miss Strangeworth secretly warn people of "possible evil"?
- **A** She leaves messages for the police to tell them of "possible evil" in the community.
- **B** She gossips to people about other people's actions.
- **C** She gives roses only to people whom she feels are good.
- **D** She sends people unsigned letters that hint at evil actions in town.

2 What is Miss Strangeworth's view of human nature?
- **A** She knows that there are many good people in the world.
- **B** She believes there are many wicked people in the world.
- **C** She thinks that wicked people cannot be helped.
- **D** She is convinced of people's desire to be kind.

3 The phrase "it was Miss Strangeworth's duty to keep her town alert to [evil]" (line 220) tells you that Miss Strangeworth feels that she —
- **A** is failing to alert people to the possibility of evil
- **B** deserves to be paid to warn people about evil in town
- **C** knows that she is the most important person in town
- **D** has a moral reason to warn people of evil

4 The sentence "Besides, Miss Strangeworth liked writing her letters" (lines 224–225) reveals that she —
- **A** has several different motivations for her actions
- **B** likes writing friendly letters
- **C** sends letters only to people she likes
- **D** expects her letters to be appreciated

The Teacher Who Changed My Life
Essay by Nicholas Gage

Who has made you a BETTER person?

Sometimes one person can have a powerful effect on your life. When you look back, you realize how much you have benefited from his or her influence. In "The Teacher Who Changed My Life," Nicholas Gage fondly recalls his seventh-grade teacher, Miss Hurd.

LIST IT   In a small group, discuss what makes a person an inspiration. What makes people an inspiration to others? Make a list of the common character traits of inspiration figures from your discussion.

Text Analysis: Characterization in Nonfiction

When characterizing a real person, nonfiction writers are limited to the facts. However, nonfiction writers can shape the reader's attitude toward the person by using the same methods of **characterization** used in fiction. The chart below shows different methods of characterization an author can use.

Character Traits of Inspirational Figures

1. _____

2. _____

3. _____

4. _____

5. _____

6. _____

METHODS OF CHARACTERIZATION	EXAMPLE
the author's direct comments about the character	Enrique's active imagination often got him into trouble.
the physical appearance of the character	Sheri flashed a smile as bright as her new red dress.
the character's own thoughts, speech, and actions	"Am I the *only* one who knows how to play this game?" Elena thought critically.
other characters' reactions to and comments about the character	James's friends were shocked that the quiet, upstanding man they knew had plotted a complex bank robbery.

Reading Skill: Author's Purpose

An **author's purpose** is what the writer hopes to achieve in a particular work. For example, the title of Gage's essay suggests that he wants to inform you about how a teacher influenced his life. Other purposes for writing can be:

- to persuade (the author wants you to believe or act a certain way)

- to entertain (to make you laugh or smile)

- to express ideas or emotions (to make you understand a concept or a feeling)

Use a chart to record how Gage's purposes affect his choice of words and details, and how they affect his **tone,** or attitude, toward his topic.

Purpose	How Purpose Affects Writing
To show influence of Miss Hurd	Describes how she pushed him to write about his experiences

Vocabulary in Context

Note: Words are listed in the order in which they appear in the selection.

mentor (mĕn′tôr′) *n.* a wise and trusted counselor or teacher
I've learned a lot from my **mentor.**

tact (tăkt) *n.* an understanding of the proper thing to do or say around others
They handled the awkward situation with great **tact.**

isolated (ī′sə-lā′tĭd) *adj.* separated from others
The defeat left him lonely and **isolated.**

avidly (ăv′ĭd-lē) *adv.* with great eagerness and enthusiasm
He participated willingly and **avidly.**

catalyst (kăt′l-ĭst) *n.* something or someone that brings about change
We need a **catalyst** *to send us in a new direction.*

emphatically (ĕm-făt′ĭk-lē) *adv.* with strong emphasis
She **emphatically** *endorsed the candidate.*

Vocabulary Practice

Work with a partner to discuss ways in which a teacher could change someone's life. Write your answer below, using at least two vocabulary words.

_____

_____

_____

**SET A PURPOSE
FOR READING**

Read to determine how
Nicholas Gage's life was
changed by a teacher who
influenced and inspired
him.

The Teacher Who Changed *My Life*

Essay by

NICHOLAS GAGE

BACKGROUND Nicholas Gage was born
in Lia, a village in northern Greece. After
World War II, Gage, his mother, Eleni, and
his four sisters found themselves caught
in Greece's civil war between Communists
and royalists. Fearing for her children,
Eleni made arrangements for her family to
flee. Gage and three of his sisters escaped,
but Eleni and one sister were left behind.
The Communists arrested Eleni, put her
on trial, and executed her. Gage and his
siblings were eventually reunited with
their father, who had been working in the
United States.

**Ⓐ CHARACTERIZATION IN
NONFICTION**
In lines 1–8, underline the details
that describe Marjorie Hurd.
Based on this first paragraph,
how much of an influence did
she have on Gage's life?

_____

_____

_____

The person who set the course of my life in the new land I
entered as a young war refugee—who, in fact, nearly dragged
me onto the path that would bring all the blessings I've received in
America—was a salty-tongued, no-nonsense schoolteacher named
Marjorie Hurd. When I entered her classroom in 1953, I had been
to six schools in five years, starting in the Greek village where I
was born in 1939. Ⓐ

When I stepped off a ship in New York Harbor on a gray
March day in 1949, I was an undersized 9-year-old in short
10 pants who had lost his mother and was coming to live with the
father he didn't know. My mother, Eleni Gatzoyiannis,[1] had
been imprisoned, tortured and shot by Communist guerrillas for

---

1. **Eleni Gatzoyiannis** (ĕ-lĕ′nē gät′zô-yän′ĭs).

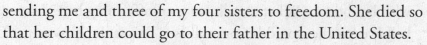
sending me and three of my four sisters to freedom. She died so that her children could go to their father in the United States.

The portly, bald, well-dressed man who met me and my sisters seemed a foreign, authoritarian figure. I secretly resented him for not getting the whole family out of Greece early enough to save my mother. Ultimately, I would grow to love him and appreciate how he dealt with becoming a single parent at the age of 56, but 20 at first our relationship was prickly, full of hostility. **B**

As Father drove us to our new home—a tenement in Worcester, Mass.—and pointed out the huge brick building that would be our first school in America, I clutched my Greek notebooks from the refugee camp, hoping that my few years of schooling would impress my teachers in this cold, crowded country. They didn't. When my father led me and my 11-year-old sister to Greendale Elementary School, the grim-faced Yankee principal put the two of us in a class for the mentally retarded. There was no facility in those days for non-English-speaking 30 children.

By the time I met Marjorie Hurd four years later, I had learned English, been placed in a normal, graded class and had even been chosen for the college preparatory track in the Worcester public school system. I was 13 years old when our father moved us yet again, and I entered Chandler Junior High shortly after the beginning of seventh grade. I found myself surrounded by richer, smarter and better-dressed classmates, who looked askance at my strange clothes and heavy accent. Shortly after I arrived, we were told to select a hobby to pursue during "club hour" on 40 Fridays. The idea of hobbies and clubs made no sense to my immigrant ears, but I decided to follow the prettiest girl in my class—the blue-eyed daughter of the local Lutheran minister. She led me through the door marked "Newspaper Club" and into the presence of Miss Hurd, the newspaper adviser and English teacher who would become my **mentor** and my muse.

A formidable, solidly built woman with salt-and-pepper hair, a steely eye and a flat Boston accent, Miss Hurd had no patience

B CHARACTERIZATION IN NONFICTION
What methods of characterization does Gage use to explain his initial impression of his father in lines 15–20? Refer to the chart on page 76 to review the methods of characterization.

_____

_____

_____

_____

_____

_____

_____

_____

_____

mentor (mĕn′tôr′) *n.* a wise and trusted counselor or teacher

ⓒ CHARACTERIZATION IN NONFICTION

In lines 48–52, why might Gage have chosen to quote Miss Hurd's actual words? What can you tell about her from her comments?

_____

_____

_____

_____

_____

ⓓ AUTHOR'S PURPOSE

Reread lines 53–64. Which **details** support Gage's purpose of explaining Miss Hurd's influence on him? Record them in the chart below and then explain how the author's purpose affected his writing.

Purpose: To show influence of Miss Hurd
Supporting Details:
How Purpose Affects Writing:

with layabouts. "What are all you goof-offs doing here?" she bellowed at the would-be journalists. "This is the Newspaper Club!
50 We're going to put out a *newspaper*. So if there's anybody in this room who doesn't like work, I suggest you go across to the Glee Club now, because you're going to work your tails off here!" ⓒ

I was soon under Miss Hurd's spell. She did indeed teach us to put out a newspaper, skills I honed during my next 25 years as a journalist. Soon I asked the principal to transfer me to her English class as well. There, she drilled us on grammar until I finally began to understand the logic and structure of the English language. She assigned stories for us to read and discuss; not tales of heroes, like the Greek myths I knew, but stories of
60 underdogs—poor people, even immigrants, who seemed ordinary until a crisis drove them to do something extraordinary. She also introduced us to the literary wealth of Greece—giving me a new perspective on my war-ravaged, impoverished homeland. I began to be proud of my origins. ⓓ

One day, after discussing how writers should write about what they know, she assigned us to compose an essay from our own experience. Fixing me with a stern look, she added, "Nick, I want you to write about what happened to your family in Greece." I had been trying to put those painful memories behind me and
70 left the assignment until the last moment. Then, on a warm spring afternoon, I sat in my room with a yellow pad and pencil and stared out the window at the buds on the trees. I wrote that the coming of spring always reminded me of the last time I said goodbye to my mother on a green and gold day in 1948.

I kept writing, one line after another, telling how the Communist guerrillas occupied our village, took our home and food, how my mother started planning our escape when she learned that the children were to be sent to re-education camps[2] behind the Iron Curtain[3] and how, at the last moment, she
80 couldn't escape with us because the guerrillas sent her with a

---

2. **re-education camps:** camps where people were forced to go to be indoctrinated with Communist ideas and beliefs.

3. **behind the Iron Curtain:** on the Communist side of the imaginary divide between the democracies of Western Europe and the Communist dictatorships of Eastern Europe; in this case, the camps were in Albania.

group of women to thresh wheat in a distant village. She promised she would try to get away on her own, she told me to be brave and hung a silver cross around my neck, and then she kissed me. I watched the line of women being led down into the ravine and up the other side, until they disappeared around the bend—my mother a tiny brown figure at the end who stopped for an instant to raise her hand in one last farewell. **PAUSE & REFLECT**

PAUSE & REFLECT

Reread lines 70–87. Why might it have been a relief for Gage to write about his mother?

_____

_____

_____

_____

_____

_____

I wrote about our nighttime escape down the mountain, across the minefields and into the lines of the Nationalist soldiers, who
90 sent us to a refugee camp. It was there that we learned of our mother's execution. I felt very lucky to have come to America, I concluded, but every year, the coming of spring made me feel sad because it reminded me of the last time I saw my mother.

I handed in the essay, hoping never to see it again, but Miss Hurd had it published in the school paper. This mortified me at first, until I saw that my classmates reacted with sympathy and <u>tact</u> to my family's story. Without telling me, Miss Hurd also submitted the essay to a contest sponsored by the Freedoms Foundation at Valley Forge, Pa., and it won a medal. The
100 Worcester paper wrote about the award and quoted my essay at length. My father, by then a "five-and-dime-store chef," as the paper described him, was ecstatic with pride, and the Worcester Greek community celebrated the honor to one of its own.

For the first time I began to understand the power of the written word. A secret ambition took root in me. One day, I vowed, I would go back to Greece, find out the details of my mother's death and write about her life, so her grandchildren would know of her courage. Perhaps I would even track down the men who killed her and write of their crimes. Fulfilling that
110 ambition would take me 30 years.

tact (tăkt) *n.* an understanding of the proper thing to do or say around others

In what way might Gage's classmates have shown **tact** in the way they reacted to his essay about his mother?

_____

_____

_____

_____

ⓔ CHARACTERIZATION IN NONFICTION
What do the father's actions in lines 124–131 tell you about his feelings for his son?

_____

_____

_____

_____

_____

_____

isolated (i′sé-la′tĭd) *adj.*
separated from others

Meanwhile, I followed the literary path that Miss Hurd had so forcefully set me on. After junior high, I became the editor of my school paper at Classical High School and got a part-time job at the Worcester *Telegram and Gazette*. Although my father could only give me $50 and encouragement toward a college education, I managed to finance four years at Boston University with scholarships and part-time jobs in journalism. During my last year of college, an article I wrote about a friend who had died in the Philippines—the first person to lose his life working for the

120 Peace Corps—led to my winning the Hearst Award for College Journalism. And the plaque was given to me in the White House by President John F. Kennedy.

For a refugee who had never seen a motorized vehicle or indoor plumbing until he was 9, this was an unimaginable honor. When the Worcester paper ran a picture of me standing next to President Kennedy, my father rushed out to buy a new suit in order to be properly dressed to receive the congratulations of the Worcester Greeks. He clipped out the photograph, had it laminated in plastic and carried it in his breast pocket for the rest of his life

130 to show everyone he met. I found the much-worn photo in his pocket on the day he died 20 years later. **ⓔ**

In our **isolated** Greek village, my mother had bribed a cousin to teach her to read, for girls were not supposed to attend school beyond a certain age. She had always dreamed of her children receiving an education. She couldn't be there when I graduated from Boston University, but the person who came with my father and shared our joy was my former teacher, Marjorie Hurd. We celebrated not only my bachelor's degree but also the scholarships that paid my way to Columbia's Graduate School of Journalism.

140 There, I met the woman who would eventually become my wife. At our wedding and at the baptisms of our three children, Marjorie Hurd was always there, dancing alongside the Greeks.

By then, she was Mrs. Rabidou, for she had married a widower when she was in her early 40s. That didn't distract her from

her vocation of introducing young minds to English literature, however. She taught for a total of 41 years and continually would make a "project" of some balky student in whom she spied a spark of potential. Often these were students from the most troubled homes, yet she would alternately bully and charm each one with
150 her own special brand of tough love until the spark caught fire. She retired in 1981 at the age of 62 but still **avidly** follows the lives and careers of former students while overseeing her adult stepchildren and driving her husband on camping trips to New Hampshire. **F**

Miss Hurd was one of the first to call me on Dec. 10, 1987, when President Reagan, in his television address after the summit meeting with Gorbachev,[4] told the nation that Eleni Gatzoyiannis's dying cry, "My children!" had helped inspire him to seek an arms agreement "for all the children of the world."
160 "I can't imagine a better monument for your mother," Miss Hurd said with an uncharacteristic catch in her voice.

Although a bad hip makes it impossible for her to join in the Greek dancing, Marjorie Hurd Rabidou is still an honored and enthusiastic guest at all our family celebrations, including my 50th birthday picnic last summer, where the shish kebab was cooked on spits, clarinets and *bouzoukis*[5] wailed, and costumed dancers led the guests in a serpentine line around our Colonial farmhouse, only 20 minutes from my first home in Worcester.

My sisters and I felt an aching void because my father was
170 not there to lead the line, balancing a glass of wine on his head while he danced, the way he did at every celebration during his 92 years. But Miss Hurd was there, surveying the scene with quiet satisfaction. Although my parents are gone, her presence was a consolation, because I owe her so much. **G**

This is truly the land of opportunity, and I would have enjoyed its bounty even if I hadn't walked into Miss Hurd's classroom in 1953. But she was the one who directed my grief and

avidly (ăv'ĭd-lē) *adv.* with great eagerness and enthusiasm

F AUTHOR'S PURPOSE
Reread lines 143–154. Underline the words and details in this paragraph that help Gage pay tribute to Miss Hurd.

G AUTHOR'S PURPOSE
Reread lines 169–174. What purpose is suggested by Gage's **tone,** or attitude, in this paragraph?

___

4. **summit meeting with Gorbachev** (gôr'bə-chôf'): a high-level meeting between U.S. president Ronald Reagan and Mikhail Gorbachev, the last president of the Soviet Union.
5. *bouzoukis* (bŏŏ-zōō'kēz): traditional Greek stringed instruments resembling mandolins.

catalyst (kăt′l-ĭst) *n.* something or someone that brings about change

emphatically (ĕm-făt′ĭk-lē) *adv.* with strong emphasis

PAUSE & REFLECT

What does Gage mean by "this remembrance instead" in line 190?

_____

_____

_____

_____

_____

pain into writing, and if it weren't for her, I wouldn't have become an investigative reporter and foreign correspondent, recorded the
180 story of my mother's life and death in *Eleni* and now my father's story in *A Place for Us*, which is also a testament to the country that took us in. She was the <u>**catalyst**</u> that sent me into journalism and indirectly caused all the good things that came after. But Miss Hurd would probably deny this <u>**emphatically**</u>.

A few years ago, I answered the telephone and heard my former teacher's voice telling me, in that won't-take-no-for-an-answer tone of hers, that she had decided I was to write and deliver the eulogy at her funeral. I agreed (she didn't leave me any choice), but that's one assignment I never want to do. I hope, Miss Hurd, that you'll
190 accept this remembrance instead. **PAUSE & REFLECT**

Text Analysis: Characterization in Nonfiction

Gage uses a variety of methods to create a portrait of Miss Hurd. For each method of characterization in the chart, give an example of how Gage uses it to convey Miss Hurd's personality.

Method of Characterization	Example from Text	What It Reveals about Miss Hurd
Words and Actions		
Physical Appearances		
Gage's Comments		

Which method gives you the most vivid impression of Miss Hurd? Explain your answer.

_____

_____

_____

_____

Reading Skill: Author's Purpose

Look at the chart you completed while reading "The Teacher Who Changed My Life." Decide the main purpose of Gage's essay, and support your answer with evidence from the text.

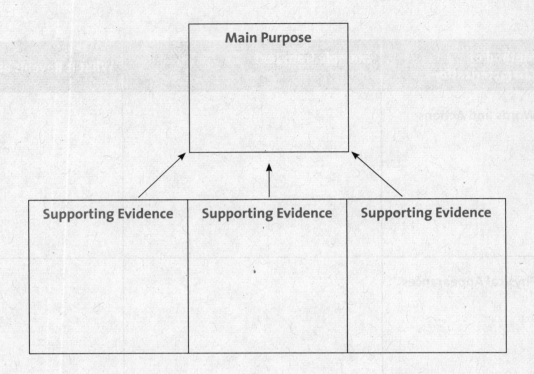

Main Purpose

Supporting Evidence   **Supporting Evidence**   **Supporting Evidence**

Who has made you a **BETTER** person?

How can a teacher inspire you to improve yourself?

_____

_____

_____

Vocabulary Practice

Write an **S** if words are synonyms (words with similar meanings) and an **A** if words are antonyms (words with opposite meanings).

_____ **1.** mentor/advisor

_____ **2.** tact/insensitivity

_____ **3.** isolated/united

_____ **4.** avidly/enthusiastically

_____ **5.** catalyst/observer

_____ **6.** emphatically/wearily

Academic Vocabulary in Speaking

| dynamic | individual | motive | seek | undergo |

TURN AND TALK In a small group, discuss why it is important for a person to be grateful for the help he or she has received from others. Think about the **individual** attention that Nicholas Gage received from Marjorie Hurd and how this motivated him. Use at least one Academic Vocabulary word in your discussion. Definitions for these terms are listed on page 57.

Assessment Practice

DIRECTIONS Use "The Teacher Who Changed My Life" to answer questions 1–6.

1 Nicholas Gage came to the United States because —

- (A) his parents wanted him to attend school in America
- (B) only Communists could leave Greece
- (C) his family was escaping from the Communists
- (D) his father was killed by the Communists

2 According to the selection, Miss Hurd encouraged Gage to write an essay about —

- (A) President Reagan's television address
- (B) his father's job at the "five-and-dime"
- (C) what happened to his family in Greece
- (D) his friend who died in the Philippines

3 Which of the following statements best describes the influence Miss Hurd had on Gage's career?

- (A) She set a "literary path" for him that led to his career.
- (B) She helped Gage's family move to the United States.
- (C) She convinced the Worcester *Telegram and Gazette* to hire Gage.
- (D) She told Gage that he would have a career in reporting.

4 What led Miss Hurd to take a special interest in Gage when he was her student?

- (A) She expected that he would fail her class.
- (B) She was told to give him extra help.
- (C) She wanted him to stay in the newspaper club.
- (D) She realized he had great potential.

5 Marjorie Hurd's mentoring style is not typical because she —

- (A) gives easier homework to Nicholas Gage than to other students
- (B) uses "tough love," rather than a soft approach
- (C) uses a "soft" approach rather than challenging students
- (D) tells Nicholas Gage to forget about what happened in Greece

6 What did Nicholas Gage understand better after his essay was published?

- (A) the reasons for his mother's death
- (B) the need for revenge
- (C) the tremendous power of writing
- (D) the purpose of a rough draft

A Marriage Proposal
Drama by Anton Chekhov

Why do people argue over SILLY THINGS?

When two stubborn people have very different opinions about something unimportant, a silly argument is likely to erupt. Such pettiness is displayed by the characters in *A Marriage Proposal*, who can't seem to agree on anything, even when they share the same goal.

QUICKWRITE Think about a time when you had a silly argument with someone—a friend or a family member, perhaps. What was the argument about? How was it resolved? Write your thoughts in the notebook at left.

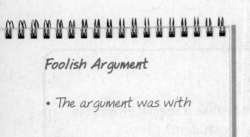

Foolish Argument

• The argument was with

_____

_____

• We argued about

_____

_____

• The argument ended when

_____

_____

Text Analysis: Characters in a Farce

A **farce** is a humorous play that includes ridiculous situations and dialogue. Characters in a farce are usually comical stereotypes who are defined by a single trait or who display a single pattern of behavior. Read the following example from a play, including the stage directions.

John *(rolling his eyes). Yes, Pat your idea is the best one I've heard yet.*

The stage directions suggest that John doesn't want to talk to Pat and does not think that Pat's idea is good. In this speech from *A Marriage Proposal*, notice how a character's trait is exaggerated for comic effect:

I have a weak heart, continual palpitation, and I'm very sensitive and always getting excited.

As you read the play, you will be asked to identify traits of different characters. Record details that help you identify the character's main trait or pattern of behavior. See the example below.

Lomov:
• weak heart
• very sensitive

Reading Skill: Reading a Play

To understand a play, you will need to read **stage directions** that describe the scenery and props, the actions of characters, or the tone in which dialogue should be delivered. Sometimes a stage direction will indicate one of the following:

- an **aside**—a short speech directed to the audience or to a character but not heard by the other characters onstage

- a **monologue**—a long speech that is usually delivered by a character who is alone onstage

Asides and monologues can be used to reveal a character's private thoughts and feelings. As you read *A Marriage Proposal*, you will be prompted to answer questions about the stage directions that give you information about the characters. See the chart below for an example.

Character	Line Number and Stage Direction	What the Stage Direction Tells About the Character
Ivan Vassiliyitch Lomov	*Line 13: (composing himself)*	*It shows that Lomov is flustered and anxious.*

Vocabulary in Context

Note: Words are listed in the order in which they appear in the play.

meditate (měd'ĭ-tāt') *v.* to consider for a long time
   *I need to **meditate** on this issue awhile before deciding.*

usurper (yōō-sûrp'ər) *n.* someone who wrongfully takes possession of something
   *The scheming **usurper** tried to seize the king's throne.*

glutton (glŭt'n) *n.* a person who eats too much
   *Please don't be a **glutton** at the dinner table.*

contrary (kŏn'trĕr'ē) *adj.* stubbornly uncooperative or contradictory
   *You insist on being **contrary** just to be different.*

Vocabulary Practice

Review the vocabulary words and their definitions. Then, choose two words and write a sentence for each on the lines below.

_____

_____

**SET A PURPOSE
FOR READING**

Read this play to find out
how a marriage proposal
turns ugly.

A Marriage PROPOSAL

Drama by
ANTON CHEKHOV

BACKGROUND *A Marriage Proposal*
takes place on a country estate in late-
19th-century Russia. The characters are
members of the privileged class known
as the gentry. These wealthy landowners
employed peasants to work their fields,
which allowed them to enjoy a life of
leisure. Writers of farces often poked
fun at the habits of the gentry, including
their tendency to marry for economic
gain rather than affection.

Ⓐ READING A PLAY
What information in the **stage
directions** helps you visualize the
setting of the play?

_____

_____

_____

_____

_____

_____

CHARACTERS

**Stepan Stepanovitch
Tschubukov** (styĭ-pän′ styĭ-
pän′əv-yĭch chü-bü′kəf), a
country farmer

Natalia Stepanovna (nə-täl′yə
styĭ-pä-nôv′nə), his daughter
(aged 25)

Ivan Vassiliyitch Lomov
(ĭ-vän′ vəs-yēl′yĭch lô′məf),
Tschubukov's neighbor

SCENE

The reception room in
Tschubukov's country home
in Russia. Tschubukov
discovered as the curtain rises.
Enter Lomov, wearing a dress
suit. Ⓐ

Time

The present [1890s]

Tschubukov (*going toward him and greeting him*). Who is this I see? My dear fellow! Ivan Vassiliyitch! I'm so glad to see you! (*shakes hands*) But this is a surprise! How are you?

Lomov. Thank you! And how are you?

Tschubukov. Oh, so-so, my friend. Please sit down. It isn't right to forget one's neighbor. But tell me, why all this ceremony? Dress clothes, white gloves, and all? Are you on your way to some engagement, my good fellow?

Lomov. No, I have no engagement except with you, Stepan
10 Stepanovitch.

Tschubukov. But why in evening clothes, my friend? This isn't New Year's!

Lomov. You see, it's simply this, that— (*composing himself*) I have come to you, Stepan Stepanovitch, to trouble you with a request. It is not the first time I have had the honor of turning to you for assistance, and you have always, that is—I beg your pardon, I am a bit excited! I'll take a drink of water first, dear Stepan Stepanovitch. (*He drinks.*)

Tschubukov (*aside*). He's come to borrow money! I won't give
20 him any! (*to Lomov*) What is it, then, dear Lomov? **B**

Lomov. You see—dear—Stepanovitch, pardon me, Stepan— Stepan—dearvitch—I mean—I am terribly nervous, as you will be so good as to see—! What I mean to say—you are the only one who can help me, though I don't deserve it, and—and I have no right whatever to make this request of you.

Tschubukov. Oh, don't beat about the bush, my dear fellow. Tell me!

Lomov. Immediately—in a moment. Here it is, then: I have come to ask for the hand of your daughter, Natalia Stepanovna.

Tschubukov (*joyfully*). Angel! Ivan Vassiliyitch! Say that once
30 again! I didn't quite hear it!

Lomov. I have the honor to beg—

Tschubukov (*interrupting*). My dear, dear man. I am so happy that everything is so—everything! (*embraces and kisses him*) I have wanted this to happen for so long. It has been my dearest wish! (*He represses a tear.*) And I have always loved you, my dear fellow,

B READING A PLAY
Reread lines 1–20 and think about the way Tschubukov speaks to Lomov. What does Tschubukov's **aside** in lines 19–20 reveal about his actual opinion of Lomov?

_____

_____

_____

_____

_____

_____

_____

_____

as my own son! May God give you his blessings and his grace and—I always wanted it to happen. But why am I standing here like a blockhead? I am completely dumbfounded with pleasure, completely dumbfounded. My whole being—! I'll call Natalia—

40 **Lomov.** Dear Stepan Stepanovitch, what do you think? May I hope for Natalia Stepanovna's acceptance?

Tschubukov. Really! A fine boy like you— and you think she won't accept on the minute? Lovesick as a cat and all that—! (*He goes out, right.*)

Lomov. I'm cold. My whole body is trembling as though I was going to take my examination! But the chief thing is to settle matters! If a person **meditates** too much, or hesitates, or talks about it, waits for an ideal or for true love, he never gets it. Brrr! It's cold! Natalia is an excellent housekeeper, not at all bad

50 looking, well educated—what more could I ask? I'm so excited my ears are roaring! (*He drinks water.*) And not to marry, that won't do! In the first place, I'm thirty-five—a critical age, you might say. In the second place, I must live a well-regulated life. I have a weak heart, continual palpitation, and I am very sensitive and always getting excited. My lips begin to tremble and the pulse in my right temple throbs terribly. But the worst of all is sleep! I hardly lie down and begin to doze before something in my left side begins to pull and tug, and something begins to hammer in my left shoulder—and in my head, too! I jump up like a

60 madman, walk about a little, lie down again, but the moment I fall asleep I have a terrible cramp in the side. And so it is all night long! (*Enter* Natalia Stepanovna.) **C**

Natalia. Ah! It's you. Papa said to go in: there was a dealer in there who'd come to buy something. Good afternoon, Ivan Vassiliyitch.

Lomov. Good day, my dear Natalia Stepanovna.

Natalia. You must pardon me for wearing my apron and this old dress: we are working today. Why haven't you come to see us oftener? You've not been here for so long! Sit down (*They sit down.*) Won't you have something to eat?

70 **Lomov.** Thank you, I have just had lunch.

---

meditate (mĕd´ĭ-tāt´) *v.* to consider for a long time

C CHARACTERS IN A FARCE
Reread lines 45–62. Now that Lomov is in the room, he talks to himself. What main trait does Lomov exhibit in his **monologue**?

_____
_____
_____
_____
_____
_____
_____
_____
_____
_____
_____
_____

Natalia. Smoke, do, there are the matches. Today it is beautiful, and only yesterday it rained so hard that the workmen couldn't do a stroke of work. How many bricks have you cut? Think of it! I was so anxious that I had the whole field mowed, and now I'm sorry I did it, because I'm afraid the hay will rot. It would have been better if I had waited. But what on earth is this? You are in evening clothes! The latest cut! Are you on your way to a ball? And you seem to be looking better, too—really. Why are you dressed up so gorgeously? **D**

80 **Lomov** (*excited*). You see, my dear Natalia Stepanovna—it's simply this: I have decided to ask you to listen to me—of course it will be a surprise, and indeed you'll be angry, but!— (*aside*) How fearfully cold it is!

Natalia. What is it? (*a pause*) Well?

Lomov. I'll try to be brief. My dear Natalia Stepanovna, as you know, for many years, since my childhood, I have had the honor to know your family. My poor aunt and her husband, from whom, as you know, I inherited the estate, always had the greatest respect for your father and your poor mother. The Lomovs and
90 the Tschubukovs have been for decades on the friendliest, indeed the closest, terms with each other, and furthermore my property, as you know, adjoins your own. If you will be so good as to remember, my meadows touch your birch woods.

Natalia. Pardon the interruption. You said "my meadows"—but are they yours?

Lomov. Yes, they belong to me.

Natalia. What nonsense! The meadows belong to us—not to you!

Lomov. No, to me! Now, my dear Natalia Stepanovna!

Natalia. Well, that is certainly news to me. How do they belong
100 to you?

Lomov. How? I am speaking of the meadows lying between your birch woods and my brick earth.[1]

Natalia. Yes, exactly. They belong to us.

---

1. **brick earth:** clay suitable for making bricks.

D **CHARACTERS IN A FARCE**
In lines 71–79, what pattern of behavior is Natalia showing? How is her behavior stereotypical?

_____

_____

_____

_____

_____

_____

_____

_____

_____

_____

_____

_____

_____

_____

_____

_____

_____

_____

_____

ⓔ READING A PLAY
Reread lines 94–110. Remember that Lomov intends to ask Natalia to marry him. What do they start arguing about instead?

_____

_____

_____

_____

_____

_____

_____

_____

_____

_____

_____

_____

_____

_____

_____

_____

Lomov. No, you are mistaken, my dear Natalia Stepanovna, they belong to me.

Natalia. Try to remember exactly, Ivan Vassiliyitch. Is it so long ago that you inherited them?

Lomov. Long ago! As far back as I can remember they have always belonged to us.

110 **Natalia.** But that isn't true! You'll pardon my saying so. ⓔ

Lomov. It is all a matter of record, my dear Natalia Stepanovna. It is true that at one time the title to the meadows was disputed, but now everyone knows they belong to me. There is no room for discussion. Be so good as to listen: my aunt's grandmother put these meadows, free from all costs, into the hands of your father's grandfather's peasants for a certain time while they were making bricks for my grandmother. These people used the meadows free of cost for about forty years, living there as they would on their own property. Later, however, when—

120 **Natalia.** There's not a word of truth in that! My grandfather, and my great grandfather, too, knew that their estate reached back to the swamp, so that the meadows belong to us. What further discussion can there be? I can't understand it. It is really most annoying.

Lomov. I'll show you the papers, Natalia Stepanovna.

Natalia. No, either you are joking or trying to lead me into a discussion. That's not at all nice! We have owned this property for nearly three hundred years, and now all at once we hear that it doesn't belong to us. Ivan Vassiliyitch, you will pardon me, but I
130 really can't believe my ears. So far as I'm concerned, the meadows are worth very little. In all they don't contain more than five acres, and they are worth only a few hundred rubles,[2] say three hundred, but the injustice of the thing is what affects me. Say what you will, I can't bear injustice.

Lomov. Only listen until I have finished, please! The peasants of your respected father's grandfather, as I have already had the

---

2. **rubles** (rōo'bəlz): units of Russian money.

honor to tell you, baked bricks for my grandmother. My aunt's grandmother wished to do them a favor—

Natalia. Grandfather! Grandmother! Aunt! I know nothing of
140 them. All I know is that the meadows belong to us, and that ends the matter.

Lomov. No, they belong to me!

Natalia. And if you keep on explaining it for two days and put on five suits of evening clothes, the meadows are still ours, ours, ours! I don't want to take your property, but I refuse to give up what belongs to us!  🅕

Lomov. Natalia Stepanovna, I don't need the meadows, I am only concerned with the principle. If you are agreeable, I beg of you, accept them as a gift from me!

150 **Natalia.** But I can give them to you, because they belong to me! That is very peculiar, Ivan Vassiliyitch! Until now we have considered you as a good neighbor and a good friend; only last year we lent you our threshing machine so that we couldn't thresh until November, and you treat us like thieves! You offer to give me my own land. Excuse me, but neighbors don't treat each other that way. In my opinion, it's a very low trick—to speak frankly—

Lomov. According to you I'm a <u>usurper</u>, then, am I? My dear lady, I have never appropriated other people's property, and I shall permit no one to accuse me of such a thing! (*He goes quickly to the*
160 *bottle and drinks water.*) The meadows are mine!

Natalia. That's not the truth! They are mine!

Lomov. Mine!

Natalia. Eh? I'll prove it to you! This afternoon I'll send my reapers into the meadows.

Lomov. W—h—a—t?

Natalia. My reapers will be there today!

Lomov. And I'll chase them off!

Natalia. If you dare!

🅕 **CHARACTERS IN A FARCE**
Reread lines 125–146. How does Natalia respond to Lomov? What pattern of behavior is evident in her responses?

_____
_____
_____
_____
_____
_____
_____
_____
_____
_____

usurper (yōō-sûrp′ər) *n.* someone who wrongfully takes possession of something

Complete the following sentence. Lomov says that Natalia accuses him of being a **usurper** because . . .

_____
_____
_____
_____
_____

G CHARACTERS IN A FARCE

In lines 165–176, how is Lomov's behavior pattern similar to Natalia's?

_____

_____

_____

_____

_____

_____

_____

_____

_____

_____

_____

_____

_____

_____

_____

_____

_____

_____

Lomov. The meadows are mine, you understand? Mine!

170 **Natalia.** Really, you don't need to scream so! If you want to scream and snort and rage you may do it at home, but here please keep yourself within the limits of common decency.

Lomov. My dear lady, if it weren't that I were suffering from palpitation of the heart and hammering of the arteries in my temples, I would deal with you very differently! (*in a loud voice*) The meadows belong to me! **G**

Natalia. Us!

Lomov. Me! (*Enter* Tschubukov, *right*.)

Tschubukov. What's going on here? What is he yelling about?

180 **Natalia.** Papa, please tell this gentleman to whom the meadows belong, to us or to him?

Tschubukov (*to* Lomov). My dear fellow, the meadows are ours.

Lomov. But, merciful heavens, Stepan Stepanovitch, how do you make that out? You at least must be reasonable. My aunt's grandmother gave the use of the meadows free of cost to your grandfather's peasants; the peasants lived on the land for forty years and used it as their own, but later when—

Tschubukov. Permit me, my dear friend. You forget that your grandfather's peasants never paid, because there had been a 190 lawsuit over the meadows, and everyone knows that the meadows belong to us. You haven't looked at the map.

Lomov. I'll prove to you that they belong to me!

Tschubukov. Don't try to prove it, my dear fellow.

Lomov. I will!

Tschubukov. My good fellow, what are you shrieking about? You can't prove anything by yelling, you know. I don't ask for anything that belongs to you, nor do I intend to give up anything of my own. Why should I? If it has gone so far, my dear man, that you really intend to claim the meadows, I'd rather give them to 200 the peasants than you, and I certainly shall!

Lomov. I can't believe it! By what right can you give away property that doesn't belong to you?

Tschubukov. Really, you must allow me to decide what I am to do with my own land! I'm not accustomed, young man, to have people address me in that tone of voice. I, young man, am twice your age, and I beg you to address me respectfully.

Lomov. No! No! You think I'm a fool! You're making fun of me! You call my property yours and then you expect me to stand quietly by and talk to you like a human being. That isn't the
210 way a good neighbor behaves, Stepan Stepanovitch! You are no neighbor, you're no better than a land grabber. That's what you are! **⊕**

Tschubukov. Wh—at? What did he say?

Natalia. Papa, send the reapers into the meadows this minute!

Tschubukov (*to* Lomov). What was that you said, sir?

Natalia. The meadows belong to us, and I won't give them up! I won't give them up! I won't give them up!

Lomov. We'll see about that! I'll prove in court that they belong to me.

220 **Tschubukov.** In court! You may sue in court, sir, if you like! Oh, I know you, you are only waiting to find an excuse to go to law! You're an intriguer,³ that's what you are! Your whole family were always looking for quarrels. The whole lot!

Lomov. Kindly refrain from insulting my family. The entire race of Lomov has always been honorable! And never has one been brought to trial for embezzlement, as your dear uncle was!

Tschubukov. And the whole Lomov family were insane!

Natalia. Every one of them!

Tschubukov. Your grandmother was a dipsomaniac,⁴ and the
230 younger aunt, Nastasia Michailovna, ran off with an architect. **①**

---

3. **intriguer** (ĭn-trē′gər): a schemer.
4. **dipsomaniac** (dĭp′sə-mā′nē-ăk′): an alcoholic.

⊕ CHARACTERS IN A FARCE
Lomov continues to argue and gets more and more worked up. What does his behavior suggest about his character?

_____

_____

_____

_____

_____

_____

_____

① CHARACTERS IN A FARCE
Reread lines 220–230. Underline details in the dialogue in which Chekhov uses exaggeration to create humor.

glutton (glŭt'n) *n.* a person who eats too much

Lomov. And your mother limped. (*He puts his hand over his heart.*) Oh, my side pains! My temples are bursting! Lord in heaven! Water!!

Tschubukov. And your dear father was a gambler—and a <u>glutton</u>!

Natalia. And your aunt was a gossip like few others.

Lomov. And you are an intriguer. Oh, my heart! And it's an open secret that you cheated at the elections—my eyes are blurred! Where is my hat?

Natalia. Oh, how low! Liar! Disgusting thing!

240 **Lomov.** Where's my hat? My heart! Where shall I go? Where is the door? Oh—it seems—as though I were dying! I can't—my legs won't hold me— (*goes to the door*)

Tschubukov (*following him*). May you never darken my door again!

Natalia. Bring your suit to court! We'll see! (Lomov *staggers out, center.*)

Tschubukov (*angrily*). The devil!

Natalia. Such a good-for-nothing! And then they talk about being good neighbors!

Tschubukov. Loafer! Scarecrow! Monster!

250 **Natalia.** A swindler like that takes over a piece of property that doesn't belong to him and then dares to argue about it!

Tschubukov. And to think that this fool dares to make a proposal of marriage!

Natalia. What? A proposal of marriage? **PAUSE & REFLECT**

Tschubukov. Why, yes! He came here to make you a proposal of marriage.

Natalia. Why didn't you tell me that before?

PAUSE & REFLECT
In line 254, Natalia seems surprised to hear of the marriage proposal. How do you think she will react?

_____

_____

_____

_____

_____

Tschubukov. That's why he had on his evening clothes! The poor fool!

260 **Natalia.** Proposal for me? (*falls into an armchair and groans*) Bring him back! Bring him back!

Tschubukov. Bring whom back!

Natalia. Faster, faster, I'm sinking! Bring him back! (*She becomes hysterical.*)

Tschubukov. What is it? What's wrong with you? (*his hands to his head*) I'm cursed with bad luck! I'll shoot myself! I'll hang myself!

Natalia. I'm dying! Bring him back!

Tschubukov. Bah! In a minute! Don't bawl! (*He rushes out, center.*)

Natalia (*groaning*). What have they done to me? Bring him back!
270 Bring him back!

Tschubukov (*comes running in*). He's coming at once! The devil take him! Ugh! Talk to him yourself, I can't!

Natalia (*groaning*). Bring him back!

Tschubukov. He's coming, I tell you! "Oh, Lord! What a task it is to be the father of a grown daughter!" I'll cut my throat! I really will cut my throat! We've argued with the fellow, insulted him, and now you've thrown him out!—and you did it all, you! **ⓙ**

Natalia. No, you! You haven't any manners, you are brutal! If it weren't for you, he wouldn't have gone!

280 **Tschubukov.** Oh, yes, I'm to blame! If I shoot or hang myself, remember *you'll* be to blame. You forced me to do it! (Lomov *appears in the doorway.*) There, talk to him yourself! (*He goes out.*)

Lomov. Terrible palpitation! My leg is lamed! My side hurts me—

Natalia. Pardon us, we were angry, Ivan Vassiliyitch. I remember now—the meadows really belong to you.

Lomov. My heart is beating terribly! My meadows—my eyelids tremble—(*They sit down.*) We were wrong. It was only the

ⓙ CHARACTERS IN A FARCE
How does Tschubukov respond to his daughter's request. Is this behavior typical of him? Explain.

_____

_____

_____

_____

_____

_____

_____

_____

K CHARACTERS IN A
FARCE
Reread lines 284–285 and
290. How serious is Natalia's
commitment to principle?
Explain.

_____

_____

_____

_____

_____

_____

_____

_____

_____

_____

L READING A PLAY
Reread lines 293–315. What
pattern of behavior starts again
with Natalia's aside on line 293?

_____

_____

_____

_____

_____

principle of the thing—the property isn't worth much to me, but
the principle is worth a great deal.

290 **Natalia.** Exactly, the principle! Let us talk about something else. **K**

Lomov. Because I have proofs that my aunt's grandmother had,
with the peasants of your good father—

Natalia. Enough, enough. (*aside*) I don't know how to begin. (*to*
Lomov) Are you going hunting soon?

Lomov. Yes, heath cock shooting, respected Natalia Stepanovna.
I expect to begin after the harvest. Oh, did you hear? My dog,
Ugadi, you know him—limps!

Natalia. What a shame! How did that happen?

Lomov. I don't know. Perhaps it's a dislocation, or maybe he was
300 bitten by some other dog. (*He sighs.*) The best dog I ever had—to
say nothing of the price! I paid Mironov a hundred and twenty-
five rubles for him.

Natalia. That was too much to pay, Ivan Vassiliyitch.

Lomov. In my opinion it was very cheap. A wonderful dog!

Natalia. Papa paid eighty-five rubles for his Otkatai, and Otkatai
is much better than your Ugadi!

Lomov. Really? Otkatai is better than Ugadi? What an idea!
(*He laughs.*) Otkatai better than Ugadi!

Natalia. Of course he is better. It is true Otkatai is still young; he
310 isn't full grown yet, but in the pack or on the leash with two or
three, there is no better than he, even—

Lomov. I really beg your pardon, Natalia Stepanovna, but you
quite overlooked the fact that he has a short lower jaw, and a dog
with a short lower jaw can't snap.

Natalia. Short lower jaw? That's the first I ever heard that! **L**

Lomov. I assure you, his lower jaw is shorter than the upper.

Natalia. Have you measured it?

Lomov. I have measured it. He is good at running though.

Natalia. In the first place, our Otkatai is pure-bred, a full-blooded
320 son of Sapragavas and Stameskis, and as for your mongrel, nobody
could ever figure out his pedigree; he's old and ugly and skinny as
an old hag.

Lomov. Old, certainly! I wouldn't take five of your Otkatais for
him! Ugadi is a dog, and Otkatai is—it is laughable to argue
about it! Dogs like your Otkatai can be found by the dozens at
any dog dealer's, a whole pound full!

Natalia. Ivan Vassiliyitch, you are very **contrary** today. First our
meadows belong to you, and then Ugadi is better than Otkatai. I
don't like it when a person doesn't say what he really thinks. You
330 know perfectly well that Otkatai is a hundred times better than
your silly Ugadi. What makes you keep on saying he isn't?

Lomov. I can see, Natalia Stepanovna, that you consider me either
a blind man or a fool. But at least you may as well admit that
Otkatai has a short lower jaw!

Natalia. It isn't so!

Lomov. Yes, a short lower jaw!

Natalia (*loudly*). It's not so!

Lomov. What makes you scream, my dear lady?

Natalia. What makes you talk such nonsense? It's disgusting!
340 It is high time that Ugadi was shot; and you compare him with
Otkatai!

Lomov. Pardon me, but I can't carry on this argument any longer.
I have palpitation of the heart!

Natalia. I have always noticed that the hunters who do the most
talking know the least about hunting.

Lomov. My dear lady, I beg of you to be still. My heart is
bursting! (*He shouts.*) Be still!

Natalia. I won't be still until you admit that Otkatai is better!
(*Enter* Tschubukov.) **PAUSE & REFLECT**

---

contrary (kŏn′trĕr′ē) *adj.*
stubbornly uncooperative or
contradictory

Underline the examples Natalia
gives to prove that Lomov is
being **contrary**. Then explain
what she means on the lines
below.

_____

_____

_____

_____

_____

_____

_____

PAUSE & REFLECT
At this point, do you think that
Natalia and Lomov would make
a good married couple? Why or
why not?

_____

_____

_____

_____

_____

350 **Tschubukov.** Well, has it begun again?

Natalia. Papa, say frankly, on your honor, which dog is better: Otkatai or Ugadi?

Lomov. Stepan Stepanovitch, I beg of you, just answer this: has your dog a short lower jaw or not? Yes or no?

Tschubukov. And what if he has? Is it of such importance? There is no better dog in the whole country.

Lomov. My Ugadi is better. Tell the truth now!

Tschubukov. Don't get so excited, my dear fellow! Permit me. Your Ugadi certainly has his good points. He is from a good
360 breed, has a good stride, strong haunches, and so forth. But the dog, if you really want to know, has two faults; he is old and he has a short lower jaw.

Lomov. Pardon me, I have a palpitation of the heart!—Let us keep to facts—just remember in Maruskins's meadows, my Ugadi kept ear to ear with Count Rasvachai and your dog was left behind.

Tschubukov. He was behind, because the count struck him with his whip.

Lomov. Quite right. All the other dogs were on the fox's scent, but Otkatai found it necessary to bite a sheep.

370 **Tschubukov.** That isn't so!—I am sensitive about that and beg you to stop this argument. He struck him because everybody looks on a strange dog of good blood with envy. Even you, sir, aren't free from sin. No sooner do you find a dog better than Ugadi than you begin to—this, that—his, mine—and so forth! I remember distinctly.

Lomov. I remember something, too!

Tschubukov (*mimicking him*). I remember something, too! What do you remember?

Lomov. Palpitation! My leg is lame—I can't—

380 **Natalia.** Palpitation! What kind of hunter are you? You ought to stay in the kitchen by the stove and wrestle with the potato peelings and not go fox hunting! Palpitation!

Ⓜ READING A PLAY

What does the stage direction for lines 377–378 tell you about Tschubukov?

_____

_____

_____

_____

Tschubukov. And what kind of hunter are you? A man with your disease ought to stay at home and not jolt around in the saddle. If you were a hunter! But you only ride round in order to find out about other people's dogs and make trouble for everyone. I am sensitive! Let's drop the subject. Besides, you're no hunter.

Lomov. You only ride around to flatter the count! My heart! You intriguer! Swindler!

390 **Tschubukov.** And what of it? (*shouting*) Be still!

Lomov. Intriguer!

Tschubukov. Baby! Puppy! Walking drugstore!

Lomov. Old rat! Jesuit![5] Oh, I know you!

Tschubukov. Be still! Or I'll shoot you—with my worst gun, like a partridge! Fool! Loafer!

Lomov. Everyone knows that—oh, my heart!—that your poor late wife beat you. My leg—my temples—heavens—I'm dying—I—

Tschubukov. And your housekeeper wears the pants in your house!

Lomov. Here—here—there—there—my heart has burst! My
400 shoulder is torn apart. Where is my shoulder? I'm dying! (*He falls into a chair.*) The doctor! (*faints*)

Tschubukov. Baby! Half-baked clam! Fool!

Natalia. Nice sort of hunter you are! You can't even sit on a horse. (*to* Tschubukov) Papa, what's the matter with him? (*She screams.*) Ivan Vassiliyitch! He is dead!

Lomov. I'm ill! I can't breathe! Air!

Natalia. He is dead! (*She shakes* Lomov *in the chair.*) Ivan Vassiliyitch! What have we done! He is dead! (*She sinks into a chair.*) The doctor—doctor! (*She goes into hysterics.*)

410 **Tschubukov.** Ahh! What is it? What's the matter with you?

Natalia (*groaning*). He's dead! Dead!

N CHARACTERS IN A FARCE

In lines 407–410, what is ridiculous about Natalia's reaction?

_____

_____

_____

_____

_____

_____

_____

---

5. **Jesuit** (jĕzh′o͞o-ĭt): a member of a Roman Catholic religious order that was suppressed in Russia because of its resistance to the authority of the czar, the ruler of Russia. At the time, the term had the negative meaning of "one who schemes or plots."

CHARACTERS IN A FARCE
What does Tschubukov's reaction tell you about him?

_____

_____

_____

_____

_____

_____

_____

_____

_____

_____

_____

_____

_____

_____

_____

_____

_____

_____

_____

_____

_____

_____

Tschubukov. Who is dead? Who? (*looking at* Lomov) Yes, he is dead! Good God! Water! The doctor! (*holding the glass to* Lomov's *lips*) Drink! No, he won't drink! He's dead! What a terrible situation! Why didn't I shoot myself? Why have I never cut my throat? What am I waiting for now? Only give me a knife! Give me a pistol! (Lomov *moves.*) He's coming to! Drink some water—there!

Lomov. Sparks! Mists! Where am I?

420 **Tschubukov.** Get married! Quick, and then go to the devil! She's willing! (*He joins the hands of* Lomov *and* Natalia.) She's agreed! Only leave me in peace!

Lomov. Wh—what? (*getting up*) Whom?

Tschubukov. She's willing! Well? Kiss each other and—the devil take you both!

Natalia (*groans*). He lives! Yes, yes, I'm willing!

Tschubukov. Kiss each other!

Lomov. Eh? Whom? (Natalia *and* Lomov *kiss.*) Very nice! Pardon me, but what is this for? Oh, yes, I understand! My heart—sparks—I am happy. Natalia Stepanovna. (*He kisses her hand.*) My
430 leg is lame!

Natalia. I'm happy too!

Tschubukov. Ahhh! A load off my shoulders! Ahh!

Natalia. And now at least you'll admit that Ugadi is worse that Otkatai!

Lomov. Better!

Natalia. Worse!

Tschubukov. Now the domestic joys have begun. Champagne!

Lomov. Better!

Natalia. Worse, worse, worse!

440 **Tschubukov** (*trying to drown them out*). Champagne, champagne!

Translated from the Russian by

Hilmer Baukhage and Barrett H. Clark

Text Analysis: Characters in a Farce

Natalia's arguments with Lomov are the major conflict in *A Marriage Proposal*.
Write a statement about Lomov's main character trait or pattern of behavior
in the chart below. How does Natalia provoke or cause Lomov to become
more excited? Write specific examples in the boxes below.

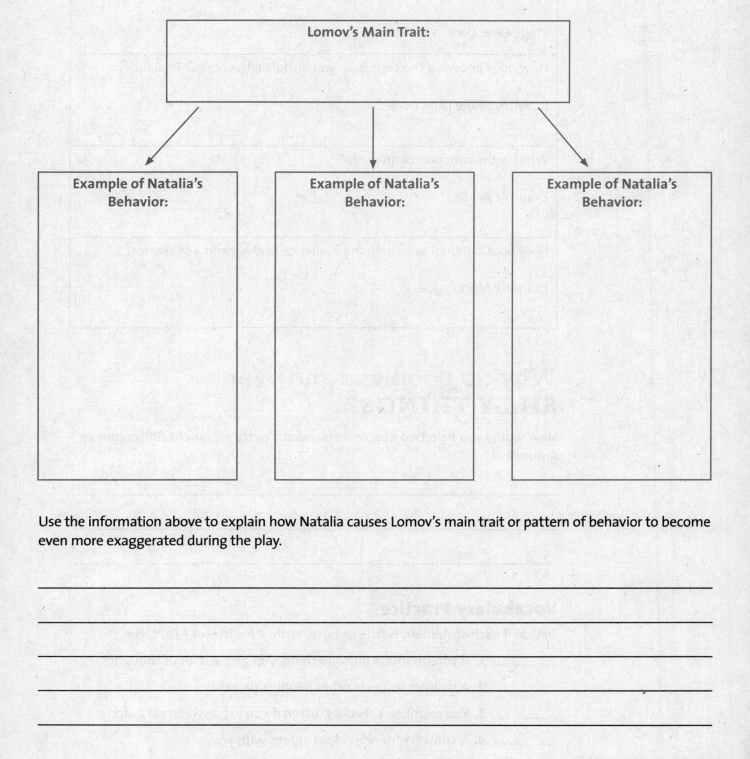

Lomov's Main Trait:

Example of Natalia's Behavior:

Example of Natalia's Behavior:

Example of Natalia's Behavior:

Use the information above to explain how Natalia causes Lomov's main trait or pattern of behavior to become
even more exaggerated during the play.

_____

_____

_____

_____

_____

Reading Skill: Reading a Play

Use the notes you took as you read to help you answer the questions below. For each answer, provide an example from the text.

How do stage directions help you understand the actions of the characters?   Stage Direction:
How does knowing the tone help you visualize the scene? Explain.   Example Stage Direction:
What is the function of an aside?   Example Aside:
How does a monologue help the audience understand a character?   Example Monologue:

Why do people argue over SILLY THINGS?

How would you help two people involved in a petty argument find common ground?

_____

_____

Vocabulary Practice

Decide if each statement is true or false. Write *T* for true or *F* for false.

_____ 1. If you **meditate** on something, you give it a lot of thought.

_____ 2. A **usurper** respects other people's property.

_____ 3. You might be called a **glutton** if you eat a whole pie quickly.

_____ 4. A **contrary** friend seldom agrees with you.

Academic Vocabulary in Writing

dynamic	individual	motive	seek	undergo

What **motives** do people have for arguing? Are they always trying to reach a goal or do they just find it exciting to argue? Use at least one Academic Vocabulary word in your response. Definitions for these terms are listed on page 57.

_____

_____

_____

_____

_____

_____

Assessment Practice

DIRECTIONS Use *A Marriage Proposal* to answer questions 1–4.

1 What two topics lead to petty arguments between Lomov and Natalia?

- **A** Lomov's illnesses and Tschubukov's dog
- **B** money lending and land ownership
- **C** Lomov's proposal and Natalia's acceptance
- **D** meadow ownership and dog quality

2 One way that stage directions help readers is by —

- **A** giving a detailed summary of monologues
- **B** reviewing the actions the characters have taken
- **C** describing the tone in which dialogue should be delivered
- **D** supporting the action with lengthy asides

3 What does this play suggest about Chekhov's attitude toward this class of landowners?

- **A** Chekhov supports the arguments of these people.
- **B** Chekhov thinks these landowners are greedy and petty.
- **C** Chekhov believes that these landowners are happy.
- **D** Chekhov knows these people marry for love.

4 Lomov's monologue in lines 45–62 allows the reader to —

- **A** appreciate Natalia's feelings toward Lomov
- **B** prepare to read the other characters' monologues
- **C** determine Tschubukov's opinion about Lomov
- **D** understand Lomov's neurotic character without interruption

UNIT 3

A Writer's Choice
NARRATIVE DEVICES

Be sure to read the Text Analysis Workshop on pp. 302–307 in *Holt McDougal Literature*.

Academic Vocabulary for Unit 3

Preview the following Academic Vocabulary words. You will encounter these words as you work through this book and will use them as you write and talk about the selections in this unit.

consequent (kŏn'sĭ kwent') *adj.* following as an effect or result
*What **consequent** events do you think will result from the character's actions?*

crucial (krōō'shəl) *adj.* extremely important; critical
*The setting of this story in the distant future is **crucial** to its plot.*

initial (ĭ-nĭsh'əl) *adj.* occurring at the beginning
*My **initial** impression of the character was negative, but I grew to like him as I continued reading the story.*

shift (shĭft) *v.* to change course; to move or transfer
*In this story, the point of view **shifts** when a different narrator begins describing events.*

survive (sər-vīv) *v.* to live longer than expected; to remain in existence
*Will any of the characters be able to **survive** the devastating war?*

Think of a time when your **initial** response to a person, a place, or a situation turned out to be very different from your final judgment. What caused your feelings to change? Write your response on the lines below, using at least two Academic Vocabulary words.

_____

_____

_____

_____

By the Waters of Babylon
Short Story by Stephen Vincent Benét

Does **KNOWLEDGE** come at a price?

How much knowledge should a person or a society have? When, if ever, should our pursuit of knowledge be limited? In "By the Waters of Babylon," you'll meet John, a character who learns through a difficult journey that knowledge can be very costly.

DISCUSS Think about a time when your desire to know something got you into a tough situation. See the example at the left and then add an example from your own life to the chart. Share your chart with a small group of classmates, and then discuss whether some things are better left unknown.

What I Wanted to Know

Who my older sister liked

What I Did to Find Out

Read her electronic journal

What Happened

I found out we both liked the same guy.

Text Analysis: First-Person Point of View

Point of view refers to the perspective from which a story is told. The author creates point of view by choosing a **narrator**—the voice that tells the story. The narrator may be a character in the story or an outside observer. In a story told from the **first-person point of view,** the narrator is a character in the story. The chart below provides more information about first-person point of view.

FIRST-PERSON POINT OF VIEW	STRATEGIES FOR ANALYSIS
The narrator • is a main or minor character in the story • refers to him- or herself as *I* or *me* • presents his or her own thoughts, feelings, and interpretations • lacks direct access to the thoughts of other characters • creates a subjective tone, or a personal attitude toward events in the story	**Consider the source.** You may feel connected to a first-person narrator because he or she seems to be talking directly to you. However, don't trust everything the narrator says. Ask yourself: • Is the narrator trustworthy? Does he or she know enough to describe things accurately? • How might the narrator's opinions or beliefs affect what he or she says about other characters, events, and situations?

"By the Waters of Babylon" is a short story told from the first-person point of view. Everything in the story is presented through the eyes of a character named John. At times, John does not fully understand what he sees or experiences. Such a narrator is called a **naive narrator.** However, remember that the author and the narrator are not the same person. The author uses John's naive perspective to reveal the **tone,** or the author's attitude toward the subject of the story.

As you read "By the Waters of Babylon," notice how the point of view affects what you learn about the story's characters, events, and tone.

Reading Skill: Make Inferences

When a character narrates a story, you know only as much as that character knows. By **making inferences,** or educated guesses, you can figure out information that the narrator does not tell you. Use the following strategies to make inferences about the setting of "By the Waters of Babylon":

• Notice the names of places.

• Think about how these places resemble places that you know.

As you read the story, you'll be prompted to jot down important details that help you understand the different places John visits on his journey. The chart below provides an example.

Places	Important Details	My Inferences
1. Dead Places	Only priests and sons of priests can visit.	There are lots of rules in this society.
2. the great river		
3. the Place of the Gods		

**SET A PURPOSE
FOR READING**

Read the story to find out where John's desire for knowledge leads him.

By the Waters of Babylon

by **STEPHEN VINCENT BENÉT**

BACKGROUND The title of this story is an **allusion,** or reference, to Psalm 137 in the Bible. The psalm expresses the sorrow of the Jews over their enslavement in Babylon and the destruction of Zion, their homeland. The psalm begins: "By the waters of Babylon, there we sat down and wept, when we remembered thee, O Zion."

Ⓐ POINT OF VIEW
Reread lines 1–11 and underline the sentence that expresses the narrator's **tone,** or attitude, toward the rules of his society. As you continue reading, think about how his beliefs affect the way he describes events and situations.

The north and the west and the south are good hunting ground, but it is forbidden to go east. It is forbidden to go to any of the Dead Places except to search for metal, and then he who touches the metal must be a priest or the son of a priest. Afterwards, both the man and the metal must be purified. These are the rules and the laws; they are well made. It is forbidden to cross the great river and look upon the place that was the Place of the Gods—this is most strictly forbidden. We do not even say its name, though we know its name. It is there that spirits live, and demons—it is there that there
10 are the ashes of the Great Burning. These things are forbidden—they have been forbidden since the beginning of time. Ⓐ

My father is a priest; I am the son of a priest. I have been in the Dead Places near us, with my father—at first, I was afraid. When my father went into the house to search for the metal, I stood by the door, and my heart felt small and weak. It was a dead man's house, a spirit house. It did not have the smell of man, though there were old bones in a corner. But it is not fitting that a priest's son should show fear. I looked at the bones in the shadow and kept my voice still. **B**

20   Then my father came out with the metal—a good, strong piece. He looked at me with both eyes, but I had not run away. He gave me the metal to hold—I took it and did not die. So he knew that I was truly his son and would be a priest in my time. That was when I was very young—nevertheless, my brothers would not have done it, though they are good hunters. After that, they gave me the good piece of meat and the warm corner by the fire. My father watched over me—he was glad that I should be a priest. But when I boasted or wept without a reason, he punished me more strictly than my brothers. That was right.

30   After a time, I myself was allowed to go into the dead houses and search for metal. So I learned the ways of those houses—and if I saw bones, I was no longer afraid. The bones are light and old—sometimes they will fall into dust if you touch them. But that is a great sin.

I was taught the chants and the spells—I was taught how to stop the running of blood from a wound and many secrets. A priest must know many secrets—that was what my father said. If the hunters think we do all things by chants and spells, they may believe so—it does not hurt them. I was taught how to read in
40 the old books and how to make the old writings—that was hard and took a long time. My knowledge made me happy—it was like a fire in my heart. Most of all, I liked to hear of the Old Days and the stories of the gods. I asked myself many questions that I could not answer, but it was good to ask them. At night, I would lie awake and listen to the wind—it seemed to me that it was the voice of the gods as they flew through the air.

We are not ignorant like the Forest People—our women spin wool on the wheel; our priests wear a white robe. We do not eat grubs from the tree; we have not forgotten the old writings,

B MAKE INFERENCES
What **inferences** can you make so far about the setting of the story? Write details about the Dead Places and your inferences in the chart below.

Details About Dead Places

↓

My Inferences

C POINT OF VIEW
The **first-person point of view** gives you direct access to the narrator's thoughts and feelings. Reread lines 35–53 and underline details that help you get to know the narrator as a character. Then describe his traits on the lines below.

_____

_____

_____

_____

_____

_____

_____

50 although they are hard to understand. Nevertheless, my knowledge and my lack of knowledge burned in me—I wished to know more. When I was a man at last, I came to my father and said, "It is time for me to go on my journey. Give me your leave." **C**

He looked at me for a long time, stroking his beard; then he said at last, "Yes. It is time." That night, in the house of the priesthood, I asked for and received purification. My body hurt, but my spirit was a cool stone. It was my father himself who questioned me about my dreams.

He bade me look into the smoke of the fire and see—I saw 60 and told what I saw. It was what I have always seen—a river, and, beyond it, a great Dead Place and in it the gods walking. I have always thought about that. His eyes were stern when I told him—he was no longer my father but a priest. He said, "This is a strong dream."

"It is mine," I said, while the smoke waved and my head felt light. They were singing the star song in the outer chamber, and it was like the buzzing of bees in my head.

He asked me how the gods were dressed, and I told him how they were dressed. We know how they were dressed from the book, 70 but I saw them as if they were before me. When I had finished, he threw the sticks three times and studied them as they fell.

"This is a very strong dream," he said. "It may eat you up."

"I am not afraid," I said and looked at him with both eyes. My voice sounded thin in my ears, but that was because of the smoke.

He touched me on the breast and the forehead. He gave me the bow and the three arrows.

"Take them," he said. "It is forbidden to travel east. It is forbidden to cross the river. It is forbidden to go to 80 the Place of the Gods. All these things are forbidden."

"All these things are forbidden," I said, but it was my voice that spoke and not my spirit. He looked at me again.

"My son," he said. "Once I had young dreams. If your dreams do not eat you up, you may be a great priest. If they eat you, you are still my son. Now go on your journey." **D**

I went fasting, as is the law. My body hurt but not my heart. When the dawn came, I was out of sight of the village. I prayed and purified myself, waiting for a sign. The sign was an eagle. It flew east.

Sometimes signs are sent by bad spirits. I waited again on the flat rock, fasting, taking no food. I was very still—I could feel the sky above me and the earth beneath. I waited till the sun was beginning to sink. Then three deer passed in the valley, going east—they did not wind me or see me. There was a white fawn with them—a very great sign.

I followed them, at a distance, waiting for what would happen. My heart was troubled about going east, yet I knew that I must go. My head hummed with my fasting—I did not even see the panther spring upon the white fawn. But, before I knew it, the bow was in my hand. I shouted, and the panther lifted his head from the fawn. It is not easy to kill a panther with one arrow, but the arrow went through his eye and into his brain. He died as he tried to spring—he rolled over, tearing at the ground. Then I knew I was meant to go east—I knew that was my journey. When the night came, I made my fire and roasted meat.

It is eight suns' journey to the east, and a man passes by many Dead Places. The Forest People are afraid of them, but I am not. Once I made my fire on the edge of a Dead Place at night, and next morning, in the dead house, I found a good knife, little rusted. That was small to what came afterward, but it made my heart feel big. Always when I looked for game, it was in front of my arrow, and twice I passed hunting parties of the Forest People without their knowing. So I knew my magic was strong and my journey clean, in spite of the law. **E**

Toward the setting of the eighth sun, I came to the banks of the great river. It was half a day's journey after I had left the god road—we do not use the god roads now, for they are falling apart

90

100

110

120

D MAKE INFERENCES
Why does the narrator's father allow him to travel to the Place of the Gods, even though it is forbidden?

_____

_____

_____

_____

_____

_____

E POINT OF VIEW
Reread lines 93–117 and underline details that show the narrator still feels uneasy about traveling east. What makes him conclude that he is doing the right thing in breaking his society's laws?

_____

_____

_____

_____

_____

_____

_____

F MAKE INFERENCES
Reread lines 118–134 and underline details that describe the great river and the Place of the Gods. Do these places look like any places you know? Explain.

Great river:

_____

_____

_____

Place of the Gods:

_____

_____

_____

into great blocks of stone, and the forest is safer going. A long way off, I had seen the water through trees, but the trees were thick. At last, I came out upon an open place at the top of a cliff. There was the great river below, like a giant in the sun. It is very long, very wide. It could eat all the streams we know and still be thirsty. Its name is Ou-dis-sun, the Sacred, the Long. No man of my tribe had seen it, not even my father, the priest. It was magic, and I prayed.

Then I raised my eyes and looked south. It was there, the Place of the Gods.

130 How can I tell what it was like—you do not know. It was there, in the red light, and they were too big to be houses. It was there with the red light upon it, mighty and ruined. I knew that in another moment the gods would see me. I covered my eyes with my hands and crept back into the forest. **F**

Surely, that was enough to do, and live. Surely it was enough to spend the night upon the cliff. The Forest People themselves do not come near. Yet, all through the night, I knew that I should have to cross the river and walk in the places of the gods, although the gods ate me up. My magic did not help me at all, and yet there 140 was a fire in my bowels, a fire in my mind. When the sun rose, I thought, "My journey has been clean. Now I will go home from my journey." But, even as I thought so, I knew I could not. If I went to the Place of the Gods, I would surely die, but, if I did not go, I could never be at peace with my spirit again. It is better to lose one's life than one's spirit, if one is a priest and the son of a priest.

Nevertheless, as I made the raft, the tears ran out of my eyes. The Forest People could have killed me without fight, if they had come upon me then, but they did not come. When the raft was made, I said the sayings for the dead and painted myself for 150 death. My heart was cold as a frog and my knees like water, but the burning in my mind would not let me have peace. As I pushed the raft from the shore, I began my death song—I had the right. It was a fine song.

"I am John, son of John," I sang. "My people are the Hill People. They are the men.

*I go into the Dead Places, but I am not slain. I take the metal
from the Dead Places, but I am not blasted.*

*I travel upon the god roads and am not afraid. E-yah! I have
killed the panther; I have killed the fawn!*

160 *E-yah! I have come to the great river. No man has come there before.*

*It is forbidden to go east, but I have gone, forbidden to go on the
great river, but I am there.*

Open your hearts, you spirits, and hear my song.

Now I go to the Place of the Gods; I shall not return.

*My body is painted for death and my limbs weak, but my heart is
big as I go to the Place of the Gods!"* **PAUSE & REFLECT**

All the same, when I came to the Place of the Gods, I was
afraid, afraid. The current of the great river is very strong—it
gripped my raft with its hands. That was magic, for the river itself
170 is wide and calm. I could feel evil spirits about me, in the bright
morning; I could feel their breath on my neck as I was swept
down the stream. Never have I been so much alone—I tried to
think of my knowledge, but it was a squirrel's heap of winter nuts.
There was no strength in my knowledge anymore, and I felt small
and naked as a new-hatched bird—alone upon the great river, the
servant of the gods.

Yet, after a while, my eyes were opened, and I saw. I saw both
banks of the river—I saw that once there had been god roads
across it, though now they were broken and fallen like broken
180 vines. Very great they were, and wonderful and broken—broken
in the time of the Great Burning when the fire fell out of the sky.
And always the current took me nearer to the Place of the Gods,
and the huge ruins rose before my eyes.

I do not know the customs of rivers—we are the People of
the Hills. I tried to guide my raft with the pole, but it spun
around. I thought the river meant to take me past the Place of the
Gods and out into the Bitter Water of the legends. I grew angry
then—my heart felt strong. I said aloud, "I am a priest and the
son of a priest!" The gods heard me—they showed me how to

PAUSE & REFLECT
What does John's death song
tell you about him? Underline
details in the text that reveal his
character, and then write your
overall impression on the lines
below.

G **POINT OF VIEW**
Reread lines 184–191. Underline details that suggest John is a **naive narrator,** or one who does not fully understand his surroundings.

H **MAKE INFERENCES**
Reread lines 192–210. Underline details that describe what John sees in the Place of the Gods. What can you infer about the events that happened there?

_____

_____

_____

_____

_____

190 paddle with the pole on one side of the raft. The current changed itself—I drew near to the Place of the Gods. **G**

When I was very near, my raft struck and turned over. I can swim in our lakes—I swam to the shore. There was a great spike of rusted metal sticking out into the river—I hauled myself up upon it and sat there, panting. I had saved my bow and two arrows and the knife I found in the Dead Place, but that was all. My raft went whirling downstream toward the Bitter Water. I looked after it, and thought if it had trod me under, at least I would be safely dead. Nevertheless, when I had dried my bowstring and restrung 200 it, I walked forward to the Place of the Gods.

It felt like ground underfoot; it did not burn me. It is not true what some of the tales say, that the ground there burns forever, for I have been there. Here and there were the marks and stains of the Great Burning, on the ruins, that is true. But they were old marks and old stains. It is not true either, what some of our priests say, that it is an island covered with fogs and enchantments. It is not. It is a great Dead Place—greater than any Dead Place we know. Everywhere in it there are god roads, though most are cracked and broken. Everywhere there are the ruins of the high towers of 210 the gods. **H**

How shall I tell what I saw? I went carefully, my strung bow in my hand, my skin ready for danger. There should have been the wailings of spirits and the shrieks of demons, but there were not. It was very silent and sunny where I had landed—the wind and the rain and the birds that drop seeds had done their work—the grass grew in the cracks of the broken stone. It is a fair island no wonder the gods built there. If I had come there, a god, I also would have built.

220 How shall I tell what I saw? The towers are not all broken— here and there one still stands, like a great tree in a forest, and the birds nest high. But the towers themselves look blind, for

the gods are gone. I saw a fish hawk, catching fish in the river. I
saw a little dance of white butterflies over a great heap of broken
stones and columns. I went there and looked about me—there
was a carved stone with cut letters, broken in half. I can read
230 letters, but I could not understand these. They said UBTREAS.
There was also the shattered image of a man or a god. It had
been made of white stone, and he wore his hair tied back like a
woman's. His name was ASHING, as I read on the cracked half
of a stone. I thought it wise to pray to ASHING, though I do not
know that god. ❶

    How shall I tell what I saw? There was no smell of man left,
on stone or metal. Nor were there many trees in that wilderness
of stone. There are many pigeons, nesting and dropping in the
towers—the gods must have loved them, or, perhaps, they used
240 them for sacrifices. There are wild cats that roam the god roads,
green-eyed, unafraid of man. At night they wail like demons, but
they are not demons. The wild dogs are more dangerous, for they
hunt in a pack, but them I did not meet till later. Everywhere there
are the carved stones, carved with magical numbers or words.

    I went north—I did not try to hide myself. When a god or a
demon saw me, then I would die, but meanwhile I was no longer
afraid. My hunger for knowledge burned in me—there was so
much that I could not understand. After a while, I knew that
my belly was hungry. I could have hunted for my meat, but I did
250 not hunt. It is known that the gods did not hunt as we do—they
got their food from enchanted boxes and jars. Sometimes these
are still found in the Dead Places—once, when I was a child
and foolish, I opened such a jar and tasted it and found the food
sweet. But my father found out and punished me for it strictly, for,
often, that food is death. Now, though, I had long gone past what
was forbidden, and I entered the likeliest towers, looking for the
food of the gods. ❷

    I found it at last in the ruins of a great temple in the mid-city.
A mighty temple it must have been, for the roof was painted
260 like the sky at night with its stars—that much I could see, though
the colors were faint and dim. It went down into great caves

❶ **MAKE INFERENCES**
In lines 231–235 John sees a
statue of a person. Part of his
name is ASHING (the stone that
names his is cracked.) What
famous person from U.S. history
might this be?

_____

_____

_____

_____

_____

_____

❷ **MAKE INFERENCES**
Reread lines 245–257. Why do
you think the "food of the gods"
caused death for some of John's
people?

_____

_____

_____

_____

_____

_____

PAUSE & REFLECT
What do you think John drank
that made his head swim?

_____

_____

_____

_____

_____

_____

_____

_____

_____

_____

_____

_____

_____

_____

_____

_____

_____

_____

_____

_____

_____

and tunnels—perhaps they kept their slaves there. But when I started to climb down, I heard the squeaking of rats, so I did not go—rats are unclean, and there must have been many tribes of them, from the squeaking. But near there, I found food, in the heart of a ruin, behind a door that still opened. I ate only the fruits from the jars—they had a very sweet taste. There was drink, too, in bottles of glass—the drink of the gods was strong and made my head swim. After I had eaten and drunk, I slept on the top of a stone, my bow at my side. **PAUSE & REFLECT**

When I woke, the sun was low. Looking down from where I lay, I saw a dog sitting on his haunches. His tongue was hanging out of his mouth; he looked as if he were laughing. He was a big dog, with a gray-brown coat, as big as a wolf. I sprang up and shouted at him, but he did not move—he just sat there as if he were laughing. I did not like that. When I reached for a stone to throw, he moved swiftly out of the way of the stone. He was not afraid of me; he looked at me as if I were meat. No doubt I could have killed him with an arrow, but I did not know if there were others. Moreover, night was falling.

I looked about me—not far away there was a great, broken god road, leading north. The towers were high enough, but not so high, and while many of the dead houses were wrecked, there were some that stood. I went toward this god road, keeping to the heights of the ruins, while the dog followed. When I had reached the god road, I saw that there were others behind him. If I had slept later, they would have come upon me asleep and torn out my throat. As it was, they were sure enough of me; they did not hurry. When I went into the dead house, they kept watch at the entrance—doubtless they thought they would have a fine hunt. But a dog cannot open a door, and I knew, from the books, that the gods did not like to live on the ground but on high.

I had just found a door I could open when the dogs decided to rush. Ha! They were surprised when I shut the door in their faces—it was a good door, of strong metal. I could hear their foolish baying beyond it, but I did not stop to answer them. I was in darkness—I found stairs and climbed. There were many stairs, turning around till my head was dizzy. At the top was another door—I found the knob and opened it. I was in a long small chamber—on one side of it was a bronze door that could not be opened, for it had no handle. Perhaps there was a magic word to open it, but I did not have the word. I turned to the door in the opposite side of the wall. The lock of it was broken, and I opened it and went in. **K**

Within, there was a place of great riches. The god who lived there must have been a powerful god. The first room was a small anteroom—I waited there for some time, telling the spirits of the place that I came in peace and not as a robber. When it seemed to me that they had had time to hear me, I went on. Ah, what riches! Few, even, of the windows had been broken—it was all as it had been. The great windows that looked over the city had not been broken at all, though they were dusty and streaked with many years. There were coverings on the floors, the colors not greatly faded, and the chairs were soft and deep. There were pictures upon the walls, very strange, very wonderful—I remember one of a bunch of flowers in a jar—if you came close to it, you could see nothing but bits of color, but if you stood away from it, the flowers might have been picked yesterday. It made my heart feel strange to look at this picture—and to look at the figure of a bird, in some hard clay, on a table and see it so like our birds. Everywhere there were books and writings, many in tongues that I could not read. The god who lived there must have been a wise god and full of knowledge. I felt I had a right there, as I sought knowledge also. **L**

Nevertheless, it was strange. There was a washing place but no water—perhaps the gods washed in air. There was a cooking place but no wood, and though there was a machine to cook

K **POINT OF VIEW**
Reread lines 281–304. In what way does the first-person point of view make this scene more intense and exciting for readers?

_____

_____

_____

_____

_____

_____

_____

_____

_____

_____

L **MAKE INFERENCES**
Reread lines 305–324 and underline details that describe the "place of great riches." What does this place remind you of?

_____

_____

_____

_____

_____

_____

_____

_____

Ⓜ POINT OF VIEW
Reread lines 325–340 and underline details that show John is a naive narrator.

_____

_____

_____

_____

_____

_____

_____

_____

Ⓝ MAKE INFERENCES
In what room within the "place of great riches" does John sleep? Underline details in lines 341–353 that provide clues, and write your inference on the lines below.

_____

_____

_____

_____

_____

_____

_____

_____

_____

food, there was no place to put fire in it. Nor were there candles or lamps—there were things that looked like lamps, but they had neither oil nor wick. All these things were magic, but I touched them and lived—the magic had gone out of them. Let me tell one thing to show. In the washing place, a thing said "Hot," but it was not hot to the touch—another thing said "Cold," but it was not cold. This must have been a strong magic, but the magic was gone. I do not understand—they had ways—I wish that I
340 knew. Ⓜ

It was close and dry and dusty in the house of the gods. I have said the magic was gone, but that is not true—it had gone from the magic things, but it had not gone from the place. I felt the spirits about me, weighing upon me. Nor had I ever slept in a Dead Place before—and yet, tonight, I must sleep there. When I thought of it, my tongue felt dry in my throat, in spite of my wish for knowledge. Almost I would have gone down again and faced the dogs, but I did not.

I had not gone through all the rooms when the darkness fell.
350 When it fell, I went back to the big room looking over the city and made fire. There was a place to make fire and a box with wood in it, though I do not think they cooked there. I wrapped myself in a floor covering and slept in front of the fire—I was very tired. Ⓝ

Now I tell what is very strong magic. I woke in the midst of the night. When I woke, the fire had gone out, and I was cold. It seemed to me that all around me there were whisperings and voices. I closed my eyes to shut them out. Some will say that I slept again, but I do not think that I slept. I could feel the spirits drawing my spirit out of my body as a fish is drawn on a line.
360 Why should I lie about it? I am a priest and the son of a priest. If there are spirits, as they say, in the small Dead Places near us, what spirits must there not be in that great Place of the Gods? And would not they wish to speak? After such long years? I know that I felt myself drawn as a fish is drawn on a line. I had stepped out of my body—I could see my body asleep in front of the cold fire, but it was not I. I was drawn to look out upon the city of the gods.

It should have been dark, for it was night, but it was not dark. Everywhere there were lights—lines of light—circles and blurs of light—ten thousand torches would not have been the same. The sky itself was alight—you could barely see the stars for the glow in the sky. I thought to myself "This is strong magic" and trembled. There was a roaring in my ears like the rushing of rivers. Then my eyes grew used to the light and my ears to the sound. I knew that I was seeing the city as it had been when the gods were alive.

That was a sight indeed—yes, that was a sight: I could not have seen it in the body—my body would have died. Everywhere went the gods, on foot and in chariots—there were gods beyond number and counting, and their chariots blocked the streets. They had turned night to day for their pleasure—they did not sleep with the sun. The noise of their coming and going was the noise of many waters. It was magic what they could do—it was magic what they did. **PAUSE & REFLECT**

I looked out of another window—the great vines of their bridges were mended, and the god roads went east and west. Restless, restless, were the gods and always in motion! They burrowed tunnels under rivers—they flew in the air. With unbelievable tools they did giant works—no part of the earth was safe from them, for, if they wished for a thing, they summoned it from the other side of the world. And always, as they labored and rested, as they feasted and made love, there was a drum in their ears—the pulse of the giant city, beating and beating like a man's heart.

Were they happy? What is happiness to the gods? They were great; they were mighty; they were wonderful and terrible. As I looked upon them and their magic, I felt like a child—but a little more, it seemed to me, and they would pull down the moon from the sky. I saw them with wisdom beyond wisdom and knowledge beyond knowledge. And yet not all they did was well done—even I could see that—and yet their wisdom could not but grow until all was peace. ◎

PAUSE & REFLECT
What does John mean when he says "they did not sleep with the sun." Explain.

_____

_____

_____

_____

_____

_____

_____

_____

◎ **POINT OF VIEW**
Reread lines 383–399. In what way do the narrator's comments reveal the author's **tone,** or attitude, toward the doomed civilization?

_____

_____

_____

_____

_____

_____

400   Then I saw their fate come upon them, and that was terrible past speech. It came upon them as they walked the streets of their city. I have been in the fights with the Forest People—I have seen men die. But this was not like that. When gods war with gods, they use weapons we do not know. It was fire falling out of the sky and a mist that poisoned. It was the time of the Great Burning and the Destruction. They ran about like ants in the streets of their city—poor gods, poor gods! Then the towers began to fall. A few escaped—yes, a few. The legends tell it. But, even after the city had become a Dead Place, for many years the poison

410 was still in the ground. I saw it happen; I saw the last of them die. It was darkness over the broken city, and I wept. **P**

    All this, I saw. I saw it as I have told it, though not in the body. When I woke in the morning, I was hungry, but I did not think first of my hunger, for my heart was perplexed and confused. I knew the reason for the Dead Places, but I did not see why it had happened. It seemed to me it should not have happened, with all the magic they had. I went through the house looking for an answer. There was so much in the house I could not understand— and yet I am a priest and the son of a priest. It was like being on one

420 side of the great river, at night, with no light to show the way.

    Then I saw the dead god. He was sitting in his chair, by the window, in a room I had not entered before, and for the first

P MAKE INFERENCES
What destroyed the "gods" and their city? Reread lines 400–411 and underline clues in the text. Then write your inference below.

_____

_____

_____

_____

moment, I thought that he was alive. Then I saw the skin on the back of his hand—it was like dry leather. The room was shut, hot and dry—no doubt that had kept him as he was. At first I was afraid to approach him—then the fear left me. He was sitting looking out over the city—he was dressed in the clothes of the gods. His age was neither young nor old—I could not tell his age. But there was wisdom in his face and great sadness. You could
430 see that he would have not run away. He had sat at his window, watching his city die—then he himself had died. But it is better to lose one's life than one's spirit—and you could see from the face that his spirit had not been lost. I knew that, if I touched him, he would fall into dust—and yet, there was something unconquered in the face.

That is all of my story, for then I knew he was a man—I knew then that they had been men, neither gods nor demons. It is a great knowledge, hard to tell and believe. They were men—they went a dark road, but they were men. I had no fear after that—I
440 had no fear going home, though twice I fought off the dogs and once I was hunted for two days by the Forest People. When I saw my father again, I prayed and was purified. He touched my lips and my breast; he said, "You went away a boy. You come back a man and a priest." I said, "Father, they were men! I have been in the Place of the Gods and seen it! Now slay me, if it is the law— but still I know they were men."

He looked at me out of both eyes. He said, "The law is not always the same shape—you have done what you have done. I could not have done it my time, but you come after me. Tell!"
450 I told, and he listened. After that, I wished to tell all the people, but he showed me otherwise. He said, "Truth is a hard deer to hunt. If you eat too much truth at once, you may die of the truth. It was not idly that our fathers forbade the Dead Places." He was right—it is better the truth should come little by little. I have learned that, being a priest. Perhaps, in the old days, they ate knowledge too fast. **Q**

Q POINT OF VIEW
Reread lines 436–446. Is John still a naive narrator? Explain your answer.

_____

_____

_____

_____

_____

_____

_____

_____

_____

_____

_____

PAUSE & REFLECT

Do you think John's society will be able to avoid making the mistakes that the people of "newyork" did? Explain your answer.

_____

_____

_____

_____

_____

_____

_____

_____

_____

_____

_____

_____

_____

_____

_____

_____

_____

_____

Nevertheless, we make a beginning. It is not for the metal alone we go to the Dead Places now—there are the books and the writings. They are hard to learn. And the magic tools are broken—but we can look at them and wonder. At least, we make a beginning. And, when I am chief priest, we shall go beyond the great river. We shall go to the Place of the Gods—the place newyork—not one man but a company. We shall look for the images of the gods and find the god ASHING and the others—the gods Lincoln and Biltmore[1] and Moses.[2] But they were men who built the city, not gods or demons. They were men. I remember the dead man's face. They were men who were here before us. We must build again. **PAUSE & REFLECT**

---

1. **Biltmore:** the name of a once-famous hotel in New York City.
2. **Moses:** Robert Moses (1888–1981), a New York City public official whose name appears on many bridges and other structures built during his administration.

Text Analysis: First-Person Point of View

Review the notes you took while reading "By the Waters of Babylon." Use them to answer the questions in the chart. Be sure to explain your answers and provide supporting details from the text.

Questions About Point of View	Answers
Does the narrator have enough knowledge to accurately describe his experiences in the Place of the Gods?	
How do the narrator's beliefs affect what he says about the Place of the Gods?	
How do the narrator's experiences and ideas help express the author's tone toward the doomed city and its people?	

What did Stephen Vincent Benét's choice of a narrator add to your enjoyment of "By the Waters of Babylon"? Explain what you gained from John's first-person point of view.

_____

_____

_____

Reading Strategy: Make Inferences

Now that you have read "By the Waters of Babylon," you have more background knowledge to help you make inferences about specific things described by the naive narrator. Make an inference from each detail in the chart below.

DEAD PLACES	**Detail:** *"I take the metal from the Dead Places, but I am not blasted."* (lines 156–157)
My Inference:	
THE GREAT RIVER	**Detail:** "I thought the river meant to take me past the Place of the Gods and out into the Bitter Water of the legends." (lines 186–187)
My Inference:	
THE PLACE OF THE GODS	**Detail:** ". . . it is there that there are the ashes of the Great Burning." (lines 9–10)
My Inference:	

Does KNOWLEDGE come at a price?

What are some consequences of gaining knowledge?

_____

_____

Academic Vocabulary in Writing

consequent	crucial	initial	shift	survive

How do John's experiences in the Place of the Gods change his **initial** beliefs about and feelings toward its inhabitants? Use at least two Academic Vocabulary words in your response. Definitions for these terms are listed on page 109.

_____

_____

_____

Assessment Practice

DIRECTIONS Use "By the Waters of Babylon" to answer questions 1–6.

1 Which line from the story indicates that it is written from the first-person point of view?

- **A** ". . . it is forbidden to go east." (line 2)
- **B** "Afterwards, both the man and the metal must be purified." (lines 4–5)
- **C** ". . . I am the son of a priest." (line 12)
- **D** "It was a dead man's house. . . ." (lines 15–16)

2 The Dead Places are —

- **A** rivers that flow toward the Bitter Water
- **B** places where priests go to purify themselves
- **C** areas where the hostile Forest People live
- **D** towns and cities where all the residents are dead

3 Why does John set out on his journey?

- **A** He is eager to gain more knowledge.
- **B** His father wants him to visit the Place of the Gods.
- **C** He is the only one who does not fear the Dead Places.
- **D** His people need him to collect more metal.

4 In lines 367–374, you can infer that John is describing —

- **A** a great fire
- **B** starlight illuminating a city
- **C** a city at night lit by electricity
- **D** a tribe holding a nighttime celebration

5 The allusion to Psalm 137 in the story's title is appropriate because —

- **A** John believes that New York City is the promised land of Zion from the Bible
- **B** John weeps when he dreams about the destruction of New York City in a war
- **C** the Place of the Gods is similar to New York City but is really Babylon
- **D** the author hopes his story will lead his readers to discover the Bible

6 From what John learns in the story, you can infer that the author —

- **A** wants the story to serve as a warning to modern society
- **B** feels that legends are more important than actual historical events
- **C** believes that modern society will be destroyed
- **D** thinks that modern society must return to simpler times

There Will Come Soft Rains

Short Story by **Ray Bradbury**

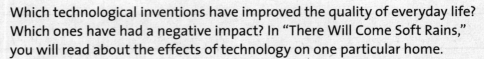

Is **TECHNOLOGY** taking over?

Which technological inventions have improved the quality of everyday life? Which ones have had a negative impact? In "There Will Come Soft Rains," you will read about the effects of technology on one particular home.

QUICKWRITE With a group, list advantages and disadvantages of technology in the notebook at left. First, write down technologies that you use in your daily life. Then write about the positive and negative effects technology has on everyday life. An example has been done for you.

Text Analysis: Chronological Order

Writers make choices about how to organize events in a story. One common way of organizing a story is to describe events in **chronological order**—the sequence in which events occur. To determine chronological order in a story look for the following.

- words that identify time
  Examples: *six o'clock, today, tomorrow, later that day*

- words that signal order
  Examples: *before, after, then, meanwhile, next, first, last*

- breaks in the chronological flow of events, such as a flashback to an earlier time
  Examples: *when I was three, a few years ago, way back when*

As you read "There Will come Soft Rains," think about the reasons Ray Bradbury might have chosen to present this science fiction story in chronological order.

Effects of Technology

Technology: Internet

_____

_____

Advantages: Easy access to
information

_____

_____

Disadvantages: Lack of human
contact

_____

_____

Reading Strategy: Draw Conclusions

A **conclusion** is a judgment based on evidence in the story and your own prior knowledge. Use the following strategies to analyze information about the house in the story:

- Analyze details about the family and their routine.
- Analyze details about the areas near the house.
- Identify changes in the performance of the house.

As you read the story, you will be prompted to record and analyze important details. Later you will draw conclusions about what happened.

Important Details	My Thoughts
It's morning and the house is empty.	The people are gone. The house still acts as though they're there.

Vocabulary in Context

Note: Words are listed in the order in which they appear in the story.

silhouette (sĭl'ōō-ĕt') *n.* an outline that appears dark against a light background
*The **silhouette** of the great oak is visible for miles.*

paranoia (păr'ə-noi'ə) *n.* an irrational fear of danger or misfortune
*Your increasing **paranoia** is making you a nervous wreck.*

manipulate (mə-nĭp'yə-lāt') *v.* to move, operate, or handle
*To **manipulate** a puppet properly requires practice.*

tremulous (trĕm'yə-ləs) *adj.* trembling, unsteady
*The sight of the rattlesnake made Don **tremulous.***

oblivious (ə-blĭv'ē-əs) *adj.* paying no attention, completely unaware
*She is **oblivious** to the mess all around her.*

sublime (sə-blīm') *adj.* supreme, splendid
*This is a **sublime** piece of cheesecake.*

SET A PURPOSE FOR READING

Read "There Will Come Soft Rains" to find out one writer's vision of the future.

THERE WILL COME Soft Rains

Short Story by

RAY BRADBURY

BACKGROUND Before 1900, electric machines were used primarily in workplaces. With the spread of electricity, however, families enjoyed modern appliances in their homes. In the early 20th century, many household machines, such as the vacuum cleaner and the toaster, became available for the first time. Science fiction writers of this period often created works featuring utopias—or ideal worlds—in which machines freed people of difficult tasks. In "There Will Come Soft Rains," Bradbury challenges this idea by presenting a society harmed by modern technology.

In the living room the voice-clock sang, *Tick-tock, seven o'clock, time to get up, time to get up, seven o'clock!* as if it were afraid that nobody would. The morning house lay empty. The clock ticked on, repeating and repeating its sounds into the emptiness. *Seven-nine, breakfast time, seven-nine!*

   In the kitchen the breakfast stove gave a hissing sigh and ejected from its warm interior eight pieces of perfectly browned toast, eight eggs sunnyside up, sixteen slices of bacon, two coffees, and two cool glasses of milk.

10   "Today is August 4, 2026," said a second voice from the kitchen ceiling, "in the city of Allendale, California." It repeated the date three times for memory's sake. "Today is Mr. Featherstone's birthday. Today is the anniversary of Tilita's

marriage. Insurance is payable, as are the water, gas, and light bills."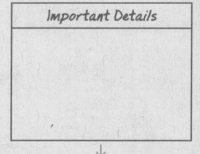

Somewhere in the walls, relays[1] clicked, memory tapes glided under electric eyes.

Eight-one, tick-tock, eight-one o'clock, off to school, off to work, run, run, eight-one! But no doors slammed, no carpets took the
20 soft tread of rubber heels. It was raining outside. The weather box on the front door sang quietly: "Rain, rain, go away; rubbers, raincoats for today . . ." And the rain tapped on the empty house, echoing.

Outside, the garage chimed and lifted its door to reveal the waiting car. After a long wait the door swung down again.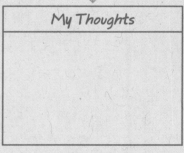

At eight-thirty the eggs were shriveled and the toast was like stone. An aluminum wedge scraped them into the sink, where hot water whirled them down a metal throat which digested and flushed them away to the distant sea. The dirty dishes were
30 dropped into a hot washer and emerged twinkling dry.

Nine-fifteen, sang the clock, *time to clean.*

Out of warrens in the wall, tiny robot mice darted. The rooms were acrawl with the small cleaning animals, all rubber and metal. They thudded against chairs, whirling their mustached runners, kneading the rug nap, sucking gently at hidden dust. Then, like mysterious invaders, they popped into their burrows. Their pink electric eyes faded. The house was clean.

Ten o'clock. The sun came out from behind the rain. The house stood alone in a city of rubble and ashes. This was the one house
40 left standing. At night the ruined city gave off a radioactive glow which could be seen for miles.

Ten-fifteen. The garden sprinklers whirled up in golden founts, filling the soft morning air with scatterings of brightness. The water pelted windowpanes, running down the charred west side where the house had been burned evenly free of its white paint. The entire west face of the house was black, save for five places. Here the <u>silhouette</u> in paint of a man mowing a lawn. Here, as in a photograph, a woman bent to pick flowers. Still farther over,

---

1. **relays:** devices that automatically turn switches in electric circuits on and off.

Monitor Your Comprehension

Ⓐ CHRONOLOGICAL ORDER
Reread lines 1–15. Which words and phrases tell you that the story is organized in chronological order? Underline them in the selection.

Ⓑ DRAW CONCLUSIONS
Which story details in lines 18–25 suggest that this is an unusual day for the family? Fill in the chart below with important details from the story and your thoughts.

Important Details

↓

My Thoughts

silhouette (sĭl'ōō-ĕt') *n.* an outline that appears dark against a light background.

⊙ DRAW CONCLUSIONS
Reread lines 38–54. Based on the story details about the city, what do you think has happened?

_____

_____

_____

_____

_____

paranoia (păr′ə-noi′ə) *n.* an irrational fear of danger or misfortune

their images burned on wood in one titanic instant, a small boy, hands flung into the air; higher up, the image of a thrown ball, and opposite him a girl, hands raised to catch a ball which never came down.

The five spots of paint—the man, the woman, the children, the ball—remained. The rest was a thin charcoaled layer. ⊙

The gentle sprinkler rain filled the garden with falling light.

Until this day, how well the house had kept its peace. How carefully it had inquired, "Who goes there? What's the password?" and, getting no answer from lonely foxes and whining cats, it had shut up its windows and drawn shades in an old-maidenly preoccupation with self-protection which bordered on a mechanical **paranoia**.

It quivered at each sound, the house did. If a sparrow brushed a window, the shade snapped up. The bird, startled, flew off! No, not even a bird must touch the house!

The house was an altar with ten thousand attendants, big, small, servicing, attending, in choirs. But the gods had gone away, and the ritual of the religion continued senselessly, uselessly.

Twelve noon.

A dog whined, shivering, on the front porch.

The front door recognized the dog voice and opened. The dog, once huge and fleshy, but now gone to bone and covered with sores, moved in and through the house, tracking mud. Behind it whirred angry mice, angry at having to pick up mud, angry at inconvenience.

For not a leaf fragment blew under the door but what the wall panels flipped open and the copper scrap rats flashed swiftly out. The offending dust, hair, or paper, seized in miniature steel jaws, was raced back to the burrows. There, down tubes which fed into the cellar, it was dropped into the sighing vent of an incinerator which sat like evil Baal[2] in a dark corner.

The dog ran upstairs, hysterically yelping to each door, at last realizing, as the house realized, that only silence was here.

---

2. **Baal** (bā′əl): an idol worshiped by certain ancient peoples of the Middle East.

It sniffed the air and scratched the kitchen door. Behind the door, the stove was making pancakes which filled the house with a rich baked odor and the scent of maple syrup.

The dog frothed at the mouth, lying at the door, sniffing, its eyes turned to fire. It ran wildly in circles, biting at its tail, spun in a frenzy, and died. It lay in the parlor for an hour.

Two o'clock, sang a voice.

90 Delicately sensing decay at last, the regiments of mice hummed out as softly as blown gray leaves in an electrical wind.

Two-fifteen.

The dog was gone.

In the cellar, the incinerator glowed suddenly and a whirl of sparks leaped up the chimney. **PAUSE & REFLECT**

Two thirty-five.

Bridge tables sprouted from patio walls. Playing cards fluttered onto pads in a shower of pips. Martinis manifested on an oaken bench with egg-salad sandwiches. Music played.

100 But the tables were silent and the cards untouched.

At four o'clock the tables folded like great butterflies back through the paneled walls.

Four-thirty.

The nursery walls glowed.

Animals took shape: yellow giraffes, blue lions, pink antelopes, lilac panthers cavorting in crystal substance. The walls were glass. They looked out upon color and fantasy. Hidden films clocked through well-oiled sprockets, and the walls lived. The nursery floor was woven to resemble a crisp, cereal meadow. Over this

110 ran aluminum roaches and iron crickets, and in the hot still air butterflies of delicate red tissue wavered among the sharp aroma of animal spoors! There was the sound like a great matted yellow hive of bees within a dark bellows, the lazy bumble of

PAUSE & REFLECT

How does the house react when the dog runs through it and sniffs at the kitchen door? What does the dog's death suggest about the house?

_____

_____

_____

_____

_____

_____

_____

_____

_____

_____

_____

_____

a purring lion. And there was the patter of okapi[3] feet and the murmur of a fresh jungle rain, like other hoofs, falling upon the summer-starched grass. Now the walls dissolved into distances of parched weed, mile on mile, and warm endless sky. The animals drew away into thorn brakes and water holes.

It was the children's hour.

120 *Five o'clock.* The bath filled with clear hot water.

Six, seven, eight o'clock. The dinner dishes <u>manipulated</u> like magic tricks, and in the study a *click*. In the metal stand opposite the hearth where a fire now blazed up warmly, a cigar popped out, half an inch of soft gray ash on it, smoking, waiting.

Nine o'clock. The beds warmed their hidden circuits, for nights were cool here. **D**

Nine-five. A voice spoke from the study ceiling:

"Mrs. McClellan, which poem would you like this evening?"

The house was silent.

130 The voice said at last, "Since you express no preference, I shall select a poem at random." Quiet music rose to back the voice. "Sara Teasdale. As I recall, your favorite. . . .

> "There will come soft rains and the
> smell of the ground,
>
> And swallows circling with their
> shimmering sound;
>
> And frogs in the pools singing at night,
> And wild plum trees in *tremulous* white;
>
> Robins will wear their feathery fire,
> 140 Whistling their whims on a low fence-wire;
> And not one will know of the war, not one
> Will care at last when it is done.

---

3. **okapi** (ō-kä′pē): an antelope-like hoofed mammal of the African jungle.

---

manipulate (mə-nĭp′yə-lāt′) *v.* to move, operate, or handle

D DRAW CONCLUSIONS
Think about the **setting** of this story. What do you learn about the society from the house's many automated features?

_____

_____

_____

_____

_____

tremulous (trĕm′yə-ləs) *adj.* trembling, unsteady

Why might the poet have used the word *tremulous* to describe the plum trees.

_____

_____

_____

_____

_____

Not one would mind, neither bird nor tree,
If mankind perished utterly;

And Spring herself, when she woke at dawn
Would scarcely know that we were gone." **E**

The fire burned on the stone hearth and the cigar fell away into a mound of quiet ash on its tray. The empty chairs faced each other between the silent walls, and the music played.

150   At ten o'clock the house began to die. **F**
        The wind blew. A falling tree bough crashed through the kitchen window. Cleaning solvent, bottled, shattered over the stove. The room was ablaze in an instant!
        "Fire!" screamed a voice. The house lights flashed, water pumps shot water from the ceilings. But the solvent spread on the linoleum, licking, eating, under the kitchen door, while the voices took it up in chorus: "Fire, fire, fire!"

PAUSE & REFLECT

What do you think will happen to the house? Use details from the text to support your answer.

_____

_____

_____

_____

_____

_____

_____

_____

_____

_____

_____

_____

_____

_____

_____

_____

_____

_____

The house tried to save itself. Doors sprang tightly shut, but the windows were broken by the heat and the wind blew and
160 sucked upon the fire.

The house gave ground as the fire in ten billion angry sparks moved with flaming ease from room to room and then up the stairs. While scurrying water rats squeaked from the walls, pistoled their water, and ran for more. And the wall sprays let down showers of mechanical rain. **PAUSE & REFLECT**

But too late. Somewhere, sighing, a pump shrugged to a stop. The quenching rain ceased. The reserve water supply which had filled baths and washed dishes for many quiet days was gone.

The fire crackled up the stairs. It fed upon Picassos and
170 Matisses[4] in the upper halls, like delicacies, baking off the oily flesh, tenderly crisping the canvases into black shavings.

Now the fire lay in beds, stood in windows, changed the colors of drapes!

And then, reinforcements.

From attic trapdoors, blind robot faces peered down with faucet mouths gushing green chemical.

The fire backed off, as even an elephant must at the sight of a dead snake. Now there were twenty snakes whipping over the floor, killing the fire with a clear cold venom of green froth.
180 But the fire was clever. It had sent flame outside the house, up through the attic to the pumps there. An explosion! The attic brain which directed the pumps was shattered into bronze shrapnel on the beams.

The fire rushed back into every closet and felt of the clothes hung there.

The house shuddered, oak bone on bone, its bared skeleton cringing from the heat, its wire, its nerves revealed as if a surgeon had torn the skin off to let the red veins and capillaries quiver in the scalded air. Help, help! Fire! Run, run! Heat snapped mirrors
190 like the first brittle winter ice. And the voices wailed Fire, fire,

---

4. **Picassos and Matisses:** paintings by the famous 20th-century artists Pablo Picasso (pǐ-kä′sō) and Henri Matisse (mə-tēs′).

run, run, like a tragic nursery rhyme, a dozen voices, high, low, like children dying in a forest, alone, alone. And the voices fading as the wires popped their sheathings like hot chestnuts. One, two, three, four, five voices died. **PAUSE & REFLECT**

In the nursery the jungle burned. Blue lions roared, purple giraffes bounded off. The panthers ran in circles, changing color, and ten million animals, running before the fire, vanished off toward a distant steaming river. . . .

Ten more voices died. In the last instant under the fire
200 avalanche, other choruses, <u>oblivious</u>, could be heard announcing the time, playing music, cutting the lawn by remote-control mower, or setting an umbrella frantically out and in the slamming and opening front door, a thousand things happening, like a clock shop when each clock strikes the hour insanely before or after the other, a scene of maniac confusion, yet unity; singing, screaming, a few last cleaning mice darting bravely out to carry the horrid ashes away! And one voice, with <u>sublime</u> disregard for the situation, read poetry aloud in the fiery study, until all the film spools burned, until all the wires withered and the circuits
210 cracked.

The fire burst the house and let it slam flat down, puffing out skirts of spark and smoke.

In the kitchen, an instant before the rain of fire and timber, the stove could be seen making breakfasts at a psychopathic rate, ten

PAUSE & REFLECT
Reread lines 186–194. Underline the words used to describe the human qualities of the house. What inventions do we have today that mimic humans?

_____

_____

oblivious (ə-blĭv′ē-əs) *adj.* paying no attention, completely unaware

sublime (sə-blīm′) *adj.* supreme, splendid

Why is the house pitiful when it shows its **sublime** disregard for the fire?

_____

_____

_____

G DRAW CONCLUSIONS
What idea about technology does Bradbury convey in the burning of the house?

_____

_____

_____

_____

_____

_____

_____

_____

_____

dozen eggs, six loaves of toast, twenty dozen bacon strips, which, eaten by fire, started the stove working again, hysterically hissing!

The crash. The attic smashing into kitchen and parlor. The parlor into cellar, cellar into sub-cellar. Deep freeze, armchair, film tapes, circuits, beds, and all like skeletons thrown in a
220 cluttered mound deep under.

Smoke and silence. A great quantity of smoke.

Dawn showed faintly in the east. Among the ruins, one wall stood alone. Within the wall, a last voice said, over and over again and again, even as the sun rose to shine upon the heaped rubble and steam: "Today is August 5, 2026, today is August 5, 2026, today is …" **G**

Text Analysis: Chronological Order

A timeline like the one below shows an order of events. Look back over the selection to complete the timeline of events below.

Time	Events
Seven o'clock	Living voice-clock sings. It's time to get up.
Seven to nine	Date and reminders announced.

Review your notes for "There Will Come Soft Rains" and your timeline. Then, consider how the references to the chronological order affected the way you read the story. Why might Bradbury have chosen to follow chronological order?

_____

_____

_____

_____

Reading Strategy: Draw Conclusions

Review the chart you filled in as you read. What has happened to the
McClellan family and the city? Complete the chart below with your conclusion
and supporting details from the selection.

Conclusion:

_____

_____

Supporting Details:

Is **TECHNOLOGY** taking over?

Are people becoming too dependent on technology?

_____

_____

_____

Vocabulary Practice

Choose the word that best completes the sentence.

1. Leon has overcome his _____ and now enjoys social activities.

2. The cellist knows how to skillfully _____ his instrument.

3. My elderly great aunt walks in a _____ manner.

4. Jenna enjoys winter activities and is _____ to the cold.

5. Critics agree that the artist's painting is her most _____ work yet.

6. The young girl left a chalky _____ of her hand on the sidewalk.

WORD LIST

manipulate

oblivious

paranoia

silhouette

sublime

tremulous

Academic Vocabulary in Writing

consequent	crucial	initial	shift	survive

Write a paragraph about technologies that you would like to see developed. Explain why you think these technologies are **crucial** to society. Consider how the technologies might help people **survive**. Use at least one Academic Vocabulary word in your response. Definitions for these terms are listed on page 109.

_____

_____

_____

_____

Assessment Practice

DIRECTIONS Use "There Will Come Soft Rains" to answer questions 1–4.

1 Three functions the house performs in this story are —

- (A) gardening, cooking, painting
- (B) cleaning, cooking, dog bathing
- (C) cooking, cleaning, gardening
- (D) cleaning, gardening, driving

2 Which statement best describes the sequence of the changes the house undergoes during the story?

- (A) First the empty house carries out its programmed tasks, then a falling tree branch causes a fire, finally the house is destroyed after trying to save itself.
- (B) First a falling tree branch causes a fire, then the house tries to save itself, finally the house is left with only the ability to tell the date.
- (C) First the family leaves for the day, then the dog comes home, finally a falling tree branch causes a fire.
- (D) First the house starts cooking dinner, then the family comes home, finally the house warms the beds.

3 What conclusion can you draw about the family and their relationship to the natural world through the description of the nursery in lines 103–118?

- (A) The family needs technology to interact with the natural world.
- (B) The family appreciates nature through technological media.
- (C) The family insists on realistic images of the natural world.
- (D) The family dislikes learning about nature.

4 What is the theme, or main message, of the story?

- (A) Technology causes problems in homes.
- (B) Technology is powerful but must be handled wisely.
- (C) Technology needs to be made less powerful.
- (D) Technology can save and protect people.

4

Message and Meaning

THEME

Be sure to read the Text Analysis Workshop on pp. 418–425 in *Holt McDougal Literature*.

Academic Vocabulary for Unit 4

Preview the following Academic Vocabulary words. You will encounter these words as you work through this book and will use them as you write and talk about the selections in the unit.

alter (ôl′tər) *v.* to change or modify some details

*An author may **alter** or revise a manuscript many times.*

layer (lā′ər) *n.* a single thickness, fold, or level

*A word can have more than one **layer** of meaning depending on the context.*

symbol (sĭm′bəl) *n.* something that represents or suggests another thing

*Authors sometimes use a flower as a **symbol** of love or innocence.*

theme (thēm) *n.* a topic or subject of a discussion or piece of writing

*Knowing the **theme** of a selection can help you understand how the details are related to each other.*

unify (yōō′ nə fī) v. to make into one; to bring together into a unit

*It is important to **unify** the ideas in a piece of writing to avoid confusing the audience.*

Think of a book you have read or a movie you have seen that includes **symbols.** Write a description of the symbols and explain why you think they were interesting or important to include. Use at least two Academic Vocabulary words in your response.

_____

_____

_____

_____

The Interlopers
Short Story by Saki

What's wrong with holding a **GRUDGE?**

Both history and literature are full of individuals who bear grudges, or feelings of great resentment, against others. In "The Interlopers," you will read about two neighboring families whose ongoing feud has serious consequences.

ROLE-PLAY With a partner, imagine a situation in which a grudge exists between the two of you. Think about what your relationship once involved—were you once teammates or best friends? Do you even remember what led to your disagreement in the first place? Write notes about this imagined grudge in the notebook on the left. Then use your ideas to role-play a chance meeting.

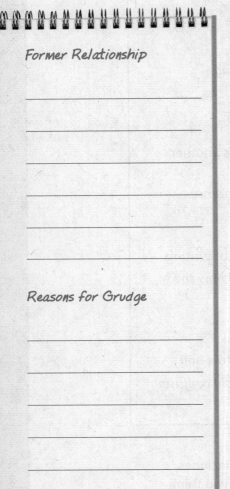

Former Relationship

_____

_____

_____

_____

_____

Reasons for Grudge

_____

_____

_____

_____

_____

Text Analysis: Theme and Setting

In a short story, a **theme** is a message about life or human nature that the writer wants to communicate to readers. Often, the **setting** of a story—where and when it takes place—helps convey this message. To understand how setting might contribute to theme, review the chart below.

SETTING
The setting's significance to the characters and the conflict can suggest the theme.
• How does the setting influence the characters?
• How does the setting affect the plot?
• What larger idea or issue might the setting represent?
• How does the setting relate to the story's main conflict?

"The Interlopers" takes place in a forest whose ownership has been disputed by two families for generations. As you read, think about what Saki is saying about human nature and how the story's setting helps make this message clear.

Reading Strategy: Monitor

Good readers automatically check, or **monitor,** their comprehension of what they read. One way they accomplish this is by **clarifying** difficult passages, or using strategies to understand the text more clearly. Strategies such as rereading, reading aloud, and summarizing can make tough parts easier to understand.

As you read "The Interlopers," you will be prompted to stop and clarify the points in the story that are confusing to you. See the chart below for an example of how to organize your ideas.

| Confusing Passage | → | How I Clarified My Understanding | → | My New Understanding |

Vocabulary in Context

Note: Words are listed in the order in which they appear in the story.

interloper (ĭn'tər-lō'pər) *n.* one that intrudes in a place, situation, or activity
*An **interloper** disturbed the club meeting by entering uninvited and making comments.*

precipitous (prĭ-sĭp'ĭ-təs) *adj.* extremely steep
*The mountain path was **precipitous** and slippery.*

acquiesce (ăk'wē-ĕs') *v.* to agree or give in to
*Parents sometimes **acquiesce** when a child asks for something at the store.*

marauder (mə-rô'dər) *n.* one who raids and loots
*The town was invaded by **marauders** who stole goods and damaged buildings.*

pinioned (pĭn'yənd) *adj.* restrained or immobilized
*During the match, the **pinioned** wrestler struggled to free her hands.*

condolence (kən-dō'ləns) *n.* an expression of sympathy
*It is common to send your **condolences** when someone you know has died.*

draft (drăft) *n.* a gulp or swallow
*The first sweet **draft** of lemonade was especially delicious.*

languor (lăng'gər) *n.* a lack of feeling or energy
*Only joy and **languor** was felt by the students on the first day of vacation.*

succor (sŭk'ər) *n.* help in a difficult situation
*The doctors provided **succor** to the people wounded in the earthquake.*

pestilential (pĕs'tə-lĕn'shəl) *adj.* likely to spread and cause disease
*Nobody in the hiking party wanted to drink the **pestilential** water in the stream.*

SET A PURPOSE FOR READING

Read this story to find out what happens when two enemies come face to face.

interloper (ĭn′tər-lō′pər) *n.* one that intrudes in a place, situation, or activity

THE
Interlopers

Short Story by **Saki**

BACKGROUND An *interloper* is someone who interferes in the affairs of others, often for selfish reasons. In the time and place of this story, two neighboring families have an ongoing feud about land ownership that has dire results.

Ⓐ THEME AND SETTING
What parts of the story's natural setting are highlighted in lines 1–8?

_____

_____

_____

_____

precipitous (prĭ-sĭp′ĭ-təs) *adj.* extremely steep

In a forest of mixed growth somewhere on the eastern spurs of the Carpathians,[1] a man stood one winter night watching and listening, as though he waited for some beast of the woods to come within the range of his vision, and, later, of his rifle. But the game[2] for whose presence he kept so keen an outlook was none that figured in the sportsman's calendar as lawful and proper for the chase; Ulrich von Gradwitz[3] patrolled the dark forest in quest of a human enemy. Ⓐ

10 The forest lands of Gradwitz were of wide extent and well stocked with game; the narrow strip of **precipitous** woodland that lay on its outskirt was not remarkable for the game it harbored or the shooting it afforded, but it was the most jealously guarded of all its owner's territorial possessions. A famous lawsuit, in the days

_____

1. **eastern spurs of the Carpathians** (kär-pā′thē-ənz): the edges of a mountain range in central Europe.
2. **game:** animals hunted for food or sport.
3. **Ulrich von Gradwitz** (ōōl′rĭкн fôn gräd′vĭts).

of his grandfather, had wrested it from the illegal possession of a neighboring family of petty landowners; the dispossessed party had never <u>acquiesced</u> in the judgment of the Courts, and a long series of poaching affrays[4] and similar scandals had embittered the relationships between the families for three generations. The neighbor feud had grown into a personal one since Ulrich had
20 come to be head of his family; if there was a man in the world whom he detested and wished ill to it was Georg Znaeym,[5] the inheritor of the quarrel and the tireless game-snatcher and raider of the disputed border-forest. The feud might, perhaps, have died down or been compromised if the personal ill-will of the two men had not stood in the way; as boys they had thirsted for one another's blood, as men each prayed that misfortune might fall on the other, and this wind-scourged winter night Ulrich had banded together his foresters to watch the dark forest, not in quest of four-footed quarry, but to keep a lookout for the prowling
30 thieves whom he suspected of being afoot from across the land boundary. The roebuck,[6] which usually kept in the sheltered hollows during a storm wind, were running like driven things tonight, and there was movement and unrest among the creatures that were wont to sleep through the dark hours. Assuredly there was a disturbing element in the forest, and Ulrich could guess the quarter from whence it came. **B**

He strayed away by himself from the watchers whom he had placed in ambush on the crest of the hill, and wandered far down the steep slopes amid the wild tangle of undergrowth, peering
40 through the tree trunks and listening through the whistling and skirling[7] of the wind and the restless beating of the branches for sight or sound of the <u>marauders</u>. If only on this wild night, in this dark, lone spot, he might come across Georg Znaeym, man to man, with none to witness—that was the wish that was uppermost in his thoughts. And as he stepped around the trunk of a huge beech, he came face to face with the man he sought.

---

4. **poaching affrays** (ə-frāz'): noisy quarrels about hunting on someone else's property.

5. **Georg Znaeym** (gā-ôrg' tsnā'ēm).

6. **roebuck:** a male roe deer.

7. **skirling:** a shrill cry or sound.

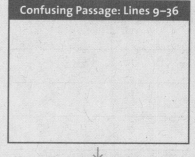

acquiesce (ăk'wē-ĕs') v. to agree or give in to

B MONITOR
Reread or read aloud lines 9–36 to **clarify** your understanding of why Ulrich and Georg are enemies. Then write your new understanding of the passage in the chart below.

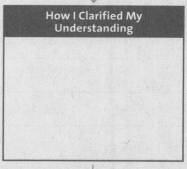

Confusing Passage: Lines 9–36

↓

How I Clarified My Understanding

↓

My New Understanding

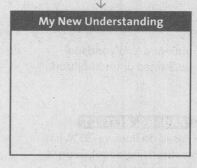

marauder (mə-rôd'ər) n. one who raids and loots

C THEME AND SETTING
How does the natural setting, particularly the fallen tree, affect Ulrich and Georg?

_____

_____

_____

_____

_____

_____

_____

_____

_____

_____

_____

_____

_____

_____

_____

_____

_____

pinioned (pĭn'yənd) *adj.*
restrained or immobilized

PAUSE & REFLECT
Based on lines 74–82, what is surprising about Georg's comment to Ulrich?

_____

_____

_____

_____

_____

_____

The two enemies stood glaring at one another for a long silent moment.

Each had a rifle in his hand, each had hate in his heart and
50 murder uppermost in his mind. The chance had come to give full play to the passions of a lifetime. But a man who has been brought up under the code of a restraining civilization cannot easily nerve himself to shoot down his neighbor in cold blood and without a word spoken, except for an offense against his hearth and honor. And before the moment of hesitation had given way to action a deed of Nature's own violence overwhelmed them both. A fierce shriek of the storm had been answered by a splitting crash over their heads, and ere they could leap aside a mass of falling beech tree had thundered down on them. Ulrich von Gradwitz
60 found himself stretched on the ground, one arm numb beneath him and the other held almost as helplessly in a tight tangle of forked branches, while both legs were pinned beneath the fallen mass. His heavy shooting boots had saved his feet from being crushed to pieces, but if his fractures were not as serious as they might have been, at least it was evident that he could not move from his present position till someone came to release him. The descending twigs had slashed the skin of his face, and he had to wink away some drops of blood from his eyelashes before he could take in a general view of the disaster. At his side, so near
70 that under ordinary circumstances he could almost have touched him, lay Georg Znaeym, alive and struggling, but obviously as helplessly **pinioned** down as himself. All around them lay a thick-strewn wreckage of splintered branches and broken twigs. **C**

Relief at being alive and exasperation at his captive plight brought a strange medley of pious thank offerings and sharp curses to Ulrich's lips. Georg, who was nearly blinded with the blood which trickled across his eyes, stopped his struggling for a moment to listen, and then gave a short, snarling laugh.

"So you're not killed, as you ought to be, but you're caught,
80 anyway," he cried; "caught fast. Ho, what a jest, Ulrich von Gradwitz snared in his stolen forest. There's real justice for you!"

And he laughed again, mockingly and savagely.

PAUSE & REFLECT

"I'm caught in my own forest land," retorted Ulrich. "When my men come to release us, you will wish, perhaps, that you were in a better plight than caught poaching on a neighbor's land, shame on you."

Georg was silent for a moment; then he answered quietly.

"Are you sure that your men will find much to release? I have men, too, in the forest tonight, close behind me, and they will be here first and do the releasing. When they drag me out from under these branches, it won't need much clumsiness on their part to roll this mass of trunk right over on the top of you. Your men will find you dead under a fallen beech tree. For form's sake I shall send my **condolences** to your family."

"It is a useful hint," said Ulrich fiercely. "My men had orders to follow in ten minutes' time, seven of which must have gone by already, and when they get me out—I will remember the hint. Only as you will have met your death poaching on my lands, I don't think I can decently send any message of condolence to your family."

"Good," snarled Georg, "good. We fight this quarrel out to the death, you and I and our foresters, with no cursed interlopers to come between us. Death . . . to you, Ulrich von Gradwitz."

"The same to you, Georg Znaeym, forest thief, game-snatcher." **D**

Both men spoke with the bitterness of possible defeat before them, for each knew that it might be long before his men would seek him out or find him; it was a bare matter of chance which party would arrive first on the scene.

Both had now given up the useless struggle to free themselves from the mass of wood that held them down; Ulrich limited his endeavors to an effort to bring his one partially free arm near enough to his outer coat pocket to draw out his wine flask. Even when he had accomplished that operation, it was long before he could manage the unscrewing of the stopper or get any of the liquid down his throat. But what a heaven-sent **draft** it seemed! It was an open winter,[8] and little snow had fallen as yet, hence the

condolence (kən-dō'ləns) *n.* an expression of sympathy

D MONITOR
Monitor your reading by rereading lines 90–93. Then, summarize in one or two sentences what each man threatens to do if rescued.

draft (drăft) *n.* a gulp or swallow

8. **open winter:** a mild winter.

captives suffered less from the cold than might have been the case at that season of the year; nevertheless, the wine was warming and reviving to the wounded man, and he looked across with
120 something like a throb of pity to where his enemy lay, just keeping the groans of pain and weariness from crossing his lips.

"Could you reach this flask if I threw it over to you?" asked Ulrich suddenly; "there is good wine in it, and one may as well be as comfortable as one can. Let us drink, even if tonight one of us dies."

"No, I can scarcely see anything; there is so much blood caked around my eyes," said Georg, "and in any case I don't drink wine with an enemy." Ulrich was silent for a few minutes and lay listening to the weary screeching of the wind. An idea was slowly
130 forming and growing in his brain, an idea that gained strength every time that he looked across at the man who was fighting so grimly against pain and exhaustion. In the pain and **languor** that Ulrich himself was feeling the old fierce hatred seemed to be dying down. **E**

"Neighbor," he said presently, "do as you please if your men come first. It was a fair compact. But as for me, I've changed my mind. If my men are the first to come, you shall be the first to be helped, as though you were my guest. We have quarreled like devils all our lives over this stupid strip of forest, where the trees
140 can't even stand upright in a breath of wind. Lying here tonight, thinking, I've come to think we've been rather fools; there are better things in life than getting the better of a boundary dispute. Neighbor, if you will help me to bury the old quarrel I—I will ask you to be my friend."

Georg Znaeym was silent for so long that Ulrich thought, perhaps, he had fainted with the pain of his injuries. Then he spoke slowly and in jerks.

"How the whole region would stare and gabble if we rode into the market square together. No one living can remember
150 seeing a Znaeym and a von Gradwitz talking to one another in friendship. And what peace there would be among the forester

languor (lăng′gər) *n.* a lack of feeling or energy

E THEME AND SETTING
In what ways are Ulrich's actions influenced by the natural setting and its conditions? Underline specific information in lines 109–134 that shows these influences.

_____

_____

_____

_____

_____

_____

_____

_____

_____

folk if we ended our feud tonight. And if we choose to make peace among our people, there is none other to interfere, no interlopers from outside. . . . You would come and keep the Sylvester night[9] beneath my roof, and I would come and feast on some high day at your castle. . . . I would never fire a shot on your land, save when you invited me as a guest; and you should come and shoot with me down in the marshes where the wildfowl are. In all the countryside there are none that could hinder if we willed to make peace. I never thought to have wanted to do other than hate you all my life, but I think I have changed my mind about things too, this last half-hour. And you offered me your wine flask. . . . Ulrich von Gradwitz, I will be your friend."

For a space both men were silent, turning over in their minds the wonderful changes that this dramatic reconciliation would bring about. In the cold, gloomy forest, with the wind tearing in fitful gusts through the naked branches and whistling around the tree trunks, they lay and waited for the help that would now bring release and **succor** to both parties. And each prayed a private prayer that his men might be the first to arrive, so that he might be the first to show honorable attention to the enemy that had become a friend.

Presently, as the wind dropped for a moment, Ulrich broke silence.

"Let's shout for help," he said; "in this lull our voices may carry a little way."

"They won't carry far through the trees and undergrowth," said Georg, "but we can try. Together, then."

The two raised their voices in a prolonged hunting call.

"Together again," said Ulrich a few minutes later, after listening in vain for an answer halloo.

"I heard something that time, I think," said Ulrich.

"I heard nothing but the **pestilential** wind," said Georg hoarsely.

There was silence again for some minutes, and then Ulrich gave a joyful cry.

Ⓕ THEME AND SETTING
Reread lines 135–173. How has the setting caused changes in the conflict between Ulrich and Georg?

_____

_____

_____

_____

_____

_____

succor (sŭk′ər) *n.* help in a difficult situation

Why do Ulrich and Georg now both expect **succor** when help arrives?

_____

_____

_____

_____

pestilential (pĕs′tə-lĕn′shəl) *adj.* likely to spread and cause disease

---

9. **Sylvester night:** New Year's Eve, the feast day of Saint Sylvester (Pope Sylvester I).

G THEME AND SETTING
How does nature get the better
of Ulrich and Georg at the end of
the story?

_____

_____

_____

_____

_____

_____

_____

_____

_____

_____

"I can see figures coming through the wood. They are
following in the way I came down the hillside."

190   Both men raised their voices in as loud a shout as they could
muster.

"They hear us! They've stopped. Now they see us. They're
running down the hill towards us," cried Ulrich.

"How many of them are there?" asked Georg.

"I can't see distinctly," said Ulrich; "nine or ten."

"Then they are yours," said Georg; "I had only seven out
with me."

"They are making all the speed they can, brave lads," said
Ulrich gladly.

200   "Are they your men?" asked Georg. "Are they your men?"

"No," said Ulrich with a laugh, the idiotic chattering laugh of
a man unstrung with hideous fear.

"Who are they?" asked Georg quickly, straining his eyes to see
what the other would gladly not have seen.

"*Wolves.*" **G**

Text Analysis: Theme and Setting

Think about the story's setting and the way it affects Ulrich and Georg. Complete the chart below with information about theme and setting in "The Interlopers."

Details About Setting:

1. _____

2. _____

3. _____

↓

How theme is related to setting:

_____

_____

_____

_____

_____

_____

Review your notes for "The Interlopers" and the chart above. Write a theme statement about holding grudges that is suggested by the surprise ending.

_____

_____

_____

_____

_____

_____

_____

Reading Strategy: Monitor

Review the notes you took while reading "The Interlopers." How has clarifying your reading helped you to better understand the story? In the chart below, write your answer and give two personal examples to support your ideas.

How has clarifying your reading helped you to better understand the story?	
Personal Example to Support Answer	Personal Example to Support Answer

What's wrong with holding a GRUDGE?

Why do you think grudges appear so often in literature?

_____

_____

_____

Vocabulary Practice

Decide whether each pair of terms are similar or different. Write *S* if they are similar or *D* if they are different.

_____ **1.** precipitous/steep

_____ **2.** acquiesce/dispute

_____ **3.** marauder/raider

_____ **4.** condolence/indifference

_____ **5.** languor/energy

_____ **6.** draft/sip

_____ **7.** succor/assistance

_____ **8.** pestilential/healthful

_____ **9.** interloper/guest

_____ **10.** pinioned/pinned down

Academic Vocabulary in Speaking

| alter | layer | symbol | theme | unify |

TURN AND TALK With a partner, discuss one **theme** of "The Interlopers." For example, one theme is that people and relationships are more important than things. Why is this an important theme, and what examples from the story support the theme? Use at least one Academic Vocabulary word in your conversation. Definitions for these terms are listed on page 145.

Assessment Practice

DIRECTIONS Use "The Interlopers" to answer questions 1–6.

1 The von Gradwitz and Znaeym families are fighting —

- (A) because of wolves
- (B) to buy land
- (C) over land ownership
- (D) to save trees

2 What do Georg and Ulrich initially say they will do when their foresters arrive?

- (A) have the foresters help them get free
- (B) have each other over for dinner
- (C) have the foresters cut down all the trees
- (D) have their foresters kill the other man

3 The storm described in the story changes the conflict between Ulrich and Georg by —

- (A) allowing them to face each other and solve their conflict through violence
- (B) forcing them to face each other and change their minds about their conflict
- (C) pushing them to hunt each other through the storm with their foresters
- (D) offering them a way to discuss their problem and still stay enemies

4 How do Ulrich and Georg change in the story?

- (A) They agree to become friends.
- (B) They decide to stay enemies.
- (C) They push each other under the falling tree.
- (D) They realize their argument is still important.

5 Which of the following is the best summary of what happens to Ulrich and Georg?

- (A) Ulrich and Georg are hunting each other, find each other by a tree, and shoot each other before talking.
- (B) Ulrich and Georg are pinned down by a tree, agree to become friends, and are rescued at the last minute by foresters.
- (C) Georg is pinned down by a tree, Ulrich agrees to become his friend, and Ulrich goes looking for help.
- (D) Ulrich and Georg are pinned down by a tree, agree to become friends, and are forced to wait for rescuers who never come.

6 What theme related to setting is expressed in the story?

- (A) Human beings control what happens in nature.
- (B) Human beings can only control nature if they work together.
- (C) Nature has ultimate control over human beings.
- (D) Nature has little effect on the lives of human beings.

When Mr. Pirzada Came to Dine

Short Story by Jhumpa Lahiri

When do world **CONFLICTS** affect us?

How do you feel when you learn about a conflict in a distant part of the world? For some people, the problem is quickly forgotten. For others, however, a faraway conflict can become very personal. In the following story, a young girl tries to lessen the worries of a man whose loved ones live in a war-torn country.

SURVEY Survey at least three people in your classroom or in your school to find out what current conflicts they are following in the news and why. Record your results in the notebook on the left. Then discuss your results in a small group. Are the people surveyed interested in current world conflicts? Explain why or why not.

Text Analysis: Theme and Character

A **theme** is an insight about human life that is revealed in a literary work. In good literature, a theme is almost never stated directly. After all, the writer of imaginative fiction does not want to preach to us. Instead the writer wants us, along with the characters, to recognize some truth about human existence. The writer wants to bring alive some segment of human life. When the writer's task is done well, theme arises naturally from the story, so that by the end of the story, we think we have discovered something—or rediscovered a truth we had forgotten.

One way to discover a theme is to analyze the thoughts, words, and actions of a story's **main character.** Keep these questions in mind as you learn about Lilia, the main character:

- What are Lilia's key traits and motivations? Consider how the writer might want readers to feel about Lilia.
- How does Lilia react to other characters?
- What conflicts does Lilia experience?
- How does the Lilia change over time?
- What lessons does Lilia learn?

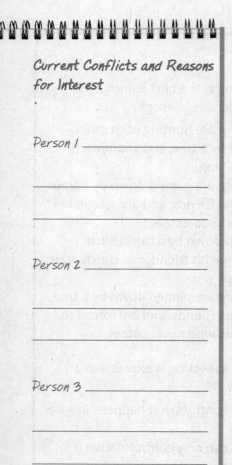

Current Conflicts and Reasons
for Interest

Person 1 _____

_____

_____

Person 2 _____

_____

_____

Person 3 _____

_____

_____

Reading Skill: Draw Conclusions

When you **draw conclusions,** you gather pieces of information—from your reading and from what you already know—to make judgments. Use the following strategies to help you draw conclusions about how the political events in Pakistan affect the story's characters:

- Note how the characters behave before and after the outbreak of violence in Pakistan.

- Identify any changes in the characters' habits.

As you read, you will be prompted to take notes in a chart like this one.

Details About Character	My Thoughts
At first, Lilia and her family share relaxed meals with Mr. Pirzada.	Lilia and her family are thoughtful to include Mr. Pirzada in their meals.

Vocabulary in Context

Note: Words are listed in the order in which they appear in the story.

ascertain (ăs'ər-tān') *v.* to discover with certainty
*The gardener could not **ascertain** who caused the damage to the garden.*

autonomy (ô-tŏn'ə-mē) *n.* freedom; independence
*Young children often struggle for more **autonomy** from the rules of adults.*

compatriot (kəm-pā'trē-ət) *n.* a person from one's own country
*It isn't unusual to find **compatriots** in different parts of the world.*

sovereignty (sŏv'ər-ĭn-tē) *n.* complete independence and self-governance
*After a nation fights for **sovereignty,** it must build a working government.*

impeccably (ĭm-pĕk'ə-blē) *adv.* perfectly, flawlessly
*The designer's new home was **impeccably** decorated.*

imperceptible (ĭm'pər-sĕp'tə-bel) *adj.* impossible or difficult to notice
*Before the bell, the students' movement toward the door was almost **imperceptible.***

assail (ə-sāl') *v.* to attack or deliver a blow
*The noise of the marching band **assailed** the ears of the audience.*

concede (kən-sēd') *v.* to admit or acknowledge, often reluctantly
*The politician **conceded** the victory to her opponent after the votes were counted.*

**SET A PURPOSE
FOR READING**

As you read, think about how a war half a world away affects the narrator and her family.

WHEN

Mr. Pirzada Came to Dine

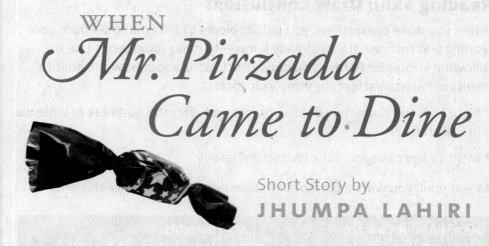

Short Story by
JHUMPA LAHIRI

BACKGROUND This story takes place in 1971, the year in which civil war erupted in Pakistan. At the time, Pakistan had two distinct parts, West Pakistan and East Pakistan, which were divided by more than a thousand miles of Indian soil. Major linguistic, cultural, and economic differences also separated the two sections. When East Pakistan demanded independence, the West Pakistan government reacted with brutal force. Thousands of people died in the fighting, and millions of refugees fled to India. From this civil war, East Pakistan became the independent nation of Bangladesh. Today, the country's biggest city is Dhaka, also spelled Dacca, as it is in Lahiri's story.

ascertain (ăs'ər-tān') *v.* to discover with certainty

autonomy (ô-tŏn'ə-mē) *n.* freedom; independence

In the autumn of 1971 a man used to come to our house, bearing confections in his pocket and hopes of **ascertaining** the life or death of his family. His name was Mr. Pirzada,[1] and he came from Dacca,[2] now the capital of Bangladesh, but then a part of Pakistan. That year Pakistan was engaged in civil war. The eastern frontier, where Dacca was located, was fighting for **autonomy** from the ruling regime in the west. In March, Dacca had been invaded, torched, and shelled by the Pakistani army. . . . By the end of the summer, three hundred thousand people were said to have died. In

10 Dacca Mr. Pirzada had a three-story home, a lectureship in botany[3] at the university, a wife of twenty years, and seven daughters

---

1. **Pirzada:** (pēr-zä'də).
2. **Dacca:** (dăk'ə).
3. **botany** (bŏt'n-ē): the science or study of plants.

between the ages of six and sixteen whose names all began with the letter A. "Their mother's idea," he explained one day, producing from his wallet a black-and-white picture of seven girls at a picnic, their braids tied with ribbons, sitting cross-legged in a row, eating chicken curry off of banana leaves. "How am I to distinguish? Ayesha, Amira, Amina, Aziza, you see the difficulty."

Each week Mr. Pirzada wrote letters to his wife, and sent comic books to each of his seven daughters, but the postal system, along
20 with most everything else in Dacca, had collapsed, and he had not heard a word of them in over six months. Mr. Pirzada, meanwhile, was in America for the year, for he had been awarded a grant from the government of Pakistan to study the foliage of New England. In spring and summer he had gathered data in Vermont and Maine, and in autumn he moved to a university north of Boston, where we lived, to write a short book about his discoveries. The grant was a great honor, but when converted into dollars it was not generous. As a result, Mr. Pirzada lived in a room in a graduate dormitory, and did not own a proper stove or a television set. And so he came to
30 our house to eat dinner and watch the evening news. **A**

At first I knew nothing of the reason for his visits. I was ten years old, and was not surprised that my parents, who were from India, and had a number of Indian acquaintances at the university, should ask Mr. Pirzada to share our meals. It was a small campus, with narrow brick walkways and white pillared buildings, located on the fringes of what seemed to be an even smaller town. The supermarket did not carry mustard oil, doctors did not make house calls, neighbors never dropped by without an invitation, and of these things, every so often, my parents
40 complained. In search of <u>compatriots</u>, they used to trail their fingers, at the start of each new semester, through the columns of the university directory, circling surnames familiar to their part of the world. It was in this manner that they discovered Mr. Pirzada, and phoned him, and invited him to our home.

I have no memory of his first visit, or of his second or his third, but by the end of September I had grown so accustomed to Mr. Pirzada's presence in our living room that one evening as

A DRAW CONCLUSIONS
Underline the details in lines 1–17 that describe Mr. Pirzada's life in Dacca. How is his life in New England different from his life in Dacca?

_____

_____

_____

_____

_____

_____

_____

_____

_____

_____

_____

compatriot (kəm-pā'trē-ət) *n.* a person from one's own country

Why did the narrator's parents search for **compatriots** in the university directory?

_____

_____

_____

_____

B DRAW CONCLUSIONS
Underline the details in
lines 45–56 that suggest that
Mr. Pirzada is a welcome guest
in Lilia's home.

PAUSE & REFLECT
Why does Lilia's father say
"Mr. Pirzada is no longer
considered Indian"?

I was dropping ice cubes into the water pitcher, I asked my mother
to hand me a fourth glass from a cupboard still out of my reach.
50 She was busy at the stove, presiding over a skillet of fried spinach
with radishes, and could not hear me because of the drone of the
exhaust fan and the fierce scrapes of her spatula. I turned to my
father, who was leaning against the refrigerator, eating spiced
cashews from a cupped fist.

"What is it, Lilia?"

"A glass for the Indian man." **B**

"Mr. Pirzada won't be coming today. More importantly,
Mr. Pirzada is no longer considered Indian," my father
announced, brushing salt from the cashews out of his trim black
60 beard. "Not since Partition.[4] Our country was divided. 1947."

When I said I thought that was the date of India's independence
from Britain, my father said, "That too. One moment we were free
and then we were sliced up," he explained, drawing an X with his
finger on the countertop, "like a pie. Hindus here, Muslims there.
Dacca no longer belongs to us." He told me that during Partition
Hindus and Muslims had set fire to each other's homes. For many,
the idea of eating in the other's company was still unthinkable.

PAUSE & REFLECT

It made no sense to me. Mr. Pirzada and my parents spoke the
same language, laughed at the same jokes, looked more or less the
70 same. They ate pickled mangoes with their meals, ate rice every
night for supper with their hands. Like my parents, Mr. Pirzada
took off his shoes before entering a room, chewed fennel seeds
after meals as a digestive, drank no alcohol, for dessert dipped
austere biscuits[5] into successive cups of tea. Nevertheless my father
insisted that I understand the difference, and he led me to a map
of the world taped to the wall over his desk. He seemed concerned
that Mr. Pirzada might take offense if I accidentally referred to
him as an Indian, though I could not really imagine Mr. Pirzada
being offended by much of anything. "Mr. Pirzada is Bengali, but
80 he is a Muslim," my father informed me. "Therefore he lives in

4. **Partition:** the division in 1947 of the Indian subcontinent into two
independent countries, India and Pakistan, after British withdrawal.
5. **biscuits:** a British term for cookies or crackers.

East Pakistan, not India." His finger trailed across the Atlantic, through Europe, the Mediterranean, the Middle East, and finally to the sprawling orange diamond that my mother once told me resembled a woman wearing a sari[6] with her left arm extended. Various cities had been circled with lines drawn between them to indicate my parents' travels, and the place of their birth, Calcutta, was signified by a small silver star. I had been there only once and had no memory of the trip. "As you see, Lilia, it is a different country, a different color," my father said. Pakistan was yellow,

90 not orange. I noticed that there were two distinct parts to it, one much larger than the other, separated by an expanse of Indian territory; it was as if California and Connecticut constituted a nation apart from the U.S.

My father rapped his knuckles on top of my head. "You are, of course, aware of the current situation? Aware of East Pakistan's fight for **sovereignty**?"

I nodded, unaware of the situation. **C**

We returned to the kitchen, where my mother was draining a pot of boiled rice into a colander. My father opened up the can

100 on the counter and eyed me sharply over the frames of his glasses as he ate some more cashews. "What exactly do they teach you at school? Do you study history? Geography?"

"Lilia has plenty to learn at school," my mother said. "We live here now, she was born here." She seemed genuinely proud of the fact, as if it were a reflection of my character. In her estimation, I knew, I was assured a safe life, an easy life, a fine education, every opportunity. I would never have to eat rationed food, or obey curfews, or watch riots from my rooftop, or hide neighbors in water tanks to prevent them from being shot, as she and my father

110 had. "Imagine having to place her in a decent school. Imagine her having to read during power failures by the light of kerosene lamps. Imagine the pressures, the tutors, the constant exams." She ran a hand through her hair, bobbed to a suitable length for her part-time job as a bank teller. "How can you possibly expect her to know about Partition? Put those nuts away."

sovereignty (sŏv′ər-ĭn-tē) *n.* complete independence and self-governance

C THEME AND CHARACTER
Reread lines 57–97. In this passage, Lilia's father shares information about India and Pakistan. Does she understand the conflict between these two nations? If not, why does she nod? Explain.

6. **sari** (sä′rē): a garment worn mostly by women of Pakistan and India, consisting of a length of fabric with one end wrapped around the waist to form a skirt and the other draped over the shoulder or covering the head.

D THEME AND CHARACTER
Do you think Lilia likes her history class? Why or why not?

_____

_____

_____

_____

_____

_____

_____

_____

_____

impeccably (ĭm-pĕk′ə-blē) *adv.*
perfectly, flawlessly

"But what does she learn about the world?" My father rattled the cashew can in his hand. "What is she learning?"

We learned American history, of course, and American geography. That year, and every year, it seemed, we began by 120 studying the Revolutionary War. We were taken in school buses on field trips to visit Plymouth Rock,[7] and to walk the Freedom Trail, and to climb to the top of the Bunker Hill Monument.[8] We made dioramas out of colored construction paper depicting George Washington crossing the choppy waters of the Delaware River, and we made puppets of King George wearing white tights and a black bow in his hair. During tests we were given blank maps of the thirteen colonies, and asked to fill in names, dates, capitals. I could do it with my eyes closed. **D**

The next evening Mr. Pirzada arrived, as usual, at six o'clock. 130 Though they were no longer strangers, upon first greeting each other, he and my father maintained the habit of shaking hands.

"Come in, sir. Lilia, Mr. Pirzada's coat, please."

He stepped into the foyer, **impeccably** suited and scarved, with a silk tie knotted at his collar. Each evening he appeared in ensembles of plums, olives, and chocolate browns. He was a compact man, and though his feet were perpetually splayed, and his belly slightly wide, he nevertheless maintained an efficient posture, as if balancing in either hand two suitcases of equal weight. His ears were insulated by tufts of graying hair that seemed 140 to block out the unpleasant traffic of life. He had thickly lashed eyes shaded with a trace of camphor,[9] a generous mustache that turned up playfully at the ends, and a mole shaped like a flattened raisin in the very center of his left cheek. On his head he wore a black fez[10] made from the wool of Persian lambs, secured by bobby

---

7. **Plymouth Rock:** a boulder in Plymouth, Massachusetts, said to be the site where the Pilgrims disembarked from the *Mayflower*.

8. **Freedom Trail . . . Bunker Hill Monument:** historic sites in Boston, which commemorate critical events in the American struggle for independence from Great Britain.

9. **camphor** (kăm′fər): a fragrant compound from an Asian evergreen tree, used in skin-care products.

10. **fez** (fĕz): a man's felt hat in the shape of a flat-topped cone, worn mainly in the eastern Mediterranean region.

pins, without which I was never to see him. Though my father always offered to fetch him in our car, Mr. Pirzada preferred to walk from his dormitory to our neighborhood, a distance of about twenty minutes on foot, studying trees and shrubs on his way, and when he entered our house his knuckles were pink with the effects
150 of the crisp autumn air.

"Another refugee, I am afraid, on Indian territory."

"They are estimating nine million at the last count," my father said.

Mr. Pirzada handed me his coat, for it was my job to hang it on the rack at the bottom of the stairs. It was made of finely checkered gray-and-blue wool, with a striped lining and horn buttons, and carried in its weave the faint smell of limes. There were no recognizable tags inside, only a hand-stitched label with the phrase "Z. Sayeed, Suitors" embroidered on it in cursive with glossy black
160 thread. On certain days a birch or maple leaf was tucked into a pocket. He unlaced his shoes and lined them against the baseboard; a golden paste clung to the toes and heels, the result of walking through our damp, unraked lawn. Relieved of his trappings, he grazed my throat with his short, restless fingers, the way a person feels for solidity behind a wall before driving in a nail. Then he followed my father to the living room, where the television was tuned to the local news. As soon as they were seated my mother appeared from the kitchen with a plate of mincemeat kebabs with coriander chutney.[11] Mr. Pirzada popped one into his mouth.

170 "One can only hope," he said, reaching for another, "that Dacca's refugees are as heartily fed. Which reminds me." He reached into his suit pocket and gave me a small plastic egg filled with cinnamon hearts. "For the lady of the house," he said with an almost **imperceptible** splay-footed bow. ❸

"Really, Mr. Pirzada," my mother protested. "Night after night. You spoil her."

"I only spoil children who are incapable of spoiling."

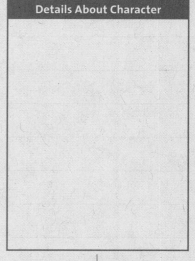

Details About Character

↓

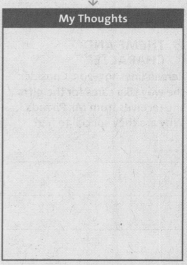

My Thoughts

imperceptible (ĭm′pər-sĕp′tə-bel) *adj.* impossible or difficult to notice

---

11. **mincemeat kebabs** (kə-bŏbz′) **. . . chutney** (chŭt′nē): an Indian or Pakistani dish consisting of pieces of spiced meat that have been placed on skewers and roasted, with an accompanying relish made of fruits, spices, and herbs.

F THEME AND CHARACTER

Why does Lilia have conflicted feelings about Mr. Pirzada? Underline details in lines 178–194 that explain her feelings.

_____

_____

_____

_____

_____

_____

_____

G THEME AND CHARACTER

Reread lines 195–205. Consider the way Lilia cares for the gifts she receives from Mr. Pirzada. Why are they special to her?

_____

_____

_____

_____

_____

_____

_____

_____

_____

It was an awkward moment for me, one which I awaited in part with dread, in part with delight. I was charmed by the presence of Mr. Pirzada's rotund elegance, and flattered by the faint theatricality of his attentions, yet unsettled by the superb ease of his gestures, which made me feel, for an instant, like a stranger in my own home. It had become our ritual, and for several weeks, before we grew more comfortable with one another, it was the only time he spoke to me directly. I had no response, offered no comment, betrayed no visible reaction to the steady stream of honey-filled lozenges, the raspberry truffles, the slender rolls of sour pastilles. I could not even thank him, for once, when I did, for an especially spectacular peppermint lollipop wrapped in a spray of purple cellophane, he had demanded, "What is this thank-you? The lady at the bank thanks me, the cashier at the shop thanks me, the librarian thanks me when I return an overdue book, the overseas operator thanks me as she tries to connect me to Dacca and fails. If I am buried in this country I will be thanked, no doubt, at my funeral." **F**

It was inappropriate, in my opinion, to consume the candy Mr. Pirzada gave me in a casual manner. I coveted each evening's treasure as I would a jewel, or a coin from a buried kingdom, and I would place it in a small keepsake box made of carved sandalwood beside my bed, in which, long ago in India, my father's mother used to store the ground areca nuts[12] she ate after her morning bath. It was my only memento of a grandmother I had never known, and until Mr. Pirzada came to our lives I could find nothing to put inside it. Every so often before brushing my teeth and laying out my clothes for school the next day, I opened the lid of the box and ate one of his treats. **G**

That night, like every night, we did not eat at the dining table, because it did not provide an unobstructed view of the television set. Instead we huddled around the coffee table, without conversing, our plates perched on the edges of our knees. From the kitchen my mother brought forth the succession of dishes: lentils[13] with fried onions, green beans with coconut, fish cooked with raisins in a yogurt sauce. I followed with the water glasses,

---

12. **areca** (ə-rē′kə) **nuts:** seeds of the betel palm, chewed as a stimulant.
13. **lentils:** cooked seeds of a beanlike plant native to southwest Asia, a staple in Indian and Pakistani cuisine.

and the plate of lemon wedges, and the chili peppers, purchased on monthly trips to Chinatown and stored by the pound in the freezer, which they liked to snap open and crush into their food.

Before eating Mr. Pirzada always did a curious thing. He took out a plain silver watch without a band, which he kept in his breast pocket, held it briefly to one of his tufted ears, and wound it with three swift flicks of his thumb and forefinger. Unlike the
220 watch on his wrist, the pocket watch, he had explained to me, was set to the local time in Dacca, eleven hours ahead. For the duration of the meal the watch rested on his folded napkin on the coffee table. He never seemed to consult it.

Now that I had learned Mr. Pirzada was not an Indian, I began to study him with extra care, to try to figure out what made him different. I decided that the pocket watch was one of those things. When I saw it that night, as he wound it and arranged it on the coffee table, an uneasiness possessed me; life, I realized, was being lived in Dacca first. I imagined Mr. Pirzada's daughters rising
230 from sleep, tying ribbons in their hair, anticipating breakfast, preparing for school. Our meals, our actions, were only a shadow of what had already happened there, a lagging ghost of where Mr. Pirzada really belonged. ⓗ

At six-thirty, which was when the national news began, my father raised the volume and adjusted the antennas. Usually I occupied myself with a book, but that night my father insisted that I pay attention. On the screen I saw tanks rolling through dusty streets, and fallen buildings, and forests of unfamiliar trees into which East Pakistani refugees had fled, seeking safety over
240 the Indian border. I saw boats with fan-shaped sails floating on wide coffee-colored rivers, a barricaded university, newspaper offices burnt to the ground. I turned to look at Mr. Pirzada; the images flashed in miniature across his eyes. As he watched he had an immovable expression on his face, composed but alert, as if someone were giving him directions to an unknown destination.

During the commercial my mother went to the kitchen to get more rice, and my father and Mr. Pirzada deplored the policies

ⓗ **THEME AND CHARACTER**
Reread lines 216–233. What "curious thing" does Mr. Pirzada do, and why? Why does Lilia study him more closely now?

assail (ə-sāl′) *v.* to attack or deliver a blow

❶ DRAW CONCLUSIONS
How does Lilia feel when she starts to understand the situation in East Pakistan?

_____

_____

_____

_____

_____

_____

_____

_____

_____

_____

_____

_____

_____

_____

_____

_____

of a general named Yahyah Khan. They discussed intrigues I did not know, a catastrophe I could not comprehend. "See, children your age, what they do to survive," my father said as he served me another piece of fish. But I could no longer eat. I could only steal glances at Mr. Pirzada, sitting beside me in his olive green jacket, calmly creating a well in his rice to make room for a second helping of lentils. He was not my notion of a man burdened by such grave concerns. I wondered if the reason he was always so smartly dressed was in preparation to endure with dignity whatever news **assailed** him, perhaps even to attend a funeral at a moment's notice. I wondered, too, what would happen if suddenly his seven daughters were to appear on television, smiling and waving and blowing kisses to Mr. Pirzada from a balcony. I imagined how relieved he would be. But this never happened. **❶**

That night when I placed the plastic egg filled with cinnamon hearts in the box beside my bed, I did not feel the ceremonious satisfaction I normally did. I tried not to think about Mr. Pirzada, in his lime-scented overcoat, connected to the unruly, sweltering world we had viewed a few hours ago in our bright, carpeted living room. And yet for several moments that was all I could think about. My stomach tightened as I worried whether his wife and seven daughters were now members of the drifting, clamoring crowd that had flashed at intervals on the screen. In an effort to banish the image I looked around my room, at the yellow canopied bed with matching flounced curtains, at framed class pictures mounted on white and violet papered walls, at the penciled inscriptions by the closet door where my father had recorded my height on each of my birthdays. But the more I tried to distract myself, the more I began to convince myself that Mr. Pirzada's family was in all likelihood dead. Eventually I took a square of white chocolate out of the box, and unwrapped it, and then I did something I had never done before. I put the chocolate in my mouth, letting it soften until the last possible moment, and then as I chewed it slowly, I prayed that Mr. Pirzada's family was safe and sound. I had never prayed for anything before, had never been taught or told to, but I decided, given the circumstances, that it was something I should do. That night when I went to the bathroom I only pretended to brush my teeth, for I feared that I would somehow rinse the prayer out as well. I wet the brush and rearranged the tube of paste to prevent my parents from asking any questions, and fell asleep with sugar on my tongue. **J**

290 No one at school talked about the war followed so faithfully in my living room. We continued to study the American Revolution, and learned about the injustices of taxation without representation, and memorized passages from the Declaration of Independence. During recess the boys would divide in two groups, chasing each other wildly around the swings and seesaws, Redcoats against the colonies. In the classroom our teacher, Mrs. Kenyon, pointed frequently to a map that emerged like a movie screen from the top of the chalkboard, charting the route of the *Mayflower*, or showing us the location of the Liberty Bell. Each week two members of the class gave a report on a particular aspect of the 300 Revolution, and so one day I was sent to the school library with my friend Dora to learn about the surrender at Yorktown. Mrs. Kenyon handed us a slip of paper with the names of three books to look up in the card catalogue. We found them right away, and sat down at a low round table to read and take notes. But I could not concentrate. I returned to the blond-wood shelves, to a section I had noticed labeled "Asia." I saw books about China, India, Indonesia, Korea. Eventually I found a book titled *Pakistan: A Land and Its People.* I sat on a footstool and opened the book. The laminated jacket crackled in my grip. I began turning the 310 pages, filled with photos of rivers and rice fields and men in military uniforms. There was a chapter about Dacca, and I began to read about its rainfall, and its jute[14] production. I was studying a population chart when Dora appeared in the aisle.

"What are you doing back here? Mrs. Kenyon's in the library. She came to check up on us."

I slammed the book shut, too loudly. Mrs. Kenyon emerged, the aroma of her perfume filling up the tiny aisle, and lifted the book by the tip of its spine as if it were a hair clinging to my sweater. She glanced at the cover, then at me.

320 "Is this book a part of your report, Lilia?" **K**

---

14. **jute:** the fiber from an Asian plant, used for sacking and cording.

J THEME AND CHARACTER
Review lines 233–288. Think about the **internal conflict,** or struggle that Lilia has. How has her interest in Pakistan changed since the beginning of the story? Who or what has caused this change?

_____

_____

_____

_____

_____

_____

_____

_____

_____

_____

K DRAW CONCLUSIONS
How has the conflict in Pakistan affected the lives of Lilia's classmates and her history teacher, Mrs. Kenyon? Explain.

_____

_____

_____

_____

_____

_____

L **DRAW CONCLUSIONS**

In lines 324–349, how does the lack of news from Dacca affect Lilia's parents and Mr. Pirzada? Fill in the chart below with your answer.

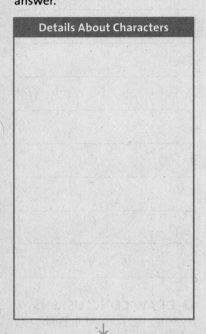

Details About Characters

↓

My Thoughts

"No, Mrs. Kenyon."

"Then I see no reason to consult it," she said, replacing it in the slim gap on the shelf. "Do you?"

As weeks passed it grew more and more rare to see any footage from Dacca on the news. The report came after the first set of commercials, sometimes the second. The press had been censored, removed, restricted, rerouted. Some days, many days, only a death toll was announced, prefaced by a reiteration of the general situation. . . . More villages set ablaze. In spite of it all, night after
330 night, my parents and Mr. Pirzada enjoyed long, leisurely meals. After the television was shut off, and the dishes washed and dried, they joked, and told stories, and dipped biscuits in their tea. When they tired of discussing political matters they discussed, instead, the progress of Mr. Pirzada's book about the deciduous trees[15] of New England, and my father's nomination for tenure, and the peculiar eating habits of my mother's American coworkers at the bank. Eventually I was sent upstairs to do my homework, but through the carpet I heard them as they drank more tea, and listened to cassettes of Kishore Kumar, and played Scrabble on
340 the coffee table, laughing and arguing long into the night about the spellings of English words. I wanted to join them, wanted, above all, to console Mr. Pirzada somehow. But apart from eating a piece of candy for the sake of his family and praying for their safety, there was nothing I could do. They played Scrabble until the eleven o'clock news, and then, sometime around midnight, Mr. Pirzada walked back to his dormitory. For this reason I never saw him leave, but each night as I drifted off to sleep I would hear them, anticipating the birth of a nation on the other side of the world. **L**

350 One day in October Mr. Pirzada asked upon arrival, "What are these large orange vegetables on people's doorsteps? A type of squash?"

---

15. **deciduous** (də-sĭj′o͞o-əs) **trees:** trees that shed or lose leaves at the end of the growing season.

"Pumpkins," my mother replied. "Lilia, remind me to pick one up at the supermarket."

"And the purpose? It indicates what?"

"You make a jack-o'-lantern," I said, grinning ferociously. "Like this. To scare people away."

"I see," Mr. Pirzada said, grinning back. "Very useful."

The next day my mother bought a ten-pound pumpkin, fat
360 and round, and placed it on the dining table. Before supper, while my father and Mr. Pirzada were watching the local news, she told me to decorate it with markers, but I wanted to carve it properly like others I had noticed in the neighborhood.

"Yes, let's carve it," Mr. Pirzada agreed, and rose from the sofa. "Hang the news tonight." Asking no questions, he walked into the kitchen, opened a drawer, and returned, bearing a long serrated knife. He glanced at me for approval. "Shall I?"

I nodded. For the first time we all gathered around the dining table, my mother, my father, Mr. Pirzada, and I. While
370 the television aired unattended we covered the tabletop with newspapers. Mr. Pirzada draped his jacket over the chair behind him, removed a pair of opal cuff links, and rolled up the starched sleeves of his shirt.

"First go around the top, like this," I instructed, demonstrating with my index finger.

He made an initial incision and drew the knife around. When he had come full circle he lifted the cap by the stem; it loosened effortlessly, and Mr. Pirzada leaned over the pumpkin for a moment to inspect and inhale its contents. My mother gave him
380 a long metal spoon with which he gutted the interior until the last bits of string and seeds were gone. My father, meanwhile, separated the seeds from the pulp and set them out to dry on a cookie sheet, so that we could roast them later on. I drew two triangles against the ridged surface for the eyes, which Mr. Pirzada dutifully carved, and crescents for eyebrows, and another triangle for the nose. The mouth was all that remained, and the teeth posed a challenge. I hesitated.

Ⓜ DRAW CONCLUSIONS
When Mr. Pirzada says in line 365, "Hang the news tonight," has he forgotten about the conflict in Pakistan? Explain.

N DRAW CONCLUSIONS
How does Mr. Pirzada react to the latest news report from Dacca? Underline the details in lines 390–412 that support your response.

_____

_____

_____

_____

_____

_____

_____

_____

_____

_____

_____

_____

_____

_____

_____

_____

_____

_____

_____

_____

_____

_____

"Smile or frown?" I asked.

"You choose," Mr Pirzada said.

390 As a compromise I drew a kind of grimace, straight across, neither mournful nor friendly. Mr. Pirzada began carving, without the least bit of intimidation, as if he had been carving jack-o'-lanterns his whole life. He had nearly finished when the national news began. The reporter mentioned Dacca, and we all turned to listen: An Indian official announced that unless the world helped to relieve the burden of East Pakistani refugees, India would have to go to war against Pakistan. The reporter's face dripped with sweat as he relayed the information. He did not wear a tie or jacket, dressed instead as if he himself were about to
400 take part in the battle. He shielded his scorched face as he hollered things to the cameraman. The knife slipped from Mr. Pirzada's hand and made a gash dipping toward the base of the pumpkin.

"Please forgive me." He raised a hand to one side of his face, as if someone had slapped him there. "I am—it is terrible. I will buy another. We will try again."

"Not at all, not at all," my father said. He took the knife from Mr. Pirzada, and carved around the gash, evening it out, dispensing altogether with the teeth I had drawn. What resulted was a disproportionately large hole the size of a lemon, so that
410 our jack-o'-lantern wore an expression of placid astonishment, the eyebrows no longer fierce, floating in frozen surprise above a vacant, geometric gaze. **N**

For Halloween I was a witch. Dora, my trick-or-treating partner, was a witch too. We wore black capes fashioned from dyed pillowcases and conical hats with wide cardboard brims. We shaded our faces green with a broken eye shadow that belonged to Dora's mother, and my mother gave us two burlap sacks that had once contained basmati rice, for collecting candy. That year our parents decided that we were old enough to roam the
420 neighborhood unattended. Our plan was to walk from my house to Dora's, from where I was to call to say I had arrived safely, and then Dora's mother would drive me home. My father equipped us

with flashlights, and I had to wear my watch and synchronize it with his. We were to return no later than nine o'clock.

When Mr. Pirzada arrived that evening he presented me with a box of chocolate-covered mints.

"In here," I told him, and opened up the burlap sack. "Trick or treat!"

430 "I understand that you don't really need my contribution this evening," he said, depositing the box. He gazed at my green face, and the hat secured by a string under my chin. Gingerly he lifted the hem of the cape, under which I was wearing a sweater and zipped fleece jacket. "Will you be warm enough?"

I nodded, causing the hat to tip to one side.

He set it right. "Perhaps it is best to stand still."

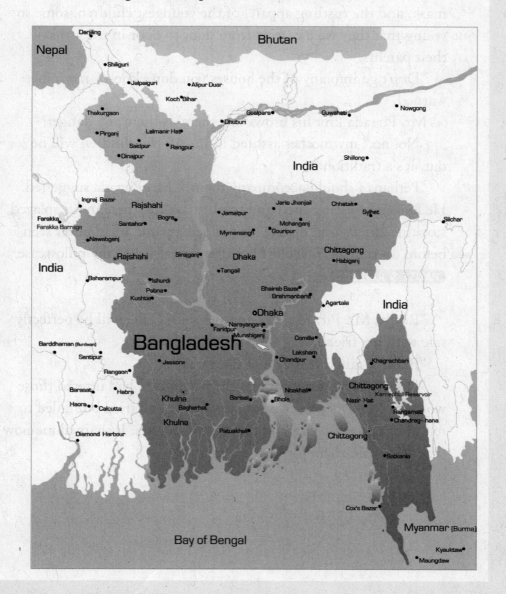

PAUSE & REFLECT

Mr. Pirzada is concerned about Lilia going out for Halloween. Is he really concerned for Lilia or worried about something else? Explain.

_____

_____

_____

_____

_____

_____

_____

_____

_____

_____

_____

_____

⊙ **THEME AND CHARACTER**

Why does Lilia feel "shamed" (line 466) when she says "Don't worry" (line 464) to Mr. Pirzada?

_____

_____

_____

_____

_____

The bottom of our staircase was lined with baskets of miniature candy, and when Mr. Pirzada removed his shoes he did not place them there as he normally did, but inside the closet instead. He began to unbutton his coat, and I waited to take it from him, but
440 Dora called me from the bathroom to say that she needed my help drawing a mole on her chin. When we were finally ready my mother took a picture of us in front of the fireplace, and then I opened the front door to leave. Mr. Pirzada and my father, who had not gone into the living room yet, hovered in the foyer. Outside it was already dark. The air smelled of wet leaves, and our carved jack-o'-lantern flickered impressively against the shrubbery by the door. In the distance came the sounds of scampering feet, and the howls of the older boys who wore no costume at all other than a rubber mask, and the rustling apparel of the youngest children, some so
450 young that they were carried from door to door in the arms of their parents.

"Don't go into any of the houses you don't know," my father warned.

Mr. Pirzada knit his brows together. "Is there any danger?"

"No, no," my mother assured him. "All the children will be out. It's a tradition."

"Perhaps I should accompany them?" Mr. Pirzada suggested. He looked suddenly tired and small, standing there in his splayed, stockinged feet, and his eyes contained a panic I had never seen
460 before. In spite of the cold I began to sweat inside my pillowcase.

PAUSE & REFLECT

"Really, Mr. Pirzada," my mother said, "Lilia will be perfectly safe with her friend."

"But if it rains? If they lose their way?"

"Don't worry," I said. It was the first time I had uttered those words to Mr. Pirzada, two simple words I had tried but failed to tell him for weeks, had said only in my prayers. It shamed me now that I had said them for my own sake. ⊙

He placed one of his stocky fingers on my cheek, then pressed it to the back of his own hand, leaving a faint green smear. "If the
470 lady insists," he <u>conceded</u>, and offered a small bow.

We left, stumbling slightly in our black pointy thrift-store shoes, and when we turned at the end of the driveway to wave good-bye, Mr. Pirzada was standing in the frame of the doorway, a short figure between my parents, waving back.

"Why did that man want to come with us?" Dora asked.

"His daughters are missing." As soon as I said it, I wished I had not. I felt that my saying it made it true, that Mr. Pirzada's daughters really were missing, and that he would never see them again.

"You mean they were kidnapped?" Dora continued. "From a
480 park or something?"

"I didn't mean they were missing. I meant, he misses them. They live in a different country, and he hasn't seen them in a while, that's all." **P**

We went from house to house, walking along pathways and pressing doorbells. Some people had switched off all their lights for effect, or strung rubber bats in their windows. At the McIntyres' a coffin was placed in front of the door, and Mr. McIntyre rose from it in silence, his face covered with chalk, and deposited a fistful of candy corns into our sacks. Several
490 people told me that they had never seen an Indian witch before. Others performed the transaction without comment. As we paved our way with the parallel beams of our flashlights we saw eggs cracked in the middle of the road, and cars covered with shaving cream, and toilet paper garlanding the branches of trees. By the time we reached Dora's house our hands were chapped from carrying our bulging burlap bags, and our feet were sore and swollen. Her mother gave us bandages for our blisters and served us warm cider and caramel popcorn. She reminded me to call my parents to tell them I had arrived safely and when I did I could
500 hear the television in the background. My mother did not seem particularly relieved to hear from me. When I replaced the phone on the receiver it occurred to me that the television wasn't on at Dora's house at all. Her father was lying on the couch, reading a magazine, with a glass of wine on the coffee table, and there was saxophone music playing on the stereo. **PAUSE & REFLECT**

concede (kən-sēd') v. to admit or acknowledge, often reluctantly

P THEME AND CHARACTER
Reread lines 471–483. According to Lilia, why is Mr. Pirzada trying to protect her? How does Lilia try to protect Mr. Pirzada?

PAUSE & REFLECT
Lilia notes that the television isn't on at Dora's house. What might this say about Dora's family?

Q DRAW CONCLUSIONS
What does Mr. Pirzada's body language in lines 517–519 suggest about the news that he has heard of the conflict in Pakistan? Explain.

_____

_____

_____

_____

_____

_____

_____

R DRAW CONCLUSIONS
Review the way Lilia's family and Mr. Pirzada behave during the 12 days of war compared with the way they acted during dinners before. How has Pakistan's civil war affected them?

_____

_____

_____

_____

_____

_____

_____

_____

_____

_____

After Dora and I had sorted through our plunder, and counted and sampled and traded until we were satisfied, her mother drove me back to my house. I thanked her for the ride, and she waited in the driveway until I made it to the door. In the glare of her headlights I saw that our pumpkin had been shattered, its thick shell strewn in chunks across the grass. I felt the sting of tears in my eyes, and a sudden pain in my throat, as if it had been stuffed with the sharp tiny pebbles that crunched with each step under my aching feet. I opened the door, expecting the three of them to be standing in the foyer, waiting to receive me, and to grieve for our ruined pumpkin, but there was no one. In the living room Mr. Pirzada, my father, and mother were sitting side by side on the sofa. The television was turned off, and Mr. Pirzada had his head in his hands. **Q**

What they heard that evening, and for many evenings after that, was that India and Pakistan were drawing closer and closer to war. Troops from both sides lined the border, and Dacca was insisting on nothing short of independence. The war was soon to be waged on East Pakistani soil. The United States was siding with West Pakistan, the Soviet Union with India and what was soon to be Bangladesh. War was declared officially on December 4, and twelve days later, the Pakistani army, weakened by having to fight three thousand miles from their source of supplies, surrendered in Dacca. All of these facts I know only now, for they are available to me in any history book, in any library. But then it remained, for the most part, a remote mystery with haphazard clues. What I remember during those twelve days of the war was that my father no longer asked me to watch the news with them, and that Mr. Pirzada stopped bringing me candy, and that my mother refused to serve anything other than boiled eggs with rice for dinner. I remember some nights helping my mother spread a sheet and blankets on the couch so that Mr. Pirzada could sleep there, and high-pitched voices hollering in the middle of the night when my parents called our relatives in Calcutta to learn more details about the situation. Most of all I remember the three of them operating during that time as if they were a single person, sharing a single meal, a single body, a single silence, and a single fear. **R**

In January, Mr. Pirzada flew back to his three-story home in Dacca, to discover what was left of it. We did not see much of him in those final weeks of the year; he was busy finishing his manuscript, and we went to Philadelphia to spend Christmas with friends of my parents. Just as I have no memory of his first visit, I have no memory of his last. My father drove him to the airport one afternoon while I was at school. For a long 550 time we did not hear from him. Our evenings went on as usual, with dinners in front of the news. The only difference was that Mr. Pirzada and his extra watch were not there to accompany us. According to reports Dacca was repairing itself slowly, with a newly formed parliamentary government. The new leader, Sheikh Mujib Rahman, recently released from prison, asked countries for building materials to replace more than one million houses that had been destroyed in the war. Countless refugees returned from India, greeted, we learned, by unemployment and the threat of famine. Every now and then I studied the map above my father's 560 desk and pictured Mr. Pirzada on that small patch of yellow, perspiring heavily, I imagined, in one of his suits, searching for his family. Of course, the map was outdated by then. **⑤**

⑤ THEME AND CHARACTER
Reread lines 543–562. How does Lilia react to Mr. Pirzada's absence?

① THEME AND CHARACTER

Why does Lilia throw away her remaining candies in line 585? Reread lines 277–284 and lines 581–584 to help you answer this question.

_____

_____

_____

_____

_____

_____

_____

_____

_____

Finally, several months later, we received a card from Mr. Pirzada commemorating the Muslim New Year,[16] along with a short letter. He was reunited, he wrote, with his wife and children. All were well, having survived the events of the past year at an estate belonging to his wife's grandparents in the mountains of Shillong. His seven daughters were a bit taller, he wrote, but otherwise they were the same, and he still could not keep their
570 names in order. At the end of the letter he thanked us for our hospitality, adding that although he now understood the meaning of the words "thank you" they still were not adequate to express his gratitude. To celebrate the good news my mother prepared a special dinner that evening, and when we sat down to eat at the coffee table we toasted our water glasses, but I did not feel like celebrating. Though I had not seen him for months, it was only then that I felt Mr. Pirzada's absence. It was only then, raising my water glass in his name, that I knew what it meant to miss someone who was so many miles and hours away, just as he had
580 missed his wife and daughters for so many months. He had no reason to return to us, and my parents predicted, correctly, that we would never see him again. Since January, each night before bed, I had continued to eat, for the sake of Mr. Pirzada's family, a piece of candy I had saved from Halloween. That night there was no need to. Eventually, I threw them away. **①**

---

16. **Muslim New Year:** an important Islamic holiday and observance that marks the Prophet Muhammad's emigration from Mecca to Medina, a turning point in Islamic history.

Text Analysis: Theme and Character

Lilia becomes more concerned about the situation in Pakistan as she gets to know Mr. Pirzada. Show Lilia's growing concern by completing the timeline below. Fill in each blank with an appropriate story detail.

TIMELINE

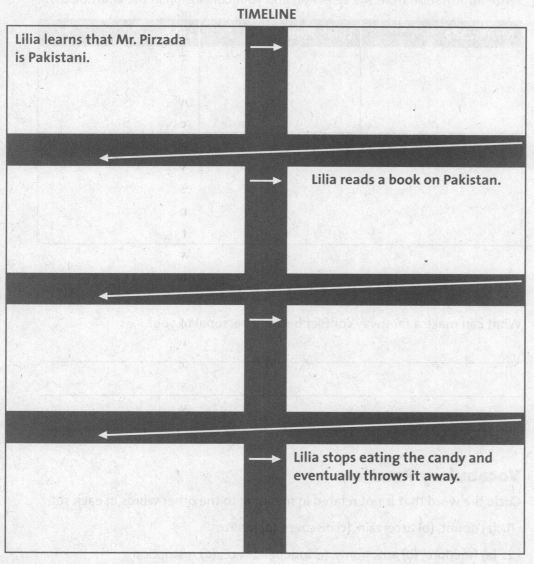

Lilia learns that Mr. Pirzada is Pakistani.

Lilia reads a book on Pakistan.

Lilia stops eating the candy and eventually throws it away.

Review your notes for "When Mr. Pirzada Came to Dine" and your completed timeline. What theme do you think the author is trying to communicate through the experiences of Lilia? Cite evidence in your answer.

_____

_____

_____

_____

Reading Skill: Draw Conclusions

Review the notes you took while reading the selection. Think about which characters are most affected by the conflict in Pakistan. Why do you think the conflict becomes a personal matter for some, but not for all of the characters? Write information from the selection and your conclusion in the chart below.

Mr. Pirzada	Lilia's Parents	Lilia
Conclusion		

When do world **CONFLICTS** affect us?

What can make a far-away conflict become personal to you?

_____

_____

_____

Vocabulary Practice

Circle the word that is not related in meaning to the other words in each set.

1. (a) doubt, (b) ascertain, (c) discover, (d) realize

2. (a) freedom, (b) autonomy, (c) independence, (d) restriction

3. (a) stranger, (b) foreigner, (c) compatriot, (d) outsider

4. (a) sovereignty, (b) dependence, (c) neediness, (d) reliance

5. (a) messily, (b) sloppily, (c) carelessly, (d) impeccably

6. (a) obvious, (b) imperceptible, (c) clear, (d) distinct

7. (a) greet, (b) assail, (c) welcome, (d) embrace

8. (a) admit, (b) allow, (c) concede, (d) correct

Academic Vocabulary in Writing

alter	layer	symbol	theme	unify

How is the candy that Mr. Pirzada gives Lilia throughout the story a **symbol** for the way he is feeling and how he misses his family? Use at least one Academic Vocabulary word in your response. Definitions for these terms are listed on page 145.

_____

_____

_____

Assessment Practice

DIRECTIONS Use "When Mr. Pirzada Came to Dine" to answer questions 1–4.

1 Mr. Pirzada begins coming to Lilia's house because —

- **A** he has known Lilia's parents for many years
- **B** Lilia's parents invite him to eat dinner and watch the TV news
- **C** he asked Lilia's parents if he could watch the TV news with them
- **D** Lilia's parents invite him to teach Lilia about Pakistan

2 How does her father's insistence that she watch the TV news report about Pakistan (lines 234–270) affect Lilia?

- **A** She is bored by the TV news coverage of the conflict.
- **B** She understands the situation in Pakistan completely.
- **C** She is angry with her father for forcing her to watch.
- **D** She loses her appetite because she is worried.

3 How has Lilia's growing awareness of world events affected her relationship with Mr. Pirzada?

- **A** She is more sensitive to the worry that Mr. Pirzada must be feeling.
- **B** She feels that she has to tell everyone about Mr. Pirzada's concerns.
- **C** She is less worried about Mr. Pirzada because she understands the situation.
- **D** She decides to teach Mr. Pirzada about the history of the United States.

4 What do the candies seem to represent for Lilia in lines 279–288?

- **A** fear that Mr. Pirzada will have to return to his family
- **B** a symbol of her prayer that Mr. Pirzada's family be safe
- **C** proof that she is thoughtful and cares about Mr. Pirzada's family
- **D** a way to help her forget her worries for Mr. Pirzada's family

Do not weep, maiden, for war is kind
Poem by Stephen Crane

the sonnet-ballad
Poem by Gwendolyn Brooks

Who are the **VICTIMS** of war?

What effect does war have on the soldiers who go into battle and on their loved ones who are left behind? The following poems show how ordinary citizens can become victims in wartime.

DISCUSS Do you know anyone who has been involved in war, either as a participant or as an observer? With a partner, brainstorm a list of the effects of war as you have heard them described or have read about them. Then, with a larger group, discuss why people have fought wars throughout history.

Text Analysis: Universal Theme

Literary works that come from different time periods and cultures often express the same message about human nature or life. These **universal themes** reflect experiences that are common to most people, such as growing older or falling in love. The poems you are about to read were written 50 years apart and are the works of two distinguished authors, Stephen Crane and Gwendolyn Brooks. As you read each poem, use the strategies in the chart below to think about the messages expressed.

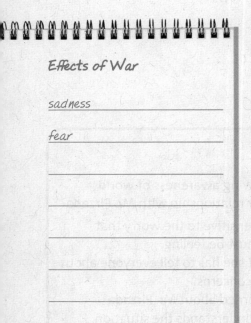

Effects of War

sadness

fear

UNIVERSAL THEME
Strategies for discovering shared messages
• Identify the **speaker,** or the voice that "talks" to the reader.
• Notice key **images** and think about their meaning.
• Identify examples of **repetition,** or words and phrases that are repeated in the poem. Think about their meaning.
• Consider the **mood,** or the overall feeling, created by the poem.

Reading Skill: Understand Verbal Irony

Unlike fiction writers, poets usually communicate their messages in little space and few words. They often use different techniques to help them write compact works of great power. One important literary technique is **verbal irony**—saying one thing but meaning the opposite. The first line of Crane's poem provides an example of verbal irony:

Do not weep, maiden, for war is kind.

As you know, war, by its definition, cannot be kind. Crane intends the reader to think something entirely different about war. Many poems, particularly those involving social criticism or protest, feature this technique. As you read the two poems, record examples in the chart below of verbal irony and explain what you think they mean.

Poem	Examples of Verbal Irony	Explanations
Crane's Poem	Do not weep, maiden, for war is kind (line 1)	War is cruel.

SET A PURPOSE
FOR READING

As you read, think about
what Stephen Crane is
really saying about war.

Do not weep, maiden, for war is kind

Poem by **STEPHEN CRANE**

BACKGROUND Although Stephen
Crane never fought in a battle, he
interviewed Civil War veterans about
their experiences. When his Civil War
novella *The Red Badge of Courage* (1895),
achieved enormous success, Stephen
Crane felt embarrassed by his lack of war
experience. However, he soon took a
job as a foreign correspondent covering
wars in Cuba and Greece and used his
experiences as a basis for his writing.

Do not weep, maiden, for war is kind.
Because your lover threw wild hands toward the sky
And the affrighted steed ran on alone,
Do not weep.
5 War is kind.

Hoarse, booming drums of the regiment,
Little souls who thirst for fight,
These men were born to drill and die.
The unexplained glory flies above them,
10 Great is the Battle-God, great, and his Kingdom—
A field where a thousand corpses lie. **A**

A **VERBAL IRONY**
Circle the image in line 3 that
conflicts with the statement
that "war is kind." Reread
lines 1–11. In what way do these
lines show verbal irony? Write
examples and explain them in
the chart on page 183.

Do not weep, babe, for war is kind.
Because your father tumbled in the yellow trenches,
Raged at his breast, gulped and died,
15 Do not weep.
War is kind.

Swift blazing flag of the regiment,
Eagle with crest of red and gold,
These men were born to drill and die.
20 Point for them the virtue of slaughter,
Make plain to them the excellence of killing
And a field where a thousand corpses lie. **PAUSE & REFLECT**

Mother whose heart hung humble as a button
On the bright splendid shroud of your son,
25 Do not weep.
War is kind. **B**

PAUSE & REFLECT
Reread stanzas 2 and 4. What repeated lines in both stanzas express the horror and inhumanity of war?

_____

_____

_____

_____

_____

_____

_____

B UNIVERSAL THEME
Reread stanzas 1, 3, and 5. Underline the **images** of war given in each stanza. What do these images have in common? Keep in mind what message the author is trying to communicate.

_____

_____

_____

_____

_____

_____

_____

_____

_____

SET A PURPOSE FOR READING

As you read, think about how this poem presents death and war as compared to the previous poem.

the sonnet-ballad

Poem by

GWENDOLYN BROOKS

BACKGROUND This poem is an example of a **dramatic monologue**—a poem in which the speaker addresses a silent or absent listener in a moment of intense emotion. The speaker's words often reveal details about his or her personality, feelings, and circumstances.

C UNIVERSAL THEME
In line 10, death is presented as "coquettish," which means "flirty." What clues does this **image** give you about theme of the poem?

_____

_____

_____

_____

_____

_____

_____

_____

Oh mother, mother, where is happiness?
They took my lover's tallness off to war,
Left me lamenting. Now I cannot guess
What I can use an empty heart-cup for.
5 He won't be coming back here any more.
Some day the war will end, but, oh, I knew
When he went walking grandly out that door
That my sweet love would have to be untrue.
Would have to be untrue. Would have to court
10 Coquettish death, whose impudent and strange
Possessive arms and beauty (of a sort)
Can make a hard man hesitate—and change.
And he will be the one to stammer, "Yes."
Oh mother, mother, where is happiness? **C**

Text Analysis: Universal Theme

In the chart below, identify the literary elements in each poem. Then use the information to state the universal theme expressed by both poems. Remember the theme of a work must be stated in at least one sentence.

	Crane's Poem	Brooks's Poem
Speaker		
Key images		
Repetition		
Mood		
Universal Theme		

Reading Skill: Understand Verbal Irony

Now that you have read both poems, review the information you recorded on page 183. Then, in the chart below, write what the use of verbal irony in the poems tells you about the writers' attitudes toward war. Support your answer with examples from the poems.

Crane's Attitude Toward War	Brooks's Attitude Toward War
Supporting Examples from Poem	**Supporting Examples from Poem**

Who are the VICTIMS of war?

How does war affect ordinary people?

_____

_____

_____

_____

Academic Vocabulary in Writing

alter	layer	symbol	theme	unify

Think about line 12 in Gwendolyn Brooks's poem, "Can make a hard man hesitate—and change." How can war and death **alter** the way people act and the kinds of decisions they make? Use at least one Academic Vocabulary word in your response. Definitions for these terms are listed on page 145.

_____

_____

_____

_____

Assessment Practice

DIRECTIONS Use "Do not weep, maiden, for war is kind" and "the sonnet-ballad" to answer questions 1–4.

1 In Crane's poem, the image of the horse that runs alone (line 3) suggests that —
- (A) the horse threw the soldier off because it was frightened
- (B) when a soldier dies, war and life go on
- (C) the soldier was glad to die in order to save the horse
- (D) the soldier jumped off the horse and ran away

2 In Brooks's poem, how does the repetition of the line "Oh mother, mother, where is happiness?" support the universal theme that war harms loved ones?
- (A) The speaker hopes that her mother can help her find happiness.
- (B) The speaker despairs because she thinks all happiness is gone.
- (C) The speaker knows that she will find happiness again.
- (D) The speaker thinks that her unhappiness is temporary.

3 Why does the line "War is kind" (lines 1, 5, 16, 26) from Crane's poem represent verbal irony?
- (A) It is repeated three times for ironic effect.
- (B) It is expressing a universal theme.
- (C) It is supporting the mood of the poem.
- (D) It is saying one thing, but meaning the opposite.

4 Which statement best expresses a universal theme of both poems?
- (A) Some wars are worth fighting despite the losses.
- (B) Mothers suffer the most from the losses of war.
- (C) War harms soldiers and their loved ones.
- (D) A soldier's death is glorious and honorable.

UNIT 5

Why Write?

AUTHOR'S PURPOSE

Be sure to read the Text Analysis Workshop on pp. 526–531 in *Holt McDougal Literature*.

Academic Vocabulary for Unit 5

Preview the following Academic Vocabulary words. You will encounter these words as you work through this book and will use them as you write and talk about the selections in this unit.

author (ô′thər) *n.* a writer; a creator of something

*The **author** of this article has also written many short stories.*

document (däk′yŏŏ mənt) *n.* something printed or written that provides a record; something that provides evidence

*A history writer must consult **documents** such as newspapers, diaries, and court records.*

goal (gōl) *n.* an aim, purpose, or specific result one tries to achieve

*The **goal** of this Web site is to provide reliable, up-to-date information on science topics.*

issue (ish′ŏŏ) *n.* a concern or problem

*What is this writer's position on the **issue** of universal health care?*

vision (vizh′ ən) *n.* a mental or imaginative image; something seen in a dream or trance

*The story presents a horrifying **vision** of a world in which everyone is the same.*

If you were a professional writer, what **goal** would you want to achieve through your writing? Write your response on the lines below, using at least two Academic Vocabulary words.

_____

_____

_____

The Plot Against People
Humorous Essay by **Russell Baker**

When are little things a BIG DEAL?

Keys get lost. Computers crash. Every day, we have to deal with minor problems and inconveniences. In the following essay, Russell Baker proposes an interesting theory about why such things happen.

QUICKWRITE What are some things that annoy you when they break down, don't work, or get lost? Write them in the list at left. Then circle the one that annoys you the most and explain why to a classmate.

Text Analysis: Tone and Diction

While reading an essay, you might notice that the writer seems serious, sarcastic, or sentimental. This quality of the writing is known as the **tone,** or the writer's attitude toward his or her subject. One way a writer creates tone is through **diction**—the choice of specific words and their **syntax,** or the way words are arranged in sentences. The chart shows an example from Russell Baker's essay. As you read the essay, notice the diction and syntax Baker uses to create tone.

Passage from Baker's Essay	Details About Diction and Syntax
The goal of all inanimate objects is to resist man and ultimately to defeat him, and the three major classifications are based on the method each object uses to achieve its purpose.	• Instead of the word *things*, Baker writes "inanimate objects." • Baker's sentence structure is long and complicated. The passage reads like a scientific paper.

↓

Tone
The contrast between Baker's formal style and the everyday topic creates a humorous tone.

Annoyances

1. *School bus breaks down*

2. *Locker won't open*

3. _____

4. _____

5. _____

6. _____

Reading Skill: Recognize Classification

A **pattern of organization** is the way ideas and information are arranged in a text. Common patterns of organization include

- **cause and effect**
- **chronological order** (in time order)
- **comparison and contrast** (similarities and differences)
- **classification** (characteristics)

To **classify** is to sort ideas or objects into groups that share common characteristics. In his thesis statement, Baker reveals that he is using classification to organize his essay: "Inanimate objects are classified scientifically into three major categories—those that don't work, those that break down, and those that get lost."

The chart below shows the three categories that Baker mentions. As you read, you will be prompted to add more information to this chart.

Category	Examples	Characteristics
Things that don't work		
Things that break down	*car,*	*create maximum frustration for people;*
Things that get lost		

SET A PURPOSE FOR READING

Read this humorous essay to find out why Russell Baker thinks objects plot against people.

The Plot Against People

Humorous Essay by
RUSSELL BAKER

BACKGROUND "The Plot Against People" is a humorous essay that reveals a truth about human life. The writer uses the format of a scientific report to describe how inanimate, or nonliving, objects attempt to defeat their human owners.

WASHINGTON, June 17—Inanimate objects are classified scientifically into three major categories—those that don't work, those that break down, and those that get lost.

The goal of all inanimate objects is to resist man and ultimately to defeat him, and the three major classifications are based on the method each object uses to achieve its purpose. As a general rule, any object capable of breaking down at the moment when it is most needed will do so. The automobile is typical of the category.

10   With the cunning typical of its breed, the automobile never breaks down while entering a filling station with a large staff of idle mechanics. It waits until it reaches a downtown intersection in the middle of the rush hour, or until it is fully loaded with family and luggage on the Ohio Turnpike. **Ⓐ**

    Thus it creates maximum misery, inconvenience, frustration, and irritability among its human cargo, thereby reducing its owner's life span.

    Washing machines, garbage disposals, lawn mowers, light bulbs, automatic laundry dryers, water pipes, furnaces, electrical
20 fuses, television tubes, hose nozzles, tape recorders, slide projectors—all are in league with the automobile to take their turn at breaking down whenever life threatens to flow smoothly for their human enemies. **PAUSE & REFLECT**

    Many inanimate objects, of course, find it extremely difficult to break down. Pliers, for example, and gloves and keys are almost totally incapable of breaking down. Therefore, they have had to evolve a different technique for resisting man.

A Plausible Theory

They get lost. Science has still not solved the mystery of how they do it, and no man has ever caught one of them in the act of
30 getting lost. The most plausible theory is that they have developed a secret method of locomotion which they are able to conceal the instant a human eye falls upon them.

    It is not uncommon for a pair of pliers to climb all the way from the cellar to the attic in its single-minded determination to raise its owner's blood pressure. Keys have been known to burrow three feet under mattresses. Women's purses, despite their great weight, frequently travel through six or seven rooms to find hiding space under a couch. **Ⓑ**

Monitor Your Comprehension

Ⓐ TONE AND DICTION
Notice Baker's choice of the words "cunning" and "breed" in line 10. What unusual image of a car does this word choice create for readers? Complete the sentence below.

I imagine a car that is _____

_____

_____

_____

PAUSE & REFLECT
This essay was written in 1968. If Baker were writing it today, what other devices might he include in the category of "objects that break down"?

_____

_____

_____

_____

_____

_____

Ⓑ CLASSIFICATION
Starting in line 24, Baker moves from discussing the first category to describing the second. Circle some examples of objects that get lost. Underline details that describe their characteristics. Then add this information to the chart on page 193.

C TONE AND DICTION
Reread lines 42–46, underlining formal words and phrases that Baker uses. Is his tone serious? Explain.

_____

_____

_____

_____

_____

_____

_____

_____

_____

D CLASSIFICATION
Reread lines 56–70, circling examples of objects that don't work and underlining their characteristics. Add this information to the chart on page 197. Why is this category of objects "the most curious of all"?

_____

_____

_____

_____

_____

_____

_____

Scientists have been struck by the fact that things that break
40 down virtually never get lost, while things that get lost hardly ever
break down.

A furnace, for example, will invariably break down at the
depth of the first winter cold wave, but it will never get lost. A
woman's purse, which after all does have some inherent capacity
for breaking down, hardly ever does; it almost invariably chooses
to get lost. **C**

Some persons believe this constitutes evidence that inanimate
objects are not entirely hostile to man, and that a negotiated peace
is possible. After all, they point out, a furnace could infuriate
50 a man even more thoroughly by getting lost than by breaking
down, just as a glove could upset him far more by breaking down
than by getting lost.

Not everyone agrees, however, that this indicates a conciliatory
attitude among inanimate objects. Many say it merely proves that
furnaces, gloves, and pliers are incredibly stupid.

The third class of objects—those that don't work—is the
most curious of all. These include such objects as barometers, car
clocks, cigarette lighters, flashlights, and toy-train locomotives. It
is inaccurate, of course, to say that they never work. They work
60 once, usually for the first few hours after being brought home,
and then quit. Thereafter, they never work again.

In fact, it is widely assumed that they are built for the purpose
of not working. Some people have reached advanced ages without
ever seeing some of these objects—barometers, for example—in
working order.

Science is utterly baffled by the entire category. There are
many theories about it. The most interesting holds that the things
that don't work have attained the highest state possible for an
inanimate object, the state to which things that break down and
70 things that get lost can still only aspire. **D**

They Give Peace

They have truly defeated man by conditioning him never to expect anything of them, and in return they have given man the only peace he receives from inanimate society. He does not expect his barometer to work, his electric locomotive to run, his cigarette lighter to light, or his flashlight to illuminate, and when they don't, it does not raise his blood pressure.

He cannot attain that peace with furnaces and keys and cars and women's purses as long as he demands that they work for their keep. **E**

E **TONE AND DICTION**
Reread lines 71–79. How do Baker's **diction** and **syntax,** or sentence structure, contribute to the humor in this passage?

_____

_____

_____

_____

_____

_____

_____

_____

_____

_____

Text Analysis: Tone and Diction

Review the notes you took while reading "The Plot Against People." In the chart below, provide some examples of diction and syntax that make Baker's essay read like a scientific report. Also note some memorable images, or mental pictures you formed based on details in the text. Then write a sentence that describes the overall tone of the essay.

Elements That Create Tone	Examples from Essay
Formal Diction	
Complicated Syntax	
Images	

$\downarrow$

Overall Tone of Essay

Reading Skill: Recognize Classification

In the essay, Baker first describes things that break down, then things that get lost, and finally things that don't work. Why do you think he chose to discuss them in that order? (Hint: Review the text to see how he introduces each new category.)

_____

_____

_____

When are little things a **BIG DEAL?**

How do you respond to life's annoyances? What are the advantages to responding with humor?

_____

_____

_____

Academic Vocabulary in Speaking

author	document	goal	issue	vision

TURN AND TALK With a partner, role-play a discussion between two scientists about the three categories of inanimate objects. How does each object achieve its **goals**? Use at least one Academic Vocabulary word in your discussion. Definitions for these terms are listed on page 191.

Assessment Practice

DIRECTIONS Use "The Plot Against People" to answer questions 1–4.

1 The main idea of Baker's essay is that —
  - (A) people take inanimate objects for granted
  - (B) losing one's keys is the most frustrating human experience
  - (C) the goal of inanimate objects is to defeat people
  - (D) cars are more highly evolved than furnaces

2 The essay is organized by classification because it —
  - (A) sorts objects into three categories
  - (B) shows a preference for objects that don't work
  - (C) uses words appropriate for a scientific report
  - (D) is divided into sections and paragraphs

3 Which of the following contributes most to the tone of the essay?
  - (A) long sentences used to classify inanimate objects
  - (B) serious discussion of stress in everyday life
  - (C) scientific diction used to describe fanciful events
  - (D) vivid images of events from the author's life

4 The overall tone of the essay is —
  - (A) sincere and helpful
  - (B) light and humorous
  - (C) concerned and sad
  - (D) annoyed and resentful

Why Leaves Turn Color in the Fall
Essay by Diane Ackerman

Can **BEAUTY** be captured in words?

How would you describe a beautiful sunset to someone who had not seen it? Would a scientific explanation take away from the sunset's beauty? In the following essay, Diane Ackerman describes the colors of autumn leaves in both poetic and scientific terms.

DISCUSS Recall a beautiful scene from nature that you experienced. In the notebook at left, record as many details as you can remember. Then describe the scene to a classmate. Afterward, discuss how easy (or hard) it was to find the right words to help your partner visualize the scene.

A Beautiful Scene from Nature

What I saw:

Details:

Text Analysis: Author's Purpose

An **author's purpose** is a writer's reason for writing something. For example, an author may write to explain a process, to describe a scene, or to reflect on an idea. Diane Ackerman does all of these things in her essay, though her overall purpose is to explain why leaves turn color and fall from trees. The chart below provides examples of how she achieves two of her purposes.

Author's Purpose	Technique Used to Achieve Purpose	Example from Essay
To explain a process	The author uses scientific terms.	*A corky layer of cells forms at the leaves' slender petioles, then scars over. Undernourished, the leaves stop producing the pigment chlorophyll, and photosynthesis ceases.*
To describe natural beauty	The author uses poetic language and **imagery,** or words and phrases that re-create sensory experiences by appealing to readers' senses of sight, hearing, touch, taste, and smell.	*They glide and swoop, rocking in invisible cradles. They are all wing and may flutter from yard to yard on small whirlwinds or updrafts, swiveling as they go.*

As you read the essay, determine the purpose of each paragraph—to explain, to describe, or to reflect.

Reading Skill: Patterns of Organization

Ackerman uses at least three **patterns of organization** to present her ideas in the following essay:

- **cause and effect,** to explain a process

- **comparison and contrast,** to show likenesses and differences

- **main idea and supporting details,** to present her reflections and insights

As you read, look for cause-and-effect organization. You'll be prompted to fill out a cause-and-effect chain like the one below.

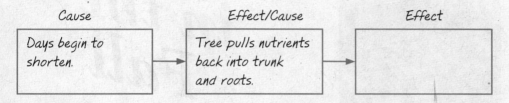

Cause	Effect/Cause	Effect
Days begin to shorten.	Tree pulls nutrients back into trunk and roots.	

Vocabulary in Context

Note: Words are listed in the order in which they appear in the essay.

stealth (stĕlth) *n.* a concealed manner of acting
*The shark moved with **stealth** until it was close enough to attack.*

edict (ē′dĭkt′) *n.* a command issued by an authority
*Everyone in the courtroom had to obey the judge's **edict.***

robustly (rō-bŭst′lē) *adv.* in a strong, powerful way
*The athlete was tall and **robustly** built.*

predisposed (prē′dĭ-spōzd′) *v.* inclined to something in advance
*As the son of two painters, he was **predisposed** to be an artist.*

adaptation (ăd′ăp-tā′shən) *n.* the process of adjusting to suit one's surroundings
*This animal has made a perfect **adaptation** to its environment.*

capricious (kə-prĭsh′əs) *adj.* impulsive, unpredictable
*Due to its **capricious** behavior, the monkey made an unpredictable pet.*

Vocabulary Practice

Use at least two vocabulary words to describe something you might see during a walk in the woods.

_____

_____

**SET A PURPOSE
FOR READING**

Read this essay to find out why leaves change color and fall off trees in the autumn.

Why Leaves Turn Color in the Fall

Essay by

DIANE ACKERMAN

BACKGROUND The selection that follows is a poetic essay. The writer uses both scientific terms and poetic diction and imagery in her work. Diane Ackerman's interest in science began at a young age. Today, she is an accomplished poet and nature writer.

stealth (stělth) *n.* a concealed manner of acting

What does the author mean when she says that autumn acts with **stealth**?

_____

_____

_____

_____

_____

The **stealth** of autumn catches one unaware. Was that a goldfinch perching in the early September woods, or just the first turning leaf? A red-winged blackbird or a sugar maple closing up shop for the winter? Keen-eyed as leopards, we stand still and squint hard, looking for signs of movement. Early-morning frost sits heavily on the grass, and turns barbed wire into a string of stars. On a distant hill, a small square of yellow appears to be a lighted stage. At last the truth dawns on us: Fall is staggering in, right on schedule, with its baggage of chilly nights, macabre 10 holidays, and spectacular, heart-stoppingly beautiful leaves. Soon the leaves will start cringing on the trees, and roll up in clenched fists before they actually fall off. Dry seedpods will rattle like tiny gourds. But first there will be weeks of gushing color so bright, so pastel, so confettilike, that people will travel up and down the East Coast just to stare at it—a whole season of leaves. **Ⓐ**

Where do the colors come from? Sunlight rules most living things with its golden <u>edicts</u>. When the days begin to shorten, soon after the summer solstice on June 21, a tree reconsiders its leaves. All summer it feeds them so they can process sunlight, but 20 in the dog days of summer the tree begins pulling nutrients back into its trunk and roots, pares down, and gradually chokes off its leaves. A corky layer of cells forms at the leaves' slender petioles,[1] then scars over. Undernourished, the leaves stop producing the pigment chlorophyll, and photosynthesis[2] ceases. Animals can migrate, hibernate, or store food to prepare for winter. But where can a tree go? It survives by dropping its leaves, and by the end of autumn only a few fragile threads of fluid-carrying xylem[3] hold leaves to their stems. **Ⓑ**

A turning leaf stays partly green at first, then reveals splotches 30 of yellow and red as the chlorophyll gradually breaks down. Dark green seems to stay longest in the veins, outlining and defining them. During the summer, chlorophyll dissolves in the heat and light, but it is also being steadily replaced. In the fall, on the other hand, no new pigment is produced, and so we notice the other colors that were always there, right in the leaf, although chlorophyll's shocking green hid them from view. With their camouflage gone, we see these colors for the first time all year, and marvel, but they were always there, hidden like a vivid secret beneath the hot glowing greens of summer.

40 The most spectacular range of fall foliage occurs in the northeastern United States and in eastern China, where the leaves are <u>robustly</u> colored, thanks in part to a rich climate. European maples don't achieve the same flaming reds as their American relatives, which thrive on cold nights and sunny days. In Europe,

---

1. **petioles:** the stalks of leaves.
2. **chlorophyll . . . photosynthesis:** Chlorophyll is the green pigment in plants that is necessary for photosynthesis, the process by which plants use sunlight, water, and carbon dioxide to produce food.
3. **xylem:** plant tissue through which water and nutrients are conducted.

Ⓐ AUTHOR'S PURPOSE
Ackerman's purpose in the first paragraph is to describe the arrival of autumn. Reread lines 1–15 and underline sensory details she uses to create imagery.

edict (ē'dĭkt') *n.* a command issued by an authority

Ⓑ PATTERNS OF ORGANIZATION
In lines 16–28, the pattern of organization switches from main idea and details to cause and effect. Complete the cause-and-effect chain below to show why leaves fall.

Tree pulls nutrients back into its trunk and roots.

↓

↓

↓

↓

robustly (rō-bŭst'lē) *adv.* in a strong, powerful way

C **AUTHOR'S PURPOSE**
Using scientific **diction,** or word choice, helps Ackerman explain the pigments that make leaves turn color. Reread lines 46–55 and circle the two scientific terms for pigments. How do these pigments differ from each other?

_____

_____

_____

_____

_____

_____

_____

_____

_____

predisposed (prē′dĭ-spōzd′) *v.*
inclined to something in advance

adaptation (ăd′ăp-tā′shən) *n.*
the process of adjusting to suit one's surroundings

the warm, humid weather turns the leaves brown or mildly yellow. Anthocyanin, the pigment that gives apples their red and turns leaves red or red-violet, is produced by sugars that remain in the leaf after the supply of nutrients dwindles. Unlike the carotenoids, which color carrots, squash, and corn, and turn leaves orange and yellow, anthocyanin varies from year to year, depending on the temperature and amount of sunlight. The fiercest colors occur in years when the fall sunlight is strongest and the nights are cool and dry (a state of grace scientists find vexing to forecast). This is also why leaves appear dizzyingly bright and clear on a sunny fall day: The anthocyanin flashes like a marquee.[4] **C**

Not all leaves turn the same colors. Elms, weeping willows, and the ancient gingko all grow radiant yellow, along with hickories, aspens, bottlebrush buckeyes, cottonweeds, and tall, keening poplars. Basswood turns bronze, birches bright gold. Water-loving maples put on a symphonic display of scarlets. Sumacs turn red, too, as do flowering dogwoods, black gums, and sweet gums. Though some oaks yellow, most turn a pinkish brown. The farmlands also change color, as tepees of cornstalks and bales of shredded-wheat-textured hay stand drying in the fields. In some spots, one slope of a hill may be green and the other already in bright color, because the hillside facing south gets more sun and heat than the northern one.

An odd feature of the colors is that they don't seem to have any special purpose. We are **predisposed** to respond to their beauty, of course. They shimmer with the colors of sunset, spring flowers, the tawny buff of a colt's pretty rump, the shuddering pink of a blush. Animals and flowers color for a reason—**adaptation** to their environment—but there is no adaptive reason for leaves to color so beautifully in the fall any more than there is for the sky or ocean to be blue. It's just one of the haphazard marvels the planet bestows every year. We find the sizzling colors thrilling, and in a sense they dupe us. Colored like living things, they signal death and disintegration. In time, they will become fragile and, like the body, return to dust. They are as we hope our own fate will be when we die: Not to vanish, just to sublime[5] from one beautiful

4. **marquee:** a lighted billboard, such as those used at movie theaters.
5. **sublime:** to transform directly into another state.

state into another. Though leaves lose their green life, they bloom with urgent colors, as the woods grow mummified day by day, and Nature becomes more carnal, mute, and radiant. **D**

We call the season "fall," from the Old English *feallan,* to fall, which leads back through time to the Indo-European *phol*, which also means to fall. So the word and the idea are both extremely ancient, and haven't really changed since the first of our kind needed a name for fall's leafy abundance. As we say the word, we're reminded of that other Fall, in the garden of Eden, when
90 fig leaves never withered and scales fell from our eyes. Fall is the time when leaves fall from the trees, just as spring is when flowers spring up, summer is when we simmer, and winter is when we whine from the cold.

Children love to play in piles of leaves, hurling them into the air like confetti, leaping into soft unruly mattresses of them. For children, leaf fall is just one of the odder figments of Nature, like hailstones or snowflakes. Walk down a lane overhung with trees in the never-never land of autumn, and you will forget about time and death, lost in the sheer delicious spill of color. Adam and Eve
100 concealed their nakedness with leaves, remember? Leaves have always hidden our awkward secrets. **PAUSE & REFLECT**

But how do the colored leaves fall? As a leaf ages, the growth hormone, auxin, fades, and cells at the base of the petiole divide. Two or three rows of small cells, lying at right angles to the axis of the petiole, react with water, then come apart, leaving the petioles hanging on by only a few threads of xylem. A light breeze, and the leaves are airborne. They glide and swoop, rocking in invisible cradles. They are all wing and may flutter from yard to yard on small whirlwinds or updrafts, swiveling as
110 they go. Firmly tethered[6] to earth, we love to see things rise up and fly—soap bubbles, balloons, birds, fall leaves. They remind us that the end of a season is <u>capricious</u>, as is the end of life. We especially like the way leaves rock, careen, and swoop as they fall. Everyone knows the motion. Pilots sometimes do a maneuver

---

6. **tethered:** fastened, as if with a rope.

D AUTHOR'S PURPOSE
Reread lines 76–83. Here Ackerman reflects on the deaths of living things, including human beings. What does she say we hope for ourselves? Underline the sentence in the text that answers this question, and then restate her idea in your own words below.

PAUSE & REFLECT
Reread lines 97–101. What role does Ackerman think beauty plays in human life?

capricious (kə-prĭsh′əs) *adj.* impulsive, unpredictable

E AUTHOR'S PURPOSE
Reread lines 122–132 and underline examples of poetic language and imagery. What is Ackerman's purpose in this paragraph?

_____

_____

_____

_____

_____

_____

_____

_____

_____

called a "falling leaf," in which the plane loses altitude quickly and on purpose, by slipping first to the right, then to the left. The machine weighs a ton or more, but in one pilot's mind it is a weightless thing, a falling leaf. She has seen the motion before, in the Vermont woods where she played as a child. Below her the

120 trees radiate gold, copper, and red. Leaves are falling, although she can't see them fall, as she falls, swooping down for a closer view.

At last the leaves leave. But first they turn color and thrill us for weeks on end. Then they crunch and crackle under foot. They *shush*, as children drag their small feet through the leaves heaped along the curb. Dark, slimy mats of leaves cling to one's heels after a rain. A damp, stuccolike mortar[7] of semidecayed leaves protects the tender shoots with a roof until spring, and makes a rich humus.[8] An occasional bulge or ripple in the leafy mounds signals a shrew or a field mouse tunneling out of sight. Sometimes one

130 finds in fossil stones the imprint of a leaf, long since disintegrated, whose outlines remind us how detailed, vibrant, and alive are the things of this earth that perish. **E**

---

7. **stuccolike mortar:** a bonding material that is like a soft, sticky plaster.
8. **humus:** decomposed organic matter that provides nutrients for plants.

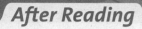

Text Analysis: Author's Purpose

In which parts of her essay is Ackerman's purpose to explain? to describe? to reflect? Use the notes you took while reading to complete the chart below.

Author's Purpose	Parts of Essay with Each Purpose
To explain	
To describe	• Lines 1–15 describe the arrival of autumn.
To reflect	

Do you think all these purposes work together well in the essay? Explain.

_____

_____

_____

_____

_____

_____

_____

_____

Reading Skill: Patterns of Organization

You have already noted the cause-and-effect organization Ackerman uses to explain why leaves fall from trees. Now review the two paragraphs in lines 84–101, in which she uses a main-idea-and-details pattern to organize her reflections. In the outline below, write the main idea of each paragraph and several supporting details from the text. Remember that the main idea of a paragraph is often not stated directly; you must infer it from the details.

I. _____

   A. _____

   B. _____

   C. _____

II. _____

   A. _____

   B. _____

   C. _____

Can **BEAUTY** be captured in words?

How do you define beauty?

_____

_____

_____

Vocabulary Practice

Write the word from the list that best completes each sentence.

1. With great _____, the lioness tracked her prey.

2. Try not to be _____; think before you act!

3. Our teacher's _____ was that tardy students would be locked out.

4. _____ to a new environment ensures the survival of a species.

5. He shook my hand _____, showing great enthusiasm.

6. As an animal lover, I am _____ to veterinary school.

WORD LIST
adaptation
capricious
edict
predisposed
robustly
stealth

Academic Vocabulary in Writing

author	document	goal	issue	vision

In what ways is Ackerman's essay different from a scientific **document** about the processes that occur in leaves? Use at least two Academic Vocabulary words in your response. Definitions for these terms are listed on page 191.

_____

_____

_____

Assessment Practice

DIRECTIONS Use "Why Leaves Turn Color in the Fall" to answer questions 1–6.

1 The author's main purpose in the essay is to —

- Ⓐ explain why leaves change color in autumn
- Ⓑ reflect on the meaning of the word *fall*
- Ⓒ describe the fall colors in a tree-lined lane
- Ⓓ inform readers about photosynthesis

2 In lines 10–15, Ackerman uses sensory details to —

- Ⓐ suggest that beauty is more powerful than death
- Ⓑ explain the natural processes that happen each fall
- Ⓒ create images of autumn in readers' minds
- Ⓓ describe an experience from her own childhood

3 Which pattern of organization does the author use in lines 102–107?

- Ⓐ main idea and details
- Ⓑ comparison and contrast
- Ⓒ order of importance
- Ⓓ cause and effect

4 Why do leaves appear green in the summer?

- Ⓐ Leaves stop producing anthocyanin in the summer.
- Ⓑ Strong sunlight makes the leaves look greener than they really are.
- Ⓒ Sugars in the leaves produce a vibrant green color.
- Ⓓ Chlorophyll hides the other pigments in the leaves.

5 According to Ackerman, fall colors may allow people to hope that —

- Ⓐ nature has no awkward secrets
- Ⓑ the comforts of winter will soon arrive
- Ⓒ death is just a lovely transformation
- Ⓓ the days are starting to get longer

6 Which of the following is described by the image "They glide and swoop, rocking in invisible cradles" (lines 107–108)?

- Ⓐ children jumping in piles of leaves
- Ⓑ leaves falling from a tree
- Ⓒ field mice tunneling under leaves
- Ⓓ trees engaging in photosynthesis

How a Leaf Works

Textbook Diagrams

Background

In Diane Ackerman's essay "Why Leaves Turn Color in the Fall," you read a poetic yet scientific description of the changes that occur in leaves each autumn. Now you will study a few well-designed graphic aids to learn why leaves are green in the first place.

Standards Focus: Interpret Graphic Aids

A **graphic aid** is a visual illustration of a verbal statement where information that could be stated in sentences is instead presented in a picture. Graphic aids include photographs, diagrams, maps, and equations. Well-made graphics clarify the text they accompany, making complex information easier to understand. They also add to the visual appeal of a page by breaking up large blocks of text or adding lines, shapes, and color to an otherwise dull page. You can use the following guidelines to interpret and to evaluate most graphic aids:

- Read the title, headings, and captions first to get the main idea of the graphic.

- Look for a key or legend to see how colors, shadings, and symbols are used.

- Use the obvious meanings of symbols such as arrows to help you read the visual information.

- Pay attention to labels that identify specific details.

- Study the information in the graphic, looking for patterns or basic concepts.

- Ask yourself, "Is this graphic clear? Does it help explain the text or add visual appeal?"

As you read the pages that follow, complete the chart below. State in your own words what each graphic aid shows.

Type of Graphic Aid	What It Shows
Magnified photograph of a leaf cell	
Cutaway diagram of a chloroplast	
Schematic drawing of photosynthesis	
Chemical equation for photosynthesis	
Cutaway diagram of a leaf	

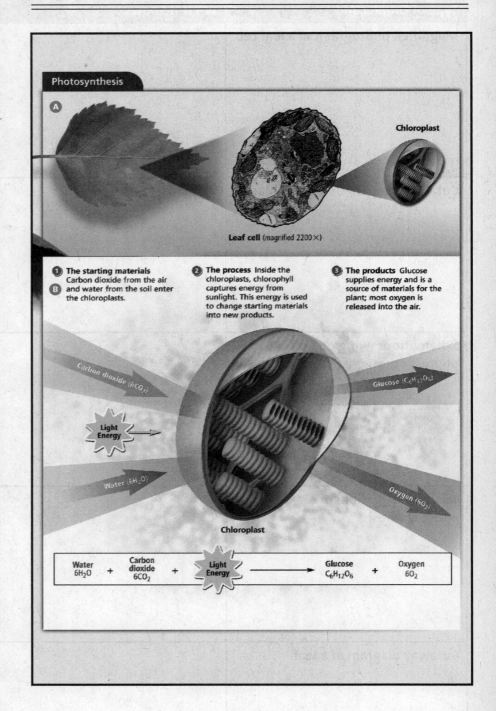

Photosynthesis

A

Chloroplast

Leaf cell (magnified 2200×)

1 **The starting materials** Carbon dioxide from the air and water from the soil enter the chloroplasts.

B

2 **The process** Inside the chloroplasts, chlorophyll captures energy from sunlight. This energy is used to change starting materials into new products.

3 **The products** Glucose supplies energy and is a source of materials for the plant; most oxygen is released into the air.

Carbon dioxide ($6CO_2$)

Glucose ($C_6H_{12}O_6$)

Light Energy

Water ($6H_2O$)

Oxygen ($6O_2$)

Chloroplast

| Water $6H_2O$ | + | Carbon dioxide $6CO_2$ | + | Light Energy | → | Glucose $C_6H_{12}O_6$ | + | Oxygen $6O_2$ |

A INTERPRET GRAPHIC AIDS

Science textbooks often include **photographs** of structures magnified to many times their actual size. What does this photo of a leaf cell show you about chloroplasts? Write your answer in the chart on page 211.

B INTERPRET GRAPHIC AIDS

A **schematic diagram** uses lines, symbols, and words to help readers picture processes or objects not normally seen. What do the arrows in this schematic diagram communicate?

_____

_____

_____

_____

_____

_____

_____

Inside a Leaf

The leaf is an organ that produces sugars. It is made up of different types of cells and tissues.

Cells at the surface produce a waxy cuticle that keeps the leaf from losing water.

Most chloroplasts are located in cells of the upper layer of the leaf.

Xylem transports water and nutrients up from the roots.

Phloem transports energy-rich compounds made in the leaf down to other parts of the plant.

Carbon dioxide, oxygen, and water vapor move into and out of the leaf through stomata.

PAUSE & REFLECT

C INTERPRET GRAPHIC AIDS

A **cutaway diagram** shows an object with the outer part removed to reveal the interior. Notice the different layers of cells in this cutaway diagram of a leaf. Circle the label that tells where the chloroplasts are located. What do the chloroplasts look like?

_____

_____

_____

_____

_____

_____

PAUSE & REFLECT

Does the information presented on page 212 make this cutaway diagram more meaningful? Explain.

_____

_____

_____

_____

_____

_____

_____

HOW A LEAF WORKS   **213**

Practicing Your Skills

Review your notes for "How a Leaf Works," including the chart you completed on page 211. Think about each graphic aid and the way it presents information. Is it clear and easy to understand? Does it leave you with any unanswered questions? Evaluate each graphic and write ideas for improvement in the chart below.

Graphic Aid	Does It Present Information Clearly?	How Could It Be Improved?
Magnified photograph of a leaf cell		
Cutaway diagram of a chloroplast		
Schematic drawing of photosynthesis		
Chemical equation for photosynthesis		
Cutaway diagram of a leaf		

Consider the information you gained from all five graphic aids. How did the graphics increase your understanding of the way a leaf works?

_____

_____

_____

_____

_____

_____

Academic Vocabulary in Writing

author	document	goal	issue	vision

What are some of the **goals** a writer can achieve by including graphic aids in a text? Use at least two Academic Vocabulary words in your response. Definitions for these terms are listed on page 191.

_____

_____

_____

_____

Assessment Practice

DIRECTIONS Use "How a Leaf Works" to answer questions 1–6.

1 In which part of a leaf does photosynthesis take place?
- Ⓐ xylem
- Ⓑ chloroplasts
- Ⓒ phloem
- Ⓓ stomata

2 What does a plant do with the glucose it produces through photosynthesis?
- Ⓐ uses it for food
- Ⓑ releases it through the stomata
- Ⓒ transports it through the xylem
- Ⓓ turns it into a waxy cuticle

3 What are the starting materials of photosynthesis?
- Ⓐ water and carbon dioxide
- Ⓑ water and oxygen
- Ⓒ chloroplasts and chlorophyll
- Ⓓ chloroplasts and light energy

4 Together, the five graphic aids explain —
- Ⓐ what a leaf looks like under a microscope
- Ⓑ why light energy is essential to photosynthesis
- Ⓒ how a leaf is structured and how it carries out photosynthesis
- Ⓓ the parts of a chloroplast and how they work together to make glucose

5 From the cutaway diagram, you can infer that stomata are —
- Ⓐ slender tubes inside a leaf
- Ⓑ cells in the upper layer of a leaf
- Ⓒ bundles of xylem and phloem
- Ⓓ small openings on the surface of a leaf

6 Which part of the schematic diagram tells where plants get the water they need for photosynthesis?
- Ⓐ caption
- Ⓑ illustration
- Ⓒ arrow
- Ⓓ equation

And of Clay Are We Created

Short Story by Isabel Allende

Can reporters always stay OBJECTIVE?

Should journalists remain detached and objective when reporting a tragedy? Or should they express their feelings and try to help victims? In the story you are about to read, a reporter finds himself deeply involved in the tragic story he is covering.

DEBATE Imagine you are a reporter at the scene of a natural disaster. Should you just report the facts, or should you get involved and try to help the victims? Write your ideas at left. Then pick a side and hold a debate with a group of classmates.

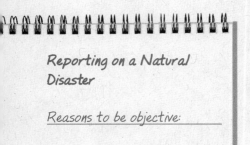

Reporting on a Natural Disaster

Reasons to be objective:

_____

_____

_____

_____

Reasons to get involved:

_____

_____

_____

Text Analysis: Author's Perspective

An **author's perspective** is the unique blend of feelings, values, and beliefs that a writer brings to a subject. "And of Clay Are We Created" contains many echoes of Isabel Allende's own life experiences as a former journalist. Read about her background in the chart below. Then, as you read her short story, use what you know about her life to help you understand her perspective.

Isabel Allende's Life Experiences
Creative Storyteller Allende remembers having "acquired the vice of storytelling at a rather early age." She became a respected magazine and television journalist in her native Chile, but she once admitted, "I could never be objective. I exaggerated and twisted reality. . . ."
Political Exile In 1973, Allende's uncle Salvador Allende, the president of Chile, was assassinated. A military government seized control, and a period of terror and violence began. Allende's family went into exile, moving to Venezuela. Later, Allende moved to the United States. She found it hard to get work as a journalist and eventually turned to creative writing.
A Mother's Loss In 1991, Allende's daughter Paula was stricken with an incurable disease. Allende began a memoir for her daughter, who eventually died. In *Paula*, Allende explores sickness, loss, and tragedy. She says that the book may have been "written with tears, but [they were] very healing tears."

Reading Strategy: Monitor

When you **monitor** your reading, you check your understanding as you read and adjust your reading strategies to improve comprehension. The following strategies may be helpful:

- **adjust your reading rate**—that is, read more slowly

- **reread**—go back over the text to clarify what you've read

- **visualize**—picture characters, events, or settings

- **question**—ask yourself questions about events or characters and then review the text to find answers

Use the following process to clarify passages you find confusing.

What I Don't Understand: where the mud came from	
I Should Probably: _____ *adjust reading rate*	✔ *reread/clarify*
_____ *visualize*	_____ *question*
I Now Understand:	

Vocabulary in Context

Note: Words are listed in the order in which they appear in the story.

tenacity (tə-năs′ĭ-tē) *n.* the quality of holding persistently to something
*Do you have the **tenacity** to keep working until the task is completed?*

fortitude (fôr′tĭ-tōōd′) *n.* strength of mind; courage
*Doing the right thing in a difficult situation requires **fortitude**.*

resignation (rĕz′ĭg-nā′shən) *n.* passive acceptance of something; submission
*Behind by 20 points, the team had a feeling of **resignation**.*

pandemonium (păn′də-mō′nē-əm) *n.* a wild uproar or noise
***Pandemonium** broke out as people ran screaming from the fire.*

embody (ĕm-bŏd′ē) *v.* to give shape to or visibly represent
*A great leader should **embody** the values of honesty and courage.*

stupor (stōō′pər) *n.* a state of mental numbness, as from shock
*The doctor was in a **stupor** after treating disaster victims for two days straight.*

stratagem (străt′ə-jəm) *n.* a clever trick or device for obtaining an advantage
*His **stratagem** to avoid answering a question was to ask another question.*

tribulation (trĭb′yə-lā′shən) *n.* great distress or suffering
*Victims of the earthquake suffered great **tribulation**.*

AND OF *Clay* ARE WE *Created*

Short Story by
ISABEL ALLENDE

BACKGROUND On November 13, 1985, the Nevado del Ruiz volcano in Colombia erupted. The intense heat from the eruption melted the mountain's icecap and sent a torrent of water, ash, mud, and rocks into the valley below and onto the town of Armero. More than 20,000 people died. Omayra Sánchez, a 13-year-old girl trapped in the mud, became the focus of a lot of media attention. In the following story, the trapped girl is named Azucena and the man that attemps to rescue her is journalist Rolf Carlé.

They discovered the girl's head protruding from the mud pit, eyes wide open, calling soundlessly. She had a First Communion name,[1] Azucena.[2] Lily. In that vast cemetery where the odor of death was already attracting vultures from far away, and where the weeping of orphans and wails of the injured filled the air, the little girl obstinately clinging to life became the symbol of the tragedy. The television cameras transmitted so often the unbearable image of the head budding like a black squash from the clay that there was no one who did not recognize her and 10 know her name. And every time we saw her on the screen, right behind her was Rolf Carlé,[3] who had gone there on assignment, never suspecting that he would find a fragment of his past, lost thirty years before.

---

1. **First Communion name:** a name traditionally given to a Roman Catholic child at the time of the child's first participation in the rite of Holy Communion.
2. **Azucena** (ä-sōō-sĕ'nə).
3. **Rolf Carlé** (rälf kär'lä).

First a subterranean[4] sob rocked the cotton fields, curling them like waves of foam. Geologists had set up their seismographs[5] weeks before and knew that the mountain had awakened again. For some time they had predicted that the heat of the eruption could detach the eternal ice from the slopes of the volcano, but no one heeded their warnings; they sounded like the tales of frightened old women. The towns in the valley went about their daily life, deaf to the moaning of the earth, until that fateful Wednesday night in November when a prolonged roar announced the end of the world, and walls of snow broke loose, rolling in an avalanche of clay, stones, and water that descended on the villages and buried them beneath unfathomable meters of telluric[6] vomit. As soon as the survivors emerged from the paralysis of that first awful terror, they could see that houses, plazas, churches, white cotton plantations, dark coffee forests, cattle pastures—all had disappeared. Much later, after soldiers and volunteers had arrived to rescue the living and try to assess the magnitude of the cataclysm,[7] it was calculated that beneath the mud lay more than twenty thousand human beings and an indefinite number of animals putrefying in a viscous soup.[8] Forests and rivers had also been swept away, and there was nothing to be seen but an immense desert of mire. **(A)**

When the station called before dawn, Rolf Carlé and I were together. I crawled out of bed, dazed with sleep, and went to prepare coffee while he hurriedly dressed. He stuffed his gear in the green canvas backpack he always carried, and we said goodbye, as we had so many times before. I had no presentiments. I sat in the kitchen, sipping my coffee and planning the long hours without him, sure that he would be back the next day. **(B)**

He was one of the first to reach the scene, because while other reporters were fighting their way to the edges of that morass in jeeps, bicycles, or on foot, each getting there however he could, Rolf Carlé had the advantage of the television helicopter, which

---

4. **subterranean** (sŭb′tə-rā′nē-ən): underground.
5. **seismographs** (sīz′mə-grăfs′): instruments that record the intensity and duration of earthquakes.
6. **telluric** (tĕ-lŏŏr′ĭk): relating to the earth.
7. **cataclysm** (kăt′ə-klĭz′əm): a violent and sudden change in the earth's crust.
8. **putrefying** (pyōō′trə-fī′ĭng) **in a viscous soup:** rotting in a thick soup.

(A) AUTHOR'S PERSPECTIVE
Think about Allende's former job as a journalist. Reread lines 14–35 and underline details in the writing that reflect Allende's background as a reporter. Then briefly describe your findings below.

_____

_____

_____

_____

_____

_____

_____

_____

_____

_____

_____

(B) MONITOR
Reread lines 36–42 and underline clues that help you identify the narrator. Who is telling this story?

_____

_____

_____

tenacity (tə-năs′ĭ-tē) *n.* the quality of holding persistently to something; firm determination

fortitude (fôr′tĭ-tōōd′) *n.* strength of mind; courage

C AUTHOR'S PERSPECTIVE
Reread lines 58–62 and underline the words that describe the effect of the camera lens on Rolf Carlé. What do you think is Allende's perspective on news reporting?

_____
_____
_____
_____
_____
_____
_____
_____
_____
_____
_____
_____
_____
_____

flew him over the avalanche. We watched on our screens the footage captured by his assistant's camera, in which he was up to his knees in muck, a microphone in his hand, in the midst of a bedlam of lost children, wounded survivors, corpses, and devastation. The story came to us in his calm voice. For years he had been a familiar figure in newscasts, reporting live at the scene of battles and catastrophes with awesome **tenacity.** Nothing could stop him, and I was always amazed at his equanimity in the face of danger and suffering; it seemed as if nothing could shake his **fortitude** or deter his curiosity. Fear seemed never to touch him, although he had confessed to me that he was not a courageous man, far from it. I believe that the lens of a camera had a strange effect on him; it was as if it transported him to a different time from which he could watch events without actually participating in them. When I knew him better, I came to realize that this fictive distance seemed to protect him from his own emotions. **C**

Rolf Carlé was in on the story of Azucena from the beginning. He filmed the volunteers who discovered her, and the first persons who tried to reach her; his camera zoomed in on the girl, her dark face, her large desolate eyes, the plastered-down tangle of her hair. The mud was like quicksand around her, and anyone attempting to reach her was in danger of sinking. They threw a rope to her that she made no effort to grasp until they shouted to her to catch it; then she pulled a hand from the mire and tried to move but immediately sank a little deeper. Rolf threw down his knapsack and the rest of his equipment and waded into the quagmire, commenting for his assistant's microphone that it was cold and that one could begin to smell the stench of corpses.

"What's your name?" he asked the girl, and she told him her flower name. "Don't move, Azucena," Rolf Carlé directed, and kept talking to her, without a thought for what he was saying, just to distract her, while slowly he worked his way forward in mud up to his waist. The air around him seemed as murky as the mud.

It was impossible to reach her from the approach he was attempting, so he retreated and circled around where there seemed to be firmer footing. When finally he was close enough, he took the rope and tied it beneath her arms, so they could pull her out. He smiled at her with that smile that crinkles his eyes and makes him look like a little boy; he told her that everything was fine, that he was here with her now, that soon they would have her out. He signaled the others to pull, but as soon as the cord tensed, the girl screamed. They tried again, and her shoulders and arms appeared, but they could move her no farther; she was trapped. Someone 90 suggested that her legs might be caught in the collapsed walls of her house, but she said it was not just rubble, that she was also held by the bodies of her brothers and sisters clinging to her legs. **D**

"Don't worry, we'll get you out of here," Rolf promised. Despite the quality of the transmission, I could hear his voice break, and I loved him more than ever. Azucena looked at him but said nothing.

During those first hours Rolf Carlé exhausted all the resources of his ingenuity to rescue her. He struggled with poles and ropes, but every tug was an intolerable torture for the imprisoned girl. 100 It occurred to him to use one of the poles as a lever but got no result and had to abandon the idea. He talked a couple of soldiers into working with him for a while, but they had to leave because so many other victims were calling for help. The girl could not move, she barely could breathe, but she did not seem desperate, as if an ancestral **resignation** allowed her to accept her fate. The reporter, on the other hand, was determined to snatch her from death. Someone brought him a tire, which he placed beneath her arms like a life buoy, and then laid a plank near the hole to hold his weight and allow him to stay closer to her. As it was impossible 110 to remove the rubble blindly, he tried once or twice to dive toward her feet but emerged frustrated, covered with mud, and spitting gravel. He concluded that he would have to have a pump to drain the water, and radioed a request for one but received in return a message that there was no available transport and it could not be sent until the next morning.

"We can't wait that long!" Rolf Carlé shouted, but in the **pandemonium** no one stopped to commiserate. Many more

D MONITOR
Reread lines 80–92 and underline details that help you **visualize** Azucena, Rolf, and the others. Why can't the rescuers pull Azucena out?

_____

_____

_____

_____

_____

_____

_____

_____

resignation (rĕz′ĭg-nā′shən) *n.* passive acceptance of something; submission

How does Azucena's **resignation** contrast with Rolf's attitude and actions?

_____

_____

_____

_____

pandemonium (păn′də-mō′nē-əm) *n.* a wild uproar or noise

AND OF CLAY ARE WE CREATED   **221**

hours would go by before he accepted that time had stagnated and reality had been irreparably distorted.

120   A military doctor came to examine the girl and observed that her heart was functioning well and that if she did not get too cold she could survive the night.

"Hang on, Azucena, we'll have the pump tomorrow," Rolf Carlé tried to console her.

"Don't leave me alone," she begged.

"No, of course I won't leave you."

Someone brought him coffee, and he helped the girl drink it, sip by sip. The warm liquid revived her, and she began telling him about her small life, about her family and her school, about how

130   things were in that little bit of world before the volcano erupted. She was thirteen, and she had never been outside her village. Rolf Carlé, buoyed by a premature optimism, was convinced that everything would end well: the pump would arrive, they would drain the water, move the rubble, and Azucena would be transported by helicopter to a hospital where she would recover rapidly and where he could visit her and bring her gifts. He thought, She's already too old for dolls, and I don't know what would please her; maybe a dress. I don't know much about women, he concluded, amused, reflecting that although he had

140   known many women in his lifetime, none had taught him these details. To pass the hours he began to tell Azucena about his travels and adventures as a news hound, and when he exhausted his memory, he called upon imagination, inventing things he thought might entertain her. From time to time she dozed, but he kept talking in the darkness, to assure her that he was still there and to overcome the menace of uncertainty.

That was a long night. **PAUSE & REFLECT**

Many miles away, I watched Rolf Carlé and the girl on a television screen. I could not bear the wait at home, so I went to National

150   Television, where I often spent entire nights with Rolf editing programs. There, I was near his world, and I could at least get a feeling of what he lived through during those three decisive days.

PAUSE & REFLECT
What do you think will happen to Azucena? Explain.

I called all the important people in the city, senators, commanders of the armed forces, the North American ambassador, and the president of National Petroleum, begging them for a pump to remove the silt, but obtained only vague promises. I began to ask for urgent help on radio and television, to see if there wasn't *someone* who could help us. Between calls I would run to the newsroom to monitor the satellite transmissions that periodically brought new
160 details of the catastrophe. While reporters selected scenes with most impact for the news report, I searched for footage that featured Azucena's mud pit. The screen reduced the disaster to a single plane and accentuated the tremendous distance that separated me from Rolf Carlé; nonetheless, I was there with him. The child's every suffering hurt me as it did him; I felt his frustration, his impotence. Faced with the impossibility of communicating with him, the fantastic idea came to me that if I tried, I could reach him by force of mind and in that way give him encouragement. I concentrated until I was dizzy—a frenzied and futile activity. At times I would
170 be overcome with compassion and burst out crying; at other times, I was so drained I felt as if I were staring through a telescope at the light of a star dead for a million years. **E**

I watched that hell on the first morning broadcast, cadavers[9] of people and animals awash in the current of new rivers formed overnight from the melted snow. Above the mud rose the tops of trees and the bell towers of a church where several people had taken refuge and were patiently awaiting rescue teams. Hundreds of soldiers and volunteers from the civil defense were clawing through rubble searching for survivors, while long rows of ragged specters
180 awaited their turn for a cup of hot broth. Radio networks announced that their phones were jammed with calls from families offering shelter to orphaned children. Drinking water was in scarce supply, along with gasoline and food. Doctors, resigned to amputating arms and legs without anesthesia, pled that at least they be sent serum and painkillers and antibiotics; most of the roads, however, were impassable, and worse were the bureaucratic obstacles that stood in the way. To top it all, the clay contaminated by decomposing bodies threatened the living with an outbreak of epidemics. **F**

9. **cadavers** (kə-dăv′ərz): dead bodies.

E MONITOR
What does the narrator attempt to do in lines 164–172, and how does the effort make her feel? Use the chart below to select a monitoring strategy and to record your answer after you have applied the strategy.

What I Don't Understand
what the narrator tries to do and how it makes her feel

I Should Probably
_____ adjust reading rate
_____ reread/clarify
_____ visualize
_____ question

I Now Understand

F AUTHOR'S PERSPECTIVE
Reread lines 153–186, underlining clues that suggest Allende's perspective on politicians and other officials. Then complete the sentence below.

Allende seems to believe

politicians are _____

_____

_____

_____

_____

embody (ĕm-bŏd′ē) v. to give shape to or visibly represent

Azucena was shivering inside the tire that held her above the
190 surface. Immobility and tension had greatly weakened her, but she
was conscious and could still be heard when a microphone was held
out to her. Her tone was humble, as if apologizing for all the fuss.
Rolf Carlé had a growth of beard, and dark circles beneath his eyes;
he looked near exhaustion. Even from that enormous distance I
could sense the quality of his weariness, so different from the fatigue
of other adventures. He had completely forgotten the camera; he
could not look at the girl through a lens any longer. The pictures we
were receiving were not his assistant's but those of other reporters
who had appropriated Azucena, bestowing on her the pathetic
200 responsibility of **embodying** the horror of what had happened
in that place. With the first light Rolf tried again to dislodge the
obstacles that held the girl in her tomb, but he had only his hands
to work with; he did not dare use a tool for fear of injuring her. He
fed Azucena a cup of the cornmeal mush and bananas the army was
distributing, but she immediately vomited it up. A doctor stated
that she had a fever but added that there was little he could do:
antibiotics were being reserved for cases of gangrene.[10] A priest also
passed by and blessed her, hanging a medal of the Virgin around
her neck. By evening a gentle, persistent drizzle began to fall.
210 "The sky is weeping," Azucena murmured, and she, too,
began to cry.

"Don't be afraid," Rolf begged. "You have to keep your
strength up and be calm. Everything will be fine. I'm with you,
and I'll get you out somehow." **PAUSE & REFLECT**

Reporters returned to photograph Azucena and ask her the same
questions, which she no longer tried to answer. In the meanwhile,
more television and movie teams arrived with spools of cable, tapes,
film, videos, precision lenses, recorders, sound consoles, lights,
reflecting screens, auxiliary motors, cartons of supplies, electricians,
220 sound technicians, and cameramen: Azucena's face was beamed to
millions of screens around the world. And all the while Rolf Carlé
kept pleading for a pump. The improved technical facilities bore
results, and National Television began receiving sharper pictures

PAUSE & REFLECT
Do you think Rolf still believes he will be able to get Azucena out? Explain your answer.

_____

_____

_____

_____

_____

_____

_____

10. **gangrene:** death and decay of body tissue, usually resulting from injury or disease.

and clearer sound, the distance seemed suddenly compressed, and I had the horrible sensation that Azucena and Rolf were by my side, separated from me by impenetrable glass. I was able to follow events hour by hour; I knew everything my love did to wrest the girl from her prison and help her endure her suffering; I overheard fragments of what they said to one another and could guess the rest; I was present when she taught Rolf to pray and when he distracted her with the stories I had told him in a thousand and one nights beneath the white mosquito netting of our bed. **G**

When darkness came on the second day, Rolf tried to sing Azucena to sleep with old Austrian folk songs he had learned from his mother, but she was far beyond sleep. They spent most of the night talking, each in a **stupor** of exhaustion and hunger and shaking with cold. That night, imperceptibly, the unyielding floodgates that had contained Rolf Carlé's past for so many years began to open, and the torrent of all that had lain hidden in the deepest and most secret layers of memory poured out, leveling before it the obstacles that had blocked his consciousness for so long. He could not tell it all to Azucena; she perhaps did not know there was a world beyond the sea or time previous to her own; she was not capable of imagining Europe in the years of the war. So he could not tell her of defeat, nor of the afternoon the Russians had led them to the concentration camp to bury prisoners dead from starvation. Why should he describe to her how the naked bodies piled like a mountain of firewood resembled fragile china? How could he tell this dying child about ovens and gallows? Nor did he mention the night that he had seen his mother naked, shod in stiletto-heeled red boots, sobbing with humiliation. There was much he did not tell, but in those hours he relived for the first time all the things his mind had tried to erase. Azucena had surrendered her fear to him and so, without wishing it, had obliged Rolf to confront his own. There, beside that hellhole of mud, it was impossible for Rolf to flee from himself any longer, and the visceral terror he had lived as a boy suddenly invaded him. He reverted to the years when he was the age of Azucena and younger, and, like her, found himself trapped in a pit without escape, buried in life, his head barely above ground; he saw before his eyes the boots and legs of his father, who

G **AUTHOR'S PERSPECTIVE**
Reread lines 215–232. What details suggest that Allende is critical of the media for having access to technical resources when the victims do not? Underline these details in the text.

stupor (stōō'pər) *n.* a state of mental numbness, as from shock

Why are Azucena and Rolf in a "**stupor** of exhaustion"?

_____
_____
_____
_____
_____
_____
_____

had removed his belt and was whipping it in the air with the never-forgotten hiss of a viper coiled to strike. Sorrow flooded through him, intact and precise, as if it had lain always in his mind, waiting. He was once again in the armoire[11] where his father locked him to punish him for imagined misbehavior, there where for eternal hours he had crouched with his eyes closed, not to see the darkness, with his hands over his ears to shut out the beating of his heart, trembling, huddled like a cornered animal. Wandering in the mist of his memories he found his sister, Katharina, a sweet, retarded

270 child who spent her life hiding, with the hope that her father would forget the disgrace of her having been born. With Katharina, Rolf crawled beneath the dining room table, and with her hid there under the long white tablecloth, two children forever embraced, alert to footsteps and voices. Katharina's scent melded with his own sweat, with aromas of cooking, garlic, soup, freshly baked bread, and the unexpected odor of putrescent[12] clay. His sister's hand in his, her frightened breathing, her silk hair against his cheek, the candid gaze of her eyes. Katharina . . . Katharina materialized before him, floating on the air like a flag, clothed in the white tablecloth,

280 now a winding sheet, and at last he could weep for her death and for the guilt of having abandoned her. He understood then that all his exploits as a reporter, the feats that had won him such recognition and fame, were merely an attempt to keep his most ancient fears at bay, a **stratagem** for taking refuge behind a lens to test whether reality was more tolerable from that perspective. He took excessive risks as an exercise of courage, training by day to conquer the monsters that tormented him by night. But he had to come face to face with the moment of truth; he could not continue to escape his past. He was Azucena; he was buried in the clayey mud; his terror

290 was not the distant emotion of an almost forgotten childhood, it was a claw sunk in his throat. In the flush of his tears he saw his mother, dressed in black and clutching her imitation-crocodile pocketbook to her bosom, just as he had last seen her on the dock when she had come to put him on the boat to South America. She had not come to dry his tears, but to tell him to pick up a shovel: the war was over and now they must bury the dead. Ⓗ

stratagem (străt′ə-jəm) *n.* a clever trick or device for obtaining an advantage

Ⓗ MONITOR
Reread lines 255–296. What terrible memories does Rolf have from his childhood in a defeated Austria after World War II? List three below.

_____

_____

_____

_____

_____

_____

11. **armoire** (ärm-wär′): a large wardrobe or cabinet.
12. **putrescent** (pyoō-trĕs′ənt): rotting and foul-smelling.

"Don't cry. I don't hurt anymore. I'm fine," Azucena said when dawn came.

"I'm not crying for you," Rolf Carlé smiled. "I'm crying for
300 myself. I hurt all over." ❶

The third day in the valley of the cataclysm began with a pale light filtering through storm clouds. The president of the republic visited the area in his tailored safari jacket to confirm that this was the worst catastrophe of the century; the country was in mourning; sister nations had offered aid; he had ordered a state of siege; the armed forces would be merciless; anyone caught stealing or committing other offenses would be shot on sight. He added that it was impossible to remove all the corpses or count the thousands who had disappeared; the entire valley would be
310 declared holy ground, and bishops would come to celebrate a solemn mass for the souls of the victims. He went to the army field tents to offer relief in the form of vague promises to crowds of the rescued, then to the improvised hospital to offer a word of encouragement to doctors and nurses worn down from so many hours of **tribulations**. Then he asked to be taken to see Azucena, the little girl the whole world had seen. He waved to her with a limp statesman's hand, and microphones recorded his emotional voice and paternal tone as he told her that her courage had served as an example to the nation. Rolf Carlé interrupted to ask for a
320 pump, and the president assured him that he personally would attend to the matter. I caught a glimpse of Rolf for a few seconds kneeling beside the mud pit. On the evening news broadcast, he was still in the same position; and I, glued to the screen like a fortune teller to her crystal ball, could tell that something fundamental had changed in him. I knew somehow that during the night his defenses had crumbled and he had given in to grief; finally he was vulnerable. The girl had touched a part of him that he himself had no access to, a part he had never shared with me. Rolf had wanted to console her, but it was Azucena who had given
330 him consolation.

I recognized the precise moment at which Rolf gave up the fight and surrendered to the torture of watching the girl die.

tribulation (trĭb′yə-lā′shən) *n.* great distress or suffering

I was with them, three days and two nights, spying on them from the other side of life. I was there when she told him that in all her thirteen years no boy had ever loved her and that it was a pity to leave this world without knowing love. Rolf assured her that he loved her more than he could ever love anyone, more than he loved his mother, more than his sister, more than all the women who had slept in his arms, more than he loved me, his
340 life companion, who would have given anything to be trapped in that well in her place, who would have exchanged her life for Azucena's, and I watched as he leaned down to kiss her poor forehead, consumed by a sweet, sad emotion he could not name. I felt how in that instant both were saved from despair, how they were freed from the clay, how they rose above the vultures and helicopters, how together they flew above the vast swamp of corruption and laments. How, finally, they were able to accept death. Rolf Carlé prayed in silence that she would die quickly, because such pain cannot be borne.

350   By then I had obtained a pump and was in touch with a general who had agreed to ship it the next morning on a military cargo plane. But on the night of that third day, beneath the unblinking focus of quartz lamps and the lens of a hundred cameras, Azucena gave up, her eyes locked with those of the friend who had sustained her to the end. Rolf Carlé removed the life buoy, closed her eyelids, held her to his chest for a few moments, and then let her go. She sank slowly, a flower in the mud.

PAUSE & REFLECT

Is the ending of the story tragic, hopeful, both, or neither? Explain your answer.

You are back with me, but you are not the same man. I often accompany you to the station, and we watch the videos of
360 Azucena again; you study them intently, looking for something you could have done to save her, something you did not think of in time. Or maybe you study them to see yourself as if in a mirror, naked. Your cameras lie forgotten in a closet; you do not write or sing; you sit long hours before the window, staring at the mountains. Beside you, I wait for you to complete the voyage into yourself, for the old wounds to heal. I know that when you return from your nightmares, we shall again walk hand in hand, as before. **PAUSE & REFLECT**

Translated by Margaret Sayers Peden

Text Analysis: Author's Perspective

Review the notes you took while reading and consider how Isabel Allende's life experiences have affected her perspective. In the chart below, describe how each of Allende's life experiences is reflected in "And of Clay Are We Created." Cite specific details from the story.

Allende's Life Experiences	Details from Story
She worked as a journalist in her native Chile.	
She was exiled from Chile after her uncle was assassinated and a military government took control.	
Knowing that her daughter Paula was dying, she wrote a memoir for her.	

Who do you think would be more objective in this story—the narrator or Rolf Carlé? Explain your answer using details from the text.

_____

_____

_____

_____

_____

_____

Reading Strategy: Monitor

As you monitored your comprehension of Allende's story, which strategy—adjusting your reading rate, rereading and clarifying, visualizing, or questioning—did you use most often? Review your notes and write your answer in the chart below. Then explain how the strategy helped you improve your understanding.

Strategy I Used	How It Helped Me

Can reporters always stay OBJECTIVE?

Should a reporter's duty to remain objective, or unbiased, always take priority over other considerations? Explain.

_____

_____

_____

_____

Vocabulary Practice

Decide whether the words in each pair are synonyms (words with similar meanings) or antonyms (words with opposite meanings). Write **S** if they are synonyms or **A** if they are antonyms.

_____ **1.** tenacity/laziness

_____ **2.** fortitude/weakness

_____ **3.** resignation/acceptance

_____ **4.** pandemonium/chaos

_____ **5.** stupor/enthusiasm

_____ **6.** embody/represent

_____ **7.** stratagem/scheme

_____ **8.** tribulation/hardship

ACADEMIC VOCABULARY IN WRITING

author	document	goal	issue	vision

How can the writer of a fictional story bring a real-world **issue,** or concern, to life for readers? Use at least one Academic Vocabulary word in your response. Definitions for these terms are listed on page 191.

_____

_____

_____

_____

Assessment Practice

DIRECTIONS Use "And of Clay Are We Created" to answer questions 1–4.

1 Rolf Carlé is sent to Azucena's town to —
- **A** locate a pump to rescue Azucena
- **B** report on the disaster that has occurred
- **C** convince local politicians to do more
- **D** comfort Azucena during her last hours

2 What happens to Rolf Carlé during the second night he stays with Azucena?
- **A** He realizes that he would like to have a daughter of his own.
- **B** He relives the painful memories he has tried to repress for many years.
- **C** He comes up with a new plan for digging Azucena out of the mud.
- **D** He tries to reach the narrator by focusing his mind on her.

3 The story's narrator follows what is happening with Azucena and Rolf Carlé by —
- **A** talking to Rolf on his cell phone
- **B** reporting on the story herself
- **C** watching news coverage on television
- **D** communicating with high-level officials

4 At the end of the story, the narrator says Rolf Carlé is "not the same man" because —
- **A** his experiences have made him bitter and cruel
- **B** he is lost in his painful past and needs time to heal
- **C** he has changed careers and is no longer a journalist
- **D** his love for the narrator has been replaced by love for Azucena

UNIT

6

Making a Case

ARGUMENT AND PERSUASION

Be sure to read the Text Analysis Workshop on pp. 632–637 in *Holt McDougal Literature*.

Academic Vocabulary for Unit 6

Preview the following Academic Vocabulary words. You will encounter these words as you work through this book and will use them as you write and talk about the selections in this unit.

cite (sīt) *v.* to quote from some source such as a book, Internet article, or speech

*In your research paper, be sure to **cite** all the sources from which you gathered information.*

controversy (kän′trə vər′se) *n.* a debate or quarrel over opposing opinions

*Strong arguments can be made on both sides of this **controversy**.*

convince (kən vins′) *v.* to overcome any doubts with argument or persuasion

*Did the writer **convince** you to accept her point of view?*

objective (əb-jĕk′tĭv) *n.* something worked toward or striven for

*The advertisement's **objective** is to persuade people to buy this brand of cookie.*

statistic (stə tis′tik) *n.* a numerical fact or quantity

*I'm not sure I believe the **statistic** that 90 percent of students favor a longer school day!*

Think of a story or a movie that features some kind of **controversy** that divides the characters. What is the controversy about, and what do the characters do about it? Write your response on the lines below, using at least two Academic Vocabulary words.

_____

_____

_____

Doing Nothing Is Something

Persuasive Essay by **Anna Quindlen**

How should you spend your FREE TIME?

What is your typical day like? After school homework, and other activities, such as jobs, sports practice, and family chores, you may not have much time left over for leisure. In this essay, Anna Quindlen explores whether young people might be too busy for their own good.

DISCUSS If you had more free time, how would you spend it? In the notebook at left, make a list of things you would do—or not do! Then discuss with a partner how you would benefit from the extra free time.

Free Time

1. Draw cartoons

2. Take long walks

3. _____

4. _____

5. _____

6. _____

Text Analysis: Argument

An **argument** is speech or writing that takes a position on an issue and gives evidence to back it up. At the heart of every argument is a **claim,** the writer's position on the issue. To convince readers that a claim is valid, a writer must offer **support,** which may consist of

- reasons that explain or justify an action, a belief, or a decision
- evidence in the form of facts, statistics, examples, or the views of experts

This diagram shows the basic structure of an argument.

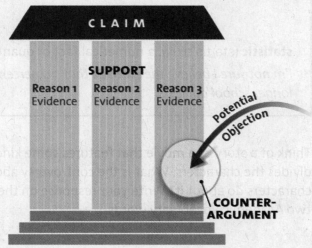

CLAIM

SUPPORT

Reason 1
Evidence

Reason 2
Evidence

Reason 3
Evidence

Potential Objection

COUNTER-ARGUMENT

In "Doing Nothing Is Something," Anna Quindlen takes a position on the issue of how leisure time is used in contemporary U.S. society. As you read, look for the claim she makes and the reasons and evidence she offers as support.

Reading Skill: Distinguish Fact from Opinion

A **fact** is a statement that can be proved, such as "Most U.S. households have Internet access." An **opinion** is a statement of belief, such as "I think people rely too much on the Internet."

Words and phrases such as *I think, I believe, perhaps,* and *maybe* often signal opinions. To identify opinions that lack these clue words, remember that an opinion cannot be proved. At best, an opinion can only be supported. As you read Quindlen's essay, you will be prompted to note examples of facts and opinions.

Fact	Opinion
Most U.S. households have Internet access.	I think people rely too much on the Internet.

Vocabulary in Context

Note: Words are listed in the order in which they appear in the essay.

hiatus (hī-ā′təs) *n.* a gap or break in continuity
*Each weekend provides a brief **hiatus** from school and work.*

deficit (dĕf′ĭ-sĭt) *n.* a shortfall or deficiency
*After studying all night for the test, I suffered from a **deficit** of sleep.*

prestigious (prĕ-stē′jəs) *adj.* having a great reputation; highly respected
*His story won a **prestigious** award from a well-known literary journal.*

contemptuous (kən-tĕmp′chōō-əs) *adj.* scornful or disrespectful
*Her **contemptuous** manner suggested that she did not want to hear any ideas that conflicted with her own.*

laudable (lô′də-bəl) *adj.* worthy of high praise
*Improving your math grade next semester is a **laudable** goal.*

Vocabulary Practice

Review the vocabulary words and their meanings. Then use at least two vocabulary words to explain why having more free time is important.

_____

_____

_____

**SET A PURPOSE
FOR READING**
Read this essay to find out why the author claims that "doing nothing" can be valuable.

Doing *Nothing* *Is* Something

by Anna Quindlen

BACKGROUND As a prize-winning columnist for the *New York Times,* Anna Quindlen has earned widespread acclaim for her ability to address important social issues through her personal experiences. Her writing is filled with family events, both significant and incidental.

Summer is coming soon. I can feel it in the softening of the air, but I can see it, too, in the textbooks on my children's desks. The number of uncut pages at the back grows smaller and smaller. The loose leaf is ragged at the edges, the binder plastic ripped at the corners. An old remembered glee rises inside me. Summer is coming. Uniform skirts in mothballs.

Pencils with their points left broken. Open windows. Day trips to the beach. Pickup games. Hanging out.

How boring it was.

10　Of course, it was the making of me, as a human being and a writer. Downtime is where we become ourselves, looking into the middle distance, kicking at the curb, lying on the grass or sitting on the stoop and staring at the tedious blue of the summer sky. I don't believe you can write poetry, or compose music, or become an actor without downtime, and plenty of it, a <u>hiatus</u> that passes for boredom but is really the quiet moving of the wheels inside that fuel creativity.

And that, to me, is one of the saddest things about the lives of American children today. Soccer leagues, acting

20　classes, tutors—the calendar of the average middle-class kid is so over the top that soon Palm handhelds will be sold in Toys "R" Us. Our children are as overscheduled as we are, and that is saying something.

This has become so bad that parents have arranged to schedule times for unscheduled time. Earlier this year the privileged suburb of Ridgewood, N.J., announced a Family Night, when there would be no homework, no athletic practices and no after-school events. This was terribly exciting until I realized that this was not one night a week,

30　but one single night. There is even a free-time movement, and Web site: familylife1st.org. Among the frequently asked questions provided online: "What would families do with family time if they took it back?" Ⓐ

Let me make a suggestion for the kids involved: how about nothing? It is not simply that it is pathetic to consider

hiatus (hī-āʹtəs) *n.* a gap or break in continuity

Ⓐ **DISTINGUISH FACT FROM OPINION**
Reread lines 18–33. In the chart below, record one fact and one opinion that Quindlen presents.

Fact

Opinion

B ARGUMENT

In many arguments, the author's claim is not directly stated in a single sentence. Based on what you have read so far, what is Quindlen's claim about the way American children should spend their summers?

_____

_____

_____

_____

_____

deficit (dĕf′ĭ-sĭt) *n.* a shortfall or deficiency

C ARGUMENT

What support does Quindlen provide in lines 46–53 for her claim? Underline three pieces of evidence in this paragraph.

prestigious (prĕ-stē′jəs) *adj.* having a great reputation; highly respected

the lives of children who don't have a moment between piano and dance and homework to talk about their day or just search for split ends, an enormously satisfying leisure-time activity of my youth. There is also ample psychological
40 research suggesting that what we might call "doing nothing" is when human beings actually do their best thinking, and when creativity comes to call. Perhaps we are creating an entire generation of people whose ability to think outside the box, as the current parlance[1] of business has it, is being systematically stunted by scheduling. **B**

A study by the University of Michigan quantified[2] the downtime **deficit**; in the last 20 years American kids have lost about four unstructured hours a week. There has even arisen a global Right to Play movement: in the Third World
50 it is often about child labor, but in the United States it is about the sheer labor of being a perpetually busy child. In Omaha, Neb., a group of parents recently lobbied for additional recess. Hooray, and yikes. **C**

How did this happen? Adults did it. There is a culture of adult distrust that suggests that a kid who is not playing softball or attending science-enrichment programs—or both—is huffing or boosting cars: if kids are left alone, they will not stare into the middle distance and consider the meaning of life and how come your nose in pictures
60 never looks the way you think it should, but instead will get into trouble. There is also the culture of cutthroat and unquestioning competition that leads even the parents of preschoolers to gab about **prestigious** colleges without a trace of irony: this suggests that any class in which you do not enroll your first grader will put him at a disadvantage in, say, law school.

---

1. **parlance** (pär′ləns): a particular manner of speaking.
2. **quantified**: expressed as a number or quantity.

Finally, there is a culture of workplace presence (as opposed to productivity). Try as we might to suggest that all these enrichment activities are for the good of the
70 kid, there is ample evidence that they are really for the convenience of parents with way too little leisure time of their own. Stories about the resignation of presidential aide Karen Hughes unfailingly reported her dedication to family time by noting that she arranged to get home at 5:30 one night a week to have dinner with her son. If one weekday dinner out of five is considered <u>laudable</u>, what does that say about what's become commonplace? **D**

Summer is coming. It used to be a time apart for kids, a respite from the clock and the copybook, the organized day.
80 Every once in a while, either guilty or overwhelmed or tired of listening to me keen[3] about my monumental boredom, my mother would send me to some rinky-dink park program that consisted almost entirely of three-legged races and making things out of Popsicle sticks. Now, instead, there are music camps, sports camps, fat camps, probably thin camps. I mourn hanging out in the backyard. I mourn playing Wiffle ball in the street without a sponsor and matching shirts. I mourn drawing in the dirt with a stick.

Maybe that kind of summer is gone for good. Maybe this
90 is the leading edge of a new way of living that not only has no room for contemplation but is <u>contemptuous</u> of it. But if downtime cannot be squeezed during the school year into the life of frantic and often joyless activity with which our children are saddled while their parents pursue frantic and often joyless activity of their own, what about summer? Do most adults really want to stand in line for Space Mountain or sit in traffic to get to a shore house that doesn't have

laudable (lô′də-bəl) *adj.* worthy of high praise

D DISTINGUISH FACT FROM OPINION
Reread lines 67–77. What fact does Quindlen include to support her opinion that parents have too little leisure time? Underline it in the text.

contemptuous (kən-tĕmp′chōō-əs) *adj.* scornful or disrespectful

---

3. **keen:** cry out in grief.

PAUSE & REFLECT

Do you think the sense of humor that Quindlen displays in her essay strengthens or weakens her argument? Explain.

enough saucepans? Might it be even more enriching for their children to stay at home and do nothing? For those
100 who say they will only watch TV or play on the computer, a piece of technical advice: the cable box can be unhooked, the modem removed. Perhaps it is not too late for American kids to be given the gift of enforced boredom for at least a week or two, staring into space, bored out of their gourds, exploring the inside of their own heads. "To contemplate is to toil, to think is to do," said Victor Hugo. "Go outside and play," said Prudence Quindlen. Both of them were right.

PAUSE & REFLECT

Text Analysis: Argument

Use the notes you took while reading to help you complete the following chart with details about Anna Quindlen's argument in "Doing Nothing Is Something." Remember that the claim is a very basic statement of the writer's position on an issue. Reasons and evidence support the claim and complete the argument.

Claim

Reasons	Evidence

Were you convinced by Quindlen's argument? Explain why or why not.

_____

_____

_____

_____

_____

Reading Skill: Distinguish Fact from Opinion

Decide whether each statement in the chart is a fact or an opinion. In each case, explain how you know which it is.

Statement	Fact or Opinion? How Do You Know?
"I don't believe you can write poetry, or compose music, or become an actor without downtime . . ." (lines 14–15)	
"And that, to me, is one of the saddest things about the lives of American children today. . . . Our children are as overscheduled as we are . . ." (lines 18–23)	
". . . in the last 20 years American kids have lost about four unstructured hours a week." (lines 47–48)	

How should you spend your FREE TIME?

Do you think you need to spend more time doing nothing? Explain.

_____

_____

_____

Vocabulary Practice

Circle the word that is most different in meaning from the others. If necessary, use a dictionary to check the precise meanings or words you are unsure of.

1. (a) prestigious, (b) reputable, (c) infamous, (d) eminent
2. (a) hiatus, (b) gap, (c) respite, (d) renewal
3. (a) surplus, (b) excess, (c) sufficiency, (d) deficit
4. (a) despicable, (b) admirable, (c) laudable, (d) commendable
5. (a) disdainful, (b) deferential, (c) scornful, (d) contemptuous

Academic Vocabulary in Speaking

cite	controversy	convince	objective	statistic

TURN AND TALK With a partner, role-play a conversation in which you try to **convince** a parent or guardian that you need more time for doing nothing. Use at least one Academic Vocabulary word in your discussion. Definitions for these terms are listed on page 233.

Assessment Practice

DIRECTIONS Use "Doing Nothing Is Something" to answer questions 1–6.

1 Quindlen's main claim in her essay is that —

- **A** families spend too little time together
- **B** children spend too much of their summer vacations doing useless activities
- **C** children need to have downtime to become creative, developed people
- **D** parents need to do a better job of scheduling their children's activities

2 Which of the following does Quindlen use to support a claim she makes about children's lives?

- **A** a story about a presidential aide who resigned because of family duties
- **B** the idea that kids will commit more crimes if they aren't enrolled in sports programs
- **C** examples that show how much better summer camps are now than when she was a child
- **D** a study that shows American children have less unscheduled time than they did 20 years ago

3 Who or what does Quindlen hold responsible for the way children's lives are scheduled?

- **A** teachers
- **B** parents
- **C** children
- **D** schools

4 Which of the following is a fact?

- **A** "Our children are as overscheduled as we are, and that is saying something."
- **B** "Earlier this year . . . Ridgewood, N.J., announced a Family Night, when there would be no homework. . . ."
- **C** "Perhaps we are creating an entire generation of people whose ability to think outside the box . . . is being systematically stunted by scheduling."
- **D** "Maybe this is the leading edge of a new way of living that not only has no room for contemplation but is contemptuous of it."

5 Quindlen says many adults worry that a child who is not in a structured activity will —

- **A** stare into the middle distance
- **B** come up with creative ideas
- **C** become bored and unhappy
- **D** get into trouble

6 Quindlen says her own "boring" summers —

- **A** made her a more competitive adult
- **B** showed her the value of structured camp programs
- **C** created a lot of tension between her and her mother
- **D** fueled her creativity as a writer

I Acknowledge Mine
Essay by Jane Goodall

Do animals have **RIGHTS?**

People express their love for animals by pampering them or contributing to wildlife preservation organizations. But we may also buy products that were tested on animals—tests that can cause the suffering or even the death of animals. In this selection, Jane Goodall raises questions about the importance of animal rights.

DEBATE Should our society recognize animal rights? With a group, record a position statement for this issue and a list of reasons for your position in the notebook on the left. Then debate the topic with another group.

Text Analysis: Persuasive Techniques

Writers use **persuasive techniques** to help convince readers to think a certain way about an issue. Even when you know how to evaluate an argument, it's easy to be swayed by appeals that bypass your brain and go straight to your heart. You should be aware of how powerful language and **emotional appeals**—statements intended to stir up strong feelings—can be used to enhance strong arguments or distract you from holes in weak ones.

In her essay, Jane Goodall includes disturbing details and emotionally charged words to persuade readers to feel pity. As you read, pay attention to the use of persuasive techniques, such as the ones in the chart below.

Technique	Example
Emotional Appeals	
Appeal to Pity, Fear, or Vanity Uses strong feelings, rather than facts and evidence to persuade	Abandoned. Hungry. Frightened. Your donation can help find homes for these puppies.
Appeal to Values	
Ethical Appeal Taps into people's values or moral standards	If you believe in education, vote against cutting after-school programs. With your help we can keep these programs running.
Word Choice	
Loaded Language Uses words with positive or negative connotations to stir people's emotions	**Destroyed** by **hatred,** the war-torn landscape looked like something from a **nightmare.**

Should our society recognize animal rights?

Position Statement:

We think that

because

Reading Strategy: Summarize

When you **summarize** an argument, you briefly restate the text's main ideas and important information. A summary is a brief retelling of the main facts; it is not meant as an evaluation. When you summarize, you should

- present ideas and information in the same order in which they appear in the text

- leave out examples and details that are not essential for understanding the writer's key points

- not critique, or evaluate, the writer's ideas

As you read, you will be prompted to write summaries by first recording the main idea and important details of parts of the text. See the example below.

Main Ideas	Details
Chimpanzees in the lab suffered from over crowding and isolation.	The youngest were kept in pairs in small, dark cages. Older ones lived alone, without any companionship or stimulation.

Vocabulary in Context

Note: Words are listed in the order in which they appear in the selection.

stark (stärk) *adj.* harsh or grim
*The **stark** room was cold, almost empty, and painted a dull brown.*

boisterous (boi'stər-əs) *adj.* noisy and lacking in restraint or discipline
*The students moved in **boisterous** groups through the hallways between classes.*

alleviate (ə-lē'vē-āt') *v.* to make easier or provide relief
*The workers tried to **alleviate** the stress of the animals displaced by the storm.*

stridently (strīd'nt-lē) *adv.* harshly; conspicuously
*The activist **stridently** opposed using animals for medical testing.*

complicity (kəm-plĭs'ĭ-tē) *n.* association or partnership in a crime or offense
*The man did not admit his own **complicity** in the theft, but blamed someone else.*

SET A PURPOSE FOR READING

As you read, think about why Jane Goodall has written this essay.

I Acknowledge Mine

Essay by

JANE GOODALL

BACKGROUND About 98 percent of chimpanzees' genetic material is identical to ours. For this reason, they have long been used by researchers for studying the progression and treatment of human diseases. The use of chimpanzees in research has grown increasingly controversial. Jane Goodall is a leading authority on chimpanzee behavior. Famous for her work studying wild chimpanzees in Africa, she writes here about the situation of chimpanzees in laboratories.

It was on December 27, 1986, that I watched the videotape that would change the pattern of my life. I had spent a traditional Christmas with my family in Bournemouth, England. We all sat watching the tape, and we were all shattered. Afterward, we couldn't speak for a while. The tape showed scenes from inside a biomedical research laboratory, in which monkeys paced round and round, back and forth, within incredibly small cages stacked

one on top of the other, and young chimpanzees, in similar tiny prisons, rocked back and forth or from side to side, far gone in
10 misery and despair. I had, of course, known about the chimpanzees who were locked away in medical research laboratories. But I had deliberately kept away, knowing that to see them would be utterly depressing, thinking that there would be nothing I could do to help them. After seeing the video I knew I had to try. . . . Ⓐ

The videotape had revealed conditions inside Sema, a federally funded laboratory in Maryland. Goodall took action, criticizing Sema for violating government standards and causing psychological harm to chimpanzees. The president of Sema denied these charges. Several months after Goodall first viewed the videotape, she received
20 *permission to visit the laboratory.*

Even repeated viewing of the videotape had not prepared me for the <u>stark</u> reality of that laboratory. I was ushered, by white-coated men who smiled nervously or glowered, into a nightmare world. The door closed behind us. Outside, everyday life went on as usual, with the sun and the trees and the birds. Inside, where no daylight had ever penetrated, it was dim and colorless. I was led along one corridor after another, and I looked into room after room lined with small, bare cages, stacked one above the other. I watched as monkeys paced around their tiny prisons, making
30 bizarre, abnormal movements.

Then came a room where very young chimpanzees, one or two years old, were crammed, two together, into tiny cages that measured (as I found out later) some twenty-two inches by twenty-two inches at the base. They were two feet high. These chimp babies peered out from the semidarkness of their tiny cells as the doors were opened. Not yet part of any experiment, they had been waiting in their cramped quarters for four months. They were simply objects, stored in the most economical way, in the smallest space that would permit the continuation of life. At least they had
40 each other, but not for long. Once their quarantine was over they would be separated, I was told, and placed singly in other cages, to be infected with hepatitis or AIDS or some other viral disease. And all the cages would then be placed in isolettes. Ⓑ

Ⓐ **SUMMARIZE**
How would you summarize the information in lines 1–14? Where are the monkeys Goodall describes and what are the "tiny prisons" in which they are trapped?

_____

_____

_____

_____

_____

stark (stärk) *adj.* harsh or grim

Why does Goodall say that she isn't prepared for the "stark reality" of the laboratory?

_____

_____

_____

Ⓑ **SUMMARIZE**
Reread lines 31–43. Underline the words Goodall uses to describe the lives of laboratory chimpanzees. What main idea about animal rights does she imply?

_____

_____

_____

_____

_____

_____

_____

Reread lines 44–53. Goodall included **rhetorical questions**—questions that do not require answers—in this passage. Underline the questions in the text. How does Goodall answer these questions?

_____

_____

_____

_____

_____

_____

_____

_____

_____

_____

D PERSUASIVE TECHNIQUES

To what does Goodall compare the chimpanzees in lines 60–68? Circle examples of **loaded language,** words used to appeal to your emotions.

_____

_____

_____

_____

_____

_____

_____

What could they see, these infants, when they peered out through the tiny panel of glass in the door of their isolette? The blank wall opposite their prison. What was in the cage to provide occupation, stimulation, comfort? For those who had been separated from their companions—nothing. I watched one isolated prisoner, a juvenile female, as she rocked from side to side,

50 sealed off from the outside world in her metal box. A flashlight was necessary if one wanted to see properly inside the cage. All she could hear was the constant loud sound of the machinery that regulated the flow of air through vents in her isolette. **C**

A "technician" (for so the animal-care staff are named, after training) was told to lift her out. She sat in his arms like a rag doll, listless, apathetic. He did not speak to her. She did not look at him or try to interact with him in any way. Then he returned her to her cage, latched the inner door, and closed her isolette, shutting her away again from the rest of the world.

60 I am still haunted by the memory of her eyes, and the eyes of the other chimpanzees I saw that day. They were dull and blank, like the eyes of people who have lost all hope, like the eyes of children you see in Africa, refugees, who have lost their parents and their homes. Chimpanzee children are so like human children, in so many ways. They use similar movements to express their feelings. And their emotional needs are the same—both need friendly contact and reassurance and fun and opportunity to engage in wild bouts of play. And they need love. **D**

Dr. James Mahoney, veterinarian at the Laboratory for

70 Experimental Medicine and Surgery in Primates (LEMSIP), recognized this need when he began working for Jan Moor-Jankowski.[1] Several years ago he started a "nursery" in that lab for the infant chimpanzees when they are first taken from their mothers. It was not long after my visit to Sema that I went for the first of a number of visits to LEMSIP.

Once I was suitably gowned and masked and capped, with paper booties over my shoes, Jim took me to see his nursery. Five young chimps were there at the time, ranging in age from about

---

1. **Jan Moor-Jankowski:** director of LEMSIP.

nine months to two years. Each one was dressed in children's
80 clothes—"to keep their diapers on, really," said the staff member
who was with them. (Someone is always with them throughout
the day.) The infants played vigorously around me as I sat on
the soft red carpet, surrounded by toys. I was for the moment
more interesting than any toy, and almost immediately they had
whisked off my cap and mask. Through a window these infants
could look into a kitchen and work area where, most of the time,
some human activity was going on. They had been taken from
their mothers when they were between nine and eighteen months
old, Jim said. He brings them into the nursery in groups, so that
90 they can all go through the initial trauma together, which is why
some were older than others. And, he explained, he tries to do
this during summer vacation so that there will be no shortage of
volunteer students to help them over their nightmares. Certainly
these **boisterous** youngsters were not depressed.

I stayed for about forty minutes, then Jim came to fetch me. He
took me to a room just across the corridor where there were eight
young chimpanzees who had recently graduated from the nursery.
This new room was known as "Junior Africa," I learned. Confined
in small, bare cages, some alone, some paired, the youngsters could
100 see into the nursery through the window. They could look back into
their lost childhood. For the second time in their short lives, security
and joy had been abruptly brought to an end through no fault of
their own. Junior Africa: the name seems utterly appropriate until
one remembers all the infants in Africa who are seized from their
mothers by hunters, rescued and cared for in human families, and
then, as they get older, banished into small cages or tied to the ends
of chains. Only the reasons, of course, are different. Even these very
young chimpanzees at LEMSIP may have to go through grueling
experimental procedures, such as repeated liver biopsies[2] and the
110 drawing of blood. Jim is always pleading for a four-year childhood
before research procedures commence, but the bodies of these
youngsters, like those of other experimental chimps, are rented out

boisterous (boi'stər-əs) *adj.*
noisy and lacking in restraint
or discipline

**Is Goodall using the word
boisterous to describe the
chimps in a negative way?
Explain.**

_____

_____

_____

_____

_____

_____

---

2. **biopsies:** removals of tissue samples from a living body for examination.

E PERSUASIVE TECHNIQUES

In lines 115–123, Goodall revisits Josh in "Junior Africa." How has this chimp changed? How does this story help persuade readers to think about Goodall's concerns?

_____

_____

_____

_____

_____

_____

_____

_____

_____

_____

_____

_____

_____

_____

_____

to researchers and pharmaceutical companies. The chimpanzees, it seems, must earn their keep from as early an age as possible.

During a subsequent visit to LEMSIP, I asked after one of the youngsters I had met at the nursery, little Josh. A real character he had been there, a born group leader. I was led to one of the cages in Junior Africa, where that once-assertive infant, who had been so full of energy and zest for life, now sat huddled in the corner of
120 his barred prison. There was no longer any fun in his eyes. "How can you bear it?" I asked the young woman who was caring for him. Her eyes, above the mask, filled with tears. "I can't," she said. "But if I leave, he'll have even less." **E**

This same fear of depriving the chimpanzees of what little they have is what keeps Jim at LEMSIP. After I had passed through Junior Africa that first day, Jim took me to the windowless rooms to meet ten adult chimps. No carpets or toys for them, no entertainment. This was the hard, cold world of the adult research chimps at LEMSIP. Five on each side of the central corridor,
130 each in his own small prison, surrounded by bars—bars on all sides, bars above, bars below. Each cage measured five feet by five feet and was seven feet high, which was the legal minimum cage size at that time for storing adult chimpanzees. Each cage was suspended above the ground, so that feces and food remains would fall to the floor below. Each cage contained an old car tire and a chimpanzee. That was all.

JoJo's cage was the first on the right as we went in. I knelt down, new cap and mask in place, along with overalls and plastic shoe covers and rubber gloves. I looked into his eyes and talked to
140 him. He had been in his cage at least ten years. He had been born in the African forest. . . . Could he remember, I wondered? Did he sometimes dream of the great trees with the breeze rustling through the canopy, the birds singing, the comfort of his mother's arms? Very gently JoJo reached one great finger through the steel bars and touched one of the tears that slipped out above my mask, then went on grooming the back of my wrist. So gently. Ignoring

the rattling of cages, the clank of steel on steel, the violent sway of imprisoned bodies beating against the bars, as the other male chimps greeted the veterinarian. **PAUSE & REFLECT**

150   His round over, Jim returned to where I still crouched before JoJo. The tears were falling faster now. "Jane, please don't," Jim said, squatting beside me and putting his arm around me. "Please don't. I have to face this every morning of my life."

    I also visited [the pharmaceutical company] Immuno's two labs in Austria. The first of these, where hepatitis research is conducted and where chimpanzees are used to test batches of vaccine, was built some time ago. There I got no farther than the administration building. I was not allowed into the chimpanzee rooms because I had not had a hepatitis shot. And—how
160 unfortunate!—the closed-circuit TV monitors could not, for some reason, be made to work that day. In the lobby, though, there were two demonstration cages, set there so the public could see for itself the magnificent and spacious housing that Immuno was planning for its chimpanzee colony. (This they felt was necessary because of all the criticisms that were being made about the small size of the existing cages, dangerous criticisms leading to expensive lawsuits.) The present cages, I knew, were not very large. The new ones looked identical to those at LEMSIP. . . .

    To my mind, it should be required that all scientists working
170 with laboratory animals, whatever the species, not only know something about the animals and their natural behavior, but see for themselves how their protocols[3] affect individual animals. Researchers should observe firsthand any suffering they cause, so that they can better balance the benefit (or hoped-for benefit) to humanity against the cost in suffering to the animal. Laboratory chimpanzees are prisoners, but they are guilty of no crimes. Rather, they are helping—perhaps—to **alleviate** human suffering. Yet in some of the labs I have described, and in others around the

alleviate (ə-lē′vē-āt′) *v.* to make easier or provide relief

---

3. **protocols** (prō′tə-kôlz′): plans for scientific experiments.

F SUMMARIZE

Briefly restate the key point that Goodall makes in lines 169–180.

_____

_____

_____

_____

_____

_____

_____

_____

_____

_____

_____

_____

_____

_____

_____

_____

_____

_____

world, they are subjected to far harsher treatment than we give to
180 hardened criminals. Surely we owe them more than that. **F**

Even if all research labs could be redesigned to provide the best possible environment for the chimpanzee subjects, there would still be one nagging question—should chimpanzees be used at all? . . . Of course I wish I could wave a wand and see the lab cages standing empty. Of course I hate the suffering that goes on behind the closed doors of animal labs. I hate even more the callous attitude that lab personnel so often show toward the animals in their power—deliberately cultivated, no doubt, to try to protect themselves from any twinge of guilt. . . . Our children
190 are gradually desensitized to animal suffering. ("It's all right, darling; it's only an animal.") The process goes on throughout school, culminating in the frightful things that zoology, psychology, veterinary, and medical students are forced to do to animals in the process of acquiring knowledge. They have to quell empathy if they are to survive in their chosen fields, for scientists do things to animals that, from the animals' point of view, are torture and would be regarded as such by almost everyone if done by nonscientists.

Animals in labs are used in different ways. In the quest for
knowledge, things are done to them to see what happens. To test
the safety of various products, animals are injected with or forced
to swallow different amounts to see how sick they get, or if they
survive. The effectiveness of medical procedures and drugs are
tried out on animals. Surgical skills are practiced on animals.
Theories of all sorts, ranging from the effects of various substances
to psychological trauma, are tested on animals. What is so shocking
is the lack of respect for the victims, the almost total disregard for
their living, feeling, sometimes agonizing bodies. And often the
tortures are inflicted for nothing. There is an angry debate, ongoing
and abrasive, about the role of animals in medicine. Even though
I am not qualified to judge a dispute of this magnitude, which
has become so polarized, it seems obvious that extremists on both
sides are wrong. The scientists who claim that medical research
could never have progressed at all without the use of animals are as
incorrect as the animal-rights activists who declare **stridently** that
no advances in medicine have been made due to animal research. **G**

Let me return to chimpanzees and to the question of
whether we are justified in using them in our search for medical
knowledge. Approximately three thousand of them languish in
medical research laboratories around the world, somewhat more
than half this number (about one thousand eight hundred) in
the United States. Today, as we have seen, they are primarily used
in infectious-disease research and vaccine testing; even though
they have seldom shown even minor symptoms of either AIDS
or hepatitis, the experimental procedures are often stressful, the
conditions in which they are maintained typically bleak. . . .

Humans are a species capable of compassion, and we should
develop a heightened moral responsibility for beings who are so
like ourselves. Chimpanzees form close, affectionate bonds that
may persist throughout life. Like us, they feel joy and sorrow
and despair. They show many of the intellectual skills that until
recently we believed were unique to ourselves. They may look
into mirrors and see themselves as individuals—beings who have
consciousness of "self." Do they not, then, deserve to be treated

G PERSUASIVE TECHNIQUES
In lines 199–216, what
information does Goodall
present about animals in labs?
What is her main point about
the use of these animals?

_____

_____

_____

_____

_____

_____

stridently (strīd'nt-lē) *adv.*
harshly; conspicuously

Are activists who present their
ideas **stridently** more or less
likely to gain the sympathy of
their audience? Explain.

_____

_____

_____

_____

_____

_____

_____

_____

_____

Ⓗ SUMMARIZE

In lines 227–244, Goodall attempts to determine whether experiments on chimpanzees are justified. Use the chart below to summarize Goodall's proposal.

Main Idea:

Details:

Summary:

with the same kind of consideration that we accord to other highly sensitive, conscious beings—ourselves? Granted, we do not always show much consideration to one another. That is why there is so much anguish over human rights. That is why it makes little sense to talk about the "rights" of chimpanzees. But at least where

240 we desist from doing certain things to human beings for ethical reasons, we should desist also from doing them to chimpanzee beings. We no longer perform certain experiments on humans, for ethical reasons. I suggest that it would be logical to refrain also from doing these experiments on chimpanzees. Ⓗ

Why do I care so much? Why, in order to try to change attitudes and actions in the labs, do I subject myself repeatedly to the personal nightmare of visiting these places, knowing that I shall be haunted endlessly by memories of my encounters with the prisoners there? Especially in their eyes, those bewildered or

250 sad or angry eyes. The answer is simple. I have spent so many years in the forests of Gombe, being with and learning from the chimpanzees. I consider myself one of the luckiest people on earth. It is time to repay something of the debt I owe the chimpanzees, for what they have taught me about themselves, about myself, about the place of humans and chimpanzees in the natural world.

When I visit JoJo in his tiny steel prison I often think of David Greybeard, that very special chimpanzee who, by his calm acceptance of my presence, first helped me to open the door into the magic world of the chimpanzees of Gombe. I learned so

260 much from him. It was he who introduced me to his companions, Goliath and Mike and the Flo family and all the other unique, fascinating personalities who made up his community at that time. David even allowed me to groom him. A fully adult male chimpanzee who had lived all his life in the wild actually tolerated the touch of a human hand.

There was one especially memorable event. I had been following David one day, struggling through dense undergrowth near a stream. I was thankful when he stopped to rest, and I sat near him. Close by I noticed the fallen red fruit of an oil nut palm, a favorite

270 food of chimpanzees. I picked it up and held it out to David on the palm of my hand. For a moment I thought he would ignore

my gesture. But then he took the nut, let it fall to the ground and, with the same movement, very gently closed his fingers around my hand. He glanced at my face, let go of my hand, and turned away. I understood his message: "I don't want the nut, but it was nice of you to offer it." We had communicated most truly, relying on shared primate signals that are deeper and more ancient than words. It was a moment of revelation. I did not follow David when he wandered off into the forest. I wanted to be alone, to ponder

280 the significance of what had happened, to enshrine those moments permanently in my mind. **PAUSE & REFLECT**

And so, when I am with JoJo, I remember David Greybeard and the lessons he taught me. I feel deep shame—shame that we, with our more sophisticated intellect, with our greater capacity for understanding and compassion, have deprived JoJo of almost everything. Not for him the soft colors of the forest, the dim greens and browns entwined, or the peace of the afternoon when the sun flecks the canopy and small creatures rustle and flit and creep among the leaves. Not for him the freedom to choose,

290 each day, how he will spend his time and where and with whom. Nature's sounds are gone, the sounds of running water, of wind in the branches, of chimpanzee calls that ring out so clear and rise up through the treetops to drift away in the hills. The comforts are gone, the soft leafy floor of the forest, the springy branches from which sleeping nests can be made. All are gone. Here, in the lab, the world is concrete and steel; it is loud, horrible sounds, clanging bars, banging doors, and the deafening volume of chimpanzee

300 calls confined in underground rooms. It is a world where there are no windows, nothing to look at, nothing to play with. A world where family and friends

PAUSE & REFLECT

In your own words, described the "significance" of Goodall's encounter with David Greybeard.

_____

_____

_____

_____

_____

_____

_____

_____

_____

_____

_____

_____

_____

_____

_____

_____

❶ **PERSUASIVE TECHNIQUES**

In lines 282–306, underline the words and images that appeal to your emotions.

complicity (kəm-plĭs′ĭ-tē) *n.* association or partnership in a crime or offense

PAUSE & REFLECT

Reread lines 282–311. Why does Jane Goodall feel that she needs to pay back a debt to chimpanzees by speaking out on behalf of their rights?

_____

_____

_____

_____

_____

are torn apart and where sociable beings are locked away, innocent of crime, into solitary confinement. ❶

It is we who are guilty. I look again into JoJo's clear eyes. I acknowledge my own **complicity** in this world we have made, and I feel the need for forgiveness. He reaches out a large, gentle
310 finger and once again touches the tear trickling down into my mask. **PAUSE & REFLECT**

Some of the laboratories discussed in this selection have changed their practices, partly in response to Jane Goodall's criticism and recommendations. For example, Sema, which is now called Diagnon, no longer keeps chimpanzees in isolettes. The chimpanzees now live in more spacious, well-lit cubicles, and they are sometimes allowed to have contact with other chimpanzees.

Text Analysis: Persuasive Techniques

Review the notes you took about the persuasive techniques Jane Goodall uses in her essay. Then complete the chart below.

Technique	Examples from Essay
Emotional Appeals	
Appeal to Pity, Fear, or Vanity Uses strong feelings, rather than facts and evidence to persuade	
Appeal to Values	
Ethical Appeal Taps into people's values or moral standards	
Word Choice	
Loaded Language Uses words with positive or negative connotations to stir people's emotions	

Review your notes for "I Acknowledge Mine" and your examples of persuasive techniques above. Does Jane Goodall use **emotional appeals** appropriately in her argument by avoiding **logical fallacies**—that is, appeals to false situations, appeals to pity, or personal attacks?

_____

_____

_____

_____

Reading Strategy: Summarize

In the chart below, provide details from the selection to support the main idea about the treatment of chimpanzees in laboratories. Then write a brief summary of Goodall's ideas.

Main Idea: The treatment of chimpanzees in laboratories must be improved.	
Supporting Detail	**Supporting Detail**
Briefly summarize Goodall's proposals to improve the treatment of chimpanzees in laboratories.	

Do animals have **RIGHTS?**

Should it be against the law to perform medical research on animals?

_____

_____

_____

Vocabulary Practice

Decide whether each statement is true or false. Write **T** for true and **F** false.

_____ 1. To **alleviate** a problem is to make it worse.

_____ 2. A **boisterous** child may disrupt a quiet restaurant.

_____ 3. If you have **complicity** in a crime, you had involvement in it.

_____ 4. An elegantly decorated room can be described as **stark.**

_____ 5. To speak **stridently** is to ask in a sweet, quiet manner.

Academic Vocabulary in Speaking

cite	controversy	convince	objective	statistic

TURN AND TALK With a partner, discuss the **controversy** that Jane Goodall presents in this essay. Did her arguments **convince** you to accept her position? Use at least one Academic Vocabulary word in your conversation. Definitions for these terms are listed on page 233.

Assessment Practice

DIRECTIONS Use "I Acknowledge Mine" to answer questions 1–5.

1 The title most likely refers to Goodall's —
 (A) vast knowledge of chimp behavior
 (B) part in a society that saves animals
 (C) sympathy toward lab workers
 (D) special relationship with chimpanzees

2 Which of the following is the best example of an emotional appeal?
 (A) "The chimpanzees . . . must earn their keep. . . ." (lines 113–114)
 (B) "JoJo's cage was the first on the right as we went in." (line 137)
 (C) "I remember David Greybeard and the lessons he taught me." (lines 282–283)
 (D) "He . . . touches the tear trickling down into my mask." (lines 309–311)

3 Reread lines 234–236. Goodall most likely asks this rhetorical question because —
 (A) she thinks the answer is self-evident
 (B) she thinks it is unanswerable
 (C) she believes it has many answers
 (D) it is a question no one has considered

4 How does the example of Goodall's experiences with David Greybeard support her arguments in the essay?
 (A) It proves that chimps are unable to interact with human beings.
 (B) It demonstrates a logical fallacy and faulty reasoning.
 (C) It shows that chimps are intelligent with advanced social skills.
 (D) It gives a confusing message about chimps' social skills.

5 To support the essay's main idea, Jane Goodall draws upon —
 (A) studies of chimps in laboratories around the world
 (B) personal experiences with chimpanzees in Africa and in laboratories
 (C) veterinary papers concerning the use of animals in research
 (D) studies published by laboratories not using animals

Use of Animals in Biomedical Research

Position Paper by **the American Medical Association**

Do the **ENDS** justify the means?

Jane Goodall and other advocates for animal welfare object to some aspects of animal research. In "Use of Animals in Biomedical Research," the American Medical Association addresses the issue of whether improving human health outweighs the suffering of animals in medical laboratories.

DISCUSS Think of a situation in which an unpleasant action (such as experimenting on animals) may lead to a worthy outcome. In the notebook at left, jot down the possible benefits and harm of this action. Share your notes with a classmate, and discuss whether the possible benefits outweigh the harm.

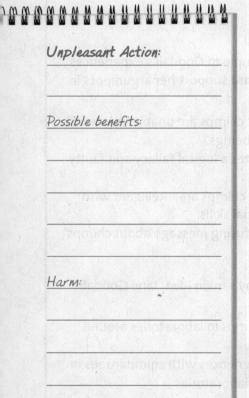

Unpleasant Action:

Possible benefits:

Harm:

Text Analysis: Counterarguments

A **counterargument** is a brief argument in which the writer refutes an objection to his or her claim that an opponent might raise. A counterargument is usually brief and negates any claims "the other side" is might present. In the following position paper, the American Medical Association expresses its support of using animals in research. To strengthen its case, it also states some opposing viewpoints and disputes them with counterarguments. The chart below shows an example.

Opposing Viewpoint	Counterargument	Support for Counterargument
Animal experimentation isn't needed.	Most modern medical advances have required such experiments.	Many Nobel Prizes have been awarded for medical research involving animals.

As you read "Use of Animals in Biomedical Research," look for more examples of counterarguments.

Reading Strategy: Summarize and Critique

In "Use of Animals in Biomedical Research," the authors summarize several opposing arguments and then critique them. The chart below shows the major differences between a summary and a critique.

Summary	Critique
When you **summarize** an argument, you • restate the argument's main points • include only information that appears in the original text—not your own opinions	When you **critique** an argument, you • discuss your opinions about or criticisms of the argument • back up your ideas with examples and evidence

As you read the selection, you'll be prompted to practice this strategy by summarizing the American Medical Association's arguments and developing your own critique.

Vocabulary in Context

Note: Words are listed in the order in which they appear in the selection.

rhetoric (rĕt′ər-ĭk) *n.* grand but empty talk
   *The politician's **rhetoric** sounded good, but she had no specific ideas.*

speculative (spĕk′yə-lə-tĭv) *adj.* based on guesses and theories rather than fact
   *My answer is only **speculative** because I don't know all the facts.*

proponent (prə-pō′nənt) *n.* a person who pleads for or supports a cause
   ***Proponents** of the new law called voters to try to win their support.*

impede (ĭm-pēd′) *v.* to obstruct or hinder
   *A lack of funds **impeded** the school's plan to build a new science laboratory.*

Vocabulary Practice

Review the vocabulary words and their meanings. Then use at least two vocabulary words to describe a debate between two scientists.

_____

_____

_____

_____

SET A PURPOSE FOR READING
Read this paper to understand the American Medical Association's position on using animals for medical research.

Use of Animals in Biomedical Research

American Medical Association

BACKGROUND The position paper you are about to read is published by the American Medical Association. Founded in Philadelphia in 1847, the American Medical Association (AMA) is the largest professional organization for physicians in the United States. The AMA identifies its core purpose as the promotion of "the science and art of medicine and the betterment of public health."

Animals have been used in experiments for at least 2,000 years, with the first reference made in the third century B.C. in Alexandria, Egypt, when the philosopher and scientist Erisistratus used animals to study body functions.

Five centuries later, the Roman physician Galen used apes
and pigs to prove his theory that veins carry blood rather
than air. In succeeding centuries, animals were employed
to discover how the body functions or to confirm or
disprove theories developed through observation. Advances
10 in knowledge made through these experiments included
Harvey's demonstration of the circulation of blood in
1622, the effect of anesthesia on the body in 1846, and the
relationship between bacteria and disease in 1878.

Today, animals are used in experiments for three general
purposes: (1) biomedical and behavioral research, (2)
education, (3) drug and product testing. . . . Biomedical
research increases understanding of how biological systems
function and advances medical knowledge. . . . Educational
experiments are conducted to educate and train students
20 in medicine, veterinary medicine, physiology,[1] and general
science. In many instances, these experiments are conducted
with dead animals. . . . Animals also are employed to
determine the safety and efficacy[2] of new drugs or the
toxicity[3] of chemicals to which humans or animals may
be exposed. Most of these experiments are conducted by
commercial firms to fulfill government requirements. . . . Ⓐ

Use of Animals Rather than Humans

A basic assumption of all types of research is that man should
relieve human and animal suffering. One objection to the use
of animals in biomedical research is that the animals are used
30 as surrogates for human beings. This objection presumes the
equality of all forms of life; animal rights advocates argue
that if the tests are for the benefit of man, then man should

Ⓐ **SUMMARIZE AND CRITIQUE**
Lines 14–26 outline information
that will be discussed in more
detail later in the paper. Reread
the paragraph, underlining the
most important information.
Then summarize the paragraph
on the lines below.

_____

_____

_____

_____

_____

_____

_____

_____

_____

_____

_____

---

1. **physiology** (fĭz′ē-ŏl′ə-jē): a branch of biology that deals with the
   functioning of organisms.
2. **efficacy** (ĕf′ĭ-kə-sē): the capacity to produce a desired effect.
3. **toxicity** (tŏk-sĭs′ĭ-tē): the quality of being poisonous or harmful.

B COUNTERARGUMENTS
Circle the opposing viewpoint summarized in lines 31–33. Then underline the counterargument that the authors present in the rest of the paragraph.

C SUMMARIZE AND CRITIQUE
In the chart below, summarize the information in lines 47–55. Then write a critique that an animal rights advocate might make of this information.

Summary
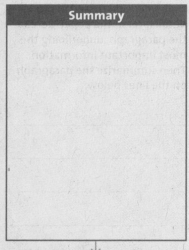

↓

Critique
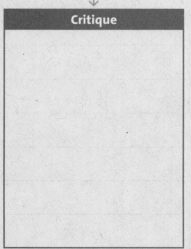

serve as the subject of the experiments. There are limitations, however, to the use of human subjects both ethically, such as in the testing of a potentially toxic drug or chemical, and in terms of what can be learned. The process of aging, for instance, can best be observed through experiments with rats, which live an average of two to three years, or with some types of monkeys, which live 15 to 20 years.
40 Some experiments require numerous subjects of the same weight or genetic makeup or require special diets or physical environments; these conditions make the use of human subjects difficult or impossible. By using animals in such tests, researchers can observe subjects of uniform age and background in sufficient numbers to determine if findings are consistent and applicable to a large population. **B**

Animals are important in research precisely because they have complex body systems that react and interact with stimuli much as humans do. The more true this is with a particular
50 animal, the more valuable that animal is for a particular type of research. One important property to a researcher is discrimination—the extent to which an animal exhibits the particular quality to be investigated. The greater the degree of discrimination, the greater the reliability and predictability of the information gathered from the experiment. **C**

For example, dogs have been invaluable in biomedical research because of the relative size of their organs compared to humans. The first successful kidney transplant was performed in a dog, and the techniques used to save the lives
60 of "blue babies," babies with structural defects in their hearts, were developed with dogs. Open-heart surgical techniques, coronary bypass surgery,[4] and heart transplantation all were developed using dogs.

---

4. **coronary bypass surgery:** open-heart surgery to improve the blood supply to the heart.

Another important factor is the amount of information available about a particular animal. Mice and rats play an extensive role in research and testing, in part because repeated experiments and controlled breeding have created a pool of data to which the findings from a new experiment can be related and given meaning. Their rapid rate of
70 reproduction also has made them important in studies of genetics and other experiments that require observation over a number of generations. Moreover, humans cannot be bred to produce "inbred strains"[5] as can be done with animals; therefore, humans cannot be substituted for animals in studies where an inbred strain is essential.

Scientists argue repeatedly that research is necessary to reduce human and animal suffering and disease. Biomedical advances depend on research with animals, and not using them would be unethical because it would
80 deprive humans and animals of the benefits of research. . . .

PAUSE & REFLECT

Benefits of Animal Experimentation

The arguments advanced by animal rights activists in opposing the use of animals in biomedical research . . . are scientific, emotional, and philosophic. . . . The scientific challenge raised by animal rights activists goes to the heart of the issue by asking whether animal experiments are necessary for scientific and medical progress and whether all the experiments being performed and all the animals being used are justified and required. Scientists insist that they are; animal rights activists insist that they are not.

---

5. **inbred strains:** groups of animals produced by the mating of siblings over at least 20 generations, resulting in individuals as genetically similar as possible.

PAUSE & REFLECT
Explain how animals might benefit from research on other animals. Does this fact strengthen the case for experimenting on animals? Why?

SUMMARIZE AND CRITIQUE

Underline the argument that the article summarizes in lines 90–94. What critique do the animal rights activists offer in response?

_____

_____

_____

_____

_____

_____

_____

_____

_____

_____

_____

_____

_____

_____

_____

_____

_____

_____

90   Scientists justify use of animals in biomedical research on two grounds: the contribution that the information makes to human and animal health and welfare, and the lack of any alternative way to gain the information and knowledge. Animal rights activists contest experiments that utilize animals on both these grounds and assert that this practice no longer is necessary because alternative methods of experimentation exist for obtaining the same information.

In an appearance on the *Today* show in 1985, Ingrid Newkirk, representing People for the Ethical Treatment of Animals (PETA), stated: "If it were such a valuable way to gain knowledge, we should have eternal life by now." This statement is similar in spirit to one made in 1900 by an antivivisectionist[6] who stated that, given the number of experiments on the brain done up to then, the insane asylums of Washington, D.C. should be empty. **D**

Scientists believe that such assertions miss the point. The issue is not what *has not* been accomplished by animal use in biomedical research, but what *has* been accomplished. A longer life span has been achieved, decreased infant mortality[7] has occurred, effective treatments have been developed for many diseases, and the quality of life has been enhanced for mankind in general.

One demonstration of the critical role that animals play in medical and scientific advances is that 54 of 76 Nobel Prizes awarded in physiology or medicine since 1901 have been for discoveries and advances made through the use of experimental animals. Among these have been the Prize awarded in 1985 for the studies (using dogs) that documented the relationship between cholesterol and heart disease; the 1966 Prize for the studies (using chickens) that linked viruses

---

6. **antivivisectionist** (ăn′tē-vĭv′ĭ-sĕk′shən-ĭst): someone opposed to the act of operating on live animals for science experiments.

7. **infant mortality:** the death rate during the first year of life.

and cancer; and the 1960 Prize for studies (using cattle, mice, and chicken embryos) that established that a body can be taught to accept tissue from different donors if it is inoculated[8] with different types of tissue prior to birth or during the first year of life, a finding expected to help simplify and advance organ transplants in the future. Studies using animals also resulted in successful culture of the poliomyelitis[9] virus; a Nobel Prize was awarded for this work in 1954. The discovery of insulin and treatment of diabetes, achieved through
130 experiments using dogs, also earned the Prize in 1923.

In fact, virtually every advance in medical science in the 20th century, from antibiotics and vaccines to antidepressant drugs and organ transplants, has been achieved either directly or indirectly through the use of animals in laboratory experiments. The result of these experiments has been the elimination or control of many infectious diseases—smallpox, poliomyelitis, measles—and the development of numerous life-saving techniques—blood transfusions, burn therapy, open-heart and brain surgery. This has meant a longer,
140 healthier, better life with much less pain and suffering. For many, it has meant life itself. Often forgotten in the **rhetoric** is the fact that humans *do* participate in biomedical research in the form of clinical trials. They experience pain and are injured, and in fact, some of them die from this participation. Hence, scientists are not asking animals to be "guinea pigs" alone for the glory of science. . . . **E**

Scientists feel that it is essential for the public to understand that had scientific research been restrained in the first decade of the 20th century as antivivisectionists and
150 activists were then and are today urging, many millions of

---

E COUNTERARGUMENTS
In lines 131–146, two opposing viewpoints are disputed. Draw a line to show where the response to the first argument ends and the response to the second begins. Then, write a sentence summarizing the opposing arguments that the author is responding to.

_____

_____

_____

_____

_____

_____

_____

rhetoric (rĕt′ər-ĭk) *n.* grand but empty talk

---

8. **inoculated** (ĭ-nŏk′yə-lā′tĭd): injected.
9. **poliomyelitis** (pō′lē-ō-mī′ə-lī′tĭs): a highly infectious viral disease that generally affects children and may lead to paralysis and deformity. Also called *polio.*

Americans alive and healthy today would never have been born or would have suffered a premature death. Their parents or grandparents would have died from diphtheria, scarlet fever, tuberculosis, diabetes, appendicitis, and countless other diseases and disorders. . . .

The Danger of Restricting Research

The activities and arguments of animal rights and animal welfare activists and organizations present the American people with some fundamental decisions that must be made regarding the use of animals in biomedical research.

160   The fundamental issue raised by the philosophy of the animal rights movement is whether man has the right to use animals in a way that causes them to suffer and die. To accept the philosophical and moral viewpoint of the animal rights movement would require a total ban on the use of animals in any scientific research and testing. The consequences of such a step were set forth by the Office of Technology Assessment (OTA) in its report to Congress: "Implementation of this option would effectively arrest most basic biomedical and behavioral research and toxicological

170   testing in the United States." The economic and public health consequences of that, the OTA warned Congress, "are so unpredictable and <u>speculative</u> that this course of action should be considered dangerous." **F**

No nation and no jurisdiction within the United States has yet adopted such a ban. Although . . . laws to ban the use of animals in biomedical research have been introduced into a number of state legislatures, neither a majority of the American people nor their elected representatives have ever supported these bills.

180   Another aspect of the use of animals in biomedical research that has received little consideration is the economic

---

F SUMMARIZE AND CRITIQUE
In lines 160–173, underline the critique of the idea of a total ban on research that causes animals to suffer and die. Is this critique effective? Why?

_____

_____

_____

_____

_____

_____

_____

speculative (spĕk′yə-lə-tĭv) *adj.* based on guesses and theories rather than fact

consequences of regulatory change. Clearly, other nations are not curtailing the use of animals to any significant degree. Some of these, like Japan, are major competitors of the United States in biomedical research. Given the economic climate in the United States, our massive trade imbalance, and our loss of leadership in many areas, can the United States afford not to keep a leading industry, i.e., biomedical science, developing as rapidly as possible? Many nations are in positions to assume
190 leadership roles, and the long-term economic impact on our citizens could be profound. This economic impact would be expressed in many ways, not the least of which would certainly be a reduction in the quality and number of health services available for people who need them.

Through polls and by other means, the American people have indicated that they support the use of animals in research and testing. At the same time they have expressed a strong wish that the animals be protected against any unnecessary pain and suffering. The true question, therefore, is how to
200 achieve this without interfering with the performance of necessary research. Scientists already comply with a host of federal, state, municipal, and institutional guidelines and laws. However, in this era of cost containment, they fear that overregulation will become so costly that research progress will suffer. Scientists emphasize that a reasonable balance must be achieved between increased restrictions and increased cost.

PAUSE & REFLECT

What must be recognized, say scientists, is that it is not possible to protect all animals against pain and still conduct meaningful research. No legislation and no standard of
210 humane care can eliminate this necessity. The only alternative is either to eliminate the research, as animal rights adherents

PAUSE & REFLECT
Do you think most people could agree on a "reasonable balance" between making research progress and protecting animals from unnecessary suffering? Explain why or why not.

_____

_____

_____

_____

_____

_____

_____

_____

_____

_____

_____

proponent (prə-pō'nənt) *n.*
a person who pleads for or
supports a cause

impede (ĭm-pēd') *v.* to obstruct
or hinder

⊙ COUNTERARGUMENTS
In lines 215–221, what
counterargument is made in
response to the animal welfare
movement? Summarize this
counterargument below.

_____

_____

_____

_____

_____

_____

_____

_____

_____

_____

_____

urge, and forego the knowledge and the benefits of health-
related research that would result, or to inflict the pain and
suffering on human beings by using them as research subjects.

The desire by animal welfare **proponents** to ensure
maximum comfort and minimal pain to research animals is
understandable and appeals to scientists, the public, and to
legislators. But what also must be recognized and weighed
in the balance is the price paid in terms of human pain and
220 suffering if overly protective measures are adopted that **impede**
or prevent the use of animals in biomedical research. **⊙**

In short, the American people should not be misled by
emotional appeals and philosophic rhetoric on this issue.
Biomedical research using animals is essential to continued
progress in clinical medicine. Animal research holds the
key for solutions to AIDS, cancer, heart disease, aging, and
congenital defects.[10] In discussing legislation concerning
animal experimentation, the prominent physician and
physiologist Dr. Walter B. Cannon stated in 1896 that
230 ". . . the antivivisectionists are the second of the two types
Theodore Roosevelt described when he said, 'Common
sense without conscience may lead to crime, but conscience
without common sense may lead to folly, which is the
handmaiden of crime.'"

The American Medical Association has been an outspoken
proponent of biomedical research for over 100 years, and
that tradition continues today. The Association believes
that research involving animals is absolutely essential to
maintaining and improving the health of the American people.
240 The Association is opposed to any legislation or regulation that
would inappropriately limit such research, and actively supports
all legislative efforts to ensure the continued use of animals in
research, while providing for their humane treatment.

10. **congenital defects:** defects present at birth.

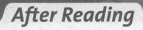

Text Analysis: Counterarguments

The chart below summarizes the AMA's main claim and several of the opposing viewpoints mentioned in the position paper. Review your notes and the selection to find a counterargument for each opposing viewpoint. Then briefly describe the support provided for each counterargument.

Claim: Using animals in medical research is necessary and should not be limited by more regulations.		
Opposing Viewpoint	**Counterargument**	**Support for Counterargument**
If an experiment will benefit humans, then the experiment should be done on human subjects, not animals.		
Animal testing must not be very effective, because scientists have conducted countless experiments and still many diseases have not been cured.		
Animals have rights, and using them in a way that causes suffering and death violates their rights and must be banned.		

Did the inclusion of opposing viewpoints and counterarguments strengthen the AMA's argument? Explain.

_____

_____

_____

_____

_____

Reading Strategy: Summarize and Critique

Find each of the passages mentioned in the chart and write a summary of the argument stated there. Then write a critique of the argument. If your own view of the argument is not critical, write your critique from the perspective of an animal rights advocate.

Summary	Critique
Lines 64–75	
Lines 180–194	

Do the **ENDS** justify the means?

Are humans justified in using animals in medical research? Why or why not?

_____

_____

_____

Vocabulary Practice

Write the word from the list that best completes each sentence.

1. Until we get the facts from the proper sources, everything is _____.

2. Concrete actions speak louder than empty _____.

3. As a _____ of conservation, she signed a petition for the preservation of wetlands.

4. I do not want to _____ your work, so please let me know if I'm a distraction.

WORD LIST

impede

proponent

rhetoric

speculative

Academic Vocabulary in Speaking

cite	controversy	convince	objective	statistic

TURN AND TALK Why is there so much **controversy** over the issue of animal research? Discuss this question with a classmate. Use at least one Academic Vocabulary word in your discussion. Definitions for these terms are listed on page 233.

Assessment Practice

DIRECTIONS Use "Use of Animals in Biomedical Research" to answer questions 1–6.

1 The AMA's position is that the use of animals in medical research is —

- **A** not as painful as animal rights activists claim
- **B** the best way for scientists to win Nobel Prizes
- **C** essential for the health of the American people
- **D** justifiable only in the case of deadly diseases

2 In the earliest known cases of animal research, scientists used animals to study —

- **A** the spread of infectious diseases
- **B** similarities between human and dog kidneys
- **C** the effects of new medicines
- **D** the functions of the body

3 Which of the following is a counterargument to the idea that animal research is not necessary to advance our scientific knowledge?

- **A** Nearly every advance in medical science in the 20th century was made using animal research.
- **B** Humans do not have the right to inflict pain and death on animals for their own benefit.
- **C** There are alternative methods that yield the same information as animal testing.
- **D** Banning animal research would have devastating results for the American economy.

4 Which of the following is a summary of Ingrid Newkirk's statement in lines 100–101?

- **A** Animal research has not led to any effective treatments for human diseases.
- **B** If animal research continues, someday people will find the secret to eternal life.
- **C** The value of animal research is proven by the many successes it has achieved.
- **D** Animal research must not be very effective because people still get sick and die.

5 Accepting the idea of animal rights would mean —

- **A** involving animals in clinical trials
- **B** taking steps to reduce animal suffering
- **C** ending research that causes animal deaths
- **D** banning all animal research

6 According to the AMA, which two factors need to be balanced?

- **A** people's health and the health of the economy
- **B** scientific progress and the humane treatment of animals
- **C** regulation of research practices and total bans on animal research
- **D** animal testing and human clinical trials

Be sure to read the Text Analysis Workshop
on pp. 770–777 in *Holt McDougal Literature*.

Academic Vocabulary for Unit 7

Preview the following Academic Vocabulary words. You will encounter these words as you work through this book and will use them as you write and talk about the selections in this unit.

abstract (ab-strakt) *adj.* thought of or stated without reference to a specific instance

*The poem suggests that love is more than an **abstract** idea; love becomes real only when one experiences it.*

•

device (dĭ-vīs') *n.* a literary technique used to achieve a particular effect

*The poet uses the **device** of parallelism to suggest a similarity between the two situations.*

•

form *n. a* method of arranging elements in a literary work

*A sonnet is a poetic **form** with a fixed pattern of rhyme.*

•

literal (lĭt'ər-əl) *adj.* limited to the simplest or most obvious meaning of a word or words

*To understand this poem, you must look beyond the **literal** meanings of the words.*

•

tradition (trə-dĭsh'ən) *n.* a set of customs and usages passed down from generation to generation that sets an example for present behavior

*This poet writes in the **tradition** of epic poetry dating back to ancient Greece.*

What is your favorite literary **form**—short story, essay, novel, epic poem, free verse, or something else? What do you like about it? Write your response on the lines below, using at least two Academic Vocabulary words.

_____

_____

_____

There Will Come Soft Rains
Poem by Sara Teasdale

Meeting at Night
Poem by Robert Browning

The Sound of Night
Poem by Maxine Kumin

What is our place in
NATURE?

People change landscapes, drive other species to extinction, and generally use nature for their own ends. Are humans more powerful than nature? Or are humans actually insignificant in the face of nature's power?

DISCUSS Think about a recent encounter you had with nature. What was your attitude in that moment—admiration? boredom? Jot down some notes in the notebook at left. Then, with a small group of classmates, discuss your overall attitudes toward nature.

Text Analysis: Sound Devices

Prosody, the rhythm and rhyme of a poem, can give one poem a brisk, urgent beat and another poem the sound of an everyday conversation. Poets use techniques called sound devices to affect the way their poems sound when read aloud. **Rhyme,** the repetition of sounds at the ends of words, is one common sound device.

A **rhyme scheme** is a pattern of end rhymes in a poem. A rhyme scheme is noted by assigning a letter of the alphabet, beginning with *a*, to each line. Lines that rhyme are given the same letter. Notice the rhyme scheme of the first four lines of this poem.

> *There will come soft rains and the smell of the ground,*   a
> *And swallows circling with their shimmering sound;*   a
>
> *And frogs in the pools singing at night,*   b
> *And wild plum-trees in tremulous white;*   b

—from "There Will Come Soft Rains" by Sara Teasdale

An Encounter with Nature

Where I Was: _____

_____

What Happened: _____

_____

_____

My Attitude: _____

_____

_____

_____

The following chart shows other kinds of sound devices used in poetry.

Sound Device	Definition	Example
End rhyme	Rhyme at the ends of lines	*Whose woods these are I think I <u>know</u>.* *His house is in the village <u>though</u>.* —from "Stopping by Woods on a Snowy Evening" by Robert Frost
Alliteration	The repetition of consonant sounds at the beginnings of words	*<u>Dr</u>oning a <u>dr</u>owsy syncopated tune* —from "The Weary Blues" by Langston Hughes
Onomatopoeia	The use of words that imitate sounds	*The <u>buzz</u> saw <u>snarled</u> and <u>rattled</u> in the yard* —from "Out, Out—" by Robert Frost

As you read the following poems, you'll be prompted to note examples of sound devices. The chart below shows an example.

Title	End Rhyme	Alliteration	Onomatopoeia
"There Will Come Soft Rains"	ground/sound (lines 1 and 2)		

Reading Strategy: Reading Poetry

When you read poetry, you must pay attention not only to the meaning of the words but also to the way they look and sound. The following strategies will help you:

- Notice how the lines are arranged on the page. Are they long lines, or short? Are they grouped into regular stanzas or irregular stanzas, or are they not divided into stanzas at all? (A **stanza** is a group of lines similar to a paragraph in prose writing. The start of a new stanza usually signals the start of a new idea.)

- Pause in your reading where punctuation marks appear, just as you would when reading prose. Note that in poetry, punctuation does not always occur at the end of a line; a thought may continue for several lines.

- Read a poem aloud several times. As you read, notice whether the rhythm is regular or varied. Is there a **rhyme scheme,** or regular pattern of end rhyme? For example, you'll notice that "There Will Come Soft Rains" is written in **couplets,** two-line units with an *aa* rhyme scheme. Regular patterns of rhythm and rhyme give a musical quality to poems.

SET A PURPOSE
FOR READING
Read this poem to discover
one possible scenario of
life without humankind.

There Will Come Soft Rains

Poem by
SARA TEASDALE

BACKGROUND "There Will Come Soft
Rains" is a lyric poem. Lyric poems are
short poems with one speaker who
expresses a thought or feeling about a
person or subject. Sara Teasdale wrote
this poem in reaction to World War I.

A READING POETRY
Read the first stanza aloud. Circle
the rhyming words that make it
a rhymed **couplet.**

B SOUND DEVICES
What examples of **alliteration**
can you find in lines 1–6?
Underline consonants that are
repeated at the beginnings of
words.

There will come soft rains and the smell of the ground,
And swallows circling with their shimmering sound; **A**

And frogs in the pools singing at night,
And wild plum-trees in tremulous white;

5　Robins will wear their feathery fire
Whistling their whims on a low fence-wire; **B**

And not one will know of the war, not one
Will care at last when it is done.

Not one would mind, neither bird nor tree
10　If mankind perished utterly;

And Spring herself, when she woke at dawn,
Would scarcely know that we were gone.

Meeting at Night

Poem by
ROBERT BROWNING

BACKGROUND Robert Browning was a master at capturing the complexity of different personalities. Using **dramatic monologue,** a poem addressed to a silent listener, he conveyed the personalities of both fictional and historical figures.

SET A PURPOSE FOR READING
Read the poem to find out whom the speaker is meeting, and where.

Monitor Your Comprehension

1

The gray sea and the long black land;
And the yellow half-moon large and low;
And the startled little waves that leap
In fiery ringlets from their sleep,
5 As I gain the cove[1] with pushing prow,[2]
And quench its speed i' the slushy sand. **C**

2

Then a mile of warm sea-scented beach;
Three fields to cross till a farm appears;
A tap at the pane, the quick sharp scratch
10 And blue spurt of a lighted match,
And a voice less loud, through its joys and fears,
Than the two hearts beating each to each!

PAUSE & REFLECT

C READING POETRY
Read the first stanza aloud. What **rhyme scheme** do you notice? Use the letters *a, b,* and *c* to label the pattern of end rhyme in lines 1–6.

PAUSE & REFLECT
Where does the speaker arrive, and what happens once he is there?

_____

_____

_____

_____

_____

1. **cove:** a small, partly enclosed body of water.
2. **prow** (prou): the front part of a boat.

**SET A PURPOSE
FOR READING**

Read this poem to find out
how the poet describes
the sound—or the many
sounds—of night.

The Sound of Night

Poem by

MAXINE KUMIN

BACKGROUND Through her poetry,
Maxine Kumin explores changes in
nature, people's relationships to the land
and its creatures, and human mortality,
loss, and survival. She once told an
interviewer that for her, writing poetry
is a mystical process; she knows it's time
to write because she gets a prickle at the
base of her neck.

D SOUND DEVICES
Read the first stanza aloud. Then
reread lines 1–9 and underline
examples of **onomatopoeia** that
you notice. What does this sound
device add to the poem?

_____

_____

_____

_____

_____

_____

_____

_____

_____

And now the dark comes on, all full of chitter noise.
Birds huggermugger[1] crowd the trees,
the air thick with their vesper[2] cries,
and bats, snub seven-pointed kites,
5 skitter across the lake, swing out,
squeak, chirp, dip, and skim on skates
of air, and the fat frogs wake and prink
wide-lipped, noisy as ducks, drunk
on the boozy black, gloating chink-chunk. **D**

---

1. **huggermugger:** disorderly.
2. **vesper:** pertaining to the evening; a type of swallow that sings in the
   evening.

10 And now on the narrow beach we defend ourselves from dark.
   The cooking done, we build our firework
   bright and hot and less for outlook
   than for magic, and lie in our blankets
   while night nickers around us. Crickets
15 chorus hallelujahs; paws, quiet
   and quick as raindrops, play on the stones
   expertly soft, run past and are gone;
   fish pulse in the lake; the frogs hoarsen.

   Now every voice of the hour—the known, the supposed, the
        strange,
20 the mindless, the witted, the never seen—
   sing, thrum, impinge,[3] and rearrange
   endlessly; and debarred[4] from sleep we wait
   for the birds, importantly silent,
   for the crease of first eye-licking light,
25 for the sun, lost long ago and sweet.
   By the lake, locked black away and tight,
   we lie, day creatures, overhearing night. **PAUSE & REFLECT**

PAUSE & REFLECT
What are the people in this poem doing, and how do they feel about their natural surroundings?

_____

_____

_____

_____

_____

_____

3. **impinge** (ĭm-pĭnj′): to strike or push upon.
4. **debarred:** prevented or hindered.

Text Analysis: Sound Devices

Review the notes you took while reading the poems. In the chart below, describe the stanza structure and the rhyme scheme of each poem. Also list examples of alliteration and onomatopoeia that you found especially effective.

	Stanzas	Rhyme Scheme	Alliteration	Onomatopoeia
"There Will Come Soft Rains"				
"Meeting at Night"				
"The Sound of Night"				

Reading Skill: Reading Poetry

What qualities of nature are conveyed in each poem? How do the sound devices suggest these qualities?

_____

_____

_____

_____

_____

_____

_____

What is our place in NATURE?

Do you think humans are part of nature? Why or why not?

_____

_____

Academic Vocabulary in Writing

abstract	device	form	literal	tradition

Which poem makes the most effective use of sound **devices** to convey its
message? Use at least two Academic Vocabulary words in your response.
Definitions for these terms are listed on page 275.

_____

_____

_____

_____

Assessment Practice

DIRECTIONS Use "There Will Come Soft Rains," "Meeting at Night," and
"The Sound of Night" to answer questions 1–4.

1 An example of alliteration from Teasdale's
poem is —

  (A) "There will come soft rains" (line 1)
  (B) "Robins will wear their feathery fire" (line 5)
  (C) "If mankind perished utterly" (line 10)
  (D) "at dawn, / . . . were gone" (lines 11–12)

2 In "Meeting at Night," what is the object of the
speaker's journey?

  (A) He is returning home to his farm.
  (B) He is going to meet his beloved.
  (C) He is exploring a new cove in his boat.
  (D) He is enjoying the moonlight along
      the beach.

3 What is the rhyme scheme of "Meeting
at Night"?

  (A) abcabc defdef
  (B) abacdc efeghg
  (C) abccba deffed
  (D) abbcca deeffd

4 Which of the following words from "The Sound
of Night" are onomatopoetic?

  (A) chitter, squeak, chink-chunk
  (B) snub, skim, skates
  (C) strange, mindless, witted
  (D) light, tight, night

Sonnet 18
Poem by **William Shakespeare**

Sonnet XXX of *Fatal Interview*
Poem by **Edna St. Vincent Millay**

What makes a good LOVE POEM?

How do you describe something you cannot see, taste, or touch? Like a love song, a love poem uses familiar objects and experiences to make sense of the mysterious feelings of love. As you'll see in the following sonnets, the results can be as different as day and night.

BRAINSTORM In a group, brainstorm a list of comparisons you might use to describe how it feels to be in love. Think of song lyrics you know or poems you have read. Record your ideas in the notebook at left. Then review your list and discuss what aspect or quality of love each comparison communicates.

Being in Love Is Like . . .

1. _____

2. _____

3. _____

4. _____

5. _____

Poetic Form: Sonnet

The sonnet has been a popular poetic form for centuries. Traditionally, sonnets have been about love. While different types of sonnets have been developed by various poets, some characteristics are common to all sonnets.

- Typically, the **sonnet** is a 14-line lyric poem written with a strict pattern of rhyme and rhythm. (A lyric poem has a single speaker who expresses personal thoughts and feelings.)

- The **English,** or **Shakespearean, sonnet** has a rhyme scheme of *abab cdcd efef gg*. Notice how this divides the poem into four distinct line groups: three **quatrains,** or four-line units, followed by a **couplet**—a pair of rhymed lines.

- The **meter,** or the repeated pattern of rhythm, in each line of a sonnet is typically **iambic pentameter.** Read more about iambic pentameter on the next page.

- Each rhythmic unit of a meter is known as a **foot.** The most commonly used metrical foot is an **iamb,** which is an unstressed syllable followed by a stressed syllable, as in the word *hello.* Note the iambs in the following example from Shakespeare's "Sonnet 18":

  So long as men can breathe, or eyes can see,

  So long lives this, and this gives life to thee.

- In each line, notice that there are five iambs. When a line contains five feet, it is called **pentameter.** Therefore, this meter is called iambic pentameter.

As you read the two sonnets in this lesson, pay attention to their rhyme schemes and meter.

Reading Strategy: Reading Sonnets

To understand the complex ideas expressed in a sonnet, you first need to understand the poem's structure. These strategies will help you:

1. Identify the situation, problem, or question introduced at the beginning of the poem.

2. Identify the turning point, if there is one. This is when the poem shifts from describing the problem to solving the problem, for example.

3. Determine how the situation is clarified, the problem resolved, or the question answered.

As you read, apply these strategies and record your results in the chart below.

Strategy	Sonnet 18	Sonnet XXX
Situation, Problem, or Question		
Turning Point		
Solution, Resolution, or Answer		

SONNET 18

Poem by

WILLIAM SHAKESPEARE

BACKGROUND Although Shakespeare is best
known for his plays, he was also a brilliant poet.
When Shakespeare began his career in the 1590s,
the sonnet was a literary fashion. Sonnets were
usually written as a longing tribute to a faraway
love. Many of Shakespeare's sonnets are addressed
to a "dark lady" whose identity has never been
discovered. First published in 1609, "Sonnet 18" is
one poem in a series of 154 sonnets.

A READING SONNETS
Reread the second **quatrain**
(lines 5–8). What situation does
it describe? Record your answer
in the chart on page 285.

B READING SONNETS
Underline the lines where the
speaker shifts from describing a
situation to starting to resolve
it. In the chart on page 285,
identify the turning point and
the resolution.

Shall I compare thee to a summer's day?
Thou art more lovely and more temperate:[1]
Rough winds do shake the darling buds of May,
And summer's lease hath all too short a date:
5 Sometime too hot the eye of heaven shines,
And often is his gold complexion dimmed;
And every fair from fair sometime declines,
By chance or nature's changing course untrimmed;[2] **A**
But thy eternal summer shall not fade,
10 Nor lose possession of that fair thou owest;[3]
Nor shall Death brag thou wander'st in his shade,
When in eternal lines to time thou growest:
    So long as men can breathe, or eyes can see,
    So long lives this, and this gives life to thee. **B**

---

1. **temperate** (tĕm′pər-ĭt): moderate, mild.
2. **untrimmed**: stripped of beauty.
3. **thou owest** (thou ō′ĭst): you own; you possess.

Sonnet XXX
OF FATAL INTERVIEW

Poem by
**EDNA
ST. VINCENT
MILLAY**

BACKGROUND Edna St. Vincent Millay was only 19 when her poem "Renascence" made her an instant celebrity. In 1923 she became the first woman to win the Pulitzer Prize in poetry. Eight years later, Millay published *Fatal Interview,* a collection of 52 sonnets. "Sonnet XXX" also goes by the title "Love is not all."

SET A PURPOSE FOR READING
Read this poem to find out how much the speaker values love.

Love is not all: it is not meat nor drink
Nor slumber nor a roof against the rain;
Nor yet a floating spar¹ to men that sink
And rise and sink and rise and sink again;
5 Love can not fill the thickened lung with breath,
Nor clean the blood, nor set the fractured bone;
Yet many a man is making friends with death
Even as I speak, for lack of love alone. **C**
It well may be that in a difficult hour,
10 Pinned down by pain and moaning for release,
Or nagged by want² past resolution's power,
I might be driven to sell your love for peace,
Or trade the memory of this night for food.
It well may be. I do not think I would. **PAUSE & REFLECT**

1. **spar:** a pole used to support a ship's sails.
2. **want:** need.

C SONNET
Reread lines 1–8 and use the letters *a, b, c,* and so on to mark the **rhyme scheme.**

PAUSE & REFLECT
What value does the speaker place on love?

_____

_____

_____

_____

Poetic Form: Sonnet

Complete the chart below with information about the two sonnets. Refer to the notes you took while reading and the chart you completed on page 285.

	"Sonnet 18"	"Sonnet XXX"
What is the rhyme scheme of the poem?		
Mark the stressed and unstressed syllables in these lines to show iambic pentameter.	Shall I compare thee to a summer's day? Thou art more lovely and more temperate:	Love is not all: it is not meat nor drink Nor slumber nor a roof against the rain;
Summarize the situation presented in the poem and how it is resolved.		
What does the poem say about love?		

Reading Skill: Reading Poetry

Is Millay's poem a Shakespearean sonnet? Explain why or why not.

_____

_____

_____

What makes a good LOVE POEM?

Do the two sonnets agree with your own ideas about love? Explain.

_____

_____

_____

Academic Vocabulary in Speaking

abstract	device	form	literal	tradition

TURN AND TALK Is the sonnet a good poetic **form** in which to explore the topic of love? Discuss this question with a classmate. Use at least two Academic Vocabulary words in your discussion. Definitions for these terms are listed on page 275.

Assessment Practice

DIRECTIONS Use "Sonnet 18" and "Sonnet XXX" to answer questions 1–4.

1 In "Sonnet 18," the speaker compares his beloved to —
- **A** the "darling buds" of springtime
- **B** a summer day
- **C** a day that is uncomfortably warm
- **D** the cycle of nature

2 In "Sonnet 18," the speaker says that his beloved's "eternal summer shall not fade" because —
- **A** she died before she could grow old
- **B** he will always remember how lovely she is
- **C** she is equally beautiful in all seasons
- **D** he has immortalized her beauty in the poem

3 The rhymed couplet in "Sonnet 18" —
- **A** introduces a situation that is explored throughout the sonnet
- **B** leaves readers with an unanswered question to consider
- **C** resolves the situation described in the first two quatrains
- **D** is a turning point that begins to resolve the situation

4 The speaker in "Sonnet XXX" believes that love is —
- **A** less important than food and drink
- **B** the most precious thing in life
- **C** all a person needs to survive
- **D** a constant torment for most people

Lord Randall
Anonymous Ballad

Ballad/Balada
Poem by Gabriela Mistral

Midwinter Blues
Poem by Langston Hughes

When does poetry SING?

Have you ever found yourself singing a song you'd forgotten you knew? As you'll see in this lesson, poems based on music can be as catchy as song lyrics.

QUICKWRITE With a small group, write out the lyrics of a well-known song. Discuss the patterns you notice in the song, such as repetition and rhyme. Then, in the notebook at left, write a sentence or two explaining what qualities make a poem "songlike."

Poetic Form: Ballad

A **ballad** is a story told in song, using the voice and language of everyday people. The earliest ballads were composed orally, and singers often added or changed details to make the songs meaningful for their audiences. These early ballads, typical of the medieval period, are known as **folk ballads.**

Like a work of fiction, a ballad has characters, setting, and dialogue. Like a song, it uses repetition and has regular rhyme and meter. A **traditional ballad**—such as "Lord Randall," the written version of an older folk ballad—has these characteristics:

• consists of four-line stanzas with a simple rhyme scheme

• narrates a single tragic event through dialogue

A ballad's rhyme scheme may be very loose or seem inconsistent. A loose rhyme scheme gave the singer more freedom to improvise lyrics. And, because pronunciations change over time, words that once rhymed may no longer sound alike.

As you read "Ballad" and "Midwinter Blues," consider how these poems expand the traditional ballad form.

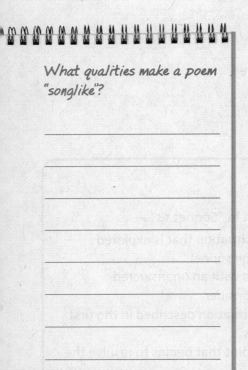

What qualities make a poem "songlike"?

Reading Skill: Understand Dialect

People who live in a particular region or who belong to a particular social or ethnic group may speak in a **dialect,** a variation of a language. Their speech may differ in pronunciation, vocabulary, and grammar from the standard form of the language.

Dialect often provides clues about a poem's setting, as in "Lord Randall," which uses an 18th-century Scottish dialect. It can also reveal information about the speaker's identity, such as ethnicity and social class. This is the case with "Midwinter Blues."

As you read "Lord Randall" and "Midwinter Blues," use the charts below to record key passages written in dialect and to restate them in standard English. An example is provided.

Title: "Lord Randall"	
Speaker's English	**Standard English**
What gat ye to your dinner?	What did you eat?

Title: "Midwinter Blues"	
Speaker's English	**Standard English**

SET A PURPOSE
FOR READING
Read this ballad to find out
why the mother's son is so
weary.

Lord Randall
ANONYMOUS BALLAD

BACKGROUND "Lord Randall" is one of
the oldest and best-known ballads in the
English language. It is found in countless
variations throughout the British Isles and
North America, but the dialogue structure
and basic story is always the same. Although
most scholars believe that "Lord Randall"
has its roots in an Italian ballad of the 1600s,
one scholar has suggested that Lord Randall
was Randolph, the sixth Earl of Chester, who
was poisoned by his wife in 1232.

Ⓐ DIALECT
Reread lines 1–4. Underline
words and phrases that are
written in the **dialect** of the two
speakers. Then add line 4 to the
chart on page 291 and restate it
in standard English.

"Oh where ha'e ye[1] been, Lord Randall my son?
O where ha'e ye been, my handsome young man?"
"I ha'e been to the wild wood: mother, make my bed soon,
For I'm weary wi'[2] hunting, and fain[3] wald[4] lie down." Ⓐ

5 "Where gat ye[5] your dinner, Lord Randall my son?
Where gat ye your dinner, my handsome young man?"
"I dined wi' my true love: mother, make my bed soon,
For I'm weary wi' hunting, and fain wald lie down."

---

1. **ha'e ye** (hā' yē'): have you.
2. **wi'** (wǐ): with.
3. **fain** (fān): gladly, eagerly.
4. **wald** (wǎld): would.
5. **gat ye** (gǎt yē): did you get.

"What gat ye to your dinner, Lord Randall my son?
10 What gat ye to your dinner, my handsome young man?"
"I gat eels boiled in broo:⁶ mother, make my bed soon,
For I'm weary wi' hunting and fain wald lie down."

"What became of your bloodhounds, Lord Randall my son?
What became of your bloodhounds, my handsome young man?"
15 "O they swelled and they died: mother, make my bed soon,
For I'm weary wi' hunting and fain wald lie down."

"O I fear ye are poisoned, Lord Randall my son!
O I fear ye are poisoned, my handsome young man!"
"Oh yes, I am poisoned: mother, make my bed soon,
20 For I'm sick at the heart, and I fain wald lie down." **B**

B BALLAD
Reread lines 17–20 and compare this stanza to previous ones. How does the ballad's pattern of repetition change in the last stanza?

_____

_____

_____

_____

_____

_____

_____

_____

_____

_____

---

6. **broo** (broo): brew, broth.

SET A PURPOSE
FOR READING
Read this ballad (written in
both English and Spanish)
to learn why the speaker
feels betrayed.

Ballad

Poem by
GABRIELA MISTRAL

BACKGROUND Chilean poet Gabriela Mistral
wrote about the lives of everyday people. She
believed the poet has a duty to speak for his or
her own people and age. She once remarked,
"What soul is to the body, so is the artist to his
people." Many of Mistral's poems grapple with
the suicide of her fiancé, Romelio Ureta, who
left Mistral prior to his death.

He passed by with another;
I saw him pass by.
The wind ever sweet
and the path full of peace.
5 And these eyes of mine, wretched,
saw him pass by!

He goes loving another
over the earth in bloom.
The hawthorn[1] is flowering
10 and a song wafts by.
He goes loving another
over the earth in bloom! **C**

He kissed the other
by the shores of the sea.
15 The orange-blossom moon
skimmed over the waves.
And my heart's blood did not taint[2]
the expanse of the sea!

C BALLAD
Reread lines 1–12. Circle words,
phrases, and lines that are
repeated.

---

1. **hawthorn:** a spring-flowering shrub.
2. **taint** (tānt): contaminate.

He will go with another
20 through eternity.
Sweet skies will shine.
(God wills to keep silent.)
And he will go with another
through eternity! **PAUSE & REFLECT**

Translated by Doris Dana

PAUSE & REFLECT
How does the speaker feel at the end of the poem? Explain.

Balada

Poem by
GABRIELA MISTRAL

El pasó con otra;
yo le vi pasar.
Siempre dulce el viento
y el camino en paz.
5 ¡Y estos ojos míseros
le vieron pasar!

El va amando a otra
por la tierra en flor.
Ha abierto el espino;
10 pasa una canción.
¡Y él va amando a otra
por la tierra en flor!

El besó a la otra
a orillas del mar;
15 resbaló en las olas
la luna de azahar.
¡Y no untó mi sangre
la extensión del mar!

El irá con otra
20 por la eternidad
Habrá cielos dulces.
(Dios quiere callar.)
¡Y él irá con otra
por la eternidad!

SET A PURPOSE FOR READING

Read this ballad to find out who is suffering from the "midwinter blues" and why.

Midwinter Blues

Poem by

LANGSTON HUGHES

BACKGROUND Langston Hughes was a central figure of the Harlem Renaissance, a cultural movement of the 1920s and 1930s that celebrated African-American artistic expression. He was one of the first artists to champion the beauty of blues songs, which he called music from "black, beaten, but unbeatable throats." Blues songs and the "low-down folks" who sang them were a lifelong inspiration for Hughes, who drew on their rhythms, motifs, and themes in his writing.

D BALLAD
Reread lines 1–6 and underline the repeating words and phrases.

E DIALECT
Reread lines 1–12 and circle words and phrases that are written in dialect. Then add to the chart on page 291. What does the dialect tell you about the speaker's identity?

_____

_____

_____

In the middle of the winter,
Snow all over the ground.
In the middle of the winter,
Snow all over the ground—
5 'Twas the night befo' Christmas
My good man turned me down. **D**

Don't know's I'd mind his goin'
But he left me when the coal was low.
Don't know's I'd mind his goin'
10 But he left when the coal was low.
Now, if a man loves a woman
That ain't no time to go. **E**

He told me that he loved me
But he must a been tellin' a lie.
15 He told me that he loved me.
He must a been tellin' a lie.
But he's the only man I'll
Love till the day I die.

I'm gonna buy me a rose bud
20 An' plant it at my back door,
Buy me a rose bud,
Plant it at my back door,
So when I'm dead they won't need
No flowers from the store. **PAUSE & REFLECT**

PAUSE & REFLECT
Why do you think the speaker
wants a rose bud planted at her
back door?

_____

_____

_____

_____

Poetic Form: Ballad

Review the notes you took while reading "Lord Randall" and "Ballad." Then complete the following chart to compare how the elements of a traditional ballad are used in both poems.

Ballad Characteristics	"Lord Randall"	"Ballad"
Single tragic event		
Repetition		
Dialogue		
Four-line stanzas		
Regular rhyme and meter		

How does Mistral's poem depart from the traditional ballad form?

_____

_____

_____

Reading Skill: Analyze Dialect

Review the dialect chart you made on page 291. How does dialect help characterize the speakers in "Lord Randall" and "Midwinter Blues"?

_____

_____

_____

When does poetry SING?

Why are poems and songs so often about love and loss?

_____

_____

_____

Academic Vocabulary in Writing

abstract	device	form	literal	tradition

Why do traditional ballads often contain dialect? Recall what you learned about the history of the ballad **form** on page 290, and use at least two Academic Vocabulary words in your response. Definitions for these terms are listed on page 275.

_____

_____

_____

Assessment Practice

DIRECTIONS Use "Lord Randall," "Ballad," and "Midwinter Blues" to answer questions 1–4.

1 Which detail from "Lord Randall" most clearly hints at what will happen to Randall?

  (A) "'I ha'e been to the wild wood'" (line 3)
  (B) "'I dined wi' my true love'" (line 7)
  (C) "'I gat eels boiled in broo'" (line 11)
  (D) "'O they swelled and they died'" (line 15)

2 The story of "Lord Randall" is told in the form of —

  (A) a monologue in which a man tells of his weariness
  (B) a narrative that describes a man hunting in the woods
  (C) a dialogue between a man and his mother
  (D) a letter from a man to his true love

3 What is the situation of the speaker in "Ballad"?

  (A) She loves a man who loves someone else.
  (B) She enjoys the beauty of nature.
  (C) She is losing her eyesight.
  (D) She yearns to fling herself into the sea.

4 The speaker in Hughes's poem has the blues because —

  (A) the harsh winter weather is making her sad
  (B) there is no coal left to heat her house
  (C) she cannot afford to buy flowers at the store
  (D) her man left her on Christmas Eve

8 Signatures

AUTHOR'S STYLE AND VOICE

Be sure to read the Text Analysis Workshop on pp. 850–855 in *Holt McDougal Literature*.

Academic Vocabulary for Unit 8

Preview the following Academic Vocabulary words. You will encounter these words as you work through this book and will use them as you write and talk about the selections in the unit.

clarify (klăr′ə fī′) *v.* to make clear or easier to understand
*A reader uses the author's words to help **clarify** ideas in a selection.*

●

feature (fē′chər) *n.* a special quality or characteristic of something
*One unusual **feature** of this poem is the way the words are arranged on the page to make a picture.*

●

precise (prĭ-sīs′) *adj.* exact; accurately defined or stated
*The language in a selection is not always **precise,** which means that the reader must interpret the work's message.*

●

style (stīl) *n.* a distinctive or original manner of expression
*Every author has a particular **style** that makes his or her writing unique.*

●

transmit (trăns-mĭt′) *v.* to communicate; to send or hand off to others
*Sometimes, writers try to **transmit** ideas about a topic or theme in a poem or short story.*

Think of the different **styles** in books that you've read or movies that you've seen. Are there certain **features** that you look for when choosing a book or movie? Write a few sentences about styles that you like or dislike. Use at least two Academic Vocabulary words in your response.

_____

_____

_____

_____

The Pit and the Pendulum
Short Story by Edgar Allan Poe

What breeds TERROR?

What causes your heart to race and your palms to sweat? Perhaps it's a deserted alley, a snarling dog, or a shadowy stranger. In the following story, you'll read about both the physical and the psychological effects of fear.

LIST IT In the notebook at left, list things that terrify people. What distinguishes the fear of snakes from the fear of being buried alive, for example? Why are some people afraid and others fearless?

Things That Terrify People

1. _____
   _____
2. _____
   _____
3. _____
   _____

Text Analysis: Poe's Style

A writer's **style** is the particular way he or she uses language to communicate ideas. Edgar Allan Poe has a distinctive style that helped create the genre of modern horror literature. The elements in the chart below are characteristics of his style that you should look out for as you read. Examples from the story are provided in the column at right.

Characteristics of Poe's Style	Examples
• a **first-person point of view** in which the narrator expresses emotional intensity, creating a **tone** of horror and terror	*I was sick—sick unto death with that long agony . . .*
• repeated or italicized words	the pit—*whose horrors had been destined for so bold a recusant as myself*—the pit
• unusual choice of words, phrases, and expressions	*the madness of a memory which busies itself among forbidden things*
• long sentences or sentences with interruptions	*They appeared to me white—whiter than the sheet upon which I trace these words—and thin even to grotesqueness; thin with the intensity of their expression of firmness—of immoveable resolution—of stern contempt of human torture.*
• strange or grotesque **sensory images**	

As you read "The Pit and the Pendulum," think about how Poe's choice of narrator affects the tone of the work.

Reading Strategy: Paraphrase

Poe's works can be challenging because they often feature unfamiliar words and complex sentences. One way that you can make sense of his writing as you read is to **paraphrase,** or restate information in your own words. A paraphrase is usually the same length as the original text but contains simpler language.

Poe's Words	Paraphrase
"VERY suddenly there came back to my soul motion and sound" (lines 80–81)	I very quickly regained consciousness and was able to see and hear.

Vocabulary in Context

Note: Words are listed in the order in which they appear in the story.

indeterminate (ĭn′dĭ-tûr′mə-nĭt) *adj.* not precisely known or determined
*It was difficult to plan the fair because of the **indeterminate** weather forecast.*

eloquent (ĕl′ə-kwənt) *adj.* vividly expressive
*The student gave an **eloquent** speech when he received the award.*

lucid (lōō′sĭd) *adj.* clear; mentally sound
*Her **lucid** retelling of the events during the hurricane helped me visualize the storm.*

pervade (pər-vād′) *v.* to spread throughout
*A feeling of joy **pervaded** the family after they heard the good news.*

supposition (sŭp′ə-zĭsh′ən) *n.* something supposed; an assumption
*The **supposition** is that people are innocent until they are proven guilty.*

insuperable (ĭn-sōō′pər-ə-bəl) *adj.* impossible to overcome
*The high, **insuperable** barrier of the mountains blocked the travelers' road.*

lethargy (lĕth′ər-jē) *n.* prolonged sluggishness; unconsciousness
*A feeling of **lethargy** overcame the students on the bus after the big track meet.*

confound (kən-found′) *v.* to confuse or astonish
*The math teacher was **confounded** when every student passed the quiz.*

pertinacity (pûr′tn-ăs′ĭ-tē) *n.* unyielding persistence or adherence
*The **pertinacity** of the players was shown by the number of hours they practiced.*

voracity (vô-răs′ĭ-tē) *n.* greed for food
*The puppies ate the food with great **voracity** until they were full.*

SET A PURPOSE
FOR READING

As you read, note the characteristics of the story's narrator.

The Pit and the Pendulum

Short Story by

EDGAR ALLAN POE

BACKGROUND "The Pit and the Pendulum" is set in the Spanish city of Toledo during the grim age of the Spanish Inquisition. Since the late 15th century, the Inquisition, a court of the Roman Catholic Church, punished people whose beliefs were opposed to church teachings. The punishments often involved torture—physical or mental. In this story, the narrator is a prisoner of the Inquisition. As the story opens, he is brought into the court to hear the judges pass sentences on him.

Ⓐ POE'S STYLE
Read the meaning of the Latin poem in footnote 1. What effect does starting the story with a quatrain in Latin have on your impression of the story?

_____

_____

_____

_____

_____

_____

_____

_____

_____

_____

Impia tortorum longos hic turba furores
Sanguinis innocui, non satiata, aluit.
Sospite nunc patriâ, fracto nunc funeris antro,
Mors ubi dira fuit vita salusque patent.[1]

[Quatrain composed for the gates of a market to be erected upon the site of the Jacobin[2] Club House at Paris.] Ⓐ

I was sick—sick unto death with that long agony; and when they at length unbound me, and I was permitted to sit, I felt that my senses were leaving me. The sentence—the dread sentence of death—was the last of distinct accentuation which reached my ears. After that, the sound of the inquisitorial voices seemed merged in one dreamy <u>indeterminate</u> hum. It conveyed to my soul the idea of *revolution*—perhaps from its association in fancy with the burr of a millwheel. This only for a brief period; for presently I heard no more. Yet, for a while, I saw; but with how

---

1. **Impia . . . patent** *Latin*: Here the wicked crowd of tormentors, unsated, fed their long-time lusts for innocent blood. Now that our homeland is safe, now that the tomb is broken, life and health appear where once was dread death.
2. **Jacobin** (jăk′ə-bĭn): belonging to a radical French political group famous for its terrorist policies during the French Revolution.

indeterminate (ĭn′dĭ-tûr′mə-nĭt) *adj.* not precisely known or determined

10 terrible an exaggeration! I saw the lips of the black-robed judges. They appeared to me white—whiter than the sheet upon which I trace these words—and thin even to grotesqueness; thin with the intensity of their expression of firmness—of immoveable resolution—of stern contempt of human torture. I saw that the decrees of what to me was Fate, were still issuing from those lips. I saw them writhe with a deadly locution.[3] I saw them fashion the syllables of my name; and I shuddered because no sound succeeded. I saw, too, for a few moments of delirious horror, the soft and nearly imperceptible waving of the sable draperies which 20 enwrapped the walls of the apartment.[4] And then my vision fell upon the seven tall candles upon the table. At first they wore the aspect of charity, and seemed white slender angels who would save me; but then, all at once, there came a most deadly nausea over my spirit, and I felt every fiber in my frame thrill as if I had touched the wire of a galvanic[5] battery, while the angel forms became meaningless specters, with heads of flame, and I saw that from them there would be no help. And then there stole into my fancy, like a rich musical note, the thought of what sweet rest there must be in the grave. The thought came gently and stealthily, 30 and it seemed long before it attained full appreciation;[6] but just as my spirit came at length properly to feel and entertain it, the figures of the judges vanished, as if magically, from before me; the tall candles sank into nothingness; their flames went out utterly; the blackness of darkness supervened; all sensations appeared swallowed up in a mad rushing descent as of the soul into Hades.[7] Then silence, and stillness, and night were the universe. **B**

I had swooned;[8] but still will not say that all of consciousness was lost. What of it there remained I will not attempt to define, or even to describe; yet all was not lost. In the deepest slumber—no! 40 In delirium—no! In a swoon—no! In death—no! even in the grave all *is not* lost. Else there is no immortality for man. Arousing

---

3. **locution** (lō-kyōō′shən): speech.
4. **apartment**: room.
5. **galvanic** (găl-văn′ĭk): electric.
6. **attained full appreciation**: was fully understood.
7. **Hades** (hā′dēz): the underworld in Greek mythology.
8. **swooned**: passed out from weakness or distress.

B PARAPHRASE
The narrator sees the judges say his name but does not hear what they say. Paraphrase lines 27–36. What are the narrator's thoughts, and how do these thoughts affect him?

eloquent (ĕl'ə-kwənt) *adj.* vividly expressive

PAUSE & REFLECT
In lines 37–60, the narrator compares fainting, dreaming, and death. What does the narrator seem to think they have in common?

_____

_____

_____

_____

lucid (lōō'sĭd) *adj.* clear; mentally sound

Explain the phrase "**lucid** reason of a later epoch." Use a dictionary to help you.

_____

_____

_____

_____

from the most profound of slumbers, we break the gossamer web of *some* dream. Yet in a second afterward, (so frail may that web have been) we remember not that we have dreamed. In the return to life from the swoon there are two stages; first, that of the sense of mental or spiritual; secondly, that of the sense of physical, existence. It seems probable that if, upon reaching the second stage, we could recall the impressions of the first, we should find these impressions **eloquent** in memories of the gulf beyond. And

50 that gulf is—what? How at least shall we distinguish its shadows from those of the tomb? But if the impressions of what I have termed the first stage, are not, at will, recalled, yet, after long interval, do they not come unbidden, while we marvel whence[9] they come? He who has never swooned, is not he who finds strange palaces and wildly familiar faces in coals that glow; is not he who beholds floating in midair the sad visions that the many may not view; is not he who ponders over the perfume of some novel flower—is not he whose brain grows bewildered with the meaning of some musical cadence which has never before arrested

60 his attention.   **PAUSE & REFLECT**

Amid frequent and thoughtful endeavors to remember; amid earnest struggles to regather some token of the state of seeming nothingness into which my soul had lapsed, there have been moments when I have dreamed of success; there have been brief, very brief periods when I have conjured up remembrances which the **lucid** reason of a later epoch assures me could have had reference only to that condition of seeming unconsciousness. These shadows of memory tell, indistinctly, of tall figures that lifted and bore me in silence

70 down—down—still down—till a hideous dizziness oppressed me at the mere idea of the interminableness of the descent. They tell also of a vague horror at my heart, on account of that heart's unnatural stillness. Then comes a sense of sudden motionlessness throughout all things; as if those who bore me (a ghastly train!) had outrun, in their descent, the limits of the limitless, and paused from the wearisomeness of their toil. After this I call to mind flatness and dampness; and that all is

_____

9. **whence:** from where.

madness—the madness of a memory which busies itself among forbidden things.

80   VERY suddenly there came back to my soul motion and sound—the tumultuous motion of the heart, and, in my ears, the sound of its beating. Then a pause in which all is blank. Then again sound, and motion, and touch—a tingling sensation **pervading** my frame. Then the mere consciousness of existence, without thought—a condition which lasted long. Then, very suddenly, *thought,* and shuddering terror, and earnest endeavor to comprehend my true state. Then a strong desire to lapse into insensibility. Then a rushing revival of soul and a successful effort to move. And now a full memory of the trial, of the judges, of
90   the sable draperies, of the sentence, of the sickness, of the swoon. Then entire forgetfulness of all that followed; of all that a later day and much earnestness of endeavor have enabled me vaguely to recall. **C**

So far, I had not opened my eyes. I felt that I lay upon my back, unbound. I reached out my hand, and it fell heavily upon something damp and hard. There I suffered[10] it to remain for many minutes, while I strove to imagine where and *what* I could be. I longed, yet dared not to employ my vision. I dreaded the first glance at objects around me. It was not that I feared to look upon
100   things horrible, but that I grew aghast lest there should be *nothing* to see. At length, with a wild desperation at heart, I quickly unclosed my eyes. My worst thoughts, then, were confirmed. The blackness of eternal night encompassed me. I struggled for breath. The intensity of the darkness seemed to oppress and stifle me. The atmosphere was intolerably close. I still lay quietly, and made effort to exercise my reason. I brought to mind the inquisitorial proceedings, and attempted from that point to deduce my real condition. The sentence had passed; and it appeared to me that a very long interval of time had since elapsed. Yet not for a
110   moment did I suppose myself actually dead. Such a **supposition,** notwithstanding what we read in fiction, is altogether inconsistent

---

10. **suffered:** allowed.

pervade (pər-vād′) *v.* to spread throughout

C PARAPHRASE
Use the chart below to record Poe's words from line 80 through the word *frame* in line 84. Then paraphrase the lines in the next box.

Poe's Words

↓

Paraphrase

supposition (sŭp′ə-zĭsh′ən) *n.* something supposed; an assumption

D POE'S STYLE
Reread lines 120–132. Underline
the **unusual words and phrases**
that express the narrator's dread
of the dungeon. What is "the
most hideous of fates"?

_____

_____

_____

_____

_____

E PARAPHRASE
Finish the paraphrase of
lines 133–142 started below.

Now as I stepped carefully

forward, I suddenly

remembered the rumors

I had heard about the

dungeons in Toledo.

_____

_____

_____

_____

_____

_____

_____

_____

_____

with real existence;—but where and in what state was I? The
condemned to death, I knew, perished usually at the *autos-da-fé*,[11]
and one of these had been held on the very night of the day of
my trial. Had I been remanded to my dungeon, to await the next
sacrifice, which would not take place for many months? This I at
once saw could not be. Victims had been in immediate demand.
Moreover, my dungeon, as well as all the condemned cells at
Toledo, had stone floors, and light was not altogether excluded.

120   A fearful idea now suddenly drove the blood in torrents
upon my heart, and for a brief period, I once more relapsed
into insensibility. Upon recovering, I at once started to my feet,
trembling convulsively in every fiber. I thrust my arms wildly
above and around me in all directions. I felt nothing; yet dreaded
to move a step, lest I should be impeded by the walls of the *tomb*.
Perspiration burst from every pore and stood in cold big beads on
my forehead. The agony of suspense grew at length intolerable,
and I cautiously moved forward, with my arms extended, and my
eyes straining from their sockets, in the hope of catching some
130 faint ray of light. I proceeded for many paces; but still all was
blackness and vacancy. I breathed more freely. It seemed evident
that mine was not, at least, the most hideous of fates. **D**

    And now, as I still continued to step cautiously onward, there
came thronging upon my recollection a thousand vague rumors
of the horrors of Toledo. Of the dungeons there had been strange
things narrated—fables I had always deemed them—but yet
strange, and too ghastly to repeat, save in a whisper. Was I left
to perish of starvation in the subterranean world of darkness; or
what fate, perhaps even more fearful, awaited me? That the result
140 would be death, and a death of more than customary bitterness, I
knew too well the character of my judges to doubt. The mode and
the hour were all that occupied or distracted me. **E**

    My outstretched hands at length encountered some solid
obstruction. It was a wall, seemingly of stone masonry—very
smooth, slimy, and cold. I followed it up! stepping with all the
careful distrust with which certain antique narratives had inspired

---

11. *autos-da-fé* (ou'tōz-də-fā') *Portuguese:* acts of faith—public executions of
people tried by the Inquisition, carried out by the civil authorities.

me. This process, however, afforded me no means of ascertaining the dimensions of my dungeon; as I might make its circuit, and return to the point whence I set out, without being aware of the fact; so perfectly uniform seemed the wall. I therefore sought the knife which had been in my pocket, when led into the inquisitorial chamber; but it was gone; my clothes had been exchanged for a wrapper of coarse serge.[12] I had thought of forcing the blade in some minute crevice of the masonry, so as to identify my point of departure. The difficulty, nevertheless, was but trivial; although, in the disorder of my fancy, it seemed at first **insuperable**. I tore a part of the hem from the robe and placed the fragment at full length, and at right angles to the wall. In groping my way around the prison I could not fail to encounter this rag upon completing the circuit. So, at least I thought: but I had not counted upon the extent of the dungeon, or upon my own weakness. The ground was moist and slippery. I staggered onward for some time, when I stumbled and fell. My excessive fatigue induced me to remain prostrate; and sleep soon overtook me as I lay.

UPON awakening, and stretching forth an arm, I found beside me a loaf and a pitcher with water. I was too much exhausted to reflect upon this circumstance, but ate and drank with avidity. Shortly afterward, I resumed my tour around the prison, and with much toil, came at last upon the fragment of the serge. Up to the period when I fell I had counted fifty-two paces, and upon resuming my walk, I counted forty-eight more;—when I arrived at the rag. There were in all, then, a hundred paces; and, admitting two paces to the yard, I presumed the dungeon to be fifty yards in circuit. I had met, however, with many angles in the wall, and thus I could form no guess at the shape of the vault; for vault I could not help supposing it to be. **G**

I had little object—certainly no hope—in these researches; but a vague curiosity prompted me to continue them. Quitting the wall, I resolved to cross the area of the enclosure. At first I proceeded with extreme caution, for the floor, although seemingly

insuperable (ĭn-sōō′pər-ə-bəl) *adj.* impossible to overcome

What does the narrator think will be **insuperable**?

_____

_____

_____

G POE'S STYLE
In lines 165–176, the narrator seems more focused than in earlier passages. What elements of Poe's style did you find in previous paragraphs that you do not find here?

_____

_____

_____

_____

_____

_____

_____

_____

_____

12. **serge** (sûrj): a woolen cloth.

G POE'S STYLE
Reread lines 187–205. Look for Poe's use of **sensory images**—words and phrases that appeal to the senses. Circle the details that help you envision the pit. Then write a description of the pit in your own words.

_____

_____

_____

_____

_____

_____

_____

_____

_____

_____

_____

_____

_____

_____

_____

_____

_____

_____

of solid material, was treacherous with slime. At length, however, I took courage, and did not hesitate to step firmly; endeavoring to cross in as direct a line as possible. I had advanced some ten or twelve paces in this manner, when the remnant of the torn hem of my robe became entangled between my legs. I stepped on it, and fell violently on my face.

In the confusion attending my fall, I did not immediately apprehend a somewhat startling circumstance, which yet, in a few seconds afterward, and while I still lay prostrate, arrested
190 my attention. It was this—my chin rested upon the floor of the prison, but my lips and the upper portion of my head, although seemingly at a less elevation than the chin, touched nothing. At the same time my forehead seemed bathed in a clammy vapor, and the peculiar smell of decayed fungus arose to my nostrils. I put forward my arm, and shuddered to find that I had fallen at the very brink of a circular pit, whose extent, of course, I had no means of ascertaining at the moment. Groping about the masonry just below the margin, I succeeded in dislodging a small fragment, and let it fall into the abyss. For many seconds I hearkened to its
200 reverberations as it dashed against the sides of the chasm in its descent; at length there was a sullen plunge into water, succeeded by loud echoes. At the same moment there came a sound resembling the quick opening, and as rapid closing of a door overhead, while a faint gleam of light flashed suddenly through the gloom, and as suddenly faded away. **G**

I saw clearly the doom which had been prepared for me, and congratulated myself upon the timely accident by which I had escaped. Another step before my fall, and the world had seen me no more. And the death just avoided, was of that very character
210 which I had regarded as fabulous and frivolous in the tales respecting the Inquisition. To the victims of its tyranny, there was the choice of death with its direst physical agonies, or death with its most hideous moral horrors. I had been reserved for the latter. By long suffering my nerves had been unstrung, until I trembled

at the sound of my own voice, and had become in every respect a fitting subject for the species of torture which awaited me.

Shaking in every limb, I groped my way back to the wall; resolving there to perish rather than risk the terrors of the wells, of which my imagination now pictured many in various positions 220 about the dungeon. In other conditions of mind I might have had courage to end my misery at once by a plunge into one of these abysses; but now I was the veriest of cowards. Neither could I forget what I had read of these pits—that the *sudden* extinction of life formed no part of their most horrible plan. **H**

Agitation of spirit kept me awake for many long hours; but at length I again slumbered. Upon arousing, I found by my side as before, a loaf and a pitcher of water. A burning thirst consumed me, and I emptied the vessel at a draft. It must have been drugged; for scarcely had I drunk, before I became irresistibly 230 drowsy. A deep sleep fell upon me—a sleep like that of death. How long it lasted of course, I know not; but when, once again, I unclosed my eyes, the objects around me were visible. By a wild sulphurous luster,[13] the origin of which I could not at first determine, I was enabled to see the extent and aspect of the prison.

IN its size I had been greatly mistaken. The whole circuit of its walls did not exceed twenty-five yards. For some minutes this fact occasioned me a world of vain trouble;[14] vain indeed! for what could be of less importance, under the terrible circumstances 240 which environed me, than the mere dimensions of my dungeon? But my soul took a wild interest in trifles, and I busied myself in endeavors to account for the error I had committed in my measurement. The truth at length flashed upon me. In my first attempt at exploration I had counted fifty-two paces, up to the period when I fell; I must then have been within a pace or two of the fragments of serge; in fact, I had nearly performed the circuit of the vault. I then slept, and upon awaking, I must have returned upon my steps—thus supposing the circuit nearly double what it

H PARAPHRASE
Finish the paraphrase started below of lines 217–224. Think about the narrator's opinion of himself. Do you agree or disagree with his view?

Shaking all over, I felt my way back to the wall, deciding to die there rather than fall into one of the pits, which I now imagined around me.

---

13. **sulphurous** (sŭl'fə-rəs) **luster:** fiery glow.
14. **occasioned . . . trouble:** caused me a great deal of useless worry.

lethargy (lĕth′ər-jē) *n.* prolonged sluggishness; unconsciousness

❶ POE'S STYLE
In lines 252–269, Poe uses **personification** to describe the pit. Underline the words in this passage that describe the pit as a person. Then explain what effect this style has on the image that is created.

_____

_____

_____

_____

_____

_____

_____

_____

_____

_____

_____

_____

_____

actually was. My confusion of mind prevented me from observing
250 that I began my tour with the wall to the left, and ended it with
the wall to the right.

I had been deceived, too, in respect to the shape of the
enclosure. In feeling my way around I had found many angles, and
thus deduced an idea of great irregularity; so potent is the effect
of total darkness upon one arousing from **lethargy** or sleep! The
angles were simply those of a few slight depressions, or niches, at
odd intervals. The general shape of the prison was square. What I
had taken for masonry seemed now to be iron, or some other metal,
in huge plates, whose sutures or joints occasioned the depression.
260 The entire surface of this metallic enclosure was rudely daubed
in all the hideous and repulsive devices to which the charnel
superstitions[15] of the monks has given rise. The figures of fiends
in aspects of menace, with skeleton forms, and other more really
fearful images, overspread and disfigured the walls. I observed
that the outlines of these monstrosities were sufficiently distinct,
but that the colors seemed faded and blurred, as if from the effects
of a damp atmosphere. I now noticed the floor, too, which was of
stone. In the center yawned the circular pit from whose jaws I had
escaped; but it was the only one in the dungeon. ❶

270 ALL this I saw distinctly and by much effort: for my personal
condition had been greatly changed during slumber. I now lay
upon my back, and at full length, on a species of low framework
of wood. To this I was securely bound by a long strap resembling
a surcingle.[16] It passed in many convolutions about my limbs and
body, leaving at liberty only my head, and my left arm to such
extent that I could, by dint[17] of much exertion, supply myself with
food from an earthen dish which lay by my side on the floor. I
saw, to my horror, that the pitcher had been removed. I say to my
horror; for I was consumed with intolerable thirst. This thirst it
280 appeared to be the design of my persecutors to stimulate: for the
food in the dish was meat pungently seasoned.

---

15. **charnel** (chär′nəl) **superstitions:** ghastly irrational beliefs.
16. **surcingle** (sûr′sĭng′gəl): a band used to tie a pack or saddle to a horse.
17. **dint:** force.

Looking upward I surveyed the ceiling of my prison. It was some thirty or forty feet overhead, and constructed much as the side walls. In one of its panels a very singular figure riveted my whole attention. It was the painted figure of Time as he is commonly represented, save that, in lieu of a scythe, he held what, at a casual glance, I supposed to be the pictured image of a huge pendulum such as we see on antique clocks. There was something, however, in the appearance of this machine which caused me to

290 regard it more attentively. While I gazed directly upward at it (for its position was immediately over my own) I fancied that I saw it in motion. In an instant afterward the fancy was confirmed. Its sweep was brief, and of course slow. I watched it for some minutes, somewhat in fear, but more in wonder. Wearied at length with observing its dull movement, I turned my eyes upon the other objects in the cell.

A slight noise attracted my notice, and, looking to the floor, I saw several enormous rats traversing it. They had issued from the well, which lay just within view to my right. Even then, while

300 I gazed, they came up in troops, hurriedly, with ravenous eyes, allured by the scent of the meat. From this it required much effort and attention to scare them away. **J**

It might have been half an hour, perhaps even an hour, (for I could take but imperfect note of time) before I again cast my eyes upward. What I then saw **confounded** and amazed me. The sweep of the pendulum had increased in extent by nearly a yard. As a natural consequence, its velocity was also much greater. But what mainly disturbed me was the idea that it had perceptibly *descended*. I now observed—with what horror it is

310 needless to say—that its nether extremity was formed of a crescent of glittering steel, about a foot in length from horn to horn; the horns upward, and the under edge evidently as keen as that of a razor. Like a razor also, it seemed massy and heavy, tapering from the edge into a solid and broad structure above. It was appended to a weighty rod of brass, and the whole *hissed* as it swung through the air.

J PARAPHRASE
The narrator has just given a detailed description of his cell. What position does he find himself in now? What else is in the room? Paraphrase lines 282–302.

_____

_____

_____

_____

_____

_____

_____

_____

_____

confound (kən-found′) *v.* to confuse or astonish

K POE'S STYLE
In lines 303–329, underline the various **italicized words** that Poe includes. What do these words emphasize?

_____

_____

_____

_____

_____

PAUSE & REFLECT
What besides the idea of a painful death fills the narrator with fear and begins to drive him insane in lines 330–340?

_____

_____

_____

_____

_____

_____

_____

_____

_____

_____

I could no longer doubt the doom prepared for me by monkish ingenuity in torture. My cognizance of the pit had become known to the inquisitorial agents—*the pit* whose horrors had been destined for so bold a recusant[18] as myself—*the pit*, typical of hell, and regarded by rumor as the Ultima Thule[19] of all their punishments. The plunge into this pit I had avoided by the merest of accidents, and I knew that surprise, or entrapment into torment, formed an important portion of all the grotesquerie of these dungeon deaths. Having failed to fall, it was no part of the demon plan to hurl me into the abyss; and thus (there being no alternative) a different and a milder destruction awaited me. Milder! I half smiled in my agony as I thought of such application of such a term. **K**

What boots it[20] to tell of the long, long hours of horror more than mortal, during which I counted the rushing vibrations of the steel! Inch by inch—line by line—with a descent only appreciable at intervals that seemed ages—down and still down it came! Days passed—it might have been that many days passed—ere it swept so closely over me as to fan me with its acrid breath. The odor of the sharp steel forced itself into my nostrils. I prayed—I wearied heaven with my prayer for its more speedy descent. I grew frantically mad, and struggled to force myself upward against the sweep of the fearful scimitar.[21] And then I fell suddenly calm, and lay smiling at the glittering death, as a child at some rare bauble. **PAUSE & REFLECT**

THERE was another interval of utter insensibility; it was brief; for, upon again lapsing into life there had been no perceptible descent in the pendulum. But it might have been long; for I knew there were demons who took note of my swoon, and who could have arrested the vibration at pleasure. Upon my recovery, too, I felt very—oh, inexpressibly sick and weak, as if through long

---

18. **recusant** (rĕk'yə-zənt): a religious dissenter; heretic.
19. **Ultima Thule** (ŭl'tə-mə thōō'lē): according to ancient geographers, the most remote region of the habitable world—here used figuratively to mean "most extreme achievement; summit."
20. **what boots it:** what good is it.
21. **scimitar** (sĭm'ĭ-tər): a curved, single-edged Asian sword.

inanition.[22] Even amid the agonies of that period, the human nature craved food. With painful effort I outstretched my left arm as far as my bonds permitted, and took possession of the small remnant which had been spared me by the rats. As I put a portion of it within my lips, there rushed to my mind a half formed thought of joy—of hope. Yet what business had I with hope? It was, as I say, a half formed thought—man has many such which are never completed. I felt that it was of joy—of hope; but I felt also that it had perished in its formation. In vain I struggled to perfect—to regain it. Long suffering had nearly annihilated all my ordinary powers of mind. I was an imbecile—an idiot. **PAUSE & REFLECT**

The vibration of the pendulum was at right angles to my length. I saw that the crescent was designed to cross the region of the heart. It would fray the serge of my robe—it would return and repeat its operations—again—and again. Notwithstanding its terrifically wide sweep (some thirty feet or more) and the hissing vigor of its descent, sufficient to sunder these very walls of iron, still the fraying of my robe would be all that, for several minutes, it would accomplish. And at this thought I paused. I dared not go farther than this reflection. I dwelt upon it with a **pertinacity** of attention—as if, in so dwelling, I could arrest *here* the descent of the steel. I forced myself to ponder upon the sound of the crescent as it should pass across the garment—upon the peculiar thrilling sensation which the friction of cloth produces on the nerves. I pondered upon all this frivolity until my teeth were on edge.

Down—steadily down it crept. I took a frenzied pleasure in contrasting its downward with its lateral velocity. To the right—to the left—far and wide—with the shriek of a . . . spirit; to my heart with the stealthy pace of the tiger! I alternately laughed and howled as the one or the other idea grew predominant.

Down—certainly, relentlessly down! It vibrated within three inches of my bosom! I struggled violently, furiously, to free my left arm. This was free only from the elbow to the hand. I could reach the latter, from the platter beside me, to my mouth, with great effort, but no farther. Could I have broken the fastenings

---

22. **inanition** (ĭn′ə-nĭsh′ən): wasting away from lack of food.

PAUSE & REFLECT
In lines 352–353, the narrator says that "a half formed thought of joy—of hope" rushes into his mind. What do you think it means that he uses the words "joy" and "hope"?

_____

_____

_____

_____

_____

_____

_____

pertinacity (pûr′tn-ăs′ĭ-tē) *n.* unyielding persistence or adherence

Complete the following sentence: The narrator focuses on the pendulum with **pertinacity** because _____

_____

_____

_____

_____

_____

_____

❶ POE'S STYLE
Reread lines 373–395. Which stylistic devices help communicate the narrator's growing fear? If you need help, review the meaning of each stylistic device introduced on page 302 and then look for examples in the passage.

above the elbow, I would have seized and attempted to arrest the pendulum. I might as well have attempted to arrest an avalanche!

Down—still unceasingly—still inevitably down! I gasped and struggled at each vibration. I shrunk convulsively at its every sweep. My eyes followed its outward or upward whirls with the eagerness of the most unmeaning despair; they closed themselves spasmodically at the descent, although death would have been a relief, oh! how unspeakable! Still I quivered in every nerve to think how slight a sinking of the machinery would precipitate that keen, glistening axe upon my bosom. It was *hope* that prompted the nerve to quiver—the frame to shrink. It was *hope*—the hope that triumphs on the rack[23]—that whispers to the death-condemned even in the dungeons of the Inquisition. ❶

I saw that some ten or twelve vibrations would bring the steel in actual contact with my robe, and with this observation there suddenly came over my spirit all the keen, collected calmness of despair. For the first time during many hours—or perhaps days—I *thought*. It now occurred to me that the bandage, or surcingle, which enveloped me, was *unique*. I was tied by no separate cord. The first stroke of the razor-like crescent athwart[24] any portion of the band, would so detach it that it might be unwound from my person by means of my left hand. But how fearful, in that case, the proximity of the steel! The result of the slightest struggle how deadly! Was it likely, moreover, that the minions[25] of the torturer had not foreseen and provided for this possibility! Was it probable that the bandage crossed my bosom in the track of the pendulum? Dreading to find my faint, and, as it seemed, my last hope frustrated, I so far elevated my head as to obtain a distinct view of my breast. The surcingle enveloped my limbs and body close in all directions—*save in the path of the destroying crescent.*

Scarcely had I dropped my head back into its original position, when there flashed upon my mind what I cannot better describe than as the unformed half of that idea of deliverance to which I have previously alluded, and of which a moiety[26] only floated

---

23. **rack:** a device for torturing people by gradually stretching their bodies.
24. **athwart:** across.
25. **minions** (mĭn'yənz): followers; servants.
26. **moiety** (moi'ĭ-tē): half.

indeterminately through my brain when I raised food to my burning lips. The whole thought was now present—feeble, scarcely sane, scarcely definite,—but still entire. I proceeded at once, with the nervous energy of despair, to attempt its execution.

For many hours the immediate vicinity of the low framework upon which I lay, had been literally swarming with rats. They were wild, bold, ravenous; their red eyes glaring upon me as if they waited but for motionlessness on my part to make me their prey. "To what food," I thought, "have they been accustomed in the well?" ⓜ

They had devoured, in spite of all my efforts to prevent them, all but a small remnant of the contents of the dish. I had fallen into an habitual see-saw, or wave of the hand about the platter, and, at length, the unconscious uniformity of the movement deprived it of effect. In their **voracity** the vermin frequently fastened their sharp fangs into my fingers. With the particles of the oily and spicy viand[27] which now remained, I thoroughly rubbed the bandage wherever I could reach it; then, raising my hand from the floor, I lay breathlessly still. ⓝ

At first the ravenous animals were startled and terrified at the change—at the cessation of movement. They shrank alarmedly back; many sought the well. But this was only for a moment. I had not counted in vain upon their voracity. Observing that I remained without motion, one or two of the boldest leaped upon the framework, and smelt at the surcingle. This seemed the signal for a general rush. Forth from the well they hurried in fresh troops. They clung to the wood—they overran it, and leaped in hundreds upon my person. The measured movement of the pendulum disturbed them not at all. Avoiding its strokes they busied themselves with the anointed bandage. They pressed—they swarmed upon me in ever accumulating heaps. They writhed upon my throat; their cold lips sought my own; I was half stifled by their thronging pressure; disgust, for which the world has no name, swelled my bosom, and chilled, with a heavy clamminess, my heart. Yet one minute, and I felt that the struggle would be

420

430

440

450

27. **viand** (vī'ənd): food.

ⓜ **POE'S STYLE**
How do Poe's sensory images in the description of the rats in lines 422–427 affect you as the reader?

_____

_____

_____

_____

_____

voracity (vô-răs'ĭ-tē) n. greed for food

ⓝ **PARAPHRASE**
Paraphrase lines 428–436. Why does the narrator rub the binding with the meat? What does he expect will happen?

_____

_____

_____

_____

_____

_____

_____

⊙ POE'S STYLE

Reread lines 456–484. How does Poe's use of the first-person point of view affect what you know?

_____

_____

_____

_____

_____

_____

_____

_____

_____

_____

_____

_____

_____

_____

_____

_____

_____

_____

_____

over. Plainly I perceived the loosening of the bandage. I knew that in more than one place it must be already severed. With a more than human resolution I lay _still_.

Nor had I erred in my calculations—nor had I endured in vain. I at length felt that I was _free_. The surcingle hung in ribands[28] from my body. But the stroke of the pendulum already pressed upon my bosom. It had divided the serge of the robe. It had cut
460 through the linen beneath. Twice again it swung, and a sharp sense of pain shot through every nerve. But the moment of escape had arrived. At a wave of my hand my deliverers hurried tumultuously away. With a steady movement—cautious, sidelong, shrinking, and slow—I slid from the embrace of the bandage and beyond the reach of the scimitar. For the moment, at least, _I was free_.

Free!—and in the grasp of the Inquisition! I had scarcely stepped from my wooden bed of horror upon the stone floor of the prison, when the motion of the hellish machine ceased and I beheld it drawn up, by some invisible force, through the ceiling.
470 This was a lesson which I took desperately to heart. My every motion was undoubtedly watched. Free!—I had but escaped death in one form of agony, to be delivered unto worse than death in some other. With that thought I rolled my eyes nervously around the barriers of iron that hemmed me in. Something unusual—some change which at first I could not appreciate distinctly—it was obvious, had taken place in the apartment. For many minutes in a dreamy and trembling abstraction, I busied myself in vain, unconnected conjecture. During this period, I became aware, for the first time, of the origin of the sulphurous
480 light which illuminated the cell. It proceeded from a fissure, about half an inch in width, extending entirely around the prison at the base of the walls, which thus appeared, and were, completely separated from the floor. I endeavored, but of course in vain, to look through the aperture.[29] ⊙

As I arose from the attempt, the mystery of the alteration in the chamber broke at once upon my understanding. I have observed that, although the outlines of the figures upon the walls were

---

28. **ribands** (rĭb'əndz): ribbons.
29. **aperture** (ăp'ər-chər): opening.

sufficiently distinct, yet the colors seemed blurred and indefinite. These colors had now assumed, and were momentarily assuming, a startling and most intense brilliancy, that gave to the spectral and fiendish portraitures an aspect that might have thrilled even firmer nerves than my own. Demon eyes, of a wild and ghastly vivacity, glared upon me in a thousand directions, where none had been visible before, and gleamed with the lurid luster of a fire that I could not force my imagination to regard as unreal.

Unreal!—Even while I breathed there came to my nostrils the breath of the vapor of heated iron! A suffocating odor pervaded the prison! A deeper glow settled each moment in the eyes that glared at my agonies! A richer tint of crimson diffused itself over the pictured horrors of blood. I panted! I gasped for breath! There could be no doubt of the design of my tormentors—oh! most unrelenting! oh! most demoniac of men! I shrank from the glowing metal to the center of the cell. Amid the thought of the fiery destruction that impended, the idea of the coolness of the well came over my soul like balm. I rushed to its deadly brink. I threw my straining vision below. The glare from the enkindled roof illumined its inmost recesses. Yet, for a wild moment, did my spirit refuse to comprehend the meaning of what I saw. At length it forced—it wrestled its way into my soul—it burned itself in upon my shuddering reason.—Oh! for a voice to speak!—oh! horror!—oh! any horror but this! With a shriek, I rushed from the margin, and buried my face in my hands—weeping bitterly. ⓟ

The heat rapidly increased, and once again I looked up, shuddering as with a fit of the ague.[30] There had been a second change in the cell—and now the change was obviously in the form. As before, it was in vain that I, at first, endeavored to appreciate or understand what was taking place. But not long was I left in doubt. The Inquisitorial vengeance had been hurried by my two-fold escape, and there was to be no more dallying with the King of Terrors. The room had been square. I saw that two of its iron angles were now acute—two, consequently, obtuse. The fearful difference quickly increased with a low rumbling or

490
500
510
520

ⓟ **POE'S STYLE**
Reread lines 496–512. What does the **punctuation** used by Poe suggest about the narrator's emotional state?

_____

_____

_____

_____

_____

_____

_____

_____

_____

_____

---

30. **the ague** (ā′gyo͞o): a feverish illness.

PAUSE & REFLECT

Reread lines 513–538. What crisis does the narrator face after he escapes from his "bed of horror"?

_____

_____

_____

_____

_____

_____

_____

_____

_____

_____

_____

moaning sound. In an instant the apartment had shifted its form into that of a lozenge. But the alteration stopped not here—I neither hoped nor desired it to stop. I could have clasped the red walls to my bosom as a garment of eternal peace. "Death," I said, "any death but that of the pit!" Fool! might I have not known that *into the pit* it was the object of the burning iron to urge me? Could I resist its glow? or, if even that, could I withstand its
530 pressure? And now, flatter and flatter grew the lozenge, with a rapidity that left me no time for contemplation. Its center, and of course, its greatest width, came just over the yawning gulf. I shrank back—but the closing walls pressed me resistlessly onward. At length for my seared and writhing body there was no longer an inch of foothold on the firm floor of the prison. I struggled no more, but the agony of my soul found vent in one loud, long, and final scream of despair. I felt that I tottered upon the brink—I averted my eyes— **PAUSE & REFLECT**

There was a discordant hum of human voices! There was a
540 loud blast of many trumpets! There was a harsh grating as of a thousand thunders! The fiery walls rushed back! An outstretched arm caught my own as I fell, fainting, into the abyss. It was that of General Lasalle. The French army had entered Toledo. The Inquisition was in the hands of its enemies.

Text Analysis: Poe's Style

Poe has fascinated readers with his tales of horror. In the chart below, provide examples of the stylistic characteristics of "The Pit and the Pendulum."

Stylistic Characteristics	Example from "The Pit and the Pendulum"
a first-person point of view that expresses emotional intensity, creating a tone of horror and terror	
repeated or italicized words	
unusual choice of words, phrases, and expressions	
long sentences or sentences with interruptions	
strange or grotesque sensory images	

Review your notes for "The Pit and the Pendulum" and the chart above. Which of the elements of Poe's style did you enjoy the most? Explain.

_____

_____

_____

Reading Strategy: Paraphrase

Review the notes you took while reading. Paraphrase the story's conclusion in the chart below. Then, answer the question below.

My Paraphrase of lines 539–544

_____

_____

_____

_____

_____

Do you think the narrator is truly saved, or is he simply imagining a rescue as he falls? Explain.

_____

_____

_____

_____

_____

What breeds **TERROR?**

What could a person do to overcome his or her fear?

_____

_____

Vocabulary Practice

Decide whether the words in each pair are synonyms or antonyms. Write **S** for synonyms or **A** for antonyms.

_____ 1. precise/indeterminate

_____ 2. eloquent/inarticulate

_____ 3. lucid/clear

_____ 4. spread/pervade

_____ 5. supposition/evidence

_____ 6. insuperable/unconquerable

_____ 7. lethargy/excitement

_____ 8. bewilder/confound

_____ 9. reluctance/pertinacity

_____ 10. hunger/voracity

Academic Vocabulary in Writing

clarify	feature	precise	style	transmit

How do the **features** and **style** of "The Pit and the Pendulum" compare to frightening movies you have seen or books you have read? Use at least one Academic Vocabulary word in your answer. Definitions for these terms are listed on page 301.

_____

_____

_____

_____

_____

Assessment Practice

DIRECTIONS Use "The Pit and the Pendulum" to answer questions 1–4.

1 The first two dangers the narrator faces in the story are the —
- (A) scorching walls and the pit
- (B) rats and the pendulum
- (C) pit and the pendulum
- (D) pendulum and the scorching walls

2 What does the narrator fear more than the actual pain of death?
- (A) the long hours and possibly days of waiting
- (B) the lack of time to think about ways to escape
- (C) the rats swarming over him looking for food
- (D) the idea that he is being watched continuously

3 In lines 330–341, what does the punctuation used by Poe most likely suggest about the narrator's emotional state?
- (A) The narrator is hopeful that he will be released soon.
- (B) The narrator thinks that he can escape the prison if he is calm.
- (C) The narrator is frightened, but determined to fight back.
- (D) The narrator is extremely frightened and in mental anguish.

4 Who or what seems to save the narrator at the end?
- (A) The torturers decide that the man is actually innocent.
- (B) An officer of the conquering French army arrives.
- (C) The fires go out as the walls reach the well.
- (D) A friend convinces the torturers to let the narrator go.

Birches
Poem by **Robert Frost**

Mending Wall
Poem by **Robert Frost**

How can **NATURE** inspire you?

Spending time in nature can inspire us to think beyond our everyday routines. Whether it's hiking through the woods or canoeing down a river, being outside can help us appreciate our place in the world at large. In the following poems by Robert Frost, the speakers gain insights into their own lives through their experiences with nature.

QUICKWRITE Think of an outdoor activity that says something about you and what you're like—such as bird watching, fishing, playing basketball, or swimming. In the notebook at left, write a few sentences describing the activity and what it has helped you realize about yourself.

Text Analysis: Frost's Style

In many ways, Robert Frost reflects the poetry styles of both the 19th and 20th centuries. Like writers before him, Frost loved and wrote about the natural world, particularly rural New England. However, his poems contain more than his impressions of simple country life. Frost often uses humor to point to more serious matters, such as themes of solitude and isolation. See the chart below for key aspects of Frost's style.

Key Aspects of Frost's Style
• conversational or **colloquial language** (informal language)
• rich sensory **imagery** (words and phrases that evoke a picture or sensation)
• imaginative **similes** and **metaphors** (comparisons between unrelated things)
• realistic **dialogue** (people speaking to one another)
• a playful, mocking **tone** (attitude the writer takes towards its subject or audience)

As you read, notice how these stylistic techniques help make "Birches" and "Mending Wall" works of beauty and complexity.

Things I've Learned from Being Outdoors

Reading Skill: Make Inferences

In modern poetry, speakers do not often make direct statements about their viewpoints. Instead, readers must use clues in the texts to **make inferences**, or logical guesses, about the speakers' ideas and feelings. Read the following lines from "Birches" and think about what the speaker wants:

So was I once myself a swinger of birches.
And so I dream of going back to be.

The speaker is saying he once swung on birches as a small boy and he dreams of being a child again. As you read each poem, try to "read between the lines" and record your inferences in the chart below. An example has been given for you.

"Birches"		
Poem Details	**My Association**	**Inferences**
When I see birches bend to left and right / Across the lines of straighter darker trees / I like to think some boy's been swinging them. (lines 1–3)	Birches are white, flexible trees.	Seeing bent birches makes the speaker invent a playful explanation for them.

"Mending Wall"		
Poem Details	**My Association**	**Inferences**

SET A PURPOSE FOR READING

As you read, think about the views of the life that the poem conveys.

Birches

Poem by

ROBERT FROST

BACKGROUND In "Birches," Robert Frost paints a vivid picture of the skinny white-barked trees that adorn much of the countryside in New England. Their trunks are remarkably flexible—a fact that gives this poem its realistic base. Children do, in fact, climb and swing on birch trees.

Ⓐ FROST'S STYLE

Frost uses plain and **colloquial words**—such as contractions, shortened forms of words—throughout this poem. Underline one or two examples in lines 1–13. What effect do these everyday words create?

_____

_____

_____

_____

_____

_____

When I see birches bend to left and right
Across the lines of straighter darker trees,
I like to think some boy's been swinging them.
But swinging doesn't bend them down to stay
5 As ice-storms do. Often you must have seen them
Loaded with ice a sunny winter morning
After a rain. They click upon themselves
As the breeze rises, and turn many-colored
As the stir cracks and crazes their enamel.
10 Soon the sun's warmth makes them shed crystal shells
Shattering and avalanching on the snow-crust—
Such heaps of broken glass to sweep away
You'd think the inner dome of heaven had fallen. Ⓐ
They are dragged to the withered bracken[1] by the load,
15 And they seem not to break; though once they are bowed
So low for long, they never right themselves:
You may see their trunks arching in the woods

---

1. **bracken:** weedy ferns having large triangular fronds and often forming dense thickets.

Years afterwards, trailing their leaves on the ground
Like girls on hands and knees that throw their hair
20 Before them over their heads to dry in the sun. **B**
But I was going to say when Truth broke in
With all her matter-of-fact about the ice-storm
I should prefer to have some boy bend them
As he went out and in to fetch the cows—
25 Some boy too far from town to learn baseball,
Whose only play was what he found himself,
Summer or winter, and could play alone. **C**
One by one he subdued[2] his father's trees
By riding them down over and over again
30 Until he took the stiffness out of them,
And not one but hung limp, not one was left
For him to conquer. He learned all there was
To learn about not launching out too soon
And so not carrying the tree away
35 Clear to the ground. He always kept his poise[3]
To the top branches, climbing carefully
With the same pains you use to fill a cup
Up to the brim, and even above the brim.
Then he flung outward, feet first, with a swish,
40 Kicking his way down through the air to the ground. **D**
So was I once myself a swinger of birches.
And so I dream of going back to be.
It's when I'm weary of considerations,
And life is too much like a pathless wood
45 Where your face burns and tickles with the cobwebs
Broken across it, and one eye is weeping
From a twig's having lashed across it open. **E**
I'd like to get away from earth awhile
And then come back to it and begin over.

---

2. **subdued:** brought under control.
3. **poise:** balance.

B FROST'S STYLE
Circle the sensory details presented so far that help the **image** of the birches come alive for you.

C MAKE INFERENCES
Reread lines 21–27. What can you infer about the speaker? Underline details in the poem that provide clues. Then add these details to the chart on page 325 and fill in your associations and inferences.

D FROST'S STYLE
In lines 28–40, underline the words or phrases that convey Frost's playful and energetic **tone**.

E FROST'S STYLE
Identify the **simile** used in lines 41–47. What ideas beyond the literal meaning of the words does this simile convey?

_____

_____

_____

_____

_____

PAUSE & REFLECT

What feelings about nature and life does "Birches" express?

_____

_____

_____

_____

_____

50 May no fate willfully misunderstand me
And half grant what I wish and snatch me away
Not to return. Earth's the right place for love:
I don't know where it's likely to go better.
I'd like to go by climbing a birch tree,
55 And climb black branches up a snow-white trunk
Toward heaven, till the tree could bear no more,
But dipped its top and set me down again.
That would be good both going and coming back.
One could do worse than be a swinger of birches. **PAUSE & REFLECT**

SET A PURPOSE FOR READING

Read this poem to find out the speaker's attitude towards walls and neighbors.

Mending Wall

Poem by

R O B E R T   F R O S T

BACKGROUND The title "Mending Wall" refers to the act of repairing the stone walls that divide farms and fields in New England. Farmers typically build these walls with stones removed from their own land. In winter, freezing water tends to shift the stones in the wall and push up boulders from the earth.

F FROST'S STYLE

Think about Frost's decision to use the informal, plain word *something* in line 1. Can you think of another word to use there? Explain.

_____

_____

_____

_____

Something there is that doesn't love a wall,
That sends the frozen-ground-swell under it
And spills the upper boulders in the sun,
And makes gaps even two can pass abreast. **F**
5 The work of hunters is another thing:
I have come after them and made repair
Where they have left not one stone on a stone,
But they would have the rabbit out of hiding,
To please the yelping dogs.¹ The gaps I mean,
10 No one has seen them made or heard them made,

---

1. **The work . . . yelping dogs:** The speaker has replaced the stones hunters have removed from the wall when they have been pursuing rabbits.

But at spring mending-time we find them there.

I let my neighbor know beyond the hill;

And on a day we meet to walk the line

And set the wall between us once again. **G**

15 We keep the wall between us as we go.

To each the boulders that have fallen to each.

And some are loaves and some so nearly balls

We have to use a spell to make them balance:

"Stay where you are until our backs are turned!"

20 We wear our fingers rough with handling them.

Oh, just another kind of outdoor game,

One on a side. It comes to little more:

There where it is we do not need the wall:

He is all pine and I am apple orchard.

25 My apple trees will never get across

And eat the cones under his pines, I tell him.

He only says, "Good fences make good neighbors."

Spring is the mischief in me, and I wonder

If I could put a notion in his head:

30 "Why do they make good neighbors? Isn't it

Where there are cows? But here there are no cows. **H**

Before I built a wall I'd ask to know

What I was walling in or walling out,

And to whom I was like to give offense.

35 Something there is that doesn't love a wall,

That wants it down." I could say "Elves" to him,

But it's not elves exactly, and I'd rather

He said it for himself. I see him there,

Bringing a stone grasped firmly by the top

40 In each hand, like an old-stone savage armed.

He moves in darkness as it seems to me,

Not of woods only and the shade of trees.

He will not go behind his father's saying,

And he likes having thought of it so well

45 He says again, "Good fences make good neighbors." **I**

G **MAKE INFERENCES**
Describe the speaker's feeling so far about mending the stone wall. Underline words and phrases in the poem that helped you make your inference.

_____

_____

_____

H **MAKE INFERENCES**
Reread lines 23–31. Does the speaker admire his neighbor? Underline details in the text that provide clues. Then use the chart on page 325 to make and explain your inference.

I **FROST'S STYLE**
Think about Frost's **tone,** or attitude, in this poem. Do you think the poet himself likes or dislikes walls between neighbors? Explain.

_____

_____

_____

_____

_____

_____

_____

_____

Text Analysis: Frost's Style

One aspect of Frost's style is his use of imaginative **similes** and **metaphors.** A simile is a comparison between two unlike things using *like* or *as*. A metaphor is a comparison that does not use specific words of comparison. In the chart below, identify a simile and a metaphor in the poems. Explain how they convey ideas beyond the literal meaning of the words.

Examples	Explanation of Meaning
Simile	
Metaphor	

Reading Skill: Make Inferences

Review the charts you made as you read. Think about the key inferences that helped you understand the speaker of each poem. What personality traits and values does each speaker appear to have?

_____

_____

_____

How can **NATURE** inspire you?

What can nature teach you about humanity?

_____

_____

_____

Academic Vocabulary in Writing

clarify	feature	precise	style	transmit

What **features** of Frost's **style** do you find interesting and effective? **Clarify** the reasons that you like or dislike "Birches" and "Mending Wall." Support your answer with details from the poems. Use at least one Academic Vocabulary word in your response. Definitions for these terms are listed on page 301.

_____

_____

_____

_____

Assessment Practice

DIRECTIONS Use "Birches" and "Mending Wall" to answer questions 1–4.

1 In line 44 of "Birches," what does the speaker most likely mean by "And life is too much like a pathless wood"?

  A Life will be good if the speaker can swing in birches.

  B Life is unpredictable but interesting.

  C It is difficult to find a way through life's challenges.

  D Birches show the way through the woods.

2 Does the speaker in "Mending Wall" respect his neighbor's opinion that "Good fences make good neighbors"?

  A No, because the neighbor isn't a good neighbor despite the wall.

  B Yes, because it is important to pay attention to old sayings.

  C No, because the neighbor doesn't even question the need for a wall.

  D Yes, because the fence is important to keeping the crops safe.

3 What does the speaker in "Birches" mean by "May no fate willfully misunderstand me / And half grant what I wish and snatch me away / Not to return"?

  A The speaker thinks fate will cause him to die.

  B The speaker wants to continue living.

  C The speaker hopes that half the wish will be granted.

  D The speaker knows that he won't return.

4 What is one likely reason the author gives the gaps a mysterious quality in lines 10–11 of "Mending Wall"?

  A The mystery makes the reader aware that an unseen force of nature has been at work.

  B The mystery pushes the reader to ignore the gaps and focus on the neighbor's actions.

  C The mystery engages the reader in solving the puzzle before the end of the poem.

  D The mystery offers a pause from the more serious thoughts the author is conveying.

Only Daughter
Personal Essay by **Sandra Cisneros**

from Caramelo
Fiction by **Sandra Cisneros**

What is your **ROLE** in your household?

Think about the different roles that you play in your family and how you feel about them. Do you have to do certain things because you are a boy or a girl? In the following selections by Sandra Cisneros, you will learn what it means to be a daughter in a traditional Mexican-American family.

DISCUSS During the 1960s, many people began reexamining the role of women both at home and in society. Since then, ideas about the proper roles of males and females have changed dramatically. In the chart to the left, write your thoughts about the roles of males and females today. Then, in a large group, discuss gender roles at home, at school, and in the workplace.

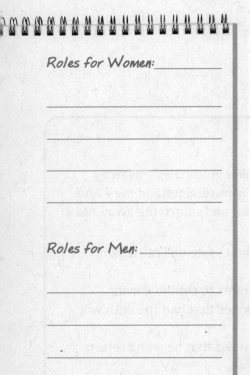

Roles for Women: _____

_____

_____

_____

Roles for Men: _____

_____

_____

_____

_____

Text Analysis: Style and Voice

Sandra Cisneros is a contemporary writer who is known for her vibrant writing style. Her work is easily recognizable because of her distinctive voice. In literature, a voice is a writer's use of language in a way that allows readers to "hear" a personality in his or her writing. Diction, tone, and imagery are elements that contribute to voice. Cisneros's use of conversational language, vivid images, and lyrical sentences gives readers a sense of her lively spirit.

ELEMENTS OF VOICE
• **Diction** includes both a writer's choice of words and his or her syntax, or arrangement of words into sentences.
• **Tone** is a writer's attitude toward a subject, as expressed through choice of words and details.
• **Imagery** consists of words and phrases that re-create sensory experiences for readers.

As you read the selections that follow, think about the stylistic elements that contribute to Cisneros's voice.

Reading Skill: Identify Author's Purpose

You may recall that an **author's purpose** is the reason he or she creates a particular work. Often, an author's purpose directly relates to the form, or genre, of a text, as well as its structural pattern. Cisneros writes poetry, nonfiction, and fiction. As you read each selection, you will be prompted to think about the author's purpose with questions like the ones below. Answers to these questions can help you draw conclusions about Cisneros's purpose in each selection.

- What is the form, or genre of this work?

- Why do writers usually write this type of work?

- Which words or phrases suggest a specific tone?

- Does the tone of the work suggest a specific purpose?

Vocabulary in Context

Note: Words are listed in the order in which they appear in the texts.

anthology (ăn-thŏl′ə-jē) *n.* a collection of written works—such as poems, short stories, or plays—in a single book or set
*A literature **anthology** is often used in a school to give students a variety of reading experiences.*

destiny (dĕs′tə-nē) *n.* the determined fate of a particular person or thing; lot in life
*Everyone thought the boy's **destiny** was to become a lawyer like his mother.*

retrospect (rĕt′rə-spĕkt′) *n.* a view or contemplation of something past
*In **retrospect,** it was a bad idea to bike 25 miles to the beach on a hot summer day.*

trauma (trô′mə) *n.* severe physical or emotional distress
*The hurricane victims experienced severe **trauma** because of the flooding and destruction.*

nostalgia (nŏ-stăl′jə) *n.* a wistful longing for the past or the familiar
*Some people feel **nostalgia** for their childhood home or country.*

Vocabulary Practice

Review the vocabulary words and think about their meanings. With a partner, write sentences for at least two of the vocabulary words.

_____

_____

SET A PURPOSE
FOR READING
Read to discover how
Sandra Cisneros feels
about being an "only
daughter."

ONLY DAUGHTER

Personal Essay by
SANDRA CISNEROS

BACKGROUND In "Only Daughter," Cisneros
describes her father's ideas about the
proper role of females. Coming from the
culture of old Mexico, Cisneros's father held
the patriarchal beliefs of many traditional
cultures—that is, he considered men the
heads of families and the leaders of society.
According to his values, a woman needed
only to "become someone's wife" and devote
herself to her home and family.

**SET A PURPOSE
FOR READING**
Read to discover how
Sandra Cisneros feels
about being an "only
daughter."

anthology (ăn-thŏl'ə-jē) *n.* a
collection of written works—
such as poems, short stories, or
plays—in a single book or set

A AUTHOR'S PURPOSE
Reread lines 1–16. What is the
subject of this personal essay?
Underline the details that helped
you draw your conclusion, and
then write your answer below.

_____

_____

_____

_____

Once, several years ago, when I was just starting out my
writing career, I was asked to write my own contributor's
note for an **anthology** I was part of. I wrote: "I am the only
daughter in a family of six sons. *That* explains everything."

Well, I've thought about that ever since, and yes, it explains a
lot to me, but for the reader's sake I should have written: "I am
the only daughter in a *Mexican* family of six sons." Or even: "I am
the only daughter of a Mexican father and a Mexican-American
mother." Or: "I am the only daughter of a working-class family of
10 nine." All of these had everything to do with who I am today.

I was/am the only daughter and *only* a daughter. Being an
only daughter in a family of six sons forced me by circumstance
to spend a lot of time by myself because my brothers felt it
beneath them to play with a *girl* in public. But that aloneness, that
loneliness, was good for a would-be writer—it allowed me time to
think and think, to imagine, to read and prepare myself. **A**

Being only a daughter for my father meant my <u>destiny</u> would lead me to become someone's wife. That's what he believed. But when I was in the fifth grade and shared my plans for college with
20 him, I was sure he understood. I remember my father saying, *"Que bueno, mi'ja,*[1] that's good." That meant a lot to me, especially since my brothers thought the idea hilarious. What I didn't realize was that my father thought college was good for girls—good for finding a husband. After four years in college and two more in graduate school and still no husband, my father shakes his head even now and says I wasted all that education.

In <u>retrospect</u>, I'm lucky my father believed daughters were meant for husbands. It meant it didn't matter if I majored in something silly like English. After all, I'd find a nice professional
30 eventually, right? This allowed me the liberty to putter about embroidering my little poems and stories without my father interrupting with so much as a "What's that you're writing?"

But the truth is, I wanted him to interrupt. I wanted my father to understand what it was I was scribbling, to introduce me as "My only daughter, the writer." Not as "This is only my daughter. She teaches." *Es maestra*[2]—teacher. Not even *profesora*.[3] **PAUSE & REFLECT**

In a sense, everything I have ever written has been for him, to win his approval even though I know my father can't read English words, even though my father's only reading includes
40 the brown-ink *Esto* sports magazines from Mexico City and the bloody *¡Alarma!* magazines that feature yet another sighting of *La Virgen de Guadalupe*[4] on a tortilla or a wife's revenge on her philandering[5] husband by bashing his skull in with a *molcajete*[6] (a kitchen mortar[7] made of volcanic rock). Or the *fotonovelas*,[8] the

---

1. *Que bueno, mi'ja* (kĕ bwĕ'nô mē'hä) *Spanish:* That's good, my daughter. (Mi'ja is a shortened form of mi hija.)
2. *Es maestra* (ĕs mä-ĕs'trä) *Spanish:* She is a teacher.
3. *profesora* (prô-fĕ-sô'rä) *Spanish:* professor.
4. *La Virgen de Guadalupe* (lä vĕr'hĕn dĕ gwä-dä-lōō'pĕ) *Spanish:* the Virgin of Guadalupe—a vision of Mary, the virgin mother of Jesus, said to have appeared on a hill outside Mexico City in 1531.
5. *philandering:* engaging in many casual love affairs.
6. *molcajete* (môl-kä-hĕ'tĕ) *Spanish.*
7. *mortar:* bowl for grinding grain.
8. *fotonovelas* (fô-tô-nô-vĕ'läs) *Spanish.*

destiny (dĕs'tə-nē) *n.* the determined fate of a particular person or thing; lot in life

Complete the following thought: The narrator says that her **destiny** is _____

retrospect (rĕt'rə-spĕkt') *n.* a view or contemplation of something past

PAUSE & REFLECT
In lines 27–36, why is the father's disinterest in Cisneros's writing both positive and negative?

trauma (trô′mə) *n.* severe physical or emotional distress

nostalgia (nŏ-stăl′jə) *n.* a wistful longing for the past or the familiar

B STYLE AND VOICE
Reread lines 50–67. Underline words or phrases that indicate Cisneros's **tone,** or attitude toward her father. How would you describe her feelings toward him?

_____

_____

_____

_____

_____

_____

_____

_____

little picture paperbacks with tragedy and <u>trauma</u> erupting from the characters' mouths in bubbles.

My father represents, then, the public majority. A public who is disinterested in reading, and yet one whom I am writing about and for and privately trying to woo.

50   When we were growing up in Chicago, we moved a lot because of my father. He suffered bouts of <u>nostalgia</u>. Then we'd have to let go our flat, store the furniture with mother's relatives, load the station wagon with baggage and bologna sandwiches, and head south. To Mexico City.

We came back, of course. To yet another Chicago flat, another Chicago neighborhood, another Catholic school. Each time, my father would seek out the parish priest in order to get a tuition break and complain or boast: "I have seven sons."

He meant siete *hijos,*[9] seven children, but he translated it as
60   "sons." "I have seven sons." To anyone who would listen. The Sears Roebuck employee who sold us the washing machine. The short-order cook where my father ate his ham-and-eggs breakfasts. "I have seven sons." As if he deserved a medal from the state.

My papa. He didn't mean anything by that mistranslation, I'm sure. But somehow I could feel myself being erased. I'd tug my father's sleeve and whisper: "Not seven sons. Six! and *one daughter.*" **B**

When my oldest brother graduated from medical school, he fulfilled my father's dream that we study hard and use this—our
70   heads, instead of this—our hands. Even now my father's hands are thick and yellow, stubbed by a history of hammer and nails and twine and coils and springs. "Use this," my father said, tapping his head, "and not this," showing us those hands. He always looked tired when he said it.

Wasn't college an investment? And hadn't I spent all those years in college? And if I didn't marry, what was it all for? Why would anyone go to college and then choose to be poor? Especially someone who had always been poor.

_____

9. **siete hijos** (syĕ′tĕ ē′hôs) *Spanish.* (*Hijos* can mean either "children" or "sons.")

Last year, after ten years of writing professionally, the financial
80 rewards started to trickle in. My second National Endowment for
the Arts Fellowship.[10] A guest professorship at the University of
California, Berkeley. My book, which sold to a major New York
publishing house.

At Christmas, I flew home to Chicago. The house was
throbbing, same as always; hot *tamales*[11] and sweet *tamales* hissing
in my mother's pressure cooker, and everybody—my mother, six
brothers, wives, babies, aunts, cousins—talking too loud and at the
same time, like in a Fellini[12] film, because that's just how we are.

I went upstairs to my father's room. One of my stories had just
90 been translated into Spanish and published in an anthology of
Chicano[13] writing, and I wanted to show it to him. Ever since he
recovered from a stroke two years ago, my father likes to spend his
leisure hours horizontally. And that's how I found him, watching a
Pedro Infante[14] movie on Galavisión[15] and eating rice pudding.

There was a glass filmed with milk on the bedside table. There
were several vials of pills and balled Kleenex. And on the floor,
one black sock and a plastic urinal that I didn't want to look at
but looked at anyway. Pedro Infante was about to burst into song,
and my father was laughing. **C**

100 I'm not sure if it was because my story was translated into
Spanish or because it was published in Mexico or perhaps because
the story dealt with Tepeyac,[16] the *colonia* my father was raised in
and the house he grew up in, but at any rate, my father punched
the mute button on his remote control and read my story.

C STYLE AND VOICE
Cisneros uses **vivid images** to give readers a sense of her spirit and to describe personal experiences for the reader. Reread lines 95–99. Why do you think Cisneros included these details of her father's room?

---

10. **National Endowment for the Arts Fellowship:** The National Endowment for the Arts (Nəā)—a U.S. government agency—awards money in the form of fellowships to artists and writers.

11. *tamales* (tä-mä′lĕs) *Spanish:* rolls of cornmeal dough filled with meat and peppers and steamed in cornhusk wrappings.

12. **Fellini:** the Italian movie director Federico Fellini (1920–1993), famous for his noisy, energetic films.

13. **Chicano:** Mexican-American.

14. **Pedro Infante** (pā′drō ĭn-fän′tā): a popular Mexican film star.

15. **Galavisión:** cable TV network that features movies and programs in Spanish.

16. **Tepeyac** (tĕ-pĕ-yäk′): a district of Mexico City.

PAUSE & REFLECT
Why is Cisneros's father finally able to appreciate her writing? Explain how Cisneros feels about her father's reaction.

_____
_____
_____
_____
_____
_____
_____
_____
_____
_____
_____
_____
_____
_____

I sat on the bed next to my father and waited. He read it very slowly. As if he were reading each line over and over. He laughed at all the right places and read lines he liked out loud. He pointed and asked questions: "Is this So-and-so?"

"Yes," I said. He kept reading.

110   When he was finally finished, after what seemed like hours, my father looked up and asked: "Where can we get more copies of this for the relatives?"

Of all the wonderful things that happened to me last year, that was the most wonderful. **PAUSE & REFLECT**

Caramelo

Fiction by
SANDRA CISNEROS

BACKGROUND As a young girl Sandra Cisneros had few friends because her family moved frequently between Chicago and Mexico. To ward off loneliness, she often read stories and wrote poetry. As a teenager, she continued to write but was careful to keep her work away from her family because they disapproved of her writing.

SET A PURPOSE FOR READING
Read to find out more about Sandra Cisneros's writing style and voice.

Acuérdate de Acapulco,
de aquellas noches,
María bonita, María del alma;
acuérdate que en la playa,
con tus manitas las estrellitas
las enjuagabas.[1]
—*"María bonita," by Augustín Lara, version sung by the composer while playing the piano, accompanied by a sweet, but very, very sweet violin*

D STYLE AND VOICE
Reread lines 1–3. Describe the narrator's voice. Why does she use such short sentences?

_____

_____

_____

_____

_____

_____

We're all little in the photograph above Father's bed. We were little in Acapulco. We will always be little. For him we are just as we were then. **D**

Here are the Acapulco waters lapping just behind us, and here we are sitting on the lip of land and water. The little kids, Lolo and Memo, making devil horns behind each other's head; the Awful Grandmother holding them even though she never held them in real life. Mother seated as far from her as politely possible; Toto slouched beside her. The big boys, Rafa, Ito, and Tikis, stand

---

1. **Acuérdate de Acapulco . . . las enjuagabas** *Spanish:* Remember Acapulco, those nights, beautiful Maria, Maria of my soul; remember that in the sand, you washed the stars with your hands.

E AUTHOR'S PURPOSE
Reread lines 4–22. Consider your own reaction to phrases such as "making devil horns" and "the Awful Grandmother." How do these descriptions help you picture the characters?

_____

_____

_____

_____

_____

_____

_____

_____

F STYLE AND VOICE
Cisneros's style often includes informal sentences that are like speech, such as those in lines 23–32. What aspect of Cisneros's own voice comes through in this type of writing?

_____

_____

_____

_____

_____

_____

_____

10 under the roof of Father's skinny arms. Aunty Light-Skin hugging Antonieta Araceli to her belly. Aunty shutting her eyes when the shutter clicks, as if she chooses not to remember the future, the house on Destiny Street sold, the move north to Monterrey.

Here is Father squinting that same squint I always make when I'm photographed. He isn't *acabado*[2] yet. He isn't *finished*, worn from working, from worrying, from smoking too many packs of cigarettes. There isn't anything on his face but his face, and a tidy, thin mustache, like Pedro Infante, like Clark Gable.[3] Father's skin pulpy and soft, pale as the belly side of a shark.

20 The Awful Grandmother has the same light skin as Father, but in elephant folds, stuffed into a bathing suit the color of an old umbrella with an amber handle. **E**

I'm not here. They've forgotten about me when the photographer walking along the beach proposes a portrait, *un recuerdo*, a remembrance literally. No one notices I'm off playing by myself building sand houses. They won't realize I'm missing until the photographer delivers the portrait to Catita's house, and I look at it for the first time and ask,—When was this taken? Where? Then everyone realizes the portrait is incomplete. It's 30 as if I didn't exist. It's as if I'm the photographer walking along the beach with the tripod camera on my shoulder asking.—*¿Un recuerdo?* A souvenir? A memory? **F**

_____

2. *acabado* (ä-kä-bä′dô) *Spanish:* finished.
3. **Clark Gable:** an American film star of the 1940s.

Text Analysis: Style and Voice

Cisneros's writing style is often marked by a use of conversational language and fragmented sentences. Complete the chart with examples from "Only Daughter" and the excerpt from *Caramelo*.

Elements of Style	Examples
Diction includes both a writer's choice of words and his or her syntax, or arrangement of words into sentences.	
Tone is a writer's attitude toward a subject, as expressed through choice of words and details.	
Imagery consists of words and phrases that re-create sensory experiences for readers.	

Review your notes for "Only Daughter" and the excerpt from *Caramelo*, as well as the chart above. How might your ideas about Cisneros and her experiences be different if the selections had been written with more formal words and sentence structures?

_____

_____

_____

_____

Reading Skill: Identify Author's Purpose

Review the notes you took as you read. In the chart below, identify Cisneros's purpose for writing each selection and then answer the question.

AUTHOR'S PURPOSE
"Only Daughter"
from Caramelo
What similarities or differences do you see between Cisneros's purpose in writing "Only Daughter" and the excerpt from *Caramelo*? Explain.

What is your **ROLE** in your household?

What has shaped the way your family members take on different roles?

_____

_____

_____

Vocabulary Practice

Write the vocabulary word that best completes each sentence.

1. Josh believed that his _____ was to become a famous actor.

2. Someone with _____ often relives happy memories of earlier times.

3. The _____ contains the works of her favorite author.

4. In _____, I wish I had done things differently.

5. The _____ of the accident would never completely leave Kyra.

WORD LIST
anthology
destiny
nostalgia
retrospect
trauma

Academic Vocabulary in Speaking

clarify	feature	precise	style	transmit

TURN AND TALK With a partner, **clarify** the gender roles that you observe in your school. Do you feel that people in your school are treated fairly when it comes to gender? Use at least one Academic Vocabulary word in your conversation. Definitions for these terms are listed on page 301.

Assessment Practice

DIRECTIONS Use "Only Daughter" and the excerpt from *Caramelo* to answer questions 1–5.

1 Cisneros went against her father's expectations because —

- **A** she failed to become a doctor
- **B** she didn't go to college to find a husband
- **C** she married her husband before going to college
- **D** she gave up writing in high school

2 Which word best describes how Sandra Cisneros felt as a child?

- **A** ostracized
- **B** content
- **C** overlooked
- **D** happy

3 In "Only Daughter," what theme about female roles does Cisneros communicate through her relationship with her father?

- **A** Girls are not as important as boys and should only go to college to find a husband.
- **B** Fathers have low expectations of their sons because they don't encourage them to go to college.
- **C** It is most important to maintain the gender roles defined by your parents.
- **D** While traditional female roles can be restrictive, a person can choose other roles and achieve her goals.

4 In the excerpt from *Caramelo*, what does the narrator's absence from the portrait described in lines 23–26 suggest about her role in the family?

- **A** She plays a significant role in her family.
- **B** She doesn't need to play with her family.
- **C** She plays an insignificant role in her family.
- **D** She doesn't like to be disturbed when playing.

5 In lines 29–32 of the excerpt from *Caramelo*, the narrator compares herself to the photographer because —

- **A** neither she nor the photographer are in the picture, but both of them created a remembrance of the family
- **B** both she and the photographer are in the picture, and the family gives each of them a copy as a remembrance
- **C** only she is missing from the picture because the photographer joins the others when she takes the picture
- **D** all of the narrator's brothers want to take the picture so that everyone remembers the day they were photographers

9 Product of the Times

HISTORY, CULTURE, AND THE AUTHOR

Be sure to read the Text Analysis Workshop on pp. 934–939 in *Holt McDougal Literature*.

Academic Vocabulary for Unit 9

Preview the following Academic Vocabulary words. You will encounter these words as you work through this book and will use them as you write and talk about the selections in the unit.

---

acknowledge (ăk-nŏl′ ĭj) *v.* to recognize and admit that something is true or accurate

*The author **acknowledged** the help she received from other people while writing the book.*

•

community (kə myōō′nĭ tē) *n.* a group of individuals with a common interest or characteristic

*A **community** of writers can review and edit each other's work to make it better.*

•

contemporary (kən-tĕm′pə-rĕr′ē) *adj.* current; modern

*Not everyone enjoys reading **contemporary** fiction and nonfiction.*

•

culture (kŭl′chər) *n.* the attitudes, behavior, or customs that characterize a group; the particular group having such attitudes, behavior, or customs

*The members of a **culture** interact over time to create their own customs.*

•

role (rōl) *n.* a character played by an actor in a performance; a function or part assumed in a process

*Some people feel that the **role** of literature is to encourage people to think about society's issues.*

Do you think contemporary works can help people understand issues and make society better? Explain, using at least two Academic Vocabulary words in your response.

_____

_____

_____

from Farewell to Manzanar

Memoir by Jeanne Wakatsuki Houston and James D. Houston

What if your government declared you the ENEMY?

What sort of government would harm innocent people just because of their race? Unfortunately, such actions have occurred in many nations, including our own. During World War II, the United States declared Japanese Americans to be enemy aliens and forced them into internment camps, a tragic event described in *Farewell to Manzanar*.

QUICKWRITE Governments often take extreme measures during times of crisis. Do you think it's ever acceptable to limit the rights of citizens or legal residents? If so, why?

Text Analysis: Cultural Characteristics

In memoirs, writers often provide information about their culture or about a particular time period in which they lived. When reading such accounts, readers can learn about the characteristics of a culture, including:

- beliefs
- values
- traditions
- customs

For example, in *Farewell to Manzanar*, Wakatsuki makes the following statement about the customs of the Japanese diet:

Among the Japanese . . . rice is never eaten with sweet foods, only with salty or savory foods.

As you read about the Wakatsuki family, identify cultural beliefs, customs, traditions, or values and how these influence the family's actions and point of view about events.

Limiting Rights, Justifiable or Not?

_____
_____
_____
_____
_____
_____
_____
_____
_____
_____
_____

Reading Strategy: Monitor

Memoirs often mix personal details with references to historical events. To help you keep track of such information, you can use techniques such as the following to **monitor** your reading:

- Ask questions about events or ideas that are unclear, and then read to find the answers.
- Clarify your understanding by rereading passages, summarizing, or slowing down your reading pace.

As you read the excerpt from *Farewell to Manzanar,* you will be prompted to use monitoring techniques to improve your comprehension of difficult passages. The following chart shows an example.

Passage	Monitoring Technique
lines 1–13	I reread the paragraph to understand more about the different locations that are mentioned.

Vocabulary in Context

Note: Words are listed in the order in which they appear in the selection.

inevitable (ĭn-ĕvʹĭ-tə-bəl) *adj.* unavoidable
*The collision was almost **inevitable** because of the icy roads.*

irrational (ĭ-răshʹə-nəl) *adj.* not possessed with reason or understanding
*The woman had an **irrational** fear of all dogs because one had knocked her down as a child.*

sinister (sĭnʹĭ-stər) *adj.* threatening or foreshadowing evil
*There was something **sinister** about the shadows cast by the moonlit trees.*

permeate (pûrʹmē-ātʹ) *v.* to spread or flow throughout
*The cold rain **permeated** the fabric of the tent and soaked the people inside.*

subordinate (sə-bôrʹdn-ātʹ) *v.* to lower in rank or importance
*The people **subordinated** their need for food because they needed water more.*

SET A PURPOSE FOR READING

Read the excerpt from this memoir to understand what life was like for Japanese Americans forced into internment camps during World War II.

Farewell *to* Manzanar

Memoir by **JEANNE WAKATSUKI HOUSTON** AND **JAMES D. HOUSTON**

BACKGROUND After the United States entered World War II, some officials feared that Japanese Americans would secretly aid Japan's war effort, although there was no evidence of their disloyalty. In February 1942, President Franklin Roosevelt signed an order that led to the removal of almost 120,000 Japanese Americans from their homes on the West Coast. With little notice, they were bused to ten "relocation" centers in Western states and Arkansas, where they were confined for the duration of the war.

The American Friends Service[1] helped us find a small house in Boyle Heights, another minority ghetto, in downtown Los Angeles, now inhabited briefly by a few hundred Terminal Island refugees.[2] Executive Order 9066 had been signed by President Roosevelt, giving the War Department authority to define military areas in the western states and to exclude from them anyone who might threaten the war effort. There was a lot of talk about internment, or moving inland, or something like that in store for all Japanese Americans. I remember my brothers sitting

10 around the table talking very intently about what we were going to do, how we would keep the family together. They had seen how quickly Papa was removed, and they knew now that he would not be back for quite a while. Just before leaving Terminal Island,

---

1. **American Friends Service:** a Quaker charity that often aids political and religious refugees and other displaced persons.
2. **Terminal Island refugees:** Shortly after Pearl Harbor was attacked, Japanese fishermen and cannery workers were forced to leave Terminal Island, which is located near Los Angeles.

Mama had received her first letter, from Bismarck, North Dakota. He had been imprisoned at Fort Lincoln, in an all-male camp for enemy aliens. Ⓐ

Papa had been the patriarch. He had always decided everything in the family. With him gone, my brothers, like councilors in the absence of a chief, worried about what should be done. The ironic
20 thing is, there wasn't much left to decide. These were mainly days of quiet, desperate waiting for what seemed at the time to be **inevitable**. There is a phrase the Japanese use in such situations, when something difficult must be endured.

You would hear the older heads, the Issei,[3] telling others very quietly, *"Shikata ga nai"* (It cannot be helped). *"Shikata ga nai"* (It must be done). Ⓑ

Mama and Woody went to work packing celery for a Japanese produce dealer. Kiyo and my sister May and I enrolled in the local school, and what sticks in my memory from those few weeks is
30 the teacher—not her looks, her remoteness. In Ocean Park my teacher had been a kind, grandmotherly woman who used to sail with us in Papa's boat from time to time and who wept the day we had to leave. In Boyle Heights the teacher felt cold and distant. I was confused by all the moving and was having trouble with the classwork, but she would never help me out. She would have nothing to do with me.

This was the first time I had felt outright hostility from a Caucasian. Looking back, it is easy enough to explain. Public attitudes toward the Japanese in California were shifting rapidly.
40 In the first few months of the Pacific war, America was on the run. Tolerance had turned to distrust and **irrational** fear. The hundred-year-old tradition of anti-Orientalism on the west coast soon resurfaced, more vicious than ever. Its result became clear about a month later, when we were told to make our third and final move.

The name Manzanar meant nothing to us when we left Boyle Heights. We didn't know where it was or what it was. We went because the government ordered us to. And, in the case of my older brothers and sisters, we went with a certain amount of relief.
50 They had all heard stories of Japanese homes being attacked,

---

3. **Issei** (ē′sā): people born in Japan who immigrate to the United States.

A MONITOR UNDERSTANDING
Reread lines 1–16. What has happened to the narrator's father?

_____

_____

_____

inevitable (ĭn-ĕv′ĭ-tə-bəl) *adj.* unavoidable

B CULTURAL CHARACTERISTICS
Reread lines 17–26. What does this passage reveal about traditional Japanese attitudes toward hardship?

_____

_____

_____

_____

irrational (ĭ-răsh′ə-nəl) *adj.* not possessed with reason or understanding

Why was the American public's fear of Japanese people **irrational**?

_____

_____

_____

_____

C CULTURAL
CHARACTERISTICS
In lines 67–82, what do you
learn about the values of the
Wakatsuki family and other
families that were moved?

of beatings in the streets of California towns. They were as
frightened of the Caucasians as Caucasians were of us. Moving,
under what appeared to be government protection, to an area less
directly threatened by the war seemed not such a bad idea at all.
For some it actually sounded like a fine adventure.

Our pickup point was a Buddhist church in Los Angeles. It
was very early, and misty, when we got there with our luggage.
Mama had bought heavy coats for all of us. She grew up in
eastern Washington and knew that anywhere inland in early
60 April would be cold. I was proud of my new coat, and I remember
sitting on a duffel bag trying to be friendly with the Greyhound
driver. I smiled at him. He didn't smile back. He was befriending
no one. Someone tied a numbered tag to my collar and to the
duffel bag (each family was given a number, and that became our
official designation until the camps were closed), someone else
passed out box lunches for the trip, and we climbed aboard.

I had never been outside Los Angeles County, never traveled
more than ten miles from the coast, had never even ridden on
a bus. I was full of excitement, the way any kid would be, and
70 wanted to look out the window. But for the first few hours the
shades were drawn. Around me other people played cards, read
magazines, dozed, waiting. I settled back, waiting too, and
finally fell sleep. The bus felt very secure to me. Almost half its
passengers were immediate relatives. Mama and my older brothers
had succeeded in keeping most of us together, on the same bus,
headed for the same camp. I didn't realize until much later what a
job that was. The strategy had been, first, to have everyone living
in the same district when the evacuation began, and then to get
all of us included under the same family number, even though
80 names had been changed by marriage. Many families weren't
as lucky as ours and suffered months of anguish while trying to
arrange transfers from one camp to another. **C**

We rode all day. By the time we reached our destination, the
shades were up. It was late afternoon. The first thing I saw was
a yellow swirl across a blurred, reddish setting sun. The bus was
being pelted by what sounded like splattering rain. It wasn't rain.
This was my first look at something I would soon know very

well, a billowing Xurry of dust and sand churned up by the wind through Owens Valley.[4]

90 We drove past a barbed-wire fence, through a gate, and into an open space where trunks and sacks and packages had been dumped from the baggage trucks that drove out ahead of us. I could see a few tents set up, the first rows of black barracks, and beyond them, blurred by sand, rows of barracks that seemed to spread for miles across this plain. People were sitting on cartons or milling around, with their backs to the wind, waiting to see which friends or relatives might be on this bus. As we approached, they turned or stood up, and some moved toward us expectantly. But inside the bus no one stirred. No one waved or spoke. They 100 just stared out the windows, ominously silent. I didn't understand this. Hadn't we finally arrived, our whole family intact? I opened a window, leaned out, and yelled happily. "Hey! This whole bus is full of Wakatsukis!" **D**

Outside, the greeters smiled. Inside there was an explosion of laughter, hysterical, tension-breaking laughter that left my brothers choking and whacking each other across the shoulders.

We had pulled up just in time for dinner. The mess halls weren't completed yet. An outdoor chow line snaked around a half-finished building that broke a good part of the wind. They 110 issued us army mess kits, the round metal kind that fold over, and plopped in scoops of canned Vienna sausage, canned string beans, steamed rice that had been cooked too long, and on top of the rice a serving of canned apricots. The Caucasian servers were thinking that the fruit poured over rice would make a good dessert. Among the Japanese, of course, rice is never eaten with sweet foods, only with salty or savory foods. Few of us could eat such a mixture. But at this point no one dared protest. It would have been impolite. I was horrified when I saw the apricot syrup seeping through my little mound of rice. I opened my mouth to complain. My mother 120 jabbed me in the back to keep quiet. We moved on through the line and joined the others squatting in the lee[5] of half-raised walls,

4. **Owens Valley:** the valley of the Owens River in south-central California west of Death Valley, where Manzanar was built. The once lush and green valley had become dry and deserted in the 1930s after water was diverted to an aqueduct supplying Los Angeles.
5. **lee:** the side sheltered from the wind.

E CULTURAL CHARACTERISTICS

How does the cultural information in lines 107–123 help you understand the experience of interned Japanese Americans?

_____

_____

_____

_____

_____

F MONITOR

What strategy would you use to clarify the information in lines 132–139? Use the chart below to record your answer.

Passage: *Lines 132–139*

Monitoring Technique:

dabbing courteously at what was, for almost everyone there, an inedible concoction. **E**

After dinner we were taken to Block 16, a cluster of fifteen barracks that had just been finished a day or so earlier—although finished was hardly the word for it. The shacks were built of one thickness of pine planking covered with tarpaper. They sat on concrete footings, with about two feet of open space between the Xoorboards and the ground. Gaps showed between the planks, 130 and as the weeks passed and the green wood dried out, the gaps widened. Knotholes gaped in the uncovered floor.

Each barracks was divided into six units, sixteen by twenty feet, about the size of a living room, with one bare bulb hanging from the ceiling and an oil stove for heat. We were assigned two of these for the twelve people in our family group; and our official family "number" was enlarged by three digits—16 plus the number of this barracks. We were issued steel army cots, two brown army blankets each, and some mattress covers, which my brothers stuffed with straw. **F**

140 The first task was to divide up what space we had for sleeping. Bill and Woody contributed a blanket each and partitioned off the first room: one side for Bill and Tomi, one side for Woody and Chizu and their baby girl. Woody also got the stove, for heating formulas.

The people who had it hardest during the first few months were young couples like these, many of whom had married just before the evacuation began, in order not to be separated and sent to different camps. Our two rooms were crowded, but at least it was all in the family. My oldest sister and her husband were 150 shoved into one of those sixteen-by-twenty-foot compartments with six people they had never seen before—two other couples, one recently married like themselves, the other with two teenage boys. Partitioning off a room like that wasn't easy. It was bitter cold when we arrived, and the wind did not abate. All they had to use for room dividers were those army blankets, two of which were barely enough to keep one person warm. They argued over whose blanket should be sacrificed and later argued about noise at night—the parents wanted their boys asleep by 9:00 P.M.—and they continued arguing over matters like that for six months, until

160 my sister and her husband left to harvest sugar beets in Idaho. It was grueling work up there, and wages were pitiful, but when the call came through camp for workers to alleviate the wartime labor shortage, it sounded better than their life at Manzanar. They knew they'd have, if nothing else, a room, perhaps a cabin of their own.

That first night in Block 16, the rest of us squeezed into the second room—Granny; Lillian, age fourteen; Ray, thirteen; May, eleven; Kiyo, ten; Mama; and me. I didn't mind this at all at the time. Being youngest meant I got to sleep with Mama. And before we went to bed I had a great time jumping up and down on the

170 mattress. The boys had stuffed so much straw into hers, we had to flatten it some so we wouldn't slide off. I slept with her every night after that until Papa came back.

We woke early, shivering and coated with dust that had blown up through the knotholes and in through the slits around the doorway. During the night Mama had unpacked all our clothes and heaped them on our beds for warmth. Now our cubicle looked as if a great laundry bag had exploded and then been sprayed with fine dust. A skin of sand covered the floor. I looked over Mama's shoulder at Kiyo, on top of his fat mattress, buried

180 under jeans and overcoats and sweaters. His eyebrows were gray, and he was starting to giggle. He was looking at me, at my gray eyebrows and coated hair, and pretty soon we were both giggling. I looked at Mama's face to see if she thought Kiyo was funny. She lay very still next to me on our mattress, her eyes scanning everything—bare rafters, walls, dusty kids—scanning slowly, and I think the mask of her face would have cracked had not Woody's voice just then come at us through the wall. He was rapping on the planks as if testing to see if they were hollow.

"Hey!" he yelled. "You guys fall into the same flour barrel
190 as us?"

"No," Kiyo yelled back. "Ours is full of Japs."

All of us laughed at this.

"Well, tell 'em it's time to get up," Woody said. "If we're gonna live in this place, we better get to work." **G**

He gave us ten minutes to dress, then he came in carrying a broom, a hammer, and a sack full of tin can lids he had scrounged somewhere. Woody would be our leader for a while now, short,

G MONITOR
How important is Woody's joking and positive attitude to the family's successful adaptation to their new living situation? To clarify, read on and check your answer.

sinister (sĭn′ĭ-stər) *adj.*
threatening or foreshadowing
evil

Is Woody's behavior at this time
sinister? Explain.

_____

_____

_____

_____

**Ⓗ CULTURAL
CHARACTERISTICS**
In lines 210–235, what does
Woody's behavior show about
his role in the family, and how
does this reflect the family's
values?

_____

_____

_____

_____

_____

_____

_____

_____

_____

_____

_____

_____

stocky, grinning behind his mustache. He had just turned twenty-four. In later years he would tour the country with Mr. Moto, the Japanese tag-team wrestler, as his **sinister** assistant Suki—karate chops through the ropes from outside the ring, a chunky leg reaching from under his kimono to trip up Mr. Moto's foe. In the ring Woody's smile looked sly and crafty; he hammed it up. Offstage it was whimsical, as if some joke were bursting to be told.

"Hey, brother Ray, Kiyo," he said. "You see these tin can lids?"

"Yeah, yeah," the boys said drowsily, as if going back to sleep. They were both young versions of Woody.

"You see all them knotholes in the floor and in the walls?"

They looked around. You could see about a dozen.

Woody said, "You get those covered up before breakfast time. Any more sand comes in here through one of them knotholes, you have to eat it off the floor with ketchup."

"What about sand that comes in through the cracks?" Kiyo said.

Woody stood up very straight, which in itself was funny, since he was only about five-foot-six.

"Don't worry about the cracks," he said. "Different kind of sand comes in through the cracks."

He put his hands on his hips and gave Kiyo a sternly comic look, squinting at him through one eye the way Papa would when he was asserting his authority. Woody mimicked Papa's voice: "And I can tell the difference. So be careful."

The boys laughed and went to work nailing down lids. May started sweeping out the sand. I was helping Mama fold the clothes we'd used for cover, when Woody came over and put his arms around her shoulder. He was short; she was even shorter, under five feet.

He said softly, "You okay, Mama?"

She didn't look at him, she just kept folding clothes and said, "Can we get the cracks covered too, Woody?"

Outside the sky was clear, but icy gusts of wind were buffeting our barracks every few minutes, sending fresh dust puffs up through the floorboards. May's broom could barely keep up with it, and our oil heater could scarcely hold its own against the drafts.

"We'll get this whole place as tight as a barrel, Mama. I already met a guy who told me where they pile all the scrap lumber." **Ⓗ**

"Scrap?"

"That's all they got. I mean, they're still building the camp, you know. Sixteen blocks left to go. After that, they say maybe we'll get some stuff to fix the insides a little bit."

240 Her eyes blazed then, her voice quietly furious. "Woody, we can't live like this. Animals live like this."

It was hard to get Woody down. He'd keep smiling when everybody else was ready to explode. Grief flickered in his eyes. He blinked it away and hugged her tighter. "We'll make it better, Mama. You watch."

We could hear voices in other cubicles now. Beyond the wall Woody's baby girl started to cry.

"I have to go over to the kitchen," he said, "see if those guys got a pot for heating bottles. That oil stove takes too long—
250 something wrong with the fuel line. I'll find out what they're giving us for breakfast."

"Probably hotcakes with soy sauce," Kiyo said, on his hands and knees between the bunks. ❶

"No." Woody grinned, heading out the door. "Rice. With Log Cabin syrup and melted butter."

I don't remember what we ate that first morning. I know we stood for half an hour in cutting wind waiting to get our food. Then we took it back to the cubicle and ate huddled around the stove. Inside, it was warmer than when we left, because Woody was
260 already making good his promise to Mama, tacking up some ends of lath[6] he'd found, stuffing rolled paper around the door frame.

Trouble was, he had almost nothing to work with. Beyond this temporary weather stripping, there was little else he could do. Months went by, in fact, before our "home" changed much at all from what it was the day we moved in—bare floors, blanket partitions, one bulb in each compartment dangling from a roof beam, and open ceilings overhead so that mischievous boys like Ray and Kiyo could climb up into the rafters and peek into anyone's life.

270 The simple truth is the camp was no more ready for us when we got there than we were ready for it. We had only the dimmest ideas of what to expect. Most of the families, like us, had moved

❶ **CULTURAL CHARACTERISTICS**
Why is Kiyo joking about the kitchen serving soy sauce with hotcakes?

---

6. **lath** (lăth): a thin strip of wood.

J CULTURAL CHARACTERISTICS

In lines 278–293, underline the information about what the people in the camp did with the clothing from the war department. What do their actions show about traditional Japanese values?

out from southern California with as much luggage as each person could carry. Some old men left Los Angeles wearing Hawaiian shirts and Panama hats and stepped off the bus at an altitude of 4000 feet, with nothing available but sagebrush and tarpaper to stop the April winds pouring down off the back side of the Sierras.[7]

The War Department was in charge of all the camps at this point. They began to issue military surplus from the First World War—olive-drab knit caps, earmuffs, peacoats, canvas leggings. Later on, sewing machines were shipped in, and one barracks was turned into a clothing factory. An old seamstress took a peacoat of mine, tore the lining out, opened and flattened the sleeves, added a collar, put arm holes in and handed me back a beautiful cape. By fall, dozens of seamstresses were working full-time transforming thousands of these old army clothes into capes, slacks, and stylish coats. But until that factory got going and packages from friends outside began to fill out our wardrobes, warmth was more important than style. I couldn't help laughing at Mama walking around in army earmuffs and a pair of wide-cuffed, khaki-colored wool trousers several sizes too big for her. Japanese are generally smaller than Caucasians, and almost all these clothes were oversize. They flopped, they dangled, they hung. **J**

It seems comical, looking back; we were a band of Charlie Chaplins[8] marooned in the California desert. But at the time, it was pure chaos. That's the only way to describe it. The evacuation had been so hurriedly planned, the camps so hastily thrown together, nothing was completed when we got there, and almost nothing worked.

I was sick continually, with stomach cramps and diarrhea. At first it was from the shots they gave us for typhoid, in very heavy doses and in assembly-line fashion: swab, jab, swab, *Move along now*, swab, jab, swab, *Keep it moving*. That knocked all of us younger kids down at once, with fevers and vomiting. Later, it was the food that made us sick, young and old alike. The kitchens were too small and badly ventilated. Food would spoil from being left out too long. That summer, when the heat got fierce, it would spoil faster. The refrigeration kept breaking down. The cooks, in

---

7. **Sierras** (sē-ĕr′əz): the Sierra Nevada mountain range in eastern California.
8. **Charlie Chaplins:** Charlie Chaplin, an actor and director, portrayed a tramp in baggy clothing in comedy films of the 1920s and 1930s.

many cases, had never cooked before. Each block had to provide
310 its own volunteers. Some were lucky and had a professional or two
in their midst. But the first chef in our block had been a gardener
all his life and suddenly found himself preparing three meals a
day for 250 people.

"The Manzanar runs" became a condition of life, and you
only hoped that when you rushed to the latrine,[9] one would be in
working order. **K**

That first morning, on our way to the chow line, Mama and
I tried to use the women's latrine in our block. The smell of it
spoiled what little appetite we had. Outside, men were working in
320 an open trench, up to their knees in muck—a common sight in
the months to come. Inside, the floor was covered with excrement,
and all twelve bowls were erupting like a row of tiny volcanoes.

Mama stopped a kimono-wrapped woman stepping past us
with her sleeve pushed up against her nose and asked, "What do
you do?"

"Try Block Twelve," the woman said, grimacing. "They have
just finished repairing the pipes."

It was about two city blocks away. We followed her over there
and found a line of women waiting in the wind outside the
330 latrine. We had no choice but to join the line and wait with them.

Inside it was like all the other latrines. Each block was built
to the same design just as each of the ten camps, from California
to Arkansas, was built to a common master plan. It was an open
room, over a concrete slab. The sink was a long metal trough
against one wall, with a row of spigots for hot and cold water.
Down the center of the room twelve toilet bowls were arranged
in six pairs, back to back, with no partitions. My mother was a
very modest person, and this was going to be agony for her, sitting
down in public, among strangers. **PAUSE & REFLECT**

340 One old woman had already solved the problem for herself by
dragging in a large cardboard carton. She set it up around one
of the bowls, like a three-sided screen. OXYDOL was printed in
large black letters down the front. I remember this well, because

---

9. **latrine:** a communal toilet in a camp or barracks.

K MONITOR
How would you summarize the
information on lines 300–316?

_____

_____

_____

_____

_____

_____

_____

_____

PAUSE & REFLECT
Is it just or fair to require
people to live in the conditions
described in lines 328–339,
particularly if they have not
been convicted of any crime?

_____

_____

_____

_____

_____

_____

_____

_____

permeate (pûr'mē-āt') *v.* to spread or flow throughout

① MONITOR
What monitoring technique would you use if you were having difficulty understanding lines 348–359? Explain why you feel it would be the best technique to use.

_____

_____

_____

_____

_____

_____

_____

subordinate (sə-bôr'dn-āt') *v.* to lower in rank or importance

PAUSE & REFLECT
What do the authors mean when they say that the experience was "a slap in the face you were powerless to challenge" (lines 381–382)?

_____

_____

_____

that was the soap we were issued for laundry; later on, the smell of it would **permeate** these rooms. The upended carton was about four feet high. The old woman behind it wasn't much taller. When she stood, only her head showed over the top.

She was about Granny's age. With great effort she was trying to fold the sides of the screen together. Mama happened to be at 350 the head of the line now. As she approached the vacant bowl, she and the old woman bowed to each other from the waist. Mama then moved to help her with the carton, and the old woman said very graciously, in Japanese, "Would you like to use it?"

Happily, gratefully, Mama bowed again and said, *"Arigato"* (Thank you). *"Arigato gozaimas"* (Thank you very much). "I will return it to your barracks."

"Oh, no. It is not necessary. I will be glad to wait."

The old woman unfolded one side of the cardboard, while Mama opened the other; then she bowed again and scurried out the door. **①**

360 Those big cartons were a common sight in the spring of 1942. Eventually sturdier partitions appeared, one or two at a time. The first were built of scrap lumber. Word would get around that Block such and such had partitions now, and Mama and my older sisters would walk halfway across the camp to use them. Even after every latrine in camp was screened, this quest for privacy continued. Many would wait in line at night. Ironically, because of this, midnight was often the most crowded time of all.

Like so many of the women there, Mama never did get used to the latrines. It was a humiliation she just learned to endure: *shikata* 370 *ga nai*, this cannot be helped. She would quickly **subordinate** her own desires to those of the family or the community, because she knew cooperation was the only way to survive. At the same time, she placed a high premium on personal privacy, respected it in others and insisted upon it for herself. Almost everyone at Manzanar had inherited this pair of traits from the generations before them who had learned to live in a small, crowded country like Japan. Because of the first, they were able to take a desolate stretch of wasteland and gradually make it livable. But the entire situation there, especially in the beginning—the packed sleeping 380 quarters, the communal mess halls, the open toilets—all this was an open insult to that other, private self, a slap in the face you were powerless to challenge. **PAUSE & REFLECT**

Text Analysis: Cultural Characteristics

Use the organizer below to record what you learned about Japanese beliefs, values, customs and traditions as you read the memoir. Give examples from the selection.

What I Learned About Japanese Culture

Review your notes for *Farewell to Manzanar* and the chart above. How did the cultural details included in the selection help you understand what the people were experiencing?

_____

_____

_____

_____

Reading Strategy: Monitor

In the chart below, place a check mark next to each monitoring technique you used while reading *Farewell to Manzanar* and explain why each one was helpful. Include examples from the memoir to support your answers.

✔	Monitoring Technique	How Technique Was Helpful
	• Asking questions and reading to find the answer	
	• rereading	
	• summarizing	
	• slowing down reading pace	

What if your government declared you the ENEMY?

Which rights would you be willing to give up during a time of national crisis?

_____

_____

_____

Vocabulary Practice

Decide whether each statement is true or false. Write *T* for true or *F* for false.

_____ 1. Something inevitable can be easily avoided.

_____ 2. A person who displays sound reasoning and judgment is irrational.

_____ 3. The stench of garbage can permeate the room.

_____ 4. A letter that talks of evil to come can be described as sinister.

_____ 5. To subordinate your feelings is to share them openly with others.

Academic Vocabulary in Speaking

acknowledge	community	contemporary	culture	role

TURN AND TALK With a partner, discuss how **contemporary culture** views **community.** Is community important in our society? What **role** does community play in supporting the people in times of crisis? Use at least one Academic Vocabulary word in your conversation. Definitions for these terms are listed on page 345.

Assessment Practice

DIRECTIONS Use the excerpt from *Farewell to Manzanar* to answer questions 1–5.

1 The Wakatsukis were sent to Manzanar because —
- **A** the Los Angeles area was too crowded and the U.S. government offered free land
- **B** during the war people were needed to help pick farm crops in the western states
- **C** Japanese Americans in California were worried for their safety during the war
- **D** the U.S. government feared that Japanese Americans would threaten the war effort

2 Of the following, what was most difficult for Mama to endure at Manzanar?
- **A** the billowing dust
- **B** the lack of personal privacy
- **C** the need to cooperate
- **D** the unfamiliar food

3 How did the administrators' lack of knowledge about Japanese culture affect conditions?
- **A** It meant that rice was served with savory foods and people had private rooms.
- **B** It allowed some people to get what they needed while others had to go without.
- **C** It led to unappetizing food and humiliating open latrines.
- **D** It forced some families to be separated even if they arrived together.

4 Jeanne and her siblings were able to adjust to life at Manzanar because —
- **A** the family had enough money to buy the things they needed
- **B** they kept their senses of humor and worked and helped each other
- **C** conditions were better than the place they had been living previously
- **D** they worked together and didn't share or help any other families

5 What does the phrase *"Shikata ga nai"* (lines 25–26)—meaning "It cannot be helped or it must be done"—reveal about traditional Japanese culture?
- **A** The culture valued patience above action.
- **B** The culture valued an aggressive attitude.
- **C** The culture valued action above patience.
- **D** The culture valued a lack of endurance.

A Eulogy for Dr. Martin Luther King Jr.
Speech

Background
Robert F. Kennedy was the younger brother of John F. Kennedy, who served as president from 1961 until his assassination in 1963. As Attorney General, Robert Kennedy was a strong supporter of the civil rights movement. In April 1968, while running his own campaign for president, he gave this eulogy on the evening of King's assassination. Just two months later, Robert Kennedy was himself killed by an assassin's bullet.

Standards Focus: Analyze Rhetorical Devices

Rhetorical devices are techniques that allow writers to communicate ideas more effectively. Rhetorical devices are commonly used in speeches because they help keep an audience's attention. By analyzing rhetorical devices, you can gain insight into what makes a speech powerful or memorable.

Writers use **diction,** or word choice, as well as **syntax,** or sentence structure, to help create rhetorical devices. Two common rhetorical devices are repetition and parallelism.

- **Repetition** is the use of a word, phrase, or sentence more than once for emphasis.

- **Parallelism** is the use of similar grammatical constructions to express related ideas.

As you read Robert F. Kennedy's speech, you'll be prompted to record examples of repetition and parallelism. The following chart shows examples from a speech delivered by Martin Luther King Jr. during the Montgomery bus boycott.

RHETORICAL DEVICES	
Repetition	Parallelism
Tired of being segregated and humiliated; tired of being kicked about by the brutal feet of oppression.	*They are protesting for the perpetuation of injustice in the community; we're protesting for the birth of justice. . . .*

SET A PURPOSE FOR READING
Read this eulogy aloud to hear the powerful language Kennedy uses to appeal to his audience.

A Eulogy for Dr. Martin Luther King Jr.

Robert F. Kennedy

On April 4, 1968, hundreds of African Americans gathered for what they thought would be an exciting political event. Presidential candidate Robert F. Kennedy was coming to speak to them. Before he was to deliver his speech, however, Kennedy was informed that Martin Luther King Jr. had been assassinated earlier that day. He nevertheless went to the rally, where he found the people upbeat in anticipation of his appearance. Realizing that they were unaware of the tragic event, he began his speech with the following words.

I have bad news for you, for all of our fellow citizens, and people who love peace all over the world, and that is that Martin Luther King was shot and killed tonight.

Martin Luther King dedicated his life to love and to justice for his fellow human beings, and he died because of that effort.

In this difficult day, in this difficult time for the United States, it is perhaps well to ask what kind of a nation we are and what direction we want to move in. For those of you 10 who are black—considering the evidence there evidently is that there were white people who were responsible—you can be filled with bitterness, with hatred, and a desire for revenge. We can move in that direction as a country, in great polarization—black people amongst black, white people amongst white, filled with hatred toward one another. **A**

Or we can make an effort, as Martin Luther King did, to understand and to comprehend, and to replace that violence, that stain of bloodshed that has spread across our land, with an effort to understand with compassion and love.

20 For those of you who are black and are tempted to be filled with hatred and distrust at the injustice of such an act, against all white people, I can only say that I feel in my own heart the same kind of feeling. I had a member of my family killed, but he was killed by a white man. But we have to make an effort in the United States, we have to make an effort to understand, to go beyond these rather difficult times. **PAUSE & REFLECT**

My favorite poet was Aeschylus. He wrote, "In our sleep, pain which cannot forget falls drop by drop upon the heart 30 until, in our own despair, against our will, comes wisdom through the awful grace of God."

A RHETORICAL DEVICES
Reread lines 7–15. Underline the examples of **parallelism** Kennedy uses to emphasize the potential for American society to become more divided? Record examples below.

Parallelism

PAUSE & REFLECT
What kind of wisdom might come from the painful experience of having a family member killed?

What we need in the United States is not division; what we need in the United States is not hatred; what we need in the United States is not violence or lawlessness but love and wisdom, and compassion toward one another, and a feeling of justice towards those who still suffer within our country, whether they be white or they be black.

So I shall ask you tonight to return home, to say a prayer for the family of Martin Luther King, that's true, but more

40 importantly to say a prayer for our own country, which all of us love—a prayer for understanding and that compassion of which I spoke.

We can do well in this country. We will have difficult times. We've had difficult times in the past. We will have difficult times in the future. It is not the end of violence; it is not the end of lawlessness; it is not the end of disorder. **B**

But the vast majority of white people and the vast majority of black people in this country want to live together, want to improve the quality of our life, and want justice for all

50 human beings who abide in our land.

Let us dedicate ourselves to what the Greeks wrote so many years ago: to tame the savageness of man and to make gentle the life of this world.

Let us dedicate ourselves to that, and say a prayer for our country and for our people. **C**

B RHETORICAL DEVICES
Reread lines 43–46 and underline examples of parallelism. To what idea does Kennedy draw attention through this use of parallelism?

_____

_____

_____

_____

_____

_____

_____

C RHETORICAL DEVICES
Reread lines 51–55 and circle the phrase that is repeated. What does Kennedy suggest through the **repetition** of this phrase?

_____

_____

_____

_____

_____

_____

_____

Practicing Your Skills

Review your notes for "A Eulogy for Martin Luther King Jr." Choose one example of repetition and one example of parallelism that you found especially effective. Record these examples in the chart below. Then explain how each one helps make the speech effective. Keep these questions in mind:

- How might Kennedy's diction, or his choice of particular words, have affected his audience?

- What important ideas does Kennedy emphasize with each rhetorical device?

Rhetorical Device	Best Example from Speech	How It Makes the Speech More Effective
Repetition		
Parallelism		

Consider how Kennedy's ideas and his rhetorical devices work together in the speech. Would the speech have been effective without either one of these elements? Explain.

_____

_____

_____

_____

Academic Vocabulary in Writing

| acknowledge | community | contemporary | culture | role |

In what ways does Kennedy **acknowledge** the impact that Dr. King's death will have on African Americans? Use at least two Academic Vocabulary words in your response. Definitions for these terms are listed on page 345.

_____

_____

_____

_____

Assessment Practice

DIRECTIONS Use "A Eulogy for Dr. Martin Luther King Jr." to answer questions 1–4.

1 Kennedy begins his speech by —
   - A quoting his favorite poet, Aeschylus
   - B announcing the death of Dr. King
   - C telling a story from his own life
   - D urging the crowd not to become violent

2 Kennedy says he can understand having feelings of hatred and distrust because —
   - A a member of his own family was assassinated
   - B his brother was killed by a black person
   - C Dr. King would have felt the same way
   - D white people and black people cannot get along

3 Kennedy quotes Aeschylus in lines 28–31 to convey the idea that —
   - A wisdom is more awful than the pain of loss
   - B truth is often revealed to people as they sleep
   - C when pain is constant, it causes despair
   - D suffering terrible pain can lead to wisdom

4 What does Kennedy ask his audience to do?
   - A make sure Dr. King's assassin is brought to justice
   - B seek comfort in poetry and other literature
   - C respond to King's death with compassion and wisdom
   - D return home and try to forget what has happened

Marriage Is a Private Affair
Short Story by **Chinua Achebe**

Whose **LIFE** is it, anyway?

Growing up means learning to make your own decisions. But parents are often reluctant to let go of their authority. In the traditional culture that Chinua Achebe portrays in his short story, even adults are expected to get parental approval for some big decisions.

BRAINSTORM What decisions are people allowed to make at different ages? With a small group, brainstorm some decisions people can make when they are 10, 16, and 21 years old. List them in the notebook at left. Then discuss whether we have too much or too little freedom to make one's own decisions at these ages.

Text Analysis: Moral Dilemma

A **moral dilemma** is a difficult decision in which either option results in violating one's moral principles. Moral dilemmas sometimes arise through cultural conflicts—a clash between competing cultures and their values. In "Marriage Is a Private Affair," a father's traditional values clash with his son's decisions about whom to marry. The chart below shows how this clash leads to a moral dilemma for the son.

Decisions People Can Make at Different Ages

10 years old: _____

_____

_____

16 years old: _____

_____

_____

21 years old: _____

_____

_____

Father (Traditional Culture)
I have found a girl who will suit you admirably—Ugoye Nweke, the eldest daughter of our neighbor, Jacob Nweke. She has a proper Christian upbringing.

Girlfriend (Modern Culture)
In the cosmopolitan atmosphere of the city it had always seemed to her something of a joke that a person's tribe could determine whom he married.

Son
Faces a moral dilemma over whom he should marry

As you read, examine the forces that create the characters' moral dilemmas and note how the characters respond to them.

Reading Strategy: Predict

You can use text clues in a story to make **predictions,** reasonable guesses about what will happen next. When making predictions,

- analyze characters' words, thoughts, and actions to gain a sense of how the characters might react in a situation
- tap into your own experiences and knowledge of human behavior

As you read, you'll be prompted to make predictions and see how they compare with actual outcomes. The chart below shows an example.

Prediction	Reason for Prediction	Actual Outcome
Nnaemeka's father will be upset about the engagement.	Nnaemeka says villagers are unhappy when they do not get to arrange an engagement.	

Vocabulary in Context

Note: Words are listed in the order in which they appear in the story.

cosmopolitan (kŏz′mə-pŏl′ĭ-tn) *adj.* containing elements from all over the world; sophisticated
*Her travels had given her a **cosmopolitan** attitude.*

vehemently (vē′ə-mənt-lē) *adv.* in a fierce, intense manner
*He **vehemently** denied any wrongdoing on his part.*

dissuasion (dĭ-swā′zhən) *n.* an attempt to deter a person from a course of action
*She would not accept attempts at **dissuasion;** her mind was set.*

deference (děf′ər-əns) *n.* polite respect; submission to someone else's wishes
*It is important to show **deference** to your elders.*

persevere (pûr′sə-vîr′) *v.* to persist in an action or belief despite difficulty
*We can still **persevere,** despite all the obstacles ahead.*

Vocabulary Practice

Review the vocabulary words and think about their meanings. Then, working with a partner, take turns writing a sentence for at least one vocabulary word.

_____

_____

SET A PURPOSE FOR READING

Read the story to learn whether Nnaemeka is justified in feeling nervous about informing his father of his engagement.

Marriage Is a PRIVATE Affair

Short Story by

CHINUA ACHEBE

BACKGROUND This story takes place in the West African country of Nigeria. It focuses on a conflict between a father and son who belong to the Ibo, one of Nigeria's largest ethnic groups. The father lives in an Ibo village where people follow traditional practices, including choosing spouses for their children. The son has moved to Lagos, a large and ethnically diverse city. In Lagos, modern practices have displaced many of the village traditions. The tension between old and new ways of life sometimes creates conflicts within families, especially between generations.

"Have you written to your dad yet?" asked Nene[1] one afternoon as she sat with Nnaemeka[2] in her room at 16 Kasanga Street, Lagos.

"No. I've been thinking about it. I think it's better to tell him when I get home on leave!"

"But why? Your leave is such a long way off yet—six whole weeks. He should be let into our happiness now."

Nnaemeka was silent for a while and then began very slowly as if he groped for his words: "I wish I were sure it would be
10 happiness to him."

"Of course it must," replied Nene, a little surprised. "Why shouldn't it?"

"You have lived in Lagos all your life, and you know very little about people in remote parts of the country."

---

1. **Nene** (nĕ′-nĕ).
2. **Nnaemeka** (ĕn-nä′ĕ-mĕ′kä).

"That's what you always say. But I don't believe anybody will be so unlike other people that they will be unhappy when their sons are engaged to marry."

"Yes. They are most unhappy if the engagement is not arranged by them. In our case it's worse—you are not even an Ibo."

20 This was said so seriously and so bluntly that Nene could not find speech immediately. In the <u>cosmopolitan</u> atmosphere of the city it had always seemed to her something of a joke that a person's tribe could determine whom he married.

At last she said, "You don't really mean that he will object to your marrying me simply on that account? I had always thought you Ibos were kindly disposed to other people."

"So we are. But when it comes to marriage, well, it's not quite so simple. And this," he added, "is not peculiar to the Ibos. If your father were alive and lived in the heart of Ibibio-land, he would be 30 exactly like my father." **A**

"I don't know. But anyway, as your father is so fond of you, I'm sure he will forgive you soon enough. Come on then, be a good boy and send him a nice lovely letter . . ."

"It would not be wise to break the news to him by writing. A letter will bring it upon him with a shock. I'm quite sure about that."

"All right, honey, suit yourself. You know your father."

As Nnaemeka walked home that evening, he turned over in his mind different ways of overcoming his father's opposition, 40 especially now that he had gone and found a girl for him. He had thought of showing his letter to Nene but decided on second thoughts not to, at least for the moment. He read it again when he got home and couldn't help smiling to himself. He remembered Ugoye³ quite well, an Amazon⁴ of a girl who used to beat up all the boys, himself included, on the way to the stream, a complete dunce at school.

I have found a girl who will suit you admirably—Ugoye Nweke, the eldest daughter of our neighbor, Jacob Nweke. She has a proper Christian upbringing. When she stopped schooling some years ago,

cosmopolitan (kŏz′mə-pŏl′ĭ-tn) *adj.* containing elements from all over the world; sophisticated

A MORAL DILEMMA
Reread lines 1–30. Underline details that reveal the cultural backgrounds of Nene and Nnaemeka. How does Nnaemeka's background contribute to his moral dilemma?

3. **Ugoye** (Ū-gō′yĕ).
4. **Amazon:** a woman who is tall, strong-willed, and aggressive.

PAUSE & REFLECT
How do you think Nnaemeka
feels about his father's letter?

_____

_____

_____

_____

_____

_____

_____

Ⓑ MORAL DILEMMA
Reread lines 59–72. Circle
details that reveal Nnaemeka's
attitude about marriage.
Underline details that reveal his
father's beliefs. What conflict
is developing between the two
sets of beliefs?

_____

_____

_____

_____

_____

_____

_____

_____

_____

50 *her father (a man of sound judgment) sent her to live in the house*
of a pastor where she has received all the training a wife could
need. Her Sunday school teacher has told me that she reads her
Bible very fluently. I hope we shall begin negotiations when you
come home in December. **PAUSE & REFLECT**

On the second evening of his return from Lagos Nnaemeka sat
with his father under a cassia tree. This was the old man's retreat
where he went to read his Bible when the parching December sun
had set and a fresh, reviving wind blew on the leaves.

"Father," began Nnaemeka suddenly, "I have come to ask for
60 forgiveness."

"Forgiveness? For what, my son?" he asked in amazement.

"It's about this marriage question."

"Which marriage question?"

"I can't—we must—I mean it is impossible for me to marry
Nweke's daughter."

"Impossible? Why?" asked his father.

"I don't love her."

"Nobody said you did. Why should you?" he asked.

"Marriage today is different . . ."

70 "Look here, my son," interrupted his father, "nothing is
different. What one looks for in a wife are a good character and a
Christian background." **Ⓑ**

Nnaemeka saw there was no hope along the present line of
argument.

"Moreover," he said, "I am engaged to marry another girl who
has all of Ugoye's good qualities, and who . . ."

His father did not believe his ears. "What did you say?" he
asked slowly and disconcertingly.

"She is a good Christian," his son went on, "and a teacher in a
80 girls' school in Lagos."

"Teacher, did you say? If you consider that a qualification
for a good wife, I should like to point out to you, Emeka, that
no Christian woman should teach. St. Paul in his letter to the

Corinthians says that women should keep silence." He rose slowly from his seat and paced forwards and backwards. This was his pet subject, and he condemned <u>vehemently</u> those church leaders who encouraged women to teach in their schools. After he had spent his emotion on a long homily, he at last came back to his son's engagement, in a seemingly milder tone.

90   "Whose daughter is she, anyway?"

"She is Nene Atang."

"What!" All the mildness was gone again. "Did you say Neneataga; what does that mean?"

"Nene Atang from Calabar.[5] She is the only girl I can marry." This was a very rash reply, and Nnaemeka expected the storm to burst. But it did not. His father merely walked away into his room. This was most unexpected and perplexed Nnaemeka. His father's silence was infinitely more menacing than a flood of threatening speech. That night the old man did not eat. **C**

100   When he sent for Nnaemeka a day later, he applied all possible ways of <u>dissuasion</u>. But the young man's heart was hardened, and his father eventually gave him up as lost.

"I owe it to you, my son, as a duty to show you what is right and what is wrong. Whoever put this idea into your head might as well have cut your throat. It is Satan's work." He waved his son away.

"You will change your mind, Father, when you know Nene."

"I shall never see her" was the reply. From that night the father scarcely spoke to his son. He did not, however, cease hoping that he would realize how serious was the danger he was heading for.

110 Day and night he put him in his prayers.

Nnaemeka, for his own part, was very deeply affected by his father's grief. But he kept hoping that it would pass away. If it had occurred to him that never in the history of his people had a man married a woman who spoke a different tongue, he might have been less optimistic. "It has never been heard," was the verdict of an old man speaking a few weeks later. In that short sentence he spoke for all of his people. This man had come with others to commiserate with Okeke[6] when news went round about his son's behavior. By that time the son had gone back to Lagos.

---

5. **Calabar:** a seaport in southeastern Nigeria.
6. **Okeke** (ō-kĕ′-kĕ).

vehemently (vē′ə-mənt-lē) *adv.* in a fierce, intense manner

C PREDICT
Will Nnaemeka's father change his mind after thinking about his son's marriage plans? Underline evidence in the text, and then write your prediction below.

_____

_____

_____

_____

_____

dissuasion (dĭ-swā′zhən) *n.* an attempt to deter a person from a course of action

What other methods of **dissuasion** might Nnaemeka's father have tried?

_____

_____

_____

_____

_____

_____

_____

_____

_____

_____

PAUSE & REFLECT
Nnaemeka's father is less superstitious than his neighbors, who believe that a traditional medicine could cure Nnaemeka of his love for Nene. If Okeke has moved away from some of the old beliefs, why does he still cling to the tradition of selecting a wife for his son?

_____

_____

_____

_____

_____

_____

_____

_____

_____

_____

_____

_____

120   "It has never been heard," said the old man again with a sad shake of his head.

"What did Our Lord say?" asked another gentleman. "Sons shall rise against their fathers; it is there in the Holy Book."

"It is the beginning of the end," said another.

The discussion thus tending to become theological, Madubogwu, a highly practical man, brought it down once more to the ordinary level.

"Have you thought of consulting a native doctor about your son?" he asked Nnaemeka's father.

130   "He isn't sick" was the reply.

"What is he then? The boy's mind is diseased, and only a good herbalist⁷ can bring him back to his right senses. The medicine he requires is _Amalile,_ the same that women apply with success to recapture their husbands' straying affection."

"Madubogwu is right," said another gentleman. "This thing calls for medicine."

"I shall not call in a native doctor." Nnaemeka's father was known to be obstinately ahead of his more superstitious neighbors in these matters. "I will not be another Mrs. Ochuba. If my son

140 wants to kill himself, let him do it with his own hands. It is not for me to help him."

"But it was her fault," said Madubogwu. "She ought to have gone to an honest herbalist. She was a clever woman, nevertheless."

"She was a wicked murderess," said Jonathan, who rarely argued with his neighbors because, he often said, they were incapable of reasoning. "The medicine was prepared for her husband, it was his name they called in its preparation, and I am sure it would have been perfectly beneficial to him. It was wicked

150 to put it into the herbalist's food and say you were only trying it out." **PAUSE & REFLECT**

Six months later, Nnaemeka was showing his young wife a short letter from his father:

---

7. **herbalist** (ûr′bə-lĭst): a person who is expert in the use of medicinal herbs.

It amazes me that you could be so unfeeling as to send me your wedding picture. I would have sent it back. But on further thought I decided just to cut off your wife and send it back to you because I have nothing to do with her. How I wish that I had nothing to do with you either.

When Nene read through this letter and looked at the mutilated picture, her eyes filled with tears, and she began to sob.

"Don't cry, my darling," said her husband. "He is essentially good-natured and will one day look more kindly on our marriage." But years passed, and that one day did not come. ◐

For eight years, Okeke would have nothing to do with his son, Nnaemeka. Only three times (when Nnaemeka asked to come home and spend his leave) did he write to him.

"I can't have you in my house," he replied on one occasion. "It can be of no interest to me where or how you spend your leave—or your life, for that matter."

The prejudice against Nnaemeka's marriage was not confined to his little village. In Lagos, especially among his people who worked there, it showed itself in a different way. Their women, when they met at their village meeting, were not hostile to Nene. Rather, they paid her such excessive **deference** as to make her feel she was not one of them. But as time went on, Nene gradually broke through some of this prejudice and even began to make friends among them. Slowly and grudgingly they began to admit that she kept her home much better than most of them.

The story eventually got to the little village in the heart of the Ibo country that Nnaemeka and his young wife were a most happy couple. But his father was one of the few people in the village who knew nothing about this. He always displayed so much temper whenever his son's name was mentioned that everyone avoided it in his presence. By a tremendous effort of will he had succeeded in pushing his son to the back of his mind. The strain had nearly killed him, but he had **persevered** and won.

Then one day he received a letter from Nene, and in spite of himself he began to glance through it perfunctorily until all of a sudden the expression on his face changed and he began to read more carefully.

◐ **MORAL DILEMMA**
Do you think there's a good way for Nnaemeka to resolve his moral dilemma? Explain your answer.

_____

_____

_____

_____

_____

_____

_____

_____

_____

_____

deference (dĕf′ər-əns) *n.* polite respect; submission to someone else's wishes

persevere (pûr′sə-vîr′) *v.* to persist in an action or belief despite difficulty

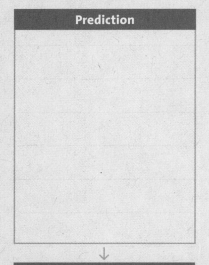

ⓔ PREDICT

How will Nnaemeka's father react to this letter? Write your prediction and your reason in the chart below. Then continue reading and fill in the last box.

Prediction

↓

Reason for Prediction

↓

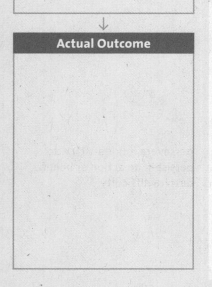

Actual Outcome

. . . Our two sons, from the day they learnt that they have a grandfather, have insisted on being taken to him. I find it impossible to tell them that you will not see them. I implore you to allow Nnaemeka to bring them home for a short time during his leave next month. I shall remain here in Lagos . . . ⓔ

The old man at once felt the resolution he had built up over so many years falling in. He was telling himself that he must not give in. He tried to steel his heart against all emotional appeals. It was a reenactment of that other struggle. He leaned against a window
200 and looked out. The sky was overcast with heavy black clouds, and a high wind began to blow, filling the air with dust and dry leaves. It was one of those rare occasions when even Nature takes a hand in a human fight. Very soon it began to rain, the first rain in the year. It came down in large sharp drops and was accompanied by the lightning and thunder which mark a change of season. Okeke was trying hard not to think of his two grandsons. But he knew he was now fighting a losing battle. He tried to hum a favorite hymn, but the pattering of large raindrops on the roof broke up the tune. His mind immediately returned to the
210 children. How could he shut his door against them? By a curious mental process he imagined them standing, sad and forsaken, under the harsh angry weather—shut out from his house.

That night he hardly slept, from remorse—and a vague fear that he might die without making it up to them.

Text Analysis: Moral Dilemma

Review the notes you took while reading. Then complete the chart with details about the moral dilemma that Nnaemeka faced in the story. An example has been done for you.

NNAEMEKA'S MORAL DILEMMA	
Possible Action	**How It Would Violate His Beliefs or Principles**
Marry Nene	*Nnaemeka wants to marry Nene but is afraid his father won't approve.*
Marry Ugoye	

NNAEMEKA'S DECISION	
What he did	
Effects on him, his father, his wife	

Okeke's feelings of remorse at the end of the story suggest that he faced a moral dilemma, too. By clinging to his traditional beliefs and refusing to associate with his son's family, what other values did he sacrifice?

_____

_____

_____

_____

Reading Strategy: Predict

What events or outcomes in the story took you by surprise? Below, write a prediction you made that turned out to be inaccurate. Then explain your reason for the prediction, what actually happened, and what clues from the text or from your own experience might have led to a correct prediction.

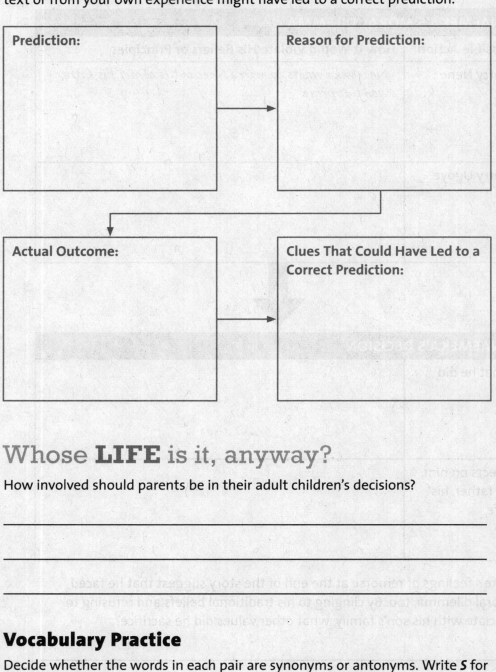

Prediction:	Reason for Prediction:

Actual Outcome:	Clues That Could Have Led to a Correct Prediction:

Whose LIFE is it, anyway?

How involved should parents be in their adult children's decisions?

_____

_____

_____

Vocabulary Practice

Decide whether the words in each pair are synonyms or antonyms. Write **S** for synonyms or **A** for antonyms.

_____ **1.** cosmopolitan/provincial   _____ **4.** deference/respect

_____ **2.** vehemently/fiercely   _____ **5.** abandon/persevere

_____ **3.** persuasion/dissuasion

Academic Vocabulary in Speaking

| acknowledge | community | contemporary | culture | role |

TURN AND TALK Compared to Okeke's traditional values, Nnaemeka's values are more **contemporary.** However, the two men still have some beliefs in common. With a partner, discuss what values Okeke and Nnaemeka share. Use at least two Academic Vocabulary words in your conversation. Definitions for these terms are listed on page 345.

Assessment Practice

DIRECTIONS Use "Marriage Is a Private Affair" to answer questions 1–6.

1 Why does Okeke oppose Nnaemeka's choice of a wife?

- **A** He does not get along with Nene's father.
- **B** He wants Nnaemeka to marry a teacher.
- **C** He believes he should choose his son's wife.
- **D** He thinks Nnaemeka should marry for love.

2 What qualities does Okeke think a wife should have?

- **A** housekeeping skills and faith in God
- **B** a loving heart and a respectable job
- **C** good character and a Christian background
- **D** cleverness and generosity

3 Nnaemeka's moral dilemma involves choosing between his love for Nene and —

- **A** his respect for his father
- **B** his belief in traditional medicine
- **C** his Christian faith
- **D** his right to privacy

4 What does Okeke do when Nnaemeka sends him a wedding photo?

- **A** He refuses to look at the photo.
- **B** He gives the photo to a native doctor.
- **C** He shares the picture with his village.
- **D** He cuts Nene out of the picture.

5 Okeke avoids hearing any news about Nnaemeka and Nene by —

- **A** forcing Nnaemeka to stay in a different house when he visits the village
- **B** refusing to read the letters that Nnaemeka sends him
- **C** moving to a different village where no one knows Nnaemeka
- **D** becoming angry when anyone mentions Nnaemeka's name

6 Okeke changes his response to his moral dilemma when he realizes that —

- **A** Nene is a better housekeeper than most Ibo women
- **B** he has sacrificed his relationship with his grandsons
- **C** his beliefs about marriage are based on superstition
- **D** Nnaemeka is suffering from Okeke's harsh treatment

UNIT 10

Upholding Honor

GREEK TRAGEDY AND MEDIEVAL ROMANCE

Be sure to read the Text Analysis Workshop on pp. 1058–1063 in *Holt McDougal Literature*.

Academic Vocabulary for Unit 10

Preview the following Academic Vocabulary words. You will encounter these words as you work through this book and will use them as you write and talk about the selection in the unit.

> **drama** (drä′mə) *n.* literature in which plot and characters are developed through dialogue and action
>
> *Many people enjoy reading a **drama** because the characters express familiar emotions and problems, but also offer new solutions.*
>
> •
>
> **emerge** (ĭ-mûrj′) *v.* to become visible; to develop or become something new
>
> *The theme of a piece of literature often **emerges** slowly through the details the author includes.*
>
> •
>
> **encounter** (ĕn-koun′tər) *n.* an unexpected meeting
>
> *An **encounter** with a tragic character in a story can draw the reader into the emotions of the character's life.*
>
> •
>
> **globe** (glōb) *n.* a round, ball-shaped model of the earth; the earth
>
> *People read and watch plays all around the **globe.***
>
> •
>
> **underlie** (ŭn′dər-lī′) *v.* to form the basis or foundation of
>
> *The craft of the author **underlies** every piece of fiction and nonfiction.*

Think of a book you've read or a movie you've seen lately in which one of the characters dreams of reaching a difficult goal. Write a couple of sentences about why dreams **underlie** the goals of many people. Use at least two Academic Vocabulary words in your response.

_____

_____

_____

_____

from Don Quixote
Novel by **Miguel de Cervantes**

Why do we admire DREAMERS?

Think of people who have pursued their dreams even when the dreams seemed impossible to achieve. What qualities do these dreamers possess?

DISCUSS With a small group, generate a list of people who have been considered dreamers. Then discuss these questions: What traits do these individuals share? Record your list and notes about your discussion in the notebook at left.

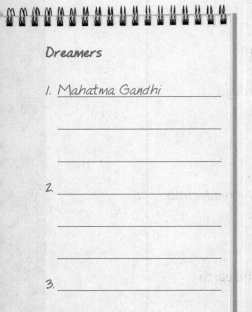

Dreamers

1. Mahatma Gandhi

2.

3.

Text Analysis: Parody

A **parody** is a comic imitation of another work or of a type of literature. A parody may include the same **archetypes,** or common features, of traditional romances, but it turns the reader's understanding of the archetypes inside out. This excerpt portrays a ridiculous hero on a hopeless quest. The following chart describes the code of chivalry, lists common features of medieval romances, and shows the comic strategies the writer uses to get his jokes across. Refer to this information as you read the selection.

Code of Chivalry	Common Features of Medieval Romances	Comic Strategies the Writer Uses
Knights — • swear allegiance to a lord • fight to uphold Christianity • seek to redress all wrongs • honor truth by word and deed • are faithful to one lady • act with bravery, courtesy, and modesty	• idealized noble characters • exaggerated behavior • a hero's journey or quest • supernatural or magical elements • unusual or exotic settings	• verbal humor, such as exaggerated descriptions, puns, and irony • language that imitates the style of a chivalric romance • absurd situations that parallel the actions of a chivalric hero

Reading Strategy: Set a Purpose for Reading

When you **set a purpose for reading,** you decide what to look for as you read. In this lesson, you are reading to analyze a novel excerpt that parodies the medieval romance. As you read, you will be prompted to note the specific ideas the writer is mocking and the techniques he uses to achieve his comic effects. See the example below.

Idea Being Mocked	Technique the Writer Is Using
a hero's journey or quest	describing an absurd situation in which the character fights against windmills

Vocabulary in Context

Note: Words are listed in the order in which they appear in the selection.

resurrect (rĕz′ə-rĕkt) *v.* to bring back to life
*The student **resurrected** his self-esteem after failing a test by studying harder.*

fictitious (fĭk-tĭsh′əs) *adj.* fabricated; created by the imagination
*The novel contained a **fictitious** account of a quest to save the world.*

affable (ăf′ə-bəl) *adj.* warm and friendly
*The hotel had an **affable** staff that made the guests feel welcome.*

burnish (bûr′nĭsh) *v.* to polish
*The boy **burnished** the stair banister with a rag soaked in lemon oil.*

incongruous (ĭn-kŏng′grōō-əs) *adj.* unsuitable; incompatible
*The baseball looked **incongruous** in the middle of the basketball court.*

enmity (ĕn′mĭ-tē) *n.* hostility and ill will
*Unfortunately, an **enmity** grew between the two friends after they argued about money.*

hapless (hăp′lĭs) *adj.* pitiful; unfortunate
*The firefighters were able to free the **hapless** dog after it became entangled in a fishing net.*

Vocabulary Practice

Explain why you think people need to dream about things even if the dreams are **fictitious.** How can dreaming about possible and impossible things help a person reach his or her goals?

_____

_____

_____

Don Quixote

Novel by
MIGUEL
DE CERVANTES

BACKGROUND Miguel de Cervantes served
as a soldier in Spain before being captured
and enslaved by pirates for five years.
After he returned home, he found himself
struggling to make a living and eventually
landing in debtor's prison. In 1605, after 25
years of failures, Miguel de Cervantes found
fame with *Don Quixote*. Written to parody
both romances and romantic ideals, the
book's inspired use of irony and realistic
details changed the way novels were written.
Today *Don Quixote* is one of the most widely
published books in the world.

**(A) SET A PURPOSE FOR
READING**
In lines 1–8, how does the
narrator describe the gentleman?

_____

_____

_____

_____

_____

_____

_____

_____

Part 1, Chapter 1

In a village of La Mancha[1] the name of which I have no desire
to recall, there lived not so long ago one of those gentlemen
who always have a lance in the rack, an ancient buckler,[2] a skinny
nag, and a greyhound for the chase. A stew with more beef
than mutton in it, chopped meat for his evening meal, scraps
for a Saturday, lentils on Friday, and a young pigeon as a special
delicacy for Sunday, went to account for three-quarters of his
income. **(A)**

The rest of it he laid out on a broadcloth greatcoat[3] and velvet
10 stockings for feast days, with slippers to match, while the other
days of the week he cut a figure in a suit of the finest homespun.

---

1. **La Mancha:** a high, flat, barren region in central Spain.
2. **buckler:** a small, round shield carried or worn on the arm.
3. **broadcloth greatcoat:** a heavy wool overcoat.

Living with him were a housekeeper in her forties, a niece who was not yet twenty, and a lad of the field and market place who saddled his horse for him and wielded the pruning knife.

This gentleman of ours was close on to fifty, of a robust constitution but with little flesh on his bones and a face that was lean and gaunt. He was noted for his early rising, being very fond of the hunt. They will try to tell you that his surname was Quijada or Quesada—there is some difference of opinion
20 among those who have written on the subject—but according to the most likely conjectures we are to understand that it was really Quejana.[4] But all this means very little so far as our story is concerned, providing that in the telling of it we do not depart one iota from the truth. **B**

You may know, then, that the aforesaid gentleman, on those occasions when he was at leisure, which was most of the year around, was in the habit of reading books of chivalry with such pleasure and devotion as to lead him almost wholly to forget the life of a hunter and even the administration of his estate. So great
30 was his curiosity and infatuation in this regard that he even sold many acres of tillable land in order to be able to buy and read the books that he loved, and he would carry home with him as many of them as he could obtain. **PAUSE & REFLECT**

Of all those that he thus devoured none pleased him so well as the ones that had been composed by the famous Feliciano de Silva,[5] whose lucid prose style and involved conceits[6] were as precious to him as pearls; especially when he came to read those tales of love and amorous challenges that are to be met with in many places, such a passage as the following, for example:
40 "The reason of the unreason that afflicts my reason, in such a manner weakens my reason that I with reason lament me of your comeliness." And he was similarly affected when his eyes fell upon such lines as these: ". . . the high Heaven of your divinity divinely fortifies you with the stars and renders you deserving of that desert your greatness doth deserve."

---

4. **Quijada** (kē-hä′dä) . . . **Quesada** (kĕ-sä′dä) . . . **Quejana** (kĕ-hä′nä).
5. **Feliciano de Silva:** a Spanish author of fictional books about knights.
6. **conceits:** lengthy, exaggerated comparisons.

B PARODY
Reread lines 1–24. Underline details in the text that describe the gentleman. In most medieval romances, the heroes are healthy, elegant, strong, and youthful. How does the gentleman in Don Quixote compare to the typical modern hero?

_____

_____

_____

_____

_____

_____

_____

PAUSE & REFLECT
What details in lines 25–33 reveal that the gentleman is completely impractical?

_____

_____

_____

_____

_____

_____

_____

_____

_____

resurrect (rĕz′ə-rĕkt′) v. to bring back to life

G PARODY
Describe the tone of lines 46–69. How does the narrator seem to view books of chivalry and Quejana's passion for them? Review the ideas listed below to help you respond to the question.

- Read the quotation from de Silva (lines 40–45) aloud and notice how ridiculous it sounds. The author compares de Silva's words to pearls but also says that Aristotle would find them difficult to understand.

- Cervantes says that Quejana would have finished writing the adventures himself, if he and "not been constantly occupied with other things" but the author does not say what those things are.

- Read footnote 10. Why does the author point out that the village curate is a "learned man" but that he also graduated from a "minor" university?

The poor fellow used to lie awake nights in an effort to disentangle the meaning and make sense out of passages such as these, although Aristotle[7] himself would not have been able to understand them, even if he had been **resurrected** for that sole
50 purpose. He was not at ease in his mind over those wounds that Don Belianís[8] gave and received; for no matter how great the surgeons who treated him, the poor fellow must have been left with his face and his entire body covered with marks and scars. Nevertheless, he was grateful to the author for closing the book with the promise of an interminable adventure to come; many a time he was tempted to take up his pen and literally finish the tale as had been promised, and he undoubtedly would have done so, and would have succeeded at it very well, if his thoughts had not been constantly occupied with other things of greater moment.

60 He often talked it over with the village curate,[9] who was a learned man, a graduate of Sigüenza,[10] and they would hold long discussions as to who had been the better knight, Palmerin of England or Amadis of Gaul; but Master Nicholas, the barber of the same village, was in the habit of saying that no one could come up to the Knight of Phoebus,[11] and that if anyone could compare with him it was Don Galaor, brother of Amadis of Gaul, for Galaor was ready for anything—he was none of your finical[12] knights, who went around whimpering as his brother did, and in point of valor he did not lag behind him. **G**

70 In short, our gentleman became so immersed in his reading that he spent whole nights from sundown to sunup and his days from dawn to dusk in poring over his books, until, finally, from so little sleeping and so much reading, his brain dried up and he went completely out of his mind. He had filled his imagination with everything that he had read, with enchantments, knightly encounters, battles, challenges, wounds, with tales of love and its

---

7. **Aristotle:** a Greek philosopher (384–322 B.C.) widely known for his wisdom.
8. **Don Belianís** (dôn bĕ-lyä-nēs′): the hero of a chivalric romance.
9. **curate** (kyŏŏr′ĭt): a religious official in charge of a parish.
10. **Sigüenza** (sē-gwĕn′sä): a "minor" university of Spain, whose graduates were often mocked.
11. **Palmerin of England . . . Amadis** (ä′mə-dĭs) **of Gaul . . . Knight of Phoebus** (fē′bəs): romance heroes who exemplified knightly perfection.
12. **finical** (fĭn′ĭ-kəl): finicky; picky.

torments, and all sorts of impossible things, and as a result had come to believe that all these <u>fictitious</u> happenings were true; they were more real to him than anything else in the world. He would
80 remark that the Cid Ruy Díaz[13] had been a very good knight, but there was no comparison between him and the Knight of the Flaming Sword,[14] who with a single backward stroke had cut in half two fierce and monstrous giants. He preferred Bernardo del Carpio,[15] who at Roncesvalles had slain Roland despite the charm the latter bore, availing himself of the stratagem which Hercules employed when he strangled Antaeus, the son of Earth, in his arms.

He had much good to say for Morgante[16] who, though he belonged to the haughty, overbearing race of giants, was of an <u>affable</u> disposition and well brought up. But, above all, he cherished
90 an admiration for Rinaldo of Montalbán,[17] especially as he beheld him sallying forth from his castle to rob all those that crossed his path, or when he thought of him overseas stealing the image of Mohammed which, so the story has it, was all of gold. And he would have liked very well to have had his fill of kicking that traitor Galalón,[18] a privilege for which he would have given his housekeeper with his niece thrown into the bargain. **PAUSE & REFLECT**

At last, when his wits were gone beyond repair, he came to conceive the strangest idea that ever occurred to any madman in this world. It now appeared to him fitting and necessary, in
100 order to win a greater amount of honor for himself and serve his country at the same time, to become a knight-errant[19] and roam

---

13. **Cid Ruy Díaz** (sēd' rwē' dē'äs): Rodrigo (or Ruy) Díaz de Vivar, known as the Cid, was an actual Spanish military leader and national hero about whom an epic poem was written.

14. **Knight of the Flaming Sword:** Amadis of Greece, a romance hero whose symbol was a red sword.

15. **Bernardo del Carpio** (kär'pyô): a legendary Spanish hero who, in some tales, killed the hero of *The Song of Roland* by strangling him in midair, as Hercules had done to the giant Antaeus.

16. **Morgante** (môr-gän'tĕ): a ferocious giant, in an Italian romantic poem, who later became sweet and loving.

17. **Rinaldo of Montalbán** (môn-täl-bän'): the hero in a series of French epic poems.

18. **Galalón** (gä-lä-lôn'): Ganelon, the stepfather and betrayer of Roland, the French epic hero.

19. **knight-errant:** a knight who wanders the countryside in search of adventure to prove his chivalry.

fictitious (fĭk-tĭsh'əs) *adj.* fabricated; created by the imagination

Underline the word that the adjective **fictitious** modifies in line 78.

affable (ăf'ə-bəl) *adj.* warm and friendly

PAUSE & REFLECT
Reread lines 87–96. What qualities in these fictional characters does the gentleman seem to admire?

PAUSE & REFLECT

Do you think that Quejana's decision to become a knight-errant in line 101 is reasonable, or is he a madman? Explain.

_____

_____

_____

_____

burnish (bûr′nĭsh) *v.* to polish

D **SET A PURPOSE FOR READING**

Use the chart below to record how Cervantes is mocking an idealized noble character in lines 111–128. Turn back to page 382 to review the techniques Cervantes uses in his writing.

Idea Being Mocked:

↓

Technique the Writer Is Using:

the world on horseback, in a suit of armor; he would go in quest of adventures, by way of putting into practice all that he had read in his books; he would right every manner of wrong, placing himself in situations of the greatest peril such as would redound[20] to the eternal glory of his name. As a reward for his valor and the might of his arm, the poor fellow could already see himself crowned Emperor of Trebizond[21] at the very least; and so, carried away by the strange pleasure that he found in such thoughts as these, he at
110 once set about putting his plan into effect. **PAUSE & REFLECT**

The first thing he did was to **burnish** up some old pieces of armor, left him by his great-grandfather, which for ages had lain in a corner, moldering and forgotten. He polished and adjusted them as best he could, and then he noticed that one very important thing was lacking: there was no closed helmet, but only a morion, or visorless headpiece, with turned up brim of the kind foot soldiers wore. His ingenuity, however, enabled him to remedy this, and he proceeded to fashion out of cardboard a kind of half-helmet, which, when attached to the morion, gave the appearance
120 of a whole one. True, when he went to see if it was strong enough to withstand a good slashing blow, he was somewhat disappointed; for when he drew his sword and gave it a couple of thrusts, he succeeded only in undoing a whole week's labor. The ease with which he had hewed it to bits disturbed him no little, and he decided to make it over. This time he placed a few strips of iron on the inside, and then, convinced that it was strong enough, refrained from putting it to any further test; instead, he adopted it then and there as the finest helmet ever made. **D**

After this, he went out to have a look at his nag; and although
130 the animal had more *cuartos,* or cracks, in its hoof than there are quarters in a real,[22] and more blemishes than Gonela's steed[23] which *tantum pellis et ossa fuit,*[24] it nonetheless looked to its

---

20. **redound:** contribute.
21. **Trebizond:** a former Greek empire, often mentioned in stories of knighthood.
22. **quarters in a real** (rā-äl′): A real was a coin worth about five cents.
23. **Gonela's steed:** the horse of the Italian court comedian Pietro Gonela, which was famous for having gas.
24. *tantum pellis et ossa fuit* Latin: was only skin and bones.

master like a far better horse than Alexander's Bucephalus or the Babieca of the Cid.[25] He spent all of four days in trying to think up a name for his mount; for—so he told himself—seeing that it belonged to so famous and worthy a knight, there was no reason why it should not have a name of equal renown. The kind of name he wanted was one that would at once indicate what the nag had been before it came to belong to a knight-errant and what its

140 present status was; for it stood to reason that, when the master's worldly condition changed, his horse also ought to have a famous, high-sounding appellation, one suited to the new order of things and the new profession that it was to follow.

After he in his memory and imagination had made up, struck out, and discarded many names, now adding to and now subtracting from the list, he finally hit upon "Rocinante," a name that impressed him as being sonorous and at the same time indicative of what the steed had been when it was but a hack, whereas now it was nothing other than the first and foremost of

150 all the hacks[26] in the world. **E**

Having found a name for his horse that pleased his fancy, he then desired to do as much for himself, and this required another week, and by the end of that period he had made up his mind that he was henceforth to be known as Don Quixote,[27] which, as has been stated, has led the authors of this veracious history to assume that his real name must undoubtedly have been Quijada, and not Quesada as others would have it. But remembering that the valiant Amadis was not content to call himself that and nothing more, but added the name of his kingdom and fatherland

160 that he might make it famous also, and thus came to take the name Amadis of Gaul, so our good knight chose to add his place of origin and become "Don Quixote de la Mancha"; for by this means, as he saw it, he was making very plain his lineage and was conferring honor upon his country by taking its name as his own.

---

25. **Alexander's Bucephalus** (byōō-sĕf′ə-ləs) **or the Babieca** (bä-byĕ′kä) **of the Cid:** famous horses. Alexander is Alexander the Great, the early conqueror of Asia.

26. **Rocinante** (rô-sĕ-nän′tĕ) **. . . foremost of all the hacks:** *Rocin* means "nag" or "hack" in Spanish; *ante* means "before" or "first." So the name Rocinante indicates that the horse is the first, or chief, nag.

27. **Quixote** (kē-hô′tĕ): The word literally denotes a piece of armor that protects the thigh.

E PARODY
What does the horse's name (line 146) imply about the hero's lofty goals? Make sure you read footnote 26 and think about the meaning of the horse's name before answering the question.

_____

_____

_____

_____

_____

_____

_____

_____

_____

_____

_____

_____

_____

_____

_____

_____

_____

F PARODY
Reread lines 151–183. What romantic conventions does Cervantes mock here? Look back at the information about medieval romance on page 382 to help you answer the question.

_____
_____
_____
_____
_____
_____
_____
_____

incongruous (ĭn-kŏng′grōō-əs) _adj._ unsuitable; incompatible

Why might Don Quixote think the name Aldonza Lorenzo would seem **incongruous** when paired with Don Quixote?

_____
_____
_____
_____
_____
_____

And so, having polished up his armor and made the morion over into a closed helmet, and having given himself and his horse a name, he naturally found but one thing lacking still: he must seek out a lady of whom he could become enamored; for a knight-errant without a ladylove was like a tree without leaves or fruit, a 170 body without a soul.

"If," he said to himself, "as a punishment for my sins or by a stroke of fortune I should come upon some giant hereabouts, a thing that very commonly happens to knights-errant, and if I should slay him in a hand-to-hand encounter or perhaps cut him in two, or, finally, if I should vanquish and subdue him, would it not be well to have someone to whom I may send him as a present, in order that he, if he is living, may come in, fall upon his knees in front of my sweet lady, and say in a humble and submissive tone of voice, 'I, lady, am the giant Caraculiambro,²⁸ lord of the 180 island Malindrania, who has been overcome in single combat by that knight who never can be praised enough, Don Quixote de la Mancha, the same who sent me to present myself before your Grace that your Highness may dispose of me as you see fit'?" **F**

Oh, how our good knight reveled in this speech, and more than ever when he came to think of the name that he should give his lady! As the story goes, there was a very good-looking farm girl who lived near by, with whom he had once been smitten, although it is generally believed that she never knew or suspected it. Her name was Aldonza Lorenzo, and it seemed to him that 190 she was the one upon whom he should bestow the title of mistress of his thoughts. For her he wished a name that should not be **incongruous** with his own and that would convey the suggestion of a princess or a great lady; and, accordingly, he resolved to call her "Dulcinea del Toboso,"²⁹ she being a native of that place. A musical name to his ears, out of the ordinary and significant, like the others he had chosen for himself and his appurtenances.³⁰

---

28. **Caraculiambro** (kä-rä-kōō-lyäm′brô).
29. **Dulcinea del Toboso** (dōōl-sē-nĕ′ä dĕl tô-bô′sô): The name comes from _dulce,_ the Spanish word for sweet.
30. **appurtenances:** appendages; accessories.

After completing his preparations, Don Quixote sets off on his first adventure, which lasts three days. He persuades an innkeeper to dub him a knight. Then he "rescues" a servant boy from his master's beating, but as soon as "our knight" leaves, the master beats the boy even harder. Next, Don Quixote mistakes a traveling group of merchants for hostile knights. After insulting the merchants for failing to swear to the beauty of Dulcinea del Toboso, he is badly beaten. A neighbor finds him on the road and carries him home, to the great relief of his family and friends. They blame Don Quixote's mad behavior on his reading habits, so for his own good they decide to burn his books.

from Part 1, Chapter 7

. . . That night the housekeeper burned all the books there were in the stable yard and in all the house; and there must have been some that went up in smoke which should have been preserved
200 in everlasting archives, if the one who did the scrutinizing had not been so indolent. Thus we see the truth of the old saying, to the effect that the innocent must sometimes pay for the sins of the guilty.

One of the things that the curate and the barber advised as a remedy for their friend's sickness was to wall up the room where the books had been, so that, when he arose, he would not find them missing—it might be that the cause being removed, the effect would cease—and they could tell him that a magician had made away with them, room and all. This they proceeded to do as
210 quickly as possible. Two days later, when Don Quixote rose from his bed, the first thing he did was to go have a look at his library, and, not finding it where he had left it, he went from one part of the house to another searching for it. Going up to where the door had been, he ran his hands over the wall and rolled his eyes in every direction without saying a word; but after some little while he asked the housekeeper where his study was with all his books.

She had been well instructed in what to answer him. "Whatever study is your Grace talking about?" she said. "There is no study, and no books, in this house; the devil took them all
220 away." **PAUSE & REFLECT**

PAUSE & REFLECT

Why does the housekeeper burn Don Quixote's books? How do his friends keep him from his books?

_____

_____

_____

_____

_____

_____

_____

_____

_____

_____

_____

_____

enmity (ĕn′mĭ-tē) *n.* hostility and ill will

G PARODY
How does Don Quixote's response in lines 238–245 sound like a traditional romance?

_____

_____

_____

_____

_____

_____

_____

hapless (hăp′lĭs) *adj.* pitiful; unfortunate

"No," said the niece, "it was not the devil but an enchanter who came upon a cloud one night, the day after your Grace left here; dismounting from a serpent that he rode, he entered your study, and I don't know what all he did there, but after a bit he went flying off through the roof, leaving the house full of smoke; and when we went to see what he had done, there was no study and not a book in sight. There is one thing, though, that the housekeeper and I remember very well: at the time that wicked old fellow left, he cried out in a loud voice that it was all on account of a secret **enmity** that he bore the owner of those books and that study, and that was why he had done the mischief in this house which we would discover. He also said that he was called Muñatón the Magician."

"Freston, he should have said," remarked Don Quixote.

"I can't say as to that," replied the housekeeper, "whether he was called Freston or Fritón;[31] all I know is that his name ended in a *tón*."

"So it does," said Don Quixote. "He is a wise enchanter, a great enemy of mine, who has a grudge against me because he knows by his arts and learning that in the course of time I am to fight in single combat with a knight whom he favors, and that I am to be the victor and he can do nothing to prevent it. For this reason he seeks to cause me all the trouble that he can, but I am warning him that it will be hard to gainsay or shun that which Heaven has ordained." . . . **G**

In the meanwhile Don Quixote was bringing his powers of persuasion to bear upon a farmer who lived near by, a good man—if this title may be applied to one who is poor—but with very few wits in his head. The short of it is, by pleas and promises, he got the **hapless** rustic to agree to ride forth with him and serve him as his squire. Among other things, Don Quixote told him that he ought to be more than willing to go, because no telling what adventure might occur which would win them an island, and then he (the farmer) would be left to be the governor of it. As a result of these and other similar assurances, Sancho Panza

---

31. **Freston** (frĕs-tôn′) **or Fritón** (frē-tôn′): Freston, a magician, was thought to be the author of *History of Belianís of Greece*.

forsook his wife and children and consented to take upon himself the duties of squire to his neighbor.

Next, Don Quixote set out to raise some money, and by selling this thing and pawning that and getting the worst of the bargain always, he finally scraped together a reasonable amount. He also asked a friend of his for the loan of a buckler and patched up his broken helmet as well as he could. He advised his squire, Sancho, of the day and hour when they were to take the road and told him to see to laying in a supply of those things that were most necessary, and, above all, not to forget the saddlebags. Sancho replied that he would see to all this and added that he was also thinking of taking along with him a very good ass that he had, as he was not much used to going on foot.

With regard to the ass, Don Quixote had to do a little thinking, trying to recall if any knight-errant had ever had a squire thus asininely[32] mounted. He could not think of any, but nevertheless he decided to take Sancho with the intention of providing him with a nobler steed as soon as occasion offered; he had but to appropriate the horse of the first discourteous knight he met. Having furnished himself with shirts and all the other things that the innkeeper had recommended, he and Panza rode forth one night unseen by anyone and without taking leave of wife and children, housekeeper or niece. They went so far that by the time morning came they were safe from discovery had a hunt been started for them. . . . ⊕

from Part 1, Chapter 8

At this point they caught sight of thirty or forty windmills which were standing on the plain there, and no sooner had Don Quixote laid eyes upon them than he turned to his squire and said, "Fortune is guiding our affairs better than we could have wished; for you see there before you, friend Sancho Panza, some thirty or more lawless giants with whom I mean to do battle. I shall deprive them of their lives, and with the spoils from this encounter we shall begin to enrich ourselves; for this is righteous warfare, and

---

32. **asininely:** foolishly; ridiculously (derived from Latin *asinus*, "ass"). The statement is both a literal description and a sly joke about Sancho's unheroic appearance.

⊕ **SET A PURPOSE FOR READING**

In lines 258–280, how is Cervantes conveying an absurd situation that parallels the actions of a knight-errant? Look back at page 382 if you need some help.

PAUSE & REFLECT
What does Don Quixote think
the windmills are? What reason
does he give for Sancho Panza
not seeing them?

_____

_____

_____

_____

_____

_____

_____

_____

_____

_____

_____

_____

_____

_____

_____

_____

_____

_____

_____

_____

_____

it is a great service to God to remove so accursed a breed from the
290 face of the earth."

"What giants?" said Sancho Panza.

"Those that you see there," replied his master, "those with the
long arms some of which are as much as two leagues in length."

"But look, your Grace, those are not giants but windmills, and
what appear to be arms are their wings which, when whirled in
the breeze, cause the millstone to go."

"It is plain to be seen," said Don Quixote, "that you have had
little experience in this matter of adventures. If you are afraid, go
off to one side and say your prayers while I am engaging them in
300 fierce, unequal combat." **PAUSE & REFLECT**

Saying this, he gave spurs to his steed Rocinante, without paying any heed to Sancho's warning that these were truly windmills and not giants that he was riding forth to attack. Nor even when he was close upon them did he perceive what they really were, but shouted at the top of his lungs, "Do not seek to flee, cowards and vile creatures that you are, for it is but a single knight with whom you have to deal!"

At that moment a little wind came up and the big wings began turning.

310 "Though you flourish as many arms as did the giant Briareus,"[33] said Don Quixote when he perceived this, "you still shall have to answer to me."

He thereupon commended himself with all his heart to his lady Dulcinea, beseeching her to succor him in this peril; and, being well covered with his shield and with his lance at rest, he bore down upon them at a full gallop and fell upon the first mill that stood in his way, giving a thrust at the wing, which was whirling at such a speed that his lance was broken into bits and both horse and horseman went rolling over the plain, very much battered 320 indeed. Sancho upon his donkey came hurrying to his master's assistance as fast as he could, but when he reached the spot, the knight was unable to move, so great was the shock with which he and Rocinante had hit the ground. **I**

"God help us!" exclaimed Sancho, "did I not tell your Grace to look well, that those were nothing but windmills, a fact which no one could fail to see unless he had other mills of the same sort in his head?"

"Be quiet, friend Sancho," said Don Quixote. "Such are the fortunes of war, which more than any other are subject to 330 constant change. What is more, when I come to think of it, I am sure that this must be the work of that magician Frestón, the one who robbed me of my study and my books, and who has thus changed the giants into windmills in order to deprive me of the glory of overcoming them, so great is the enmity that he bears me; but in the end his evil arts shall not prevail against this trusty sword of mine." **J**

I PARODY
In lines 310–323, how do Don Quixote's actions mirror what might happen in a medieval romance, and how do they differ?

J PARODY
What point is Cervantes making about using chivalry as a practical guide to life in lines 328–336?

---

33. **Briareus** (brē-ăr'yoos): a mythological giant with 100 arms.

"May God's will be done," was Sancho Panza's response. And with the aid of his squire the knight was once more mounted on Rocinante, who stood there with one shoulder half out of joint.
340 And so, speaking of the adventure that had just befallen them, they continued along the Puerto Lápice[34] highway; for there, Don Quixote said, they could not fail to find many and varied adventures, this being a much traveled thoroughfare. . . .

Translated by Samuel Putnam

---

34. **Puerto Lápice** (pwĕr′tô lä′pē-sĕ).

Text Analysis: Parody

A parody is a comic imitation of another work. *Don Quixote* parodies
the medieval romance with a bumbling hero and his ridiculous sidekick.
Complete the chart below with examples of Cervantes's use of comic
strategies in his parody.

Comic Strategies	Example from Novel Excerpt
• character traits and motivations conveyed through description	
• verbal humor, such as exaggerated descriptions, puns, and irony	
• language that imitates the style of a chivalric romance	
• absurd situations that parallel the actions of a chivalric hero	

Review your notes for the excerpt from *Don Quixote* and the chart above. How do Don Quixote's unique word
choices and speech patterns help Cervantes communicate the point of his parody?

_____

_____

_____

_____

Reading Strategy: Set a Purpose for Reading

While reading this selection, you determined specific ideas Cervantes was mocking and how he created comic effects. Now you are ready to think back about Cervantes's parody of chivalric romances. Complete the following chart.

Points of Parody	In the Novel
What motivates the main character?	
How do the main character's traits compare with those of a romance hero?	
What romance conventions are being mocked?	

Why do we admire DREAMERS?

Is it foolish or inspiring to dream about what seems impossible? Explain.

_____

_____

_____

Vocabulary Practice

Choose the word that best completes the sentence.

1. Her quirky outfit looked _____ next to the conservative clothes that others had.

2. This _____ child seems always to have bad luck.

3. That noise was loud enough to _____ the dead!

4. He was distressed and puzzled by the _____ of his rival.

5. Although they seem real, the characters in her story are _____.

6. She left orders to _____ the trophies until they gleamed.

7. People easily warm up to your _____ personality

> **WORD LIST**
> affable
> burnish
> enmity
> fictitious
> hapless
> incongruous
> resurrect

Academic Vocabulary in Speaking

drama	emerge	encounter	globe	underlie

TURN AND TALK What **underlies** the idea that Cervantes's *Don Quixote* changed the way novels were written? With a partner, discuss how the elements of the story and Cervantes's writing style remind you of modern books and stories that you have read. Include examples from your reading to make your discussion more interesting. Use at least one Academic Vocabulary word in your conversation. Definitions for these terms are listed on page 381.

Assessment Practice

DIRECTIONS Use the excerpt from *Don Quixote* to answer questions 1–5.

1 Don Quixote's family and friends feel that the cause of his madness is —

A eating too much and reading too little

B burning too many books and imagining too much

C selling too much land and getting too little money

D sleeping too little and reading too much

2 Why does Don Quixote decide to become a knight-errant?

A to show off for his ladylove and win honor for himself

B to right wrongs and win honor for himself and his country

C to earn money for the poor and build an honorable country

D to right wrongs and steal horses from other knights

3 What element of medieval romance is parodied in lines 221–233 of *Don Quixote*?

A a supernatural occurrence

B a hidden identity

C an exotic setting

D a romantic quest

4 Which of the following details does Cervantes exaggerate in his description of the horse in lines 129–150?

A the running speed of the horse and the number of its blemishes

B the fact that the horse was a thoroughbred and its new name

C the number of cracks in the horse's hoof and the number of its blemishes

D the previous ownership by Alexander and the horse's worth in reals

5 Which of the following comic strategies does Cervantes use when he describes Sancho Panza's mount in lines 270–271?

A description of character traits and motivation

B verbal humor, such as exaggerated descriptions, puns, and irony

C language that imitates the style of a chivalric romance

D absurd situations that parallel the actions of a chivalric hero

UNIT 11

Shakespearean Drama

THE TRAGEDY OF JULIUS CAESAR

Be sure to read "Shakespeare's World" on pp. 1186–1189 and the Text Analysis Workshop on pp. 1190–1197 in *Holt McDougal Literature*.

Academic Vocabulary for Unit 11

Preview the following Academic Vocabulary words. You will encounter these words as you work through this book and will use them as you write and talk about the selection in this unit.

convention (kən-vĕn′shən) *n.* a widely used and accepted device or technique

The soliloquy—a speech given by a character who is alone on the stage—is a convention that Shakespeare used often in his dramas.

highlight (hī′līt′) *v.* to make prominent; to emphasize

The character's reasons for plotting the murder were highlighted in his soliloquy.

portray (pôr-trā′) *v.* to represent dramatically, as on the stage

Shakespeare's drama portrays historical events that took place in ancient Rome.

principal (prĭn′sə-pəl) *adj.* first or highest in importance, rank, worth, or degree; chief

What is this character's principal motivation—personal ambition or a commitment to public service?

rhetorical (rī-tôr′ĭ-kəl) *adj.* relating to the art or study of using language effectively and persuasively

The speaker used rhetorical techniques to make her argument more persuasive.

If you were asked to **portray** your favorite character from a book or movie, what character traits would you **highlight?** Write your response on the lines below, using at least two Academic Vocabulary words.

_____

_____

from The Tragedy of Julius Caesar

Drama by William Shakespeare

Can your CONSCIENCE mislead you?

When you're facing a difficult decision, people may urge you to let your conscience be your guide—in other words, to rely on an internal sense of what is right and wrong. But how foolproof is your conscience? In *The Tragedy of Julius Caesar*, a man guided by the highest ideals fails to foresee the consequences of his actions.

QUICKWRITE Think of a time when you made a wrong decision, even though your intention was good. In the chart at left, briefly describe your intention, your action, and the outcome. Then explain why things did not turn out the way you had planned.

An Unexpected Outcome

My Intention:

My Action:

The Outcome:

Why Things Didn't Work Out:

Text Analysis: Shakespearean Tragedy

A **tragedy** is a drama in which a series of actions leads to the downfall of the main character, or **tragic hero.** In Shakespeare's tragedies, the hero is usually the title character. However, many critics believe that the tragic hero of *Julius Caesar* is not Caesar but another character, a prominent Roman named Brutus. As you read the following scenes from the tragedy, pay attention to the characteristics described in the chart.

CHARACTERISTICS OF A SHAKESPEAREAN TRAGEDY	
Tragic Hero	• Because the tragic hero is a person of high rank, his or her fate has an impact on all of society.
	• The hero has a **tragic flaw**—a fatal error in judgment or a weakness in character—that contributes to his or her downfall.
Soliloquy	• A **soliloquy** is a speech given by a character alone on the stage, in which the character expresses private thoughts and feelings.
	• Soliloquies may help the audience understand a character's motivation.

Blank Verse	• The dialogue in Shakespeare's tragedies is written mostly in **blank verse,** or unrhymed lines of iambic pentameter. • **Iambic pentameter** is a metrical pattern in which each line has five unstressed syllables, each followed by a stressed syllable. See pages 284–285 for further information about iambic pentameter.
Rhetorical Devices	*Julius Caesar* is about power, ambition, and betrayal. The characters are constantly trying to persuade themselves and others of the rightness of their actions. As a result, the play has many speeches full of **rhetorical devices,** or techniques used to enhance an argument and communicate more effectively. Watch for the following rhetorical devices as you read: • **Repetition** is the use of a word or phrase more than once to emphasize an idea. • **Parallelism** is the repetition of a grammatical structure to express ideas that are related or of equal importance. • **Rhetorical questions** are questions that require no answer because the speaker's rightness is assumed to be self-evident. For example: "Stop that! Do you want to hurt yourself?"

Reading Strategy: Reading Shakespearean Drama

Shakespeare's plays, with their unusual vocabulary, grammar, and word order, can be challenging for modern readers. The following reading strategies can help:

• Read the synopsis, or summary, at the beginning of each scene to get an idea of what will happen in the scene.

• Use footnotes to figure out the meanings of unfamiliar words and to learn other helpful information. However, remember that you do not need to understand every word to understand and enjoy the play.

• Rearrange sentences that have unusual word order to create a familiar sentence structure.

• Use the stage directions (which are bracketed and printed in italic type) and details in the dialogue to help you visualize the play's settings and action.

• Identify and analyze important characters in the play. As you read, you'll be prompted to note details about the principal characters.

**SET A PURPOSE
FOR READING**

Read these scenes from
Julius Caesar to find out
how a conspiracy led to a
leader's assassination.

The Tragedy of

JULIUS CÆSAR

Act One, Scene 2 and Act Three, Scene 2

Drama by

WILLIAM SHAKESPEARE

BACKGROUND In a time of chaos, a great leader rises
to power by promising to restore order. He rewards the
loyal followers who have helped him. Soon he grows so
powerful and arrogant that even his followers no longer
trust him and conspire to kill him. In the hands of William
Shakespeare, this true story from history became a great
tragic drama, *The Tragedy of Julius Caesar.*

CAST OF CHARACTERS

Julius Caesar

TRIUMVIRS AFTER THE DEATH OF JULIUS CAESAR

Octavius Caesar

Marcus Antonius

M. Aemilius Lepidus

SENATORS

Cicero

Publius

Popilius Lena

CONSPIRATORS AGAINST JULIUS CAESAR

Marcus Brutus

Cassius

Casca

Trebonius

Ligarius

Decius Brutus

Metellus Cimber

Cinna

Flavius and Marullus, *tribunes of the people*

Artemidorus of Cnidos, *a teacher of Rhetoric*

TIME

44 B.C.

A Soothsayer

Cinna, *a poet*

Another Poet

FRIENDS TO BRUTUS AND CASSIUS

Lucilius

Titinius

Messala

Young Cato

Volumnius

SERVANTS TO BRUTUS

Varro

Clitus

Claudius

Strato

Lucius

Dardanius

Pindarus, *servant to Cassius*

Calpurnia, *wife to Caesar*

Portia, *wife to Brutus*

The Ghost of Caesar

Senators, Citizens, Guards, Attendants, Servants, etc.

PLACE

Rome; the camp near Sardis; the plains of Philippi

Act One

SCENE 2 *A public place in Rome.*

At the time this story takes place, Rome has been a republic, with elected leaders, for 450 years. The play begins on February 15, the religious feast of Lupercal. The people are celebrating Caesar's return to Rome after a long civil war in which he defeated the forces of Pompey, his rival for power. Caesar now has the opportunity to take full control of Rome.

Act One, Scene 2 opens with a ceremonial footrace. Caesar instructs Antony, a strong young man running in the race, to touch Calpurnia, his wife, as he passes. Caesar believes this will cure Calpurnia's sterility, as she has not yet been able to bear Caesar a child. As Caesar and his entourage head towards the festival, a soothsayer, or fortuneteller, warns him to beware the ides of March, or March 15. (The middle day of each month was called the ides.) When Caesar leaves, Cassius and Brutus speak. Cassius tries to turn Brutus against Caesar by using flattery, examples of Caesar's weaknesses, and sarcasm about Caesar's power. Caesar passes by again, expressing his distrust of Cassius. Cassius and Brutus learn of Caesar's reluctant rejection of a crown that his friend Antony has offered him. They agree to meet again to discuss what must be done about Caesar.

[A flourish of trumpets announces the approach of Caesar. A large crowd of Commoners *has assembled; a* Soothsayer *is among them. Enter* Caesar, *his wife* Calpurnia, *Portia, Decius, Cicero, Brutus, Cassius, Casca, and* Antony, *who is stripped for running in the games.]*

Caesar. Calpurnia.

Casca.   Peace, ho! Caesar speaks.

Caesar.   Calpurnia.

Calpurnia. Here, my lord.

Caesar. Stand you directly in Antonius' way
When he doth run his course. Antonius.

5 **Antony.** Caesar, my lord?

Caesar. Forget not in your speed, Antonius,
To touch Calpurnia; for our elders say
The barren, touched in this holy chase,
Shake off their sterile curse.

Antony.   I shall remember.
10 When Caesar says "Do this," it is performed. Ⓐ

Caesar. Set on, and leave no ceremony out.

[*Flourish of trumpets.* Caesar *starts to leave.*]

Soothsayer. Caesar!

Caesar. Ha! Who calls?

Casca. Bid every noise be still. Peace yet again!

15 **Caesar.** Who is it in the press that calls on me?[1]
I hear a tongue shriller than all the music
Cry "Caesar!" Speak. Caesar is turned to hear.

Soothsayer. Beware the ides of March.

Caesar.   What man is that?

Brutus. A soothsayer bids you beware the ides of March.

20 **Caesar.** Set him before me; let me see his face.

Cassius. Fellow, come from the throng; look upon Caesar.

Caesar. What say'st thou to me now? Speak once again.

Soothsayer. Beware the ides of March.

Caesar. He is a dreamer; let us leave him. Pass. **PAUSE & REFLECT**

[*Trumpets sound. Exeunt all but* Brutus *and* Cassius.]

25 **Cassius.** Will you go see the order of the course?

Brutus. Not I.

Cassius. I pray you do.

Brutus. I am not gamesome.[2] I do lack some part
Of that quick spirit that is in Antony.

---

1. The fortuneteller (**soothsayer**) who calls out Caesar's name can hardly be heard about the noise of the crowd (**press**). Casca tells the crowd to quiet down.

2. Cassius asks if Brutus is going to watch the race (**the order of the course**), but Brutus says he is not fond of sports (**gamesome**).

Ⓐ **SHAKESPEAREAN DRAMA**
What do lines 9–10 tell you about Antony's personality and his attitude toward Caesar?

_____

_____

_____

_____

_____

_____

_____

_____

_____

_____

PAUSE & REFLECT
An omen is a sign of future good or evil. Underline the soothsayer's omen and then state it in your own words below. How might this omen affect an audience watching the play?

_____

_____

_____

_____

B SHAKESPEAREAN
DRAMA

In lines 32–36, Cassius says that
Brutus has not been very friendly
to him lately. Reread Brutus's
response in lines 36–47. Based
on what he says, what is your
impression of Brutus's character
and personality?

_____

_____

_____

_____

_____

_____

_____

_____

_____

_____

_____

_____

_____

_____

_____

_____

_____

_____

_____

_____

_____

_____

30 Let me not hinder, Cassius, your desires.
I'll leave you.

Cassius. Brutus, I do observe you now of late;
I have not from your eyes that gentleness
And show of love as I was wont to have.[3]
35 You bear too stubborn and too strange a hand
Over your friend that loves you.

Brutus.   Cassius,
Be not deceived. If I have veiled my look,
I turn the trouble of my countenance
Merely upon myself. Vexed I am
40 Of late with passions of some difference,
Conceptions only proper to myself,
Which give some soil, perhaps, to my behaviors;[4]
But let not therefore my good friends be grieved
(Among which number, Cassius, be you one)
45 Nor construe any further my neglect
Than that poor Brutus, with himself at war,
forgets the shows of love to other men. **B**

Cassius. Then, Brutus, I have much mistook your passion,
By means whereof this breast of mine hath buried
50 Thoughts of great value, worthy cogitations.[5]
Tell me, good Brutus, can you see your face?

Brutus. No, Cassius, for the eye sees not itself
But by reflection, by some other things.

Cassius. 'Tis just.
55 And it is very much lamented, Brutus,
That you have no such mirrors as will turn
Your hidden worthiness into your eye,
That you might see your shadow. I have heard
Where many of the best respect in Rome
60 (Except immortal Caesar), speaking of Brutus

---

3. **I do observe . . . to have:** Lately I haven't seen the friendliness in your face
   that I used to see.

4. **passions of some difference:** mixed emotions.

5. **I have . . . cogitations:** I have misunderstood your feelings and have kept my
   own important thoughts to myself.

And groaning underneath this age's yoke,
Have wished that noble Brutus had his eyes.[6]   **PAUSE & REFLECT**

Brutus. Into what dangers would you lead me, Cassius,
That you would have me seek into myself
65 For that which is not in me?

Cassius. Therefore, good Brutus, be prepared to hear;
And since you know you cannot see yourself
So well as by reflection, I, your glass,[7]
Will modestly discover to yourself
70 That of yourself which you yet know not of.
And be not jealous on me,[8] gentle Brutus.
Were I a common laugher, or did use
To stale with ordinary oaths my love
To every new protester; if you know
75 That I do fawn on men and hug them hard,
And after scandal them; or if you know
That I profess myself in banqueting
To all the rout, then hold me dangerous.[9]

[*Flourish and shout.*]

Brutus. What means this shouting? I do fear the people
80 Choose Caesar for their king.   **PAUSE & REFLECT**

Cassius.   Ay, do you fear it?
Then must I think you would not have it so.

Brutus. I would not, Cassius, yet I love him well.
But wherefore do you hold me here so long?

---

6. **Where . . . eyes:** Many respected citizens of Rome have wished Brutus could see what others see in him. Cassius uses the phrase "immortal Caesar" sarcastically—implying that Caesar thinks of himself as a god.

7. **glass:** mirror.

8. **jealous on:** suspicious of.

9. **Were I . . . dangerous:** I am not a fool (**common laugher**) or someone who pretends to be everyone's friend. I don't talk evil about friends (**scandal them**) or swear love to anyone who comes along. Nor do I try to win over people (**all the rout**).

PAUSE & REFLECT
In what way does Cassius flatter Brutus in lines 51–62?

PAUSE & REFLECT
Brutus hears a flourish of trumpets and shouting in the distance. How does Brutus feel about this?

C SHAKESPEAREAN
DRAMA
What evidence do you find that
Brutus is an honorable man?
Underline clues in the text, and
then explain your answer below.

_____

_____

_____

_____

_____

_____

_____

_____

_____

_____

_____

_____

_____

_____

_____

_____

_____

_____

What is it that you would impart to me?

85　If it be aught toward the general good,
　　Set honor in one eye and death i' the other,
　　And I will look on both indifferently;[10]
　　For let the gods so speed me as I love
　　The name of honor more than I fear death. **C**

90　**Cassius.** I know that virtue to be in you, Brutus,
　　As well as I do know your outward favor.[11]
　　Well, honor is the subject of my story.
　　I cannot tell what you and other men
　　Think of this life, but for my single self,

95　I had as lief not be as live to be
　　In awe of such a thing as I myself.[12]
　　I was born free as Caesar, so were you;
　　We both have fed as well, and we can both
　　Endure the winter's cold as well as he.

100　For once, upon a raw and gusty day,
　　The troubled Tiber chafing with her shores,[13]
　　Caesar said to me, "Dar'st thou, Cassius, now
　　Leap in with me into this angry flood
　　And swim to yonder point?" Upon the word,

105　Accoutered[14] as I was, I plunged in
　　And bade him follow. So indeed he did.
　　The torrent roared, and we did buffet it
　　With lusty sinews, throwing it aside
　　And stemming it with hearts of controversy.[15]

110　But ere we could arrive the point proposed,
　　Caesar cried, "Help me, Cassius, or I sink!"
　　I, as Aeneas, our great ancestor,
　　Did from the flames of Troy upon his shoulder
　　The old Anchises bear, so from the waves of Tiber

---

10. **If it . . . indifferently:** If what you have in mind concerns the general good,
　　I will not let the fear of death prevent me from doing the honorable thing.

11. **outward favor:** physical appearance.

12. **I had . . . I myself:** I would rather not live, than to live in awe of someone no
　　better than I am.

13. **troubled . . . shores:** The Tiber River was raging against the shores.

14. **accoutered:** fully armed.

15. **hearts of controversy:** spirit of competition, or fighting spirit.

115 Did I the tired Caesar.[16] And this man
     Is now become a god, and Cassius is
     A wretched creature and must bend his body
     If Caesar carelessly but nod on him.
     He had a fever when he was in Spain,
120 And when the fit was on him, I did mark
     How he did shake. 'Tis true, this god did shake.
     His coward lips did from their color fly
     And that same eye whose bend[17] doth awe the world
     Did lose his luster. I did hear him groan.
125 Ay, and that tongue of his that bade the Romans
     Mark him and write his speeches in their books,
     Alas, it cried, "Give me some drink, Titinius,"
     As a sick girl! Ye gods! it doth amaze me
     A man of such a feeble temper should
130 So get the start of the majestic world
     And bear the palm alone.[18] **D**

     [*Shout. Flourish.*]

     Brutus. Another general shout?
     I do believe that these applauses are
     For some new honors that are heaped on Caesar.

135 **Cassius.** Why, man, he doth bestride the narrow world
     Like a Colossus,[19] and we petty men
     Walk under his huge legs and peep about
     To find ourselves dishonorable graves.
     Men at some time are masters of their fates.
140 The fault, dear Brutus, is not in our stars,
     But in ourselves, that we are underlings.[20]
     "Brutus," and "Caesar." What should be in that "Caesar"?

---

16. **I, as Aeneas . . . Caesar:** Aeneas, the mythological father of Rome, carried his father, Anchises, out of the burning city of Troy, just as Cassius carried Caesar out of the water when he could no longer swim.

17. **bend:** glance.

18. **that tongue . . . alone:** The same tongue that told the Romans to memorize his speeches cried out like a sick girl. I'm amazed that such a weak man should get ahead of the rest of the world and appear as a victor (**bear the palm**) all by himself.

19. **Colossus:** a huge statue of the Greek god Apollo.

20. **The fault . . . underlings:** It is not the stars that have determined our fate; we are inferiors through our own fault.

Why should that name be sounded more than yours?
Write them together: yours is as fair a name.
145 Sound them, it doth become the mouth as well.
Weigh them, it is as heavy. Conjure with 'em:
"Brutus" will start a spirit as soon as "Caesar."
Now in the names of all the gods at once,
Upon what meat doth this our Caesar feed
150 That he is grown so great? Age, thou are shamed![21]
Rome, thou hast lost the breed of noble bloods!
When went there by an age since the great Flood
But it was famed with more than with one man?
When could they say (till now) that talked of Rome
155 That her wide walls encompassed but one man?
Now is it Rome indeed, and room enough,
When there is in it but one only man!
O, you and I have heard our fathers say
There was a Brutus once that would have brooked
160 The eternal devil to keep his state in Rome
As easily as a king.[22]

Brutus. That you do love me I am nothing jealous.
What you would work me to, I have some aim.[23]
How I have thought of this, and of these times,
165 I shall recount hereafter. For this present,
I would not (so with love I might entreat you)
Be any further moved. What you have said
I will consider; what you have to say
I will with patience hear, and find a time
170 Both meet to hear and answer such high things.
Till then, my noble friend, chew upon this:
Brutus had rather be a villager
Than to repute himself a son of Rome
Under these hard conditions as this time
175 Is like to lay upon us. **E**

E SHAKESPEAREAN DRAMA
In lines 164–167, Brutus asks for Cassius not to convince him any further. Then, Brutus reveals that he'd rather give up being a Roman citizen than live in Rome as the subject of a king. What does Brutus' request and his claim reveal about his character?

_____
_____
_____
_____
_____
_____

---

21. **Age . . . shamed:** It is a shameful time in which to be living. Cassius goes on to complain that Rome has lost its honor now that only Caesar is celebrated.

22. **There was . . . a king:** Cassius refers to an ancestor of Brutus who expelled the last king of Rome and set up the Republic.

23. **That you . . . some aim:** That you do love me I am sure and I have a guess as to what work you want me to do.

Cassius.   I am glad
That my weak words have struck but thus much show
Of fire from Brutus.

[*Voices and music are heard approaching.*]

Brutus. The games are done, and Caesar is returning.

Cassius. As they pass by, pluck Casca by the sleeve,
180 And he will (after his sour fashion) tell you
What hath proceeded worthy note today.

[*Reenter* Caesar *and his train of followers.*]

Brutus. I will do so. But look you, Cassius!
The angry spot doth glow on Caesar's brow,
And all the rest look like a chidden train.[24]
185 Calpurnia's cheek is pale, and Cicero
Looks with such ferret and such fiery eyes
As we have seen him in the Capitol,
Being crossed in conference by some senators.[25]

Cassius. Casca will tell us what the matter is.

[Caesar *looks at* Cassius *and turns to* Antony.] **F**

190 **Caesar.** Antonius.

Antony. Caesar?

Caesar. Let me have men about me that are fat,
Sleek-headed men, and such as sleep o' nights.
Yond Cassius has a lean and hungry look;
195 He thinks too much, such men are dangerous.

Antony. Fear him not, Caesar, he's not dangerous.
He is a noble Roman, and well given.[26]

Caesar. Would he were fatter! But I fear him not.
Yet if my name were liable to fear,
200 I do not know the man I should avoid
So soon as that spare Cassius. He reads much,

---

24. **chidden train:** a group of followers who have been scolded.

25. **Cicero . . . senators:** Cicero is a senator. Brutus says he has the angry look of a **ferret** (a fierce weasel-like animal), the look he gets when other senators disagree with him.

26. **well given:** Antony says that Cassius, despite his appearance, is a supporter of Caesar.

F SHAKESPEAREAN DRAMA
No one else hears the conversation between Caesar and Antony in lines 190–214. Although Caesar claims not to fear Cassius, he says that men like Cassius are dangerous. What do you learn about Caesar from this passage?

_____

_____

_____

_____

_____

_____

He is a great observer, and he looks
Quite through the deeds of men.[27] He loves no plays
As thou dost, Antony; he hears no music.
205 Seldom he smiles, and smiles in such a sort
As if he mocked himself and scorned his spirit
That could be moved to smile at anything.
Such men as he be never at heart's ease
Whiles they behold a greater than themselves,
210 And therefore are they very dangerous.
I rather tell thee what is to be feared
Than what I fear, for always I am Caesar.
Come on my right hand, for this ear is deaf,
And tell me truly what thou think'st of him. **G**

[*Trumpets sound. Exeunt* Caesar *and all his train except* Casca, *who stays behind.*]

215 **Casca.** You pulled me by the cloak. Would you speak with me?

Brutus. Ay, Casca. Tell us what hath chanced[28] today
That Caesar looks so sad.

Casca. Why, you were with him, were you not?

Brutus. I should not then ask Casca what had chanced.

220 **Casca.** Why, there was a crown offered him; and
being offered him, he put it by with the back of his
hand, thus. And then the people fell a-shouting.

Brutus. What was the second noise for?

Casca. Why, for that too.

225 **Cassius.** They shouted thrice. What was the last cry for?

Casca. Why, for that too.

Brutus. Was the crown offered him thrice?

Casca. Ay, marry, was't![29] and he put it by thrice, every time
gentler than other; and at every putting-by mine honest
230 neighbors shouted.

G SHAKESPEAREAN
DRAMA
How does Caesar compare
Antony and Cassius in this
speech?

_____

_____

_____

_____

_____

_____

_____

_____

_____

_____

_____

_____

_____

_____

_____

_____

---

27. **he looks . . . of men:** He looks through what men do and sees their secrets.

28. **hath chanced:** has happened.

29. **Ay marry, was't:** Yes, indeed it was. *Marry* was a mild oath meaning "by the Virgin Mary."

Cassius. Who offered him the crown?

Casca. Why, Antony.

Brutus. Tell us the manner of it, gentle Casca. **H**

Casca. I can as well be hanged as tell the manner of it. It was
235 mere foolery; I did not mark it. I saw Mark Antony offer him a
crown—yet 'twas not a crown neither, 'twas one of these
coronets[30]—and, as I told you, he put it by once. But for all that,
to my thinking, he would fain[31] have had it. Then he offered it to
him again; then he put it by again; but to my thinking, he was
240 very loath[32] to lay his fingers off it. And then he offered it the
third time. He put it the third time by; and still as he refused it,
the rabblement[33] hooted, and clapped their chapped hands, and
threw up their sweaty nightcaps, and uttered such a deal of
stinking breath because Caesar refused the crown that it had,
245 almost, choked Caesar; for he swounded[34] and fell down at it.
And for mine own part, I durst not laugh, for fear of opening
my lips and receiving the bad air. **PAUSE & REFLECT**

Cassius. But soft,[35] I pray you. What, did Caesar swound?

Casca. He fell down in the market place and foamed at mouth
250 and was speechless.

Brutus. 'Tis very like. He hath the falling sickness.[36]

Cassius. No, Caesar hath not it; but you, and I,
And honest Casca, we have the falling sickness.[37]

Casca. I know not what you mean by that, but I am sure Caesar
255 fell down. If the tag-rag people did not clap him and hiss him,
according as he pleased and displeased them, as they use to do
the players in the theater, I am no true man.

---

30. **coronets:** small crowns.
31. **fain:** gladly.
32. **loath:** reluctant.
33. **rabblement:** unruly crowd.
34. **swounded:** fainted.
35. **soft:** Wait a moment.
36. **falling sickness:** disease we now called epilepsy, marked by seizures.
37. **No, Caesar . . . falling sickness:** Cassius implies that he and Brutus and
    Casca have the "falling sickness" because they bow down to Caesar.

H SHAKESPEAREAN DRAMA
Consider what you know about Brutus. How do you think he would feel about Caesar being offered the crown?

_____

_____

_____

_____

_____

_____

PAUSE & REFLECT
Did Caesar refuse the crown because he felt it was the right thing to do for Rome? Reread Casca's speech in lines 234–247 and underline details that suggest how Casca would answer this question. Then write your answer below.

_____

_____

_____

_____

_____

_____

_____

_____

❶ SHAKESPEAREAN TRAGEDY

Notice that Shakespeare chose to write Casca's speeches in prose instead of **blank verse,** because Casca is very blunt. Underline evidence of his direct talk in lines 259–269. Restate the last sentence "If Caesar had stabbed their mothers, they would have done no less" in your own words.

_____

_____

_____

_____

_____

_____

_____

_____

_____

_____

_____

_____

_____

_____

_____

_____

_____

Brutus. What said he when he came unto himself?

Casca. Marry, before he fell down, when he perceived the
260 common herd was glad he refused the crown, he plucked me ope
his doublet[38] and offered them his throat to cut. An I had been a
man of any occupation, if I would not have taken him at a word
I would I might go to hell among the rogues.[39] And so he fell.
When he came to himself again, he said, if he had done or said
265 anything amiss, he desired their worships to think it was his
infirmity. Three or four wenches where I stood cried, "Alas,
good soul!" and forgave him with all their hearts. But there's no
heed to be taken of them. If Caesar had stabbed their mothers,
they would have done no less. ❶

270 **Brutus.** And after that, he came thus sad away?

Casca. Ay.

Cassius. Did Cicero say anything?

Casca. Ay, he spoke Greek.

Cassius. To what effect?

275 **Casca.** Nay, an I tell you that, I'll ne'er look you i' the face again.
But those that understood him smiled at one another and shook
their heads; but for mine own part, it was Greek to me. I could
tell you more news, too. Marullus and Flavius, for pulling scarfs
off Caesar's images, are put to silence.[40] Fare you well. There was
280 more foolery yet, if I could remember it.

Cassius. Will you sup with me tonight, Casca?

Casca. No, I am promised forth.[41]

Cassius. Will you dine with me tomorrow?

Casca. Ay, if I be alive, and your mind hold, and your
285 dinner worth eating.

Cassius. Good. I will expect you.

---

38. **ope his doublet:** open his jacket
39. **An . . . rogues:** If **(An)** I had been a worker with a proper tool, may I go
to hell if I would not have done as he asked.
40. **put to silence:** silenced by removal from office, exile, or death.
41. **I am promised forth:** I have another appointment.

Casca. Do so. Farewell both.

[*Exit.*] PAUSE & REFLECT

Brutus. What a blunt fellow is this grown to be!
He was quick mettle⁴² when he went to school.

290 **Cassius.** So is he now in execution
Of any bold or noble enterprise,
However he puts on this tardy form.
This rudeness is a sauce to his good wit,
Which gives men stomach to digest his words
295 With better appetite.⁴³

Brutus. And so it is. For this time I will leave you.
Tomorrow, if you please to speak with me,
I will come home to you; or if you will,
Come home to me, and I will wait for you.

300 **Cassius.** I will do so. Till then, think of the world.

[*Exit* Brutus.]

Well, Brutus, thou art noble; yet I see
Thy honorable mettle may be wrought
From that it is disposed.⁴⁴ Therefore it is meet
That noble minds keep ever with their likes;
305 For who so firm that cannot be seduced?
Caesar doth bear me hard,⁴⁵ but he loves Brutus.
If I were Brutus now and he were Cassius,
He should not humor me. I will this night,
In several hands, in at his windows throw,
310 As if they came from several citizens,
Writings, all tending to the great opinion
That Rome holds of his name; wherein obscurely

---

42. **mettle:** clever.

43. **So is . . . appetite:** Cassius says that Casca can still be intelligent in carrying
out an important project. He only pretends to be slow **(tardy)**. His rude
manner makes people more willing to accept **(digest)** the things he says.

44. **Thy . . . disposed:** Your honorable nature can be manipulated **(wrought)** into
something not quite so honorable.

45. **bear me hard:** hold a grudge against me.

PAUSE & REFLECT
Reread lines 234–269. What
happened to Caesar after he
refused the crown three times?
Do you think he really wants to
be king? Explain.

J SHAKESPEAREAN TRAGEDY

Reread Cassius' **soliloquy** in lines 301–315. Why would Cassius not want Brutus to hear the thoughts he expresses in this speech? Underline specific details that he would want to hide from Brutus, and then explain below.

_____

_____

_____

_____

_____

_____

_____

_____

_____

_____

_____

_____

_____

_____

_____

_____

_____

_____

_____

Caesar's ambition shall be glanced at.[46]
And after this let Caesar seat him sure,

315   For we will shake him, or worse days endure. **J**

[*Exit.*]

Act Three

SCENE 2   *The forum in Rome.*

In Act Two, Brutus decides Caesar should be killed. Though he is a close personal friend of Caesar, he thinks the Roman people will be treated very badly if Caesar's powers grow. Caesar continues to ignore bad omens warning him of coming danger. At the beginning of Act Three, Caesar enters the Capitol. There, the conspirators surround him and stab him to death. When Mark Antony, Caesar's loyal supporter, hears of Caesar's death, he pretends to join sides with the conspirators and even shakes their bloody hands. Convinced by his loyalty, Brutus grants Antony's request to take Caesar's body to the Forum and to give a speech praising and honoring him—as long as he doesn't condemn Brutus and the rest of the conspirators. Secretly, though, Antony vows to avenge Caesar's death by turning the Roman people against those who murdered Caesar.

At the beginning of Scene 2, Brutus speaks before a group of "citizens," or common people of Rome. He explains why Caesar had to be slain for the good of Rome. Then Brutus leaves and Antony speaks to the citizens. A far better judge of human nature than Brutus, Antony cleverly manages to turn the crowd against the conspirators by telling them of Caesar's good works and his concern for the people, as proven by the slain ruler's will. He has left all his wealth to the people. As Antony stirs the citizens to pursue the assassins and kill them, he learns that Octavius has arrived in Rome and that Brutus and Cassius have fled.

[*Enter* Brutus *and* Cassius *and a throng of* Citizens, *disturbed by the death of* Caesar.]

Citizens. We will be satisfied! Let us be satisfied!

46. **I will . . . glanced at:** Cassius plans to leave messages at Brutus's home that appear to be from concerned citizens of Rome.

Brutus. Then follow me and give me audience, friends.
Cassius, go you into the other street
And part the numbers.

5 Those that will hear me speak, let 'em stay here;
Those that will follow Cassius, go with him;
And public reasons shall be rendered
Of Caesar's death.[47]

First Citizen.   I will hear Brutus speak.

Second Citizen. I will hear Cassius, and compare their reasons
10 when severally we hear them rendered.

[*Exit* Cassius, *with some of the* Citizens. Brutus *goes into the pulpit.*]

Third Citizen. The noble Brutus is ascended. Silence!

Brutus. Be patient till the last.
Romans, countrymen, and lovers, hear me for my cause, and be
silent, that you may hear. Believe me for mine honor, and have
15 respect to mine honor, that you may believe. Censure me[48] in your
wisdom, and awake your senses, that you may the better judge. If
there be any in this assembly, any dear friend of Caesar's, to him I
say that Brutus' love to Caesar was no less than his. If then that
friend demand why Brutus rose against Caesar, this is my answer:
20 Not that I loved Caesar less, but that I loved Rome more. Had you
rather Caesar were living, and die all slaves, than that Caesar were
dead, to live all freemen? As Caesar loved me, I weep for him; as he
was fortunate, I rejoice at it; as he was valiant, I honor him; but—as
he was ambitious, I slew him. There is tears for his love; joy for his
25 fortune; honor for his valor; and death for his ambition. Who is
here so base that would be a bondman?[49] If any, speak, for him have
I offended. Who is here so rude[50] that would not be a Roman? If any,
speak, for him have I offended. Who is here so vile that will not
love his country? If any, speak, for him have I offended. I pause
30 for a reply. **Ⓚ**

---

47. **Cassius . . . Of Caesar's death:** Brutus tells Cassius to divide the crowd (**part the numbers**) so they can explain their reasons for killing Caesar to different groups.

48. **Censure me:** Judge me.

49. **Who is . . . bondman:** Which of you is so low that you would prefer to be a slave?

50. **rude:** uncivilized.

Ⓚ **SHAKESPEAREAN TRAGEDY**
Reread lines 12–30 of Brutus's monologue. Underline the reasons he gives for killing Caesar.

All. None, Brutus, none!

Brutus. Then none have I offended. I have done no more to Caesar than you shall do to Brutus. The question of his death is enrolled in the Capitol; his glory not extenuated, wherein he was
35 worthy, nor his offenses enforced, for which he suffered death.[51]

[*Enter* Antony *and others, with* Caesar's *body.*]

Here comes his body, mourned by Mark Antony, who though he had no hand in his death, shall receive the benefit of his dying, a place in the commonwealth, as which of you shall not? With this I depart, that, as I slew my best lover for the good of Rome, I
40 have the same dagger for myself when it shall please my country to need my death.

All. Live, Brutus! live, live!

First Citizen. Bring him with triumph home unto his house.

Second Citizen. Give him a statue with his ancestors.

45 **Third Citizen.** Let him be Caesar.

Fourth Citizen.   Caesar's better parts[52]
Shall be crowned in Brutus.

First Citizen. We'll bring him to his house with shouts and clamors.

Brutus. My countrymen—

Second Citizen.   Peace! silence! Brutus speaks.

First Citizen. Peace ho!

50 **Brutus.** Good countrymen, let me depart alone,
And, for my sake, stay here with Antony.
Do grace to Caesar's corpse, and grace his speech[53]
Tending to Caesar's glories which Mark Antony,
By our permission, is allowed to make.

---

51. **The question . . . death:** The reasons for his death are on record in the Capitol. We have not belittled (**extenuated**) his accomplishments or overemphasized (**enforced**) the failings for which he was killed.

52. **parts:** qualities.

53. **grace his speech:** Listen to him respectfully.

55 I do entreat you, not a man depart,
Save[54] I alone, till Antony have spoke.

[*Exit.*]

First Citizen. Stay, ho! and let us hear Mark Antony.

Third Citizen. Let him go up into the public chair.[55]
We'll hear him. Noble Antony, go up.

60 **Antony.** For Brutus' sake I am beholding[56] to you.

[*Goes into the pulpit.*]

Fourth Citizen. What does he say of Brutus?

Third Citizen.   He says for Brutus'
Sake he finds himself beholding to us all.

Fourth Citizen. 'Twere best he speak no harm of Brutus here!

65 **First Citizen.** This Caesar was a tyrant.

Third Citizen.   Nay, that's certain.
We are blest that Rome is rid of him.

Second Citizen. Peace! Let us hear what Antony can say.

Antony. You gentle Romans—

All.   Peace, ho! Let us hear him.

70 **Antony.** Friends, Romans, countrymen, lend me your ears;
I come to bury Caesar, not to praise him.
The evil that men do lives after them;
The good is oft interred with their bones.
So let it be with Caesar. The noble Brutus
75 Hath told you Caesar was ambitious.
If it were so, it was a grievous[57] fault,
And grievously hath Caesar answered it.
Here, under leave of[58] Brutus and the rest
(For Brutus is an honorable man;
80 So are they all, all honorable men),

---

54. **Save:** Except.
55. **public chair:** speaker's platform.
56. **beholding:** indebted.
57. **grievous:** serious.
58. **under leave of:** with the permission of.

● SHAKESPEAREAN
TRAGEDY
Recall that a **tragic hero** often
makes an error in judgment
that leads to his or her downfall.
Might Brutus's allowing Antony
to speak at Caesar's funeral be
such an error? Explain.

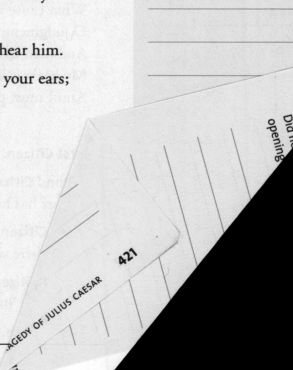

Ⓜ SHAKESPEAREAN TRAGEDY
Reread lines 74–96 and note Antony's **repetition** of the words *ambitious* and *honorable*. Underline *ambitious* wherever it appears, and circle *honorable*. Does Antony really believe Brutus is honorable?

_____

_____

_____

_____

_____

_____

_____

_____

_____

PAUSE & REFLECT
eread the first sentence of
ony's speech (lines 70–71).
follow through with his
statement? Explain.

_____

_____

_____

_____

Come I to speak in Caesar's funeral.
He was my friend, faithful and just to me;
But Brutus says he was ambitious,
And Brutus is an honorable man.
85 He hath brought many captives home to Rome,
Whose ransoms did the general coffers[59] fill.
Did this in Caesar seem ambitious?
When that the poor have cried, Caesar hath wept;
Ambition should be made of sterner stuff.
90 Yet Brutus says he was ambitious;
And Brutus is an honorable man.
You all did see that on the Lupercal
I thrice presented him a kingly crown,
Which he did thrice refuse. Was this ambition?
95 Yet Brutus says he was ambitious;
And sure he is an honorable man. Ⓜ
I speak not to disprove what Brutus spoke,
But here I am to speak what I do know.
You all did love him once, not without cause.
100 What cause withholds you then to mourn for him?
O judgment, thou art fled to brutish beasts,
And men have lost their reason! Bear with me,
My heart is in the coffin there with Caesar,
And I must pause till it come back to me. **PAUSE & REFLECT**

105 **First Citizen.** Methinks there is much reason in his sayings.

Second Citizen. If thou consider rightly of the matter,
Caesar has had great wrong.

Third Citizen. Has he, masters?
I fear there will a worse come in his place.

Fourth Citizen. Marked ye his words? He would not take the crown;
110 Therefore 'tis certain he was not ambitious.

First Citizen. If it be found so, some will dear abide it.[60]

Second Citizen. Poor soul! his eyes are red as fire with weeping.

---

59. **general coffers:** the Roman government's treasury.
    some will dear abide it: Some will pay for it dearly.

Third Citizen. There's not a nobler man in Rome than Antony.

Fourth Citizen. Now mark him. He begins again to speak.

115 **Antony.** But yesterday the word of Caesar might
Have stood against the world. Now lies he there,
And none so poor to do him reverence.[61]
O masters! If I were disposed to stir
Your hearts and minds to mutiny and rage,
120 I should do Brutus wrong, and Cassius wrong,
Who, you all know, are honorable men.
I will not do them wrong. I rather choose
To wrong the dead, to wrong myself and you,
Than I will wrong such honorable men.
125 But here's a parchment with the seal of Caesar.
I found it in his closet; 'tis his will.
Let but the commons hear this testament,
Which (pardon me) I do not mean to read,
And they would go and kiss dead Caesar's wounds
130 And dip their napkins in his sacred blood;
Yea, beg a hair of him for memory,
And dying, mention it within their wills,
Bequeathing it as a rich legacy
Unto their issue.[62] **PAUSE & REFLECT**

135 **Fourth Citizen.** We'll hear the will! Read it, Mark Antony.

All. The will, the will! We will hear Caesar's will!

Antony. Have patience, gentle friends, I must not read it.
It is not meet[63] you know how Caesar loved you.
You are not wood, you are not stones, but men;
140 And being men, hearing the will of Caesar,
It will inflame you, it will make you mad.

---

61. **And none . . . reverence:** And no one is low enough to show respect for him.
62. Antony says that if the people heard Caesar's will, they would dip their handkerchiefs (**napkins**) in his blood or beg for one of his hairs, and then upon their own deaths their children (**issue**) would inherit these valuable mementos.
63. **meet:** proper.

N SHAKESPEAREAN
TRAGEDY
Reread lines 146–160 and
underline the **rhetorical
questions** (questions with no
intended response) Antony
uses. How does he use these
questions to suggest a particular
relationship between himself
and the crowd? Cite evidence
to show whether this device
achieves the effect he wants.

'Tis good you know not that you are his heirs,
For if you should, O, what would come of it?

Fourth Citizen. Read the will! We'll hear it, Antony!
145 You shall read us the will, Caesar's will!

Antony. Will you be patient? Will you stay awhile?
I have o'ershot myself to tell you of it.[64]
I fear I wrong the honorable men
Whose daggers have stabbed Caesar; I do fear it.

150 **Fourth Citizen.** They were traitors. Honorable men!

All. The will! the testament!

Second Citizen. They were villains, murderers! The will!
Read the will!

Antony. You will compel me then to read the will?
155 Then make a ring about the corpse of Caesar
And let me show you him that made the will.
Shall I descend? and will you give me leave?

All. Come down.

Second Citizen. Descend.

160 **Third Citizen.** You shall have leave. **N**

[Antony *comes down.*]

Fourth Citizen. A ring! Stand round.

First Citizen. Stand from the hearse! Stand from the body!

Second Citizen. Room for Antony, most noble Antony!

Antony. Nay, press not so upon me. Stand far off.

165 **All.** Stand back! Room! Bear back!

Antony. If you have tears, prepare to shed them now.
You all do know this mantle.[65] I remember
The first time ever Caesar put it on.
'Twas on a summer's evening in his tent,
170 That day he overcame the Nervii.[66]

---

64. **I have . . . of it:** I have gone too far in even mentioning it to you.
65. **mantle:** Caesar's toga.
66. **the Nervii:** a Belgian tribe that Caesar defeated 13 years earlier.

Look, in this place ran Cassius' dagger through.
See what a rent[67] the envious Casca made.
Through this the well-beloved Brutus stabbed;
And as he plucked his cursed steel away,
175 Mark how the blood of Caesar followed it,
As rushing out of doors to be resolved
If Brutus so unkindly knocked or no;[68]
For Brutus, as you know, was Caesar's angel.
Judge, O you gods, how dearly Caesar loved him!
180 This was the most unkindest cut of all;
For when the noble Caesar saw him stab,
Ingratitude, more strong than traitors' arms,
Quite vanquished[69] him. Then burst his mighty heart;
And in his mantle muffling up his face,
185 Even at the base of Pompey's statue
(Which all the while ran blood) great Caesar fell.
O, what a fall was there, my countrymen!
Then I, and you, and all of us fell down,
Whilst bloody treason flourished over us.
190 O, now you weep, and I perceive you feel
The dint[70] of pity. These are gracious drops.
Kind souls, what, weep you when you but behold
Our Caesar's vesture wounded? Look you here!
Here is himself, marred, as you see, with traitors.[71]

[*Pulls the cloak off* Caesar's *body*.]   **PAUSE & REFLECT**

195 **First Citizen.** O piteous spectacle!

Second Citizen. O noble Caesar!

Third Citizen. O woeful day!

Fourth Citizen. O traitors, villains!

---

67. **rent:** tear, hole.

68. **As rushing . . . or no:** as if it rushed out of that opening to find out if it really
    was Brutus who had made the wound.

69. **vanquished:** defeated.

70. **dint:** force

71. **weep you . . . traitors:** Do you cry when you look only at his wounded clothing
    (**vesture**)? Here, look at his body!

◉ SHAKESPEAREAN DRAMA

What does Antony say would happen if he and Brutus were to switch places?

_____

_____

_____

_____

_____

_____

_____

_____

_____

_____

_____

_____

_____

_____

_____

_____

_____

_____

_____

_____

_____

_____

First Citizen. O most bloody sight!

200 **Second Citizen.** We will be revenged.

All. Revenge! About! Seek! Burn! Fire! Kill! Slay!
Let not a traitor live!

Antony. Stay, countrymen.

First Citizen. Peace there! Hear the noble Antony.

205 **Second Citizen.** We'll hear him, we'll follow him, we'll die with him!

Antony. Good friends, sweet friends, let me not stir you up
To such a sudden flood of mutiny.
They that have done this deed are honorable.
What private griefs they have, alas, I know not,

210 That made them do it. They are wise and honorable,
And will no doubt with reasons answer you.
I come not, friends, to steal away your hearts.
I am no orator, as Brutus is,
But (as you know me all) a plain blunt man

215 That love my friend; and that they know full well
That gave me public leave to speak of him.
For I have neither wit, nor words, nor worth,
Action, nor utterance, nor the power of speech
To stir men's blood. I only speak right on.

220 I tell you that which you yourselves do know,
Show you sweet Caesar's wounds, poor poor dumb mouths,
And bid them speak for me. But were I Brutus,
And Brutus Antony, there were an Antony
Would ruffle up your spirits, and put a tongue

225 In every wound of Caesar that should move
The stones of Rome to rise and mutiny. ◉

All. We'll mutiny.

First Citizen.   We'll burn the house of Brutus.

Third Citizen. Away then! Come, seek the conspirators.

Antony. Yet hear me, countrymen. Yet hear me speak.

230 **All.** Peace, ho! Hear Antony, most noble Antony!

Antony. Why, friends, you go to do you know not what.
Wherein hath Caesar thus deserved your loves?
Alas, you know not! I must tell you then.
You have forgot the will I told you of.

235 **All.** Most true! The will! Let's stay and hear the will.

Antony. Here is the will, under Caesar's seal.
To every Roman citizen he gives,
To every several man, seventy-five drachmas.[72]

Second Citizen. Most noble Caesar! We'll revenge his death!

240 **Third Citizen.** O royal Caesar!

Antony. Hear me with patience.

All. Peace, ho!

Antony. Moreover, he hath left you all his walks,
His private arbors, and new-planted orchards,
245 On this side Tiber; he hath left them you,
And to your heirs for ever—common pleasures,
To walk abroad and recreate yourselves.[73]
Here was a Caesar! When comes such another?

First Citizen. Never, never! Come, away, away!
250 We'll burn his body in the holy place
And with the brands[74] the traitors' houses.
Take up the body.

Second Citizen. Go fetch fire!

Third Citizen. Pluck down benches!

255 **Fourth Citizen.** Pluck down forms, windows, anything!

[*Exeunt* Citizens *with the body.*]

Antony. Now let it work. Mischief, thou art afoot,
Take thou what course thou wilt.[75]

---

72. **several:** individual; **drachmas:** silver coins.

73. Antony tells the crowd that Caesar has left all his private parks and gardens on this side of the Tiber River to be used by the public.

74. **brands:** pieces of burning wood.

75. **Now let . . . wilt:** Alone, Antony thinks about what has happened. Let things take their course, he says. Whatever happens, happens.

PAUSE & REFLECT

Reread Antony's statements after the angry crowd has departed, in lines 256–267. Does he seem to have a guilty conscience about inciting the crowd to violence? Explain what these lines reveal about his thoughts and feelings.

_____

_____

_____

_____

_____

_____

_____

_____

_____

_____

[*Enter a* Servant.]

How now, fellow?

260 **Servant.** Sir, Octavius is already come to Rome.

Antony. Where is he?

Servant. He and Lepidus are at Caesar's house.

Antony. And thither will I straight to visit him.[76]
He comes upon a wish. Fortune is merry,
And in this mood will give us anything.[77]

Servant. I heard him say Brutus and Cassius
265 Are rid[78] like madmen through the gates of Rome.

Antony. Belike[79] they had some notice of the people,
How I had moved them. Bring me to Octavius.

[*Exeunt.*] **PAUSE & REFLECT**

---

76. **thither . . . him:** I will go right there to see him.
77. Antony believes that Fortune, the goddess of fate, is on his side.
78. **Are rid:** have ridden.
79. **Belike:** probably.

Text Analysis: Shakespearean Tragedy

At the end of Act Three, Scene 2, Brutus and Cassius have fled Rome after the public turns against them. As the play continues, armies led by Brutus and Antony fight for control of Rome. In the end, Antony's forces are victorious, and Brutus dies a noble death. The chart below will help you create a profile of this tragic hero. Think about the decisions Brutus made and their consequences.

BRUTUS: A TRAGIC HERO	
Qualities	
Actions	
Tragic Flaw	

How does Brutus differ from Marc Antony? Why does one man stay loyal to Caesar and the other betray him? Write your thoughts based on details from the play.

_____

_____

_____

Reading Strategy: Reading Shakespearean Drama

The English language has changed a great deal since Shakespeare's time. Complete the chart below by restating the following portions of speeches by Brutus and Antony in your own words.

Speech	Your Words
Brutus: "Had you rather Caesar were living, and die all slaves, than that Caesar were dead, to live all free men? As Caesar loved me, I weep for him; as he was fortunate, I rejoice at it; as he was valiant, I honor him; but, as he was ambitious I slew him."	
Antony: "Friends, Romans, countrymen, lend me your ears; / I come to bury Caesar, not to praise him. / The evil that men do lives after them, / The good is oft interred with their bones; / So let it be with Caesar. The noble Brutus / Hath told you Caesar was ambitious. / If it were so, it was a grievous fault, / And grievously hath Caesar answered it."	

Can your CONSCIENCE mislead you?

What can you do to avoid making wrong decisions?

_____

_____

_____

Academic Vocabulary in Writing

convention	highlight	portray	principal	rhetorical

How does a dramatic **convention** like the soliloquy help Shakespeare bring figures from ancient history to life for modern audiences? Write your response on the lines below, using at least two Academic Vocabulary words. Definitions for these terms are listed on page 401.

_____

_____

_____

_____

Assessment Practice

DIRECTIONS Use *The Tragedy of Julius Caesar* to answer questions 1–4.

1 In Act One, Scene 2, both Cassius and Brutus are worried that —

  (A) their friendship is not as strong as it once was

  (B) Antony will win the Lupercal race

  (C) dangerous men threaten Rome's leaders

  (D) Caesar may become king of Rome

2 According to Casca, what happened at the Lupercal games when Antony offered Caesar a crown?

  (A) Caesar accepted the crown but then decided to give it back.

  (B) Caesar refused the crown three times, but reluctantly.

  (C) A soothsayer warned Caesar not to accept the crown until the ides of March.

  (D) A group of conspirators killed Caesar so he would not become king.

3 Cassius' soliloquy in lines 301–315 of Act One, Scene 2 reveals his plan to —

  (A) influence Brutus by sending him forged letters that support Cassius' viewpoint

  (B) continue trying to persuade Brutus, even though he cannot be manipulated

  (C) take Brutus' place as a close and trusted friend of Caesar

  (D) convince the citizens of Rome that Brutus should be their leader

4 In Act Three, Scene 2, what information does Antony share with the crowd in his funeral speech?

  (A) what Caesar left the people in his will

  (B) why Caesar was a danger to Rome

  (C) why Brutus' actions were honorable

  (D) how many captives Caesar brought to Rome

The Glossary of Academic Vocabulary in this section is an alphabetical list of the Academic Vocabulary words found in this textbook. Use this glossary just as you would use a dictionary—to find out the meanings of words used in your literature class, to talk about and write about literary and informational texts, and to talk about and write about concepts and topics in your other academic classes.

For each word, the glossary includes the pronunciation, syllabication, part of speech, and meaning. A Spanish version of each word and definition follows the English version. For more information about the words in this glossary, please consult a dictionary.

abstract (ab-strakt) *adj.* thought of or stated without reference to a specific instance
 abstracto *adj.* significa pensado o indicado sin referencia a un caso específico

acknowledge (ăk-nŏl′ ĭj) *v.* to recognize and admit that something is true or accurate
 reconocer *v.* admitir y aceptar que algo es verdadero o exacto

affect (ə-fĕkt′) *v.* to influence; to create an effect upon
 afectar *v.* influir; crear un efecto

alter (ôl′tər) *v.* to change or modify some details
 alterar *v.* cambiar o modificar algunos detalles

author (ô′thər) *n.* a writer; a creator of something
 autor *sust.* escritor; creador de algo

authoritative (ə-thôr′ĭ-tā′tĭv) *adj.* backed by evidence and showing deep knowledge
 fidedigno *adj.* que se sostiene con pruebas y que demuestra un conocimiento profundo

cite (sīt) *v.* to quote from some source such as a book, internet article, or speech
 citar *v.* mencionar parte de una fuente, como un libro, un artículo de Internet o un discurso

clarify (klăr′ə fī′) *v.* to make clear or easier to understand
 aclarar *v.* hacer que algo sea más claro o fácil de comprender

communicate (kə myōō′nĭ kāt′) *v.* to share or exchange information or ideas
 comunicar *v.* compartir o intercambiar información o ideas

community (kə myōō′nĭ tē) *n.* a group of individuals with a common interest or characteristic
 comunidad *sust.* grupo de personas con intereses o características en común

compile (kəm-pīl′) *v.* to gather things together to form a whole
 compilar *v.* reunir cosas para formar un todo

consequent (kŏn′sĭ kwĕnt′) *adj.* following as an effect or result
 consiguiente *adj.* que sigue como efecto o resultado

contemporary (kən-tĕm′pə-rĕr′ē) *adj.* current; modern
 contemporáneo *adj.* actual; moderno

controversy (kŏn′trə vûr′sē) *n.* a debate or quarrel over opposing opinions
 controversia *sust.* debate o discusión con respecto a opiniones opuestas

convention *n.* a widely used and accepted device or technique
 convención *sust.* técnica o recurso de gran uso y aceptación

convince (kən vĭns') *v.* to overcome any doubts with argument or persuasion
   convencer *v.* superar las dudas por medio de argumentos o persuasiones

crucial (krōō'shəl) *adj.* extremely important; critical
   crucial *adj.* sumamente importante; crítico

culture (kŭl'chər) *n.* the attitudes, behavior, or customs that characterize a group; the particular group having such attitudes, behavior, or customs
   cultura *sust.* actitudes, conductas o costumbres que caracterizan a un grupo; grupo particular que tiene esas actitudes, conductas o costumbres

debates (dĭ-bāts') *n.* public discussions involving opposing points
   debates *sust.* discusiones públicas sobre puntos opuestos

definite (dĕf'ə nĭt) *adj.* certain; unquestionable
   definitivo *adj.* seguro; incuestionable

device (dĭ-vīs') *n.* a literary technique used to achieve a particular effect
   recurso *sust.* técnica literaria utilizada para obtener un efecto en particular

document (dŏk'yə mənt) *n.* something printed or written that provides a record; something that provides evidence
   documento *sust.* algo impreso o escrito que sirve como registro; algo que proporciona pruebas

drama (drä'mə) *n.* literature in which plot and characters are developed through dialogue and action
   drama *sust.* literatura en la que la trama y los personajes se desarrollan mediante el diálogo y la acción

dynamic (dī năm'ik) *adj.* energetic; changing; in motion
   dinámico *adj.* enérgico; cambiante; en movimiento

encounter (ĕn-koun'tər) *n.* an unexpected meeting
   encuentro *sust.* reunión inesperada

emerge (ĭ mûrj') *v.* to develop; to become something new
   surgir *v.* desarrollarse; convertirse en algo nuevo

establish (ĭ stăb' lĭsh) *v.* to make stable or firm
   establecer *v.* hacer que algo esté estable o firme

feature (fē'chər) *n.* a special quality or characteristic of something
   rasgo *sust.* cualidad o característica especial de algo

form *n.* a method of arranging elements in a literary work
   forma *sust.* método según el cual se ordenan los elementos en una obra literaria

globe (glōb) *n.* a round, ball-shaped model of the earth; the earth
   globo *sust.* modelo redondo y con forma de pelota de la Tierra; la Tierra

goal (gōl) *n.* an aim, purpose, or specific result one tries to achieve
   meta *sust.* fin, propósito o resultado específico que se busca alcanzar

highlight *v.* to make prominent; to emphasize
   resaltar *v.* destacar o enfatizar algo

identify (ī-dĕn'tə-fī') *v.* to find or name the characteristics, nature, or qualities of someone or something
   identificar *v.* hallar o nombrar las características, la naturaleza o las cualidades de alguien o algo

individual (ĭn'də-vĭj'ōō-əl) *adj.* existing as a single, separate thing or being
   individual *adj.* que existe como cosa o ser único o singular

initial (ĭ-nĭsh'əl) *adj.* occurring at the beginning
   inicial *adj.* que ocurre al principio

inquiry (ĭn-kwīr'ē) *n.* a close examination in search for information
   averiguación *sust.* evaluación exhaustiva para buscar información

issue (ĭsh'ōō) *n.* a concern or problem
  cuestión *sust.* asunto o problema

layer (lā'ər) *n.* a single thickness, fold, or level
  capa *sust.* veta, pliegue o nivel individual

literal (lĭt'ər-əl) *adj.* limited to the simplest or most obvious meaning of a word or words
  literal *adj.* limitarse al significado más simple o más obvio de una o más palabras

motive (mō'tĭv) *n.* incentive; inner drive or desire that causes someone to act
  motivo *sust.* incentivo; impulso o deseo interno que hace que una persona actúe

objective (əb-jĕk'tĭv) *n.* something worked toward or striven for
  objetivo *sust.* finalidad del trabajo o el esfuerzo

portray *v.* to represent dramatically, as on the stage
  representar *v.* interpretar una obra dramática

precise (prĭ-sīs') *adj.* exact; accurately defined or stated
  preciso *adj.* exacto; definido o expuesto con precisión

principal *adj.* first or highest in importance, rank, worth, or degree; chief
  principal *adj.* primero o de mayor importancia, rango, valor o grado; jefe

relevant (rĕl'ə-vənt) *adj.* pertaining to a matter at hand; significance
  relevante *adj.* relacionado con un tema; importante

rhetorical *adj.* relating to the art or study of using language effectively and persuasively
  retórico *adj.* relacionado al arte o estudio del uso efectivo y persuasivo del lenguaje

role (rōl) *n.* a character played by an actor in a performance; a function or part assumed in a process
  papel *sust.* personaje que representa un actor en una obra; función o posición que se asume en un proceso

seek (sēk) *v.* to look for or try to find
  buscar *v.* rastrear o intentar hallar

shift (shĭft) *v.* to change course; to move or transfer
  correr *v.* cambiar el curso; mover o transferir

statistic (stə-tĭs'tĭk) *n.* numerical fact or quantity
  estadística *sust.* dato numérico o cantidad

style (stīl) *n.* a distinctive or original manner of expression
  estilo *sust.* forma de expresión distintiva u original

survive (sər-vīv') *v.* to live longer than expected; to remain in existence
  sobrevivir *v.* vivir más de lo esperado; conservar la existencia

symbol (sĭm'bəl) *n.* something that represents or suggests another thing
  símbolo *sust.* algo que representa o sugiere otra cosa

theme (thēm) *n.* a topic or subject of a discussion or piece of writing
  tema *sust.* materia o asunto de un debate o un escrito

tradition (trə-dĭsh'ən) *n.* a set of customs and usages passed down from generation to generation that sets an example for present behavior
  tradición *sust.* conjunto de costumbres y usos transmitidos de generación en generación que marca las pautas de las costumbres actuales.

transmit (trăns-mĭt') *v.* to communicate; to send or hand off to others
  transmitir *v.* comunicar; enviar o entregar a otros

undergo (ŭn′dər-gō′) *v.* to endure, go through, or experience

  soportar *v.* sobrellevar, vivir o experimentar

underlie (ŭn′dər-lī′) *v.* to form the basis or foundation of

  subyacer *v.* formar la base o los cimientos de algo

unify (yōō′ nə-fī′) *v.* to make into one; to bring together into a unit

  unificar *v.* unir en uno solo; juntar para formar una unidad

vision (vĭzh′ən) *n.* a mental or imaginative image; something seen in a dream or trance

  visión *sust.* imagen mental o intelectual; algo que se ve en un sueño o un trance

Pronunciation Key

Symbol	Examples	Symbol	Examples	Symbol	Examples
ă	at, gas	m	man, seem	v	van, save
ā	ape, day	n	night, mitten	w	web, twice
ä	father, barn	ng	sing, hanger	y	yard, lawyer
âr	fair, dare	ŏ	odd, not	z	zoo, reason
b	bell, table	ō	open, road, grow	zh	treasure, garage
ch	chin, lunch	ô	awful, bought, horse	ə	awake, even, pencil,
d	dig, bored	oi	coin, boy		pilot, focus
ĕ	egg, ten	ŏŏ	look, full	ər	perform, letter
ē	evil, see, meal	ōō	root, glue, through		
f	fall, laugh, phrase	ou	out, cow	**Sounds in Foreign Words**	
g	gold, big	p	pig, cap	KH	*German* ich, auch;
h	hit, inhale	r	rose, star		*Scottish* loch
hw	white, everywhere	s	sit, face	N	*French* entre, bon, fin
ĭ	inch, fit	sh	she, mash	œ	*French* feu, cœur;
ī	idle, my, tried	t	tap, hopped		*German* schön
îr	dear, here	th	thing, with	ü	*French* utile, rue;
j	jar, gem, badge	*th*	then, other		*German* grün
k	keep, cat, luck	ŭ	up, nut		
l	load, rattle	ûr	fur, earn, bird, worm		

Stress Marks

′ This mark indicates that the preceding syllable receives the primary stress. For example, in the word *language*, the first syllable is stressed: lăng′gwĭj.

′ This mark is used only in words in which more than one syllable is stressed. It indicates that the preceding syllable is stressed, but somewhat more weakly than the syllable receiving the primary stress. In the word *literature*, for example, the first syllable receives the primary stress, and the last syllable receives a weaker stress: lĭt′ər-ə-chŏŏr′.

Adapted from *The American Heritage Dictionary of the English Language,* fourth edition. Copyright © 2000 by Houghton Mifflin Company. Used with the permission of Houghton Mifflin Company.

High-Frequency Word List

Would you like to build your word knowledge? If so,

the word lists on the next six pages can help you.

These lists contain the 600 most common words in the

English language. The most common words are on the

First Hundred Words list; the next most common are on

the Second Hundred Words list; and so on.

Study tip: Read through these lists starting with the

First Hundred Words list. For each word you don't know,

make a flash card. Work through the flash cards until

you can read each word quickly.

FIRST HUNDRED WORDS

the	he	go	who
a	I	see	an
is	they	then	their
you	one	us	she
to	good	no	new
and	me	him	said
we	about	by	did
that	had	was	boy
in	if	come	three
not	some	get	down
for	up	or	work
at	her	two	put
with	do	man	were
it	when	little	before
on	so	has	just
can	my	them	long
will	very	how	here
are	all	like	other
of	would	our	old
this	any	what	take
your	been	know	cat
as	out	make	again
but	there	which	give
be	from	much	after
have	day	his	many

SECOND HUNDRED WORDS			
saw	big	may	fan
home	where	let	five
soon	am	use	read
stand	ball	these	over
box	morning	right	such
upon	live	present	way
first	four	tell	too
came	last	next	shall
girl	color	please	own
house	away	leave	most
find	red	hand	sure
because	friend	more	thing
made	pretty	why	only
could	eat	better	near
book	want	under	than
look	year	while	open
mother	white	should	kind
run	got	never	must
school	play	each	high
people	found	best	far
night	left	another	both
into	men	seem	end
say	bring	tree	also
think	wish	name	until
back	black	dear	call

THIRD HUNDRED WORDS

ask	hat	off	fire
small	car	sister	ten
yellow	write	happy	order
show	try	once	part
goes	myself	didn't	early
clean	longer	set	fat
buy	those	round	third
thank	hold	dress	same
sleep	full	tell	love
letter	carry	wash	hear
jump	eight	start	eyes
help	sing	always	door
fly	warm	anything	clothes
don't	sit	around	through
fast	dog	close	o'clock
cold	ride	walk	second
today	hot	money	water
does	grow	turn	town
face	cut	might	took
green	seven	hard	pair
every	woman	along	now
brown	funny	bed	keep
coat	yes	fine	head
six	ate	sat	food
gave	stop	hope	yesterday

FOURTH HUNDRED WORDS			
told	yet	word	airplane
Miss	true	almost	without
father	above	thought	wear
children	still	send	Mr.
land	meet	receive	side
interest	since	pay	poor
feet	number	nothing	lost
garden	state	need	wind
done	matter	mean	Mrs.
country	line	late	learn
different	large	half	held
bad	few	fight	front
across	hit	enough	built
yard	cover	feet	family
winter	window	during	began
table	even	gone	air
story	city	hundred	young
I'm	together	week	ago
tried	sun	between	world
horse	life	change	kill
brought	street	being	ready
shoes	party	care	stay
government	suit	answer	won't
sometimes	remember	course	paper
time	something	against	outside

FIFTH HUNDRED WORDS

hour	grade	egg	spell
glad	brother	ground	beautiful
follow	remain	afternoon	sick
company	milk	feed	became
believe	several	boat	cry
begin	war	plan	finish
mind	able	question	catch
pass	charge	fish	floor
reach	either	return	stick
month	less	sir	great
point	train	fell	guess
rest	cost	fill	bridge
sent	evening	wood	church
talk	note	add	lady
went	past	ice	tomorrow
bank	room	chair	snow
ship	flew	watch	whom
business	office	alone	women
whole	cow	low	among
short	visit	arm	road
certain	wait	dinner	farm
fair	teacher	hair	cousin
reason	spring	service	bread
summer	picture	class	wrong
fill	bird	quite	age

SIXTH HUNDRED WORDS			
become	themselves	thousand	wife
body	herself	demand	condition
chance	idea	however	aunt
act	drop	figure	system
die	river	case	line
real	smile	increase	cause
speak	son	enjoy	marry
already	bat	rather	possible
doctor	fact	sound	supply
step	sort	eleven	pen
itself	king	music	perhaps
nine	dark	human	produce
baby	whose	court	twelve
minute	study	force	rode
ring	fear	plant	uncle
wrote	move	suppose	labor
happen	stood	law	public
appear	himself	husband	consider
heart	strong	moment	thus
swim	knew	person	least
felt	often	result	power
fourth	toward	continue	mark
I'll	wonder	price	voice
kept	twenty	serve	whether
well	important	national	president

Acknowledgments

From *Caramelo* by Sandra Cisneros. Copyright © 2002 by Sandra Cisneros. Published by Vintage Books in paperback in 2003 and originally in hardcover by Alfred A. Knopf, Inc. Reprinted by permission of Susan Bergholz Literary Services, New York. All rights reserved.

Fairyland Music: Excerpt from the song lyric "Moon Men Mambo," words and music by Paul Parnes. Copyright © by Fairyland Music (ASCAP). All rights reserved. Reprinted by permission of Fairyland Music.

Houghton Mifflin Harcourt: Excerpt from *Farewell to Manzanar* by Jeanne W. Houston and James D. Houston. Copyright © 1973 by James D. Houston, renewed 2001 by Jeanne Wakatsuki Houston and James D. Houston. Reprinted by permission of Houghton Mifflin Harcourt Publishing Company. All rights reserved.

Doubleday and Harold Ober Associates: "Marriage is a Private Affair," from *Girls At War and Other Stories* by Chinua Achebe. Copyright © 1972, 1973 by Chinua Achebe. Used by permission of Doubleday, a division of Random House, Inc. and Harold Ober Associates Incorporated.

Viking Penguin: Excerpt from *Don Quixote* by Miguel de Cervantes Saavedra, translated by Samuel Putnam. Copyright 1949 by The Viking Press, Inc. Used by permission of Viking Penguin, a division of Penguin Group (USA) Inc.

McGraw-Hill Companies: From *Elementary Reading Instruction* by Edward Fry. Copyright 1977 by McGraw-Hill Companies, Inc. All rights reserved. Reprinted by permission of the publisher.

COVER

(tc) Teacher's Discovery, Auburn Hills, Michigan; (tr) © DEA / A. DAGLI ORTI/Getty Images; (bc) Getty Images; (c) Atlantide Phototravel/Corbis; (bl) Ken Kinzie/HMH Publishers.

HOW TO USE THIS BOOK

0 *top* © John Teate/ShutterStock; *bottom* Library of Congress, Prints and Photographs Division [6-17617-29a]; **xiv** © John Teate/ShutterStock.

UNIT 1

xxx © Fotocrisis/ShutterStock; **4–12** © Andrew Doran/ShutterStock; **4** © Solus-Veer/Corbis; **18–28** © John Teate/ShutterStock; **18, 26, 28** Library of Congress, Prints and Photographs Division [6-17617-29a]; **34–52** © Christoprudov Dmitriy Gennadievich/ShutterStock; **34** © Aleksander Bochenek/ShutterStock.

UNIT 2

56 © Darrin Klimek/Getty Images; **60–72** © Photodisc/Getty Images; **60, 70** © photostogo.com; **78–84** © Creatas Images/Jupiterimages Corporation; **78** AP/Wide World Photos; **90–104** © Kirill Belyntsev/ShutterStock; **90** © photostogo.com.

UNIT 3

108 © Liv Friis-Larsen/ShutterStock; **112–126** © Binski/ShutterStock; **112, 124** © Comstock Images/Jupiterimages Corporation; **132–140** © Maksim Nikalayenka/ShutterStock; **132, 137** © Goodshoot/Jupiterimages Corporation.

UNIT 4

144 "Civilization is a method of living, an attitude of equal respect for all men,"—Jane Addams, Speech, Honolulu, 1933. From the series *Great Ideas of Western Man* (1955), George Giusti. India ink and gouache on paper, 24 ⅞" x 18 ¹⁵⁄₁₆". Gift of the Container Corporation of America. © Smithsonian American Art Museum, Washington, D.C./Art Resource, New York; **148–154** © Robertas/ShutterStock; **148** © Nadejda Ivanova/ShutterStock; **160–178** Photo by Sharon Hoogstraten; **160** © photostogo.com; **173** © Olinchuk/ShutterStock; **177** Photo by Sharon Hoogstraten; **184–186** © Photos.com / Jupiterimages Corporation; **186** Library of Congress, Prints and Photographs Division [cwp 4a40872].

UNIT 5

190 © Brooke Fasani/Getty Images; **194–197** © Kapustin Oleg/ShutterStock; **194** © Viktor1/ShutterStock; **202–206** © Kapustin Oleg/ShutterStock; **202** © Jupiterimages Corporation; **212** *top right, bottom* Illustration by Keith Kasnot; *top center* © Biophoto Associates/Photo Researchers, Inc.; *top left* © Kapustin Oleg/ShutterStock; **213** *background* © Donna Disario/Corbis; *top left* © Photodisc/Getty Images; *center* Illustration by Debbie Maizels; **218–228** © AbleStock.com/Jupiterimages Corporation; **218** © Alejandro Rivera/photolibrary.

UNIT 6

232 Photo by Phil Coale/AP/Wide World Photos; **236** © Ekaterina Pokrovskaya/ShutterStock; **246–256** © Georgios Kollidas/ShutterStock; **246** © Michael Nichols/Getty Images; **252** © Kennan Ward/Corbis; **255** © Eric Isselée/ShutterStock; **262** © LWA-Paul Chmielowiec/Corbis.

UNIT 7

274 © AbleStock.com/Jupiterimages Corporation; **278–281** © Houghton Mifflin Harcourt; **278** © Peter Clark/ShutterStock; **279** *Moonlight Over the Sea,* Mauritx F. H. De Haas. Oil on canvas. The Lowe Art Museum, The University of Miami, Florida. © Lowe Art Museum/SuperStock; **280** © Photodisc/Getty Images; **286** *The Cathedral* (1908), Auguste Rodin. Bronze. 24 ½" x 10 ¾" x 11 ¾". Photo © Timothy McCarthy/Art Resource, New York; **287** © Corbis; **292–297** © Nata_Tata/ShutterStock; **292** *Portrait of a Young Man* (1700s), John Opie. Oil on canvas. San Diego Museum of Art, Gift of Bella Mabury in memory of Paul R. Mabury. © Bridgeman Art Library; **294** © Glowimages/PunchStock; **296, 297** © Photos.com/Jupiterimages Corporation.

UNIT 8

300 © Photodisc/PunchStock; **304–320** © dundanim/ShutterStock; **304** © Jupiterimages Corporation; **326–329** © Kuttelvaserova/ShutterStock; **326** © photostogo.com; **328** © Erin Paul Donovan/SuperStock; **334–340** © PunchStock; **334** © Photodisc/PunchStock; **339** Photo by Eric Gay/AP/Wide World Photos.

UNIT 9

344 © Timothy A. Clary/AFP/Getty Images; **348–358** © Sasha Buzko/ShutterStock; **348** © Bettmann/Corbis; **363** © Bettmann/Corbis; **370–376** © BananaStock/PunchStock; **370** © Gideon Mendel/ActionAid/Corbis.

UNIT 10

380 © Bettmann/Corbis; **384–396** © Matt Trommer/ShutterStock; **384** © Photodisc/PunchStock; **394** © Phillip Lange/ShutterStock; **396** © Photodisc/PunchStock.

UNIT 11

400 © Andrea Pistolesi/Getty Images; **404–430** © Jupiterimages Corporation; **404** © Hoberman Collection/Corbis.

Index of Authors and Titles

Architectural Design
July/August 2007

4dsoci
Interac   **nts**

Guest-edited
Lucy Bullivant

WILEY-ACADEMY

ISBN-978 0 470 31911 6
Profile No 188
Vol 77 No 4

Editorial Offices
International House
Ealing Broadway Centre
London W5 5DB

T: +44 (0)20 8326 3800
F: +44 (0)20 8326 3801
E: architecturaldesign@wiley.co.uk

Editor
Helen Castle

Production Controller
Jenna Brown

Project Management
Caroline Ellerby

Design and Prepress
Artmedia Press, London

Printed in Italy by Conti Tipocolor

Advertisement Sales
Faith Pidduck/Wayne Frost
T +44 (0)1243 770254
E fpidduck@wiley.co.uk

Editorial Board
Will Alsop, Denise Bratton, Mark Burry, André
Chaszar, Nigel Coates, Peter Cook, Teddy Cruz,
Max Fordham, Massimiliano Fuksas, Edwin
Heathcote, Michael Hensel, Anthony Hunt,
Charles Jencks, Jan Kaplicky, Robert Maxwell,
Jayne Merkel, Michael Rotondi, Leon van Schaik,
Neil Spiller, Ken Yeang

Contributing Editors
Jeremy Melvin
Jayne Merkel

Front cover: Studio Roosegaarde, Dune 4.0,
Netherlands Media Art Institute, Amsterdam, and
CBK Rotterdam, 2006–07. © Daan Roosegaarde

Requests to the Publisher should be addressed to:
Permissions Department,
John Wiley & Sons Ltd,
The Atrium
Southern Gate
Chichester,
West Sussex PO19 8SQ
England

F: +44 (0)1243 770571
E: permreq@wiley.co.uk

Subscription Offices UK
John Wiley & Sons Ltd
Journals Administration Department
1 Oldlands Way, Bognor Regis
West Sussex, PO22 9SA
T: +44 (0)1243 843272
F: +44 (0)1243 843232
E: cs-journals@wiley.co.uk

[ISSN: 0003-8504]

_AD_ is published bimonthly and is available to
purchase on both a subscription basis and as
individual volumes at the following prices.

Single Issues
Single issues UK: £22.99
Single issues outside UK: US$45.00
Details of postage and packing charges
available on request.

Annual Subscription Rates 2007
Institutional Rate
Print only or Online only: UK£175/US$315
Combined Print and Online: UK£193/US$347
Personal Rate
Print only: UK£110/US$170
Student Rate
Print only: UK£70/US$110
Prices are for six issues and include postage
and handling charges. Periodicals postage paid
at Jamaica, NY 11431. Air freight and mailing in
the USA by Publications Expediting Services
Inc, 200 Meacham Avenue, Elmont, NY 11003
Individual rate subscriptions must be paid by
personal cheque or credit card. Individual rate
subscriptions may not be resold or used as
library copies.

All prices are subject to change
without notice.

Postmaster
Send address changes to 3 Publications
Expediting Services, 200 Meacham Avenue,
Elmont, NY 11003

C O N T E N T S

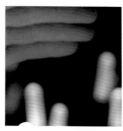

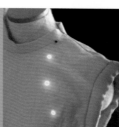

AD+

Ed Keller and Carla Leitao of A|Um Studio, SUTURE, SCI-Arc and TELIC galleries, Los Angeles, California, November 2005–January 2006
An expanded cinema installation, SUTURE at SCI-Arc encouraged visitors to experiment with media assemblage and play with the possibilities of film. A landscape of sculpted furniture and pressure sensors embedded in the floor organised circulation flows and points of view, allowing visitors to create new signal paths and new cycles between the images projected on multiple screens. By acting as catalysts, the users were able to make new connections between gestures, objects, characters, materials, spaces and narrative arcs, ultimately remixing events. A month later a parallel installation at the TELIC gallery, Los Angeles, was opened to provide an additional networked interface to SUTURE. It allowed TELIC visitors to remotely alter parameters in the programming environment at SCI-ARC, observing the results and embedding themselves as video participants in the project.

Editorial

The days in which conventional architecture was driven by a social agenda are now far behind us. They are secreted in the distant past of the most senior generation of architects when professionals worked for local authorities and housing projects were solely publicly funded. Interactive design environments are, by comparison with postwar utopian projects that could tackle large-scale urbanism such as new towns, and swathes of residential tower blocks, small-scale interventions. This is not to undermine their potency; their power to transform people's experiences and perceptions. They may not aspire to irrevocably change an individual's quality of life or life course; what they can do, however, is shift the way people interact both with those around them and also with the space around them. In an urban context, where the major cities of the world are densely populated, often with populations often over 10 million, they turn the anonymous passer-by from just another face in the crowd into an individual, and often a playful one at that. In museums, they allow the visitor to enter into a totally different relationship with works of art. Whereas conventionally the visitor is asked to stand back and view in awe a cordoned-off venerated object, with an interactive artwork touch and noise, if not a prerequisite, are generally encouraged on the visitor's part.

The aspirations of interactive art focusing largely on the experience of individuals or a small section of the public partaking in a particular project may seem modest. Its widest purpose is in an educational capacity. As Lucy Bullivant outlines in her article 'Playing with Art', digital projects that have been undertaken by London's museums and galleries have been successful in bringing a wider public both into the galleries and online. It is, however, the encouragement of sociability where the interactive is at its most potent, where it has the ability to transcend the everyday – causing the individual to pause a minute in a street corner or a gallery foyer to have fun, be playful and have occasion to smile out of unassailable joy. ∆

Helen Castle

Alice in Technoland

At their most supernatural, interactive design environments can have a transformative effect. They take the visitor to somewhere else. By actively involving the public they are both 'porous' and 'responsive', beckoning us like the rabbit in *Alice in Wonderland* to enter and participate in another world. Here **Lucy Bullivant** kicks off her introduction to this issue of *AD* by looking at an installation designed by Daan Roosegaarde for the Netherlands Media Art Institute in Amsterdam which epitomises this approach.

'We want it to learn how to behave and to become more sensitive towards the visitor,' says Dutch architect Daan Roosegaarde of his new interactive landscape, Dune 4.0. The installation consisted of two long 'bushes' of swaying, reed-like fibres fitted with microphones and presence sensors that recently lined a corridor of the Netherlands Media Art Institute in Amsterdam. 'There are several moods within the landscape; when nobody is there, it will fall asleep – glooming softly – but then as soon as you enter, light appears where you walk, as an extension of your activities,' he explains. 'When you make a lot of noise the landscape goes crazy – lightning crashes.'

Interactive design environments like Dune 4.0 promote the personalisation and customisation of not just architecture, but also of their wider physical public contexts. They assert an architecture of social relations that invites the visitor to spontaneously perform and thereby construct alternative physical, architectural, urban and social meanings. This is facilitated by the multidisciplinary ability and teamwork architects, artists and designers increasingly apply to program spaces, turning the traditional concept of ephemerality as a nature-based phenomenon into something supernatural. Through the activation of embedded, custom-designed software and responses to its effects, the identity of public space itself goes beyond its constitution through generic formal givens, and becomes porous and responsive to specific information and communication conveyed to it. The installation of Dune 4.0 in the Media Art Institute is a pilot:

Studio Roosegaarde, Dune 4.0, Netherlands Media Art Institute, Amsterdam, and CBK Rotterdam, 2006–07
The initial pilot made of fibres with concealed microphones and sensors reacts to the behaviour of visitors, its fibres lighting up in response to their sounds (30 per cent) and movements (70 per cent). A continual stimulus will after time be ignored so the work stays fresh for new human input. Another version is being planned for installation in a public place on a dyke by the River Maas in Rotterdam. Software designed with Peter de Maan, digital technology with Axis + Stuifmeel.

UVA, Volume, V&A, 2006–07
In this LED grid of 46 columns, each of which plays its own piece of music, the notes generate changing colours in real time. UVA designed the installation to work well as an experience on different scales: with no people, with one person, with less than 10 and with much larger numbers of people. They avoided determining colour according to visitor density and struck a balance between pure responsivity and controlled composition. Each visitor entered into a personal exploration of the installation, and their actions influenced others, and this was fundamental to the work, with people regularly switched from viewing to participating.

the next stage takes an evolved version of this adaptive 'bush' outdoors on to a dyke beside the River Maas in Rotterdam, where it will be a future public artwork for the municipality.

Apart from the more convincing fake nature associations possible, one of the appealing features of many interactive environments is their anthropomorphic qualities. Roosegaarde could easily be describing a pet or even a wild animal in captivity. One day he found an old lady testing Dune 4.0's sounds by barking at it. She told him she was trying to see if it would respond like her dog at home did. It is the behavioural aspects – the unpredictable, 'live' quality of installations – that is compelling and with the active involvement of visitors 'completes' the identity of the work.

The growing appetite of museums and galleries to focus on interactive installations created by artists, architects, designers and other practitioners enables a range of responsive technological applications – for instance, proximity sensing – to be evolved through public use, and even tested out in what is an ideal, controlled setting with a variety of types of visitor.

Roosegaarde usefully typifies the materials and the context as the 'hard construction', and the software and the human behaviour as the 'soft construction'. But while creating a Pavlov's Dog cybernetic model would be repetitive, a certain pattern of responsivity to the subject would seem to be more important than a work exhibiting consistent waywardness. Ultimately, each installation is a prosthetic device for human creativity, whether or not one agrees that this also opens it up to the interpretation of 'playing God'. By involving visitors and passers-by so intimately in an installation's responsive 'operating system', they too become part of the prosthetic impact, and the public space it occupies becomes, for a limited time, prosthetic, too. Roosegaarde emulates nature in a number of his works and, like an implanted field of bulrushes, Dune 4.0 has the capacity to become a new layer over the existing architecture and merging its intelligent

qualities in an ongoing game with the actively involved human body, it is hoped, avoids becoming predictable.

Works like Dune 4.0 could be perceived as a kind of second nature, interventions that make their entire environmental setting supernatural, like 'Alice in Technoland', to use Roosegaarde's phrase describing the effect of his installation. There are undoubtedly analogies with the Victorian children's story set in a fantasy realm, its unfolding narrative full of riddles and plays on meaning. In interactive environments, as in *Alice in Wonderland*, cultural codes are fluid, and function is defined as a more open-ended concept influenced by in-the-moment behaviour.

This makes them potent curatorial devices in a museum context, where handhelds are already common, but works on display to be touched and played with are rare. The cultural transformations digital technologies bring to traditional associations of a museum space are discussed in 'Playing with Art' in this issue. UVA's Volume, installed in the courtyard of the V&A last autumn, broke the customarily reserved, contemplative atmosphere of the museum. An interactive pavilion in an open garden setting that visitors could touch, push on and run through, it became, albeit temporarily, their space, perhaps a form of physical parallel to the many user-generated content sites such as MySpace proliferating daily on the Internet.

The growing appetite of museums and galleries to focus on interactive installations created by artists, architects, designers and other practitioners enables a range of responsive technological applications – for instance, proximity sensing – to be evolved through public use, and even tested out in what is an ideal, controlled setting with a variety of types of visitor. Paris-based designers Helen Evans and Heiko Hansen of HeHe did this when they built a prototype of their Mirrorspace project for remote communication, originally conceived for the interLiving project of the European Disappearing Computer initiative (2001–03) focused on communication among family members in different households. Taking the Mains d'Oeuvres gallery, the Pompidou Centre and later La Villette, all in Paris, as their venues throughout 2003, they hoped to prove that the work created a sense of shared space, overcoming the failure of many video-mediated communication systems to take proxemics into account by being designed for a specific task or a certain interpersonal distance.

As HeHe point out, artists like Dan Graham already use time-delay mechanisms in mirror-based installations to let viewers see themselves as both subject and object.[1] By presenting Mirrorspace to a broad mix of gallery visitors, HeHe found friends and relatives freely overlaying their faces on the surface, and even kissing each other. Pursuing their design-led agenda, they were able to conclude that their mirror was an ideal enabling metaphor for a new communication system. Testing showed that it was perceived at this level rather than as a video camera set up on a wall. After the exercise, the design, and the software and hardware

HeHe, Mirrorspace, Pompidou Centre, Paris, 2003
Enabling remote participants to look into each other's eyes, the work has a screen and a mini camera at its centre. This setup is repeated in a second installation, so people who look into the mirror can communicate with each other. An ultrasonic sensor calculates the physical distance that separates the spectators and, depending on how far away they are, will blur the images returned in real time. The two reflections are blended together on the surface of the mirrors, transforming the visual contact between two people and altering the space between them.

From peripheral awareness to close communication by moving towards the device.

of the device, which was connectable to similar ones in other places, could then continue to be evolved.

This common interest in user-generated input, personalisation and dynamic relations between action, space and object is shared with practitioners across various sectors including designers of wearable computing (discussed by Despina Papadopoulos in this issue), but for some artists such as Rafael Lozano-Hemmer, Scott Snibbe, Eric Schuldenfrei and Marisa Yiu, all of whose work is profiled in this publication by Maria Fernández and myself, a projection takes the place of an object. In contrast to visual art media that privilege the visual, interactive environments engage the visitor's body and assert his or her agency. In Lozano-Hemmer and Schuldenfrei and Yiu's case, although working with different social agendas, a common objective is to transform the dominant narratives of a specific building or urban setting by superimposing new audiovisual elements that recontextualise it. Snibbe invites visitors to turn the orthodoxy of linear cinema narration into a more organic interface between subject and object.

This prosthetic capacity of interactive architecture in its more design-oriented tendency can be assigned a range of innovative social roles. It may take on the form of social infrastructure, a feature typified by Flirtables, designs currently in development by Tobi Schneidler (as featured in *AD 4dspace: Interactive Architecture*, 2005). Social networking tables, intended to be assembled in a group in bars and clubs, their dimmable light surfaces contain a sensor that picks up vibrations and responds to music. Knock them with the hand and a glowing streak of light is propelled across the table. With a stronger blow it jumps to another table, but can also be specifically aimed in the direction of another individual sitting at one of the tables. This is the unique selling proposition of Flirtables: the movement of light is a social icebreaker to attract the attention of someone nearby you don't know but want to meet. For metropolitan centres like London or Stockholm where inhibitions make engineering meetings with strangers a fraught process, and singles bars are felt to possess a definite stigma, this introduces a playful new socio-spatial programme for a bar or club likely to be eagerly explored. The concept seems adaptable for other scenarios, such as informal learning environments in museums that utilise play as a means to educational involvement.

As an inventor of commercially viable design solutions straddling art and commerce, Schneidler has a kinship with other practitioners such as Jason Bruges in the UK, Scott Snibbe's Sona Research and Antenna Design in the US, the Interaction Design Lab in Italy and Daan Roosegaarde's studio in the Netherlands. Frequently adopting a laboratory-like working environment, practitioners pull together multidisciplinary teams for the research and prototyping of new concepts for widespread use in various public domains. Industry backing is clearly beginning to grow, with a more intimate public awareness being engendered by innovative initiatives of specific cultural sectors like museums and

Mirrorspace installed on an advertising hoarding in the street, showing two participants looking into each other's faces and the image sensors in the centre.

galleries. In the last 15 years these have moved away from hermetic, immersive 'black box' or kiosk models of digital spaces into ones that colonise and adapt the public spaces of these cultural places of learning on many levels.

The methodologies of interactive architecture are heavily borrowed by architects, artists and designers from interactive media art, and this process continues. But as Mark Garcia's showcasing of some new examples in this issue underlines, the field continues to evolve its own hybrid identity as solutions that are innovative in artistic, behavioural and technological terms are developed for different sectors. In an era of pervasive computing we need to think further about how humans, devices and their shared environments might coexist in a mutually constructive environment. Everyday buildings are embedded with tracking technologies that watch people. The ubiquitous presence in the environment of an invisible web of electronic activity in the form of surveillance systems, but also a wide range of electromagnetic sensitivities, can be harnessed to change people's relationships with space.

As Hugh Hart's feature on the Los Angeles-based architectural practice Electroland illuminates, they can also illicit a further feeling of ambiguity about what is happening in a positive sense, by building in custom-designed systems of responsivity that intercept occupants

and visitors and invite them to play, co-opting the tracking function of digital technologies, and turning ordinary spaces into 'stealth' art venues.

The recent full-blown evolution in interactive environment methods and means brings the need to explore the words used to describe aspects of this practice and examine the provocative counterpoints to their uses. Considering interactive architecture as an architecture of social relations and effects, it is vital to distinguish between 'interactive', 'reactive' and 'responsive', and to understand the evolution of theories of interaction and the interdisciplinary subject of cybernetics, the study of control and communication in goal-driven systems in animals and machines.

In his two articles in this issue, Usman Haque provides both a personal lexical guide to interactive art and architecture, and an assessment of the contemporary relevance to the field of Gordon Pask, one of the early proponents and practitioners of cybernetics, whose work set the foundation for authentically interactive environments. Pask's concept of Conversation Theory, a generative activity that gives identity to participants and leads to what is new, put cybernetics into a conversational frame depicted in his 'Architecture of conversations' sketches, rather than being merely a matter of communication, exchanging messages containing what is already known. His intellectual

Antenna Design, The Door, Walker Arts Centre, Minneapolis, 2000
For their commission to feature over 40 Web-based art projects, Antenna turned the solitary, 'any time, anywhere' Web experience into one that was 'here and now', requiring the visitor to physically perform in order to get results. They created a physical portal, referring to the portal metaphor of Web design, in the form of a freestanding revolving door that enabled visitors to navigate various websites simply by rotating it. When it is not used, it is a mirror-surface monolith; on pushing it, a door bell sounds, indicating that the visitor is entering a new website, which appears on the other side of the mirrored glass. The visitor can continue to interact with it via a trackpad integrated into the door handle, or continue spinning to visit the rest of the sites.

Usman Haque, Moody Mushroom Floor, Bartlett School of Architecture, UCL, London, 1996
This early work of Haque's was a field of anthropomorphically defined 'mushrooms' that developed a range of moods and aspirations in response to the ways in which visitors reacted to their outputs in the form of different lights, sounds and smells emitted at intervals. Assigned pet names including 'spoilt brat', 'sullen' and 'capricious', the responsive mushrooms tested out a range of behaviours on visitors to try to achieve their individual goal before settling on the most effective one matching their ascribed 'personality'.

frameworks and prototypes centralised the subjectivity of the observer and his or her individual knowledge within any form of scientific analysis. His work made it easy, for instance, according to Pask expert Paul Pangaro, to write software that nurtured individual learning styles.

'Increasingly, the personality of artefacts, whether objects or environments, is made up not only of appearance and materials, but also of behaviour,' say Masamichi Udagawa and Sigi Moeslinger of Antenna, the New York City-based designers. Their interactive work, ranging from public information resources (their Civic Exchange installation is discussed later in this issue), subway ticket machines, window displays and gallery installations, crosses the now no longer solid threshold between product and environment, public and private, physical and digital interfaces, and has a strong prototypical element to it. In responding to deep socio-cultural and technological changes, only a broad inclusive approach and capacity to invent new programmes,

something *4dsocial* celebrates, will do if these transformations are to be creatively interpreted in a way that opens up the civic potential of public space in a postindustrial, digital era.

The promise of our evolving supernatural facilities – thanks to a myriad imaginative prosthetic applications of digital technologies – demands that creative practitioners fully involve people in their development on both subjective and objective levels, enabling them to make their own connections between what are increasingly permeable cultural thresholds of perception and being. ∆

Note
1. Nicolas Roussel, Helen Evans and Heiko Hansen, 'Proximity as an Interface for Video Communication', IEEE Multimedia paper published by the IEEE Computer Society, 2003.

Beyond the Kiosk and the Billboard

The proliferation of commercial billboards and electronic signage in New York's Manhattan limits the possibility for interactive art sites. **Lucy Bullivant** describes how Eskyiu transformed an HSBC bank in Chinatown's Canal Street with an interactive facade and Antenna Design have created their Civic Exchange project for a site in Battery Park City.

Streets as public spaces are potent arenas for interactive installations, but art is often overtaken by commercial concerns. The other drawback is that the location potentially becomes irrelevant, something that art as well as advertising can perpetuate. However, in 1986 artist Cindy Sherman stopped the traffic in Times Square with her compelling 'Protect me from What I want' electronic signage, a specific embodiment of the city – New York City, or indeed any city – as a place of competing interests, politics and languages. These days only interactive advertising campaigns are perpetually unleashed here. The setting is physical, but in fact it could be anywhere, functioning as if it were a purely virtual advertising space; people have recently been invited by Nike's billboard to use their mobile phones to design a trainer; by Yahoo! to play a video game, by the Campaign for Real Beauty (sic) to debate 'what is beautiful?', and to make the red glowing eyes of a giant yeti (promoting Disney's latest addition to its Animal Kingdom in Florida) flash with aggressive intent.

But as the international work of video artist Rafael Lozano-Hemmer demonstrates (see Maria Fernández's article in this issue), art-based interactive installations with a well-honed political agenda continue to be invited to intervene in central urban spaces and encourage people to participate. However, external interactive art sites are rare in Manhattan – from time to time at City Hall or in Central Park, with most socially based work installed in the smaller, less commercial galleries. Given the surfeit of commercially driven interactive billboards, to the layperson interactives are predominantly recognised as an adjunct to Christmas decorations on the street, moving elements that dynamise public space, injecting playful or play-based features to otherwise predetermined built environments. It is far less common for them to be educational and place-based, with a social instrumentality,

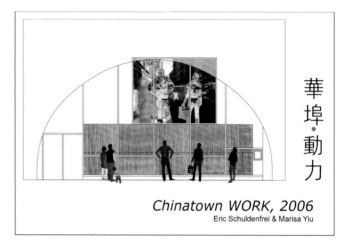

Chinatown WORK, 2006
Eric Schuldenfrei & Marisa Yiu

Postcard/flyer for the street facade-based installation. A live-feed wifi system was placed across the road from the HSBC bank, filming the movements of passers-by. Their bodies were replaced by time-lapse footage of the interiors of local garment factories and local street life, and projected on to a panel of translucent eco-resin suspended over the bank's facade.

and rarer still for artists and architects to use this hybrid discipline in a way that not only makes a political point, but also gets financial backing from public organisations.

Like a number of interactive specialists, the aim of designers Marisa Yiu and Eric Schuldenfrei, who work together under the name of Eskyiu, is to make site-specific works that underline global connections. Using time-lapse video for interactive projects they examine the ways in which the built environment and 'constructs of labour' shape social relationships, network systems and connections between participatory design and social engagement. They are concerned with issues of meaning in individual lives, and they investigate themes ranging from multinational production, sustainable food production systems and outsourcing that are central to the social restructuring brought about by the ever-expanding global free market economy.

Schuldenfrei, who studied architecture at Cornell and philosophy at Cambridge, and with Yiu teaches at the Architectural Association in London, and at Princeton and Columbia, was until a few years ago a member of the design firm D-Box, creating computer animations including Blur at the Swiss Expo 2002, Facsimile at the Moscone Convention Center, and Travelogues installed at JFK International Airport for Diller Scofidio + Renfro. Yiu trained in architecture at Columbia and Princeton, and was a panellist for the Chinatown Design Lab organised by the Rebuild Chinatown Initiative (RCI) and AAFE (Asian Americans for Equality), a leading US affordable housing association. Together they have used locally generated footage to generate a sense of the immediacy of specific community

Using time-lapse video for interactive projects they examine the ways in which the built environment and 'constructs of labour' shape social relationships, network systems and connections between participatory design and social engagement.

Marisa Yiu and Eric Schuldenfrei, Chinatown WORK, Manhattan, New York, 2006
By mounting a translucent resin screen over the facade of the bank, a light box effect is created that lends a sense of depth to the imagery projected, a mix of still images of local life in garment factories, restaurants and on the street, and time-lapse images of passers-by silhouetted against the screen.

pressures and patterns, drawing on residents' lives in the form of a video-based narrative. Their most recent interactive installation, Chinatown WORK, exhibited in New York's Chinatown in spring 2006, was a cross-disciplinary, custom-designed work and a cohesive didactive device, with the time-lapse video serving as an incisive political tool to investigate Chinatown's 'sense of place'.

Metaphorically, yet benignly turning inside spaces out into the street, the designers mixed the mobile silhouettes of pedestrians with their footage of local food markets, herb stores, pharmacies, jewellery storefronts and speciality outlets (banking, construction), garment factories, laundries and restaurants – industries that have helped establish immigrants in the city, but are typically hidden from the public.

The struggles for survival by this working community are a poignant tale of shrinking fortunes matched by a diminution in living space. In the aftermath of 9/11, not only had three-quarters of the 25,000-strong workforce of a garment factory lost their jobs, but while in 2001 there were approximately 500 garment factories in Chinatown, according to the New York State Department of Labor, there are now only about a hundred left. Clothing manufacturers, intensively affected by market dynamics, were not just losing their premises; workers were also being cut off from their foothold in the community. In 2005 the *Washington Post* reported that not only were commercial pressures eroding the number of local workplaces, they were also shrinking the availability of subsidised housing.[1] Five years later, and working closely with owners, manufacturers and employees, Yiu and Schuldenfrei filmed extensively in the area to find out more about how Chinatown was faring and to document these local private and public working environments.

The duo created a map of Lower Manhattan depicting Chinatown marked with places relevant to their research, and this was sewn on to bolts of Linea Vert fabric and a layer of translucent polyester eco-resin to aid an even distribution of light. This became the surface for a 'light box' transforming the facade of the HSBC bank on Canal Street (at 58 Bowery). Using real-time video processing software that allows a computer to generate and control matted (masked) images, they enabled their camera, set in a second-floor window across the street, to identify the motion of passers-by, to create an outline of their bodies and then replace them with the time-lapse footage. Their movements blended two scales of information: interior images of a garment factory, and exterior images of time-lapse footage of the food markets on Mott Street. The resulting composite images were projected on to the screen, changing its texture and image in real time as people walked by.

'Passers-by reactions were a mixture of surprise, intrigue and curiosity until they realised it was their own silhouette that allowed them to see the specific interior images,' explains Schuldenfrei. What might have been perceived as an anonymous, everyday space was recognised by many passers-by for the personal, familiar space that they knew. 'The bank

Chinatown WORK, 2006
Eric Schuldenfrei & Marisa Yiu

April 18th -May 21st
Free and Open to the Public
Evenings 7:30 - 11:00pm
HSBC FACADE, 58 BOWERY BRANCH

華埠
·
動力

「華埠・動力」互動裝置藝術展2006

Chinatown WORK promotional poster depicting the installation using video footage of garment factories and restaurants with their employees in Chinatown, the fabric projection screen over the front of the bank being made and images of sites that were filmed.

space was open 24 hours, so they always had the option to go inside to examine all the of the installation components in detail.'[2] Locating the work on the facade of the bank established a strong dynamic between audience and location, commerce and art, and attracted a bilingual audience who could read about the project in English and Chinese by viewing signs mounted on the glass facade.

Chinatown WORK was situated in a 'marginalised community in terms of art', and aims to correct this by emphasising Chinatown on the public art map. According to Schuldenfrei: 'It is becoming more and more difficult to find support for public art unless it is in a privately owned foyer, skyscraper or in a free space within a museum.' In developing a public artwork on a contested site in flux due to the tragedy of 9/11 as well as the impact of global systems affecting local communities, Eskyiu are 'conceptualising different levels of exploration and needs' for art to fulfil. The work was made

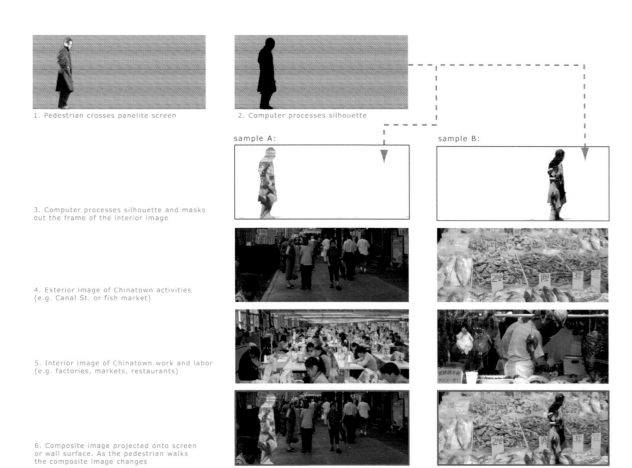

1. Pedestrian crosses panelite screen

2. Computer processes silhouette

sample A:

sample B:

3. Computer processes silhouette and masks
out the frame of the interior image

4. Exterior image of Chinatown activities
(e.g. Canal St. or fish market)

5. Interior image of Chinatown work and labor
(e.g. factories, markets, restaurants)

6. Composite image projected onto screen
or wall surface. As the pedestrian walks
the composite image changes

Diagram explanation of the composite sequence using custom-made real-time software.

A composite of time-lapse footage of passers-by and images of the interior of local garment factories and
restaurants is projected on to the facade of a Chinatown bank.

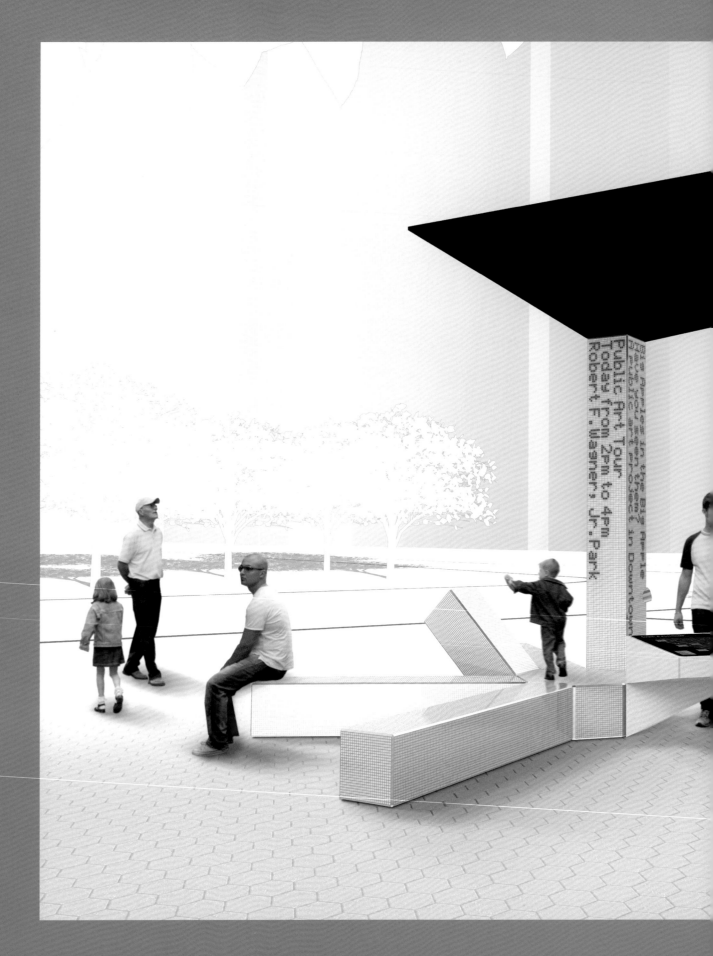

Big Apples in the Big Apple
Have you seen them?
A public art project in Downtown
Public Art Tour
Today from 2pm to 4pm
Robert F. Wagner, Jr. Park

Antenna Design, Civic Exchange, New York, 2004
Based on a 'hub' and 'spokes' system that visually embodies the notion of a tree-like gathering place, Udagawa and Moeslinger's Civic Exchange is intended to be sited at the southern end of Battery Park City. The information system is an open platform with an interactive map allowing for community participation, with an LED column serving as a public announcement screen.

The different modular configurations are surfaced in glass mosaic enclosed in a stainless-steel grid for durability, and allow for permutations of seating and information options.

with grants from the Lower Manhattan Cultural Council, Manhattan Community Arts Fund, September 11th Fund, 3-form material solutions, the Department of Cultural Affairs, and Asian American Arts Centre, with a free rein to realise the public project as a means to reflect on the roles people and visitors play in their communities, as well as the activities that are scarcely thought about by people on the street. A component of the installations was also featured at the LMCC Manhattan Arts Bash and at the Storefront for Art and Architecture in New York City in 2006, and at the Haus der Architektur in Graz, Austria.

Yiu and Schuldenfrei have since pursued other sites in Manhattan, including the now defunct Music Palace cinema in another part of Chinatown at Columbus Park, which was traditionally used by various immigrant cultures, and hope to situate a similar project somewhere in Asia.

Industrial design as a discipline applied to urban tasks is by comparison concerned with problem solving of a more tractable kind. Interactive design is now par for the course in such a multidisciplinary context, yet when Antenna Design were designing ticket-vending machines for the New York City subway they found that a large percentage of subway users were unfamiliar with touchscreens. Lacking a bank account, they had no experience with ATMs, the most common application of touchscreens at the time, so the designers gave

the now widely admired MTA/NYCT Metrocard vending machines a familiar 'Start' prompt button to anticipate people's intuitive reactions.

Antenna co-founders Masamichi Udagawa and Sigi Moeslinger, who are both professors at New York University's Interactive Telecommunications Program, see themselves as communicators and cultural commentators as much as practical problem-solvers: 'We cross the threshold between product and environment, between public and private, between physical and digital interfaces,' which they call a 'hybrid specialism'. 'New technology evokes socio-cultural change, just as socio-cultural environmental change calls for new solutions.'[3] It is, they say, these reciprocal reactions that transform everyday life.

Antenna's broad, inclusive perspective, always making context the starting point of their designs, paid off when they won the Civic Exchange competition held by the Van Alen Institute and the Architectural League of New York in 2004, a rare invitation to design a public information installation for people who live, work or visit Lower Manhattan to stimulate place-based education. The concept was to take the form of a high-profile piece of interactive street furniture to be sited at the southern end of Battery Park City. Both competition organisers are bodies that nurture critical enquiry into contemporary forms of public space and new configurations

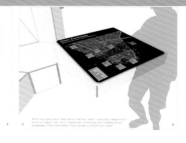

The designers envisaged various scenarios for the viewing, use and information exchange through the open platform of the installation, based around the multi-user map table that provided access to colour-coded, place-based news, events, alerts and other information, for example on shrubs growing in green spaces. Visitors can deepen their knowledge of the area, add their own landmarks or respond to local community issues.

'We cross the threshold between product and environment, between public and private, between physical and digital interfaces'

After work, on his way to the ferry he passes the Civic Exchange. From a distance he can see that there is an orange alert message on the column display.

of spatial practice. Consequently, their objective was to explore design possibilities for a new space of this kind that fostered social exchange as well as disseminated and exchanged local information.

In public spaces in cities there are very few fixed small-scale digital interactive installations people can also socially interact through. Because of the way society is organised, it is more common that what is there is simply designed to sell you a ticket or comes in the form of a bank of computers in an airport lounge with online access. Antenna's design was inspired by an image of people sitting around a tree, with a 'hub' and 'spokes' modular system clad in glass mosaic embodying this notion of a gathering place. It features multiple interactive screens incorporated into a multi-user touchscreen interactive map table. This gives the as yet unbuilt structure a familiar wayfinding feature, from which place-based news, events and alerts can be accessed. The work also includes a separate, single-user Internet terminal.

Downtown Manhattan is an area of active development, and the Civic Exchange project is intended to foster communications between members of the community,[4] so a bulletin board invited responses to local issues. A touchscreen keypad allows users, either visitors or locals, to annotate and place their own landmarks on the map. Public and emergency announcements are relayed on the large LED display of the public announcement system of a message tower. A video camera doubles up as security surveillance as well as a detector of people approaching, and triggers the LED messages. With a roof of solar panels providing back-up power and integrated seating, the exchange is a resource that can be used by both individuals and small groups at the same time.

In making the map a horizontal table, Antenna is encouraging the possibility of face-to-face communication between diverse users. The interface contains many different kinds of maps, giving it a level of depth and local relevance to its information resources analogous to an interactive

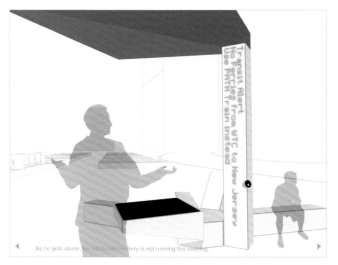

As he gets closer, he reads that his ferry is not running this evening.

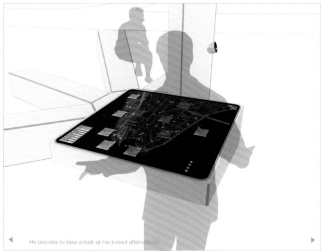

He decides to take a look at his transit alternatives.

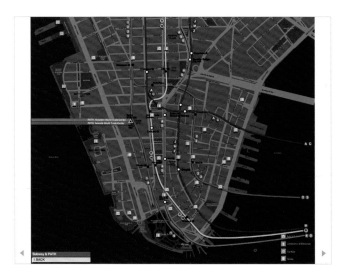

Subway & PATH
< BACK

A public announcement screen realised as an LED column relays broadcast and interactively generated content of more relevance to local workers, with the different types of information distinguished by colour and type of motion, and presenting the alert/emergency mode in a more attention-grabbing manner.

Antenna's design was inspired by an image of people sitting around a tree, with a 'hub' and 'spokes' modular system clad in glass mosaic embodying this notion of a gathering place.

themed educational museum exhibit. Civic Exchange is designed for an urban context that is frequently visited in order to fully exploit its resources. If, as is widely hoped, Civic Exchange can be realised (in 2005 the Battery Park City authority funded Antenna to undertake a feasibility study), it will be the first project of its kind in New York City and probably in any US city.

Both practices described above are category defying and threshold crossing, rooted in the research and interpretation of cultural context in a global age. As digital information systems are increasingly structuring society, reinforcing an urban sense of place by physical means is now often insufficient. The projects of these hybrid specialists rely on custom-designed digital systems, not exclusively, as in the case of other practitioners in this issue, but in the increasing number of instances where a multidisciplinary means to link physical and digital interfaces, objects and environments is vital. Site-specific design has to be inclusive enough to allow

the broad mass of people to cross these thresholds intuitively. Whether these new hybrid civic places of information are termed art or design becomes less important than the unique experience to be gained from the engagement process, which is not wholly preprogrammed, but involves participation as a means to enlarge each individual's sense of cultural context. ∆

Notes
1. *Washington Post*, 21 May 2005.
2. Interview with the author, 7 March 2007.
3. *Masamichi Udagawa + Sigi Moeslinger: Antenna*, self-published booklet, New York City, 2005.
4. As Civic Exchange competition juror Jan Abrams points out in her article 'Locus Focus on the Civic Exchange', in Jan Abrams and Peter Hall (eds), *Else/Where: Mapping New Cartographies of Networks and Territories*, University of Minnesota Design Institute, 2006.

Distinguishing Concepts
Lexicons of Interactive Art and Architecture

Interactive design has come about as a result of the intermingling of disciplines. As a consequence, the language it uses has become blurred – borrowed or stolen with little restraint from elsewhere. Though particular terms have become ubiquitous, the original concepts that lie behind them have been lost. This means that all too frequently they are no longer knowingly used. **Usman Haque** sorts the wheat from the chaff and brings clarity to bear on the vocabulary and thinking behind interactivity.

Jim Campbell, Shadow (for Heisenberg), 1993–4
If the viewer moves towards the object, the image of the object fades from view
and is replaced with the shadow of the object. The work is loosely based on
the Heisenberg Uncertainty Principle from quantum physics which states that
observation of an object determines what can be measured in that observation.

One of the consequences of the last 50 years of Western philosophy is that we are more receptive to the notion that words are not directly constrained by physical objects and that definitions themselves are fluid, mutable and dependent on the observations of individual people.[1] Still, one way that the practice of art and the practice of science have been distinguished is by ascribing to the former a certain vagueness in the use of words, while the latter is said to be more intent on precision. Design (and by extension architecture), supposedly straddled between the two, struggles to retain connections to both types of practice because such hybridity is disingenuous, and this is reflected in its capricious terminology.

Even if one does not believe that such a distinction between art and science is useful, an attempt to be more precise with words in the field of design can be viewed as pseudo-scientific. Yet without this precision, design is dismissed as arbitrary and inconsistent. Architects are notorious for naively borrowing concepts from other disciplines,[2] while language frames the debates we have and guides us towards particular

assumptions. Such phenomena are particularly evident in architecture simply because the intellectual aspect of the discipline depends to a large extent on language for its theoretical and cultural legitimacy: espoused in books, lectures, magazine descriptions and critiques.

This is particularly significant in an age where the use of technology is easily confused with the practice of art, the processes of research and design are increasingly intermingled, and the methodologies of interactive architecture are borrowing heavily from histories of interactive art.

The following text describes some common terms in the practice of interactive art and architecture, exploring the way such words have come to be used, and providing provocative counterpoints to these uses. This is not an attempt to return the true meaning to the terms under discussion. The concern here is that by wholeheartedly subscribing to the way such terms are now used, we are losing track of some of the most interesting concepts they originally offered us, which may hopefully help us conceive of further words and ideas in the future.

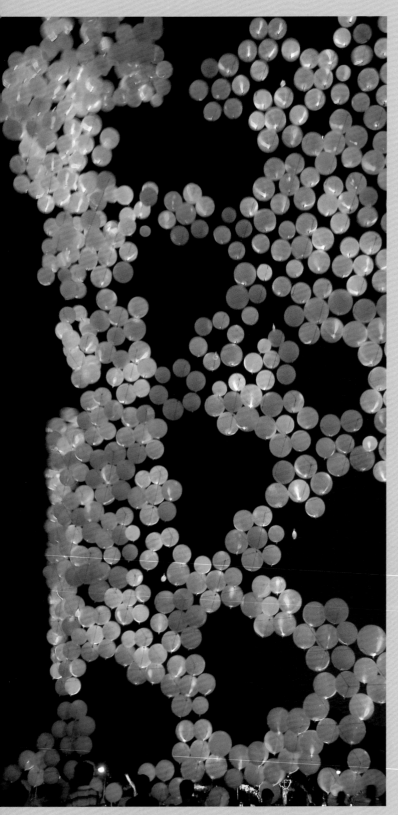

Usman Haque, Open Burble, Singapore Biennale, 2006
Participants design and construct the Burble on site. The form changes colour in response to the way that it is manipulated in real time by people holding on to the handrail down below. Their actions affect both the run-time response (changing colours) and how it responds to them (because it was they who determined the shape and configuration of the structure in the first place).

Interactive

It is often thought that the use of a dynamic/responsive system like a computer in itself enables an artwork, device or environment to open up to public participation and to be interactive. Actually, the rigidity of algorithms and input/output criteria usually employed in such systems means that they are just as autocratic as traditional media, time-based or otherwise.

'Interactive' these days is used to describe everything from software to lighting to mobile devices, confounding in particular academic institutions[3] and the creators of award categories.[4] On the one hand it is claimed that 'all art is interactive'[5] (because each viewer constructs a personal experience of it), and on the other 'to call computer media interactive is meaningless - it simply means stating the most basic fact about computers'.[6]

Artist and engineer Jim Campbell has forthrightly called his engagingly sensual works 'reactive', which is appealing because the power of his work rests on its poetic nature.[7] These days, however, leading practitioners in the field of interactive art do use the word 'interactive' in the sense of 'responsive'.[8] Interactive art and architecture premised on the notion of an artefact doing something solely in linear-causal response to actions by a person (or environment) is generally structured on preprogrammed cycles of call-and-response between human and machine. Such work invokes a mutually reactive relationship only slightly more sophisticated than that between a person and an automated cash machine.

Though it has now come to refer to anything generally reactive or responsive, a few decades ago interactive described a very different concept. By obscuring the distinction between interactive and reactive we lose a potentially fertile conceptual framework.[9] Originally, interaction was distinguished from circular 'mutual reaction': it was about affecting not just actual output (in response to input) but also about affecting the way that output is calculated.

There is a marked difference between our relationship to a cash machine and our relationship to a human bank teller, with whom we are able to enter into a conversation (concerning some news item, or a particular financial issue that requires further discussion, or a personal matter once we get to know a teller from repeated visits to the bank). This is because both the input criteria (what we can say to the teller) and the output criteria (what the teller can tell us) are dynamic, and constructed collaboratively.

To expand on this further in the context of environments and architecture, consider the rather prosaic model of the thermostat, in which input criteria (the temperature dial) and output criteria (heat) are static and predetermined. An alternative interactive implementation (in the Paskian sense)[10] might enable a person to add inputs to the temperature-regulating system as desired. These could range from 'energy consumption for last month' to 'exterior temperature for this day last year', to 'colour of my clothes today' to 'fifth letter of the second paragraph on the front

rhinoceros.mp3 | very loud | once a day | lat: 40.70851135 | lon: -73.99899292

runningBrook.mp3 | soft | once a minute | lat: 40.70851342 | lon: -73.9989901▪

sayYes.mp3 | soft | once only | lat: 40.70851342 | lon: -73.99899010

Mark Shepard, Tactical Sound Garden Toolkit, 2006
An example of a constructionally interactive system where input/output criteria are determined by participants rather
than the original designer. This open-source software platform enables anyone living within dense 802.11 wireless
(WiFi) hot zones to install a sound garden for public use. Participants plant sounds within a positional audio
environment using a WiFi-enabled mobile device (PDA, laptop or mobile phone), and wearing headphones connected
to a WiFi-enabled device people can drift though these virtual sound gardens as they move throughout the city.

page of today's newspaper'. The system would evolve
weightings for each of these input criteria in order to provide
satisfactory output, again according to criteria determined in
concert with each particular person.

Output criteria might include 'increasing thermal
comfort', 'keeping my energy bills down', 'keeping my
neighbour's energy bills down', 'minimising my hot-chocolate
drinking' or 'maximising the number of friends who come to
visit'. The system measures the input criteria and evolves
ways to act on the basis of these to produce the most
appropriate output (measured according to the output
criteria). Interaction, in this older sense, arises because a
person is able dynamically to affect the input and output
criteria *and* how they are processed. Each of the interactors
(human and machine) is able to act directly upon the other.
The person has an effect not just on the outcome, but on how
the outcome is computed (because even the input/output
criteria are not predetermined).

Crucially, in this notion of interactive, both input and
output criteria are underspecified by the designer. Instead
they are actively and iteratively constructed by other
participants of the project, and a more productive relationship
ensues between human and environment in an approach not
unlike Web 2.0 applications such as Wikipedia. It is this
constructional notion that is lost when we are content to call
interactive those things that are merely reactive.

Open Source
Several conceptual bifurcations have occurred within the term
'open source'. Originally ascribed purely to the licensing of
software, the phrase is now used to describe all sorts of
cultural production.

In the software universe, open source refers to a type of
source code, with which software is designed and built, that
is accessible or viewable by all, freely distributed as long as
it remains equally open, non-discriminatory and
technology-neutral, that allows for modification and
derivatives as long as the result is equally open, and where
patching is possible without disturbing the integrity of the
main work. Importantly, open source does not equate with
lack of copyright or authorship: it comprises a licence that
identifies potential usage, and where authors' contributions
are recursively cited.

Several designers and researchers have been particularly
interested in how these concepts might be applied to the field
of architecture.[11] There are problems with such a translation,
but it does seem that the collaborative means of production
offered by an open-source approach might have much to
contribute to a discipline that is known, particularly in the
West, for its top-down authoritarian approach.

Regrettably, however, what was once regarded as primarily
a method of production is gradually becoming instead centred
around consumption. That is, where originally an open-source

Reorient team (installation coordinated by Adam Somlai-Fischer), Reorient migrating architectures, Hungarian Pavilion, Venice Biennale, 2006
Constructed by hacking low-tech toys and gadgets and controlled by open-source hardware and software platform Arduino/Processing, the pavilion emphasises both the idea of 'borrowing' from inexpensive toys made in China, and 'sharing' by demystifying the technology and providing Web documents (www.reorient.hu and lowtech.propositions.org.uk) and a catalogue manual for others to build their own responsive systems through low-tech components.

approach was an encouragement to share, it is these days increasingly used to account for the act of borrowing. As an example of the inversion in architecture of the productive features of open source, Ole Bouman, editor-in-chief of *Volume*, suggested at the 'Game Set and Match II' conference in Delft in 2006 that architecture has long been open source because buildings have always been constructed by borrowing technology and techniques developed by other designers and disciplines.[12] Bouman described an open-source society as one 'where everybody grabs what they can'[13] and portrayed the magazine *Archis* as open source because it redistributed recipes taken from the Internet within its pages.

This idea of open source forces us to be content with the self-indulgent state of current practice, but diverts us from exploring a radically different means of architectural production, one that is explicitly designed for sharing with others – the most exciting notion behind open source in the first place. It also diverts from the possibility of an open-source architectural model in terms of constructing architectural environments that are themselves collaboratively (and iteratively) produced by people who inhabit a space.

The sharing idea of open source (within the field of architecture) is, however, being expanded in more concrete terms by, for example, Architecture for Humanity's Open Architecture Network, and Open Source Architecture for Africa (www.osafa.org), both of which are collectively constructed databases of freely available architectural design tools and projects. Taking a slightly different tack, Linden Research Inc, provider of massively popular virtual world

Second Life, recently announced that the code for its software will now be freely available under a General Public Licence, enabling anyone with requisite skills to modify the code. As cultural commentator Cory Doctorow said in announcing this news: 'Customers only ever get to love it or leave it. Citizens get to change it.'[14]

The User
One concept in the field of human–computer interaction (HCI) that has become omnipresent is the term 'the user'. Over the last 15 years there has been a marked growth in concerns for

Center for Knowledge Societies (CKS), Used In India – Media Practices from the 20th Century, 2004
Extract from a CKS publication indicating some of the ethnographic analysis undertaken.

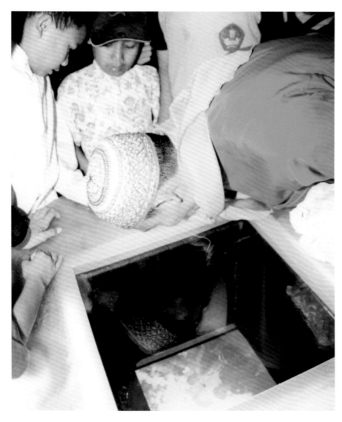

Maki Ueda, Hole in the Earth, 2004
Hole in the Earth linked Rotterdam in the Netherlands with Bandung in Indonesia by creating a video 'hole' in the planet through which people could see and hear each other in real time. The poetic nature of the installation makes this far more than a mere user-oriented video-conference system.

First, concentrating on a user or occupant often stresses the distinction between production and use and emphasises the distance between them. Second, by taking the minimum-common-denominator approach it may preclude the challenge of people learning a new skill that might open up new informational or constructional possibilities. These two factors encourage the notion of design as problem-solving (that is, the designer talks to a group of people, identifies the problems they are having and then develops a solution for them), but discourages users from proactively operating in an authentically productive capacity, potentially learning to help themselves.

This somewhat functionalist approach contrasts with the notion of design as a way to imagine and construct new ways of thinking as architects Constant Nieuwenhuis and Cedric Price were able to.[17] A particularly evocative solution to this is offered by Anne Galloway, lecturer in the Department of Sociology and Anthropology at Carleton University, and Alan Munro, research fellow in the Computer and Information Science Department at the University of Strathclyde, in their concept of 'interruption design ... that does not encourage straightforward and seamless interaction with devices ... that 'interrupts' strict notions of efficiency and usability.'[18]

Public and Private vs the Commons

Much interactive art and architecture is predicated on utopian distinctions between public and private space. Frequently sited outdoors, between buildings, in lobbies, parks and town squares, such work is said to be operating in the public sphere. Yet, the very land that such projects occupy is almost always under the dominion of a larger institution, whether it be governmental, academic or corporate.

Such areas of urban space, which carry the implication of belonging to an idealised general public, are in fact owned by these institutions and are subject to severe restrictions on the kinds of activities that can take place within their boundaries. Public space, a politely bland concept, always seeks to limit access to particular members of a community and/or selective groups of citizens, genders, behaviours or income groups.[19]

Meanwhile, the nostalgic notion of private space as a sanctuary is also fast eroding in the glare of corporations and governments using infiltration technology. Ever more detailed information about us leaks out of buildings, seeps out of our devices and is accessible to anyone with the appropriate bit of hardware or software. The data that portray our lives and lifestyles are accessible by so many individuals and organisations that they can no longer claim to lie in some private domain. Our spaces, physical and digital, are no longer exclusively our own.

Now that public and private spaces have become for many purposes indistinguishable, it may be useful to consider an older term, one that aspired to enable rather than restrict. Somewhere between the two illusory bait-and-switch concepts of public and private is a notion of space that thrives on paradox and contradiction rather than one

a design approach that is more conscious and considerate of the end user. This has been manifested in a greater desire for collaborative consultation with end users and has also resulted in a more sophisticated ethnographic approach to design. Some of the most interesting work in this area has been carried out by Aditya Dev Sood at the Centre for Knowledge Societies (CKS) in India who works with 'users in emerging markets ... [to] conduct contextual research studies to help technology companies determine the kind of devices, interfaces, features, services and power needs these groups of users require',[15] and Jan Chipchase in the User Experience Group of Nokia Research in Japan[16] who runs user studies to develop new mobile applications.

User-centred design places greater emphasis during the design process on the actual requirements of a user. In a user-centred approach, designers observe or have conversations with potential customers, test their creations on people, and are able to evaluate how first-time users can intuitively interface with them. The focus is on adopting future users' original ways of thinking rather than forcing them to adopt or learn new procedures.

There are a couple of risks with predicating design on the notion of a user, and in the field of architecture these extend to the problems with considering people as mere occupants.

all space is public: our data shadows
follow us around, leak out of buildings,
seep out of our devices... what is needed
is a truly private space... a space of absence

no phone calls
no emails
no sounds
no smells
no warm seat left behind
  by the previous visitor
no eye contact and no security cameras
no GPS signals
no 802.11 wireless networks
no microwave emissions

the idea of HOME
no longer needs to
be tied to a particular
location... it is simply
a space of absence

ALUMINUM FOIL
DEFLECTOR
BEANIE

Usman Haque, Floatables, 2004
Jellyfish-like vessels drift around cities, creating temporary, ephemeral zones of privacy: an absence of phone calls,
emails, sounds, smells and thermal patterns left behind by others. Through various electrical systems they are also
able to prevent access of GPS devices, television broadcasts, wireless networks and other microwave emissions.

that seeks to smooth these over – this is the space originally known as the 'commons'.

In Roman times the commons existed as a third category, alongside public and private space. It is a space that is defined by the rights that people have within it rather than by the restrictions that are placed upon them: it is not structured around ownership, though the actual land of the commons might be owned by someone. In the struggle between individuals and organisations, the notion of the commons dropped out of favour.

Without being nostalgic, the idea of siting design work in the commons is far more rewarding than siting it in some restricted notion of public space. Positioning design work in geographic locations that are explicitly defined by the rights that are conferred upon people – difficult though such locations may be to find – enables a wider concept of the ways that people of all kinds might engage with such work. It is premised on the notion that all our design acts are political and that we operate in a social context.[20]

Of course the concept of the commons is not limited to geospatial location; it might also consist of the 'network

commons'[21] or, as shown by the community growing around the Creative Commons Licence, the sphere of production and distribution itself.[22] Work in, on and around the commons explicitly rises to the challenge of collaborative design and it is the closest the design field can come to recognising how much of its production depends on the production of those that came before.

Further Distinctions
While 'interactive', 'open source', 'the user' and 'public and private' space are among the terms most commonly found in discussions about technology and architecture, there are of course others, and a similar exploration into these might encompass concepts behind terms such as 'technology', 'cybernetics', 'virtual' (vs 'real' – a dichotomy that is now as quaint as the 19th century's distinction between 'mind' and 'body'!),[23] 'interface', 'environment' and, of course, most complex of all, 'design' itself.

'Technology', for instance, is a usefully vague term that refers to the development of human artefacts. It is generally employed to describe recent developments (after all, it can be argued that everything developed by humans was at some point considered technological) and therefore has inherently temporal and contextual connotations. In the design world, 'technology' has an implication of newness that precludes ubiquitous distribution; it is therefore worth remembering that to work explicitly with technology is to concentrate on those artefacts that are not yet available to all.

'Cybernetics', originally concerned with the study of control and communication in animals and machines (and by extension human beings and societies), is now used to describe anything vaguely techno-biological. This is due in part to William Gibson's seminal book *Neuromancer*, in which he coined the phrase 'cyberspace' to describe a 'consensual hallucination ... a graphic representation of data abstracted from banks of every computer in the human system', and in which 'cybernetic implants' and a 'cybernetic spider' were a recurring feature. However, even before this book the term 'cybernetic' was used to denote anything vaguely sci-fi; see, for example, punk poet John Cooper Clarke referring to his alien lover's 'cybernetic fit of rage' in 1977.[24]

Clearly 'design', which operates at least partly in the cultural sphere, would only be hindered by the rigid application of definitions. Motivated as much by commercial concerns as functional and abstract obligations, design is a historical concept with very specific contextual meanings that have come to denote many things to many people. The practice of design has undergone a particularly dramatic change as it has transformed from the domain of individuals to the domain of teams, reflected in a transformation from the design of objects and environments to the design of systems of objects and environments. However, it is precisely because it thrives in a medium of ideas that it is important to consider more precisely how design is described and, equally, how it describes itself.

Again, the purpose of this exercise is not so much to pin down nostalgic meanings of words or to provide an authoritative reference guide, but rather demonstrate that there are some quite interesting and fertile conceptual frameworks in the field of interactive architectural design that can be obscured or revealed by the language we intuitively use. ∆

Notes

1 'Language frequently creates the illusion that ideas, concepts and even whole chunks of knowledge are transported from a speaker to a listener ... rather each must abstract meanings, concepts and knowledge from his or own experience.' E Von Glasersfeld, 'Editor's Introduction' in *Radical Constructivism in Mathematics Education*, Kluwer (Dordrecht), 1991, pp xiii–xx.

2 For an alternative perspective on 'reappropriation' see architect Eyal Weizman's exploration of how the Israeli military adopts language and tactics of philosophers Deleuze and Guattari, traditionally reference material for artists, architects and cultural theorists. Eyal Weizman, 'The Art of War', *Frieze* 99, 2006, http://www.frieze.com/feature_single.asp?f=1165.

3 In London, the Royal College of Art has a department that has been through at least three names in the last seven years: Design Interactions, formerly known as Interaction design, formerly known as Computer-related design.

4 See, for example, Ars Electronica who, apparently believing that the 'Interactive' category was too restrictive, introduced an even more woolly 'Hybrid' category!

5 Roy Ascott, Director, CaiiA-STAR, University of Wales College Newport and University of Plymouth, suggested in an address at the Victoria & Albert Museum, London, in May 2002 that 'we recognize that all art is interactive now, whether the work consists in the static field of a painting or a dynamic system in cyberspace'. http://www.vam.ac.uk/files/file_upload/5766_file.pdf.

6 Lev Manovich, *The Language of New Media*, MIT Press (Cambridge, MA), 2001.

7 See Campbell's exhibition entitled 'Reactive Works' at the San Jose Museum of Art, California, 1998.

8 'The standard definition of interactivity is something with feedback, where you trigger something and get a direct response' – Perry Hoberman, quoted in 'Loosen the loop', *Art Orbit* No 4, February 1999, http://artnode.se/artorbit/issue4/i_hoberman/i_hoberman.html. And 'An interactive system is a machine system which reacts in the moment, by virtue of automated reasoning based on data from its sensory apparatus', quoted in Simon Penny, 'From A to D and back again: The emerging aesthetics of Interactive Art', *Leonardo Electronic Almanac*, Vol 4, No 4, April 1996.

9 See, for example, the SAKI teaching system developed by Gordon Pask, who provides strict guidance on how to build interactive systems in a more structural sense. Gordon Pask, *An Approach to Cybernetics*, Harper & Brothers (New York), 1961; refer also to 'Paskian Environments: The Architectural Relevance of Gordon Pask' in this volume.

10 See 'Paskian Environments: The Architectural Relevance of Gordon Pask' in this volume for more on Gordon Pask and his work.

11 Brian Carroll, 'Open Source Architecture', http://www.nettime.org/Lists-Archives/nettime-bold-0006/msg00083.html; Usman Haque, 'Hardspace, Softspace and the possibilities of Open Source Architecture', http://www.haque.co.uk/papers/hardsp-softsp-open-so-arch.PDF; Dennis Kaspoori, 'A communism of ideas: towards an architectural open source practice', *Archis* No 3, 2003; Anand Bhatt, http://www.architexturez.net/; Ulrich Königs, 'Divercity', http://berlin.heimat.de/home/divercity/; Andrew Dribin, 'Copyleft Architecture', http://www.acadia.org/dde/D_055/01.html.

12 Author's notes; conference transcripts unavailable.

13 Ole Bouman, 'Open Source: Between the spirit of democracy and the law of the jungle', in proceedings of 'Game Set and Match II', TU Delft, 2006.

14 http://www.boingboing.net/2007/01/08/second_life_frees_so.html.

15 http://www.cks.in/.

16 http://www.janchipchase.com/.

17 See, for example, well-cited projects by the two: Constant's New Babylon and Price's Fun Palace.

18 Alan J Munro, Anne Galloway, Luke Skrebowski, Erik Sandelin and Simon B Larsen, 'Interruption Design: From Bovine Hordes to City Players', unpublished manuscript, 2004.

19 See, for example, the United States' use of Free Speech Zones to confine critics of authorities to carefully controlled areas, implying that territory outside these zones does not in fact allow for free speech contrary to its own constitution.

20 See Anthony Iles, 'Of Lammas Land and Olympic Dreams', *Metamute*, January 2007, http://www.metamute.org/en/Of-Lammas-Land-and-Olympic-Dreams.

21 Armin Mendosch, 'Not Just Another Wireless Utopia: Developing the Social Protocols of Free Networking', http://rixc.lv/ram/en/public07.html; and Julian Priest, 'Pico Peering Agreements', http://informal.org.uk/people/julian/resources/picopeer/PPA-english.html.

22 See the Creative Commons Licence (http://creativecommons.org/) applied by makers of all sorts of things throughout the world in order to specify ways in which their work may be shared and distributed for the common good.

23 This observation is attributed to Stephen Gage, Professor of Innovative Technology at the Bartlett School of Architecture.

24 '(I married a) Monster from outer space', performance at the Electric Circus Club in Manchester on 2 October 1977, released on 10-inch vinyl short circuit: *Live at the Electric Circus*, VCL 5003.

Playing with Art

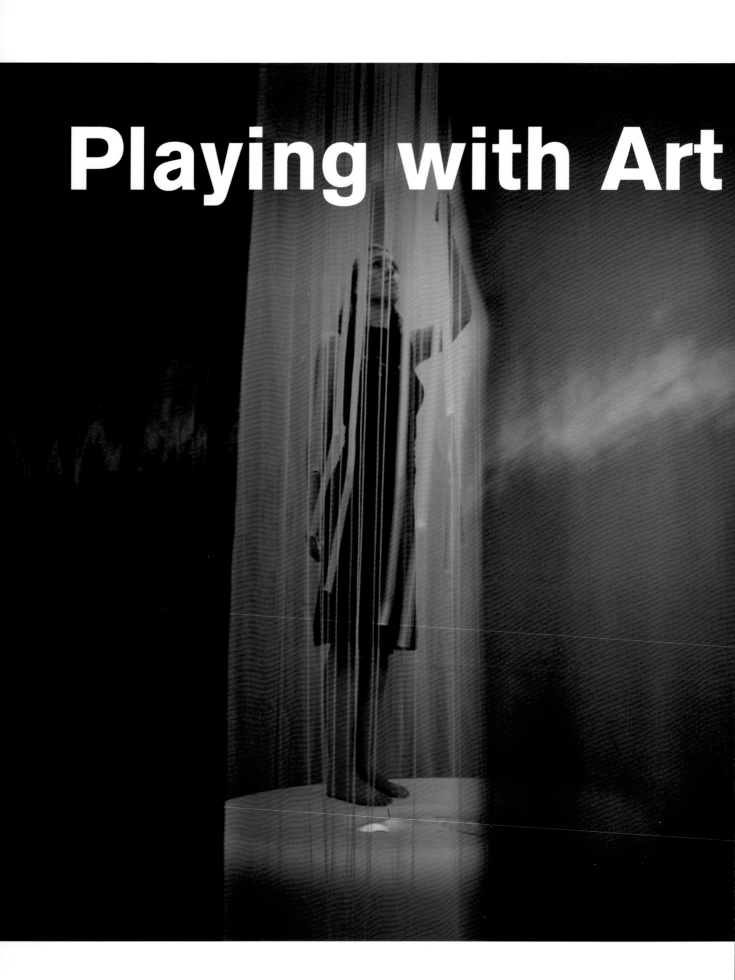

During the last decade and a half, a revolution has been under way in London's public museums and galleries. Lucy Bullivant explains how the digital has emancipated institutions from their previous physical constrictions, enabling artworks to break out from behind glass and liberating artefacts from their sealed cabinets. The perception of permanent collections is being transformed, as visitors are encouraged to make new connections between objects and break down physical distances between separate gallery spaces. Another new level of interaction is being encouraged by specially commissioned installations that encourage the user to physically engage with art.

Line Ulrika Christiansen, Stefano Mirti and Stefano Testa (with Studio Ape), Tune Me, V&A, London, 2004

Museums are increasingly active microcosms of cultural life. Their accessibility has grown in the last decade and exhibitions of the outfits of style icons – Kylie Minogue at the V&A in 2007, Jackie Kennedy at the Met in New York in 2007 – or dating evenings are now part of their populist repertoire. It is their early adoption of digital media that has given them a golden opportunity to expand definitions of art, learning and above all, who makes culture, an opportunity the UK leaders in the field have seized with both hands.

The drive to broaden the museum-going public was made easier after entrance charges to all UK national museums and galleries were scrapped by the Labour government's Department for Culture, Media and Sport in 2001 after a lengthy lobbying campaign. Tate Modern, which opened in 2000, has been such a runaway success of this open-door policy, achieving 4.1 million visitors a year, that it is now building an extension to accommodate the diversification in visual arts media as well as provide more cafés and shops for its expanding audience. This upsurge is not just physical – it is mirrored by a growth in the use of Tate Online, the Tate's website, which from 2004 to 2006 received a 56 per cent increase in traffic.

For their audiences museums compete with all forms of public entertainment providers, a key factor in the incremental shift in definitions of their role as custodians of cultural authority over the last 15 years, illustrated by the innovative proactivity of Tate, the V&A, the Science Museum and others in the evolution of handhelds, multimedia catalogues of art, and interactive installations that colonise galleries. This move to a more hybrid museum and gallery culture can be set in the wider contextual reality of the mediating impact of digital technology as a proliferator of means to learn and a customiser of content. Playing games as a means to mastery has seemingly become a ruling cultural *modus operandi* across all sectors.

By encouraging content to be customised, and art to be mediated, museums have precipitated new paradigms of informal learning and reinforced the widespread value of their public spaces as places to freely explore the personal significance of cultural value. Exhibitions using interactive elements have moved on from being hermetic, to adopting physical, experiential tactics and strategies based on the testing of visitors in their use of interactive and audiovisual elements. Event-based artworks such as Carsten Höller's Test Site, installed in Tate Modern's Turbine Hall in 2006, focus on what Höller calls the 'inner spectacle' of delight and anxiety of sliding experienced by the more intrepid visitors who elect to hurtle down his giant spiralling tubes.

The tools and the narratives now being applied by curators to amplify themes more closely both reflect and test wider cultural activities in society. In their use of digital media, participatory installations draw on longer established forms of popular culture archetypes that require physical involvement. Why make a video game playable just by pressing a button? Why not make it physically manipulable by riding a bicycle?[1]

Works parallel, mirror and build on media, old and new. A new cultural symbiosis in digital media intentions has emerged as curators actively draw from the ways in which people are already trying to develop the role of digital technologies in their lives and harness the potential they now enable for user-generated content.

By informalising their environments through innovative programming and a wider use of digital technologies, the most forward-thinking museums are addressing their rich potential as public spaces and overcoming the proprietary associations of their institutions as guardians of cultural authority as a given. The curatorial voice is still present, but the curator now acts far more as an enabler of a wider range of viewpoints and perspectives on the art being presented, which is not a static phenomenon in any case. Even a painting on a wall can now be technologically mediated. Introducing interactive works to museums and galleries raises audiences' expectations. When they work well they can be extremely popular, regarded by all ages as valuable and fun, informal educational tools, helping to broaden visitor's notions of what art – as well as the spatial identity of the institutions with responsibility for its wider mediation – can be.

The museum sector has regarded digital media as a vital weapon in advancing its public service ethos. Innovation in new resources in this field was spearheaded by the National Gallery's Micro Gallery, launched in 1991 in time for the opening of the Sainsbury Wing designed by the multimedia consultants Cogapp,[2] which immediately became regarded as a benchmark of its kind internationally. A highly effective tool for understanding in the form of a multimedia hypercard stack catalogue of the paintings with interpretative text, it was easy, responsive, fast to use – and fun. 'It encourages you to explore, to play and thus make new connections and gain new insights,' said one commentator.[3]

Eleven years later, in 2002, Tate won two BAFTA Awards for its own groundbreaking digital media adoptions. I-Map, created by Caro Howell, Special Projects Curator at Tate Modern, and Web author Daniel Porter, was the first Web-based resource for visually impaired people. It incorporated text, image enhancement and deconstruction, animation and raised images. The Multimedia Tour (July to September 2002), by contrast, was the first pilot project in the UK to use wireless technology to deliver content – videos, still images and text – to museum visitors. Developed by Tate Head of Interpretation Jane Burton in association with Antenna Audio, it enabled visitors given a wireless handheld computer to see videos and still images providing additional context for the works on display, or listen to an expert talk about details of a work that were then highlighted onscreen. Interactive screens encouraged them to respond to the art on view, for instance by answering questions or by layering a collection of sound clips to create their own soundtrack for a work.

Multitracking with the pilot's handheld was easy: visitors could record their own messages and create their own soundtracks to specific works, and the content of prepared

Jason Bruges Studio, PSP Image Cloud, V&A, London, 24 February 2006
An unconventional form of chandelier was suspended from the ceiling of the V&A's main foyer for the one-night-only Friday Late event. By splitting the video data from a Play Station console, Bruges enabled the 50 small TFT screens hanging from the ceiling to screen changing content fed up from it. This took the form of bespoke animations, but also visitors' own video material and games, giving the power to orchestrate the visual appearance of the space.

messages was there to be chosen from, not imposed. A porno-movie style soundtrack by the Chapman Brothers inevitably entertained some visitors but alienated others. According to the Multimedia Tour focus group findings, a message about Damien Hirst's *Pharmacy*, which used a 360-degree panorama of the installation as the interface for audio messages about the work, including interviews with the artists and a pharmacist, was particularly popular. Now this form of 'free choice learning' via handhelds is much more common, and virtually every major or middle-sized art museum in the world at least has an audio guide for its permanent collection, often in several languages, and many use MP3 players or PDAs. The Tate's Multimedia Tour pilot has galvanised the future development of handhelds. Its impact also supports curatorial interests in letting visitors absorb ideas and connections at random, based on their own personal interests.

The advance of museums and their relationship with art has also broken down boundaries between museums and galleries and the outside world, leading to institutions placing faith in the kinds of social evenings involving one-night-only installations that five years ago would have been customary only in nightclubs, private firms or galleries. A form of cultural club night with DJs, these events have not only nurtured new audiences, but transformed assumptions about art and design. In 2003 the V&A created the atmospheric Friday Late events, a regular series of evenings featuring live performances, guest DJs and hands-on art and design activities, and a bar in the public areas, with a sequence of some of the institution's main ground-floor galleries made open to visitors. A focus on the communal has gone hand in hand with a greater focus on the live event. The Friday Late transvision held on 24 February 2006, staged by the V&A with digital video festival directors and producers onedotzero, featured motion graphics, music videos, interactive installations by Jason Bruges Studio, Neutral, AllofUs, D-fuse, Usman Haque, United Visual Artists (UVA), the Light Surgeons and others, specifically 'to extract new meanings from museum objects and lead you through familiar and unfamiliar environments'.

If the curatorial agenda is spurring active visitor participation, it is appropriate as well, given the improvisational nature of the context, to include art engaging play or a form of 'mixing' (to use the musicians' verb). It was at one of the Friday Late evenings that Jason Bruges, an architect who has been responsible for more cutting-edge spatial interactive works for major British museums and galleries than any other individual, created PSP Image Cloud, an interactive 'chandelier' with an organically arranged array of 50 small TFT screens dangling from it in the museum's main foyer close to the DJs' turntables. Emitting a constantly changing environmental aura, it introduced into the museum the leisure-based technologies of Sony Play Station (promoting the firm as sponsor and facilitating manufacturer of artistic works). As an installation Image Cloud defied any division between rarefied museum environment and a domestic living room. Bruges hacked a portable Play Station console, and created bespoke video content that he fed into a computer, where Isadora software split the signal into components through multiple outputs up to the chandelier. Visitors were encouraged to upload their own video material and content to the PSP controlling the chandelier and experience their control of the environment through the work.

'We designed it to be accessible to an audience that may not normally engage with architecture and design in such a way,' explains Bruges. 'We overlaid the language of gaming on to the piece in the same way that Phillips AMBX technology would, utilising the idea that your gaming environment can bleed on to the environment near you. You could upload texture and mood from your PSP on to the chandelier in very much the same way you can customise your environment with something like Quake.'[4]

Another playful work commissioned by onedotzero for the V&A Friday Late transvision evening gathered visitors in the decoratively panelled 18th-century Norfolk House Music Room of the museum around a glowing table. Plink Plonk, created by digital design consultants AllofUs, used small mechanical musical boxes as playful input devices. Producing their own sound output (the tune 'You are my sunshine'), they could be moved around the table, provoking different visual narratives to respond by producing sound-reactive effects, including a glowing star scene, water drops and a sun that grew and gradually disappeared leaving a total eclipse.

Not only do interactive installations shift cultural satisfaction away from solely the static and untouchable, but as Lauren Parker, Curator of Contemporary Programmes at the V&A, where digital media has been utilised since 1999 when the contemporary programme was founded, remarks, it adds a different level or layer of communication that acts as a 'hidden colonisation' of galleries.[5]

AllofUs, Plink Plonk, V&A, London, 24 February 2006
Like an interactive board game, this installation, in the Norfolk House Music Room at the Friday Late transvision evening, had people clustered around a table. On its glowing surface they could play with small sound-input devices disguised as mechanical musical boxes. Moving them around the table provoked a range of decorative, sound reactive light effects.

UVA, Volume, V&A, London, 2006–07
Situated in the Italianate courtyard of the museum for a period of months, 46 2.5-metre (8.2-foot) columns form a grid of LED lights rigged up to an audio system, computer and separate synthesiser network for each column, which plays its own piece of music. Walking up to it increases the volume; no movement deactivates it. This simple system of rules generates complex emergent patterns as the number of people increases. The arrangement each person hears depends on his or her path through the installation, as well as the movements of the people around the individual.

Claire Wilcox, the V&A curator responsible for the 'Radical Fashion' exhibition in 2001, commissioned musician David Toop to create a collage of digital musical tracks by 12 different composers, setting a precedent at the museum for sound to intimately support the meaning of an exhibition. 'Shh! ... Sounds in Space' (2004), which Parker curated with Jonny Dawe, was not an exhibition but a personal journey that visitors embarked on through galleries of their choice, featuring a series of tracks written by artists including Jane and Louise Wilson, David Byrne, Roots Manuva and Elizabeth Fraser for particular spaces, galleries or exhibitions. Visitors were simply given a set of headphones and an MP3 player with recordings of the sound works before they set off. Trigger locations rigged up with an infrared transmitter would alter the volume, or cause a repeat or even the end of a piece. This enabled visitors to have personal, unmediated experience as well as individually chosen routes through the galleries, though complementary to those of other visitors, which could be shared on completion. While Fraser, known for her melodic singing voice on tracks by the Cocteau Twins and Massive Attack, chose the cathedral-like space hosting

the Raphael Cartoons, Cornelius, the Japanese composer, sited his electronically experimental music in the hushed enclave of the Glass Gallery.

The most recent and highly successful interactive installation in the Italian courtyard of the V&A, as a museum built in 1909 to a design by architect Aston Webb, has been Volume (2006–07), designed by UVA with sound by the band Massive Attack: 46 2.5-metre (8.2-foot) high columns that are in fact a grid of LED lights that form an 'orchestra' with modulated colour to match the changing mood of the overall piece. A digital camera with its own image-processing computer, placed high up in the courtyard, analyses the installation and figures out where people are. Walking up to a column increases the volume of its sound; walking away decreases it. If a visitor stopped moving for long enough, he or she became invisible and the column deactivated until they moved again. 'The arrangement you hear depends on your path through the installation, as well as the movements of the people around you,' explains Ash Nehru from UVA. 'It was important that the installation work as an experience on different levels.' Nehru calls it responsive rather than

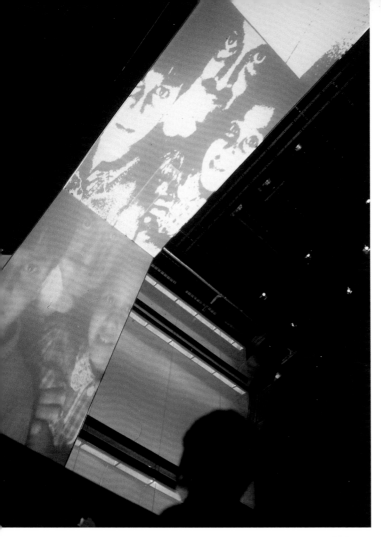

Christian Moeller, Particles, Science Museum, London, 2000
One of the first works by German-born Moeller, this projection creates silhouettes of observing visitors in the form of glowing, animated particles they can manipulate to move around the screen and change in an ongoing relationship between this technologically mediated space and the people visiting.

Tessa Elliott and Jonathan Jones-Morris, Machination, Science Museum, London, 2000
A giant banded computer screen above visitors' heads responds to their presence by interpreting it according to what it has in its memory, transmuting details into other associated objects from its neural network of domestic objects.

interactive: 'The design goals do not require that people understand the interaction model.' Physical reactions ranged from the reserved to the exuberant, trying to see what elicited a response, and people negotiating each other's space.

Jane Burton at Tate agrees that digital media is encroaching on the otherwise reserved physical world of museums. Lauren Parker points out that 'what technology is doing is enabling visitors to have individualised and more intimate experiences of museums – from audio and PDA guides, to Podcasts, to the use of RFID tags to personalise their journey through the museum'.[6]

Hannah Redler, Curator of Art Programmes at the Science Museum, also sees the potential of communal, digitally enabled experiences in museums, and argues that the coming of RFID or Bluetooth-enabled, locative pervasive technology is enabling a form of augmented reality, and moreover a seamless relationship between specialist and nonspecialist content. Networking culture, she believes, has spearheaded a growing focus on a multiplicity of voices, pushing dialogue and discussion to the forefront of art and design displays. 'Everyone is making their own media now, in control of their own data,

while subject to huge systems of control,'[7] she adds. She is aware that the challenges mounted by visitors to museums require curators to create robust internal editing processes now we all have a hand in constructing visitor experience. 'Scientists and artists layer different data sets, generate, order and use data and build complex relationships between data, but so do laypeople. Static information is dead,' she says.

The Science Museum in London was one of the earliest UK adopters of audience-focused information technology, interpreting content and communicating stories, but it has, like all of the best science museums, had an interactive – albeit more low-tech – approach to exhibition design since the 1950s when visiting children would find themselves invariably pushing buttons or turning dials. In 2000, Redler commissioned a group of new artworks for the Science Museum for a new display called 'Digitopolis'. With an overall design by Casson Mann, it examined the ways digital technologies were affecting human experiences of the world, and included Christian Moeller's Particles, a swarm of glowing animated particles projected on a screen creating a silhouette of the visitor in front of it in motion. Machination, by Tessa Elliott and Jonathan Jones-Morris, was a giant computer screen with a poetic impact that interpreted what it saw of passing visitors according to information in its custom-designed 'neural network' of domestic and decorative objects. It searched for a resemblance in its memory, thus a hand placed on the hip was relayed visually as a china cup, and the weave of a jacket as the edge of a bird's wing.

'Early interactive design really drew on the real world. To do something in the early 1990s that was an interactive display, a designer had to be a software coder, while Hypercard wasn't that accessible,'[8] observes Redler, who had her own interactive design company before becoming a curator. At this point, 'most of the small companies consulting in the field engaged a mix of people good at coding, and others who were good at graphics and animation,

Energy Ring, Energy Gallery, Science Museum, London, 2004
Above and right: The 40-metre (131-foot) long Energy Ring, a suitably
Newtonian symbol announcing the permanent Energy Gallery (designed by
Casson Mann), was a white LED screen wrapped and mounted in a 13-metre
(43-foot) aluminium circle to form a suspended ring of dynamic white light.
Four interactive terminals in the adjacent gallery, with software designed by
AllofUs, allowed visitors to send their own responses to questions on energy
to be displayed on the ring's screen, for which Soda, another consultancy,
designed the text display software. They could also 'zap' the ring from their
touch-sensitive screens, causing it to emit small flashes of light. It was a
classic of its kind: large-scale, simple and with high production values, yet
capable of engaging people at terminals in the gallery itself.

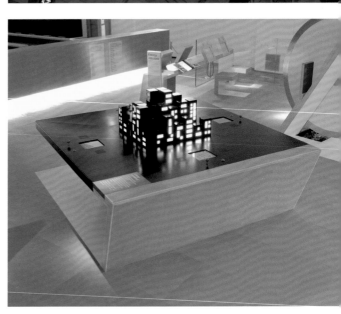

**Kitchen Rogers Design (Shona Kitchen and Ab Rogers) and Robson &
Jones (Crispin Jones and Dominic Robson), Energy Shutdown, Science
Museum, London, 2004**
This was an interactive exhibit for four players in the permanent Energy
Gallery. When visitors approached, they found a flat surface that transformed
into a rising 3-D model of a cityscape but then experienced a power cut when
all the lights on it switched off. The players had to complete a series of
games to help engineers restore power to the city, and reignite the lights.

but the early interactive installations they made conformed to
a certain orthodoxy in terms of where the buttons went.'
Specialist courses in interactive design started to emerge such
as the multidisciplinary MSc course in the subject at
Middlesex run by artists John Latham and Tessa Elliot with a
team of computer scientists, interaction designers, human
factors specialists and product designers.

In museums, as new interaction projects began to be
written in Director script, more research went into content
and scripts. Interior design by specialists such as Casson Mann
was introduced to structure results. As interactive exhibits
became successful in going beyond the screen, a more
compellingly experiential breed of interactive installations
emerged that brought people together on a physical level in a
more spontaneous way. Curators like Redler advocated
'stealth' learning, so that in order to become better
acquainted with concepts, they engaged visitors in physical
activity rather than gathering them passively around a kiosk.
The Energy Shutdown installation in the interactive Energy
Gallery, curated by Redler and designed by Casson Mann,
which opened in 2004, exemplified this mix of aspiration for
intellectual stimulation and physical activity. Designed by
Kitchen Rogers Design (KRD) and Robson & Jones, it was a
four-player table-top digital interactive exhibit with a 3-D
model cityscape. The game was based on the challenge of

Scanner (Robin Rimbaud), Sound Curtain, Science Museum, London, 2000
As visitors walked past hidden sensors in the lobby area of the museum's Wellcome Wing ground-floor toilets, their movement triggered a series of amplified sounds, ranging from the humming of a light bulb to the rush of blood through the body. Scanner intentionally chose everyday sounds that are not usually registered by our ears.

Fairground: Thrill Laboratory, Dana Centre, Science Museum, London, 2006
Curated by Brendan Walker, this interactive installation in place on specific days over a two-week period was based on three classic fairground rides: the Miami Trip, the Ghost Train and the Booster. During the day, before the rides were open to those with tickets, visitors entered a competition and the winners were eligible for the ride, for which they had to be hooked up to monitoring devices to collect data that was beamed around the room in the form of telemetric ride projections for audiences to see.

restoring energy to a city under blackout, which would zap back into life when the power returned.

Interactive installations are frequently based on gaming technologies or games of a more traditional kind, creating a kind of museum 'theme experience' with various related activities to take part in. Fairground: Thrill Laboratory (2006), curated by Brendan Walker for the Science Museum's Dana Centre, drew not upon computer games, but classic fairground rides like the Miami Trip, described as 'a party in motion'. The ride was a classic marriage of technological innovation and popular culture for audiences ready for a gravity-defying, carnivalesque thrill. Only lucky winners of the Thrill-Lab-Lotto braved the rides, whereupon they were initially hooked up to monitoring devices capturing physiological data and facial expressions. These were then beamed around the walls of the museum's lab via a wireless telemetric projection system for audience analysis.

Works also appeared in other, everyday parts of the museum, for instance sound artist Scanner (Robin Rimbaud)'s Sound Curtain (2000), which visitors discovered as they passed through the lobby area of the ground-floor toilets. Here, sensors hidden in the ceiling triggered a series of amplified sounds integral to everyday life yet scarcely registered, including the humming of a light bulb, the pulsing of sunlight or blood rushing through the human body.

Being able to sense a space more profoundly as a kinesphere is one of the chief benefits of interactive installations. Jason Bruges' Anemograph (2006), a work commissioned for the main entrance area of Sheffield's Millennium Galleries and designed to last for two years, is an artistic seismograph of changes in the weather. Its changing nature breaks down the visitor's sense of the boundaries between internal and external space as 25 balls made of polyethylene suspended in transparent acrylic tubes at the end of a long walkway gently fluctuate in height according to the speed and direction of the wind blowing outside. LED lights illuminate the colour of the balls according to their height. It is the first time the museum has commissioned an installation of this kind using light, and will also act as a wayfinder as well as a catalyst for spontaneous responses. 'While the word "interactive" can raise expectations', says Kirstie Hamilton, Head of Exhibition Programming, 'the interactive aspect of the work needs to be integral to it rather than additional.'[9]

Now that museum educators have more than 15 years' experience of realising interactive installations, and public assumptions about multimedia's role in society are constantly advancing, these new paradigms can be drawn on in a more sophisticated way. As interactivity becomes par for the course as a presentation tool, museums must demonstrate that they have the means to amplify themes readily yet imaginatively via intuitive uses of interfaces, or visitors will not pay attention.

Jason Bruges Studio, Anemograph, Millennium Galleries, Sheffield, 2006
In this suspended interactive work responding dynamically to changes in the weather, balls suspended in acrylic tubes rise
and fall depending on wind speed and direction. In turn, their changing height triggers LED lights to glow more brightly.

The V&A's 'Touch Me' exhibition (2005), a collaboration with the Wellcome Trust attended by 25,000 visitors, was a bold attempt to present a range of designs that engage with the touch senses, many via unexpected narratives of use. Around 80 per cent of the exhibition was touchable and included some surprising sensory experiences. By pushing on the Drift Table, and looking through a peephole, visitors could feel as if they were floating over the English countryside. Intimate Memory clothes by Joanna Berzowska of XS Labs (see also Despina Papadopoulos's essay on wearable computing in this issue) betrayed evidence of a whisper or a grope. And Tomoko Hayashi's Mutsugoto/Pillow Talk was a device to communicate in a more personal way long-distance messages to a lover lying on his or her bed far across the world. This required a bit of bodily organisation, as the message was relayed effectively only when the visitor's body, lying on a bed in the exhibition (having taken his or her shoes off), matched the alignment of his or her lover's silhouette.

One of the most ambitious installations free of such ritual at Touch Me was Tune Me, a screened immersive space designed by a leading group of Italian designers working in the Exhibition Unit at the Interaction Design Institute Ivrea,

who now work together in Turin as a practice – the Interaction Design Lab.[10] Inspired in part by multisensory therapy rooms designed for use by the visually impaired, deaf, blind and people with learning disabilities, it was a conceptual radio set in an egg-shaped double-layer shell to create the Faraday effect of preventing other frequencies entering the space. The radio was activated by touching silicone areas in the seating bathed in coloured light, over which long strands of tactile fabrics hung. Each interaction triggered a different experience through a pulsation from the surface of the seating.

This was an intuitive and engaging interface. Line Ulrika Christiansen of the Lab explains that people warmed to it as it was free of direct commands or buttons to press.[11] Changing the radio's channel by physical touch altered the light, sound and vibrational qualities of the overall space, creating different moods. The lighting could be adjusted to suit the tone of the FM station discovered. Although perhaps erring a little on the side of ambient without a wider application of usage, Tune Me enabled visitors to have exploratory experiences of touch as well as of the other senses, including, for this reason, people with a form of visual impairment, which was a plus. Visitors making brief visits sensed the effect of the light: more time

AllofUs, Grid, Constable exhibition, Tate Britain, London, 2006
This was one of two interactive exhibits at the exhibition using conservation x-ray techniques that illuminate an artist's working methods. The visitor's presence in front of a painting casts a shadow over it, revealing an x-ray of paint layers beneath. In this case, she can see Constable's process of 'squaring up', or starting with a small pencil sketch and ending with a 1.8-metre (6-foot) oil painting.

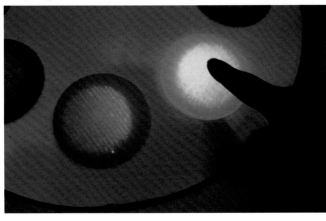

Line Ulrika Christiansen, Stefano Mirti and Stefano Testa (with Studio Ape), Tune Me, V&A, London, 2004
An immersive interactive installation at the museum's 'Touch Me' exhibition, this womb-like ambient space was based on therapy rooms for the visually impaired, and designed as an immersive 3-D radio that reacted to the visitor's touch and stimulated the sonic, visual and haptic senses through pulsations.

was needed to engage with the sonic and haptic senses. Above all, people could engage in a non-didactic way in understanding something Parker describes as having been 'neglected in so many products. Even with the newest electronic gadgets, the interaction is often primitive, brutalised, reduced to the prod of a screen or the tap of a keyboard.'[12]

The V&A's 'China Design Now' exhibition (to be staged in 2008) will feature online gaming, chat rooms, foot massage machines and a gaming parlour, establishing a smooth interdependence between physical spaces and virtual tools. While this has become an established practice, the active participation enabled by interactive technologies also allows visitors to more conventional art exhibitions to 'deconstruct' layers of the surfaces of artworks in order to better understand them. This virtual presentation of the work renders it a playful tool, a medium to enlarge interpretation of the art medium it is symbiotically entwined with. At Tate Britain, AllofUs created two interactive exhibits based on the conservation techniques already being used to analyse an artist's methods for the museum's major Constable exhibition (2006). By merely walking in front of the projected painting, the visitor casts a virtual shadow over the image, revealing a conservation x-ray of the painting underneath. The movement is the interface. A second installation, Grid, illustrated Constable's process of 'squaring up' an image in the journey from early sketches to finished work.

The evolution of sophisticated immersive experiences at one end of the scale is being matched by the policies of museums and galleries to honour their environments as public spaces for a wider social demographic, making them not just more family friendly, but developing new identities for galleries as participative art workshops. Interactive installations in their own right are not going to forge a more spontaneous environment in which social behaviours become more diverse, but rely on curatorial strategies to bring about alternative ways of thinking about museum space.

Jason Bruges Studio, Dotty Tate, Tate Britain, London, 2005
In the Octagon, 25 2-metre (6.5-foot) tall interactive wands with glowing spheres at their top turned only when touched. Bruges made a 'live painting' tracking the patterns of audience Interaction during the day.

Tate has hybrid educational resources that do this. At Tate Modern there is a new Learning Zone designed by Ab Rogers Design, a playspace made up of geometric structures in red fibreglass equipped with a range of interactives including touchscreen documentary film footage, games and quizzes on art. Tate Britain's Art Trolley, a mobile art unit on wheels equipped with a variety of materials, which sits in the middle of the gallery space near the artworks, was in fact first introduced 10 years ago. Frances Williams, Curator for Informal Activities at Tate Britain, says 'visitors not always approving responses' to this intervention 'speak so loudly about relationships towards "correct behaviour" and authority'. Yet when special days, such as BP Saturdays, are designed with drop-in workshops and interactive displays, they offer 'the possibility to experiment with different forms of social relationships to art and the environment in which it is usually shown'.[13]

Williams commissioned Jason Bruges to create a bespoke, one-day interactive installation in the Octagon, the central domed space in the middle of the Duveen Galleries. She knew that children are as affected by architectural space at Tate Britain as they are by any individual work of art, and this sometimes leads to them, and adults, feeling intimidated. Addressing an overall theme of Dottiness centred on looking for various circular motifs in works of art and in the gallery environment, Bruges made a minimal 'field' of blue LED lights set atop 25 plastic poles set 1.5 metres (5 feet) apart and

attached to the floor by vacuum suckers. As families passed through this space, they were able to touch the 'stalks', causing them to light up and gently oscillate. This movement was caught on a camera set up on the bridge above the gallery. Visitors could watch the motion their movements had created on a live monitor set up at the side of the gallery.

A mimetic work that engages touch, something that is usually prohibited in the rest of the gallery, Dotty Tate was, as Williams describes it, 'not only a "friendly" work of art that responded to being touched: in fact, it was its entire reason for being there and it would only "come alive" upon contact'.[14] She observed the particular ways in which children interpreted the piece. Many spent time watching to see how the poles worked before making their own use of them. Some children devised rhythmic games involving one or more poles to create patterns between each other. Others used them to test the limitations of the technology; how far the poles would bend, how securely they were stuck to the floor, how much violence they could withstand.

Its concept echoed that of another one-day, site-specific work Bruges created for Tate Britain that filled a gallery with 2,000 helium balloons tethered to the floor by different lengths of ribbon and light weights, with LED lights that sparked as people tested out the light patterns, giving it an unusual spatiality to be negotiated. With the day's educational theme of Fireworks, the work explored what it would be like, spatially, to have exploding light. Children's

Jason Bruges Studio, Sparkle Park, Tate Britain, London, 2006
A one-day installation in the form of a cloud of tethered interactive balloons with LED lights on their strings that sparked.
The concept here was to capture the patterns of the sparks, and as children attempted this their movements were
mapped on to a global projection as a thermal image visualising the layer of heat the whole proceedings had emitted.

movements investigating this were mapped on to a global projection, becoming one overall thermal image revealing a layer of heat over the installation.

It remains unclear how the further imaginative fusing of digital and analogue space will continue to reconstruct the social model museums and galleries represent as places of cultural authority towards one of a more participative nature. They are evolving into places where the active 'leisuretainment' of visitors, if not on a 24/7 basis then daily over a full 12-hour period, is a primary consideration. As public spaces of a particularly 21st-century kind offering both communal and individualised experiences that enjoy private-sector sponsorship, and even as social laboratories, they are attractive as they are so manipulable – unlike the wider world. However, they remain democratic places of free choice learning. Visitors are becoming attuned to touching exhibits, and this use of the senses for cultural stimulation may be on the rise. But observation in a museum or public gallery just by tuning into one's personal senses, turning off the stream of increasingly prosthetic handhelds' user-generated messages, and free of the need to add commentary of one's own to a public resource, is still also possible. ∆

Notes
1. A travelling exhibition on physics designed by AllofUs for the Science Museum and the Institute of Physics, 2005.
2. The trading name of Cognitive Applications.
3. 'The Sonic Hedgehog's Guide to Art', in *Museums News*, May 1993.
4. Interview by the author with Jason Bruges, 20 September 2006.
5. Interview by the author with Lauren Parker, 15 December 2006.
6. Interview by Line Ulrika Christiansen in *idCAST* online magazine, Interaction Design Lab, Turin, January 2007. www.interactiondesign-lab.com
7. Interview by the author with Hannah Redler, 28 September 2006.
8. Ibid.
9. Email interview by the author with Kirstie Hamilton, 1 October 2006.
10. Designed by Line Ulrika Christiansen, Stefano Mirti and Stefano Testa with Daniele Mancini and Francesca Sassaroli, and soundscapes by Rafael Monzini. These designers left the Interactive Design Institution Ivrea after its dissolution in 2005 and together established the Interaction Design Lab in Turin, Italy.
11. Email interview by the author with Line Ulrika Christiansen, 1 February 2007.
12. Lauren Parker and Hugh Aldersey-Williams, *Touch Me* exhibition guide, V&A (London), 2005.
13. Interview by the author with Frances Williams, 20 December 2006.
14. Ibid.

Otherwise Engaged

New Projects in Interactive Design

What are the possibilities of interactive technologies delivering a new level of social engagement in architecture? Taking 2002, with the ETH Ada project and Diller & Scofidio's Braincoat project, as an important watershed, Mark Garcia reviews the advances that have been made per se, and with four projects in particular, in socially interactive spatial design.

Man's specific humanity and his sociality are inextricably intertwined. Homo sapiens is always, and in the same measure, homo socius.

From Peter L Berger and Thomas Luckmann, *The Social Construction of Reality,* 1966[1]

Human life is interactive life in which architecture has long set the stage. The city remains the best arrangement for realising that human nature.

Malcolm McCullough, *Digital Ground,* 2004[2]

Since 2002 and the launch of two benchmark projects – ETH Zurich's Ada and Diller + Scofidio's[3] Braincoat – at the Swiss Expo, the promise of a socially engaged interactive architecture has begun to move from the realm of science fiction to reality. How interactive architecture should function in society, how interactive technologies should operate in more social and socially enabling ways, and how the general public, the public realm and public space should interface with these new design types are just some of the questions raised by current works in this emerging and burgeoning new field of design.

Humankind can now create lots of interactive and spectacular spaces, but are the relative social costs, benefits and risks justifiable? How do we evaluate the social impact of interactive (or for that matter any) architecture? How do we assess its social effects with respect to more conventional or more inanimate types of architectures? Can interactive architecture make space more productive, sustainable, social or meaningful? Can it create a public realm that is more flexible and adaptable to different users, activities and feelings? How do we create its content and who should maintain and manage it? What kinds of social life and social exchanges and transactions should the public realm encourage? Are these types of spaces significantly more interesting or desirable than other ways of being social, for example in bars, public squares or via the internet? What does

'social' in this context mean anyway? These types of controversial and pressing questions in the field of interactive spaces have unfortunately only been addressed in one major theoretical publication (McCullough's *Digital Ground,* 2004), and by a handful of avant-garde, conceptually driven and high-tech architecture and design schools such as the AA, ETH Zurich, Domus Academy, MIT, the Bartlett, Technical University of Delft and the Royal College of Art (RCA).

Many publicly funded academic practitioners have built or designed interactive spaces for multinational corporations (sited in private lobbies, offices and as special event features), yet these fashionable projects are generally installed for just a few weeks or months, and thus the extent to which they are useful experiments for more socially engaged works is impossible, at present, to predict. In 2004 Malcolm McCullough argued in his book *Digital Ground* that interactive technologies and design could best serve humanity and society through the design of interactive and public spaces that bore some relation to the specificity of the real places in which they were located. Many recent interactive projects in public spaces have attempted to engage the social realm and generate social interactions in the way McCullough describes, illustrating the current state of affairs in this field and addressing in very different ways the shifting issues and ideas surrounding socially engaged interactive space.

The four new projects featured here are among the most socially engaged works in their field. So how do they compare with benchmark projects such as the ETH Ada project and Diller + Scofidio's semi-realised Braincoat project for their realised Blur building? How far have we come since 2002? If, as McCullough claims, 'only when technology makes deliberative and variable response to each in a series of exchanges is it at all interactive',[4] then both Ada and the Braincoat project might seem to be as yet unsurpassed in the degree and quality of both embodied deliberation and the variety and complexity

Diller + Scofidio, Braincoat, Swiss Expo, 2002
This unrealised component of the Blur building on Lake Neuchatel proposed a wearable WiFi person-detection and identification system in which levels of affinity between personality types in individuals meeting in a blur of fog were identified through vibrating pads and a wearable electronic wireless device implanted in the plastic raincoat given to each visitor as they entered the building.

of the socially enabling, spatially embodied responses these spaces are able to create. Ada, considered to be the most intelligent real space designed to date, featured the highest levels of behavioural integration and time-varying and adaptive functionality into a single space. Ada was able to balance the flow and density of visitors as well as to identify, track, guide and group and regroup individuals and sets of people. She had a sense of vision, sound and touch and could baby-talk and play different types of games with the inhabitants as well as express her behavioural mode and emotional state using a continuous ring of video projectors.

The Braincoat project, though sadly rejected by potential corporate sponsors and thus only ever partially realised, remains an equally significant contribution to this field of research. In the proposal, visitors to the Blur building, suspended over Lake Neuchatel, would complete a detailed questionnaire before entering. Information from the questionnaire would then be fed into the Blur building's computer systems which, via a wearable electronic wireless device, would alert individuals to the proximity of other visitors with whom their personalities and tastes might compatible. Using speakers, luminous displays and vibrating pads, those in the Blur building would be able to perceive, directly and in real time, the likelihood of finding a friend or lover moving towards or away from them through the mist.

The Braincoat element of the Blur project did not achieve sponsorship and therefore could not be realised. However, as the four projects below demonstrate, the potential of this new field of design is now beginning to be realised. Not only have socially interactive projects begun to move into the public realm, they are now also receiving the financial support of both national governments and big business.

DataNatures, San Jose, California, 2005–06

Ben Hooker and Shona Kitchen

The downtown ticket installation in use. The everyday utilitarian look of the ticket printer was intended to help it meld seamlessly into the street furniture of its urban context, making this public art project an accessible, inclusive and surprising intervention into an innocuous part of city life.

The DataNatures installation produced a unique personalised ticket for each and every user shortly after they pressed the button.

DataNatures by interaction designer Ben Hooker and architect Shona Kitchen was a double site-specific electronic installation commissioned by the San Jose Public Art Program for 'ZeroOne San Jose: A Global Festival of Art of the Edge & The Thirteenth International Symposium of Electronic Art (ISEA)', 2006. It included two installations: one inside the domestic arrivals terminal inside Mineta San Jose International Airport, the other in Cesar Chavez Park, in downtown San Jose. Described by Hooker and Kitchen as an 'electronic artwork', the project was intended to 'reveal and celebrate the interconnectedness of seemingly disparate natural and manmade aspects of Mineta San Jose International Airport and its environs'. The installations took the form of 'ticket machines' linked up to a series of remote cameras placed around the airport.

On pressing a button, visitors were issued, in real time, with tickets resembling airline boarding cards that had been compiled by DataNature's custom-built software. These were a combination of a photograph of the user and both real-time and archived data (text and images) transferred via wireless systems to a PC encased within the installation. The resulting montage of information was unique to each person each time the button was pressed, and each ticket was a custom-made souvenir of that moment in San Jose. The data and images juxtaposed on the ticket were collated from websites which delivered data relating to the airport and the city of

San Jose, such as flight times, weather, noise and acoustic mappings, news stories, historical facts and narratives. Cameras located around the homes of the protected burrowing owls that live on the airport site also added images of these nocturnal residents to the tickets, highlighting concerns for their disappearing grassland habitat and focusing attention on the environmental aspects of the airport.

DataNatures was designed to identify the airport as the gateway to the San Jose community. The twin locations of the installation represent San Jose's role as the birthplace of Silicon Valley, the interconnectedness of seemingly disparate sites and the role of new technologies in bringing together formerly separate but otherwise linked places. It resulted from interviews with airport employees, research into the otherwise hidden operations of the airport, and personal observations during visits to the FAA control tower, the security communications centre, baggage processing and inspections, noise-monitoring stations, parking management systems, airport concessions, rental car and shuttle bus operations, and maintenance and cleaning routines.

The social aspects of the project lie in its value as a critical, dissenting, site-specific work of art that is active across a number of social, cultural and environmental dimensions. As an informative tool for visitors to San Jose's local and natural communities it provided a multilayered and complex, though condensed, picture of the key factors, issues and events that have made the city what it is today. More creative and sophisticated than the bland tourist pamphlets usually available at tourist kiosks, it was on the one hand a modest souvenir machine, and on the other a complex and sophisticated critique and investigation into San Jose's history, its relationship with nature and its inhabitants. As a tool to generate social interconnectedness through artistic practices, it has undoubtedly helped to raise awareness of the local natural environment and the urban pressures upon it.

However, Hooker and Kitchen agree that some data they wanted to include on the tickets was denied them. Despite all our vast, detailed and real-time information feeds and databanks, and the complex data-mining, sensing, control and communications technologies that are now available, much of the dark underbelly of the life of the city and the more sinister activities and effects of corporations, groups and of individuals remain dangerously overprotected, confidential and maliciously obscure.

While this project may not be 'traditional' architecture, Kitchen sees these smaller-scale spatial experiments as indicative of the possibility of larger architectural ideas in which spaces have layers of telematic and informational content designed into them. Their recent speculative, unrealised project Electroplex Heights (2006) is another in Hooker and Kitchen's series of ongoing projects that examine the complex and disregarded poetics of telematic living. As part of the Vitra Design Museum's 'Open House: Intelligent Living by Design' travelling exhibition of 2006, it demonstrates, albeit on a larger architectural scale, the same approach to the design process and some of the phenomenological sensibilities and ways of perceiving and managing space as those implicit in the DataNatures installation.

Electroplex Heights provides a new vision for a technologically enabled community in which residents can deploy a variety of electronic objects that can sense, communicate and control elements of the larger physical and electronic footprint of the Electroplex Heights building complex site itself. Large external display screens (wirelessly linked to cameras and other sensors positioned and controlled by the residents) take CCTV out of the security rooms and into the art world of the 21st century. This exercise in Ballardianism would, according to the designers, 'encourage a community spirit that is not entirely dependent on physical proximity (as in conventional apartment buildings), nor entirely divorced from its immediate surroundings (as in Internet chat rooms)'.

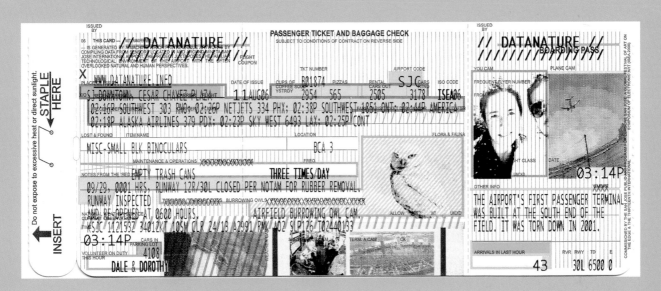

Each ticket was unique to an individual, a place and a time, the multiples representing a montage of information about the airport.

Digital Pavilion Korea, Sampang-dong, Seoul, South Korea, 2006

ONL

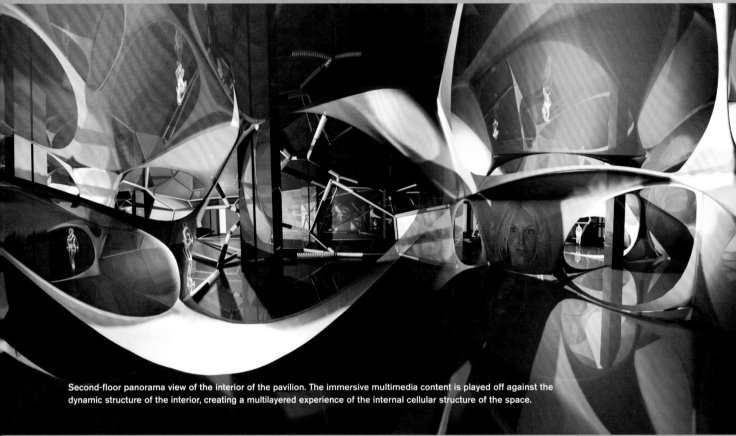

Second-floor panorama view of the interior of the pavilion. The immersive multimedia content is played off against the dynamic structure of the interior, creating a multilayered experience of the internal cellular structure of the space.

Digital panorama of the second floor. The Voronoi cell structure of the pavilion is controlled and kinetically manipulated using actuators in the beams of the structural system. The cell system breaks up into smaller, more dynamic and flexible components and spaces at key points (see centre of image) of the installation.

Kas Oosterhuis and Ilona Lenard (ONL) have designed and built some of the most famous interactive architectures in the world. As theorists, senior academic researchers and global architects they are precise about the nature of interactive spaces and the role of people within them: 'Interactive architecture is not simply responsive or adaptive to changing circumstances. On the contrary it is based on the concept of bidirectional communication, which requires two active parties. Naturally communication between two people is interactive, they both listen (input), think (process) and talk (output). But interactive architecture is not about communication between people, it is defined as the art of building relationships between built components in the first place, and building relations between people and built components in the second place.'[5]

For Oosterhuis, interactive architecture is not possible without an understanding and use of nonstandard architectural design and manufacturing processes where all the components are specific and unique to the building. Not content with buildings that are responsive or adaptive, he stresses the need for interactive architecture to be proactive and propositional (proposing and anticipating new building configurations or actions) in real time.

Interactive architecture for Oosterhuis is the 'art of conceptualising the CAS (complex adaptive system) and the art of imposing style and social behaviour on the active building materials, being aware of the fact that many of the constituting components are programmable actuators. The architect becomes an information architect … People relate themselves easier with dynamic structures than with static ones. It simply is more fun to watch live action than watching the paint dry.'[6]

This conceptualisation of interactive architecture is compelling and has been borne out in a series of immersive interactive architecture projects by ONL in conjunction with the Hyperbody Research Group, the unit for interactive architecture at the TU Delft, where Oosterhuis is a professor. The latest reincarnation in this series of projects is the Digital Pavilion Korea, located in the Digital Media City in the Sangam-dong district of Seoul. The project is an attempt by the South Korean government to produce a set of buildings to showcase the future of the country's new media, IT, software and electronics companies, and its technological strategies and economic policies . The pavilion is intended to be a five-year installation with the possible replacement of old technology on remaining hardware.

Designed as a series of interacting installations claimed to represent 'ubiquitous computing at its full potential',[7] its parametric morphology is derived from a 3-D Voronoi diagram algorithm. The surfaces of the interior are of darkened, LED-backlit glass to give the impression of an infinite, media-rich or translucent space. The beams of the Voronoi cell structure feature built-in linear actuators, able to alter the lengths of the beams in real time. The actuators, controlled via the handheld devices given to visitors, mean that users can actively control the building's internal form in real time (using the WiBro/WiMax technology embedded in the devices).

Visitors interact with the installations and the personalised, virtual content by using a handheld 4G/WiBro device into which they program personal details which are then used to configure the content they are exposed to. The handheld devices also provide dynamic maps of the positions of visitors in real time and can be used to browse through lists of exhibitors, products and embedded information about the product or information being used, which can then deliver a real-time information feed as a guide to the items selected or being viewed/experienced at the time. RFID tracking of individual visitors throughout the building is also used to build up unique profiles of the interactions of people as they wander through the pavilion. The device then stores a record of the whole trip and all of the related media content, ready for remote retrieval, via the Internet, at a later date.

Visitors can also engage in four different types of socially interactive experiences that result in alterations to the structures of the pavilion. In the middle of one of the floors of the installation, the hard kinetic pneumatic structure becomes a soft organic structure reminiscent of ONL's earlier Trans-Ports project. The interior skin of this area is composed of a point cloud of tens of thousands of programmable LEDs of variable densities in order to create a spectrum of effects for visitors ranging from low-res ambient qualities to high-res streaming text and graphics.

The four types of 'experiences', or 'game-play', offered in the interiors of the pavilion were derived from an analysis of Asian popular cultural entertainment and were selected to actively target different pavilion user groups. They are an action/shoot-em-up game, a social chat game, an adventure/mystery game and a strategy/board game, which are being developed with the help of Korean massively multiplayer, online role-playing games design companies to create dynamic and immersive team-based, as well as individual, social experiences.

The success of such highly social and interactive computer games (the Second Life game now has more than 3.3 million international 'resident' players online) seems to offer a compelling, popular precedent and model for spatially embedded and enabled social interaction, not just for the Digital Pavilion Korea but for social, interactive space design as whole.

The Digital Pavilion is an architectural hybrid between online multiplayer games and the new urban games that utilise GPS, GIS, RFID and wireless technologies (such as Geocatching and Noderunning). The question of whether this fusion of augmented reality with animate and interactive architectures will catch on as a new social pastime (a deep cross-programming of playing and shopping) remains to be seen.

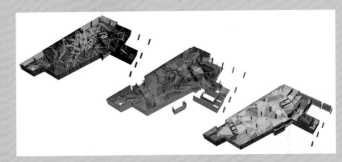

Exploded axonometric of the three floor plans showing the Voronoi cell-like structure of the building's tectonic system across each of its three storeys.

Digital image of the interior of the first floor. Made up of large, darkened, LED-backlit glass panels, the interiors of the first floor provide the perception of an infinite, media-rich or translucent space. This Postmodern fragmentation of space provides a kaleidoscopic experience of inhabiting an information-rich play-shopping crystal, a showcase for the South Korean government and entertainment and IT companies.

SPOTS, Berlin, Germany, 2005

Realities United

Ground-level view of the SPOTS media project in its urban context on Potzdammer Platz. The project converts commercial developer-style architecture into public art.

Standing in front of the Realities United SPOTS project on Potzdammer Platz in Berlin recalls the Archigram Instant City project as well as later film versions of giant, urban moving-image screens such as those which have now become stock clichés in science-fiction films like *Blade Runner* and, more recently, *Minority Report*. High-resolution screens such as in Piccadilly Circus in London and Times Square in New York are privately owned and controlled despite their dominating corporate presence in the world's most significant public spaces. More interesting are the buildings such as the Lehman Brothers' headquarters on New York's Seventh Avenue, which sports a multistorey wraparound screen across a number of the lower storeys on its facade. Sadly, though, almost all of these big public screens carry bad advertising that is mostly neither socially engaging nor at the very least aesthetically innovative. A more arts-based, democratic and populist driven content for media facades in more everyday urban settings seems more likely, however, with the launch of second-generation hypermedia skins such as the SmartSlab system by Tom Barker (www.smartslab.co.uk).

The hope afforded by these new types of more flexible, big-screen technologies is that we could all be producing and seeing more projects that come somewhere between SPOTS and the jumbotrons of Piccadilly Circus. The salient question here is more to do with whether we actually want such Las Vegas-like, Christmas-decoration style homes and streets in our cities all year round?

It seems a shame, then, that out of financial necessity, SPOTS – one of the world's few arts-content-driven, media-facade architectural projects – is such low resolution. But then pixel size is not everything. Realities United has certainly made the best of the site's limitations, and there is something poetic about this low-tech digital pointillism after all. SPOTS is dramatic in scale and fascinating in its non-intrusive simplicity and (despite its low-res nature and low-lux power) it is, as a project, arguably aesthetically superior to its high-res cousins. Its seductively self-conscious critical rejection of the full-power razzmatazz retinal circus that comes with the in-your-face high-res of jumbotron screens and its tailoring of public-arts content to the constraints and aesthetic opportunities of its low-res medium is

certainly a significant and sensitive achievement in this field. This temporary installation should therefore be made permanent.

A development on their BIX media facade for Cook and Fournier's Kunsthaus Graz in Austria, SPOTS (one of the largest media facades in the world) is scheduled to be installed for 18 months (since June 2006) on 1,350 square metres (14,531 square feet) of the facade of a converted office block. Commissioned by the Café Palermo Pubblicità agency for the client HVB Immobilien AG, the screen is made up of a large-scale matrix of 1,800 conventional fluorescent lights installed into the glass curtain wall of the building. A single computer controls the entire system and can isolate and control the brightness of each individual lamp. Text and animations can be communicated across the facade and, unusually, the underlying architecture remains largely visible through the display. Realities designer Jan Edler locates the work precisely on the boundaries of 'the transitional zones between architecture, design, art and marketing. What we are doing is the continuation of architecture by other means.'[8] Which comes as no surprise considering its location in Berlin's cultural and commercial centre, alongside such enterprises as the Neue Staatsbibliothek, Neue Nationalgalerie, Philharmonie concert hall, German parliament and the headquarters of numerous multinationals.

Though the intention is clearly to market the city as a whole, the public nature of the work is explicitly stated by the designers who explain that 'the complex needs to enrich the city more than it exploits it … it needs to satisfy the proprietary interests of the owners and likewise the public's interest in the city and in having a functioning public space'.[9] As a result, the screen broadcasts an artistic programme six days a week, with only Mondays given over to advertising with which to finance the arts-based content.

With a maximum luminous output of 67,920 watts and a maximum 'image' refresh rate of 20 luminous intensity values per second, SPOTS is not a distinctly high-tech or technically advanced system. However, its thoughtful and carefully designed content means it knocks spots off of the high-res advertising that is digitally projectile-vomited out over the public in Times Square and Piccadilly Circus.

Moving giant faces are among the most striking and recognisable content of the public arts programme broadcast via this low-res digital-media facade. The grainy, digital Benday-dot pointillism of the media screen has a poetic and critical force that contrasts effectively with most of the commonplace high-resolution advertising screens that preside over many of the world's most important public spaces.

Colour by Numbers, Stockholm, Sweden, 2006

Erik Krikortz, Milo Lavén and Loove Broms

The multicoloured lighting system being controlled via mobile phone.

An even more minimal, low-tech, urban public-arts-based interactive-lighting project reminiscent of the work of Dan Flavin and James Turrell is Colour by Numbers in Stockholm. The project is located on the facade of a converted 10-storey tower, which used to house LM Ericsson's laboratory, the site of groundbreaking experiments with microwave technology. A slim, clear landmark in the local Stockholm cityscape around Midsommarkransen, the Ericsson Tower on Telefonplan has been refurbished by designers Erik Krikortz, Milo Lavén and Loove Broms with a multicoloured set of illuminated windows. The patterns and colours of the tower vary constantly in response to numerical SMS messages sent in by the public (an acknowledgement of the history of the tower), by mobile phone or via the Internet.

The designers are explicit about the public and social nature of the project: 'Inscriptions on a publicly owned area are judged differently from signs on privately owned areas. A billboard is in a certain sense an area for sending a message in the public space, but the person paying for it controls it. Private citizens rarely get the chance to send their messages high above the houses and subway, as now at Telefonplan.'[10]

Describing their project as a form of graffiti, the apologist for this project Charlotte Bydler (a lecturer in art history at Södertorn College and Stockholm University) is modest about its impact, effects and status, noting that the public 'can't use the tower for political or commercial purposes. What remains is a playful communicative process that takes over the public space as the colours change. The tower at Telefonplan sends out a message, and for most people the message is "art" … Colour by Numbers raises issues about what democratic architecture could look like and starts a critical discussion about city planning and the use of the public space.'[11]

The sense of control in this project is intended to provide a sense of ownership. Though questions might be asked about its true social impact, about whether its low-tech systems really do count as truly interactive rather than simply 'responsive', and about for how long it is able to keep locals amused, there is no doubt that it is an improvement on what was there before. On this level the social benefits of this interactive work are purely aesthetic and fit one of the popular contemporary models of public urban art (supported by a mix of public and commercial interests) as a catalyst for regeneration.

Conclusion

While each of these four projects has undoubtedly produced new forms of poetic experience, the electronic epiphanies and techno-transcendentalism they inspire are complicated and unusual pleasures. Their 'newness' and 'strangeness' is especially compelling for those members of the public who are not exposed to interactive spaces and non-static, technologically enabled public art on a regular basis. The often low-tech, gadgety and low-budget nature of most of the projects also portrays an unfortunate aspect of this new trend in socially interactive design – the fact that this is a grossly underfunded area of research. Public bodies and research funding organisations are neglecting these types of projects in favour of less risky, less expensive ones, leaving rich multinationals to skew the capabilities of interactive architecture towards sometimes bland and barely disguised next-generation 3-D billboards and other advertising and promotional spectacles. What might a very (as opposed to a slightly) socially engaged architecture look like anyway? Is a more specifically targeted form of social engagement something these projects should or could aspire to? What might (for example) a socialist, Marxist or communist interactive architecture look like? Is (for example) a disabled, feminist, black, gay or African interactive architecture possible, or even desirable? Could interactive architecture work in the poorest residential districts of cities? Where are the critical, dissenting and interactive architectures that attempt to engage with poverty, war, bioethics, nuclear weapons, crime, drug abuse, disease, unemployment, the environment, human rights and other content?

If only corporations and public funding bodies would sit up and take notice we might all get off our sofas and, even if just for a while, enter a new type of social world.

Arguably the most sophisticated types of projects in this field are yet to be built: speculative projects such as Hooker and Kitchen's Electroplex Heights, and the work in schools of architecture where studios like Unit 14 at the Bartlett and ADS4 at the RCA in London regularly produce visionary and socially engaged architectural projects of the highest international calibre. But almost all of these 'research'-based projects remain sadly neglected and never see the light of day beyond end-of-year exhibitions and esoteric small-scale show catalogues. If only corporations and public funding bodies would sit up and take notice we might all get off our sofas and, even if just for a while, enter a new type of social world.

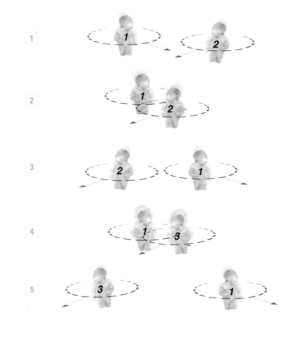

Diller + Scofidio, Braincoat, Swiss Expo, 2002
Diagram illustrating the range of possible response types across an affinity–antipathy spectrum in wearers of the Braincoat.

Whether these new worlds turn out to be more socially engaging for all of us is, as yet, too soon to tell. The most ambitious projects currently in development in this area (such as the Zaragoza Digital Mile, the multidesigner-based digitally interactive urban design project initiated by the city of Zaragoza for Spain's Zaragoza Expo of 2008) provide the opportunities to imagine that shortly, public projects will surpass the social powers of Ada or Braincoat. Δ+

Notes
1. From Peter L Berger and Thomas Luckmann, *The Social Construction of Reality: A Treatise in the Sociology of Knowledge*, Anchor Books (New York), 1966, p 5.
2. Malcolm McCullough, *Digital Ground*, MIT Press (Cambridge, MA), 2004, p xiv.
3. Now Diller Scofidio + Renfro.
4. McCullough, op cit, p 20.
5. Kas Oosterhuis, personal communication, 29 January 2007.
6. Ibid.
7. ONL, Digital Pavilion Korea Vision Document, January 2007, p 2.
8. From www.spots-berlin.com/en.
9. Ibid.
10. www.colourbynumbers.org.
11. Ibid.

The Architectural Relevance of Gordon Pask

Usman Haque reviews the contribution of Gordon Pask, the resident cybernetician on Cedric Price's Fun Palace. He describes why in the 21st century the work of this early proponent and practitioner of cybernetics has continued to grow in pertinence for architects and designers interested in interactivity.

It seems to me that the notion of machine that was current in the course of the Industrial Revolution – and which we might have inherited – is a notion, essentially, of a machine without goal, it had no goal 'of', it had a goal 'for'. And this gradually developed into the notion of machines with goals 'of', like thermostats, which I might begin to object to because they might compete with me. Now we've got the notion of a machine with an underspecified goal, the system that evolves. This is a new notion, nothing like the notion of machines that was current in the Industrial Revolution, absolutely nothing like it. It is, if you like, a much more biological notion, maybe I'm wrong to call such a thing a machine; I gave that label to it because I like to realise things as artifacts, but you might not call the system a machine, you might call it something else.

Gordon Pask[1]

Gordon Pask, cybernetician.

Gordon Pask (1928–96), English scientist, designer, researcher, academic, playwright, was one of the early proponents and practitioners of cybernetics, the study of control and communication in goal-driven systems of animals and machines. Originally trained as a mining engineer, he went on to complete his doctorate in psychology. His particular contribution was a formulation of second-order cybernetics as a framework that accounts for observers, conversations and participants in cybernetic systems.

Pask was one of the exhibitors at the 'Cybernetic Serendipity' show staged at the ICA, London, in 1968, curated by Jasia Reichardt, an exhibition that became the inspiration for many future interaction designers. The interaction loops of cybernetic systems, such as Pask's Colloquy of Mobiles (1968), where actions lead to impacts on the environment that lead to sensing and further modification of actions, are core to the notion of a Paskian environment. He is also known for his Conversation Theory, a particularly coherent and potentially the most productive theory of interaction encompassing human-to-human, human-to-machine and machine-to-machine configurations in a common framework.

There has recently been a ground swell of interest in Pask's work by architects, artists and designers,[2] though his association with architects stretched back to the 1960s, through to the early 1990s, with collaborations undertaken in particular at the Architecture Association, London, and with

the Architecture Machine Group at MIT (later to become the Media Lab). It may be argued that these collaborations were too far ahead of their time and were not fully grasped by the wider architectural community, but they did help to set the foundations for dynamic, responsive and authentically interactive environments.

The extent of Pask's research, theories and artefact design/construction was enormous.[3] As such, different groups of people find completely different tracts from his back catalogue relevant to their own work. In the 1960s, he worked with the architect Cedric Price on his Fun Palace project as

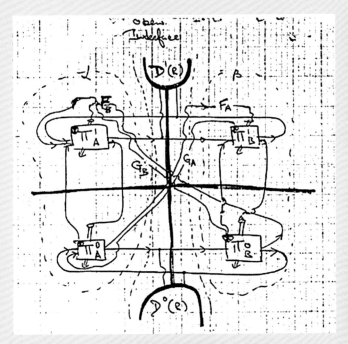

'Architecture of Conversations', sketch by Gordon Pask to annotate a conversation between two individuals (designer and co-designer) giving rise to an environment; an external observer can attribute intelligence to this environment.

Now, at the beginning of the 21st century, Pask's Conversation Theory seems particularly important because it suggests how, in the growing field of ubiquitous computing, humans, devices and their shared environments might coexist in a mutually constructive relationship.

resident cybernetician, introducing the concept of underspecified goals to architecture systems. In the 1970s, Pask's contribution to the philosophy of MIT's Architecture Machine Group was focused around the notion of architecture as an enabler of collaboration.[4] And in the 1980s and early 1990s, architects such as John Frazer at the Architecture Association were particularly interested in how Pask's adaptive systems might be applied to the architectural design process in order to evolve building forms and behaviours.

Now, at the beginning of the 21st century, Pask's Conversation Theory seems particularly important because it suggests how, in the growing field of ubiquitous computing,

humans, devices and their shared environments might coexist in a mutually constructive relationship. If we think of having conversations with our environments in which we each have to learn from each other, then Pask's early experiments with mechanical and electrochemical systems provide a conceptual framework for building interactive artefacts that deal with the natural dynamic complexity that environments must have without becoming prescriptive, restrictive and autocratic.

In this context, his teaching and conversational machines demonstrate authentically interactive systems that develop unique interaction profiles with each human participant. This approach contrasts sharply with the 'Star Trek Holodek' approach often attempted in so-called intelligent

A photo of what is believed to be the last remaining fragment of a SAKI machine. The queries and correct responses are defined by metal 'bits' placed in an array, much like punch cards were used in early computers.

environments, which presumes that we all see all things in the same way and which denies the creative-productive role of the participant in interactions with such environments. Pask recognised, for example, that interpretation and context are necessary elements in language – as opposed to locating meaning itself in language – which is particularly important to consider for any design process, not least the construction of architectural experience.

His theories on underspecified and observer-constructed goals have been a major influence on my own work. In 1996, tutored by Ranulph Glanville, former student and collaborator of Pask, and Stephen Gage, also a Pask aficionado, my final architecture school project, Moody Mushroom Floor, was an interactive floor system of sound, smell and light that determined its outputs in relation to fluctuating goals and perceived responses – no behaviour was preprogrammed.

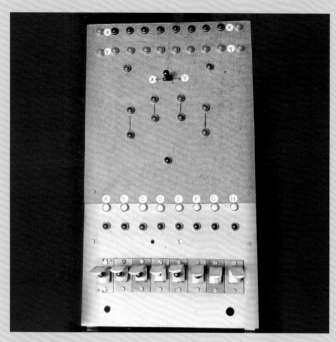

An early Paskian machine.

Gordon Pask and Robin McKinnon-Wood, MusiColour, 1953
The performance system was installed at several locations around the UK. This image shows the control system as installed at Mecca Locarno in Streatham. MusiColour appeared for a final time in 1957.

More recently, Open Burble (2006) was an attempt to build a constructional interactive system, in the sense that the participants both affected the structure, by moving it throughout a park, and constructed the way the structure responded to them by designing and assembling the modular structure themselves as they chose. Finally, the ongoing projects Paskian Environments (with Paul Pangaro, another former student and collaborator of Pask) and Evolving Sonic Environment (with Robert Davis, Goldsmiths' College) aim to provide concrete and pragmatic strategies for implementing Pask's theories in an architectural context.

What follows is an understanding of how Pask's lifetime work can be made even more relevant than ever to the practice of architecture. Pask certainly thought and wrote a lot about the field, but some of the concepts described here are founded on my interpretation of his projects, which even he may not have considered architectural. In places I simply try to extend to the field of architecture the approaches he invented; in others I use concepts that he constructed to consider alternatives to our current assumptions about architecture.

Four of Pask's projects in particular give hints about how to create richer, more engaging and stimulating interactive environments. It is worth bearing in mind that each of these predates the common digital computer and was therefore constructed mainly using analogue components. The descriptions below have been simplified, which is somewhat counter to the spirit of a Paskian approach – often necessarily complex – but it is hoped they will provoke the reader to follow up with Pask's own writings, which cover both the theories and the results of the projects he actually constructed.[5]

The MusiColour Machine,[6] constructed in 1953, was a performance system of coloured lights that illuminated in concert with audio input from a human performer (who might be using a traditional musical instrument). MusiColour should not be confused with today's multicoloured disco lights that respond directly to volume and frequency in a preprogrammed/deterministic manner. Rather, with its two inputs (frequency and rhythm) MusiColour manipulates its coloured light outputs in such a way that it becomes another performer in a performance, creating a unique (though non-random) output with every iteration.

The sequence of light outputs might depend at any one moment on the frequencies and rhythms that it can hear, but if the input becomes too continuous – for instance, the rhythm is too static or the frequency range too consistent – MusiColour will become bored and start to listen for other frequency ranges or rhythms, lighting only when it encounters those. This is not a direct translation: it listens for certain frequencies, responds and then gets bored and listens elsewhere, produces as well as stimulates improvisation, and reassembles its language much like a jazz musician might in conversation with other band members. Musicians who worked with it in the 1950s treated it very much like another on-stage participant.

The innovation in this project is that data (the light-output pattern) is provoked and produced by the participants (other musicians) and nothing exists until one of them enters into a conversation with the designed artefact. In this participant-focused constructional approach, the data evoked has no limits.

Pask constructed a system that aspires to provide enough variety to keep a person interested and engaged without becoming so random that its output appears nonsensical. How these criteria (novelty vs boredom) are measured is core to the system.[7] This calculation is constantly being reformulated on the basis of how the person responds to the response. Unlike the efficiency-oriented pattern-optimisation approach taken by many responsive environmental systems, an architecture built on Pask's system would continually encourage novelty and provoke conversational relationships with human participants.

The Self-Adaptive Keyboard Instructor (SAKI), designed by Pask and Robin McKinnon-Wood in 1956, was essentially a system for teaching people how to increase speed and accuracy in typing alphabetic and numeric symbols using a 12-key keyboard.[8]

Whereas contemporaneous teaching machines followed a learn-by-rote model, in which a student attempts to emulate and is then scored for successes, SAKI mimics the possible relationship between a human teacher and student. A teacher is able to respond directly to a student's apparent needs by focusing at times on particular aspects of the material to be studied if weaknesses are measured in these areas. This is achieved in Pask's constructed system via the dynamic modulation of three variables.

First, a record is kept for each individual item being studied with regard to the amount of time a student takes to complete this item; a student is able to return more frequently to those problems he or she finds most difficult. Second, a limited period of time is provided to respond to a query. If a student answers a query correctly, then the next time that item is tested the student is allowed less time to respond. If, however, the response is incorrect, the allowed response time for that item is subsequently increased. Third, a cue is given after a certain amount of time if there has been no response from the student. The delay for displaying this cue increases the next time this item is displayed as a student returns correct responses, and decreases as he or she returns incorrect responses. At a certain point, when a student is proficient enough with a single item, this period will be greater than the allowed response period and the student will no longer be provided with a cue.

The result is that, while presentation of test items starts out at the same rate for each item with timely cue information, gradually, as the student improves, the pace is increased and cues are withdrawn for particular items. If a student has difficulty with any individual item – manifested either by making a mistake or by responding slowly – the pace is decreased for that item alone and cue information is selectively reintroduced.

At any point, the machine responds not just to the student's actual input, but also changes the way it responds on the basis of past interactions (sometimes providing cue information, sometimes not; sometimes allowing enough time to answer, at other times cutting it back). The student responds to the machine just as the machine is responding to the student, and the nature of their goals at any point in time is dependent on the particular history of response the other has provided.

For an architecture built on sensors and actuators, SAKI provides a pragmatic strategy for constructing algorithms that have multiple dynamic environmental inputs and outputs, yet

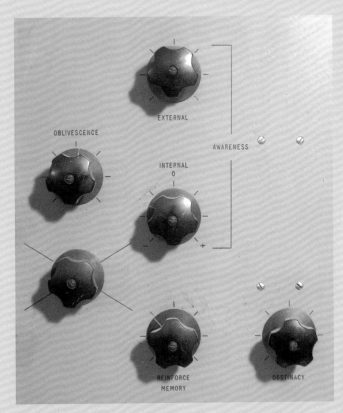

Believed to be an instrumentation panel from the Eucrates project (1955), Gordon Pask developed the system with Robin McKinnon-Wood and CEG Bailey to simulate the relationship between teacher and student. His use of variables for concepts like 'awareness', 'obstinacy' and 'oblivescence' are core to the system.

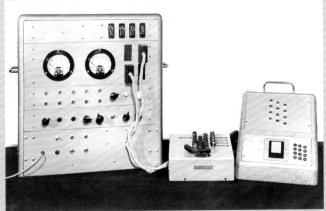

Gordon Pask and Robin McKinnon-Wood, Self-Adaptive Keyboard Instructor (SAKI), 1956
The computing unit is on the left, the middle box is the keyboard the pupil uses to make entries, and the unit on the right displays prompts and cue information.

one that is still able to account for an explicitly human contribution. It provides a model of interaction where an individual can directly adjust the way that a machine responds to him or her so that they can converge on a mutually agreeable nature of feedback: an architecture that learns from the inhabitant just as the inhabitant learns from the architecture.

Chemical computers are assemblages constructed electrochemically, that are able to compute an electrical output on the basis of electrical input. In 1958 Pask was particularly interested in how these could be used to construct analogue systems that emulated biological neural networks in their lack of specificity: they evolved behaviours over time depending on how they were trained. Such systems can modify their systemic interconnections as they grow in order to improve proficiency at calculation or pattern recognition. In effect, Pask discovered that they can grow their own sensors.

He achieved this by growing threads using a known technique of inserting powered electrodes into alcohol solutions of tin and silver. Tendrils would grow from one electrode to another, or to several if several electrodes were powered. Once a thread was broken it would spontaneously rebuild and reconfigure itself, with the break moving up the course of the thread. A sensor electrode was inserted into the thread in order to measure the output waveform generated by this arrangement.

The fascinating innovation Pask made was to reward the system with an influx of free metal ions – which enable growth of the threads – when certain output criteria were met (as measured at the electrode). The arrangement was so delicate that it was affected by all sorts of inputs including, but not limited to, physical vibration. Though several methods were employed, one in particular is interesting for its potential architectural application as an adaptive environment sensing system. A buzzer was sounded. At the moment of sounding, if the frequency of the buzzer appeared at the sensor electrode, then the system was rewarded with its metal ions. Particular arrangements of thread did occasionally detect the buzzer and replicate the electrical frequency at the sensor electrode.

As a result of the reward system – the provision of metal ions – these types of networks were allowed to survive and prosper while those that did not respond to the buzzer were starved of ions and tended to die off. In other words, by measuring the output criteria (the generated waveform) and rewarding the system when these output criteria correlated with specific input criteria (the buzzer sound), the system became better at recognising the buzzer.

The system was therefore able to evolve its own sound sensor, which would not have been possible if all components of the system had been well specified at the start of the experiment because designing and building such chemical structures would have been prohibitively complex. The underspecification of the threads meant that a much better sound sensor could be evolved and constructed. More

importantly though, by changing the input criteria, say by using electromagnetic fields rather than vibration, the system could dynamically grow a new type of sensor.

The reasoning behind Pask's interest in underspecified goals is that if a designer specifies all parts of a design and hence all behaviours that the constituent parts can conceivably have at the beginning, then the eventual identity and functioning of that design will be limited by what the designer can predict. It is therefore closed to novelty and can only respond to preconceptions that were explicitly or implicitly built into it.[9] If, on the other hand, a designed construct can choose what it senses, either by having ill-defined sensors or by dynamically determining its own perceptual categories, then it moves a step closer to true autonomy which would be required in an authentically interactive system. In an environmental sense, the human component of interaction then becomes crucial because a person involved in determining input/output criteria is productively engaging in conversations with his or her environment.

In effect, if such an embodiment has underspecified goals, it enables us to collaborate and converge on shared goals. We are able to affect both the embodiment's response and the way the response is computed.

This is a completely different notion of interaction from that used in many of today's so-called interactive systems, which are premised on unproductive and prespecified circular, deterministic reactions. In these systems, the machine contains a finite amount of information and the human simply navigates through an emerging landscape to uncover it all. I do something, the device/object/environment does something back to me; I do something else, the environment does something else back to me. The human is at the mercy of the machine and its inherent, preconfigured logical system. There is little of the conversation that a truly interactive environment should have, especially in the sense that nothing novel can emerge because all possible responses are already programmed.

The approach of these works is actually rooted in a 19th-century causal and deterministic philosophy that is easy to comprehend in the short term (because it relies on a causal relationship between human and machine – I do X, therefore machine does Y back to me), but is unsustainable in the long term because it is unable to respond to novel or unpredictable situations. Pask was more interested in creating evolving and variable interactions whose sum total is conversational in a valid sense. It is not about concealing and then revealing, but rather about creating information, just as Wikipedia enables in the context of the Web.

In an architectural context, this approach enables us to converge, agree on and thereby share each others' conceptual models of a space and what adaptations we decide it requires. With this shared conception we are better able to act upon the givens of a space in conjunction with an artefact, and do so in a constructive, engaging and ultimately satisfying manner. Such a system has to operate with underspecified

Part of Gordon Pask's Colloquy of Mobiles, showing the two 'male' figures on the left side and two of the three 'female' figures on the right. The work at the back is Peter Zinovieff's Music Computer.

Gordon Pask, Colloquy of Mobiles, ICA, London, 1968
The system was installed at the seminal exhibition 'Cybernetic Serendipity';
the 'female' bulbous forms here were designed by Yolanda Sonnabend.

sensors – either a whole collection of them, each individual sensor of which may or may not eventually be determined as useful in calculating its output and therefore rewarded by the system – or better yet, it may evolve its own sensors, through dynamically determined input criteria.[10]

In his Colloquy of Mobiles project (1968),[11] a physically constructed embodiment of Conversation Theory, Pask suspended a collection of purpose-built mechanical artefacts able to move and rotate, some directing beams of light ('females') and others using a combination of servos and mirrors to reflect light ('males').

Movement was initially random until a light beam from a female was caught by a male and reflected back to the female's light sensor. At this point, movement would cease and the light beams were locked in place as the males started oscillating their mirrors. After a period of time, the mobiles would start moving again, searching for new equilibrium arrangements.

If left alone, the males and females would continue an elaborate and complex choreography of conversations through the medium of light – one which it was not necessary or even possible to preprogramme – finding coherence every now and then as a light beam was shared between partner members of a conversation. The most interesting point came when visitors entered the scene. Some blocked pathways of light while others used handheld torches to synchronise the devices. The males and females were not able to distinguish between light created by a visitor and light reflected from a female – and had no need to. They were still able to find coherence within their own terms of reference.

Colloquy reminds us that environmental sensor/actuator systems (light beams in this case) will respond to their environment solely on their own terms. For example, a thermostat's measurement of and action upon temperature is predetermined by the designer's conceptions and is thus predicated on various assumptions, assumptions of our desire for a consistent ambient room temperature – that we know

what 21°C is, that we will not feel the fluctuations of thermal hysteresis within limits of 3°C per minute.

This makes sense for something as easy to learn and understand as a thermostat, in which there is a finite range of input conditions and a finite range of output conditions and the system attempts to map from inputs to outputs in a linear-causal way. However, it becomes problematic in complex environmental systems such as those that take into account weather predictions, energy prices and internal conditions, which are able directly to affect sunlight pathways, temperature and humidity, shading and other building management entities without genuinely understanding how Paskian conversations can be beneficial. Yet this is the approach that contemporary ubiquitous computing is taking. Also known as the 'disappearing computer' approach, this discipline aims to hide from us the complexities of technology, but in fact removes what little control we might have had over our environmental conditions and requires us to place all faith in the presumptions of the original system designers.

Such environmental systems must contain methods for ensuring that proposed outcomes of the system are actually acceptable to the human. The significant complexity and dimensions of the system must be able to improve outcomes without confounding a person with too many inappropriate or incomprehensible outcomes. Moreover, he or she must have a way to reject inappropriateness and reward those criteria that are useful. A person must be able to construct a model of action collaboratively with the environment.

This makes it clear that we need to be able to make coherent connections with our environmental systems. Rather than simply doing exactly what we tell them (which relies on us knowing exactly what we want within the terms of the machines, terms that are predetermined by the original designer) or alternatively the systems telling us exactly what they think we need (which relies on the environment interpreting our desires, leading to the usual human–machine inequality), a Paskian system would provide us with a method for comparing our conception of spatial conditions with the designed machine's conception of the space.

It is vital at this stage in the development of interactive and time-based media to reconsider Pask's model of interaction, particularly because we are no longer naive in dealing with our technological interfaces. We now expect more from them and are better able to comprehend the structures behind them. A Paskian approach to architecture does not necessarily require complexity of interaction – it relies on the creativity of the person and the machine negotiating across an interface, technological or otherwise.

In his designs, theories and constructions, Pask provides rigorous guidance on how to build such systems, with strict definitions for 'performance', 'conversation', 'interaction', 'environment' and 'participation'.

I concede that simple reactive devices designed to satisfy our creature comforts are useful for functional goals. These include systems such as those employed in Bill Gates'

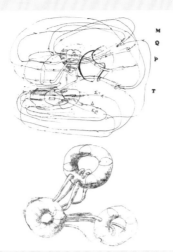

Pask was rigorous about the use of words such as 'concept', 'coherence' and 'analogy', often using sketches of 3-D toroidal forms to diagram these in the context of interaction, evolution and conversation.

technologically saturated mansion, which tracks visitors' locations to provide them with preset optimised temperatures in each room they enter. They also include building management systems that optimise sunlight distribution, rooms that change colour as people enter them, and facades that represent environmental or internal conditions on their surfaces. These satisfy very particular efficiency criteria that are determined during, and limited by, the design process. However, the key to Pask's innovative underspecified systems is that input criteria are determined dynamically; sometimes, like MusiColour by adjusting the weighting of particular input criteria – varying how important they are in the overall calculation – and sometimes, like the chemical computer, by enabling the system to select or construct its own input criteria.

This is a crucial requirement for making spaces and environments that foster engagement with their occupants. Architectural systems constructed with Paskian strategies allow us to challenge the traditional architectural model of production and consumption that places firm distinctions between designer, builder, client, owner and mere occupant. Instead we can consider architectural systems in which the occupant takes a prime role in configuring and evolving the space he or she inhabits, a bottom-up approach that enables a more productive relationship with our environments and each other. Pask's approach, if implemented, would provide a crucial counterpoint to the current pervasive computing approach that is founded on interaction loops that have been fixed by the designer and, if implemented, would have a positive impact on the design of future environments.

This interpretation of Pask's way of thinking about interactive systems does not necessarily result in technological solutions. It is not about designing aesthetic representations of environmental data, or improving online efficiency or making urban structures more spectacular. Nor is it about making another piece of high-tech lobby art that responds to flows of people moving through the space, which is just as representational, metaphor-encumbered and unchallenging as a polite watercolour landscape.

It is about designing tools that people themselves may use to construct – in the widest sense of the word – their environments and as a result build their own sense of agency. It is about developing ways in which people themselves can become more engaged with, and ultimately responsible for, the spaces they inhabit. It is about investing the production of architecture with the poetries of its inhabitants. ⚙

I would like to thank Dr Paul Pangaro for giving comments during the preparation of this article.

Notes
1 Quoted in Mary Catherine Bateson, *Our Own Metaphor: A Personal Account of a Conference on the Effects of Conscious Purpose on Human Adaptation*, Alfred A Knopf (New York), 1972.
2 See, for example, recent attempts to replicate Gordon Pask's electrochemical experiments by Peter Cariani, Tufts Medical School; collaborations by Jon Bird, University of Sussex and artist Andy Webster; Dendrite by architect Pablo Miranda, Royal Institute of Technology, Stockholm; Cornell University professor Maria Fernández, writing about Reichardt's 'Cybernetic Serendipity' exhibition at London ICA with special emphasis on Pask's installations; Andrew Pickering, historian of science from University of Illinois, preparing a book on English cyberneticians; collaboration between Omar Khan, Buffalo University and Raoul Bunschoten, Architecture Association, London.
3 Even now his archives (in both Europe and North America) have not been fully classified, though his UK archive has recently been transferred to Vienna.
4 Nicholas Negroponte, *Soft Architecture Machines*, MIT Press (Cambridge, MA), 1976.
5 In this context it is important to note the enormous contribution that Robin McKinnon-Wood, friend, collaborator and business partner, made to Pask's work; he built and helped design several of the Paskian machines described here. For more on this collaboration see Ranulph Glanville, 'Robin McKinnon-Wood and Gordon Pask: a lifelong conversation', originally published in the *Journal of Cybernetics and Human Learning*, Vol 3, No 4, 1996, now available online at www.imprint.co.uk/C&HK/vol3/v3-4rg.htm.
6 Gordon Pask, 'A Comment, a case history, a plan', in Jasia Reichardt,

Cybernetics, Art and Ideas, Studio Vista (London), 1971, pp 76–99, provides a good description of the project.
7 ibid.
8 See Gordon Pask, 'SAKI: 25 years of adaptive training into the microprocessor era', in *International Journal of Man-Machine Studies*, Vol 17, 1982, pp 69–74.
9 'Sensors and effectors determine how events in the world at large are related to the internal informational states of organisms and robotic devices. Sensors determine what kinds of distinctions (perceptual categories, features, primitives) can be made on the environment. By "evolving the sensor" perceptual repertoires can be adaptively altered and/or enlarged. To the extent that devices can adaptively choose their own feature primitives for themselves, they gain a greater measure of "epistemic autonom" vis-à-vis their designers. Such devices are useful in ill-defined situations where the designer does not know a priori what feature primitives are adequate or optimum for solving a particular task. From Peter Cariani, 'Epistemic autonomy through adaptive sensing', *Proceedings of the 1998 IEEE ISIC/CRA/ISAS Joint Conference*, IEEE (Gaithersburg, MD), 1998, pp 718–23. An expert on Paskian systems, Cariani has reconstructed Pask's sound-sensing chemical computer.
10 For more on this see 'Distinguishing Concepts: Lexicons of Interactive Art and Architecture' also in this volume.
11 See Jasia Reichardt, *Cybernetic Serendipity, Studio International* special issue, London, 1968.

Wearable Technologies, Portable Architectures and the Vicissitudes of the Space Between

The omnipresence of the iPod and mobile phone has ensured portable and wearable technologies' highly privileged position in contemporary society. They are at the top of the pile where conspicuous consumption is concerned – you only have to visit an Apple store on a Saturday afternoon to witness the degree to which this highly sought-after gadgetry has become subject to consumer frenzy and speculation. Here, **Despina Papadopoulos** reviews the particular social and cultural impact of wearable devices. She also welcomes in a new generation of interactive designers who are investigating the human and emotional potential of emergent technologies.

In a world in which technological mastery has made such rapid strides, can one not understand that the desire to feel – and to feel oneself – should arise as a compensation, necessary, even in its excesses, to our psychic survival?

Jean Starobinski, 'A short history of bodily sensations', 1989[1]

With every new artefact we create a new ideology – what are, then, the ideologies that we create and embody today? As we design and appropriate wearable technologies – garments and accessories that might have embedded sensors and computational power, can be networked and incorporate electronic textiles – we also start inhabiting a new set of ideologies. These new and emerging technologies, from our

mobile phones and iPods to the new breed of sensing, monitoring and reacting wearable devices, are not mere accessories in the form of opportunistic embellishments to new lifestyles, but physical, psychic and social prostheses.

We have come a long way from James Bond and Modesty Blaise, who wore their devices with style and pizzazz while promising a future where technology was sexy and at the service of transformation and freedom, to our current, seemingly limitless cyborgian visions of the self. In the process we have expanded our abilities to sense the world and each other, as well as our ability to represent our relationship to both the internal and external. In many ways we now stand at a threshold where cenesthesia, that internal perception of our

CuteCircuit, Hug Shirt, London, 2006
Francesca Rosella of CuteCircuit wearing the Hug Shirt that she and fellow designer Ryan Genz hope to retail by the end of 2007 for around the same price as a video iPod.

own bodies, is actualised in our transactions with ourselves and where the history of the body, its organs and substances have indeed become obtuse models of the functioning of human society. Conversely, structures and metaphors in society are becoming imprinted on the 'technological body'. Mobile phone cameras, the photo-sharing application Flickr and video blogs have become the intimate answer to surveillance cameras and radio frequency identification (RFID) tags.

Affective computing, a branch of artificial intelligence that deals with the design of devices that purport to process emotion, assumes that our galvanic skin response (GSR), our heartbeat and pulse rate are concrete and decisive, albeit algorithmically determined, signs of our emotional state. Such a reductivist reading of the self is in line with our modern fascination with reflexivity and representation. We now have garments that can monitor our function so we now can *see* what we *feel*.

What would Marcel Mauss, the French anthropologist who in 1934 talked of body techniques and habitus, make of this complex network of devices, emissions and transmissions that surround us? For Mauss, habitus involves those aspects of culture anchored in the body and its daily practices. Operating beneath the level of ideology, these patterns of motion belong to the acquired practices of the human body. What kind of body techniques are we developing today as a result of our reliance on wearable technologies? While in the past our habitus evolved over time, tradition and culture, we are now thrust into new actions and reactions engineered by labs and R&D departments. Are wearable technologies likely to become secular chasubles – portable houses that contain our relationships and fortify our neuroses?

Designers, theorists as well as market forecasters, tend to split the world of wearable technologies into military, medical, industrial, sport and fashion applications. While the first four areas have exhibited steady growth, fashion is at a loss to know how to treat technology and bring it to market. Even Hussein Chalayan, the beloved fashion designer of all wearable technologists, presented technology in his spring/summer 2007 'One Hundred and Eleven' show as a spectacle, a mythical entity that will never come to being. In the closing of the show, a series of garments were dramatically animated by a complex system of motors and wires designed by 2D:3D, the design and engineering firm that brings Harry Potter, another mythical figure, to life. While in the past Chalayan used technology to show simple interactions that accentuated the body's relationship to both social and physical space, in his latest show he presented a vision of technology that is impossible to attain and has little to do with what is possible in the seams of fabric. The complex mechanisms needed to drive the garments divorced them from anything that can actually be constructed outside a performance, thus once again presenting wearable technologies as a fantasy. But then again, fashion is about fantasy.

Going from fantasy to science fiction or to nightmare, the Future Force Warrior (FFW) initiative led by the US military at the Natick Soldier RD&E Center re-emphasises the political nature of both the body and clothes, as well as the distinct ethical and ideological dimensions of all wearable technologies. The centre's website describes the programme as follows: 'FFW notional concepts seek to create a lightweight, overwhelmingly lethal, fully integrated individual combat system, including weapon, head-to-toe individual protection, netted communications, soldier worn power sources, and enhanced human performance. The program is aimed at providing unsurpassed individual & squad lethality, survivability, communications, and responsiveness – a formidable warrior in an invincible team.'

As the remote sensing of vital organs, multi-environment dynamic camouflage, impenetrability of the body and technologically augmented senses are no longer orders of the mythical but success criteria for an ultra-human warrior, they define what our bodies could be like in the near future, and what lies between desire, fear, ability and circulation in the social.

In the world of most commercial wearable devices, the significance of sense and location is reduced to a field of RFID and GPS mechanisms – and the functional primacy of a perpetual monitoring of presence. This actualises the body as a point in a grid of 'x's and 'y's, traceable and locatable, but is devoid of meaning and the sense of serendipity that is so important to human transactions and locations. Wearable technologies, in imploding our fears of privacy and collapsing the lines between private and public and between leisure and work, are invoking a world where we are always on, always available, where everything and everyone can be accessed and traced and where the moment is perpetually postponed.

In having access to information at all times, in capturing and broadcasting the moment constantly instead of living it, we are measuring and comparing emotions instead of experiencing them. By having instant access and terminal replay loops of all of our transactions, of all our moments, we run the risk of stripping them of that which makes them: transiency. Are wearable technologies to become portable architectures of surveillance, über-functionality, commerce and invincibility?

Is this new body one we want to inhabit full time? A body without frontiers or a chimerical body that will never come to being, a tease of seduction but of no realisation? At the same time, a new direction is persistently forming, one that translocates the bounding definitions of what wearable technology is and what kind of allegiances it could make. It is in this very translocation of meaning that wearable technologies are emerging as both a practice and a metaphor, defying definition and espousing transformation, appropriation and new design interventions. Technology does not change our basic human needs, just the way they are delivered and sometimes the metaphors through which they are lived.

Francesca Rosella and Ryan Genz founded CuteCircuit, an interaction design and wearable technology company based in London, after graduating from Ivrea's Interaction Design Institute. Before meeting in Ivrea, Rosella had studied fashion while Genz had studied studio art and anthropology. Together

Mouna Andraos and Sonali Sridhar, ADDRESS, New York, 2007
Mouna Andraos wearing the GPS-enabled necklace in New York which displays the 8,686 kilometres (5,397 miles) she is away from her home in Beirut.

they create wearable technologies that are about, as Rosella says, 'good experiences, not good logos'. CuteCircuit is now in the process of bringing to the market the Hug Shirt, a shirt that allows people to send hugs over distance. Hug Shirts are fitted with sensors that feel the strength and persistence of the touch, temperature and heart rate of the sender, and actuators that re-create these sensations in the receiving shirt. They work with a Bluetooth accessory for Java-enabled mobile phones, which collects the hug data and sends them to another shirt – a kind of a wearable SMS.

The idea behind these shirts is both simple and universal: how do you send someone a hug, a powerful and direct physical constriction of the body transmitting warmth and affection? Why should some of our technologies not attempt to actuate telesensing in this way? The Hug Shirt's electronics are embedded using conductive fabrics and threads instead of wires, so the shirt is washable and form fitting. Its design and style is reminiscent of action wear, and encourages the idea of a hug on the go. While it is not yet on the market, attention from the media, and the enthusiastic response the designers get every time they show it, attests to a basic human need – that of communication. Rosella and Genz believe that the Hug Shirt also appeals to the collective imagination. The designers say that everybody sees something different in it; business people will approach it in one way while teenagers will quickly think of new uses for it. The combination of familiarity – most people know how to send SMS messages – and the sense of physical closeness turns technology to interaction design for humans craving both a hug and new platforms in which to be expressive.

While CuteCircuit uses wearable technologies to bring people together and minimise the psychological distance between them, Mouna Andraos and Sonali Sridhar, interaction designers based in New York, are creating a pendant necklace, ADDRESS, that reminds people of the distance they have travelled, and how far they are from, or close to, home. ADDRESS is a handmade, GPS-enabled pendant with an alphanumeric LED display, also fitted with a USB

connection to allow its owner to connect to a computer when they first acquire it. Users must select from an onscreen interface, either by pointing to a country or providing their zip code, the location they consider their 'anchor – where they were born or where home is'.

Once the necklace is given this location, it displays how many miles away it is from home, updating this information daily. Literal and poetic at once, ADDRESS is made of wood, encasing the LED display and GPS module, and metal. Its materials and design enable the device to transcend its electronic provenance and instead underline the crossings of global dwellers and their relationship to space. As the designers note: 'It serves as a personal connector to that special place: making the world a little smaller – or bigger.'

What ADDRESS manages to do is to use a locative technology associated with navigating space, and infuse it with meaning and personal direction. Space is then expanded and associations, journeys and connections become part of the jewellery. As the GPS unit calculates its position by its relative distance from the three satellites roaming the earth, owners of ADDRESS conduct their own emotional trilateration.

Joo Youn Paek, Free the Listening, New York, 2006
A pair of headphones that enable participation.

Joo Youn Paek invites people to share their music with her tongue-in-cheek headphones.

Joo Youn Paek, Self-Sustainable Chair, New York, 2006
Joo Youn Paek walking around New York City wearing her Self-Sustainable Chair, an inflatable dress that converts into a chair. The designer takes a rest on her chair. Minutes later it will deflate and she will have to resume her walk if she wants to rest again, a conceptual design that creates a playful cycle of action and reaction.

In addressing the emotional relationship we often have with objects and by using technology to create intersections between the visible and the invisible, the tangible and the imaginary, designers can pierce the 'digital bubble' that is sometimes encasing us and re-establish notions of serendipity and social functionality.

Joo Youn Paek, a Korean performance artist and sculptor who lives and works in New York, uses technology to twist, as she says, everyday objects and experiences. In wearing her twisted objects she wants to transform the habitual and redundant and give birth to new possibilities of interaction, or simply break up the routine of her daily course. In Free the Listening, a pair of headphones is fitted with a set of additional earpieces, but these second earpieces face out, inviting passers-by to lean over and share music. This design feature obliterates the enclosed private space that headphones usually create and invites an intimate interaction as the parasitic listener needs to lean in close to his or her host.

Paek's training as both a sculptor and interaction designer is evident in the meticulous way she constructs her objects and the effortless way in which she manipulates and transforms materials. She combines performance art, architecture, sculpture, electronic design and social commentary to create living objects, design interventions that revise the customarily constructed parameters of space and the interactions made possible within it. In another of her projects, the Self-Sustainable Chair, a dress made out of polyethylene, connected to shoes that pump air into it on each step, doubles as a chair. The dress slowly transforms into a chair with each step and when the tired flâneur requires some rest all he or she has to do is sit on the inflated dress/chair. The repose is interrupted when the chair slowly deflates, giving in to the body's weight and transforming back to a dress. In order to

inflate it again, more walking is required, creating a loop of action and reaction, and using the mechanics of the body to stimulate a game of recreational urbanism.

Another designer and artist who manipulates materials is Joey Berzowska, the founder of XS Labs, a design research studio in Montreal. XS Labs focuses on the fields of electronic textiles and wearable computing as well as what Berzowska calls 'reactive materials and squishy interfaces'. Her work, while playful and experimental, is underlined by a commitment to the adaptive and transformative properties of materials. In pushing them to their limits she also creates conceptual breakthroughs that allow her to build a new vocabulary for both computation and design. Kukia is a kinetic electronic dress, decorated with silk and felt flowers that animate by slowly opening and closing. The petals of the flowers integrate Nitinol, a shape-memory alloy, which makes the fluid, organic animation possible as it contracts. As Berzowska notes, 'The dress does not respond to proximity, mood or the stock market. Rather, it is an expressive and behavioural kinetic sculpture that develops a visceral relationship with the wearer'.

Joey Berzowska (XS Labs), Kukia electronic dress, Montreal, 2006
Close-up view of the dress as its flowers slowly start closing.

Instead of creating interactive garments, the designer experiments with the interactive relationship that develops between clothing and wearer.

In the design of another interactive garment – Vilkas – Nitinol alloy is used again, this time as part of a dress with a kinetic hemline that raises over a 30-second interval to reveal the wearer's knee and upper thigh. As the movement occurs independently of the wearer's wishes, a dialogue develops between the wearer and the dress. Berzowska thus explores the ways in which we can interact with our garments and the types of relationships that emerge from such interactions.

Garments designed by XS Labs play with the boundaries of the body and space, and at other times they become surfaces on which memories are imprinted. In Intimate Memory, an earlier work, a shirt is fitted with a microphone and a series of LEDs stitched on the front. When the microphone picks up a whisper or a soft blow, the shirt lights up, recording the intimate occurrence. The lights then slowly go off, one by one, leaving a light trail of a bygone event.

One of the greatest challenges in wearable technologies, and partly responsible for the difficulty in turning wearable technologies to a manufacturable reality, is finding ways to integrate electronic components to soft materials. Researchers, designers and artists alike, have been working for the past 10 years with conductive textiles and threads, trying to find construction techniques that would allow for washability, comfort and an aesthetic integration of microprocessors and fabrics.

Leah Buechley's research focuses not only on how to make this integration possible, but also on how to make it accessible. As part of her PhD at the Department of Computer Science at the University of Colorado at Boulder, and part of the Craft Technology Group, she is working on fabric-based printed circuit boards (PCBs) and construction kits for electronic textiles. Her work on the e-textile construction kit was detailed in a paper that won her the Best Paper award at the tenth International Symposium on Wearable Computing in 2006. Her work demonstrates how to use conductive fabrics and threads to embed microprocessors and simple electronic components on fabrics using craft techniques. Buechley loves the engineering challenges the medium presents and the

Joey Berzowska (XS Labs), Vilkas dress, Montreal, 2006
Demonstration of the animative qualities of the dress. The hemline starts rising, perhaps at an importune moment. The wearer then has to negotiate with the dress and pull it back down.

Joey Berzowska (XS Labs), Intimate Memory shirt, Montreal, 2004
The designer whispers to her clothes. A microphone on the collar of the shirt picks up whispers and soft blows which are then interpreted as light. The more intense the whisper, the brighter the lights, which then, slowly, like the feeling on the skin, start fading one by one.

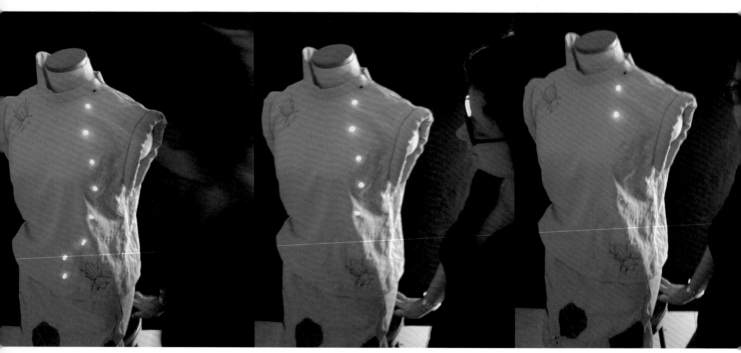

Leah Buechley, PCB fabric, Colorado, 2006
Flexible and beautiful: the PCB (printed circuit board), laser-cut conductive fabric with heat-adhesive backing is ironed on fabric.

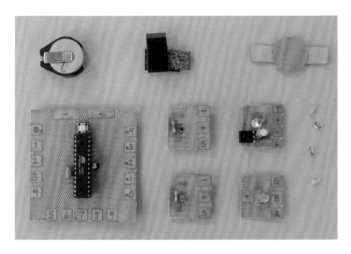

Leah Buechley, e-textiles kit, Colorado, 2006
The construction kit contains a microcontroller, an assortment of sensors and actuators, an infrared transceiver, an on/off switch and a battery pack. Each of the components is either made entirely of fabric or has been packaged so that it can be stitched directly to cloth. The e-textiles kit in action, sewn on the front of a man's shirt after assembly.

ability to combine the hardness of electronics with the softness of fabrics and in the process present the dynamic and expressive interactions that technology can make possible. Her work is both inspired and inspiring. The delight she takes in materials and her compulsion to make things, as she admits, have resulted in an uncomplicated, simple set of instructions and techniques to develop e-textiles and quickly experiment with them. Her desire to make the medium of technology more accessible, especially to women, is also driven by her desire to tackle the gender issues surrounding technology.

As Buechley notes: 'e-textiles present wonderful possibilities for changing the look, feel and culture of technology', and as the e-textile kit shows, by using craft techniques, and putting together simple electronics, designers can be empowered and actively explore the intersection of technology and its expressive potentials.

By giving access to the tools of the formative technologies that surround us to a larger group of designers and practitioners, new ways of thinking about interaction, space, social articulations and expressions can emerge. Situated outside fashion yet flirting with its possibilities and ramifications, outside architecture yet aware of its power, not quite art yet inspired by art's ability to reframe the world, we can approach wearable technologies as a series of modules that touch on all that surrounds us and inspire new possibilities for all. ⊅

Note
1. Jean Starobinski, 'A short history of bodily sensations', in Michel Feher with Ramona Naddaff and Nadia Tazi, *Fragments for a History of the Human Body*, Part Two, Zone Books (New York), 1989, p 370.

Shadow Play

The Participative Art
of Scott Snibbe

Scott Snibbe aspires to an art that aids people to abandon their bodily inhibitions and 'get out of their sense of their selves'. Lucy Bullivant profiles the work of this Californian artist and computer scientist, who is realising the potential of the ancient Chinese tradition of shadow play through an interactive digital media.

Our contemporary society relies on digital technology to facilitate on a virtual level all manner of everyday communication, transactions and play. This 'virtuality' takes the user beyond the former constraints of time and space, allowing him or her to exist in a condition that is perpetually online, and now widely wireless in nature. Digitally driven surveillance systems identify and track people through their physical presence and movement. In modern warfare it is through digital means that perpetrators can maximise distance from their targets. It is rather more rare for this 21st-century human-control weapon – or prosthesis – to demonstrate its capacity to bring about a physical sense of connection, let alone a critical awareness of the social versatility of electronic interfaces.

Yet, in the view of Scott Snibbe, the award-winning San Francisco research artist and computer scientist, electronic media has huge scope to directly engage the body of the viewer to create engaging time-based interactions. The thematic territory of Snibbe's user-friendly work is direct physical perception and the nature of the self explored in a near childlike way through the use of electronic media. It is popular because each participant's body constitutes the image, an amusing focal point if ultimately a set of mutable traces across a screen, but while in motion akin to an existentialist form of slapstick silent comedy.

Snibbe (now 37) trained as an experimental film-maker and animator as well as in computer software design, and set up his company Sona Research, now known as Snibbe Interactive, in 1997. Through the repetitiveness of projected shadow effects he stimulates a sense of first-hand unmediated visual memory. 'My artistic vocabulary relies on subtle changes in timing that unfold as projections or mechanical objects reacting to viewers,'[1] he explains. 'These changes in timing are encoded not as frames of film, but as computer instructions that constantly reinterpret and update the temporal conditions of the work.'[2] The repetitiveness of the shadow effects in each of his works stimulates a visual memory and immediate, visceral sense of presence.

The very reductive nature of Snibbe's approach helps at the same time to induce explorations that shed light on the mediated nature of our bodies. In his works, the physical body of the viewer challenges the screen by pushing it out of view – it causes the light of the screen to absorb the body's form or the shadows to eat away at the light, turning them into full-body 'motion paintings' or even becoming a character within a narrative. 'Snibbe's work radically questions familiar notions of interfaces, expanding their functionality and revealing their social impact,' says Christiane Paul, Adjunct Curator of New Media Arts, Whitney Museum of American Art.[3]

Aware of their popularity, a growing number of bodies have invited the artist to present installations. Apart from the Whitney, with its long-standing credentials in exhibiting media art, these have included New York galleries The Kitchen and Eyebeam, the city's Hall of Science in Queens, Telic in Los Angeles (an interactive art gallery) and other institutions in the US, the Tokyo Intercommunications Center, London's Institute of Contemporary Art, Ars Electronica in Austria, La Villette in Paris and South Korea's Seoul Media Art Biennial. Most of these are museums and galleries, but increasingly Snibbe's work, which manages to be both cerebral and experiential, is appearing in everyday public places such as office foyers and shopping centres.

Snibbe portrays the centrality of human interdependence by giving bodily interactions the role of main protagonists in his works. 'Many of my works do not function unless viewers actively engage with them – by touching, breathing, moving and so on – so that viewers are essential to the work's existence as art.'[4] Using technology that mimics nature, his work explores the interdependence of phenomena with their environments, even if they seem independent. The dynamic experience it creates is predictable, yet infinitely variable. Most of his work is installations, but some are online projects that are often sketches for them. His installation Cabspotting, for instance, shown at the ISEA Festival in San Jose in 2006, traces the pulsing circulatory system of San Francisco's taxi cabs as they travel through the Bay area in time lapse.

The artist's focus on the interdependence of seemingly independent phenomena with their environments is partly influenced by his Buddhist beliefs, a trait he shares with many of the Abstract Expressionist artists who adopted a similar search for the non-objective. Buddhism places emphasis on the interdependence of phenomena – no object, physical or mental, has an inherent existence in isolation from the rest of reality, whether it be parts or causes of a phenomenon, or the mind that exists and labels them as a discrete entity. Like many contemporary architects, Snibbe also draws on social psychology and complexity and network theories. The human body, he maintains, is interdependent, being composed entirely of 'non-self' elements including parents' genetic material, food and water in continual exchange with the environment and with others. Similarly, human mental structures and processes emerge from interactions with other individuals and with society.

Concentration, 2003

For more than 10 years the projects Snibbe has developed have invariably incorporated the viewer's body within a dynamic cinematic projection generated using a computer, projector and camera pointed at a floor or wall surface. 'I'm trying to expand the notion of cinema into an interactive experience, rather than a one-way delivery of story and emotion.'[5] Shadow play has been a staple part of installation art in the past, and the disruption of the visitor, or the disrupting power of the projection (in the case of Krzysztof Wodiczko's projections on to buildings that address their

status as power symbols) a standard element. Earlier media art tended to appropriate technology in order to colonise it, but often not to turn the concept of the work into an elastic one the visitor could transform by his or herself, alone or with others. However, Snibbe's particular application of technology allows the visitor's intervention to be fully folded into the concept of the work rather than just momentarily disturbing or playing with something otherwise mainly impermeable.

Boundary Functions, an early work designed and developed in 1997, and first shown at the annual Ars Electronica

emphasises the reality that personal space has an interpersonal and involuntary definition.

'What I hope for most of my pieces is to have people get out of their sense of their selves.'[6] His work is based on the transfer of bodily responses towards informing a work of art, transforming each in the process and as such adhering to phenomenological principles. As the architecture and design theorist Malcolm McCullough reminds us, phenomenology responds to mechanised abstraction with a renewed focus on presence.[7] Snibbe wants people to experience his work 'body first', he explains, with a strong visceral sensation later followed up by thought and reflection. They accordingly construct the meaning of works through a process of physical awareness. This philosophy has spurred him in 2007 to realise a public mission, to set up the Social Media Institute for Learning Experientially (SMILE), dedicated to learning through the body and through social experiences, a body operating under the aegis of Snibbe Interactive.

'None of my work is commenting on technology, but on the tradition of experimental and abstract film going back to Chinese shadow play and Plato's cave.'

Drawing on his training in this field, the history of experimental film is a major theme in Snibbe's work. 'None of my work is commenting on technology, but on the tradition of experimental and abstract film going back to Chinese shadow play and Plato's cave.'[8] Snibbe places his work in a cultural lineage based on aspirations to demediatise the media of film by encouraging the moving body to assert its primacy within the art-making process. Figures such as film-maker Len Lye, who created 'direct cinema' by putting marks on celluloid film with his body, and veteran avant-gardists Oskar Fischinger, Hans Richter and Moholy-Nagy, have been strong influences on Snibbe. What they had in common, he believes, was the ability 'to create sophisticated, time-based, emotion- and meaning-laden work without resorting to representation'.[9] What they all share is a desire to turn linear cinema narration into a more organic, post-linear form of performance.

Festival, Linz, Austria, in 1998, was later selected for the permanent collection of the new Zaha Hadid-designed Phaeno Science Museum in Wolfsburg, Germany. As people walk around a large gallery floor, the artwork projects lines between them, describing their personal space. As more people appear on foot, and perhaps with pushchairs or in wheelchairs, the spaces form a mosaic of 'tile' shapes that continue to change dynamically. When people touch, the line between them momentarily disappears, allowing them to connect without borders. This dynamically changing diagram

Boundary Functions, 2004
Using a projector, video camera, computer, retroreflective floor and Snibbe's custom software, this installation projects lines on a raised square floor, dividing each person from the others on it. As they each move, the line diagram shifts to maintain their zone of personal space in relation to the whole.

Visceral Cinema: Chien, 2005
The work draws on key moments in the Surrealist film *Un Chien Andalou* by
Salvador Dalí and Luis Buñuel, which are re-imagined as large video projections
on a wall of a man pulling a piano on a rope. Viewers' shadows interfere with
the projections, and at a certain moment cause the man's image to dissolve
into ant-like moving parts that gradually take over the whole screen.

More recently Snibbe's work has taken an increasingly narrative slant, part of his agenda to create a new medium. Visceral Cinema: Chien, a wall projection that re-imagines the Surrealist film Un Chien Andalou made by Salvador Dalí and Luis Buñuel, was Snibbe's first successful stab at a narrative work. Shown at Telic in 2005 and at the ICA, London, in 2006, it presents viewers with a large ghostly video projection of a man pulling a grand piano towards them – a poetic motif from the film that is both funny and visually arresting. When they walk between the projector and the projection, viewers' own shadows interfere with the man's actions, making his job harder. If they move between the man and the piano, the piano is pushed back, causing the man to strain harder and lose ground. If they intersect the man's shadow for long enough, he metaphorically dissolves into streams of ants that rapidly 'eat' his silhouette and gradually take over the whole screen. The two-dimensionality of the projected images is not only confronted by the physical interventions of onlookers, but the perceptual tensions arising from the interplay between the two prompt multiple readings of the work, ranging from meditations on impermanence, renewal and the notion of existential questing.

In the moment, however, the work encourages childlike engagement. 'On the experiential level, I enjoy seeing audiences get lost in the process of interaction to lose their sense of themselves and become completely intertwined with their bodies' engagement with the work and with other viewers,' says Snibbe. 'I hope that at the conceptual level the audiences will understand the inversion of media that is embodied in the works and also have some sense of their body in relation to cinema. It is the fact that we normally become completely detached from our bodies while watching cinema that I wanted to invert. I wanted to see viewers experiencing cinema body-first, and losing the sense of cinema as illusion, seeing it instead as tangible, reactive light.'[10]

Snibbe's works induce a strong spatial awareness. While the minimalist environmental art installations of the 1960s and 1970s – most notably Robert Irwin and James Turrell – explored how subtle changes in an environment can make deep impressions on the viewer, Snibbe's own constructed environments are far more pliable and mutable in relation to visitors' presence and engagement. They appear almost like literal projections of the mind, and in fact Snibbe's early encounters as a child with Turrell's work, for instance Danae (1983), in which a room was saturated with ultraviolet light, convinced him that the work is created primarily in the mind, not in the environment. It was the fact that it was a fabrication in which light was powerful but only the trigger for perception that fascinated him the most. Going one step further his gently playful works offer a form of perceptual transaction. Referring to Chien, but applicable to any of his works, he says 'it's very clear how you're affecting it'.[11]

Make Like a Tree, 2006
Employing a computer, projector, video camera and retroreflective screen and custom software, the work allows viewers' shadows to intervene in a misty forest landscape, provoking surreal humour as well as a sombre scene of the continual fading of human forms.

In each case, making an installation is for Snibbe a research process. For 'Thread: A Growing Network', a group exhibition at the ArtSpace gallery in New Haven in the US staged in 2006 on the theme of how people connect, which included online dialogue between artists and their public, Snibbe created Make Like a Tree. Visitors walking in front of a screen found their silhouettes interfering with the projected image of a misty forest. The mingled images provoked surreal humour, as a leg emerged from a tree trunk, then faded and dematerialised behind trees and into the background of layers of previous visitors' shadows, and visitors could see themselves becoming part of this now sombre yet strangely cartoon-like landscape.

Snibbe feels that his works' cultural specificity produces a respectful reaction from the public. On the other hand, they also allow people to forget their inhibitions, experiencing with their bodies what they would be unlikely to in many other public contexts. Chien has encouraged people to parade past, doing silly walks and even swaying along in conga lines. One visitor to the work expressed his relief that 'here was a machine that is not your enemy or your superior'.[12] To the more progressive curators at science museums, Snibbe's work is disarming. At the same time they support his view that a 'pure artwork' can offer a sense of the metaphysical, complementing perhaps more prosaic or text-based science exhibits that promote learning and engagement. Audience involvement is nevertheless heightened due to the appealingly simple interactive, conceptual operation of Snibbe's work,

drawing people into a subtle game with the projections that offers intrigue, a challenge to notions of representation, and emphasises his key point about interdependence. The projects work largely because they comment on ephemeral artifice while managing to avoid either ritual or moral superiority.

Concentration, made in 2003, functions on a similar conceptual basis to Boundary Functions while formally it is like the other shadow pieces. It is part of the 'Screen' series of works, each of which features a white rectangle with which the visitor's body interacts, and explores the relationships between bodies, light and shadow through various manipulations of light. In this case, it stands for energy, concentrating all the light from the projector around a visitor's body, creating a body-shaped spotlight. When other visitors arrive, only the first person remains lit. As a result they enter into a struggle to capture the halo of light, but it can only be taken by physically 'digging' deep into the heart of another visitor's shadow. There is also some kind of competition for control in Compliant (2002), another 'Screen' work, shown at the Beall Center for Art and Technology at UC Irvine, where the impact of the bodies of visitors distorts the soft white rectangle, and it continually slips away from the visitor's vain attempts to stop it, becoming part of a game that defies its purely screen-based nature. 'We push, stretch, and sculpt this amorphous non-dimensional vision, altering its size and edge with hand motions, as if light is plastic, compliant as three-dimensional clay,' wrote one visitor to the Beall Center.[13]

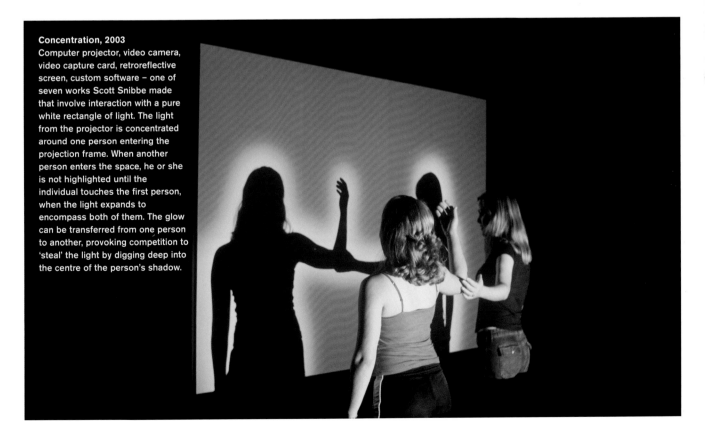

Concentration, 2003
Computer projector, video camera, video capture card, retroreflective screen, custom software – one of seven works Scott Snibbe made that involve interaction with a pure white rectangle of light. The light from the projector is concentrated around one person entering the projection frame. When another person enters the space, he or she is not highlighted until the individual touches the first person, when the light expands to encompass both of them. The glow can be transferred from one person to another, provoking competition to 'steal' the light by digging deep into the centre of the person's shadow.

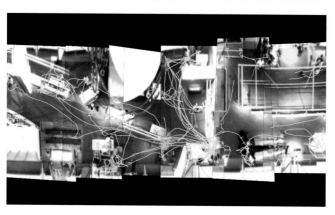

You Are Here, 2004
The project was commissioned by the New York Hall of Science. Technically Snibbe's most ambitious work to date, it uses six networked firewire cameras to track the movements of museum visitors over a 930-square-metre (10,000-square-foot) area. The paths of the last 200 visitors are shown projected on a large overhead screen. With a trackball, visitors can scroll back in time to see where they came from juxtaposed with the live video image.

In You Are Here, his most technically ambitious work to date, commissioned by the New York Hall of Science in 2004, Snibbe used six networked firewire overhead cameras and a computer to track and display the paths of visitors moving through a public space more than 930 square metres (10,000 square feet) in size. On a large screen the aggregate paths of the last 200 visitors are shown, along with the movements of people currently being tracked. The visitor's own location is highlighted with a large red arrow, a typical indicator that 'you are here'. Using a trackball, the visitor can scroll back in

Unlike surveillance systems being installed in public places, which record that reality but do not show it, this one does not collect data for security purposes.

time to see where other people came from and also look at the live video image from the networked cameras above. Snibbe's aim was to dramatise the interconnectedness of visitors to the space, giving them a sense of the accumulated presence of people over time. Unlike surveillance systems being installed in public places, which record that reality but do not show it, this one does not collect data for security purposes. The custom tracking software integrates the cameras' disparate views into a single composite data stream by correcting any lens distortion, and then transforming each image into a common coordinate system.

Snibbe feels the work makes a benevolent point about surveillance. 'It provides a visceral understanding of surveillance systems' capabilities and a sensual, visual representation of information that is normally only accessible as dry statistics.' He also explains that it 'lets you move through time as it creates time lapses like waves, giving a sense of people moving as a natural force.'[14] This exemplifies his use of technology as a medium, used to reveal the way in which it is used in the divergent mechanisms employed in experimental film and surveillance, which Snibbe harnesses to explore a social agenda.

Encounter, a challenging work about homelessness for NeoCon, an interior design trade fair in Los Angeles, gave a political edge to the moment of visitors' 'interference' with shadows as they walked back and forth in front of a wall. Entering an opulent setting with tiled walls and gold cushions, they saw ahead of them silhouettes of homeless people in downtown LA made from film footage of actual people on the streets. Inevitably they found their own shadows mingling among them, and when theirs touched those of the street people, the homeless disappeared, just as easily as their plight slips from the minds of the privileged.

Other works are overtly play mechanisms that generate a lot of excitement, often in contexts that offer few alternative facilities of this kind. The user-friendliness visitors commented on at Snibbe's 2006 exhibition at the ICA, London – which extended into the bar area with an overhead screen projecting people's shadows – is an asset when audiences are less culturally aware of media art or not in the mood for a formal artwork in the first place. Shadow Mosaic: Four by Five, a permanent installation, is positioned on the wall in a public area of the California headquarters of Yahoo! in between the company's staff café and its games room. It records people's

Encounter, 2006
The work was made in collaboration with Gensler Architects and uses a computer, projector, video camera, video capture card and retroreflective screen. In a plush setting with gold cushions and tile walls, Snibbe's photographs of the homeless on the streets of downtown LA strike a dramatic note. On the far end wall are shadow images of these sad figures. When people intersect with them, the shadows disappear.

Shadow Mosaic: Four by Five, 2006
Commissioned by Yahoo!, this installation sits in a communal area of the company's premises, between the staff café and games room, recording the moving shadows of people who walk by. It plays them back continually as small movies made directly by each person's body.

shadows as they pass by a camera installed there. As soon as they leave, everything they did plays back repeatedly in the form of anonymous silhouettes in one of 20 small rectangles. While fast trajectories past the camera are the norm, some workers come in their breaks to let down their hair and perform along with their work mates.

Perhaps fortunately for them, after a few minutes everything that has been recorded disappears as new people's movements build up on the screen. The intervention of Snibbe's works into busy everyday environments puts pressure on the simple trickery of the interface to support waves of short-term film entertainment created not by directorial intervention, but by people's movements. As his body of work proliferates, Snibbe is increasingly aware of the artistic challenge to offer a clarity of cause-and-effect in such a context, but also sufficient conceptual depth to each piece in order to induce the visitor's engagement with the work, without resorting to excessive repetition.

Like other media such as video, television or photography, which each create their own type of space, Snibbe's interactive works bring into being a mode of experience that is particular to each work. The process of experience is still the psychological and physical inhabitation that Marshall McLuhan recognised media induced.[15] What is being privileged in the process is also still 'a kind of mental involvement in process that makes the content of the item seem quite secondary'. Instead of inviting the audience to construct their own messages and challenge the authority of official media constructions, by means of new visual metaphors, as in the work of artists such as Nam June Paik, Snibbe's work is 'relational',[16] initiating encounters between onlookers. It also treats customised digital interfaces as a viable artistic element, a

medium with a versatility similar to light, which conceptual artists have long since co-opted, but also different from it.

The clear narrative cues to perform in this 'participation art' may overlook the fact that some may do so more willingly than others. Nevertheless, the installations are a fresh mix of sophisticated techniques, an accessible and performance-orientated lyricism rooted in an informed awareness of 20th-century avant-garde cinema and art. Their traces of presence may be short-lived, and the screen may need to be joined by another kind of arena if this body of work continues to expand, but what is revealed in the process – as reflections on the real – is the message. ⚙

Notes
1 Interview with the author, London, 14 May 2006.
2 Ibid.
3 Author of *Digital Art*, Thames & Hudson (London), 2003.
4 Interview with the author, London, 14 May 2006.
5 Telephone interview with the author, 15 October 2006.
6 Ibid.
7 Malcolm McCullough, *Digital Ground: Architecture, Pervasive Computing and Environmental Knowing*, MIT Press (Cambridge, MA), 2005
8 Telephone interview with the author, 15 October 2006.
9 Quote from Snibbe's written statement, 15 July 2006.
10 Interview with the author, London, 14 May 2006.
11 Telephone interview with the author, 20 November 2006.
12 Sarah Boxer, 'Art that puts you in the picture, like it or not', *New York Times*, 27 April 2005.
13 Roberta Carasso, 'Shedding a light on art', *Irvine World News*, 20 November 2003.
14 Telephone interview with the author, 15 October 2006.
15 Marshall McLuhan, *Understanding Media*, Sphere Books (Chicago, IL), 1967.
16 As defined by Nicolas Bourriaud in his book *Relational Aesthetics*, Les Presses du Réel (Dijon), 1998 (English edition, 2002).

Illuminating Embodiment
Rafael Lozano-Hemmer's Relational Architectures

Art and architecture have a strong tradition of humanism in which man and the human body are the centre and measure of all things. **Maria Fernández** describes the work of artist Rafael Lozano-Hemmer whose work transgresses and challenges these preconceptions through performance, seeking to expose the body and society's receptivity to instability, fluctuation and re-imagining.

The work of the Mexican-Canadian artist Rafael Lozano-Hemmer is concerned with creating virtual openings in architecture, the city, the body and technology. Architecture and bodies are intrinsically connected. Architecture is built for and experienced by bodies, and in the narratives of European classical architecture, architectural theorists from Vitruvius to Rudolf Wittkower have reiterated for centuries that the two are inseparably linked.[1]

Lozano-Hemmer's work challenges the supposition that buildings control bodies. This current of thought is exemplified by Jeremy Bentham's notion of the panopticon (1787) and is also evident in utopian projections of social engineering through Modern architectural design.[2] Today, powerful machine vision systems and tracking technologies supplement the regulating power of architecture. Surveillance systems are now embedded in all realms of our daily life, private and public, from door security systems to stores, banks, highways and city streets. Technologies are also playing an increasing role in the alteration and regulation of bodies in a variety of ways, from implants and telesurgery to identification by retinal scan.

Historically, societies and cities have been metaphorically conceived as bodies. For example, in his book *Policraticus* (c. 1160), Bishop John of Salisbury described the commonwealth, or society, as a body. This concept gained impetus during the Enlightenment and survived throughout the 20th century in disciplines such as sociobiology.[3] Multiple architectural theorists and practitioners including Vitruvius, Francesco di Giorgio (1439–1502) and Le Corbusier similarly theorised cities as bodies,[4] thus bodies, buildings, cities and technologies are conceptually and functionally interconnected. In his relational architectures, Lozano-Hemmer exposes the instability of these entities/concepts. Instability implies each entity's receptivity to alteration. In fact, Lozano-Hemmer declares that he is 'interested in the body as a performance, a process of becoming, of change, and less interested in physiognomy, anatomy, forensics and physical ergonomics'.[5]

Various thinkers from the 3rd Earl of Shaftesbury in 18th-century Britain to Mikhail Bakhtin in 20th-century Russia described bodies as being in the process of becoming monstrous and threatening to the social order.[6] Like Judith Butler's 'performative subversions', which are acts that can undo or at least unsettle the normative inscriptions of gender upon bodies, Lozano-Hemmer invites the spectator performatively to imagine and construct alternative bodies – physical, architectural and urban. He comments: 'I have a cursory interest in architecture when it involves utilitarian issues or permanence, symbolism or style. But if architecture is understood more widely as comprising the architecture of social relations, of surveillance, of fleeting exceptions, then count me in.[7]

In contrast to art in traditional media that privileges visuality, interactive art engages the user's body to varying degrees in the instantiation (not necessarily the creation) of the work. In Lozano-Hemmer's relational architectures the user's body activates hyperlinks to visual and auditory events predetermined by the artist. The participant's physical involvement with the work asserts his or her agency and opens the potential for a technologically compatible form of biopolitics. The artist's use of a variety of technologies including sophisticated robotically controlled projectors, widely accessible computer systems, mobile phones and radios as well as custom-made software suggests that technology can be deployed creatively at all levels.

In 1994, Lozano-Hemmer coined the term 'relational architecture' as the technological actualisation of buildings and the urban environment with alien memory. He aimed to transform the dominant narratives of a specific building or urban setting by superimposing audiovisual elements to affect it, effect it and recontextualise it.[8] He later explained that his relational architectures were 'anti-monuments for public dissimulation' (2002).[9] Such definitions simultaneously erode understandings of architecture as solid and stable, and of virtuality as independent from lived existence.

Traditionally, scholars have read buildings and monuments as material evidence for history. For the architectural historian Sir Nikolaus Pevsner, for example, buildings embodied the spirit of an age.[10] In the early 1990s many artists and theorists discussed virtuality as a digitally facilitated, purely cerebral state independent of the vicissitudes of the body. In William Gibson's novels, humans live partially in a digital domain.[11] And in his book *Mind Children* American roboticist Hans Moravec speculates that in the future people will no longer need bodies as human consciousness will be fully transferred to digital realms.[12] In recent theorisations by Elizabeth Grosz and Brian Massumi, the virtual, rather than belonging to a specific medium, is the realm of possibility, inseparable from embodiment.[13]

Distrustful of the view that all life can be reduced to simulation, Lozano-Hemmer builds anti-monuments for dis-simulation. From 1997 to 2006 he built 10 works of relational architecture beginning with Displaced Emperors and ending with under scan. The artist sometimes recognises his installation The Trace, Remote Insinuated Presence, presented at the international art fair ARCO in Spain in 1995, as his first example of relational architecture, although he did not entitle it as such.

In Displaced Emperors, Relational Architecture 2, presented at Ars Electronica in 1997, the Habsburg castle in Linz became both figure and ground for seemingly alien historical encounters. The piece provided links between two apparently unrelated historical events that connect Mexico and Austria:

The Trace, Remote Insinuated Presence, Madrid, Spain, 1995
Two participants in different locations share the same telematic space. In each location light beams and graphics on the ceiling of the room indicate the position of the remote participant.

the Mexican empire of Maximilian of Habsburg (1864–67) and a feather headdress believed to have belonged to the Aztec ruler Montezuma II, and currently part of the collection of the ethnological museum in Vienna.[14] A participant standing in a small plaza in front of one of the castle gates interacted with the building by pointing at it with his or her hand, and data from two wireless 3-D trackers placed on one arm and hand of the participant indicated the direction of his or her arm movement in real time.[15] An animated projection of a human hand appeared wherever the individual carrying the tracker pointed. The images were projected on the building using robotic motion-controlled projectors. When the participant moved his or her arm, the projected hand also moved. As the virtual hand 'caressed' the facade of the building, it wiped away the exterior wall revealing interior rooms matched to the exterior so as to appear to be inside the Linz castle.

The virtual hand also activated music sequences, which seemed to emanate from the rooms in view. The superimposed images were in fact interiors at Chapultepec castle, the main residence of Maximilian and his wife Carlota during the Habsburg rule in Mexico. In addition, for 10 schillings, other participants could interrupt the interaction of the person with the tracker by pressing the Montezuma button located in a makeshift souvenir shop in front of the castle. Pressing the button elicited an enormous image of Montezuma's headdress accompanied by a Mexican music track.

A searchlight with the cultural property symbol, a sign displayed in buildings and monuments recognised as cultural property by the international treaty of The Hague, followed the participant who had the tracker.

Through these witty layerings the work encourages the viewer to explore the interdependence of European and Mexican history, even at the level of a shared cultural heritage. Despite repeated attempts by the Mexican government to have Montezuma's headdress returned to Mexico, the object remains in Austria as part of the country's cultural treasures. Similarly, in Mexico the Habsburg's castle, transformed into a museum, is considered a national monument. In Displaced Emperors, even the body of the participant becomes vulnerable to appropriation as it is tracked by the cultural property symbol.

In the opinion of philosopher Elizabeth Grosz, the outside is 'the place that one can never occupy, for it is always other, different at a distance from where one is'. In her view, the outside of architecture may be technologies, bodies, fantasies, politics and economics that it plays on but does not direct or control.[16] Displaced Emperors literally and figuratively brings in elements from the outside – projections, texts, music and participants – that transform the building. These elements provide pleasurable sensual experiences for the participants and create surprising associations between distant geographical and historical settings, stimulating the user to meditate on other buildings, other histories, and other ways of cultural commemoration.

Modern cities are predicated on the erosion of public space and the proliferation of spectacular media. Baron Haussmann's modernisation of Paris in the 19th century and the later city plans of Le Corbusier and CIAM favoured commerce and production over socially oriented activities. In the mid-20th century in North American cities, commercial spaces such as malls gradually replaced traditional public squares, contributing to the disappearance of public space. The dissemination of these models throughout the globe transformed the world's cities to greater or lesser extents.

As Gilles Deleuze recognised, and Paul Virilio tirelessly stresses, from the Second World War industrialised societies shifted from disciplinary societies where control was exercised in determinate spaces, to societies of control where power is invisible and control is both technologically facilitated and predicated on the operations of markets.[17] In these societies surveillance and regulation of all space, especially commercial space, is paramount. Are We There Yet? a nomadic performance by the American tactical art collective Critical Art Ensemble presented throughout Florida in 1992 poignantly illustrated this state of affairs. A performer played with toy cars in non-obstructive locations at selected shopping malls and public places such as freeway rest stops. Invariably, the police suppressed the activity.

In recent years, architecture in many cities across the globe appears dematerialised by the influx of large screens within central urban environments. Building facades exhibit constantly changing imagery producing the impression of instability. Like earlier light and neon signs, one of the major purposes of city screens is advertisement. Occasionally screens are used for live transmission of sports and cultural events, which as the BBC's Big Screen in Birmingham demonstrates creates a collective experience for a heterogeneous public. Although architects, artists and hackers have devised creative solutions for interactive building facades, the selection of visual content is tightly regulated and large screens are still too pricey for most individual artists.

In his work Body Movies: Relational Architecture 6 (2001), Lozano-Hemmer challenged this passive spectatorship of the mediated city with projection. Although the use of projections is not new, what set this work apart from previous interventions by other artists was not only the technology employed, but also ensuing forms of public interaction. The artist partially anticipated the effects of Body Movies because of audience responses to his previous work, Re:Positioning Fear, Relational Architecture 3 presented at the Film and Architektur Biennale in Graz, Austria, in 1997. Here Lozano-Hemmer projected the participants' shadows on the exterior walls of the Landeszeughaus, originally one of Europe's largest military arsenals, to metaphorically connote fear. To his surprise, rather than being intimidated, participants often played with their shadows. This unexpected behaviour encouraged the artist to further explore shadows as expressive elements.

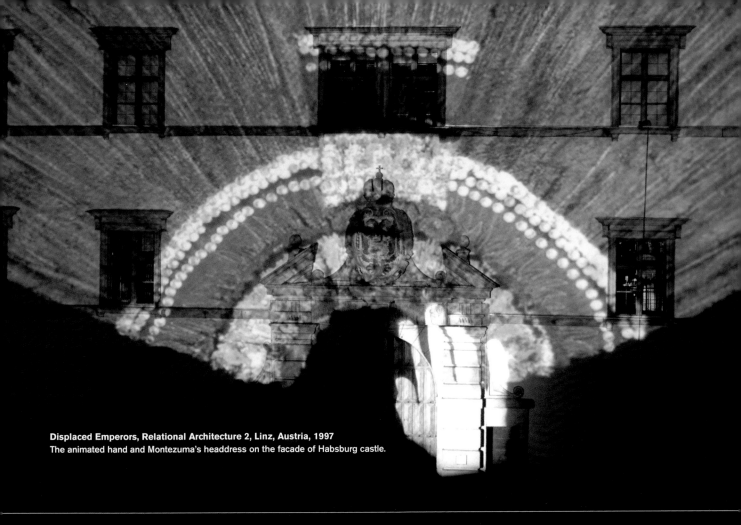

Displaced Emperors, Relational Architecture 2, Linz, Austria, 1997
The animated hand and Montezuma's headdress on the facade of Habsburg castle.

The projected hand moved across the facade of the Habsburg castle in Linz
revealing interior spaces at the Habsburg castle in Mexico.

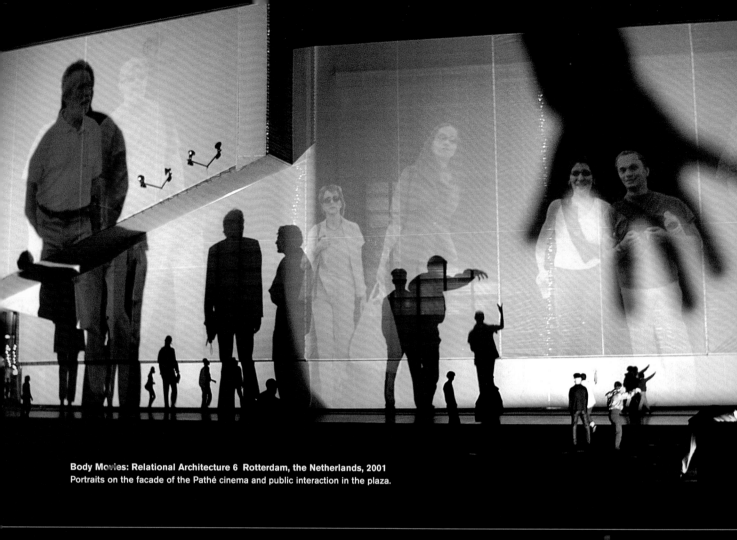

Body Movies: Relational Architecture 6 Rotterdam, the Netherlands, 2001
Portraits on the facade of the Pathé cinema and public interaction in the plaza.

Shadows of participants and passer-by on the cinema facade.

Re:Positioning Fear, Relational Architecture 3, Graz, Austria, 1997
The shadow of the participant is amplified on the facade of the
Landeszeughaus.

In Body Movies, a thousand portraits taken in the streets of
Montreal, Rotterdam and Mexico City were projected on the
facade of the Pathé cinema in Rotterdam where the work was
first presented. Three networked computers controlled the
installation: a camera server, video tracker and a robotic
controller cued by MIDI signals. The portraits were muted by
two xenon light sources located at ground level. Passers-by
saw their shadows projected on the facade. The portraits only
became visible inside a shadow between 2 and 25 metres (6
and 82 feet) high, depending on how far people were from the
light sources. Participants could match or embody a portrait
by walking around the square to adjust the size of their
silhouette. When shadows matched all the portraits a
computer selected a new set. A video projection on the square
displayed the tracking interface.

Most people's attention focused less on the portraits than
on their shadows. Participants with large shadows could
overpower, threaten or play with small shadows; those with
small shadows could interact with each other, challenge or
'tickle' the larger silhouettes. Spontaneous skits were
generated among strangers and a carnivalesque atmosphere
reigned in the plaza for the duration of the piece. The work
demonstrated that even societies of control are capable of
playful, if ephemeral, engagements.

As Lozano-Hemmer rightfully cautions, there is no
guarantee that a work will function in the same way
everywhere. The artist explains that when Body Movies was
exhibited in Lisbon, 'I thought of the stereotypical "Latino"
who loves to be out in the streets, partying and hugging
affectionately so I expected a lot of this type of interaction
with the piece. However what we saw was people trying their
best not to overlap with other people's shadows. In contrast,
when we presented the piece in England, where I had thought
we would see considerable modesty and moderation, people
got drunk, took off their clothes and acted out a variety of
orgiastic scenes.'[18] In Rotterdam, neighbourhood residents
regarded the piece as a wonderful revitalisation of the plaza
as it allowed people who did not know each other to meet
and, better yet, to play with each other, 'like children'.[19]

Cultural theorists Elizabeth Grosz and Brian Massumi
conceptualise the body as a two-dimensional topological
figure, a membrane open to the outside.[20] In Massumi's
opinion this means that we do not live in Euclidean space, but
in between dimensions.[21] Most people, however, still think of
their bodies as stable and independent entities. Lozano-
Hemmer's work perversely 'opens' the body of the participant
to beings and events outside of it using the same logic of
technologically facilitated relationality as in his relational
architecture pieces. The body's shadow becomes the medium
of contagion. In Lozano-Hemmer's view, the shadow functions
as a disembodied body part, inseparable from the body but
not of it.[22] In Body Movies, the participant could choose to
embody the portrait of a stranger. Because of the two-
dimensionality and immobility of the portraits, interaction
with them was limited.

Body Movies: Relational Architecture 6, Hong Kong, China, 2006
Projections and public interaction on the facade of the Hong Kong
Museum of Art.

under scan, Relational Architecture 11, Nottingham, UK, 2006
A pedestrian elicits a video portrait with his shadow.

under scan, Relational Architecture 11, Leicester, UK, 2006
The work was achieved with the assistance of a large group of contributors including ArtReach production and Stage Right staging.

By contrast, in under scan, Relational Architecture 11 (2005–06), commissioned by the East Midlands Development Agency in the UK, a set of portraits became the principal focus for interaction. Thousands of 'video portraits' taken in Derby, Leicester, Lincoln, Northampton and Nottingham, of ordinary people chosen at random in the street, were projected on to the ground of the main squares and pedestrian thoroughfares of these cities with the permission of the individuals involved.

A tracking system predicted the future position of a pedestrian according to his or her trajectory. As in Body Movies, the portraits were washed out by a powerful light projection. As people walked, their projected shadows revealed the video portraits. This time, the individual inside the shadow slowly turned to look at the spectator and then engaged in various behaviours. Some 'portraits' slept, others danced, mimicked or threatened the viewers. The interaction ended when the shadow moved away from the portrait. Every seven minutes, the tracking mechanism of the piece was revealed by a projection of the surveillance matrix on the floor. Here the shadow, and by implication the body, of the participant hosts another body – the body of a stranger. This goes beyond the realm of hospitality: it is an invasion of the self. The work encourages the participant to imagine what it might be like to be that other. Yet the guest eventually leaves and the individual's shadow returns to its familiar shape. Unaccustomed to such an intimate

interaction with strangers, many participants reported having preferred watching the light matrix to interacting with the portraits.[23] As is the case with all of Lozano-Hemmer's works, this piece was achieved with a large group of collaborators and assistants.

In the 1960s sociologist Henri Lefevre argued against previous understandings of space as either a mathematical or a linguistic concept. For him, social activities constructed and gave meaning to space.[24] Lefevre's teachings were fundamental for the Situationists and for later tactical performances by artists' collectives such as Critical Art Ensemble, RTMARK and the Institute for Applied Autonomy. Both before and since Lefevre's work became known, numerous writers and artists have attributed to specific technologies the generation of particular spaces of interaction, for example radiophonic and digital spaces. Brian Massumi currently argues that the body in movement produces space. Consequently, space is coeval with, not anterior to, the body.[25] Although these theorisations differ in focus and method, all conceptualise space as active and not as an inert receptacle for social activity. Lozano-Hemmer's work is informed by histories of art, science, technology and diverse philosophical currents. Because of its conceptual complexity it cannot be described as an illustration of any specific school or theory, yet consistently it reveals 'the fullness of space' in relation to both the body and technology.

under scan, Relational Architecture 11, Lincoln, UK, 2005
General view.

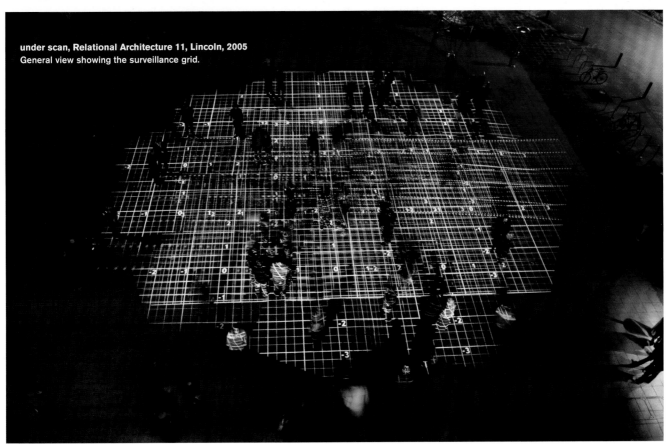

under scan, Relational Architecture 11, Lincoln, 2005
General view showing the surveillance grid.

Frequency and Volume, Relational Architecture 9, Laboratorio de Arte Alameda, Mexico City, 2003
By positioning his shadow on the wall of the exhibition space, a participant makes communications from a police radio audible to the public in the gallery.

participation of the viewer in order to manifest and behave, but the artist's design is what allows him or her to discern the complex cultural signification of these phenomena. The richness of this particular piece of Lozano-Hemmer's is not just that radio frequencies become audible, but that their perception by participants and viewers reveals to them the charged contestation of our aural environments. It makes it clear that radio signals may be captured and surveyed not only by the user, but also by other parties, and one interpretation that can be made of the work is that it suggests our voluntary or involuntary coexistence with alien presences.

Most of the work Lozano-Hemmer has produced and installed in a number of global locations from Mexico City to Sydney during his 15 years as a practising artist employs tracking technologies. Consistently he reveals the works' surveillance mechanisms either by using plasma screens that display the tracking matrix with an overlay of data showing the position of the users in the installation space (Body Movies), or by projecting the surveillance matrix on the floor (under scan). The works watch the viewer and simultaneously reveal their technological apparatus of sight. These behaviours stimulate meditations and interventions from the user that could potentially transcend the specific contexts of the artwork.

By admitting elements extraneous to their own physical constitution Lozano-Hemmer's relational architectures render architecture, the city, the body, space and technology vulnerable to the outside. The performativity of the participant as well as of the technology ensures that both play a part in their own remaking. The users of his pieces become more aware of their surroundings, of their own physicality, affective complexity and perhaps momentarily glimpse at their possible complicities with the machines. △D

This interpretation is exemplified by Frequency and Volume, first exhibited at the Laboratorio de Arte Alameda in Mexico City in 2003. Participants scan the radio spectrum of the city with their bodies, and the shadows of the participants are projected on a large interior wall. The location of each shadow, as detected by a video tracking system, specifies a frequency (between 150 kHz to 1.5 GHz) on one of several radio wavebands. A computer system coordinates the tuning of radio receivers for various bands, including air-traffic control, shortwave radio, mobile phones, police, taxi dispatch and personal pagers, while the size of the shadow determines the volume of the specific channel. The result is an unpredictable sound environment controlled by the visitor's movements.

Functioning metaphorically as a moving antenna, the visitor's body elicits normally imperceptible phenomena from its surrounding space. Cultural theorist Mark Hansen maintains that all digital art engages the body of the participant to make digitally encoded information sensually apprehensible.[26] Interactive digital art requires the bodily

Radios and computer system showing the position of participants.

under scan, Relational Architecture 11, Leicester, 2006
Projection of the surveillance matrix.

Notes

1. See George Dodds and Robert Tavernor (eds), *Body and Building: Essays on the Changing Relation of Body and Architecture*, MIT Press (Cambridge, MA), 2002.

2. Miran Bozovic (ed), *The Panopticum Writings*, Verso (London), 1995.

3. Richard Sennett, *Flesh and Stone: The Body in Western Civilization*, Norton (New York), 1996, pp 23–4 and 255–70. Joseph Rykwert, *The Dancing Column: On Order in Architecture*, MIT Press (Cambridge, MA), 1996, p 38.

4. Rykwert, op cit, pp 63–5; Sennett, op cit, p 108; David Pinder, *Visions of the City: Utopianism, Power and Politics in Twentieth-Century Urbanism*, Routledge (New York), 2005, pp 100–06.

5. Rafael Lozano-Hemmer and David Hill (eds), *under scan: Rafael Lozano-Hemmer*, draft of forthcoming publication, courtesy of the artist, p 34.

6. Anthony Ashley Cooper, 3rd Earl of Shaftebury, *Characteristics of Men, Manners, Opinions, Times*, J Purser (London), 1732. 3 vols II, ii 136. Mikhail Bakhtin, *Rabelais and His World*, trans Helene Iswolsky, MIT Press (Cambridge, MA), 1968, pp 316–18.

7. Lozano-Hemmer and Hill, op cit, p 35. Judith Butler, *Gender Trouble: Feminism and the Subversion of Identity*, Routledge (New York), 1989, pp 128ff.

8. Rafael Lozano-Hemmer, 'Relational Architecture, General Concept' *Nettime*, 30 January 1998. At that time, *Nettime* was a closed, moderated electronic mailing list. Archives are now at www.nettime.org.

9. *Rafael Lozano-Hemmer 'Subsculptures': A conversation between José Luis Barrios and Rafael Lozano-Hemmer*, catalogue of the exhibition 'Subsculptures', Galerie Guy Bärtschi, Geneva, 5 November–14 January 2006, pp 15, 18.

10. See Sir Nikolaus Pevsner, *An Outline of European Architecture*, Charles Scribner's Sons (New York), 1948, and *Pioneers of Modern Design*, Penguin (New York), 1960.

11. William Gibson, *Neuromancer*, Ace Science Fiction Books (New York), 1984, and *Count Zero*, Grafton (London), 1987.

12. Hans Moravec, *Mind Children: The Future of Robot and Human Intelligence*, Harvard University Press (Cambridge, MA), 1988.

13. Elizabeth A Grosz, *Architecture from the Outside: Essays on Virtual and Real Space*, MIT Press (Cambridge, MA), 2001, p 12; Brian Massumi, *Parables for the Virtual: Movement, Affect, Sensation*, Duke University Press (Durham, NC), 2002, p 30.

14. Although there is no evidence that this headdress belonged to Montezuma, it has special significance for Mexicans as a pre-Hispanic symbol of political and religious power.

15. The tracker (Gesture and Media System GAMS) and most of the software used in this piece were created and developed by Will Bauer and Rafael Lozano-Hemmer.

16. Grosz, op cit, p xiv.

17. Gilles Deleuze, 'Postscript on the Societies of Control', *October*, 59, Winter 1992, pp 3–7.

18. Lozano-Hemmer, *Subsculptures*, p 16.

19. Amsterdam resident, *Body Movies: Relational Architecture 6*, videotape produced by Rafael Lozano-Hemmer 2001, courtesy of the artist.

20. Elizabeth Grosz, *Volatile Bodies: Toward a Corporeal Feminism*, Allen & Unwin (St Leonards, Australia), 1994, pp 15–19, 23. Massumi, op cit, p 202.

21. Massumi, op cit, pp 178, 180.

22. Rafael Lozano-Hemmer, *Re:Positioning Fear, Relational Architecture 3* (http://rhizome.org/artbase/2398/fear/).

23. Lozano-Hemmer and Hill, op cit, p. 31.

24. Henri Lefevre, *The Production of Space*, trans Donald Nicholson-Smith, Blackwell Publishers (Oxford, UK), 1991.

25. Massumi, op cit, pp 178, 180.

26. Mark Hansen, *New Philosophy for New Media*, MIT Press (Cambridge, MA), 2004, pp 12, 52, 60.

I am a Camera: Electroland

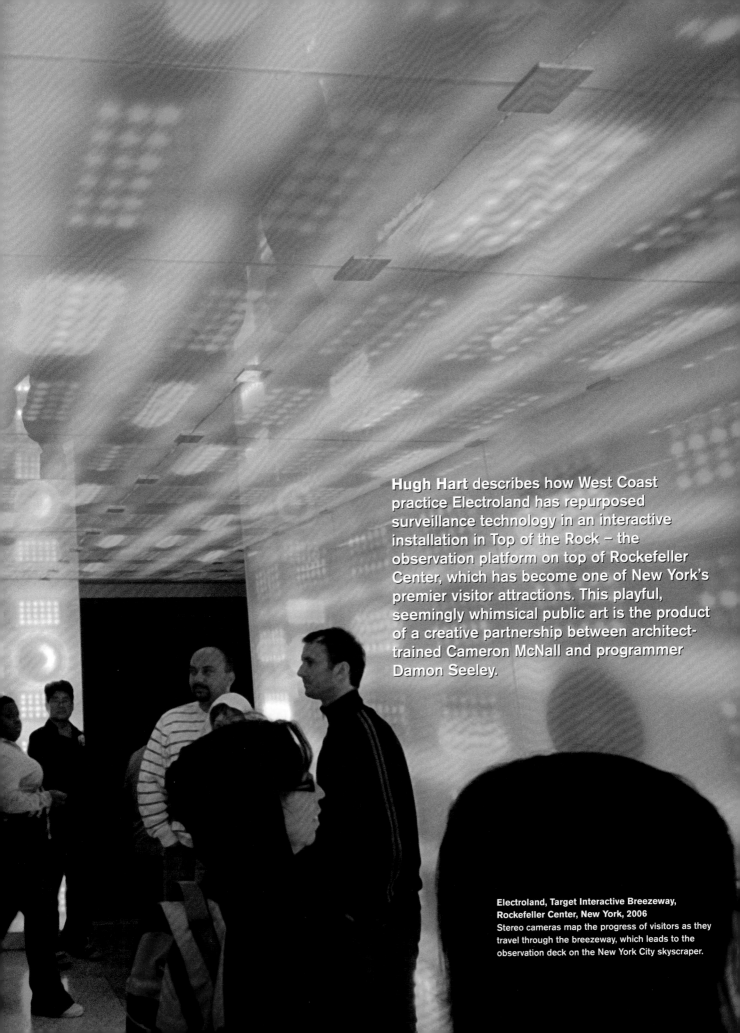

Hugh Hart describes how West Coast practice Electroland has repurposed surveillance technology in an interactive installation in Top of the Rock – the observation platform on top of Rockefeller Center, which has become one of New York's premier visitor attractions. This playful, seemingly whimsical public art is the product of a creative partnership between architect-trained Cameron McNall and programmer Damon Seeley.

Electroland, Target Interactive Breezeway, Rockefeller Center, New York, 2006
Stereo cameras map the progress of visitors as they travel through the breezeway, which leads to the observation deck on the New York City skyscraper.

Electroland, Target Interactive Breezeway, Rockefeller Center, New York, 2006
LED lights programmed to track visitors' movements line Electroland's breezeway atop Rockefeller Center in Manhattan.
The breezeway leads to an observation deck that reopened in autumn 2005 as Manhattan's second-highest observatory,
renovated for $75 million under the direction of designer/architect Michael Gabellini of Gabellini Associates.

From their studio in a quiet, bungalow-lined neighbourhood in Los Angeles, Cameron McNall and Damon Seeley can keep a close eye on events unfolding 4,200 kilometres (2,600 miles) to the east. On a recent afternoon, the soft-spoken partners of Electroland logged on to one of the two matching computers anchoring their spartan office to take a look at visitors traipsing through the Target Interactive Breezeway at Rockefeller Center in New York City.

The 69th-floor breezeway is housed in the tallest building in the multistructure complex. It leads to an observation deck that offers 360-degree views of the city rivalling those of the Empire State Building. Visitors arrive at the breezeway after taking an elevator to the 68th floor followed by an escalator to the 69th floor where observation decks, separated by a 'slice' of the building, have been built on the north and south sides. The Breezeway is one of two places where guests can walk through the building to get from one deck to the other.

On their way to the roof-top eyrie, tourists move along the passageway that Electroland has outfitted with a 10-centimetre (4-inch) layer of intelligent skin. Translucent white glass containing 9,000 white LEDs provides an ambient white glow while more than 18,000 addressable RGB-capable LEDs produce a range of patterns and immersive light effects.

But this is no random light show. The lights, prompted by data feeds from four stereo cameras, follow each individual visitor via a 'persistence tracking' program. McNall explains: 'Most systems only see warm bodies and can't distinguish between one individual and the next. With our 3-D Vision System we are able to assign a personality to each person that enters. The system can separately track and persist with 30 different behaviours, so we know when one person has been there a long time and can modify [the system's] behaviours to reward their presence.'

Curious about public reaction to their interactive handiwork, Seeley and McNall monitored a real-time video feed depicting the tourists as they strolled through the skyway. Some seem oblivious to the rectangles of coloured lights hovering above them on the ceiling. Others appear bemused once they catch on to the fact that their movements are being shadowed by the motion-sensitive smart lights. 'The challenge in most of our work,' McNall says, 'is that there's no sign that says, "You are now entering the art zone. Do this or do that." We insist on a gadget-free and instruction manual-free interface.'

While a measure of benign surveillance figures in most Electroland projects, the designers are more interested,

Tourists enjoy a view of the ceiling at Electroland's breezeway installation in Manhattan.

Partygoers enjoy the ambience at Electroland's Target Interactive Breezeway.

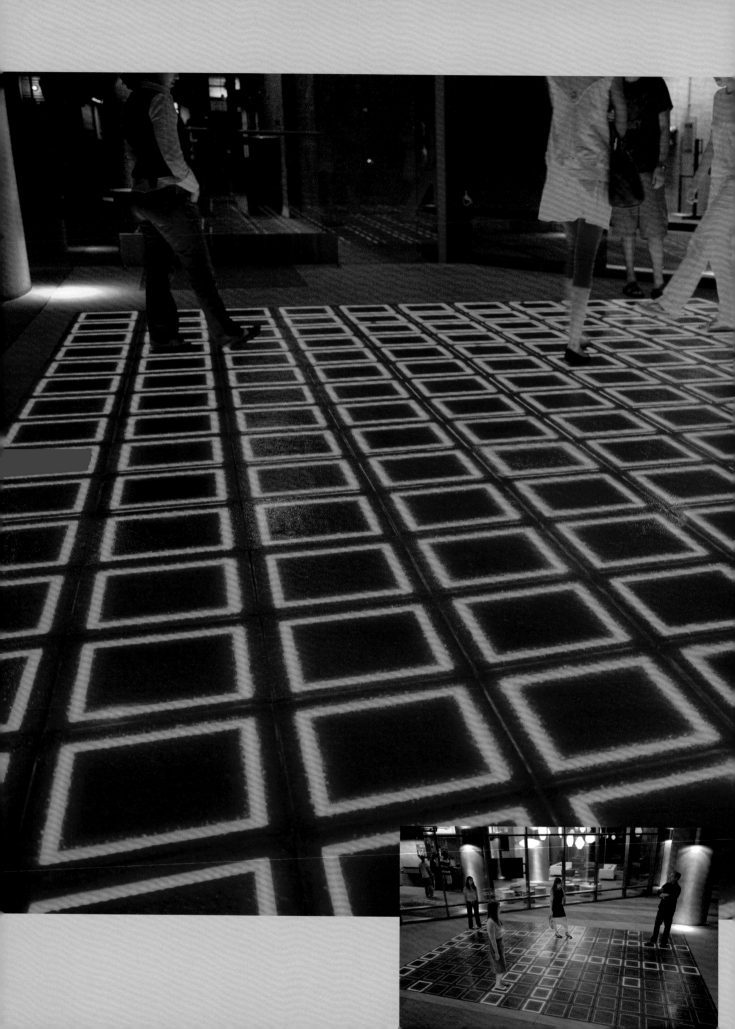

Electroland, EnterActive Carpet, Met Lofts, Los Angeles, California, 2006
The Enteractive Carpet installation at Met Lofts at its Flower Street location.

according to McNall, in the 'cybernetic notion of a neural awareness that surrounds everything. Our mantra is making manifest the vast, invisible web of electronic activity. We explore fun ways to make these things visible, and look at how this pervasiveness can change people's relationships to buildings and spaces.' The tools used to effect those goals often draw from unexpected sources, according to Seeley, who handles most of Electroland's programming tasks: 'One of my primary activities has been to maintain a very broad understanding of hundreds of technologies and industries across a variety of fields, and re-purpose those technologies in ways they were never intended to be used.'

The tracking technology Electroland used at Rockefeller Center originated in a research lab funded by industrialist-types who wanted to make sure their employees do not get run over by robots. As Seeley puts it: 'When we look at the possibilities of a technology like that, we see an almost unlimited opportunity for turning the tracking of people into a wonderful experience.'

Recent and upcoming Electroland projects offer ingenious variations on the team's smart environment theme. At the Met Lofts apartment building, designed by Johnson Fain Partners and located near Los Angeles' burgeoning downtown district, McNall and Seeley embedded entrance tiles with a grid of weight-sensitive sensors and red LED lights that pulse underfoot as residents and their guests cross from the sidewalk towards the lobby. The idea is to engage a 'distracted audience', McNall says. 'We're trying to create these gentle overlays of experience and give them some depth in a way that should be environmental and free-flowing and easy to learn.'

Additionally, the designers dramatise the intersection of public and private space at Met Lofts by amplifying the pedestrian traffic in the lobby to a grand scale: red squares flicker across a six-storey grid of LED panels melded on to the building's facade, mimicking the patterns on the ground floor. A pole-mounted video camera facing Met Lofts from across the street transmits the illuminated building exterior back to a plasma screen in the lobby, where visitors can see the impact of their footwork on commuters sailing by on the nearby 110 Freeway. 'We find that spectacle is fun,' McNall adds.

NoHo Commons, a mixed-use residential commercial complex being built in North Hollywood, aims to enliven the neighbourhood via Electroland's motion-sensitive signage. On the building's facade, an electronic vitrine facing the street will display 'wipes' of alphanumeric messages activated by passing cars. Electroland's 2008 Indianapolis Airport pedway project will literally connect the dots between travellers, who have been assigned overhead discs of light as they travel to and from the parking lot. LUMEN, the interactive stairway installation housed at Cooper-Hewitt, National Design Museum in New York, greets each visitor with a wash of polyphonic sound and a travelling troupe of playfully percolating light patterns.

Featured in the National Design Triennial 'Design Life Now' exhibition (running to 29 July 2007), LUMEN wraps the gallery's 6-metre (20-foot) wide staircase in a translucent Plexiglass barrier concealing seven Alpine speakers and 65 programmable light fixtures. McNall notes: 'When you arrive at the stairs, six lights shoot ahead of you to mark your entrance.' Alert patrons may notice three hot spots that glow with extra intensity. 'If you stand in front of them for a few seconds, you trigger much larger patterns,' McNall says. Additionally, guests are in for a surprise should they inadvertently step on an undisclosed 'Easter egg'. 'There's a hidden spot on the stairs. There's no warning whatsoever, but if you find it you trigger an overwhelming event for the whole thing.'

For 'Design Life Now' curator Ellen Lupton, 'the beauty of the piece is that it's not entirely predictable. There's some ambiguity as to whether the bulbs are responding to the person or to each other, so it's not totally obvious to the visitor what the rules are.' However, she says, 'there is a general motion up the stairs. LUMEN encourages a kind of behaviour that is quite effective for us in the museum because we've always had trouble getting people to go upstairs.'

In Lupton's view, Electroland consistently explores architecture's relationship to social interaction by designing

Electroland's 'NoHo' scale study demonstrates interaction between a pedestrian and the cryptic letterform vitrine currently being built in North Hollywood.

Electroland, LUMEN, Cooper-Hewitt, National
Design Museum, New York, 2006
Visitors prompt light patterns from Electroland's
LUMEN installation as they round the stairs.

Plexiglass-wrapped 'smart lights' track guests' movements.

spaces 'that overtly respond to people. We constantly find ourselves in environments that track and record (our activity). In Electroland's environments, it becomes obvious that the building is watching, and at the same time it invites play and enjoyment.'

Prior to co-founding Electroland, McNall earned a Master of Architecture at Harvard Graduate School of Design, devised navigable 3-D space for a CD-ROM company, and began teaching in 1991 at UCLA's Design/Media Arts Department. There he met Seeley, who was working on a BA in Design/Media Arts. In the 1990s, Seeley programmed artificial intelligence projects shown at Los Angeles' Museum of Contemporary Art, and in Germany, Italy and Austria.

Electroland's public art commissions have enabled Seeley to expand his digital canvas. He recalls: 'I was frustrated with

seeing media arts trapped, in a sense, in these university research labs where a lot of cutting-edge technology work was being done. What excited me was figuring out how interaction design could be used to enliven these much broader public spaces with a sense of whimsy and play.'

Citing mid-century PoP art as a key influence in their ongoing effort to celebrate 'urban spectacle', McNall traces Electroland's conceptual roots to ideas pioneered by the Archigram group in the UK and other forward-thinking architects from the 1960s. 'They talked about these plug-in cities and temporary situations,' he notes. 'Now, through electronics and the ability to program, you can make things invisible, they can appear, disappear – the concept of ephemerality operates on a whole other level than anyone could have thought of at that time.'

For their first collaboration in 2001, a year before officially forming Electroland, McNall and Seeley devised RGB for the Southern California Institute of Architecture (SCI-Arc). The installation enabled mobile-phone users to punch in numbers on their keypad that, in turn, activated waves of red, green and blue lights stretched out along the exterior windows of a quarter-mile-long campus building. In its way, RGB anticipated Electroland's continued fascination with transforming normally ordinary environments into stealth art venues charged with glimmers of visual poetry. 'We try to make work that's accessible to everybody,' McNall said one evening as he watched visitors to the Met Lofts building respond to its interactive carpet by breaking into spontaneous bouts of hopscotch. 'If, through the cleverness of the project, we can then make the experience more profound, that's great, but there is that baseline: people have to get it.' ᗺ

Contributors

Lucy Bullivant, the guest-editor of this issue, is an exhibition and events curator, author and critic, and formerly Heinz Curator of Architectural Programmes at the Royal Academy of Arts, London. She is Renaissance Advocate to Yorkshire Forward (2007–09), and is currently curating a major international touring exhibition on interactive environments, and a series of symposia on urban design. Her books include *Responsive Environments* (V&A Contemporary, 2006) and *Anglo Files: UK Architecture's Rising Generation* (Thames & Hudson, 2005), and she was also guest-editor of *AD 4dspace: Interactive Architecture* (Jan/Feb 2005). She is a correspondent to *Domus*, *The Plan*, *AND*, *a+u*, *Architectural Record*, *Indesign* and *Volume*.

Maria Fernández is Assistant Professor of Art History at Cornell University. Her research interests include the history and theory of digital art, postcolonial studies, Latin American art and architecture, and the intersections of these fields. She has published essays in multiple journals including *Art Journal*, *Third Text*, *nparadoxa*, *Fuse* and *Mute*. With Faith Wilding and Michelle Wright she edited the anthology *Domain Errors: Cyberfeminist Practices* (Autonomedia, 2002).

Mark Garcia is the MPhil/PhD Research Co-ordinator in the Department of Architecture, and the Research Manager in the Department of Industrial Design Engineering, at the Royal College of Art (RCA). He has worked for Branson Coates Architecture and has taught spatial design theory and design research methodologies on the RCA-wide MPhil/PhD Research Methods Course. He has published writings on Superstudio, architectural glass and transparency, the future of London, patterns in architecture, and play, games and toys in architecture. He was the guest-editor of AD Architextiles (Nov/Dec 2006) and is co-founder of the multidisciplinary RCA Architextiles project. He is currently editing a critical anthology of the theory and design of diagrams in interior, architectural, urban and landscape design.

Usman Haque is an architect specialising in responsive environments, interactive installations, digital interface devices and mass-participation performances. His skills include the design of both physical spaces and the software and systems that bring them to life. As well as directing the work of Haque Design + Research, he has also taught in the Interactive Architecture Workshop at the Bartlett School of Architecture, London.

Hugh Hart is a Los Angeles-based writer. He blogs about new media for Wired News, runs the website www.hughhart.com, and covers art, architecture, design, theatre, television and film for the *New York Times*, *Los Angeles Times* and *San Francisco Chronicle*. His work will appear this summer in Oxford University Press's *English as a Second Language* anthology series.

Despina Papadopoulos is the founder of Studio 5050, a design collective based in New York. She holds Masters degrees in philosophy and interaction design, and teaches 'Personal Expression and Wearable Technologies' and 'The Softness of Things: Technology in Space and Form' at NYU's Interactive Telecommunications Program. She is currently working on Creatures, a set of simple networked devices for Day-for-Night, a modular, reconfigurable dress made of 500 white circuit boards.

C O N T E N T S

Modular
Mountain
Retreat

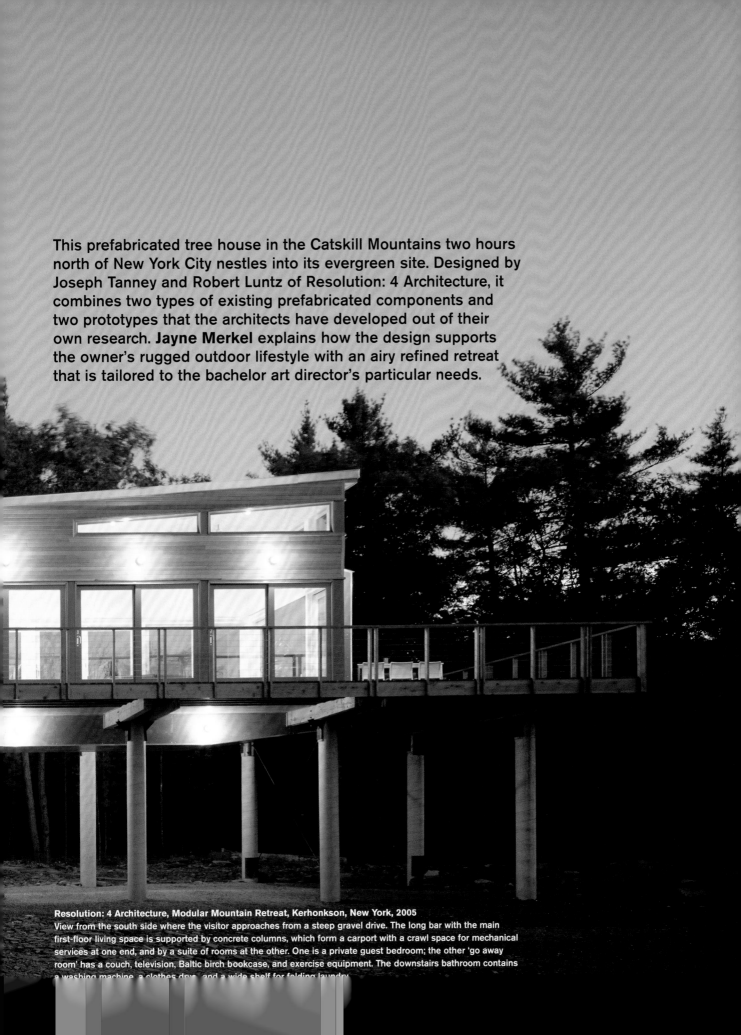

This prefabricated tree house in the Catskill Mountains two hours north of New York City nestles into its evergreen site. Designed by Joseph Tanney and Robert Luntz of Resolution: 4 Architecture, it combines two types of existing prefabricated components and two prototypes that the architects have developed out of their own research. **Jayne Merkel** explains how the design supports the owner's rugged outdoor lifestyle with an airy refined retreat that is tailored to the bachelor art director's particular needs.

Resolution: 4 Architecture, Modular Mountain Retreat, Kerhonkson, New York, 2005
View from the south side where the visitor approaches from a steep gravel drive. The long bar with the main first-floor living space is supported by concrete columns, which form a carport with a crawl space for mechanical services at one end, and by a suite of rooms at the other. One is a private guest bedroom; the other 'go away room' has a couch, television, Baltic birch bookcase, and exercise equipment. The downstairs bathroom contains a washing machine, a clothes dryer, and a wide shelf for folding laundry.

The focal point of the main living area is a tall, flat fireplace wall covered with 14-gauge hot-rolled black-steel panelling. Windows in the corner and along both side walls bring the surrounding evergreen landscape visually inside at the level of the tree tops. Decks on both sides literally open the living areas to the outdoors. One has an outdoor staircase leading to a hot tub, outdoor seating and a grill below.

Getting there is almost half the fun. The short trip from Manhattan involves a steady progression from intense urbanity through open highways to small towns, past charming old farmhouses and various examples of old modular construction – a rusting Airstream trailer, several ageing 'mobile homes' (bigger, more permanent, boxy trailers), some new manufactured sheds, and two recent, traditionally styled houses made of modular components. Then the land gets steep. Houses are tucked away from view on wooded plots, the road twists and turns, and a steep gravel driveway leads up to a knoll where a long narrow house, sheathed in cedar siding and dark-grey synthetic panelling, stands perched on concrete columns and a suite of ground-floor rooms.

An enclosed staircase, in a separate panellised structure and attached to the blocks containing the living spaces, runs along the north side of the house. Sheathed inside and out in grey Cebonit (which is similar to cement board), it leads from the front door on the ground floor to the main living spaces

among the tree tops. The client, who loves mountain biking and rock climbing, camped out on the hill top when the architects were siting the house in order to find the best spot, angle and orientation. He decided to have the fireplace wall face west (and the sunset) so that one long living-room wall would run along the south side and the southern sun would light the mountains behind the other long wall on the north.

Then the architects blasted away the rocky terrain to insert pylons, a well and a septic tank. They could have carted the big rocks away, but that would have been expensive and would have changed the character of the land. Instead they scattered big chunks of rock around the site and used them for outdoor seating and entry steps, emphasising the nature of the site and giving the house a vigour compatible with the client's pursuits.

By cladding the first outside wall one sees when reaching the summit, and the first interior wall one encounters when entering the house, in rugged Cebonit panelling, attached with visible stainless-steel studs, the architects signal that it is time to trade in your Manolos for Merrills. You are in the country now.

But you are still within the New York axis. The discipline the architects have acquired over the last 17 years inserting residential lofts into commercial buildings – what Tanney calls 'thinking inside the box' – has paid off here. The modules with the 'essential elements of domesticity' that they have developed for cramped city spaces adapt ideally to the constraints of modular housing where the sizes of components are determined by the dimensions of loads that trucks can carry down a highway. Although the architects are currently designing 50 different modular houses around the country, when they built this one two years ago they had only done two, including one for *Dwell* magazine which they had won a competition to design. Now mass-produced, the *Dwell* House has brought them national recognition.

In the main living space of the Mountain Retreat, which is 18 metres (60 foot) long, they inserted the same 1.2 x 2.4-metre (4 x 8-foot) kitchen island they have used in numerous lofts. It is big enough to hold a professional stove (which is vented under the floor), a large Baltic birch work surface, cabinets, and places for four people to have breakfast. Stools can be tucked under the table top.

Only here, instead of urban loft-like living and dining

The main living space contains a sitting area around the fireplace on the 4-metre (13-foot) tall end wall, with dark-grey wool geometric sofas and square, cherry-topped, stainless-steel coffee tables from Room & Board. A dining area in the middle of the space, where ceiling heights are about 3 metres (10 feet), is adjacent to the 2.4-metre (8-foot) tall kitchen with work surfaces, storage and seating for guests to keep the cook company. The room has bamboo floors throughout.

areas confined by interior walls with maybe windows at one end, there are walls of glass on both sides, even glass in the corners, and a clerestory to flood the space with light from above. The big long box of the main living space has a sloped 'butterfly' roof that that is attached on site. It contains the clerestory windows and allows ceiling heights to rise from 2.4 to 3.9 metres (8 to 13 feet). Decks line both long walls, making it possible to open the entire room to the outdoors. Plain white duck-cotton curtains on exposed stainless-steel hospital tracks provide privacy and protection from the sun when desired.

The no-nonsense detailing is completely consistent with the simple modern furnishings, cabinetry and fixtures that the architects are finally getting the modular housing manufacturers to supply. When they started out they had to specify the architectural finishes, fixtures and details that the factories did not offer. But over time, working with the factory owners, they have managed to convince them to offer the plain cedar-trimmed double-paned Andersen windows, solid core TruStile doors with translucent panels, maple Merillat cabinets, modern Kohler taps, Lutron light switches, Baltic birch countertops, bamboo floors and other architectural features they require. So the detailing of the house is consistent – and in the houses being built now, much of it comes right from the factory. Like many things these architects do, the Mountain Retreat is both a work of architecture and an experiment, a mass-produced product and a unique design.

Most of the American architects working with prefabricated construction today are trying to create houses that can be mass produced – products they hope many clients will want to buy. Resolution's approach, which they call 'mass customisation', is to create prototypes that can be adapted to different sites, clients' needs and budgets, but which are still largely factory built. The Mountain Retreat combines two prototypical schemes they had developed earlier as case

The bedroom at the eastern end of the elevated main floor has a butterfly roof with clerestory windows and pre-engineered trusses like the main living space. Though it had to be added on site, the space arrived almost complete with the sheet-rock walls, windows, wiring and closets. Only the skirting had to be added later after the bamboo flooring was installed.

The 167-square-metre (1,800-square-foot) Mountain Retreat is what Tanney calls a 'blur' of two prototypes that the architects had previously developed during their research on modular building – the Beach House (on the left) with its glass-walled living area set up on stilts, decks on each side, and slanted 'hat' with clerestories, and the Suburban (on the right) with its cedar siding, grey Cebonit panelling, and staircase in a separate but attached panellised structure along one side.

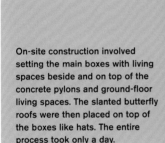

On-site construction involved setting the main boxes with living spaces beside and on top of the concrete pylons and ground-floor living spaces. The slanted butterfly roofs were then placed on top of the boxes like hats. The entire process took only a day.

studies: the Suburban (which has the same cladding) and the Beach House (which has the same elevated living areas and sloped 'hat' with clerestory windows). The retreat actually has butterfly roofs on both ends, so the master bedroom also has a tall, sloped ceiling and light from above.

This approach gives clients the cost savings and quality control of mass production in houses tailored to their programmes: the kinds of rooms they want, their configuration, their character and their cost. Resolution's houses cost about a third less than standard construction, and the costs are predictable, which is a very important factor for many clients. Factory-produced components are not only of higher and more consistent quality than those made on site, but the energy and material savings are considerable too. Woods are ordered to the lengths that are employed, and all scraps are salvaged for blocking. The process is also much faster. A house can be built in a factory in a week, in any kind of weather, and it can be assembled on site in a day.

Still, the four phases involved in designing and building a prefabricated house take about a year. The first is design – choosing from the standardised options available and deciding how to combine them and meet the client's needs.

The second phase involves documentation, engineering and coordination with the factory, where parts are selected and ordered from various manufacturers. Also during this phase, the architects are doing site work and getting local code approvals. All this can take several months. The third phase consists of construction in the factory after everything that has been ordered has arrived, which takes only a week. A day is required to ship the house to its site, and another to put it in place. Then it takes another three or four months for all the hook-ups and finishing; the time varies with the schedules of various contractors. The Mountain Retreat took only 12 weeks, but most houses take 16, though the work could be done in six if contracting could be organised efficiently.

Many Resolution: 4 Architecture clients take some time to furnish their houses, even with the off- the-rack furniture they usually choose, due to limited budgets. But most maintain a crisp modern aesthetic that lets the architecture and the setting shine through. Δ+

Concert Hall, Bruges

Jeremy Melvin describes how Robbrecht en Daem Architecten's concert hall in Bruges provides one of the most exemplary medieval Flemish cities with a 'window to modernity'. Exceeding mere juxtaposition of old and new, the architects have created a wholly sensory experience for their concert-going audience, which embraces the ephemeral quality of musical performance with the physicality of architecture.

Robbrecht en Daem's concert hall in Bruges pinpoints a clutch of the ambiguities that lie in the term 'culture', subjects them to scrutiny and offers new insights into them. The city itself perfectly embodies the ideas of culture as a preserved historic artefact. Where its Flemish neighbours either evolved into contemporary cities like Antwerp, were destroyed like Ypres or acquired a Modernist tower by Henry van de Velde as did Ghent, Bruges remained an exemplar of medieval urbanism. That was enough for AWN Pugin in the 19th century, countless Japanese tourists in the 21st, and the authorities who designated the city European capital of culture for 2002 – until they realised that the most modern performance spaces were medieval churches, appropriate perhaps for composers of Josquin des Prez's vintage, but less suitable for more recent work.

The need for a new concert hall introduced another dimension of culture, raising the possibility of a contrast

Robbrecht en Daem Architecten, Concert Hall, Bruges, Belgium, 2003
The subtly sculpted concert hall is on the edge of historic Bruges, its form and colour echoing but not aping its context.

Main hall interior: the inclined side walls came from Robbrecht's intuition that he wanted a sense of protection, but also aid the acoustic strategy.

The entrance to the concert hall is neatly tucked into the angle between the recital tower (nearest the camera) and the main hall.

between historic and contemporary architecture, between the ephemera of performance and the longevity of building, between tradition and innovation.

Paul Robbrecht has developed a reputation for working amid contemporary culture. He has collaborated with artists like Juan Munoz and Cristina Iglesias and designed the Aue Pavilions for the 1992 Kassel Documenta. The concert hall was an opportunity to see how architecture might relate to music, as these collaborations investigated its relationship with other visual arts. Its setting and function added new dimensions. Robbrecht's collaborations with living artists are explicit interfaces between contemporary art and architecture, where a concert hall might have Monteverdi one day and Messaien the next, and could also swing across the spectrum from popular to esoteric music. And there was the inescapable presence of Bruges, the historic museum city for which this building was to provide a window to modernity. Fortunately Robbrecht is as sensitive to the subtleties of Flemish culture as he is to contemporary art, and the concert hall is one of several projects where they come together.

The location evokes the shifting pattern of urban development. It saw many of the activities that traditionally take place on the city fringe, historically a cattle market and, in the 19th century, a grand railway terminus. As methods of transport and food supply changed, culture and leisure began to take their place. What was the shambles is now a large urban square, fringed on one side with a parade of cafés and restaurants. At one end is the concert hall, once the site of the former station, which moved further out when Bruges became a through route rather than a terminal. The line of the tracks has become a 'green' swathe, bringing nature into the city.

The building's form illustrates Robbrecht's skill as an intuitive and subtle designer. As the main concert hall has to adapt to an opera house, it needed a fly tower, and there is a secondary performance space also in the shape of a tower, giving two strong vertical elements. In the hands of Denys Lasdun or an unashamed functionalist, they would be expressed as raw shapes. Robbrecht sculpts them into a form which, though it may not be entirely homogenous or have the mathematical coherence of a surface generated by parametric design, has a unity of a different, visually determined sort. It is an architecture of the eye, of sensory experience rather than of abstract theory. The towers are clearly expressed, but the planes and angles of the roofs around them soften their impact and suggest that they belong in the wider urban fabric. At this level they echo the city's medieval towers and surrounding roofscape, which similarly seem to belong together. The same sensibility helps to form the entrance, which is sheltered in a right angle between the two performance spaces, yet is contiguous with the large public square.

Such elements give the exterior of the building an intriguing quality. It is a large presence, but sensitively fitted into its context. Its terracotta tile cladding stands out amid the grey and white surroundings, but recalls perhaps the autumn leaves of the swathe of nature that leads to it. Robbrecht confesses to being intrigued by the possibilities of colour as a means of expression in architecture, though he has not yet fully explored its implications.

All these elusive qualities make the concert hall a place where culture itself can be contemplated. It belongs both to the architectural culture of Bruges and Flanders more generally, as well as to the community of performance spaces.

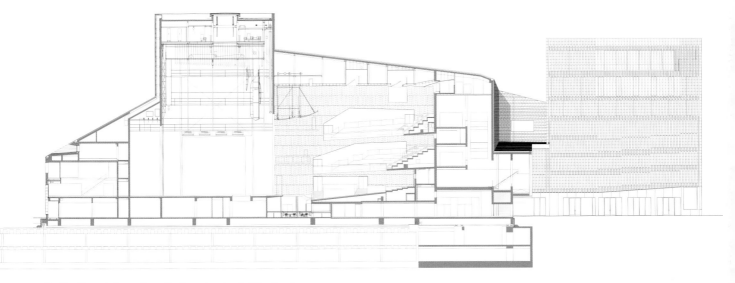

Section through the main auditorium, chamber hall in elevation.

The recital room invites all sorts of possibilities for performance and configuration. It also brings natural light into the space.

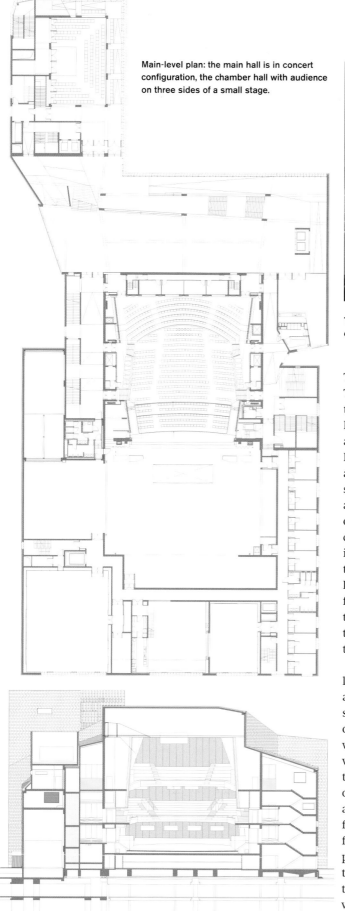

Main-level plan: the main hall is in concert configuration, the chamber hall with audience on three sides of a small stage.

Cross-section through the main auditorium.

The foyers have a rich dynamic and sense of movement that belies the austerity of their materials, and also give intriguing internal and external views

The interior makes some of these conditions more explicit. The entrance foyer is a dramatic, multilevel space, itself proof that concrete may be austere but is not necessarily forbidding. However, it is the angles, routes and views across the space and out of the building that make it really memorable. Moving from the entrance to either of the performance spaces affords all sorts of opportunities to look backwards at selective views of the city. Similarly, the journey from the auditoria back to the ground level reintroduces the physicality of architecture after the ephemera of performance, and what connects them is not a didactically determined system but individuals' perceptions and impressions, and how those of the building and performance might merge. Cristina Iglesias' Ligeti Benches capture these qualities in microcosm. Simple in form, they are coloured in strips of varying width, translating the chromatic and dissonant possibilities of music into visual terms. Like the building they mix functional possibilities with the promise of intellectual challenge.

The two auditoria are themselves magnificent spaces. The larger, seating 1,300, manages the difficult task of being adaptable to symphonic concerts or opera performances. The stage can change its configuration, opening to reveal an orchestra pit for opera, or coming forward into the auditorium with the backstage shut off for orchestral concerts. Robbrecht wanted to incline the two side walls inwards towards the top to give the sense of a protective enclosure to the back and top of the auditorium. Happily, this intuitive idea coincided with acoustic theory, which needs hard surfaces closer to seats the further they are from the stage to reinforce direct sound with first reflected sound. As well as working functionally, here the physical form responds to a psychological condition – it seems to define a protective cocoon where individual members of the audience can have their own experience of living and viewing performance. Comfort in this context does not need the opulence so favoured in 19th-century auditoria like the Opera Garnier in Paris or Vienna's Musikverein. And its

The concert hall's bulk, mass and form give definition to the large public space in front of it.

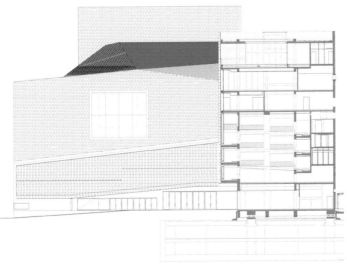

Section through the chamber music hall.

relative austerity makes it equally suitable for traditional classics or contemporary music.

The second space, the chamber music hall, is less conventional in layout. It can seat up to 300 on three levels, but its configuration is more like a Shakespearean theatre than a conventional concert hall, with a gallery surrounding a more or less square stage. Daylight also gives it an unusual quality, and some contact with the exterior. Its basic shape seems to invite numerous different types of performance in various configurations. Some types of music might suggest reversing the spatial relationship between sound and listeners, placing the audience at the lower level while performers or speakers throw sound up, across and around the galleries.

It would be naive to suggest that the concert hall is a microcosm of the city. Bruges as a historical artefact, and performance as a cultural experience, are both far too complicated for that. But the concert hall adds not just to the stock of Bruges' architectural heritage: it also extends its cultural possibilities, just as its presence in a historic city means that it is more than purely a venue for performance. Δ+

3+1 architects

Without the predominance of a single presiding tradition of modern architecture in Estonia, the way has been clear for a younger generation of architects to make their mark. **Andres Kurg** describes the work of 3+1 architects, who launched their career in the mid-1990s with an Estonian Embassy in Vilnius, Lithuania. Through their trend-setting domestic work, they have proved able to appeal to a new wealthy client base, while also developing their own interests in programme and architecture's relationship to the physical landscape.

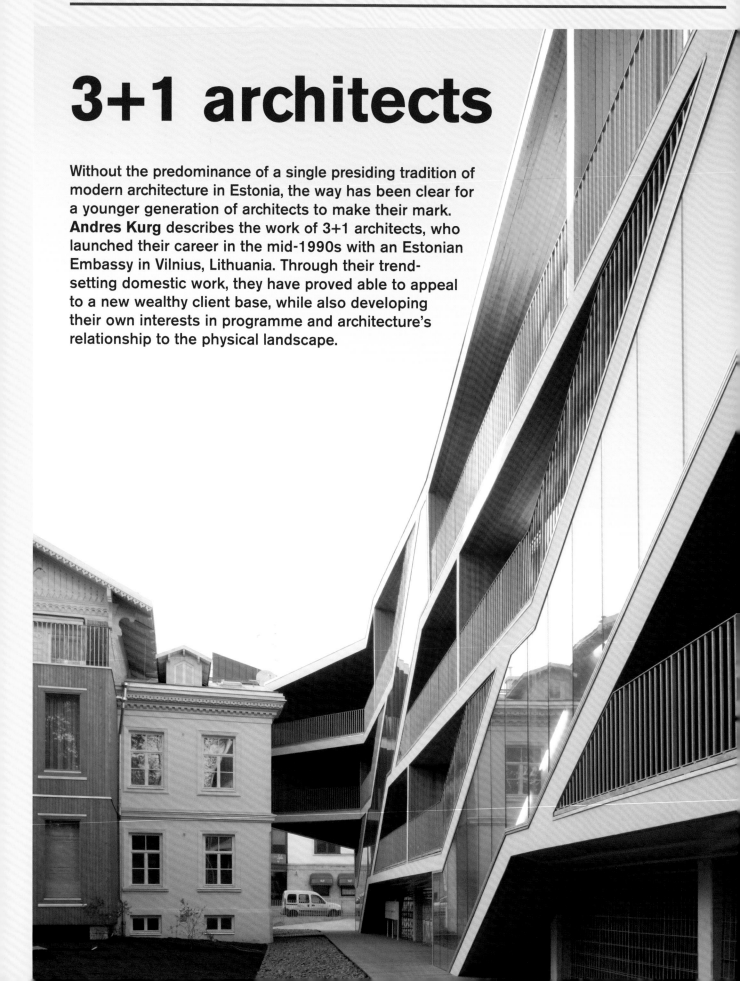

The works of 3+1 architects appear chic and stylish: formally refined and precisely detailed they are mostly constructed of simple materials such as transparent glass and untreated concrete; in their unabashed modernity these are projects that call to mind abstract sculptures or the backdrops for fashion shoots. Yet closer inspection shows that these apparently simple structures have been put together in a complex way, in many cases by experimenting with typology or applying a conceptual means to designing the programme. In addition to revealing the practice's broad rethinking of architectural conventions, a glance at the status of the clientele for their houses affords a fascinating insight into the nature of Estonia's rapidly evolving society and into the country where the architects are based.

On the face of it, the start-up of the 3+1 office appears a typical one, established as it was in 1994 by Markus Kaasik, Andres Ojari and Ilmar Valdur, the three partners who had all studied together at the Estonian Academy of Art in Tallinn.

Estonian Embassy, Vilnius, Lithuania, 1998
The facade is clad in limestone – a traditional building material widely used in Estonia – but the architects have obscured this straightforward symbolic gesture by colouring the stone with a light-blue tone, as if to avoid making too direct an association.

Apartment building, Kadriorg, Tallinn, 2005

Two years later the office (which then also included Inga Raukas) won their first major competition – for the new Estonian Embassy in Vilnius, Lithuania – and so got the chance to design one of the first significant public projects in the newly independent country. The Vilnius embassy was exceptional in many respects. It was quite different from the Neo-Modernist compositions that predominated in Estonia at that time in that it applied a more pragmatic approach to the site, yet it also had to fulfil a symbolic role as the physical representative of one small Baltic country within another. The architects' solution was a straightforward one: the building, which is situated in a centrally located old residential area, has been divided into two parts, with the limestone-clad formal streetfront following the volume of neighbouring structures and carrying the symbolic load, and the all-glass, more flexible garden facade having a separate lower volume extending out from it, accommodating a hall space. Limestone was a conscious choice for the facade, because in 1992 it was declared an Estonian national stone. Yet the architects decided to add a twist to this material and coloured the stone light blue (intended perhaps to echo the blue of the Estonian national flag), as if suspicious of the all-too-easy ways of imposing meaning through architecture.

The embassy's programme combined offices and ambassador's residence, differentiated in the interior by dislocated floor levels that produced a flexible half-floor system and so avoided the need for long corridors. In the Vilnius project, the architects can already be seen to have treated site and programme in a idiosyncratic way, the resulting structure depending less on a chosen style or sculptural form than on the application of an overall system to generate the building's final mode of construction. In the embassy building, for example, the dislocated rhythm of windows on the facade indexes the shift of floor levels within, the stone-clad volume seeming to stand apart from the building's internal functions.

This inherently disciplined approach to architecture, one that prefers system to spectacle, is further demonstrated in a series of single-family dwellings dating from the end of the 1990s and the beginning of the 2000s. By then, Estonia's burgeoning economy had produced a group of young home-owners who were open to new ideas and interested in dialogue with the architect. Their preferences were not governed by the precedent of historic architecture and they were willing to search for new models. In Estonia, the status of contemporary architecture had always been relatively high: in the 1920s, during the country's first period of independence, it was Modernism that helped define the young nation and proclaim its difference, and hence separation, from Germany and Russia. During the 1960s, as part of the Soviet Union, Finnish postwar architecture was influential in Estonia and offered a counterbalance to Soviet industrialisation and conformist building production. Yet

In City, Tallinn, Estonia, 2004

Set in a centrally located residential area in a neighbourhood of early 20th-century one- and two-storey wooden dwellings, this single-family house is composed of 3-metre (9.8-foot) modules, each of which has a different length, height and function. The modules form clusters according to their programme – after the entrance area comes the kitchen and dining area, then living and sleeping/playing areas – following a plan of 3+3+3+3+1. The interior of the building consists of a single linear wall-less space that is differentiated into functional zones by the changing shape and lighting of the modules: the high and light kitchen changes to a transparent dining area, part of which extends to the garden; this in turn mutates into a lower and closed module with a fireplace. The house is placed on the edge of the site and the character imposed by the different modules also structures the garden in front of it. The main garden area in front of the kitchen, dining and living areas is followed by a raised level at the height of the sleeping zone, with a small terrace in front of the bedroom. In this context, the low fragmented building is more reminiscent of a shed or hut than of a full-sized dwelling and so avoids producing what would be a strongly discordant contrast between old and new structures in this neighbourhood.

In Suburb House, Tallinn, 2000
The house is set in an area of traditional single-family homes; its ground plan is made up of 15 equally sized rectangles that follow the measurements of Japanese *tatami* rooms.

there was never only one dogma or father figure that dictated how architecture should be done, nor any definitive judgement as to what constituted 'good' architecture (as, for example, was the case with Scandinavian Modernism). Thus, at the outset of the 21st century, this relative absence of a historical architectural continuum produced a certain freedom for experimentation and innovation among young architects, as well as a receptiveness to their originality of approach on the part of their clients.

This openness to new forms is well illustrated by 3+1's In Suburb House (2000), a self-enclosed two-storey structure in a densely populated area on the outskirts of Tallinn. The architects compare it to a 'displaced apartment', a living space that has been removed to a neighbourhood with solid, single-family dwellings. The ground plan of the house is composed of 15 equally sized rectangles, or 'space particles', as the architects call them that take their measurements from Japanese *tatami* rooms. Some of the rectangles are functionally defined, as bathroom, sauna or storage room; in the living room and kitchen, on the other hand, the particles are articulated by doors that slide to divide the space to form differing configurations. The influence of Japanese art and architecture that this house demonstrates stems from the interests of Markus Kaasik and Andres Ojari who, while studying at Tallinn's Academy of Art, also attended lectures by artist Tõnis Vint, a man fascinated by Far Eastern symbols and

compositions. In their everyday practice, however, the architects have disconnected these signs from their transcendent meanings and used them as a basis for the programme, as a way to rethink how form and function are related in the finished work.

In the Black House (2002) near Tallinn, the living room, kitchen and study areas are all part of one continuous circular space set around the central service volume that includes a glass-walled sauna looking into the living area and to the garden (through its glass wall). The rigid box-like main volume is here contrasted with the unarticulated space that looks almost self-organising and the radically 'open' sauna (which was the client's wish, not the architects' whim). In E-Farm (2002), a suburban home that combines a living space and a working area for clients involved in software programming, the long and narrow rectangular volume is subdivided into a 'public plaza' that faces the street and a more enclosed living area with an atrium-like terrace at one end. Recently, the architects have used a formal structure for the programme in a single-family house in Tallinn – In City (2004) – where the building is made up of 3-metre (9.8-foot) modular boxes that vary in height and length, and are placed next to one another. This, however, is not only a formal solution, but fits in with the surrounding wooden housing of the area: typologically, the house blends into the vernacular cityscape of temporary sheds or courtyard buildings that have been added next to one another piecemeal over the years.

In all of these single-family houses the formal regular structure allows for a certain flexibility that would be unattainable within the parameters of a purely functionalist approach; a surplus space that is open to changes over time and to manipulation by future users. In this case form neither fixes use nor dictates the type of activity that could take place inside; rather, it contains and houses the patterns of daily living that, to a certain degree, operate independently from it.

Another interest of 3+1 architects has been the relationship of a building to the physical landscape in which it is located. In Villa V (2000), a two-storey dwelling in suburban Tallinn, the house becomes a piece of the topography of the pine forest, being partly cut into the landscape at ground floor level and 'growing' a terrace to the first-floor bedroom wing. The construction materials seem to stress this connection: the house is as if turned inside out, with wooden boarding on the outside and uncovered concrete in the interior.

The possibility of continuing or articulating a cityscape through a building is explored in the winning entry for the competition to design the city library in Pärnu (1999). Situated on a Soviet-era square, the building attempts to act as a connection between the fortified zone of the old city and the parts that date from the 1950s with a ramp leading from the central square to the library. The transparent facades on all sides of the building serve to emphasise the effect of undivided urban topography and allow for visual linkages between inside and out. With its protruding cantilevers and complex system of ramps, 3+1's library is also evidence of the

Apartment building, Kadriorg, Tallinn, 2005

Located in a traditional residential area in Tallinn, this apartment building replaces a 19th-centry courtyard structure with an insistently modern structure that contrasts with the architectural historicism of the adjoining street. The building's sculptural volume, visible from the street, is wrapped in thin sheet metal; the entrances, windows and balconies are all turned towards the garden in the courtyard. The garden facade itself is dominated by two glass staircases leading to the apartments; the staircases have intervening balconies, a device suggestive of gallery apartments. This unusual solution is reinforced by the common garden in front of the building.

As a result of bitter memories of their Soviet-era past, collectivity is still a dirty word for Estonians and new apartment buildings are usually designed with little attention to common spaces. Here, however, communal areas function as an extension of the personal living spaces and add value to the inner-city apartment in what is an innovative attempt to rethink this subject. The design of the garden by Berlin-based Atelier Le Balto, with their interest in both the everyday and the 'wild', further supports these attempts.

In the interior the apartments are divided into three sections, with kitchens, bathrooms and saunas placed at the site's outer perimeter and lit by small glass tiles in the fire wall, with living rooms and bedrooms situated in the middle and balconies at the front.

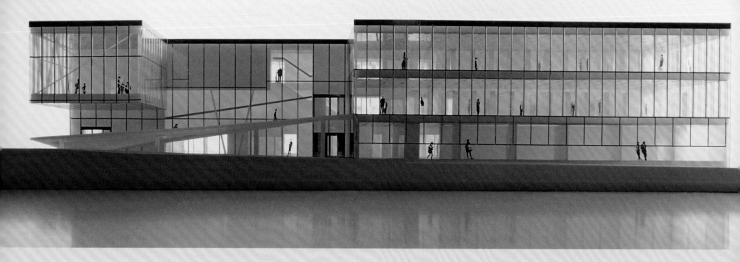

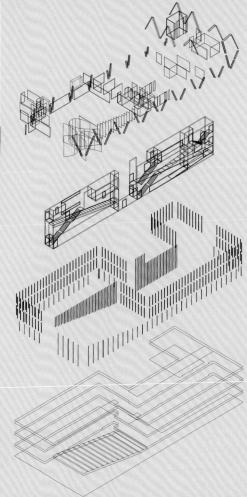

City Library, Pärnu, Estonia, due for completion 2008

The library is situated in a central square in the city of Pärnu, next to a 1960s theatre building and close to the city's 17th-century fortifications. The square itself was designed during the 1950s to replace buildings damaged by bombing during the Second World War. Thus the library is framed by a different view from each direction. In order to link it to its context, the all-glass building has a smaller plaza in front that leads to the entrance; the outside space is continued inside the building and transparent walls allow for visual continuity between them. The interior is arranged largely as an undivided continuum that serves to reinforce the idea of a single coherent space extending through the library from the theatre square to the edge of the old town. As the city of Pärnu is a popular summer resort, the building has to meet not only year-round local requirements, but also cater for the interests of a large visiting public. In addition to designated reading areas, the library is equipped with conference rooms, exhibition spaces and an Internet café.

strong influence of Dutch architecture in Estonia in the 1990s. Construction of the library has unfortunately been a long, drawn-out process as the municipality of Pärnu decided to build the structure in two stages. Due to constantly rising construction costs during the property boom of the early 2000s, private clients tried hard to finish their buildings as fast as possible; unfortunately, due to lack of resources, the municipality was only prepared to finance the building of storage space for the books and totally neglected the public function of the library. Only in 2007 have the architects finally been able to sign a contract for the completion of their project.

Recently 3+1 has been involved in large-scale projects that in addition to the design have involved broader spatial analysis or research on the potential future development of their work. One example here is the E-Piim Dairy Cheese Factory in Põlva, southern Estonia, for which the architects designed production facilities in 2005. Further, the client was interested in the possibility of developing the site for cheese tourism by adding a leisure centre with a cheese museum and a restaurant to the industrial area. The design proposed the location of a visitors' centre above the production area, with views opening down to the factory from between the sloping forms of the wooden wall and floor panels. In this way tourists would not disturb the workforce and, as the architects who were now well acquainted with the technology of cheese-

making assured their client, the manufacturing process is most attractive when viewed from above. The project is significant in many ways, for not only does it show how industrial production in Estonia is becoming so exceptional that it attracts tourists, it also exemplifies how the role of the architect entrusted with such a design brief is changing. First and foremost, the architect is expected to come up with a landmark design, to create an attraction that will stand out in a former industrial area, city environment or suburban sprawl. In an attempt to meet this requirement, it is all too easy for the architect to fall into the advertising trap, satisfying the client with an eye-catching image or stylish gesture rather than a strong programme. 3+1 architects, with their interest in abstract programmes and view of architecture as a complex system, is in a prime position to resist this tendency. ⟁+

Andres Kurg is an architectural historian and a researcher at the Estonian Academy of Arts in Tallinn. He studied art history at the Estonian Academy of Arts in Tallinn and architectural history at the Bartlett School of Architecture. He has recently published works on post-socialism and the city, on the relationship between art and architecture in the 1970s, and co-edited with Mari Laanemets A User's Guide to Tallinn (2002). He is currently preparing a PhD on alternative art spaces in 1970s Estonia.

Resumé

3+1 architects

1994
3+1 architects founded in Tallinn, Estonia

1995
Central Glass International competition for Guest House, Japan: honourable mention

1996
Estonian Embassy, Vilnius, Lithuania. Competition entry (with Inga Raukas): first prize

1998
Estonian Embassy, Vilnius, Lithuania
Blue and Green single-family dwellings, Tallinn

1999
City library, Pärnu, Estonia. Competition entry: first prize. Due for completion 2008

2000
Villa V, In Forest and In Suburb single-family dwellings, Tallinn
Participation in exhibitions '10 Years After', Architectural Association, London; and '4 architectures', Galerie d'Architecture, Paris

2001
Annual award for architecture, Estonian Cultural Endowment

2002
E-Farm and Black House single-family dwellings, Tallinn

2003
Housing in Viimsi, Estonia. Competition entry: first prize

2004
In City single-family house, Tallinn

2005
Office and residential building, Tallinn. Competition entry: first prize. Due for completion 2008
E-Piim Dairy Cheese Factory building, Põlva, southern Estonia
Apartment building, Kadriorg, Tallinn
On Hill single-family house, Tallinn
Participation in 'Emerging identities – East' exhibition, Deutsches Architektur Zentrum, Berlin, Germany

2006
Design for a series of prefabricated wooden single-family dwellings for Kopkop. Due for completion 2007

3+1 architects (from left): Markus Kaasik, Andres Ojari and Ilmar Valdur.

It's All Inside My Head

The physical manifestations of built architecture are often discussed in terms of a single architect's inspiration, overemphasising and romanticising the intellectual contribution of the signature architect. Here Neil Spiller describes the extraordinary departure that Marcos Novak is undertaking at the University of California's Santa Barbara campus, where Novak's own scanned brain becomes a literal, reflexive generating force in the formation of a spatial environment.

In the early 1990s a few architects, including myself, started to think out of the box in relation to what might happen to architecture in the wake of digital technology. Nowadays things seem to have settled down: funny-shaped buildings, unreadable diagrams and non-orthogonal cladding seem to be the current, but fading, fetishism. One of the small number of architects not attempting to put lipstick on the gorilla of rampant global capitalism seems to be Marcos Novak.

Novak was at the coalface of the architectural digital right from the near beginning, learning from computer scriptwriters and musicians simultaneously. His new work, AlloBrain@AlloSphere, really strikes at the centre of what a 'personal' architecture might be. The AlloSphere, a building currently in the throes of construction at the University of California's Santa Barbara campus, is in principle one of those 'cave' things in which you can be visually engulfed as it wraps itself around your cone of vision and plays you virtual environments. The technology is funky, but the important thing is how Novak is using it. His brain is being scanned while he is viewing and interacting with his own virtual creations. He then views his brain and the spaces within and around it as a fluxing complex architecture conditioned by external stimuli. The brain then becomes another of Novak's self-generated environments which are then re-viewed, and a feedback cycle is formed, a reflexive system – biological yet digital, 'transverged' as Novak would say. The feedback loop between brain, experience, pattern and form thus creates an ongoing digital ecology.

The brain and its complexity of support networks can be modelled in numerous ways, for example blood flows and volumes can be used by Novak to create other ways of viewing his own responses to aesthetics, vicariously creating aesthetics themselves. Virtually he can change void into mass and therefore 'inhabit' his own brain or extrapolate interesting pieces of it as architectural models – a limitless store of inspirations. This is an original piece of architectural research and will set the scene for much of what might be considered to legitimate architectural practices and processes of the near future.

The Surrealist can start to imagine all manner of weird products, spaces and architectures based on this premise: lung-shaped ashtrays that contract or darken like the owner's smoke-filled lungs used as an aid to giving up smoking; the geometry of fear as a useful shape for dentists' chairs, or finding a way out of the lacuna when creatively blocked by taking inspiration from the shape of your own block – a 'chip off the old block'.

Novak likens his creation to the ongoing virtuality of Boulée's Cenotaph for Newton, indeed the AlloSphere built form is not dissimilar. And with Novak's, and perhaps mine or your brain inside, his creation might well have more impact on architecture than Boulée's paper sphere. Novak has opened up a new seam in architecture and its relationship with the body. He describes his creation thus: 'This history of art is replete with instances of the portrait, and, especially, the artist's own self-portrait. Likewise architecture has a long history of drawing upon the human body as a model for its organisation. Here the two are combined as one – a living self-portrait not of the surface but of the inner fact and function of the architect as artist, used as both the source and content of an architecture never before possible, both virtually and actually.'

Makes you think, doesn't it? D+

Neil Spiller is Professor of Architecture and Digital Theory and Vice Dean at the Bartlett, University College London.

Marcos Novak, AlloSphere, Santa Barbara campus, University of California, 2007
Spaces and terrains are formed by the creation of a feedback loop, between the virtual and the actual. As Novak's brain is scanned, he perceives those scans (his brain is rescanned ad infinitum) and a virtual shifting landscape is produced. The illustrations here show different stages in the evolution of the terrain.

The US Solar Decathlon 2007

As the focus in the UK turns to the London Olympics in 2012, the Eco-Maestro **Ken Yeang** brings our attention to an event on the other side of the Atlantic – the US Solar Decathlon – that offers teams of young designers the opportunity to flex their ecological muscles.

One of the most important architectural competitions today must be the US Solar Decathlon. The competition takes place every two years (this year's event is to be held at the National Mall, Washington DC, from 12 to 20 October), seeking out the newest and best innovations in solar architecture and encouraging cutting-edge research into the design of highly efficient and commercially cost-effective solar-powered housing.

The Virginia Polytechnic Institute and State University's energy-efficient, solar-powered house won the Architecture and Dwelling contests at the 2005 Solar Decathlon, also held at the National Mall in Washington DC.

Each of the teams selected by the US Department of Energy receives $100,000 to design, transport, assemble and demonstrate their solar-powered house at the Decathlon, coupled with the further challenge of disassembling it after the event.

As in the Olympic Decathlon, 10 events test the architectural, engineering, energy efficiency, energy production and other aspects of the designs, which must be powered exclusively by the sun and generate sufficient electricity to run a typical modern household. In addition to being aesthetically pleasing and easy to live in, the houses must integrate solar and energy efficiency technologies, maintain a specified comfortable temperature, provide attractive and adequate lighting, power household appliances for cooking and cleaning, power home electronics, provide hot water and provide power for an electric vehicle to meet household transportation needs.

The teams begin with bioclimatic design, optimising the ambient energies of the locality and connecting the built form with the natural environment to take advantage of heat and light from the sun, prevalent cooling breezes and seasonal variations, adopting as far as possible strategies such as solar shading, thermal insulation, appropriate orientation and built form configuration.

Their next challenge is to look at the technological possibilities for building on these natural advantages, by seeking out and using the latest products and systems on the market in ingenious ways to make the limited amount of solar energy captured by the house as efficient as possible to meet all the competition's performance criteria.

The 10 contests are: Architecture, Engineering, Market Viability, Communications, Comfort Zone, Appliances, Hot Water, Lighting, Energy Balance and Getting Around (transportation), all of which contribute towards making the solar house a reality for mass housing – a step crucial if we are to reduce the threat of serious climate change and enhance our sustainable future.

The Architecture (Design and Livability) contest, for instance, evaluates how the house minimises its impact on the natural environment, and maximises the well-being of its occupants. Points are assigned to each of Vitruvius' three points of architecture: 'Firmness' (strength, suitability and materials appropriateness), 'Commodity' (ease of entry and circulation; accommodation of the technologies needed to operate the house; generosity and sufficiency of space), and 'Delight' (surprises, for example unusual use of ordinary materials, or use of extraordinary materials).

The Engineering contest evaluates engineering design and implementation, including the building envelope, indoor environmental control, and the mechanical, electrical and plumbing systems. Here the use of computational energy simulations is encouraged, as experts evaluate the teams' use of simulation tools to inform their design decisions and predict annual energy performance.

The Market Viability contest focuses on how the house designs can be brought to market; for example, their market appeal, suitability for everyday living, ability to accommodate a variety of potential homeowner-types, and economic viability, all of which again bring such solar-powered housing closer to full-scale adoption in the commercial world of home building.

The Communications contest assesses the teams' ability to communicate the technical aspects of their designs to a wide audience through websites and public as well as virtual tours, and to deliver clear and consistent messages and images that represent the vision, process and results of their projects.

However, the crucial challenge is being able to meet the various energy-performance criteria. The Comfort Zone contest requires the houses to maintain a steady and narrow temperature range of between 72°F (22.2°C) and 76°F (24.4°C), with relative humidity from 40 per cent to 55 per cent. In the Appliances contest, during the competition the teams must maintain temperatures of between −20°F (−28.9°C) and 5°F (−1.5°C) in refrigerators and freezers, wash and dry 12 towels for two days, cook and serve meals for four days, clean dishes using a dishwasher for four days, operate a TV/video player for up to six hours and a computer for up to eight hours for five days. The Hot Water contest requires the successful provision of a 'shower' that delivers 15 gallons of hot water (110°F/43.3°C) in 10 minutes or less, and the Lighting contest looks at the functionality, energy efficiency and aesthetic aspects of the lighting systems, and how these meet the needs of a particular space.

The Energy Balance contest assesses the use of only the solar-generated electric (photovoltaic) systems during the competition to provide electricity for all 10 contests. Full points are awarded if the energy to the batteries is at least as much as the energy removed from them during the course of the event. In the Getting Around contest, the houses must provide sufficient electricity to charge commercially available electric vehicles, and also assesses the number of miles achieved.

In addition to encouraging innovation, another useful outcome of the Decathlon event is public education, boosting public awareness of the increasing viability of solar housing (more than 100,000 people visited the solar villages at the 2002 and 2005 Decathlons).

The 2007 teams are from: Carnegie Mellon University, Cornell University, Georgia Institute of Technology, Kansas State University, Texas A&M University, Universidad Politécnica de Madrid, Universidad de Puerto Rico, University of Colorado, Lawrence Technological University, University of Cincinnati, New York Institute of Technology, Santa Clara University, University of Illinois, Pennsylvania State University, University of Texas at Austin, University of Maryland, Team Montréal (École de Technologie Supérieure, Université de Montréal, McGill University), Technische Universität Darmstadt.

Why is it that none of the Ivy League universities such as Harvard, Yale or Princeton participate? **Δ+**

Kenneth Yeang is a director of Llewelyn Davies Yeang in London and TR Hamzah Yeang in Kuala Lumpur, Malaysia. He is author of many articles and books on ecodesign, including *Ecodesign: A Manual for Ecological Design* (Wiley-Academy, 2006).

Lighting the Cavern

'Alvar Aalto: Through the Eyes of Shigeru Ban', Barbican Art Gallery, Barbican Centre, London, 22 February to 13 May 2007

Michael Spens has an intimate working knowledge of the buildings of Alvar Aalto having supported a restoration programme for Aalto's Viipuri Library in Russia between 1993 and 1997, which involved professionals from Russia and Finland. Here he offers his thoughts on the recent Aalto exhibition at the Barbican.

Alvar Aalto in later life.

This exhibition was timely, coming as it did almost a decade after the Centenary Exhibition on Aalto at the Museum of Modern Art, New York. Shigeru Ban is a distinguished architect himself, in Japan, and his approach to Aalto – as from a different generation – is refreshing and original.

Ban selected 15 projects, a most difficult process, but did well to adopt wide focus. By including such key works as the Experimental House, Muuratsalo (1952–53), the House of Culture, Helsinki (1952–58), Saynatsalo Town Hall (1948–52) and MIT's Baker House Dormitory at Cambridge, Massachusetts (1946–49), and the National Pensions Institute, Helsinki (1952–57), he revealed his particular interest in the materiality that Aalto so much espoused and developed: indeed, it could be said that such works had the greatest influence on postwar British architects. The early, innovative modern period

likewise is well represented by the iconic Viipuri Library (1927–35) and the Paimio Tuberculosis Sanatorium (1929–33).

All these buildings exhibit the growth and maturing of Aalto's innate humanist philosophy. This also separated him from the established CIAM elite, of course, but enabled him to develop a unique ethos and vocabulary of design.

Among the other important works selected by Ban were the Jyvaskyla Workers Club (1924–25), the New York World's Fair Finnish Pavilion (1937), that key masterpiece the Villa Mairea (1937–39), and the Church of the Three Crosses, Imatra (1955–58). However, his major contribution to spreading Aalto knowledge to the wider world was the inclusion of the AA-System Houses project (1937–45). This project was interrupted by, but also sprang out of a need created by, wars, especially the Continuation War of 1941–45 between Finland and the Soviet Union, here as a direct response to a crisis in housing caused by refugees from the former Eastern Finland and Karelia who were driven from their homeland.

The houses were an example of the flexible standardisation of building parts, which Aalto saw as living cells. They also included the latest technology for thermal insulation: the frame was thermally suited to the severity of the Finnish winters, and represented a marked advance on traditional techniques. Aalto was modest about this work (for example, it was not included in the three-volume *Oeuvre Complete* published postwar). Ban, however, with his own experience of disaster housing, had the insight to include it in the exhibition. As an *architettura minore*, it has its place in any appraisal of housing of the period.

Mindful of the high priority Aalto gave to lighting in his projects, for the exhibition Ban insisted that the lighting in the cavernous Barbican galleries was of a superlative standard, and as a result the superb models on show became real exhibits of architecture in their own right, rather than simply being 'dumped' adjacent to photographic and drawn documentation.

One note of reservation is the selection of the late work the North Jutland Art Museum (1966–72), which was executed in collaboration with Jean-Jacques Baruel, a former assistant. It was close to a beech forest near Aalborg and great

Alvar Aalto, Villa Mairea, Noormarku, Finland, 1938–39
Main entrance canopy supported by compound timber columns. The outer set are bound together, providing a slightly archaic tectonic effect. A single column in the forward set of columns is eccentrically splayed outwards by Aalto to enhance the tree-like character of the assembly.

Contemporary view of the entrance elevation and portico.

The closed frame chair designed for the Paimio Tuberculosis Sanatorium, Finland, 1932. The chair is fabricated with a bent birchwood frame and mahogany seat, and Aalto designed it to provide the patient with maximum comfort, at the same time optimising the angle that would most ease the patient's breathing.

Alvar Aalto, Workers Club, Jyvaskyla, Finland, 1924–25
Handrail to the main stairway. This demonstrates that Aalto was already moving into a modern idiom, even though the building itself was lightly classical.

Alvar Aalto, Savoy Vase, glass, 1937.

consideration was thus given to all aspects of the gallery's lighting. However, as a building the scheme does not really rank as high as other projects not included, one of which, as indeed Colin St John Wilson points out in his catalogue essay, is 'one of Aalto's last and most beautiful buildings'.[1] Among Aalto's last works, the Benedictine Monastery Library at Mount Angel, Oregon, would have enhanced Ban's choice, complemented his critique, and represented Aalto's continuity from the Viipuri Library of the 1930s.

Hereby hangs a tale. The late Colin Rowe, a brilliant writer and critic, had been taken for the first time to visit Mount Angel just prior to his flying back to London to receive the RIBA Gold Medal. He was accompanied by James Tice, a former student. Rowe was a Le Corbusier devotee, but his visit to Mount Angel represented for him something of an eleventh-hour conversion. He duly related this experience in his Gold Medal Address (1995), placing Aalto in pole position among

the modern masters, and subsequently documented it. Above all else, the exhibition demonstrates the way in which Aalto's groundbreaking humanism in modern architecture, whose canons and tradition he quietly amended to suit an evolving society, continues to offer lessons for future generations. Δ+

Michael Spens is guest-editor of *AD Landscape Architecture: Site/Non-Site* (March/April 2007). He is University Reader in Architecture at Dundee University, and has a particular interest in the relationship between architecture and the landscape.

Note
1. Juhani Pallasmaa and Tomoko Sato (eds), *Alvar Aalto: Through the Eyes of Shigeru Ban*, exhibition catalogue, Black Dog Publishing (London), 2007, p 19.

McLean's Nuggets

Programmable Paint: The Medium is the Message

At a recent talk in London, science writer Phillip Ball, author of *The Self-Made Tapestry: Pattern Formation in Nature* (Oxford University Press, 1998), showed images of what appeared to be a kind of proto stripy paint. This patterned paint media was in fact a series of Belousov–Zhabotinsky (BZ) reactions, or nonlinear chemical oscillators. These are fluid mixtures which, with chemical stimuli, can develop patterns through self-organisation. Boris Belousov's initial discovery of these liquids in 1951 has since been further developed by Anatol Zhabotinsky and the resulting BZ 'cocktails' can create concentric, stripy and spiral formations that will disappear when the liquid is shaken. Also described as spatiotemporal oscillators, the chemical oscillation can be tuned to 'switch' the visual qualities of the liquid at a given time period, for instance from clear to coloured or from clear to fluorescent. The mathematician and famous code-breaker Alan Turing theoretically explored pattern formation by a chemical reaction/diffusion in his famous paper 'The Chemical Basis for Morphogenesis' (Royal Society, 1951), explaining that patterns in nature could be replicated by a rudimentary chemical reaction. A little speculation and some technology re-purposing, and a fully programmable self-organising paint media is not as unlikely as the 'tartan paint' joke of one's youth. Programmable paint would avoid the print-media process of artwork to printer to substrate (paper etc), with digitised artwork directly uploaded into a can of liquid media. Initially available as a two-colour suspension, artwork is scaled to suit based on square-metre coverage, and then downloaded into the paint tin before application. As with any paint application, you may or may not need to reapply for the desired finish, or you may choose to more liberally decorate a surface in the manner of a 1950s action painter, well illustrated in the motion picture *The Rebel* (1960) starring aspiring artist and Nuevo beatnik Anthony Hancock, who when asked in the film how he likes to mix his paint replied – 'in a bucket with a big stick'. Reported in 2002, Philips Research, Eindhoven, was working on a 'paintable display'[1] in a process entitled 'photo-enforced stratification of a liquid crystal–polymer mix'. This research was subsequently discontinued.

Chemical wave structures in the Belousov–Zhabotinsky reaction, Department of Biophysics, Otto-von-Guericke University Magdeburg, Germany.

I Am Not Stopping

As the unfeasibly premature crocuses break through the grass-covered platform ends at Poulton-le-Fylde, the municipal apparatchiks of nearby Blackpool may reflect upon their recent failure to secure the filthy lucre of the polished proverbial known as the 'super casino'. One wonders what a direct rail link from London might do for the Northwest's capital of delights, or does the economic regenerator of mass gambling have to come first? I am not exactly sure of the tangible by-products or benefits of the casino; with horse and dog racing you get fresh-air spectator sports, social interaction and events that do not owe everything to chance. At the very least one hopes that a city without a decent rail link and indeed a decent station will get the transport system it deserves rather than depend on the gambler's investment. At present there are North and South Blackpool stations, but Second World War damage and Beeching put paid to the central station, which closed in 1964 and was later demolished.

Further down the line after the required change at Preston, I catch a glimpse of British Rail's proto high-speed Advanced Passenger Train (APT-P), circa 1980, currently being operated as a semi-abandoned moss farm on the outskirts of Dario Gradi's Crewe. Again the failure of medium- and long-term transport planning is left visibly rotting in a railway siding. So what of the economic benefits that high-speed rail links and decent stations may bring? In a recent application under the Transport and Works Act 1992 for the proposed East Midlands Parkway railway station,[2] and as part of a land acquisition order to 'secure the railway system as a part of multi-modal transportation improvements', it was noted by the then Secretary of State that: 'Economic benefits would outweigh the scheme's costs and it would produce a positive return on investment over 25 years, being cash positive in 11 years.' The station is due to open in 2008. An ability to absorb the capital costs of new infrastructure measured against social benefit seems useful, although how social benefit is measured is a very different challenge, explored in some detail by the Department of Transport in a report entitled 'Multi-modal transport appraisal investment'.[3] The report examines the disjunction between models of cost benefit analysis (CBA) and willingness to pay (WTP) calculus in appraising the economic and social benefits of new transport infrastructure.

PYRAMID SCHEMES

The construction and logistics of vast (and ancient) projects such as the Great Pyramids of Giza continue to intrigue scientists, anthropologists and technologists. Marcus Chown, writing in *New Scientist* (27 October 2001), described in some detail Californian software consultant Maureen Clemmons' theory that the vast Egyptian constructions of 3,000 years ago used giant kites to elevate and position blocks of stone. Inspired by a hieroglyph, which appeared to show a row of men holding a giant bird aloft with cables, Clemmons began to practically test her unusual theory. Working with Morteza Gharib, Professor of Aeronautics and Bioengineering at the California Institute of Technology, the pair set themselves the challenge of lifting a 3.5-tonne column (obelisk), which they did using a 40-square-metre (430-square-foot) rectangular sail. On this basis they calculated that it would be possible to move a 300-tonne obelisk with 40 men and five sails. In another attempt to fathom the constructional mysteries of ancient Egypt, writer Andrew Collins says that he has 'compelling evidence' that sound was used to move stone blocks in the building of the Great Pyramid.[4] Using a sustained vibration or resonance, the large blocks are sympathetically excited until they begin to resonate and are then merely guided into place. Collins makes reference to the work of technologist Christopher Dunn, who in his book *The Giza Power Plant: Technologies of Ancient Egypt* (Bear & Company, 1998) puts forward a theory of the Great Pyramid that it serves not only as an electromagnetic power plant, but that it is itself a huge musical instrument. The effects of resonance on building fabric are well documented, with the Tacoma Narrows bridge disaster of 1940 the most commonly used example. The use of tuned-mass dampers in high-rise buildings is commonplace to counteract the sway of large structures with equal and opposite force. The active use of resonance or vibration to construct our environment might seem unusual, but it is used, for example, to drive steel sheet piling[5] into the earth. By attaching what in essence is a large

Will McLean and Bruce McLean, Coloured 'Resonating Rock' experiment, Mala Garba, Majorca, 2001.

motor to the top of a sheet pile, a specific frequency of vibration will cause liquefaction of the earth, reducing friction between sheet and pile and letting the weight of the steel and attached driver push the steel into the ground. At a smaller scale, a high-frequency welding process that generates heat is used to weld plastics. ∆+

'McLean's Nuggets' is an ongoing technical series inspired by Will McLean and Samantha Hardingham's enthusiasm for back issues of *AD*, as explicitly explored in Hardingham's *AD* issue *The 1970s is Here and Now* (March/April 2005).
Will McLean is joint coordinator of technical studies (with Peter Silver) in the Department of Architecture at the University of Westminster.

Notes
1. IDG News Service press release, 2 April 2002.
2. www.dft.gov.uk/pgr/twa/dl/eastmidlandspar kwaystationla5629.
3. www.dft.gov.uk/pgr/economics/rdg/multimo daltransportappraisal3096? page=1#1000.
4. Dalya Alberge, arts correspondent, 'Pyramids built "by Egypt's big noises"', Times Newspaper, 10 November 1999.
5. www.sbe.napier.ac.uk/projects/retwall/help/ plant.htm#no5.

The Crystal at the Royal Ontario Museum

Sean Stanwick, the co-author of *Design City Toronto*, describes Daniel Libeskind's crystalline centrepiece for Toronto, which has become a catalyst for the city's cultural and architectural renaissance.

Toronto can be characterised by a fusion of culture, attitude and a desire to discover and explore. Yet for the past two decades the Royal Ontario Museum (ROM) seemed more of a forbidding fortress – the massive stone edifice and blackened windows largely impenetrable – rather than a welcoming institution of experience, knowledge and exploration. At the time of writing, as the new cubic and crystalline addition by Daniel Libeskind with Bregman + Hamann Architects nears completion, our perception of the city's cultural grande dame and ultimately the city of Toronto is about to be forever changed.

Asserting itself as a key protagonist in the city's architectural renaissance, the massive expansion initiative is designed to reconnect Canada's largest museum with its culturally and architecturally burgeoning host city. The geometric shapes of the Crystal (actually the Michael Lee-Chin Crystal, so named for its benefactor's generous financial contribution) were inspired by the prismatic natural objects found in the ROM's extensive gem and mineralogy galleries. The concept of offset transparent cubes was actually first set to paper by Libeskind on a ROM café napkin while touring the existing buildings.

In reality, the notion of a fully transparent crystal is somewhat misleading, as an anodised aluminium skin covers 75 per cent of the structure, with the remaining 25 per cent being a random pattern of slices and wedges of charcoal-tinted glass. Nevertheless, the effect of a shimmering urban beacon is still quite powerful as five massive cubes pierced by refracted spears of light interlock with each other and wrap around the brawny 1914 and 1933 stone wings before spilling out on to the Bloor streetscape.

Created in 1914 and home to nearly six million beautiful and remarkable objects in its collections, the ROM is North America's fifth-largest museum and a significant architectural fixture. Featuring Canada's culture and natural history, it also conducts important scientific research, placing it among the world's leading knowledge producers.

The largest, central crystal defines the museum's new entrance and acts as the datum from which a collection of gallery and public spaces will radiate, including restored wings devoted to China, Japan and Korea as well as a new gallery for Canadian First Peoples. At the point where the cubes intersect, the dramatic Crystal Court multistorey atrium is punctuated by a network of perilous catwalks and illuminated by two massive skylights that protrude awkwardly down into the space and direct beams of light to the floor below. The dramatic final act, though, is saved for the top where the Crystal Five Bistro Bar (C5) opens itself up to offer signature views of the city skyline in the distance, sumptuous meals and fine wine.

Libeskind's scheme also works to restore axial sightlines and reprogrammes existing spaces. This is what the ROM desperately needed as previous renovations had all but destroyed the original flows between galleries, subdivided its great halls and buried intricate historic stone details.

With four existing galleries newly renovated, the interior is no longer dark and maze-like as windows have been stripped of their blackout paint, ceilings have been pulled down and walls removed to create a beautiful open and naturally lit space. One also begins to understand that Libeskind's crystal vision is more than simply the assemblage of giant cubes. Inside the newly created Korea and China galleries, visitors are transported deep within a giant gemstone as the reclaimed natural light refracts through the sequence of all-glass parallelogram display cases whose layout mimics the same jagged knife style as the new building.

One of the most recognisable renovated spaces is the Rotunda, a spectacular arched dome that has served as the main entrance since 1933. No longer crowded and noisy, it is transformed into the Rotunda Café, a magical room set out with decorative stained-glass windows, inlaid animal motifs and a spectacular domed ceiling, covered in Venetian-glass mosaic tiles and animated with intricate figures and historical symbols in rich hues of gold, bronze, vivid reds and blues. Another familiar space to receive a face-lift is the Samuel Hall/Currelly Gallery. Once a dark transitional space leading to the major galleries, the majestic hall now flows into the Crystal Court. Here visitors can relax with a book, or simply enjoy the history of the space.

Beyond providing a fantastic urban spectacle, what the ROM aspires to most is to affect the way we view and experience not just singular buildings, or specific moments, but the city as a whole. According to Libeskind: 'Architecture at its deepest sense is about creating space that has never been there, and giving people a kind of vista … as if one would see the city in a very different way through this new space (interview with the author, June 2006).' It is actually difficult to tell which is more exciting – watching the massive interlocking steel skeleton rise and tilt precariously overhead, or the anticipation of the cultural changes yet to come. **Δ**+

Based in Toronto, Sean Stanwick is a regular contributor to *AD* and has a particular interest in contemporary architecture and design. He is the co-author of *Design City Toronto* (Wiley-Academy, 2007) and co-author of *Wine by Design* (Wiley-Academy, 2005). He is currently an associate with Farrow Partnership Architects.

Design City Toronto by Sean Stanwick and Jennifer Flores was published in April 2007 by Wiley-Academy, an imprint of John Wiley & Sons. For more details see www.Wiley.com

Five massive cubes pierced by refracted spears of light interlock with each other and wrap around the historic 1914 and 1933 stone wings before spilling out on to the Bloor streetscape, to create a new shimmering urban beacon. At the project's core is the Crystal Court, a multilevel space created at the intersection between the crystals. Rising the full height from basement to roof, the space will be pierced by a network of catwalks crisscrossing at various levels.

Subscribe Now

As an influential and prestigious architectural publication, *Architectural Design* has an almost unrivalled reputation worldwide. Published bimonthly, it successfully combines the currency and topicality of a newsstand journal with the editorial rigour and design qualities of a book. Consistently at the forefront of cultural thought and design since the 1960s, it has time and again proved provocative and inspirational – inspiring theoretical, creative and technological advances. Prominent in the 1980s and 1990s for the part it played in Postmodernism and then in Deconstruction, in the 2000s Δ has leveraged a depth and level of scrutiny not currently offered elsewhere in the design press. Topics pursued question the outcomes of technical innovations as well as the far-reaching social, cultural and environmental challenges that present themselves today in a period of increasing global uncertainty. Δ

SUBSCRIPTION RATES 2007
Institutional Rate (Print only or Online only): UK£175/US$315
Institutional Rate (Combined Print and Online): UK£193/US$347
Personal Rate (Print only): UK £110/US$170
Discount Student* Rate (Print only): UK£70/US$110

*Proof of studentship will be required when placing an order. Prices reflect rates for a 2007 subscription and are subject to change without notice.

TO SUBSCRIBE
Phone your credit card order:
+44 (0)1243 843 828

Fax your credit card order to:
+44 (0)1243 843 232

Email your credit card order to:
cs-journals@wiley.co.uk

Post your credit card or cheque order to:
John Wiley & Sons Ltd.
Journals Administration Department
1 Oldlands Way
Bognor Regis
West Sussex PO22 9SA
UK

Please include your postal delivery address with your order.

All Δ volumes are available individually. To place an order please write to:
John Wiley & Sons Ltd
Customer Services
1 Oldlands Way
Bognor Regis
West Sussex PO22 9SA

Please quote the ISBN number of the issue(s) you are ordering.

Δ is available to purchase on both a subscription basis and as individual volumes

○ I wish to subscribe to Δ *Architectural Design* at the **Institutional rate of** (Print only or Online only *(delete as applicable)* £175/us$315.

○ I wish to subscribe to Δ *Architectural Design* at the **Institutional rate of** (Combined Print and Online) £193/us$347.

○ I wish to subscribe to Δ *Architectural Design* at the **Personal rate of £110/us$170.**

○ I wish to subscribe to Δ *Architectural Design* at the **Student rate of £70/us$110.**

○ Δ *Architectural Design* is available to individuals on either a calendar year or rolling annual basis; Institutional subscriptions are only available on a calendar year basis. Tick this box if you would like your Personal or Student subscription on a rolling annual basis.

Payment enclosed by Cheque/Money order/Drafts.
Value/Currency £/US$ _____

○ Please charge £/US$ _____ to my credit card.
Account number:
☐☐☐☐☐☐☐☐☐☐☐☐☐☐☐☐

Expiry date:
☐☐☐☐☐☐

Card: Visa/Amex/Mastercard/Eurocard *(delete as applicable)*

Cardholder's signature _____
Cardholder's name _____
Address _____
_____
_____ Post/Zip Code _____

Recipient's name _____
Address _____
_____
_____ Post/Zip Code _____

I would like to buy the following issues at £22.99 each:

○ Δ 188 *4dsocial: Interactive Design Environments*, Lucy Bullivant
○ Δ 187 *Italy: A New Architectural Landscape*, Luigi Prestinenza Puglisi
○ Δ 186 *Landscape Architecture: Site/Non-Site*, Michael Spens
○ Δ 185 *Elegance*, Ali Rahim + Hina Jamelle
○ Δ 184 *Architextiles*, Mark Garcia
○ Δ 183 *Collective Intelligence in Design*, Christopher Hight + Chris Perry
○ Δ 182 *Programming Cultures: Art and Architecture in the Age of Software*, Mike Silver
○ Δ 181 *The New Europe*, Valentina Croci
○ Δ 180 *Techniques and Technologies in Morphogenetic Design*, Michael Hensel, Achim Menges + Michael Weinstock
○ Δ 179 *Manmade Modular Megastructures*, Ian Abley + Jonathan Schwinge
○ Δ 178 *Sensing the 21st-Century City*, Brian McGrath + Grahame Shane
○ Δ 177 *The New Mix*, Sara Caples and Everardo Jefferson
○ Δ 176 *Design Through Making*, Bob Sheil
○ Δ 175 *Food + The City*, Karen A Franck
○ Δ 174 *The 1970s Is Here and Now*, Samantha Hardingham
○ Δ 173 *4dspace: Interactive Architecture*, Lucy Bullivant
○ Δ 172 *Islam + Architecture*, Sabiha Foster
○ Δ 171 *Back To School*, Michael Chadwick
○ Δ 170 *The Challenge of Suburbia*, Ilka + Andreas Ruby
○ Δ 169 *Emergence*, Michael Hensel, Achim Menges + Michael Weinstock
○ Δ 168 *Extreme Sites*, Deborah Gans + Claire Weisz
○ Δ 167 *Property Development*, David Sokol
○ Δ 166 *Club Culture*, Eleanor Curtis
○ Δ 165 *Urban Flashes Asia*, Nicholas Boyarsky + Peter Lang